TENNESSEE
HANDBOOK

TENNESSEE
HANDBOOK

INCLUDING NASHVILLE, MEMPHIS, THE GREAT SMOKY MOUNTAINS, AND NUTBUSH

SECOND EDITION

JEFF BRADLEY

MOON
TRAVEL
HANDBOOKS

917.68
Bra

TENNESSEE HANDBOOK
SECOND EDITION

Published by
Moon Publications, Inc.
P.O. Box 3040
Chico, California 95927-3040, USA

Printed by
Colorcraft

ISBN: 1-56691-147-8
ISSN: 1091-3343

Editor: Michael Sigalas
Copy Editor: Valerie Sellers Blanton
Production & Design: Carey Wilson
Cartography: Chris Folks and Mike Morgenfeld
Index: Sondra Nation

Front cover photo by Roy Gumpel. Courtesy of Liaison Agency, Inc.

All photos by Jeff Bradley unless otherwise noted.
All illustrations by Bob Race unless otherwise noted.

Distributed in the United States and Canada by Publishers Group West

Printed in China

Please send all comments,
corrections, additions,
amendments, and critiques to:

TENNESSEE HANDBOOK
MOON TRAVEL HANDBOOKS
P.O. BOX 3040
CHICO, CA 95927-3040, USA
e-mail: travel@moon.com
www.moon.com

Printing History
1st edition—1997
2nd edition—July 1999
5 4 3 2 1 0

To George and Irene Bradley,
for not buying a farm in Pennsylvania—
or anywhere else outside of Tennessee

CONTENTS

Cross-references in **bold type** within the text of the book refer to citations in the general index.

CHATTANOOGA 218-240

SPECIAL TOPICS

SPECIAL TOPICS

MAKE THIS A BETTER BOOK

My in-laws used to take big camping trips out West, and in their eagerness to get from one place to another they would often take pictures out the window of a car going 60 miles per hour or faster. In the resulting prints, some items came out sharp, others were fuzzy, and some—particularly telephone poles—were downright distorted.

So it is in writing a travel book.

Restaurants come and go, a new Elvis impersonator comes to the theater outside the Smokies, and other places open and close. If you are using this book and find an error or run across something that ought to be in it, please let us know. *Tennessee Handbook* will be updated from time to time, and we greatly appreciate hearing from readers.

Tell us what should go in, what should come out, and let us hear what you think about this book. Address your cards and letters to:

> *Tennessee Handbook*
> Moon Publications, Inc.
> P.O. Box 3040
> Chico, CA 95927-3040

> Or drop us some e-mail at: travel@moon.com

ACCOMMODATIONS RATINGS

All accommodations in this book are rated by price category, based on double-occupancy, high-season rates. Categories used are:

> **Budget:** under $35
> **Inexpensive:** $35-60
> **Moderate:** $60-85
> **Expensive:** $85-110
> **Premium:** $110-150
> **Luxury:** $150 and up

MAPS

TENNESSEE CHAPTER DIVISIONS

Johnson City

NASHVILLE 7

Crossville

KNOXVILLE

Gatlinburg

Jackson

Murfreesboro

MEMPHIS

CHATTANOOGA

1. FIRST FRONTIER
2. KNOXVILLE
3. GATEWAYS TO THE SMOKIES
4. GREAT SMOKY MOUNTAINS NATIONAL PARK
5. HILLS AND PLATEAUS

6. CHATTANOOGA
7. NASHVILLE
8. HEARTLAND
9. MEMPHIS
10. WESTERN PLAINS

© MOON PUBLICATIONS, INC.

MAP SYMBOLS

		Interstate	⬭			
Superhighway	═══	US Highway	⬭	Sight	•	
Main Road	───	State Highway	○	Lodging	•	
Other Road	───	County Road	□	Mountain	▲	
Trail	-------	City	○	Campground	Λ	
State Border	─·─·─	Town	○	Airport	✈	
		Water	▬			

© MOON PUBLICATIONS, INC.

ABBREVIATIONS

B&B—Bed and Breakfast
CDT—central daylight time
CST—central standard time
EDT—eastern daylight time

EST—eastern standard time
Hwy.—highway
NAACP—National Association
  for the Advancement of
  Colored People

Pkwy.—Parkway
TVA—Tennessee Valley
  Authority
UT—University of Tennessee

ACKNOWLEDGMENTS

While a first edition of a travel guide is always a *tabula rasa*, the task of writing a second edition begins with a list of new material to include and mistakes to be fixed. A great many people helped me in this effort.

Once again, Fredric Koeppel made his way through the nightclubs and restaurants of Memphis. Two kind souls who demand anonymity ably worked up Nashville. Suzanne Hall divined the culinary mysteries of Chattanooga, and "Bonnie Appetit" applied her sauciness to Knoxville eateries and danceries.

Several Tennessee travel officials went above and beyond the call of duty. Denise DuBois Taylor and Valerie Parker of Memphis, Greer Broemel of Nashville, Landon Howard of Chattanooga, and Linda Caldwell of Etowah were most helpful.

Mike Sigalas capably edited this book, fresh from writing one of his own on South Carolina. Karen Bleske's work on the first edition continues to shine.

Robert Cogswell, the folklorist for the state of Tennessee, held forth on a variety of topics, from where to get the best barbecue in Murfreesboro to the finer points of cultural tourism. Tennessee is lucky to have him. Franklin Jones in Cambridge remains a source of wisdom about West Tennessee. Fiona Soltes and Sandy Smith shared their knowledge of Middle Tennessee, and Patsy Weiler helped with music.

My wife, Marta, and sons Truman and Walker have listened patiently to trivial and not-so-trivial matters about Tennessee, put up with my absences, and understood when I ignored beautiful Colorado days to work inside.

My inspiration for assembling this mass of information is David Harkness of Knoxville, truly a gentleman and a scholar, whose encyclopedic knowledge about Tennessee is exceeded only by his love for the state.

INTRODUCTION

THE LAND

GEOLOGY

The state of Tennessee cuts across the grain of geologic features in the southeastern part of North America, and thus displays a variety of land forms that have shaped the history of the state and provide a change of landscape for the modern-day traveler motoring, bicycling, or flying across the state.

The Tennessee River, which begins above Knoxville, flows southwest from that point into Alabama and then returns some 140 miles west to cross the state heading north. The river divides the state into three sections, from east to west the Appalachian highlands, the interior lowlands, and the gulf coastal plain.

The Appalachian Highlands

The highlands begin with the crest of the Appalachian Mountains, which came into being when the North American continent bumped up

against the African plate. This took place more than a billion years ago in Precambrian times and thrust up mountains that since have worn down into the shapes that visitors see today. The **highest point** in Tennessee is the Great Smoky Mountains National Park's Clingmans Dome, which rises to an elevation of 6,643 feet. This ridge of mountains marks the **Eastern Continental Divide,** with water on the Tennessee side eventually flowing to the Gulf of Mexico.

The mountains here are a series of ridges that line up on a northeast/southwest axis. This, not surprisingly, is the direction that most of the rivers run. Just west of the mountains is the 45-mile-wide **Great Valley** of East Tennessee, which contains the richest farmland in this section. Farther west is the **Cumberland Plateau,** which at an elevation of 2,000 feet is 1,000 feet higher than the Great Valley. At the Kentucky border it is 55 miles wide, but by the time it gets to the Georgia border it measures only 38 miles across. Formed when forces pushed up what had been flat-lying stone, this plateau proved such a barrier to early settlers that to get to Middle Tennessee they usually traveled through Kentucky to get around it.

Coves, caves, and waterfalls mark the Appalachian highlands. Coves are relatively flat areas that are surrounded by mountains. They were highly prized by early settlers for their rich soil and easy-to-farm conditions; the best known of these areas is the Smoky Mountains' Cades Cove, now a part of the national park.

East Tennessee has a lot of limestone, and water passing though it has created caves and caverns over the centuries. Many of these, such as Bristol Caverns, Appalachian Caverns, and Tuckaleechee Caverns, have been commercialized, but others await spelunking clubs and others who enjoy exploring these underground delights.

The Cumberland Plateau, with its layers of easily eroded sandstone, produces many waterfalls. Fall Creek Falls, in the state park with the same name, is the most prominent of these. Taller than Niagara Falls at 256 feet, it is the highest waterfall east of the Mississippi River.

Interior Lowlands
The lowlands include the **Eastern Highland Rim,** the **Central Basin,** and the **Western Highland Rim.** The Eastern Highland Rim, while 1,000 feet lower than the Cumberland Plateau to the east, sits about 300 feet higher than the Central Basin, which is bounded on the west by the Western Highland Rim—also 300 feet above the Basin.

Neither of the highland rims has very good soil, but the Central Basin between them contains some of the most productive farmland in the state. Here stand Nashville and most of Tennessee's antebellum mansions. This is the land of Walking Horses and, it is said, more bluegrass than all of Kentucky.

Like the Cumberland Plateau to the east, the Eastern Highland Rim has its share of waterfalls. Burgess Falls, in a state park of the same name, plunges 130 feet into the Central Basin. Middle Tennessee has a lot of caves as well, including McMinnville's Cumberland Caverns, said to be the largest cave in the southeastern United States.

Gulf Coastal Plain
The coastal plain begins just west of the Tennessee River Valley and extends all the way to the Mississippi River. This is the flattest section of the state, and here vast amounts of cotton and soybeans grow. The plain is broken occasionally with riverbottoms, which snake their way across to the Mississippi.

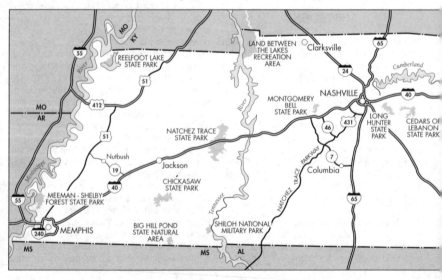

Much of the soil here—for there aren't many rocks—has come from somewhere else. The counties of Tennessee that border the Mississippi River contain sediment washed down from both the Rocky Mountains and the Appalachians. Some of the soil is loess—material blown in from points west. Several of these counties have no naturally occurring rocks larger than a child's fist.

It was in this region during the winter of 1811-12 that the most powerful **earthquakes** in U.S. history occurred. Alleged to be so intense that they stopped clocks in Boston, these earth tremors caused the land to sink and the Mississippi River to rush in and create Reelfoot Lake, which alone of Tennessee's large lakes is natural.

Memphis sits above the Mississippi River on a bluff that prevents the city from being flooded. Until the Mississippi and its tributaries were dammed, flooding was a constant threat in this region, explaining why no cities other than Memphis sit directly on the river.

GEOGRAPHY

Tennessee looks like a ship steaming toward the Atlantic, with Bristol up on the bow and the propeller coming out down at Memphis. Though only the 34th state in total area—about 42,250 square miles—it manages to touch eight other states, a feat matched only by neighboring Missouri.

As anyone who has ever driven the length of the state can testify, it is a long haul from Bristol to Memphis—500 miles in all. Bristol is closer to Canada than it is to Memphis, and Memphis is closer to the Gulf of Mexico than to Bristol.

The Tennessee River divides the state into three parts, known as the "grand divisions of Tennessee." Indeed, until a few years ago signs along the highways coming into the state welcomed visitors to "the three states of Tennessee."

This greeting was dropped in the 1980s in an effort to promote a more unified state, but the geographic divisions—exacerbated by the length of the state—help explain the differences in accents, food, music, and points of view that have emerged over the years across the state. People in West Tennessee have a deeper Southern accent than do their East Tennessee counterparts, who speak with more of an Appalachian twang. Catfish is a staple of "country cooking" in West Tennessee, while no decent restaurant in East Tennessee would think of serving breakfast without offering country ham. When Tennessee voted to secede from the Union, some East Tennesseans wanted to secede from the secessionists. One of the reasons for this was the small size of East Tennessee farms, which had few slaves.

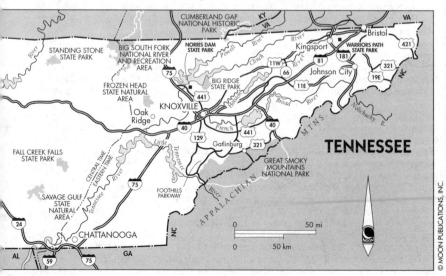

TENNESSEE "OFFICIALS"

Nickname: The Volunteer

State Bird: mockingbird

Game bird: bobwhite quail

Wildflower: passion flower

Gem: Tennessee River pearl

Insects: firefly and ladybug

Rocks: limestone and agate

Songs: "My Homeland, Tennessee," "When It's Iris Time in Tennessee," "The Tennessee Waltz," "Rocky Top," "Tennessee"

Wild animal: raccoon

The great distances from the mountains to the Mississippi account for the fact that many Tennesseans are not very well-traveled in their own state. The vast majority of East Tennesseans have never been to Memphis, while, with the exception of those who are driving to points east and north, few West Tennesseans get past the Great Smoky Mountains National Park.

Geography can even account for the differences in music across the state. East Tennessee, isolated from the rest of the state until modern highways cut through, preserved Elizabethan ballads that had come from England and the British Isles. West Tennessee had and has the highest concentration of blacks in Tennessee, and it was from them that the blues emerged. Nashville, a center of commerce in the middle of the state, had money for advertising on radio shows and thus was a perfect place for the music industry to emerge.

CLIMATE

Tennessee is a Southern state, but it has more variety in its weather than most of its Dixie neighbors. As a general rule, West Tennessee is hotter than East Tennessee, and East Tennessee gets more snow than the rest of the state combined.

Winters in the eastern part of the state can be rough, with temperatures spiking down to 15° below zero (Fahrenheit). From December through February, mountain roads, particularly in the Great Smoky Mountains National Park, are often closed by snow. A far more pernicious form of bad weather is "black ice," created when rain freezes on roadways and is not visible on the pavement. Black ice is more hazardous than a foot of snow.

Springtime is a delight across the state, although it comes with a lot of rain. Travelers should keep in mind, particularly in the mountains, that rain at a lower elevation can become snow a few thousand feet up. Spring is the best time to visit Memphis and West Tennessee, and this is when the locals hold their biggest outdoor festivals.

Summertime is hot in Tennessee. Temperatures easily reach the 90s in all but the highest places. When the humidity readings come close to those of the thermometer, it can be downright miserable.

Fall brings another round of festivals to West Tennessee and beautiful foliage all over the state. This is usually a relatively dry time, with warm days and chilly evenings.

FLORA

Trees

When settlers came across the mountains from the east, they found a land almost entirely covered by hardwood forests—trees they had to chop down to make room for fields and pastures. Tennessee remains a diversely forested state, and forest products contribute mightily to the state's economy.

In the east, the Great Smoky Mountains National Park supports more species of trees than all of Europe. As the elevation climbs to 6,000 feet, changes in the trees, a gradual shift from **hardwoods** to a **conifer forest,** reflect the variations one might see while traveling north through North America. At the top, the **spruce fir** forests resemble those found in Canada.

Across the state, the hardwoods produce a pleasing set of colors in the fall, and visitors flock to the scenic highways to enjoy the views. Reelfoot Lake and the riverbottoms of West Tennessee contain **cypress** trees, a water-dwelling plant whose knobby "knees" rise out of the water.

Wildflowers

Tennessee is noted for wildflowers, not only for their beauty but the uses to which the Indians and early settlers put them. **Yarrow** is a member of the sunflower family whose leaves have a blood-clotting component. **Bloodroot** gets its name from the fact that Indians used it to make red dye, and **trilliums** grow along many roads and trails in the mountains.

Kudzu drapes the Tennessee countryside

SCOTT TEEPLE

Kudzu

Perhaps the most amazing plant in Tennessee, found the length of the state, is kudzu, a vinelike organism with enormous leaves and a prodigious growth rate—under optimal conditions, a foot or more per day. Brought in from Asia, this plant was loosed on the South in the 1930s in an effort to control erosion. It certainly helped do that, then promptly set about controlling trees, abandoned buildings, and anything standing still. Although the plant has some practical uses—cattle will eat it when grass is scarce—the plant is largely regarded at best as a nuisance and at worse as an enemy of forestry. Kudzu climbs trees and then kills them by blocking out the sun.

Left alone, kudzu creates fantastic landscapes of vine-draped trees, totally covering buildings and cars and sprouting tendrils that hang threateningly from wires that cross roads and highways. Kudzu has captured the imaginations of Tennesseans and other Southerners, showing up in songs and in literature, and on a website: www.sa.ua.edu/cptr/kudzu.

FAUNA

Mammals

The biggest wild animals in Tennessee are **black bears,** which live in the eastern part of the state. The bears of the Smokies are the most famous, for they have the most contact with people. While black bears have a gentle reputation, they can be dangerous if cornered or if a person gets between a mother bear and her cubs. People should never feed bears. Doing so causes the animals to lose their innate fear of humans. When this happens, they often cause problems and have to be killed.

Deer live all over Tennessee, as do **raccoons, muskrats, red foxes, squirrels,** and smaller animals. Dead **possums** often grace Tennessee roads.

Birds

With its many woodlands and wetlands, Tennessee is home to a wide variety of birds. Furthermore, parts of the Mississippi and the Atlantic flyways cross the state, bringing birds that are just passing through.

Bald eagles winter at Reelfoot Lake in northwestern Tennessee. **Wild turkeys** appear in the Smokies and across the state. **Ruffed grouse** and **bobwhites** are found throughout the state, as are **barred owls** and **barn owls. Crows** live all over, as do **pileated woodpeckers**—the largest members of the woodpecker family. **Turkey vultures,** almost always called "buzzards" hereabouts, often feast on roadkill.

ANNE LONG LARSEN

Never feed a wild bear.

Waterfowl such as **Canada geese, mallards, and black ducks** live beside **great blue herons** and **belted kingfishers.**

Reptiles and Amphibians

With its temperate climate and many bodies of water, Tennessee harbors a great many reptiles and amphibians. The Smokies alone contain 23 varieties of **snakes,** only two of which—rattlesnakes and copperheads—are poisonous, and 27 species of **salamanders.**

ENVIRONMENTAL ISSUES

Historically, Southern states in general and Tennessee in particular welcomed industry and gave little thought to the pollution that accompanied jobs and an inflow of capital. Attitudes have changed, however, and Tennessee's air and water are in better shape than they were just a few decades ago. Nonetheless, paper mills and other industrial sites belch chemicals—and smells—to an extent that is noticeable by visitors.

Coal-fired power plants are another source of pollution. Since the prevailing winds blow from west to east, the Great Smoky Mountains National Park suffers a great deal from particulates borne by the wind. Visibility from the peaks has decreased something like 30% during the past three decades. And Chattanooga's Rock City, which for years has claimed that visitors can "see seven states," rarely has skies clear enough to do so.

Tennessee's Oak Ridge was one of the key sites of the atomic age, and at one time the Tennessee Valley Authority had the most ambitious nuclear power plant construction program in the world. Oak Ridge is now undergoing an extensive cleanup of radioactive materials, and, as in other places in the U.S., fission-based power plants have not arrived at a good solution for their nuclear waste.

HISTORY

THE INDIANS

The earliest evidence of people in what is now Tennessee comes from artifacts left by Ice Age hunters. Little is known of their culture, but they left fluted points, scraping tools, and other items that suggest they were nomadic hunters.

Anthropologists call the next group to inhabit Tennessee the **Archaic Indians,** who came upon the scene about 6000 B.C. These people built the first Tennessee towns, usually along rivers, where they fished using hooks and nets. Excavations of burial sites have revealed that they made jewelry from shells, bones, and copper.

The next inhabitants, the **Woodland Indians,** came about 3,000 to 2,500 years ago and set the pattern for Indian groups to follow. They cultivated corn, fashioned pottery out of clay, and used bows and arrows. They were the first people to alter the Tennessee landscape with the construction of mounds. Woodland Indian burial mounds, structures that grew in height as subsequent bodies were buried in them, exist all over the state. This group is thought to have built the "Old Stone Fort" outside Manchester.

A subsequent group, the **Early Mississippian Indians,** built some of the highest earthen structures in the United States. Coming to Tennessee about 1,000 years ago, they erected mounds for ceremonial purposes. Pinson Mounds, south of Jackson in West Tennessee, contains one pile of soil that reaches more than seven stories tall.

For all the native people who lived in Tennessee, the land proved a most hospitable place. The forests teemed with game and the rivers and streams with fish, and the rich soil readily grew corn, beans, potatoes, pumpkins, and tobacco. The Indians here, unlike some of their western counterparts who had to struggle with a hostile environment, had time to focus on matters of art, government, and games.

When Europeans arrived, they met several tribes in what is now Tennessee. Hernando de Soto reported finding large towns of Indians on the bluffs that are now Memphis. The **Chickasaw** lived in what is now Mississippi, but they considered large amounts of Tennessee their territory. The **Creek** lived farther east, the **Shawnee** inhabited the Cumberland River Valley, and a small group called the **Yuchi** lived in the east.

The Cherokee

The most powerful tribe, the one whose word "Tanasi" for the largest river in the area became "Tennessee," was the Cherokee. In the early 18th century they waged war on the Creek, Yuchi, and Shawnee, and drove them out of the region. When the settlers arrived, the Cherokee were the Indians with whom they had to deal.

The Cherokee lived in towns collected around the junction of what is now Tennessee, Georgia, North Carolina, and South Carolina. The Tennessee towns became known to settlers as the "overhill towns," since they were across the Appalachian Mountains from the settlements in North Carolina.

In their towns, the Cherokee lived in permanent dwellings made of logs. Each family belonged to one of seven clans, and together the clans governed the village. Each village had a council house, some of which could hold more than 500 people, and had designated places for each clan.

The Cherokee had a national chief who had various advisors and a bureaucracy that dealt with civic, religious, and wartime affairs. During times of combat, women took part in the government, most notably in the role of "Honored Woman," a person who could decide the fate of captives and who could make the decision of whether or not to go to war.

Game and fish were plentiful, and the Cherokee grew corn and other crops. They lived reasonably comfortable lives, but zealously defended their hunting grounds and vigorously repelled any tribe who attempted to encroach on them. At least one path over which they traveled to wage war was known as the Warrior's Path, and they kept it worn down.

EXPLORERS AND PIONEERS

Trade and War

As mentioned earlier, Hernando de Soto's expedition was the first group of Europeans to see what is now Tennessee. This group, which single-mindedly sought gold, found none and made no effort to exploit any of the territory's other riches. The English arrived in Jamestown, Virginia, in 1607 and gradually began to explore the new world before them, recording their first contact with the Cherokee in 1673. The English were eager to trade with the Cherokee, as were the French, who approached the Indians from the Mississippi River. The traders sought deerskins, which the Indians had in abundance, and in return offered them articles of clothing, metal tools such as hoes and axes, and—most desired by the Indians—guns, ammunition, and whiskey.

As France and England began to wrestle for control of the new land, each saw the advantage of having Indian tribes as allies. The British embarked on an all-out campaign to win over the Cherokee, alternately wooing them with gifts and goods and then seeking to put fear in them with mighty displays of force. Perhaps the most extraordinary gesture during this campaign was a 1730 voyage to London undertaken by six young Cherokee men. These Indians met the king and created quite a stir in England. The voyage so impressed one of them, Attakullakulla, a.k.a. "The Little Carpenter," that he became a friend of the English colonists for life.

The British built Fort Loudoun along the Tennessee River in 1756 in response to Cherokee demands for protection from the French army. This cemented the partnership for a time with the Cherokee and kept the French at bay as well. Unfortunately, relations between the English and their Indian allies deteriorated, with both sides committing massacres and British armies sacking several Cherokee towns. Finally, the war with the French was settled by the Treaty of Paris in 1763. English control of this part of North America was set, and the empire turned its attention elsewhere. In an effort to keep a lid on further troubles with the Cherokee, the British forbade any of their subjects from settling on the western side of the Appalachians. This outraged colonists who were hungry for land, particularly those who had fought for the British during the long war and thought they were due something for their efforts. And from what they heard, the other side of the mountains was very alluring indeed.

The "Long Hunters"

For years a number of individuals, the kind who would later be called "mountain men" in the American West, made their own fur-gathering exploits into Tennessee. Dubbed the "long hunters" because they were gone a long time, they traveled into Middle Tennessee, amassed furs, and either brought them back or built boats and floated all the way to New Orleans. Kasper Mansker, Daniel Boone, Timothy Demonbreun, and other long hunters, whenever (and in some cases, if ever) they returned, brought back tales of rich land and plentiful game. One came back telling of herds of buffalo so thick that he was afraid to get off his horse.

Self-Government

The first recorded settler in what is now Tennessee was William Bean, who built a log cabin in 1768 along the Watauga River in East Tennessee. He and his family were quickly joined by others along the Watauga and other rivers. The Cherokee were persuaded to lease these lands for 10 years, and the residents set about providing themselves with a system of government. The document they drew up, the Watauga "Written Articles of Association," was both an attempt to maintain order so far away from established authorities and a stab at self-governance.

In 1775, Richard Henderson engineered a massive land purchase from the Cherokee at Sycamore Shoals near present-day Elizabethton. The head of the Cherokee, handling their end of the negotiations, was Attakullakulla, who still fondly recalled his trip to England. A dissident faction was led by Dragging Canoe, a warrior who stalked out of the negotiations threatening to make the territory "a dark and bloody ground." A year after the Henderson purchase, the land that is now Tennessee became an official part of North Carolina. The entire area was called Washington County.

Henderson's chief focus was Kentucky, and he hired Daniel Boone to head a group of axemen cutting a road from the Long Island of the Holston River through the Cumberland Gap and into Kentucky. Part of his purchase, however, included the land on which Nashville now stands, and James Robertson resolved to build a settlement there.

The Cumberland Plateau made it all but impossible to go due west, so Robertson divided his party into two groups. Leaving in 1779, 200 men and boys drove livestock and walked 400 miles to Middle Tennessee through Kentucky. Meanwhile, William Donelson led a flotilla of flatboats bearing women and small children on a treacherous four-month voyage down the Holston and Tennessee Rivers and up the Ohio and Cumberland—an incredibly arduous trip.

The place they settled was called Nashborough, and here the settlers drew up the Cumberland Compact, a document of self-government. This compact outlined procedures for recalling an elected official—the first such provisions in U.S. history.

The Revolution

Settlers on the western side of the Appalachians could have sat out the Revolutionary War. They had little contact with the British and certainly enjoyed no government services from them. An arrogant British officer, however, sent word that if the people on the west of the mountains aided the warring colonials he would "lay their country to waste with fire and sword." This was all it took to get the future Tennesseans in the war. They assembled at Sycamore Shoals near present-day Elizabethton, marched over the mountains, and utterly thrashed the British army at the Battle of Kings Mountain.

STATEHOOD

With the creation of the United States, North Carolina offered in 1784 to cede its western lands to the federal government, but the fledgling country was occupied by other matters and didn't immediately accept the offer. This left the future Tennesseans greatly annoyed, for they felt themselves abandoned—without any say in the matter—by North Carolina. To remedy this situation they formed the state of Franklin and sought admission to the Union. Hearing of this, North Carolina rescinded the law that had given the western lands away and refused to recognize Franklin.

Finally North Carolina did give away Tennessee, though not before granting a great deal of its land to veterans of the Revolutionary War. The United States accepted the land, gave it the laborious name "The Territory of the United States South of the River Ohio," and made William Blount governor. He moved his capital to Knoxville in 1792. Four years later Tennessee became the 16th state. Andrew Jackson was one of the people who helped write the state's constitution, a document that Thomas Jefferson pronounced "the least imperfect and most republican."

THE GROWING STATE

Clearing out the Indians

The War of 1812 brought Andrew Jackson, a prominent figure in Tennessee, to national attention. He first gained victories against the Creek who had allied themselves with the British. Based on his successes there, he was put at the head of an army that defeated the British at Mobile, Pensacola, and, most famously, at the Battle of New Orleans. In 1818 he invaded Spanish Florida in pursuit of the Seminoles, and this further contributed to his national reputation.

When Tennessee became a state, three-fourths of the land was still owned by the Cherokee and the Chickasaw. Through treaties and purchases, the Indians slowly gave up their property. All of West Tennessee was opened up when the Chickasaw were persuaded to sell their lands in 1818. The next year Andrew Jackson and other land speculators established the town of Memphis.

The final treaty, signed in 1835, signaled the end of the Cherokee presence in Tennessee. The remaining members of the tribe moved across the state line into Georgia, which began its own efforts to move them west. These culminated in 1838 in the Cherokee's forced removal to Oklahoma. Initiated by federal troops and Georgians, the infamous Trail of Tears marched the Cherokee one last time through Tennessee on their way to their reservation in Oklahoma.

Clearing the Land

The removal of the Indians led to a population surge in Tennessee. Planters with gangs of slaves cleared the hardwood forests and set up enormous plantations in Middle and West Tennessee. The invention of the steamboat made cities such as Nashville and Memphis big trading centers connected by water to New Orleans and the world. The eastern part of the state, however, plagued by rough water on the Tennessee River below Chattanooga and at Muscle Shoals, grew slowly until the coming of the railroad in the 1850s.

Andrew Jackson was elected president in 1828 and again in 1832. He so dominated national politics that he virtually handpicked Martin Van Buren, his successor. David Crockett's exploits became a part of the nation's folklore during those years. He and other Tennesseans, among them Sam Houston, left Tennessee to take part in the birth of Texas.

The Volunteer State

When the Mexican War broke out in 1848—under the administration of Tennessean and president James K. Polk—residents of his state were so eager to fight that they were insulted to learn that Tennessee was asked to send only three regiments of troops. Some decamped for other states to volunteer, others paid for the privilege, and to be fair to everyone the military had to hold a lottery. This willingness to fight led people to call Tennessee "The Volunteer State," a nickname it proudly adopted.

The 1850s marked a time of capital improvements. New roads radiated out of Nashville, railroads connected the larger cities, and the state made important strides in education and agriculture. Democrat Andrew Johnson was elected governor in 1853 and again in 1855.

A State Divided

The final half of the decade marked turbulent times in Tennessee as the clouds of war gathered. East Tennesseans were neutral on the slavery issue, but in Middle and West Tennessee the pro-slavery fires burned hot. Surprisingly enough, Tennesseans of all stripes favored loyalty to the Union—as late as February 9, 1861, they voted to stay in the Union—but this changed drastically with the March 4 inauguration of Abraham Lincoln. Southern states, one by one, began to secede from the Union. Fort Sumter fell on April 13, and Tennessee left the Union June 8.

In the same election that catapulted Lincoln into the White House, Andrew Johnson was voted in as one of Tennessee's U.S. senators on the Democratic ticket. He went to Washington and, alone among the Southern senators, kept his seat even though his state left the Union. He was strongly supported by East Tennesseans, who sent thousands of volunteers to join Lincoln's armies.

THE CIVIL WAR

The War Between the States is covered in greater detail in other places in this book. Tennessee witnessed more battles than any state except Virginia. The state was the center of the "Western theater" of the war, and it was here that U.S. Grant made a name for himself with battles in 1862 at Fort Donelson and Shiloh. Shiloh was the first big battle of the war, where in two days more men died than in the Revolutionary War, the War of 1812, and the Mexican War combined.

Nashville and Memphis were captured by Union troops rather quickly. The new year of 1863 brought the battle of Stones River in Murfreesboro, and Confederate troops under Braxton Bragg were driven through Chattanooga and into Georgia. There they turned on their pursuers at Chickamauga, where the Union army was defeated. U.S. Grant came to the rescue, however, and beat the Confederates at Chattanooga. Tennessee was almost totally in Union hands by this time and stayed so until Sherman took Atlanta. In a desperate move, Southern General John Bell Hood tried to invade Nashville, but his army was badly beaten at the Battle of Franklin and later at Nashville.

Several Tennesseans played prominent historical roles during the war. Lincoln appointed Andrew Johnson the military governor of the state, while Confederate General Nathan Bedford Forrest, a former slave trader who had no military background, became the greatest cavalry commander of the entire war. Admiral David Farragut won important Union victories at New Orleans and Mobile.

RECONSTRUCTION

The assassination of Abraham Lincoln made Andrew Johnson president, and Tennessee became the first Confederate state to formally return to the Union. A radical Republican, William G. Brownlow, became the state's first post-war governor, and his hostility toward former Confederates was ill-concealed. Although Tennessee never went though the formal Reconstruction process, the actions of Brownlow were almost as punitive. The climate created by Brownlow and others led to the 1865 creation of the Ku Klux Klan in Pulaski, and the secret organization quickly spread across the state to the extent that nine counties were placed under martial law because of Klan activities.

Tennessee's experiences under the Republicans caused West and Middle Tennessee to stay Democratic for more than 100 years. East Tennessee remained a stronghold of the Republican Party, but the GOP seldom mustered enough votes to prevail in statewide elections. Andrew Johnson, who had been impeached by the Congress and who had escaped conviction in the Senate by one vote, won election to that body in 1876—the only former president to do so.

THE NEW SOUTH

One of the reasons the South lost the Civil War was a lack of industry, and this led Tennesseans to actively seek Northern capital and factories in the years after the war. The movement to reduce the dependency on agriculture and to embrace the industrialization of the North was called The New South.

Because railroads became more favored than steamboats, Knoxville and Chattanooga were ideally positioned to ship goods north and south, and in the post-Civil War years both of these cities' growth rates outpaced those of Nashville and Memphis. In the 1870s Memphis was hit with a yellow fever epidemic so severe that for a time it gave up its charter and ceased to be a city.

Other parts of Tennessee prospered. Nashville built a replica of the Parthenon in 1896 for an exposition held there. The 1890s also saw the departure of Adolph Ochs from Chattanooga to New York City, where he bought *The New York Times* and brought it up to Tennessee journalistic standards.

The state's population topped two million in 1900, and the turn of the century brought some reforms that afflict travelers today. A 1904 law

---

THE CIVIL WAR ON THE WEB

A wonderful place to begin surfing for information on the Civil War is www.cwc.lsu.edu/civlink.htm. This site connects to sites covering every major battle, as well as amazingly arcane matters. My favorite: "Documentation of Socks for the Army of Tennessee."

Prepare to lose an unbelievable amount of time.

prohibited the sale of alcoholic beverages in towns of fewer than 5,000 souls. Tennessee voted for the 18th "Prohibition" Amendment, thus putting several fine distilleries out of business, but voted to repeal it by passing the 21st Amendment. Rural areas in the state still tend to be "dry," to the mutual satisfaction of bootleggers and Baptists.

GROWING DISTINCTION

The 1920s began with Tennessee's ratification of the 19th Amendment, which gave women the right to vote. Tennessee was the 36th state to do so, fulfilling the constitutional requirement and thus making it law.

During the rest of that decade, Tennessee took on some of the attributes that are simultaneously a source of pride and yet a tad embarrassing.

Nashville got its first radio station in 1922, and in 1925 saw the beginning of the Grand Ole Opry, a show featuring country music bands who were encouraged to perform using names such as "The Possum Hunters" or "The Fruit Jar Drinkers." This cornball image was reinforced the same year the Tennessee legislature passed a law prohibiting the teaching of evolution. The resulting Scopes "monkey trial" showed the world a state seemingly populated by a majority of backwoods yahoos. In a makeshift studio in Bristol in 1927, the voices of Jimmy Rogers and the Carter Family began the country music recording business. Cornball or not, the musical culture of Tennessee found an accepting market that never looked back.

THE DEPRESSION AND WORLD WAR II

The TVA

All the New South speeches and factories in Tennessee cities did little to benefit the rural population, many of whom eked out their existences on poor land whose productivity was hurt by bad farming practices. Only one out of 30 farms, for instance, had electricity as late as 1935. The Great Depression hit these people hard, and their plight attracted the attention of the federal government under the administration of Franklin D. Roosevelt.

The Tennessee Valley Authority was created in 1933 to accomplish several goals—to create cheap electrical power and deliver it to rural areas, to control floods, to develop cheap fertilizers, and to build water treatment and sewage plants. In 1934 Congress established the Great Smoky Mountains National Park. The Civilian Conservation Corps simultaneously constructed trails, dams, and other infrastructure that benefitted parks and small towns. All these projects needed workers and paid wages that improved the lives of urban and country dwellers alike.

The Atomic Age

Tennessee was judged to be safe from German bombers, and the war years brought the Manhattan Project to Oak Ridge, the Arnold Engineering Center outside Tullahoma, large military bases in the state, and big contracts for existing factories. The post-war education benefits enabled more Tennesseans to take high-paying positions running these new operations.

MODERN TIMES

On July 5, 1954, a young man walked into Sun Studios in Memphis and recorded a song called "That's Alright." Elvis Presley revolutionized popular music, and his decision to continue living in Memphis emphasized the state's rich musical talent. The prosperity of the post-war years led more and more tourists to come to the Great Smoky Mountains National Park and other Tennessee attractions. The law that forbade teaching evolution was repealed in 1967.

Tennessee, like the rest of the South, struggled through the Civil Rights movement, but not with the virulence witnessed in other places. National Guard troops were called in to help integrate a high school in Clinton, and in 1964 the first black man since Reconstruction was elected to the statehouse. The worst period in race relations came in 1968, when Martin Luther King Jr. was assassinated as he stood on the balcony of the Lorraine Motel in Memphis.

During the 1970s, Tennessee Valley Authority (TVA) came under attack for the pollution caused by its coal-fired power plants. Activists in East Tennessee and Kentucky also criticized the agency for the strip-mining that supplied coal to the plants. TVA had to cut back on its ambitious

Elvis in concert, 1957

nuclear power building program, which proved too costly for electrical consumers. In 1974 the Big South Fork National River and Recreation Area was authorized by Congress. Elvis Presley died at Graceland on August 16, 1977.

In October of 1980, after intense competition among Tennessee and other states, Nissan selected Smyrna, a Middle Tennessee town south of Nashville, as the site for a truck plant. A few years later GM picked nearby Spring Hill for a Saturn car factory. Knoxville held a world's fair in 1982, the same year that Graceland opened to the public.

The Great Smoky Mountains National Park continues to be the top-drawing national park in the country, and in recent years Tennessee has tried to lure more tourists. The opening of Opryland in Nashville and the rebirth of Beale Street in Memphis have attracted visitors, and when the state celebrated its bicentennial in 1996, many small-town museums were opened or refurbished.

GOVERNMENT

Tennessee's governor serves a four-year term and is allowed to serve two terms in a row before stepping down. The state legislature consists of the Senate and House of Representatives. Tennessee's constitution specifies that the House have 99 members but says only that the Senate cannot exceed one-third of the House membership. The Senate, then, has 33 members.

The Tennessee legislature has a distinguished history; all three of the Tennesseans who became presidents of the country first served there. Present-day senators and representatives, however, have been known to have a good time while producing laws. An aged senator from Knoxville once proposed that some petrified organism be declared the official fossil of Tennessee. A colleague modified the bill so as to designate the senator the state's official fossil. According to another legendary tale, the Tennessee Senate used to begin each day by introducing any noteworthies in the gallery, and at one time these introductions were performed by an extremely nearsighted soul. Some of his colleagues brought in a notorious Nashville stripper, one instantly recognizable to a good number of the senators. She dressed for the occasion, was assigned a fictitious name, and was duly introduced to much applause.

Tennessee is divided into nine congressional districts, and the representatives from them, many of whom have done time in the Tennessee legislature, have so far not carried their prankish traditions to Washington, D.C.

Politics

Tennessee has not sent anyone to the White House since Andrew Johnson, but it has provided individuals who made significant contributions on the national scene, mostly in the U.S. Senate.

Cordell Hull, after service as a congressman and senator, was Franklin Roosevelt's secretary of state from 1933 to 1944, the longest tenure of anyone in that job. Displaying an international interest far beyond his upbringing in Byrdstown, Hull worked to strengthen U.S. ties with Latin America and championed an organization in which nations could come together to work out their problems. Dubbed "the father of the United Nations," he received the Nobel Peace Prize in 1945. Hull enjoyed slipping into a Tennessee vernacular in telling stories about his home state and was said to have thoroughly cussed out the Japanese diplomats who were in his office in 1941 when word came that Pearl Harbor had been attacked.

Estes Kefauver, a Yale-educated Chattanooga lawyer, was elected to the U.S. Senate in 1948 as a Democrat. His appearance and intelligence distinguished him from the James Eastland and Strom Thurmond models of mush-mouthed, filibustering, segregationist caricatures of Southern senators, and his televised hearings on organized crime brought him to the attention of the rest of the country. Kefauver was Adlai Stevenson's running mate in the 1956 election.

Albert Gore Sr., born and raised in Carthage, served as a senator from Tennessee for three terms beginning in 1952. Like Kefauver, he was a progressive Democrat who was not afraid to challenge party politics to do what he thought was right. In the late 1960s he questioned the Vietnam War, and this and other issues made voters think he was too liberal to represent them. Gore lost his seat to a Republican in 1970. He died in late 1998.

Howard Baker Jr., who came from Huntsville, used to tell people that he went to law school at the University of Tennessee because the line was shorter than the one for engineering school. He came from a political family—his father and stepmother served in Congress—and married the daughter of Illinois senator Everett Dirksen. Baker won his Senate seat in 1966 and came to national attention with his statesmanlike behavior as the ranking Republican on the Senate Watergate Committee. He became the minority leader and then the majority leader in the Senate, in which he served three terms. Baker ran for president in 1980 and was considered for a vice-

presidential slot several times, but he never made it. He served as President Reagan's chief of staff, then returned home to Huntsville.

Lamar Alexander, a native of Maryville, became governor in 1978 after donning a plaid shirt, boots, and jeans and walking across the state. The Republican was elected to two terms and then became the president of the University of Tennessee, and then George Bush's secretary of education. Alexander ran for president in 1996 in the same costume that had brought him victory in Tennessee, but it didn't work outside the state.

Albert Gore Jr., vice president during the Clinton administration, spent much of his boyhood in Washington, D.C., where his father, Albert Gore Sr., was a senator. He spent his summers in Carthage, however, and worked for a time for the Nashville *Tennessean.* Elected to Congress in 1977, he served four terms, then became one of Tennessee's senators. Chosen by Bill Clinton as his running mate in 1992, Gore made a name for himself as an advocate for the environment and a champion of the Internet.

ECONOMY

Almost half of the people in Tennessee make their living from manufacturing or service jobs. Tennessee factories produce chemicals, transportation equipment, and industrial machinery. A big component of services is health care, and heading this category is the nation's largest for-profit health care services company, Columbia-HCA in Nashville. Tourism also provides an important proportion of service jobs.

While less than one percent of the dollars earned by Tennesseans come from agricultural jobs, the products of farm work are an important piece of the state's economy. Cotton, soybeans, and corn are the chief crops, while cattle and horses are the leading livestock.

THE PEOPLE

The introduction to *Roy Blount's Book of Southern Humor* has a wonderful couple of sentences that aptly describe Tennessee: ". . . The South was originally settled not predominantly by Anglo-Saxons (as was the North) but by wild, oral, whiskey-loving, unfastidious, tribal, horse-racing, government-hating, WASP-scorned Irish and Welsh and pre-Presbyterian Scots. Who then brought in Africans."

Although there are wondrous things to see in Tennessee, the absolute best reason to go there is the people. As a general rule, they are friendly, polite, and happy to talk to outlanders. They will generally ask where their conversationalist is from, make some favorable comment about that place, and, if possible, ask if the speaker "knows so-and-so's brother there—no, he doesn't live there anymore, he got to thinking he was Elvis and they had to put him in a home." And on from there.

kicking up their heels at the Museum of Appalachia's Tennessee Fall Homecoming

One of the reasons that Tennesseans do so well in the military is that they don't have to be trained to say "sir" and "ma'am." It just comes out automatically. Tennesseans often appear inordinately polite to each other and to strangers, whether they deserve it or not.

TELLING STORIES AND COLORFUL SPEECH

Many Southerners are great storytellers, and Tennesseans are no exception. Stories are woven into everything—directions, accounts of what happened the day before, and answers to the simple query, "How are you?"

It's entirely appropriate that the National Storytelling Festival is in Tennessee, but visitors don't have to pay money to hear tales. Just engage someone in conversation, or sit in with several natives talking among themselves, and the stories will gradually emerge. One would never ask to hear stories, no more than one would go to Manhattan and ask the inhabitants there to be surly.

Some Tennesseans are simultaneously proud of and embarrassed by the way they speak. Natives of The Volunteer State who live in the northern United States often exist in a kind of linguistic schizophrenia, masking their Tennessee accent at work yet cheerfully letting it emerge when in the company of other Tennesseans or fellow Southerners. Part of this feeling comes from derogatory images of Tennessee and the South that come from television and other sources. The *Beverly Hillbillies* and *Petticoat Junction* television shows of the 1960s are to blame, but the all-time worst offender was *Hee Haw*, a show on which the "Fruit Jar Drinkers" of the early Grand Ole Opry would have felt right at home.

Careful listeners who travel across Tennessee can hear differences in the way the natives speak. East Tennesseans speak with an Appalachian twang. Some of their archaic words are said to date to Elizabethan times, but actually come from proper British speech of the 1700s. Examples of this include saying "knowed" for the past tense of

IT'S APPA-LATCH-IA, DAMMIT!

The name of Tennessee's easternmost mountains and the region in which they occur is frequently mispronounced as "AppaLAYchia." It should be said "AppaLATCHia," and those who say otherwise immediately mark themselves as outlanders and persons on whom natives can sharpen their fabrication skills.

"know" or leaving the "g" off "-ing" and thus saying "fishin'" or "huntin'." Moving across the state, particularly entering West Tennessee, visitors will hear speech that more resembles the Southern accent of the Deep South.

Tennesseans can be sensitive about their accents and colorful way of speaking. Perhaps the quickest way to make Southern hospitality vanish is to laugh at the way someone from Tennessee speaks.

THE BUCKLE ON THE BIBLE BELT

Tennesseans will seldom ask where a person went to college, as New Englanders do, although they may inquire where he or she goes to church. This is not done as any sort of probing, personal inquisition, but as a means of seeking connection with that person.

Religion has a powerful influence on Tennessee, one often expressed in music. Many Tennesseans who wound up shouting the blues or fronting a rock band cut their musical teeth in church. Elvis would warm up in his all-night recording sessions by singing gospel harmony, and Tina Turner had a spot in her church choir. Sun Studio's Sam Philips was once recorded arguing theology with Jerry Lee Lewis between musical takes.

Tennessee is indeed the buckle on the Bible Belt, and travelers will notice this in several ways. The farther one gets from the big cities, the more museums and restaurants will tend to be closed on Sunday. Bed-and-breakfast owners may matter-of-factly prohibit alcohol in their establishments, and the tonier restaurants in the boondocks have to pretend they are private clubs to permit legal drinking.

From time to time, some pontificator announces that the United States is becoming a dreary, homogenous place where everyone speaks the same way and listens to the same things. Those individuals should turn on a radio in Tennessee to the AM band on Sunday morning. In almost any part of the state, a twist on the knob will bring forth an out-of-breath preacher pouring it on, perhaps punctuating his sentences with a rhythmic "Hah!" The truly adventurous can see this sort of thing in the flesh by stopping off on Sunday morning at small churches—anything with "Holiness" or "Pentecostal" on the sign will provide.

The other side of all this religion in Tennessee is what might be called the joy of sin. It's the conspiratorial pouring of bourbon into a Coke at a University of Tennessee football game, the sidelong glance as one steps from the heat of the day into the darkened coolness of a Memphis bar, or going straight from a lecture on cholesterol to a barbecue place and blissfully biting into a Pig Pile sandwich.

The conniptions and carryings-on of the faithful, whether of the televised or more local variety, are almost always entertaining. One married Tennessee preacher, unfamiliar with the new telephone system his church installed, made a covert call to his girlfriend, unaware that his sweet nothings were being broadcast over the public address system, to the intense interest of the youth group meeting in the building. Southern Baptists, who for decades shielded their youth groups and college students from the wickedness of fox-trots or similar cheek-to-cheek activities, prompted the following joke, guaranteed to be appreciated all over the state.

Why don't Baptists make love standing up?

Somebody might see 'em and think they're dancing.

FINDING YOUR NOTCH ON THE BIBLE BELT

Going to Tennessee and not going to church is like going to Ireland and never entering a pub. To find the denomination of your choice, go on the Internet to www.churchsurf.com. At the last electronic count, Nashville led Memphis in number of denominations available, 47-35.

ON THE ROAD
OUTDOOR RECREATION

Tennessee has so many opportunities for recreation that the visitor can take years sampling them. The Great Smoky Mountains National Park offers beautiful mountain ranges, superb backcountry camping, and trout fishing. The Big South Fork National River and Recreation Area, while less spectacular than the Smokies, is a lot less crowded and has wonderful canyons, hiking, and whitewater.

The 49 state parks offer a wide variety of activities, from hiking and bicycling to birding and backcountry camping. Seven of them have lodges, and even more offer cabins and camping. Many of the rooms—particularly the cabins—are booked as much as a year in advance.

Fishing

Tennessee offers a wide variety of fishing experiences—fly-fishing for trout in the wilderness of the Smokies, sitting on the bank of a river, or taking a boat onto one of the state's many lakes. The fish themselves vary from sparkling mountain rainbow trout to Tennessee River catfish three or four feet long.

Guide services are available near the Smokies, and bait shops provide good advice, the right

---

WHEN TO SEE THE FALL FOLIAGE

The Great Smokies contain over 100 species of trees whose leaves erupt into beautiful colors in the fall. As a general rule, the leaves begin changing at the highest elevations in September, then move down the mountainsides and reach a crescendo during the last three weeks in October and into November.

Several factors figure into this annual show, however, such as temperature and amount of rainfall, so predicting the peak of the fall foliage is more of an art than a science. Call the Sugarlands Visitor Center at the National Park at (423) 436-1291 for accurate information.

PLAYING BY THE RULES

Fishing Licenses

Tennessee requires that all anglers over age 13 have a license to fish. An "all-species" out-of-state fishing license costs $20.50 for three days, $30.50 for 10 days, and $51 for the year. The hunting and fishing year, for license purposes, begins March 1.

Those from out of state who wish to fish for anything but trout pay less—$10.50 for three days, $15.50 for 10 days, and $26 for the year. With both kinds of licenses, the three-day and 10-day periods are consecutive days.

Anglers ages 13-15 are eligible for a junior hunting and fishing license, which costs $6 annually.

Licenses are available at most bait shops, marinas, and hardware stores. For complete fishing regulations, call the Tennessee Wildlife Resources Agency at (615) 781-6500.

Hunting Licenses

Anyone born after January 1, 1969, wishing to hunt in Tennessee must show proof that he or she has completed a hunter safety course. A seven-day small game and waterfowl hunting license for out-of-state residents costs $30.50. An annual one costs $56. Hunters ages 13-15 can buy an annual junior hunting and fishing license for $6.

An "all-game" license costs out-of-state residents $105.50 for seven days and $156 annually. The junior license does not apply for "all-game" licenses; hunters of any age must buy the same one.

With both kinds of licenses, the seven-day periods are consecutive days. Licenses are sold at most gun shops and hardware stores. For complete information on hunting regulations, call the Tennessee Wildlife Resources Agency at (615) 781-6500.

---

bait, and—occasionally—rental equipment. The major TVA lakes have marinas that rent boats, and along the Tennessee River some resorts cater exclusively to anglers. Reelfoot Lake, in the state's northwest corner, has so many fish that commercial fisheries operate there.

Bicycling

As a general rule, the farther west one goes in Tennessee, the easier the bike riding gets. East Tennessee's mountains and hills can provide a workout, then reward the rider with a thrilling downhill descent. Middle Tennessee, with its rolling hills, is perhaps the best compromise. Many cyclists take advantage of the Natchez Trace Parkway for long hauls. Bicycles are a wonderful way to tour Civil War battlefields such as Shiloh or Chickamauga. Of Tennessee's large cities, Memphis is the best suited for two-wheelers. Take a good lock.

In some rural places, drivers act surprised to see bikes. If a vehicle refuses to pass, it's a good idea to pull over and let it go by. When riding in the country—particularly in hilly terrain—putting a tall

The rivers of East Tennessee can challenge even the most experienced whitewater fans.

MURRAY LEE, COURTESY TENNESSEE TOURIST DEVELOPMENT

TENNESSEE FESTIVALS

The following thumbnail sketches illustrate the wide variety of festivals celebrated by the people of Tennessee. More details—dates, phone numbers, and costs—are described under the appropriate towns.

Winter
Elvis Presley's Birthday Tribute honors the King January 6-8 at Graceland in Memphis.

Memphis's **Beale Street Zydeco Fest** in February features Louisiana's liveliest music.

Grand Junction's **National Field Trials** test canines in mid-February, a time when dog fanciers come from all over to watch bird dogs work. Most of them watch from "the gallery"—hundreds of people follow the action on horseback.

Spring
Paris hosts the **World's Biggest Fish Fry** during the last full week in April, when approximately 100,000 people come to town to consume more than 13,000 pounds of fish. Between meals, they watch a parade, go to a rodeo, listen to music, attend the "Down & Dirty Dirt Dance," see crafts shows, and attend a beauty pageant.

The **Ramp Festival,** held on the first Sunday in May in Cosby, celebrates the onionlike plant with music, crafts, good food, and a beauty pageant.

Summer
Nashville's **International Country Music Fan Fair** in June lets fans press the flesh with some of the biggest names in country music. It lasts for a week and includes concerts, photo and autograph opportunities, and a fiddling competition.

Uncle Dave Macon Days the second week in July brings more than 30,000 people together in Murfreesboro for three days of old-time music, dance, and arts and crafts competitions, along with a bike race, good food, and children's activities.

Gatlinburg's **Craftsmen's Fairs,** held in July and October, bring 150 high-quality craftspeople to this resort town.

The **Folk Medicine Festival** in Red Boiling Springs in late July brings together old hippies and those versed in herbs, alternative medicine, and new approaches to healthy living. Music, storytelling, country dancing, and Cherokee dancers round out the offerings.

The **Rugby Pilgrimage** the first week in August celebrates the days of old by opening private homes which were built during the colony's heyday. Admission is charged.

The second week in August brings to Memphis **Elvis Week,** a.k.a. "Death Week," which culminates on the date Elvis died—August 16 (in 1977). Elvis movies, impersonators, and a candlelight vigil mark the King's passing.

The **Memphis Blues Festival,** on the second Saturday in August, brings hot licks to a hot summer night on the banks of the Mississippi. Bands play from several stages.

Shelbyville's **Tennessee Walking Horse National Celebration** honors Tennessee's famous breed on the 10 days preceding the Saturday night of Labor Day Weekend. The events culminate in the selection of the year's Grand Champion Tennessee Walking Horse.

Fall
The **Museum of Appalachia Tennessee Fall Homecoming,** held for four days in October outside Norris, brings together big names in bluegrass and traditional music, crafts demonstrations, good food, and a whole bunch of fine folks.

Jonesborough's **National Storytelling Festival** is always held on the first weekend in October and fills the town with tall tales, ghost stories, "sacred telling," and the "Swappin' Ground." Reservations are a good idea.

flag on the bike is not a bad idea. Even worse, unleashed dogs often see cyclists as wheeled invaders who must be chased. Teeth bared, the dogs charge out onto the road—usually just as the cyclist has topped a hill. Sometimes dog owners, appreciative of the ensuing entertainment, sit on the porch and enjoy the race.

Whitewater

The 1996 Summer Olympics kayaking competition was held on the Ocoee River on the Tennessee/Georgia border. Whitewater rafting is concentrated on the eastern end of the state on the following rivers: Nolichucky, Big Pigeon, Little Pigeon, Big South Fork, Clinch, Obed, Hiwassee, French Broad, Watauga, Sequatchie, and Ocoee.

The experience that one has on these rivers can vary tremendously depending on the amount of water flowing at any given time. Many of the professional whitewater outfits have toll-free telephone numbers and can give rafters an idea of what to expect.

A word to the wise: Some of this water is very cold, particularly in the spring. If an outfitter recommends wetsuits or rain gear, don't be cheap and turn it down. Being wet and cold is never much fun, particularly for children.

Skiing

Tennessee gets a fair amount of snow, but not enough to have very good skiing. For that, travelers should go to the mountains of North Carolina or, better yet, fly to Colorado.

ARTS AND ENTERTAINMENT

MUSIC

From the high tenor of bluegrass in the east and the mainstream country of Nashville to Memphis blues, rock, and gospel, Tennessee has to be the most musical state in the country.

Visitors to Tennessee should promise themselves to attend at least one live musical performance. An individual can have the finest sound system in the world, but hearing and seeing live performers is unlike anything else. In the best concerts, performers and the audience build on each other's energy until the event reaches wonderfully joyous peaks.

The venues for hearing live music in Tennessee are as varied as the music itself. These range from slick productions—the Grand Ole Opry in Nashville and the theaters around the Smokies— to much more downhome offerings such as those of the Bell Witch Opry over in Adams. Tennessee also has a strong tradition of sacred

music, and church choirs and gospel concerts should be included on visitors' itineraries as well.

CRAFTS

Handmade items have been cherished in Tennessee since pioneer days. Here are some places noted for the high quality of their crafts.

The town of **Woodbury** has a collection of craftspeople living in and around town who make baskets, chairs, and quilts. A local arts center displays the work and gives directions to the homes of people who make things.

The **Great Smoky Arts and Crafts Community,** east of Gatlinburg on roads that wind through the hills, consists of people who produce brooms, woodcarvings, paintings, pottery, and photographs.

Newberry and Sons Chairs are fifth-generation chairmakers in the Middle Tennessee community of Willette. They fashion chairs of oak, walnut, and cherry wood and put woven hickory bark bottoms and backs on some of them.

The **Arrowmont Shop** in Gatlinburg sells high-quality crafts from members of the Southern Highland Craft Guild.

Boones Creek Potter's Gallery, between Kingsport and Johnson City, carries pottery, sculpture, and stained and blown glass, as well as works in wood and iron.

HOW TO BEHAVE AT A MUSICAL GATHERING

By Patsy Weiler

In Tennessee, traditional music festivals pop up across the state like roadside weeds after a rain. Primarily in the summer and fall months, these local events celebrate everything from catfish to cotton.

Very few take place without showcasing the musical heritage of the community where they are held. Most tunes you'll hear either feature the faster tempo bluegrass style of songs or the calmer, gentler sound of old-time mountain melodies.

How do you tell the difference? Watch the banjo player's hand. Lots of plastic or metal picks on his or her fingers usually means bluegrass. An old-time music performer normally doesn't use picks and plays in a downward strumming motion.

When you're visiting one of these fun-filled festivals, the most important thing to do is have a good time and enjoy yourself. Leave the technical differences to the musicians. But if you've brought your instrument along, or come laden with enough cameras and recorders to shoot a documentary, a few cultural hints might come in handy before you cross the line of observer to participant. When in doubt on what to do, the most obvious (but greatly overlooked) solution is to politely ask. Most folks will tell you what is acceptable.

Keep in mind if an artist or group has recordings for sale, they might not smile about having their performance taped. A lot depends on whether you're pointing your video camera or tape player toward a group of friends who gather to play music for fun or on a group of professionals who depends on their sales to eat.

You'll hear good music from most stages, but the really good stuff takes place under shade trees, on porches, or tucked inside a cool building. This is where the local folks gather. Sometimes you may have to hunt a little, but it is worth the effort. These clusters of homegrown talent are where you can experience the true taste of a community.

Want to hear your favorite song? No matter how much you love *Blue Moon of Kentucky,* don't shout requests to someone on stage. Instead, find a group of casual musicians playing off stage. If they know the song you want to hear, most will be happy to oblige.

Want to join in a jam? Don't start playing without being asked. Be patient. Get out your instrument, be in tune, look eager, pay attention, and before long someone will invite you to join in the merriment.

Requests Most Likely to Cause a Bluegrass or Old-Time Player to Commit Murder

The scene: a group of old-time musicians at, say, the Museum of Appalachia, who are playing traditional music. They finish an instrumental number and, amid the applause, some guy wearing a University of Alabama T-shirt bellows out "Play 'Bonnie and Clyde!'" The observer watching the musicians may see a certain gritting of the teeth.

Some songs have been played so often that musicians would like to put a moratorium on them. Here is a list of songs to NOT to yell out at a concert or jam session. This doesn't mean they are bad songs; they're simply ones that have been overdone. In no particular order, avoid:

"Dueling Banjos"—popularized by the movie *Deliverance*

"Rocky Top"—the University of Tennessee band has played this one to death.

"Foggy Mountain Breakdown"—the song from *Bonnie and Clyde.*

"The Ballad of Jed Clampett"—the theme to TV's *The Beverly Hillbillies.*

"The Orange Blossom Special"—often pronounced "Arnge Blossom Special,"—a show-off fast fiddle piece.

ACCOMMODATIONS AND FOOD

WHERE TO STAY

In addition to listing approximate rates for most lodgings, all are rated by price using Moon's classification system. Rooms rated "Budget" are under $35; "Inexpensive" rooms are $35-60; "Moderate" category rooms cost $60-85; "Expensive" means rates of $85-110; "Premium" rooms go for $110-150; and a "Luxury" rating means rooms cost over $150. All ratings are based on high-season, double-occupancy prices, but room rates may possibly go higher during special events.

Bed and Breakfasts and Inns

The large number of fine old homes and growing numbers of upscale tourists have led to an explosion of bed and breakfasts in Tennessee. Some are bona fide inns, while others consist of a spare bedroom in a large house. Many welcome families and pets, while others forbid children, animals, drinking, and smoking. It's always a good idea to call ahead.

The biggest change in bed and breakfasts since this book first came out is the explosion of B&B information on the Web. Now you can use the Internet to examine the interior and exterior of a particular inn and check out three or four places in a matter of minutes. Some B&B owners report that they get 80% of their new business from Web users. One of the services that gets used a lot is **Bed & Breakfast Inns Online,** at www.bbonline.com/tn/index.

Several services can make it easier to choose an inn or B & B. The **Tennessee Bed & Breakfast Innkeepers Association,** 5431 Mountain View Rd., Ste. 150, Antioch, TN 37013, tel. (800) 820-8144, includes about 70 member inns across the state. Find it online at www.bbonline.com/tbbia/index.

If visitors belong to the horsey set, this association can point to places that come with private baths and stables: **Tennessee Equestrian Bed & Breakfast Association,** 5436 Leipers Creek Rd., Franklin, TN 37064, tel. (615) 791-0333, Internet: www.bbonline.com/tn/equestrian.

Travelers who can't bear to leave their Schnauzer at home can check out www.indogswetrust.com for a list of Tennessee lodging establishments that welcome four-legged guests.

Motorists who anticipate cruising down the Natchez Trace can call the **Natchez Trace Bed & Breakfast Reservation Service,** P.O. Box 193, Hampshire, TN 3846, tel. (800) 377-2770.

The Chains

As in most of America, motels in Tennessee cluster near each other at interstate highway exits as if seeking protection from the countryside. The usual chains—Holiday Inn, Motel 6, Hampton Inn, Days Inn, Comfort Inn, etc.—lie across the state, while the more upscale hotel chains—Hilton, Hyatt, Radisson, and Marriott—are well represented in the major cities. Away from the interstates, small towns have motels that are less homogenous and harder to classify. Some are just fine and others make the 40-mile drive back to the interstate well worth it.

Travelers who prefer to stay in one of the ubiquitous national chains can call their reservation services toll-free. The services will quote prices, book rooms, and offer advice about what might be open in the next town on the visitor's itinerary. Prices vary depending on whether the guest is a member of an automobile club, is a senior citizen, or qualifies for corporate rates; on length of stay and whether it's a weekend or holiday; and on seasonal events. The chains and their toll-free reservation numbers:

Best Western, tel. (800) 528-1234
Budgetel Inn, tel. (800) 428-3438
Comfort Inn, tel. (800) 221-2222
Days Inn, tel. (800) 329-7466
Econo Lodge, tel. (800) 55-ECONO (32666)
Fairfield Inn, tel. (800) 228-2800
Family Inns of America, tel. (800) 251-9752
Hampton Inn, tel. (800) 426-7866
Hilton Hotels, tel. (800) 445-8667
Holiday Inn, tel. (800) 465-4329
Howard Johnson Lodge, tel. (800) 654-2000
Hyatt Hotels, tel. (800) 233-1234
Knight's Inn, tel. (800) 424-4777
La Quinta Motor Inn, tel. (800) 531-5900

Marriott Hotels and Resorts, tel. (800) 321-2211
Quality Inn, tel. (800) 228-5151
Radisson Hotels, tel. (800) 333-3333
Ramada Inn, tel. (800) 272-6232
Red Roof Inn, tel. (800) 843-7663
Scottish Inns, tel. (800) 251-1962
Super 8 Motel, tel. (800) 800-8000
Sleep Inn, tel. (800) 62-SLEEP (75337)
Sheraton Hotels, tel. (800) 325-3535

FOOD AND DRINK

Country Cooking

The recent visitor to Tennessee was aghast. "What is the matter with these people?" she railed. "Haven't they heard of cholesterol and heart disease and all these problems? Why do they continue to eat like that?"

She was referring to Southern cooking, items such as fried chicken, fried catfish, ribs, country ham, hushpuppies, biscuits served with butter and preserves, okra, pinto beans, green beans or collard greens cooked with salt pork, and fried pies. (She probably would have done back flips at the thought of having to sample a fried baloney and egg biscuit or chocolate gravy at Forty Three and More outside of Middle Tennessee's Loretto.)

This sort of food, referred to throughout this book as "country cooking," utterly dominates the culinary landscape in Tennessee. From country clubs to small-town eateries, Southern cooking has withstood attacks from dieticians, heart specialists, vegetarians, and other well-meaning folks who just don't understand: Southern cooking persists because it tastes so good. When confronted with the healthiness or unhealthiness of the food, a Tennessean might reply with a variant of the following excuse: "Now listen here. My (insert name of beloved, venerable relative) ate like that all her life and lived to be 97. And she dipped snuff as well. I'm going to eat what I want, and even if it cuts off a few years, it'll be worth it. I'll die happy."

It's hard to argue with that.

In recent years, however, a number of restaurants that emphasize lighter fare have opened in Tennessee and enjoy great success. These have been duly noted herein along with every possible barbecue shack. Someone once said that a truly good barbecue place should have

---

THINGS TO EAT

Country Ham can be served at any meal but is particularly good for breakfast. It is a ham that has been rubbed with salt and cured for a year or so in a smokehouse. Akin to prosciutto, it has a distinctive salty taste.

Catfish is served most frequently in West Tennessee and is almost always dipped in batter and deep-fried. Cognoscenti ask for either fillets or "fiddlers"—whole fish minus the heads.

Grits are perhaps the most misunderstood Southern dish. Grits—there is no such thing as a grit—are ground corn boiled in water until soft. The only difference between cornmeal and grits is the size of the pieces of cracked corn. Eaten by themselves, grits taste dull. The proper way to eat them is with butter, pieces of country ham, the runny yolk of fried eggs, or gravy. Then they are sublime.

Barbecue has spawned entire books. Suffice to say that barbecue is almost always pork in Tennessee, and it has been cooked for a long time over low heat. A pulled pork sandwich contains meat so tender that it can be pulled by hand off the bone. The meat is good in and of itself but can be adorned with barbecue sauces of varying heat. Ribs are the top of the line.

---

burned down at least once in the past three years, and some of these have done just that.

Sweet Tea and Alcohol

Religious fundamentalists in Tennessee believe that Jesus and the disciples drank iced tea—sweetened—at The Last Supper. From Mountain City to Memphis, iced tea is served every day of the year at lunch and dinner, even if a blizzard is raging outside. Moreover, in most places the tea will come already sweetened—sometimes to the extent that it is called 30-weight tea in reference to motor oil viscosity.

When it comes to alcoholic beverages, however, tastes aren't so uniform. In the bigger cities, microbreweries proudly exist along with restaurants whose bartenders are knowledgeable about single malt scotches. The farther one goes into the hinterlands, however, the more complicated it gets. Some counties and towns ban alcoholic beverages entirely. Others permit consumption in "private clubs," which, while including bona fide watering holes of such organizations as the Moose or the Benevolent and Protective Order of Elks, also encompass otherwise normal-looking restaurants. To become a member of such clubs, one usually pay a nominal fee—perhaps $5—that may be refunded upon ordering a meal costing more than that. Visitors should ask how each place operates. It's a strange system, but it seems to work.

Some restaurants cannot legally sell alcoholic beverages, but they can serve ones that cus-tomers bring in themselves. This practice is referred to as "brown-bagging." One brings the bottle in a bag—brown or otherwise, discreetly hands it to the waiter, and awaits the steady hand to pour it in the glass.

Visitors should never assume they can bring alcoholic beverages into a restaurant. If visitors must have a chardonnay with their catfish and hushpuppies, they should ask before showing up and pulling out the bottle. Some establishments—including bed and breakfasts—forbid alcohol. This book has tried to indicate which ones do so.

PRACTICALITIES

TRANSPORTATION

Major Airports
The largest airports in Tennessee, to no surprise, are the ones serving the larger cities: Chattanooga, Knoxville, Memphis, and Nashville. The latter two have international airports. Nashville usually has the lowest fares into Tennessee, but travelers on a budget should also consider flying to Atlanta, which is only 115 miles from Chattanooga or 243 miles from Nashville. Sometimes the reduction in airline fare can more than pay for the additional miles of driving. Travelers headed for the eastern part of the state might consider flying into Charlotte, North Carolina, which is 241 miles from Knoxville.

Bus Service
Greyhound Lines, Inc. offers bus service to more than 20 cities and towns in Tennessee, mostly those along the interstate highways that cross the state. The exception is along Hwys. 51 and 45 in West Tennessee. Travelers can connect to the state from other American cities. To learn about schedules, routes, and prices, call (800) 231-2222 or visit www.greyhound.com.

Main Highways
Tennessee is a long and lean state, and the only interstate highway that runs the length is I-40, which goes from the Great Smoky Mountains National Park past Memphis. I-81 connects to I-40 and heads northeast to exit the state at Bristol. Interstates 65 and 24 make a large "X" at Nashville, and I-75 winds down from Kentucky and then goes toward Knoxville and Chattanooga, whereupon, like Union General Sherman, it heads for Atlanta.

Travelers who have Internet access should check out www.mapsonus.com, a service that will construct a map to any address or help you find a hard-to-locate destination. Or there's www.expediamaps.com or www.mapquest.com.

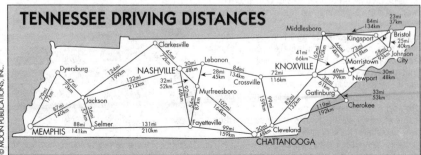

© MOON PUBLICATIONS, INC.

Firearms, Alcohol, and Cigarettes

Strictly speaking, travelers who carry firearms and who want to obey the law should notify every state they enter that they possess weapons. In practice, few people do this in Tennessee, but they *should* follow these guidelines. Store the firearm—unloaded—in a locked area away from passengers. Store the ammunition separately. Most of the people who get in trouble for possessing a gun get pulled over for a traffic violation—speeding, for instance—and the officer happens to see the gun.

Like all states, Tennessee taxes alcoholic beverages, and for this reason permits travelers to bring no such beverages into the state. Visitors who keep their case of Georgia muscadine wine out of sight in the trunk will have no problems unless they do something that might give a law enforcement officer a reason to search the car. Travelers who lash their case of Jim Beam bourbon onto the back of their motorcycles, however, can expect to have their whiskey confiscated.

Tennessee sits beside North Carolina, where most of the cigarettes in the country are manufactured and sold at relatively low prices. Travelers coming into Tennessee from North Carolina or any state may bring two cartons of cigarettes per person with them. These cannot be sold to anyone else in the state.

HEALTH AND SAFETY

Poisonous Plants

Tennessee contains several plants, including mushrooms, that can cause problems if eaten. Visitors who go around eating unknown plants in strange places are an example of Darwinism at work, and the plants to avoid ingesting will not be listed here.

Travelers may unknowingly come in contact with Tennessee's three plants that can cause skin irritation. **Poison ivy,** the most prevalent, is a vine that grows on the ground and climbs up trees. Its shiny leaves grow in clusters of three, and the oil on the leaves can cause skin irritation and itching. **Poison oak** and **poison sumac** can have the same effects. It takes about 20 minutes from the time of contact for the chemicals in these plants to enter the skin. People who think they have touched one should wash the affected area with soap and

water and also change clothes. If itching begins, calamine lotion may offer relief.

Problem-Causing Animals and Insects

Probably the unhealthiest thing one can do in Tennessee is eat too much barbecue and not enough salads, but there are a few natural denizens that the traveler should keep in mind.

Rabies occurs in wild animals as well as dogs and cats. Avoid any animal acting erratically, particularly a wild one. It is not normal, for instance, for raccoons or foxes to approach humans, and such behavior should be regarded with great suspicion.

Tennessee has several kinds of poisonous **snakes,** but most visitors will never encounter any of them. Timber rattlesnakes and eastern diamondback rattlesnakes sometimes give a warning rattle, which sounds more like a buzzing noise. Copperheads, which live all over the state, are brown-mottled snakes that tend to live around rural outbuildings as well as the backcountry. Water moccasins, a.k.a. cottonmouths, live in western Tennessee in creeks, rivers, swamps, and lakes.

The basic precaution for snakes is simple—visitors should carefully watch where they put their feet and hands. If they do see a snake, they should leave it alone. Like any wild animals, snakes will bite if pursued and cornered. Anyone who gets bitten should not attempt the longtime remedy of cutting into the afflicted member and sucking out the poison. The best thing is to stay calm and head for the nearest hospital.

Visitors are far more likely to become victims of ticks and chiggers. **Ticks** lurk on branches of trees or other plants and hitch a ride on passing animals or humans. Once aboard, they seek

Eastern diamondback rattlers sometimes buzz to signal their intentions.

a place to attach themselves and suck their host's blood. A once-a-day head-to-toe check can usually find any ticks, which should be removed with tweezers.

Chiggers are more nefarious. These almost invisible insect larvae burrow into the skin, raising a bump that itches profusely. For some reason, chiggers seem to always lurk in blackberry patches. Sufferers of acute chigger attacks may consider going after the little beasts with an ice pick, but a better remedy is commercial itch relievers. Prevention, as always, is the best cure, and the usual insect repellents work on chiggers as well.

Tennessee has two poisonous **spiders**—the brown recluse and the black widow. As with snakes, the vast majority of visitors have nothing to fear from these spiders, which inhabit basements and other dark places around buildings—including outhouses. Black widows are said to particularly like the areas around the seat of such places, so users would do well not to spend any more time than necessary there.

MONEY AND TAXES

Automatic Teller Machines (ATMs) are spreading through Tennessee as thoroughly as through any other state. Visitors should check their cash supply before venturing into the more remote areas, however, where ATMs might be scarce.

Tennessee has never seen the wisdom of an income tax, and thus relies on a very high sales tax of 6.5%. Counties and cities add to this tax, pushing it close to 10% in some places. Visitors from out of state who wish to buy things should ask if the item can be ordered later by phone, because items shipped out of Tennessee are not charged the sales tax. Depending on the purchase, the tax savings will more than pay for the shipping and leave the traveler free of one more package.

TELEPHONE NUMBERS

American telephone numbers have 10 numbers. The first three are the area code and do not have to be dialed if the dialer is within the area. For example, if you're standing in the bus station in Nashville and calling Ernest Tubb's Record Shop's Midnight Jamboree, which is in Nashville, you do not have to dial the (615) of the phone number, which is (615) 885-0028. If, however, you're calling Ernest Tubb's from Graceland in Memphis, the (615) area code is necessary.

TOURIST INFORMATION

Tennessee has a variety of organizations promoting tourism throughout the state. Although every effort has been made here to provide a source of local information for every town in the state, sometimes these regional organizations prove to be very helpful. Some areas of the state have overlapping associations, while some parts of the state have none at all. The **Tennessee Department of Tourist Development,** tel. (615) 741-2158, provides information about the entire state.

East
Chattanooga Area Convention & Visitor's Bureau, tel. (423) 756-8687 or (800) 322-3344

East Tennessee Heritage and Community Tourism Development, Knoxville, tel. (423) 594-5500

Knoxville Convention and Tourist Bureau, tel. (423) 523-7263

Middle East Tennessee Tourism Council, Knoxville, tel.(423) 584-8553

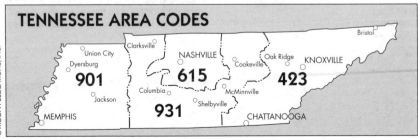

TENNESSEE AREA CODES

Bristol

Union City
Clarksville
NASHVILLE
Oak Ridge
KNOXVILLE
Dyersburg
Cookeville

901
615
423

Jackson
Columbia
McMinnville

MEMPHIS
931
Shelbyville
CHATTANOOGA

Northeast Tennessee Tourism Association, Jonesborough, tel. (800) 468-6882, ext. 25, or (423) 753-4188

Southeast Tennessee Tourism Association, Chattanooga, tel. (423) 756-8687

Tennessee Overhill Experience, Etowah, tel. (423) 263-7232

Middle

Back Roads Heritage Association, Wartrace, tel. (615) 389-6131

Cumberland Mountains/Lakeland Travel Development Association, Cookeville, tel. (615) 520-1088

Greater Nashville Regional Tourism Council, tel. (615) 862-8828

Middle Tennessee Heritage and Community Tourism Development, Nashville, tel. (615) 741-9045

Nashville Convention & Visitors Bureau, tel. (615) 259-4700

Tennessee Natchez Trace Corridor Association, Franklin, tel. (615) 794-5555

West

Give Me Memphis Hotline, tel. (901) 681-1111 or (800) 820-3035

Jackson/Madison County Convention and Visitors Bureau, tel. (800) 498-4748 or (901) 425-8333

Memphis Visitors Information Center, tel. (901) 543-5333 or (800) 447-8278

Memphis Delta Tourism Organization, tel. (901) 543-5333

Northwest Tennessee Tourism Organization, Martin, tel. (901) 587-4215

Tourism Association of Southwest Tennessee, Wildersville, tel. (901) 968-6026

West Tennessee Heritage and Community Development, Jackson, tel. (901) 426-0888

Web Sites

Chattanooga: http://dir.yahoo.com/Regional/U_S__States/Tennessee/Cities/Chattanooga/Entertainment_and_Arts/.

Knoxville: http://dir.yahoo.com/Regional/U_S__States/Tennessee/Cities/Knoxville/Entertainment_and_Arts/.

Memphis: www.memphistravel.com/

Nashville: Nashville Music City Vacation Guide, nashville.musiccityusa.com/tour

One site serves as a collection point for a wide variety of Nashville Web sites. Go to yeehaw. Nashville.net/

PHOTOGRAPHY

The man and woman in the Great Smoky Mountains National Park wanted a great picture to show the folks back home. She held the camera while he fed marshmallows to a black bear that had come out of the forest. When she had enough shots, he tried to wrap up the marshmallows and return to the car. The hungry bear had other ideas, however, and the next time the man appeared in a photographer's viewfinder he was in the emergency room.

Most residents of Tennessee, ursine or otherwise, do not object to having their pictures taken, if the photographer displays good manners and good sense. Members of the Amish villages in the middle of the state, however, do not appreciate being photographed, and visitors should respect those groups' wishes.

TIME

The eastern and central time zone boundary cuts through Tennessee. Generally, it's fairly safe to assume that East Tennessee is in the eastern time zone and everything else is in central time. When in the vicinity of Crossville and Rugby and towns that are close to the line, it's a good idea to confirm under which time zone a particular place operates. Tennessee observes daylight saving time.

THE FIRST FRONTIER

INTRODUCTION

If there's any part of Tennessee where one can come close to seeing the same views and vistas that the Indians enjoyed, this is it. The very mountains that held back settlers from the east resisted change, encouraging people to move farther west.

This was the country's first frontier, and the brave souls who left civilization and made their way across the Appalachians clearly understood that they were on their own. They lived beyond the bounds of government, beyond protection from the Indians, and beyond the fledgling commerce of the colonies.

What they found was a land rich in game, soil, and timber. A family willing to work could have a good life on the west side of the mountains. Individually, they learned to be self-reliant. Together, they developed a fierce independence whose intensity would utterly surprise the British in the Revolutionary War.

As the more western parts of Tennessee were settled, the towns and villages of the First Frontier became routes that connected points west

with the rest of the country. Presidents and other national leaders traveled through Rogersville, Kingsport, Jonesborough, and Greeneville; several of the places in which they ate and slept are still there.

Visitors to the First Frontier will hear a twangy accent that differs from voices farther south and west. To some inhabitants, a word pronounced "flare" can mean a burning device that warns motorists of dangers ahead, the blossoming part of a plant, and the chief ingredient of bread.

When cars are backed up in the Great Smoky Mountains National Park, when the trails are clogged, and the air in Gatlinburg smells of fresh exhaust, the mountains here are seldom crowded.

HISTORY

West of the Mountains
As the American colonies grew in the 1700s, a pattern emerged: Settlers moved too far west,

FIRST FRONTIER

got into trouble with the Indians, and then appealed to the British army for help. Hoping to hold down expenses, King George III in 1763 ordered all settlers to come back and stay on the eastern side of the Appalachian Mountains.

Few paid any attention to this. In 1770 a young man named James Robertson crossed the mountains to investigate the territory. He came back home so enthusiastic about what he found that he convinced a group of families to move to Sycamore Shoals of the Watauga River—later the site of Elizabethton. By 1772 there were almost 85 farms along the Watauga and Holston Rivers, and the inhabitants all thought they were living in Virginia. When surveyors proved that this was not the case, the locals realized they were literally beyond the law. Considering that the law was British, that was not so bad, but they also had no statutes to help them with practical matters like marriages, land transactions, and wills.

They decided they needed some kind of government, so in May of 1772 a call went out for all men over age 21. Those who showed up formed the Watauga Association, an organization loosely based on Virginia law. This was the first constitution west of the mountains.

Dealings with the Cherokee

The second realization from the survey was that every one of these farms was on Indian land. The British might huff and puff and express annoyance at those who defied them, but the Indi-

ans posed a very real problem, one the settlers solved using a modern-day technique. They offered to lease the land for 10 years, paying its owners several thousand dollars' worth of merchandise. The Cherokee who brokered the deal was Attakullakulla, a.k.a. "Little Carpenter," who years earlier had traveled to London and met the king.

When North Carolinians back on the eastern side heard that the Cherokees would deal, they decided to go for a much larger transaction. Richard Henderson and a group of investors summoned the Cherokees and began negotiations for the entire Cumberland Valley and the southern half of the Kentucky Valley, a piece of real estate almost the size of South Dakota.

This was a staggering amount of land—more than 20 million acres—comprising a big part of what would become Tennessee and Kentucky. The Cherokees began gathering at Sycamore Shoals to discuss Henderson's offer of 2,000 English pounds in cash and 8,000 pounds' worth of goods. In March of 1775, more than a thousand of them listened as Attakullakulla, by then 80 years old, made his case for accepting the deal.

He was opposed by Dragging Canoe, his son, who insisted that this was the beginning of the end for their people. He argued that the whites would not be happy with this purchase, and that other Indian lands were now gone. Attakullakulla won the debate, however, and the deal was consummated.

When he saw that his side had lost, Dragging Canoe stalked out of the gathering and stated that the settlers might buy the land, but they would find it a "dark and bloody ground." He spent the rest of his life making that prophecy come to pass.

Revolution

Then came the Revolutionary War. The Wataugans and others west of the mountains could have ignored the entire thing; surviving and making a living were challenge enough. Although they expressed support for their colleagues farther north and east in the war, it took a letter from an arrogant British commander to stir them to action. Major Patrick Ferguson threatened to march his own men over the mountains, "hang their leaders, and lay their country to waste with fire and sword."

These words so incensed the recipients that they called for volunteers to assemble at Syca-

more Shoals in September of 1780, prepared to fight. After a stirring prayer by Rev. Samuel Doak, roughly 1,000 men and boys set off tramping over the mountains. A month later they found Ferguson and a force numbering about the same size as their own on top of a narrow ridge named, appropriately enough, Kings Mountain.

It was not to remain the king's mountain for long. Using hunting skills they had honed all their lives, the mountain men picked off the British one by one, forcing them to surrender in a little more than an hour. Ferguson lay dead among his 353 casualties.

Up until that battle things had not been going very well for the Americans in the war, and Kings Mountain proved to be the turning point of the war in the South—some claim the entire war. The Overmountain Men, as they now were called, jubilantly marched home in time to celebrate Christmas.

MUST-SEE HIGHLIGHTS

Carter Family Fold is just across the line from Kingsport in Virginia, but this musical descendant of the Carter Family preserves old-time picking and singing in a priceless setting—you'll find cloggers, toothless old men in the audience, and the two-of-a-kind Joe and Janette Carter.

Elizabethton's **Sycamore Shoals State Historical Area,** with its replica of a frontier fort, gives a good perspective on the early days of the state. Kids love it.

Kingsport's **Bays Mountain Nature Preserve** combines a natural-history museum with a gem-like lake, all on top of a mountain.

The **Abraham Lincoln Museum** at Lincoln Memorial University in Harrogate shows a distinctly human side of the Civil War president.

Roan Mountain, when the rhododendrons are blooming, is the loveliest place in the state.

Down Home in Johnson City is the best place for live music on this end of the state. Bluegrass, blues, rock—on one night or the other this place will have it all.

Downtown Greeneville, with the General Morgan Inn joining the Andrew Johnson National Historic Site, is a history-filled place to visit.

THE LEE HIGHWAY

One of the most famous "blue highways" on the East Coast is Rt. 11, the Lee Highway. Following the old stage routes through Virginia, the road splits in Bristol into 11 West and 11 East before rejoining in Knoxville. Those are the routes, with a few diversions, that this chapter will follow. We'll begin far up in the point of Tennessee in each case.

Highway 11 West

This is a well-traveled path. Stagecoaches passed up and down here carrying people such as Andrew Jackson, who while president once stopped to go to church in the little town of Blountville. A tavern along the way at Bean Station was said to have the finest wine cellar between Baltimore and New Orleans.

Until I-81 was completed, this stretch of the Lee Highway rumbled day and night with trucks going from the Eastern Seaboard to points south and west. Hank Williams, whose final day is recalled in the Knoxville chapter, probably breathed his last on this stretch of road. With the interstate traffic gone, it remains a good way to slow down and see some of the history of East Tennessee.

Highway 11 East

The southern swing of the old Lee Highway never had as much traffic as its northern branch, but it passes through towns of greater historic significance.

Driving west along Hwy. 11 East, the traveler follows the path of settlers coming into Tennessee. First come high mountain towns, Elizabethton and Fort Watauga, then Jonesborough and its tales of Andrew Jackson. The land gets flatter and more suited for farming as Greeneville swings into view, and the historic houses, reflecting the growing prosperity of the people, get bigger and bigger. These places cannot hold a candle to the magnificent plantations of Middle Tennessee, but a modern-day traveler can certainly see where things were headed.

MOUNTAIN CITY AND VICINITY

Sitting at an elevation of 2,350 feet, the county seat of Johnson County is the highest town in the state. It is also the town where movies come to die.

A successful Hollywood movie might have 2,000 or more prints when first released. As the film moves from first run theaters to second-run houses and then to video, the demand for prints decreases. When a print is ready to be recycled, it comes to Mountain City, where most of it is chopped up into flakes and sold as an ingredient for fuel pellets.

Nearby, some scientists claim, lies the basis for the American cranberry industry. During the last ice age, glaciers 3,000 feet thick ground through Massachusetts and other northern states where cranberries are now commercially grown, effectively wiping out the red berries—and virtually every other plant. The glaciers moved so slowly, however, that cranberries carried by birds grew just ahead of the ice in cool, wet climates. These traveling cranberries found a home in Shady Valley, where a Canadian-type climate enabled them to flourish. When the glaciers retreated, birds carried the berries north, there to grow and wait for the Pilgrims to eat them at Thanksgiving.

The Tennessee cranberries survived glaciers, but the U.S. Corps of Engineers just about killed them off by straightening a stream in Shady Valley. Fortunately, the botanical and historical value of the tart berries has been recognized, and efforts are under way to preserve them and, in the case of the Cranberry Festival, to celebrate them.

WHERE TO STAY

Bed and Breakfasts
The Butler House Bed and Breakfast has an upstairs porch just dandy for looking over the 15 acres of lawn and gardens. The 1870s house is on the National Register, and rates are $60-70 and include breakfast. Call (423) 727-4119 or write 309 North Church St., Mountain City, TN 37683 for reservations and information. Moderate. **Prospect Hill B&B Inn,** 801 W. Main St.,

Mountain City, TN 37683, tel. (423) 727-0139, occupies an 1889 house built by a Civil War colonel. This place, which has been totally renovated, has large rooms, some with whirlpool baths, and a tennis court. Rates are $100-200. Expensive-Luxury.

Motels
Mountain City has two motels, both south of town on Hwy. 421: **Days Inn,** tel. (800) 329-7466, offers rooms for $70 (Moderate), while the larger **Mountain Empire Motel,** tel. (423) 727-7777, has rooms for $54 (Inexpensive).

The **K & R Motel,** southwest of Mountain City in the Doeville Community at the intersection of Hwy. 67 and Hwy. 167, tel. (423) 727-2500, offers nine rooms for $30-40 per night. Budget-Inexpensive.

The **Callalantee Mountain Development,** on Hwy. 421 South in Mountain City, tel. (423) 727-5756, offers townhouses and condos for rent. Three-bedroom, two-bath units go for $150 a night. Luxury.

MORE PRACTICALITIES

Food
Suba's, above the Days Inn, is run by a young couple who received their culinary training in Charleston, SC. They offer soups, sandwiches, and pasta for lunch, while dinnertime brings forth chicken, steak, barbecued ribs, and a wonderful smoked trout cake. Call (423) 727-5657 for information.

Mountain City offers a cluster of fast-food emporiums, but locals prefer the country cuisine of **Cooks Cafeteria,** right beside the Mountain Empire Motel. Cooks serves three meals a day Mon.-Sat. and breakfast and lunch on Sunday.

Shopping
The **Stanly Knitting Mills Outlet, 2009 Hwy. 421,** tel. (423) 727-5323, offers women's sportswear at savings of up to 50% off retail prices.

Sports fans will like the **Bike Athletic Wear Outlet,** on the corner of Church and Main Sts., tel. (423) 727-8850, offering caps, jerseys, and other athletic gear sporting the names of top college and professional teams.

Tours and Information
The **Johnson County Welcome Center** on Hwy. 421, tel. (423) 727-5800, offers exhibits, information, and a campground on the premises. The Web site is www.pages.preferred.com/~jcwc.

EAST OF MOUNTAIN CITY

Laurel Bloomery
This little town up in the point of Tennessee is the birthplace of Frank Proffitt (1913-65), whose singing and playing of traditional mountain ballads brought them to much wider audiences.

When song collectors first came to the mountains, Proffitt eagerly contributed the ones he knew, among them "Tom Dooley," which he said was the first song he remembered hearing his father play on a banjo. The song tells the tale of a man who kills the woman he loves and is sentenced to hang—not exactly cheerful stuff. In the late '50s, the Kingston Trio released its interpretation of the old song, a version that sold three million copies and helped launch the folk music boom of the '60s. In *An Encyclopedia of East Tennessee,* Jim Stokely tells of Proffitt hearing the song on television, walking outside his house, and crying. Late in his life he did receive some of the attention he deserved, performing in folk festivals and recording two albums.

Trade
This little town holds two distinctions: it's the oldest unincorporated community in Tennessee as well as the eastern-most one. When the Europeans first came to these parts, this was the place where they traded—hence the name—gunpowder, furs, and whiskey with the Indians. Following the route of an ancient Indian trail, Daniel Boone, an early highway contractor, cut a road over the mountains and came right through Trade. Locals can point out remnants of Boone's road that exist as country lanes today.

banjo

During the last week in June the town rouses to celebrate **Trade Days,** a gathering of Indians and locals who engage in tomahawk and knife throwing contests—not at each other—shooting matches, period dancing, old-time games, and the more conventional demonstrations of agricultural pursuits such as milking, spinning, churning, plowing, and horse shoeing. For information, call (423) 727-5800.

The **Tennessee Rose Bed and Breakfast** sits amid 50 acres of gardens, streams, and ponds. The two guest rooms have private baths, a common sitting area, and a private kitchen/dining space. Call (423) 727-6574, or write to 843 Wallace Rd., Trade, TN 37691. Rates run $60-70. Moderate.

SHADY VALLEY

Highway 421 leads 10-15 miles north out of Mountain City over Iron Mountain to a great view of Shady Valley, a relatively flat farmland that got its name from the thick forest that used to cover the land. The **Cranberry Festival,** a Friday and Saturday event held the second week in October at the intersection of Hwy. 421 and Hwy. 133, attracts 5,000-7,000 people who turn out to chow down at the Cranberry Bean Dinner and enjoy live performances of bluegrass and gospel music, clogging exhibitions, children's events, a parade, and demonstrations of weaving and pottery. Call (423) 727-5800 for information.

Shady Valley is home to the **Shady Valley Trading Company,** tel. (423) 739-9393, a combination restaurant, museum, gallery, farmer's market, general store, and RV Park. The museum features artifacts from Alaska, various animal skins, and a 2,500-year-old Alaskan knife. The gallery has Indian artifacts, prints, and sculptures. The first Saturday of the good weather months—generally April through October—brings a free concert to the stage out front, and a Gospel Jubilee takes place over Labor Day weekend. The restaurant offers country cooking for lunch and dinner, with a breakfast buffet on weekends. The entire operation is closed on Monday.

Turning right onto Hwy. 133 leads the visitor to one of the oddest geological formations in the state. **Backbone Rock** is a natural stone wall standing 75 feet high. The formation averages 20 feet thick and was pierced in 1901 for a railroad. Now the highway goes through what is sometimes called "the shortest tunnel in the world." The rock is surrounded by a park with a picnic area and 13 campsites. The campground is open from mid-April through October. To get the exact dates, call (423) 735-1500.

BRISTOL AND VICINITY

LAND AND HISTORY

Bristol is one of the few cities where Johnny Cash could literally walk the line. Bristol, Tennessee, and Bristol, Virginia, meet at the state line, which runs right down the middle of the street. The two Bristols are now proud of this unusual juxtaposition, but early in this century it took a Supreme Court decision to help straighten out the problems that come from having two towns too close.

Bristol lies in an area called The Great Valley, an easily traveled route that served as a pathway into Tennessee from the northeast. In 1771 an enormous fort covering an acre and a half was built from which to conduct trade and protect settlers. More than 100,000 people came through during the 1780s.

Industry

An enterprising gent named James King calculated that all those new residents would soon need nails, so he built an ironworks and eventually supplied the frontier with the products of 29 furnaces. Seeking an easy way to ship his heavy goods, he traveled 25 miles to the Holston River, where he built King's Port—the beginning of Kingsport.

King's early industry set a pattern for Bristol, which was named for a British industrial city. Bristol was a natural place for the railroad to come through in 1853, and by the time a 35-year-old New Yorker named Ralph Peer got off the train in the summer of 1927, the city produced steel, paper, furniture, leather goods, and mine cars.

Musical Gold

Peer was interested in none of those products. He was looking for music. The wide sales of phonographs had tapped an insatiable market for music—any kind of music: classical; Tin Pan Alley; and, especially for rural customers, ballads and string music from the South. At first the record companies had brought blues and traditional musicians to New York to record, but this proved expensive, inefficient, and sometimes outright disastrous, especially when bright lights, the big city, and strong drink combined. Peer had the inspiration to dispatch recording crews to the places where musicians lived, and that's what he had in mind when he got off that train. Having placed an ad in the local newspapers, he waited in a makeshift studio at 408-410 State St. to see who would show up. Ernest "Pop" Stoneman was one of the first artists to record there, a man whose "Wreck of the Titanic" had sold a million copies in 1924.

On August 1 and 2, Peer hit even bigger gold. Over those two days he made music history with four people who answered his ad. The first three were the Carter Family, and the fourth was Jimmy Rodgers, a Mississippi-born singer who happened to be performing in the area when he learned of Peer's sessions.

The Carter Family was A.P. Carter, his wife Sara, and A.P.'s sister-in-law, Maybelle. Their honest and simple tunes—songs such as "Wildwood Flower," "Will the Circle Be Unbroken?," and "Keep on the Sunny Side"—were instantly popular and have remained so for 60 years.

The trio broke up in 1943 after recording more than 300 songs, and Maybelle Carter went on to found a musical dynasty, recording with her daughters as "Mother Maybelle and the Carter Sisters." One of those daughters, June, married Johnny Cash, and their daughter—Carlene—carries on today, taking country music to places the original Carters would never have imagined.

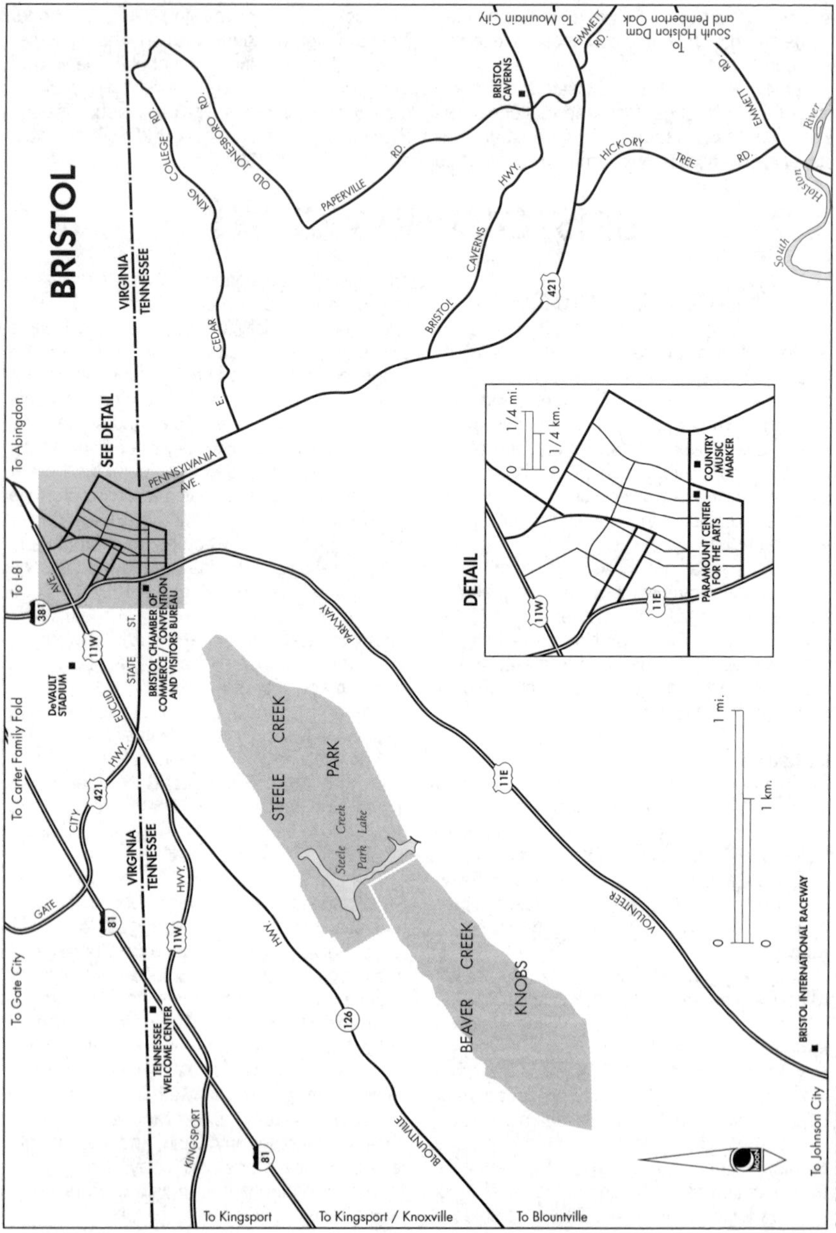

BRISTOL

VIRGINIA
TENNESSEE

SEE DETAIL

To Abingdon

To I-81

To Carter Family Fold

DeVAULT STADIUM

BRISTOL CHAMBER OF COMMERCE / CONVENTION AND VISITORS BUREAU

To Gate City

TENNESSEE WELCOME CENTER

VIRGINIA
TENNESSEE

STATE ST.

PENNSYLVANIA AVE.

E. CEDAR

KING COLLEGE RD.

OLD JONESBORO RD.

PAPERVILLE RD.

BRISTOL CAVERNS HWY

421

BRISTOL CAVERNS

HICKORY TREE RD.

EMMETT RD.

To Mountain City

To South Holston Dam and Pemberton Oak

Holston River

South

To Kingsport

To Kingsport / Knoxville

To Blountville

KINGSPORT

BLOUNTVILLE HWY

126

BEAVER CREEK KNOBS

STEELE CREEK PARK

Steele Creek Park Lake

PARKWAY

VOLUNTEER

11E

11W

11W

GATE CITY

HWY

421 HWY

EUCLID AVE.

381

BRISTOL INTERNATIONAL RACEWAY

To Johnson City

DETAIL

11W

11E

PARAMOUNT CENTER FOR THE ARTS

COUNTRY MUSIC MARKER

0   1/4 mi.
0   1/4 km.

0   1 mi.
0   1 km.

Jimmy Rodgers was the first musical superstar. Blending the black blues he had grown up with in Mississippi with the hillbilly music of Tennessee, he burst on the national scene with an outpouring of recordings that included railroad songs, "blue yodels," sweet ballads, honky-tonk numbers, and cowboy and corny songs. Stricken with tuberculosis before he ever began recording, his career came to an end after fewer than four years; he died at age 35 in 1933. He was the first person voted into the Country Music Hall of Fame, where his plaque reads "The Father of Country Music."

Other important music figures have also come out of Bristol. In the days when live performances were a staple of radio stations, WCYB in Bristol featured the Stanley Brothers, second only to Bill Monroe in bluegrass annals; Mac Wiseman; Jim and Jesse McReynolds; along with Earl Scruggs and Lester Flatt and the Foggy Mountain Boys. Radio station WOPI had a young announcer named Ernie Ford who, later known as "Tennessee" Ernie Ford, helped bring country music to mainstream America. His most popular song was "Sixteen Tons," a snappy, almost jazz-like song that became a 1955 hit.

Hometown Pride

Like most decent-sized cities, Bristol has been malled, leaving the downtown to scramble to keep its head above water. The old train station became Trainstation Marketplace for a while, but still hasn't found the right formula for success. State Street has fared better, with an eclectic mixture of shops and restaurants and a large mural at State and 8th commemorating Bristol's fortuitous role in country music history. Bristol's trademark sign, "Bristol Va Tenn A Good Place To Live," ever cheerful, presides over it all.

SIGHTS AND RECREATION

A year-round favorite of visitors is **Bristol Caverns,** a long cave with a long history. It seems that the local Indians used the caverns as a way of sneaking up on unsuspecting settlers and then mysteriously disappearing when chased. The section of the cave now open to visitors has walkways and stairs and the requisite named formations. This is a good place for children. The caverns are open daily year-round except Thanksgiving and Christmas; tours depart approximately every 20 minutes. Admission is $8 for those 13 years old and up, $4 for ages five to 12, and free for those four and under. They are five miles southeast of Bristol on Hwy. 435, tel. (423) 878-2011.

Most people think of dams as huge, concrete structures. Nearby **South Holston Dam,** one of the many built by the Tennessee Valley Authority, is made of earth and is the third largest such structure in the world. The top of the dam has a visitors center, and the land around the dam offers picnicking and fishing; bring your own boat. To get there, take Hwy. 435 out of Bristol toward Mountain City. Turn right at the sign that says "TVA South Holston Dam."

Farther along Hwy. 421 stands the **Pemberton Oak,** a historic tree an estimated 700-800 years old, which marks the place where locals gathered and trained before joining forces with other colonials and thrashing the British at Kings Mountain, South Carolina. To view this arboreal connection with history, drive 3.1 miles past Emmett Rd. and look for a historical marker. The tree is visible from this point, but if visitors want to examine it further, they can drive down Pemberton Road to Pemberton Farm.

Steele Creek Park has than 2,000 acres containing a children's park with a half-mile scenic train ride and paddleboats. The park offers 25 miles of hiking trails, as well as a nature center and nine-hole golf course. To get there go west from Bristol on Hwy. 11 West and turn left on the Blountville Highway. The entrance to the park will be on the left.

ENTERTAINMENT AND EVENTS

The Carter Family Memorial Music Center

The Carter Center isn't in Tennessee, but it's significant enough and close enough to Tennessee to be mentioned in this book. The Carter family came from Southwest Virginia; A.P. and Sara lived in Maces Spring and raised their family here between road trips and broadcasts on far-flung radio stations. After the couple retired from show business, A.P. operated a grocery store here until his death in 1960.

In 1974 their youngest daughter, Janette, who had appeared on stage with her parents as a buck dancer at age six and an autoharp player at age 12, began performing again at the Carter Family Store. The acoustic music she brought forth, true to the Carter tradition, drew such crowds that two years later she, her sister Gladys, and her brother Joe built the Carter Family "Fold," a shed seating 800-1,000 people. The name comes from the biblical parable of sheep returning to the fold.

Music lovers from all over the world and just down the road gather here, some to listen and some to raise the dust with traditional dances on the floor right in front of the stage. Bluegrass and folk music, with the occasional country performance, is all one will hear at the Fold. No electrical instruments are permitted. Shows are presented every Saturday night at 7:30 p.m. Admission is a wonderfully low $4 per adult, $1 for children 6-12, with impressionable children under six getting in for free. This is possibly the biggest entertainment bargain in the entire book. No advance tickets are sold, but the huge Fold rarely sells out.

The adjacent store now makes up the Carter Family Museum, where one can view the family's 78 rpm records, fancy "show clothes" worn in performances, photos, books, and other memorabilia. The museum is open every Saturday 5-7 p.m. Admission is 50 cents. Children accompanied by parents get in free.

On the first weekend in August a festival commemorates the historic Carter Family 1927 recording session. Continuous live music plays daily 2-11 p.m., with a headliner such as Mac Wiseman or John McCutcheon. A nearby meadow becomes a small village of tents in which local artists sell crafts and local cooks sell food.

Cautionary note: Unlike some bluegrass festivals, Mama don't 'low no drinking round here. Anyone tippling or who has toppled will find that the Carter Family circle will be broken—quickly. For information on weekly shows or the festival, call (540) 386-9480. To get to the Carter Center, take Exit 1 off I-81 in Virginia. Follow Hwy. 58/421 West to the town of Hiltons, then take Rt. 709 to Rt. 614—now named "A.P. Carter Highway"—East about three miles to Maces Spring. Find info on the Internet at www.donjon.fmp.com/carter.

Highlander Theater is a dinner theater located not far from the Tri-Cities Airport. Look under Kingsport for a complete listing.

Other Cultural Diversions

Dance, theater, concerts, and other events take place at the **Paramount Center for the Arts,** 512 State St., tel. (423) 968-7546, a restored 1931 art deco movie palace.

Theatre Bristol produces eight shows a year, a mixture of straight plays and musicals as well as children's theater. Performances take place either at the Theatre Bristol's Art Space at 506 State Street or at the Paramount Center for the Arts. Tickets and information are dispensed at the company's office at 512 State Street, tel. (423) 968-4977.

The World of Speed

For most people, NASCAR racing exists in a kind of parallel universe; they are only vaguely aware of its presence. Stock car racing grew up in the South, and though its appeal now spans the country, the South remains the hotbed of interest. The **Bristol International Raceway,** at

TENNESSEE TOURIST DEVELOPMENT

The NASCAR races at Bristol International Speedway attract thousands of stock-car fans.

.533 miles long, is the shortest major racecourse in the country. The 36° high-banked track poses special challenges for drivers, who must constantly fight the effects of a relentless centrifugal force. These circumstances, however, prove advantageous for fans, who can clearly see all of the competitors all of the time, a situation not possible at some of the larger racetracks.

Big races in Bristol attract more than 135,000 people, who happily fill up all the lodging in the area and stay as far away as Knoxville. NASCAR sets the race dates, but Bristol usually has a big race on the first or second weekend in April and the next-to-last weekend in August. Visitors to the First Frontier, even those who wouldn't know Richard Petty from Tom Petty, should keep this in mind.

To get to the Bristol International Raceway, take Hwy. 11 East toward Johnson City. Or just follow the crowd. Tickets cost $70-75 for Winston Cup races, and fans can obtain them by calling the Raceway at (423) 764-1161.

Racing fans who prefer their competition on the straight and narrow need only go to an adjacent drag strip, the **Bristol International Dragway.** Situated in the appropriately named Thunder Valley, the stands seat 30,000. Local drag races run every other weekend. You can get tickets by calling (423) 764-3724. Don't forget the ear plugs.

Baseball

Baseball fans turn out to cheer for the **Bristol White Sox,** a farm team for the Chicago White Sox. The team plays at DeVault Memorial Stadium, which is off I-81 at Exit 3. Follow Commonwealth Ave. to Euclid Ave., then go right for a half-mile. The standard game time is 7 p.m. For information, call (540) 645-7275. Except when there's a rare advance sellout, tickets are always available at the stadium before games.

WHERE TO STAY

Bed and Breakfasts

New Hope Bed & Breakfast, 822 Georgia Ave., tel. (423) 989-3343 or (888) 989-3343, sits in an 1892 house built by the older brother of R. J. Reynolds—of tobacco fame—and the father of R.S. Reynolds of Reynolds Aluminum. The house

---

RACING FOR ACCOMMODATIONS

While NASCAR stock car racing may not be every traveler's cup of tea, visitors to the First Frontier who want a hotel room on certain weekends should pay close attention to the activities at the Bristol Motor Speedway.

Big races in Bristol attract in excess of 135,000 people, who fill up all the lodging in the area and rent rooms as far away as Knoxville. Furthermore, local hostelries, hoping to cash in on life in the fast lane, often raise their rates precipitously. Winston Cup dates are set by NASCAR, but Bristol usually has a big race on the first or second weekend in April and the next-to-last weekend in August.

To get the exact dates, call the Raceway at (423) 764-1161.

---

has four rooms, all of which have private baths, and guests can borrow the inn's bicycles to explore the neighborhood. Rates are $105-120. The Internet address is www.bbonline.com/tn/newhope. html. Expensive-Premium.

Motels

Sitting beside I-81, Bristol has a good selection of franchise motels from which to choose. Some are in Virginia and some in Tennessee; if travelers are tired enough it doesn't really matter.

In Tennessee, try the **Days Inn,** 536 Volunteer Pkwy., tel. (423) 968-2171. Right off the interstate is the biggest cluster of lodgings: try the **Holiday Inn I-81,** at I-81 and Hwy. 11 West (Exit 74B), tel. (423) 968-1101. A dozen or so more options sit just across the state line in Virginia along the Lee Highway—11-19.

Camping

Observation Knob Park, 553 Knob Park Rd., tel. (423) 878-5561, is a county park on South Holston Lake where visitors can, among other things, fish from a wheelchair-accessible fishing pier. The park has 191 campsites plus overflow. To get there from northbound I-81, take Exit 1 in Virginia and get on Hwy. 421 South. Follow it through Bristol to Rt. 44. Take a left on Rt. 44 and go two miles. Turn right at the sign. It's open for camping April 1-Nov. 1.

FOOD

Barbecue

Anyone this close to the **Ridgewood Restaurant,** tel. (423) 538-7543, should know about it. Frequently described as the best barbecue place in East Tennessee, it is about nine miles from Bristol on Hwy. 19 East, between Elizabethton and Bluff City. Lunch and dinner are available every day but Monday. On Friday and Saturday night, the place is packed. Go there and taste the beef or pork barbecue and see why. Oddly enough, it doesn't serve ribs.

Steak and Seafood

The **Athens Steak House,** 105 Goodson St. in Virginia, tel. (540) 466-8271, is open for three meals Mon.-Saturday. Greek salads and great shish-kabob are the specialties here.

Troutdale Dining Room, 412 6th St., tel. (423) 968-9099, serving dinner Mon.-Sat., is one of the best restaurants at this end of the state. Although renowned for trout—it keeps a 750-gallon aquarium full of them—this place offers leading-edge American and international dishes such as veal, lamb, venison, and quail. The menu changes depending on what is fresh and seasonal. "We make everything here except the butter," comes the report from the kitchen. Reservations, especially on weekends, are a good idea.

The Vineyard Restaurant & Lounge, 603 Gate City Hwy., tel. (540) 466-4244, offers three meals a day every day, featuring steaks, seafood, Italian dishes, and chicken.

Ethnic

Mad Greek Restaurant, 2419 Volunteer Pkwy., tel. (423) 968-4848, is open Mon.-Sun. for lunch and dinner and features gyros, kabobs, and mouth-watering baklava.

Lighter Fare

Bella's Pizza, 1351 Lee Hwy., VA, tel. (540) 466-3281, open for lunch and dinner every day of the week, offers beer with homemade pizzas that are as honest as Carter Family lyrics.

The Feed Room, 620 State St., tel. (423) 764-0545, in the historic H.P. King Building, is a lunch spot offering sandwiches, soups, and salads Monday through Friday.

Martin's K.P. Duty, at 520 State St., tel. (423) 764-3889, is open for lunch Mon.-Sat. and dinner Friday and Saturday. Located right beside the Paramount Center for the Arts, Martin's offers sandwiches, specialty salads, and a wide choice of desserts. The **Gourmet Shoppe and Cafe** inside Martin's features quiche and soup.

Nana's Kitchen, 16 Sixth St., tel. (423) 968-3887, open Mon.-Fri. 8 a.m.-3 p.m., serves sandwiches, specials, and homemade desserts.

INFORMATION

The Greater Bristol Area Chamber of Commerce has its office at the corner of State St. and Volunteer Parkway. Write P.O. Box 519, Bristol, TN/VA 24203-0519, or call (423) 968-4399. Or drop by during business hours. Get information online at www.bristolva.org.

An excellent source of information for a much wider part of the state is the **Tennessee Welcome Center** on I-81 off the southbound lanes at Exit 1 in Virginia, tel. (423) 764-5821.

BLOUNTVILLE

This little town, the county seat of Sullivan County, is said to have more original log homes along its main street than any other town in Tennessee. Whether this is true or not, Blountville's historic district has 20 structures that are on the National Register. Among them are the Deery Inn, whose guests included the Marquis de Lafayette and Presidents James K. Polk, Andrew Johnson, and Andrew Jackson.

Jackson, while president, came through Blountville in 1836 on a Sunday morning and decided to go to church. His party stopped at the Blountville Presbyterian Church just as the sermon was beginning. The surprised minister halted the service, announced the new arrivals, led a hymn, and resumed his sermon. Not one Secret Service agent was present.

Sights

Blountville's Historic Society's headquarters are in the **Anderson Townhouse,** a two-story log cabin that is 200 years old. It sits across from the courthouse and beside the Blountville Presbyterian Church. Visitors can go there from April 15 through Labor Day 10 a.m.-4 p.m. to hear a little bit about the town and obtain a map for the walking tour.

When one log house begins to look too much like another, it is time to retire to **Countryside Vineyards and Winery** for sustenance. Fourteen wines are made from the grapes grown here: four reds, six whites, and four dessert wines. One of the dessert wines, the Golden Muscat, won an award in 1993 for the Best Grape Growing and Wine Making in Tennessee. Tours and samples are available whenever visitors drop by.

Hours at the winery are Mon.-Sat. 10 a.m.-6 p.m., Sunday 1-6 p.m. To get there take Exit 63 off I-81 and go past Sam's Club and a water tower. Follow the signs to Henry Harr Rd., the third road on the left. The winery is approximately 1.5 miles from Exit 63.

Highlander Theater is a dinner theater located not far from the Tri-Cities Airport. Look under Kingsport for a more complete listing.

Appalachian Caverns

Those interested in a more bracing experience should decamp for these nearby caves, Cave Hill Rd., tel. (423) 323-2337. Tennessee has all manner of caves and caverns, most operated as funnels through which to pour visitors into gift shops. This place is different. First of all, it is operated by the Appalachian Caverns Foundation, whose profits are spent cleaning up solid waste dumps in cave openings and underground drainages. Before this particular cave was opened, 162 tons of garbage had to be removed.

The work was worth the effort. Highlights include a "great room" measuring 1,400 feet long, 100 feet wide, and 135 feet high. The cave also has a seemingly bottomless pool—divers came back after going down 145 feet without finding the end. This cave does not have some of the intricate and large formations—and the accompanying imaginative and not so imaginative names—that characterize other commercial caves. But it does have more than 10,000 bats representing five species, which are utterly uninterested in their human visitors.

Visitors can take a conventional tour with almost a mile of walkways, or they can show up with old clothes and a flashlight for a Wild Tour—three and a half hours of off-the-path genuine caving. This experience, which is available evenings by appointment only, costs $300 for a group, with a $2.50 rental fee for each helmet. Participants on the Wild Tour may get very muddy, so a change of clothes or trash bags to line vehicle seats are highly recommended.

Appalachian Caverns is south of Blountville off Hwy. 37. Take Exit 69 from I-81 and go south on Hwy. 37 through Blountville for 2.5 miles to Feathers Chapel. Turn right onto Buncombe Road for 1.5 miles to Cave Hill Road. Go left for a half mile. The caverns are open March 2-Sept. 30 Mon.-Sat. 9 a.m.-6 p.m., Sunday 1-6 p.m. From October 1 to March 1 the hours are 11 a.m.-6 p.m. The caverns are closed Thanksgiving Day and Dec. 20-Jan. 10. Admission is $9 for ages 12 and over, $5 for ages 4-11, with kids under four getting in free. Senior citizens pay only $7.65.

Where to Stay

Smithhaven Bed & Breakfast, 2357 State Rd. 37, tel. (423) 323-8554, occupies a house built between 1848 and 1851. A large porch complete with rocking chairs wraps around the house. The three rooms have private baths, and rates are $75-145. Moderate-Premium.

Those who prefer to camp will find both of Blountville's campgrounds at Exit 63 of I-81. The way to each is amply marked with signs. **KOA Campground,** 425 Rocky Branch Rd., tel. (423) 323-7790, has 73 sites and six cabins. **Rocky Top Campground,** a little closer to the interstate at 496 Pearl Ln., tel. (423) 323-2535, offers 35 sites and a handful of cabins. Both are open year-round.

KINGSPORT AND VICINITY

LAND AND HISTORY

A Sacred Place

The Cherokee had long cherished an island in the south fork of the Holston River, for it was near an intersection of war paths. They used it as a sacred place to negotiate treaties with other tribes, and they wouldn't even kill animals there.

Settlers also used it as a gathering place. Bristol's James King established a port here from which he shipped his iron products, thus giving the town its name. Daniel Boone and his company of axemen began their Wilderness Road to Cumberland Gap and into Kentucky in 1775 from here, and various Revolutionary War militias used it as a rendezvous. When the Cherokee decided to wipe out all of the interlopers, they knew where to come.

In 1776 Dragging Canoe, a Cherokee who vehemently opposed white people, led a force of warriors toward the island. Having been warned by Nancy Ward, a Cherokee who befriended the settlers, the locals readily repelled the attackers. The Battle of Island Flats, as it came to be known, marked the end of all-out warfare on the part of the Cherokee. They would still engage in skirmishes, but upper east Tennessee was now relatively safe for settlers, and some of them began to think of moving even farther west.

If they decided to move on, King's Port offered access to a river flowing in the right direction, and the inhabitants helped travelers build boats and shove off downstream. In 1779 the founders of Nashville set forth from here. (Their story is recounted in the Nashville chapter.) As settlers made their way back for business or government reasons, they tended to travel this way and very often spent the night at the Netherland Inn.

A Model City

Over time King's Port became Kingsport. The town grew slowly through the 19th century; a couple of skirmishes took place during the Civil War, but the town escaped any real damage. It took the arrival of the railroad in 1909 to make Kingsport shift gears. The men at the throttle, New Yorker John B. Dennis and local boy J. Fred Johnson, set out to create a modern industrial city.

They began by drumming up business for the new railroad. They based their plan on an abundance of raw materials, plenty of hardworking people who had never heard of unions, and industries that would complement each other.

To make everything work right, they commissioned a Massachusetts planner to design America's first "model city." The plan was simple: line the rivers with factories, put houses on the hills, and let commercial districts fill up the land between. To set up a school system, the city fathers pulled in Columbia University professors as consultants.

It worked beyond their wildest dreams, especially when representatives of George Eastman of Kodak fame bought a defunct factory and founded the Eastman Chemical Company. During World War II, the company set up and ran Holston Ordinance Works, which produced RDX, a powerful explosive. Today Eastman, although no longer a part of Kodak and no longer running the explosives plant, is the 12th-largest chemical company in the country and occupies 6,097 acres. It produces more than 300 industrial chemicals, most of the cigarette filters used by American tobacco companies, and three kinds of plastic. Visit at www.eastman.com.

One thing the planners never gave a thought to was pollution, which the various industries produced in spades. After reaching a low point in the '60s and '70s, Kingsport's air and water are cleaner than they used to be, but it remains a town where one doesn't need a weatherman to know which way the wind blows.

A positive legacy of the top-down planning of Kingsport is a willingness to volunteer that permeates the city. Whether the project is a parade, a festival, or whatever, the factories and other businesses enthusiastically support it and encourage their employees to do likewise.

The King Played Here

Kingsport deserves a footnote in Tennessee's musical history, for it was here in 1955 that Elvis played the last concert in which he was an opening act. As recounted by Kingsport author Vince Staton, Elvis appeared at a country music show between the Louvin Brothers and Cowboy

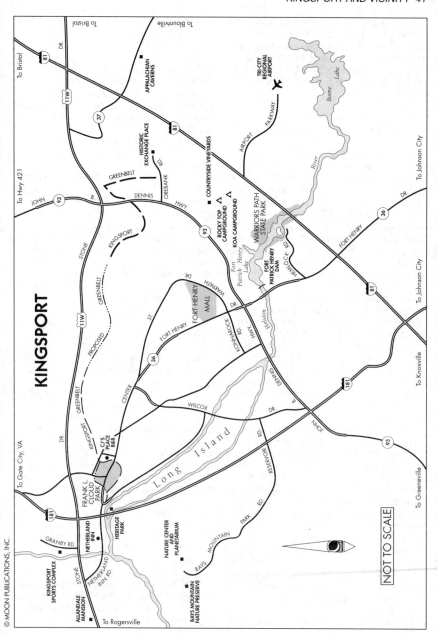

KINGSPORT

NOT TO SCALE

© MOON PUBLICATIONS, INC.

Copas, sang for a half hour—collecting $37 and change for his efforts—and then went "cruising" on Broad St. with some local teenage girls. He went home with one of them, met her parents and had a cup of coffee, then climbed into his pink Cadillac and headed back to Memphis and history.

SIGHTS AND RECREATION

Bays Mountain Nature Reserve
At 3,000 acres, the reserve is a jewel. Sitting above Kingsport on Bays Mountain, the city-owned park offers hiking and a museum/planetarium that interprets the local flora and fauna for visitors. Set around a 44-acre lake, the park has deer so tame that they often do not run when people pass by. A few animals such as foxes, a raccoon, and a bear are kept in cages, while waterfowl, deer, otters, and wolves are kept in larger—and separate—enclosures.

The most fascinating are the wolves. Large, gray wolves with yellow eyes, they cause visitors to linger the longest. Squeamish visitors may be shocked to see wolves gnawing on a deer head, which usually comes from road kill. These animals don't live on Puppy Chow. The most playful animals are the otters, whose enclosure has a pool where they slide, swim, and splash.

The park has trails ranging from a few hundred feet to 4.8 miles. Mountain bikes are permitted on the gravel roads, but riders should check in with park personnel first.

The visitors center is a good place to go anytime, but is especially good for children when the weather is bad. Inside are interesting exhibits, a planetarium, and an artificial cave through which kids love to crawl. The Harry Steadman Mountain Heritage Farmstead is a large building with antiques and old farming implements arranged in haphazard order. A new addition is the Habitat Hub, a simulated cliff that contains an exhibit of snakes, a classroom, and handicapped-accessible bathrooms. Nature programs ranging from barge rides on the lake to moonlit hikes are abundant; one can easily spend the day here. Visitors should bring their own food, for there is nothing available at the top.

Admission is $3 per car or $15 per bus. The Nature Interpretive Center itself is free, but planetarium shows, barge rides, or other programs cost $1.50 per person. For further information call (423) 229-9447.

The park lies at the end of a series of confusing, twisting roads. Pay attention to the signs. To get to the park from downtown Kingsport, come out Wilcox Drive and turn right onto Reservoir Road. Turn right again at Bays Mountain Park Rd. and follow the signs. From Hwy. 181, get off at Exit 51 and follow the signs. Find them on the Web at home.tricon.net/baysmtn.

Older Kingsport
Each of the American colonies had its own currency, so early travelers coming from Virginia were obliged to exchange one kind of money for another when they crossed boundaries. The **Exchange Place** was where they performed this monetary transaction. Once the center of a 2,000-acre plantation, the restored house and outbuildings provide a fascinating look at the past. Consisting of eight buildings dating 1820-50—six of them original to the site—the Exchange Place and the adjacent Preston Farm frequently offer demonstrations of crafts, farming methods, musket shooting, and household activities.

The Exchange Place/Preston Farm, 4812 Orebank Rd., tel. (423) 288-6071, offers group tours by a costumed guide for a small fee. Call to get information on special events.

An older establishment sits on the bank of the Holston River in a section of the city known as "Old Kingsport." Across from the western end of Long Island, the three-story **Netherland Inn,** 214 Netherland Inn Rd., tel. (423) 247-3211, was established as an inn and tavern in 1818, where it sheltered and quenched the thirst of three presidents and served as a hub of commerce for the nearby boatyard.

The first-floor tavern, second-floor family quarters, and third-floor guest rooms now look like they must have 150 years ago. Visitors can easily cross the road in front of the inn and then walk over a swinging bridge to Long Island. A small part of the island has been given back to the Cherokee, who have placed a monument there.

Picnicking sites lie nearby, and visitors can take a walking tour of the neighborhood. Most of the old homes in the area are still lived in and not open to the public.

The Netherland Inn Museum House and Boatyard Complex is open May-Oct., Sat.-Sun. 2-4:30 p.m.; admission is $3 for adults, $2 for seniors, $1 for students, and free for children under six.

A climb from the inn to a small promontory gives a very good view of the confluence of the North and South Forks of the Holston. Sunset is the best time to see this. From this place one can also see Kingsport's most striking historic home, Rotherwood Mansion. It was built in 1820 as a home for Frederick Ross, a man of wealth and taste who once persuaded local farmers to go into the silkworm business. To promote his enterprise, for several summers he wore a suit made of woven silk. He lost his shirt on a cotton mill investment, however, and silk suits, which hadn't exactly caught on, disappeared from the scene. The house is privately owned and is not open to the public.

Allandale

Out-of-towners leaving Kingsport and heading west on Hwy. 11 West sometimes find themselves staring twice at a large home on the right that bears more than a passing resemblance to the White House. This is Allandale, built in 1950 by Harvey and Ruth Brooks, who set their sights on erecting what locals call a "show place." Hiring prominent landscape architects to shape the 500-acre farm and filling the house with elegant furniture, they achieved their goal.

Twenty-five acres of the estate and the mansion are now owned by the city of Kingsport. The barn has a hayloft for dancing, concerts, and wedding receptions. The house is rented out for weddings, receptions, Murder Mystery Dinners, and whatever the city can think of to help maintain the place. The public can tour Allandale during the first weekend in December and can enjoy ice cream there during Fun Fest (see "Events" below). For additional information, call the Kingsport Convention and Visitor's Bureau at (423) 392-8820.

ENTERTAINMENT

Beechwood Music Center 441 Horton Hwy., tel. (423) 348-7321, offers bluegrass and country music every Friday and Saturday night at 8 p.m. Half of the experience here is seeing the crowd. Sometimes an old man wearing bib overalls will step onto the dance floor down front and, as locals put it, "cut a shine" with flatfoot dancing. The shows run for three hours.

The Carter Family Fold, the most significant music destination in this part of the world (described more fully under Bristol) is actually closer to Kingsport as the crow flies. To get there, take US 23 north toward Gate City and turn right on US 58 and go to Hiltons, Virginia. For a taste of genuine Appalachian music, this place is unsurpassed.

Highlander Theater, 3520 Hwy. 75, tel. (423) 323-1468 is a dinner theater with a Scottish theme. Located not far from the Tri-Cities Airport, Highlander's waiters and waitresses wear kilts, and opening nights always feature bagpipes. Tickets cost $25 per person, and patrons should bring their own alcoholic beverages, preferably a good single malt. To get there, take the Johnson City highway, TN 36, south of Kingsport and turn left on TN 75. Cross Patrick Henry Lake, and the theater is on the left.

the Tennessee White House

Baseball lovers gravitate to Kingsport's new ballpark to see the **Kingsport Mets,** part of the New York Mets farm system. The Mets play at the Kingsport Sports Complex; take Exit 57 off I-81 to Hwy. 181 North, then take the W. Stone Dr. exit. Go left on W. Stone Dr., then right on Granby Road. For schedule information, call (423) 247-7181. The usual starting time for games is 7 p.m.

The **Showboat Dinner Theatre,** 2808 John B. Dennis Bypass, tel. (423) 288-7827, combines community talent with dinner on weekend nights. Brown-bagging is permitted. Tickets cost $23 per person.

EVENTS

First Night, an alcohol-free celebration of New Year's Eve, takes place downtown and involves dozens of events and performances. The action takes place in churches, outdoors, and in tents, and ranges from Cherokee dancing to electric blues. Participants buy a First Night button that covers all admission fees, but doesn't always guarantee admission. Some events fill up quickly. For further information, call (423) 246-2017.

Almost every town and city in Tennessee has some sort of local festival; Kingsport's **Fun Fest** is one of the best. The reason is money. The city's business community, led by Eastman Chemicals, heavily subsidizes this July celebration. Typical of the more than 100 events are country, rock, gospel, and folk concerts; hot air balloon races; athletic events such as a 5K run; and puppet theater for children. Some events have admission fees, but most are free. Fun Fest takes place between the last weekend in July and the first weekend in August. Call (423) 392-8820 for further information.

WHERE TO STAY

Bed and Breakfasts
C.J.'s Place, 634 Arch St., tel. (423) 378-3517, caters primarily to traveling professionals. Patrons have a choice of four bedrooms or a suite, all with a private bath, telephone, and cable TV. The place is furnished in Queen Anne-style cherry furniture and antiques. Rooms cost $54-110. Inexpensive-Expensive.

C.J.'s Too!, 415 Roller St., tel. (423) 378-3517, is one of the very few B & Bs in Tennessee that caters to smokers. Here lovers of the tobacco weed can smoke to their heart's content in all of the four bedrooms, each of which has cable TV, a phones, and a private baths. Rates are $54-110. Inexpensive-Expensive.

Warrior's Rest , 1000 Colonial Heights Rd., tel. (423) 239-8838, is outside of Kingsport and very close to Warrior's Path State Park. The three guestrooms here, named for various railroads, all have private baths. Rates are $65-85. Moderate.

Motels
Kingsport has a new conference center and hotel that usually has room for passersby. Meadowview Conference Resort and Convention Center, 1901 Meadowview Parkway, tel. (423) 578-6600 or (800) 820-5055, is operated by Marriott and has 195 guest rooms, 73 of which have various business-related amenities. The place features an 18-hole golf course, outdoor pool, hot tub, and tennis court, and lies close to Bays Mountain Nature Reserve.

Most of the other motels in Kingsport lie along Stone Drive—Hwy. 11 West. Good franchise choices where one can rest are the **Days Inn Downtown,** 805 Lynn Garden Dr., tel. (423) 246-7126; **Howard Johnson's,** 700 Lynn Garden Dr., tel. (423) 247-3133; **Comfort Inn,** 100 Indian Center Court, tel. (423) 378-4418; **Econo Lodge,** 1740 E. Stone Dr., tel. (423) 245-0286; and **Ramada Inn,** 2005 La Masa Dr., tel. (423) 245-0271.

Camping
Most campers head for **Warrior's Path State Park,** covered below.

FOOD

Kingsport's restaurant scene runs heavily toward upscale chain establishments; they come and go—often in the same buildings—with great regularity. Residents seem to think that their eateries, like the leaves, should change at least once a year.

Top of the Heap

Skoby's, 1001 Konnarock Rd., tel. (423) 245-2761. Now in its fifth decade, this place doesn't look all that special on the outside, but within are delightful theme rooms: The Butcher Shop, Oriental Room, the Diner, the Tavern, and so on. They offer steaks, seafood, pasta, and a very good salad bar. Prices range from $10 to $20. If diners don't have time to stay, Skoby's has barbecue takeout available at the end of the building. Skoby's serves dinner only, although **The Pantry,** also in the building, has lunch and takeout barbecue. **The Back Room** features a happy hour beginning at 4:30 p.m.

A little farther afield but worth the trip is the **Harmony Grocery,** tel. (423) 348-6183, which features Creole and Cajun cuisine. This is the place for shrimp Creole and sausage or seafood gumbo, as well as fresh seafood and steaks. Brown-bagging is permitted. The restaurant is open Tues.-Sun. for dinner, and Sunday noon-2:30 p.m.

Directions to the Harmony Grocery are complicated. From Kingsport, take I-181 south to Exit 45—Eastern Star Road. Go right at the end of the road and drive one mile to a stop sign at a T intersection. This is Kincheloe Mill Road. Follow it one mile to the right to another T intersection. Go left onto Harmony Road. (By this point you are probably into the brown bag, but hang in there.) Go a little less than two miles, and Harmony Grocery is on the right. Call for further directions.

The Meadows, 1901 Meadowview Parkway, tel. (423) 578-6632 or (800) 820-5055, occupies the Meadowview Conference Resort and Convention Center. Open for all three meals seven days a week, it features a Friday night seafood buffet, Saturday prime rib buffet, and Sunday brunch. Menu items include steak, seafood, pasta, and chicken, as well as a full bar.

Easier on the Wallet

Amato's, 121 Jack White Dr., tel. (423) 245-4043, offers Italian and American lunches and dinners plus a full bar.

Giuseppe's, 2539 E. Stone Dr., tel. (423) 288-5680, serves prime rib, Italian, and seafood for lunch and dinner—dinner only on Saturday. It also offers a low-cholesterol line.

Downright Reasonable

Tennesseans love cafeterias, and two of the more popular ones here are **Piccadilly Cafeteria,** in the mall at 2101 Fort Henry Dr., tel. (423) 246-7001, which serves lunch and dinner every day; and **Wright's Country Cuisine,** 109 Jack White Dr., tel. (423) 245-2565, open for lunch and dinner every day but Sunday, when lunch only is served.

Pal's restaurants are the kinds of establishments that many towns had before the invasion of the golden arches. With five locations—1120 E. Stone Dr., tel. (423) 246-2309; 4224 Fort Henry Dr., tel. (423) 239-3442; 1316 Lynn Garden Dr., tel. (423) 245-2871; 327 Revere St., tel. (423) 246-9761; and 1735 Fort Henry Dr., tel. (423) 247-3360—these hamburger/hot dog/root beer joints seem straight out of the '50s.

Tucked under a hardware store, **Motz's Italian Restaurant,** 4231 Fort Henry Dr., tel. (423) 239-9560, serves unpretentious but tasty Italian and American food for lunch and dinner every day. The fresh bread alone is worth a stop.

Sharon's Barbecue and Burgers, 301 W. Center St., tel. (423) 247-5588, has a retro '50s look that proves a perfect setting for its offerings of burgers and barbecue. If Elvis is alive and ever walks in, he'll feel right at home. It's open seven days a week 11 a.m.-8 p.m.

MORE PRACTICALITIES

Shopping

Like almost every Tennessee city, Kingsport has suffered the effects of shopping malls. The silver lining to this particular cloud is the large number of antique stores that have appeared downtown. Broad Street alone has five stores, offering furniture as well as collectibles.

Up Against the Wall Gallery, 316 East Market St., tel. (423) 246-7210, is in itself worth a trip downtown. It began as a custom frame shop and now offers original works from regional and national artists: paintings, sculpture, jewelry, and pottery. The store carries a large collection of prints—over 1,000 by P. Buckley Moss alone.

Information

The **Kingsport Convention and Visitor's Bureau** dispenses information from 151 E. Main

Street. Call (800) 743-5282 or (423) 392-8820, or find them on the Web at kingsport.tricon.net

WARRIOR'S PATH STATE RECREATIONAL PARK

This 950-acre park was carved out of land surrounding TVA's Patrick Henry Lake, and aquatic pursuits are the chief focus here. Pleasure boating and water-skiing are very popular, as is fishing. Boats are available for rent at the marina, as are paddleboats.

The water, coming as it does from the bottom of upstream Boone Lake, tends to be on the chilly side for swimming, but bathers can cavort in one of the largest outdoor pools in the state or slide down a water slide. Both operate from early summer through Labor Day.

Nine miles of hiking trails wind through the park, and park stables offer trail rides through the woods. The park has an 18-hole golf course and driving range.

The year-round campground, close by the swimming pool, has 135 sites, all with tables and grill. Ninety-four come with water and electrical hookups. The park does not accept reservations; campsites are offered on a first-come, first-served basis.

To get to Warrior's Path State Park from I-81, take Exit 59 and go north on Hwy. 36 to Hemlock Road. Turn right and continue to the park entrance. From Kingsport, take Fort Henry Dr. south to Hemlock Road. For more information call (423) 239-8531 or check the Web at www.tnstateparks.com.

TO THE GAP

ROGERSVILLE

Home to one of the more unusual springs in the world and to a historic inn, Rogersville also boasts a downtown largely spared from progress.

If one were to list the various destroyers of small-town architecture, shopping malls come first to mind. In Tennessee, however, less obvious villains over the years have been four-lane streets. When two-lane streets get widened, historic buildings and that special small-town feel usually bite the dust.

Highway 11 West used to go through downtown Rogersville, and when the two-lane road became inadequate to carry the growing traffic, some good soul decided to bypass the town and build a wider road in the fields north of town. Thus today's visitor can enjoy a town full of history and historic structures.

Rogersville came into being in 1787, only 10 years after Davy Crockett's grandparents had been killed by the original inhabitants. Local farmers plowing their fields still turn up arrowheads and other Indian relics. Like Blountville and other towns, Rogersville flourished from people coming from and going to points west. In 1791, it became the site of the first newspaper in Tennessee, the *Knoxville Gazette*. This seeming mix-up of names came about because the publisher had his eyes on Knoxville, which he knew would be named the state capital. He set up his press and began publication in Rogersville a year before moving to Knoxville. There is no record of anyone in town objecting to the slight.

Historic Sights
The **Hawkins County Courthouse,** erected in 1836, is the oldest operating courthouse in Tennessee. Its main courtroom resembles Independence Hall in Philadelphia, an architectural point probably unappreciated by the miscreants who find themselves doing business there.

Rogersville was the location of several institutions of higher learning. Rogersville Synodical College, a Presbyterian woman's school, was established in 1850. In 1883 Swift College, a high school for black girls, joined Rogersville's academic roster. It eventually became a college, and in the 1950s moved south to Mississippi.

Rogersville has an excellent walking tour to show off its significant buildings. Free copies of a brochure that points them out are available in various locations, among them the **Depot Museum,** 415 S. Depot St., tel. (423) 272-1961. This restored Southern Railway depot serves as a visitors center as well. It's open Tues.-Thurs. 10 a.m.-4 p.m. and other days by appointment.

A three-story building right in the middle of downtown, the 1824 **Hale Springs Inn** is Tennessee's oldest continuously operating one, and well worth a stop. Like similar places in Kingsport and Blountville, this one hosted Presidents Jackson, Polk, and Johnson. (These three are mentioned so often in this book that to some it must seem as if they traveled together like the Wise Men. But Jackson died the year Polk became president, and Polk died 16 years before Johnson moved into the White House.) Unlike the Netherland Inn or similar places, where the modern-day traveler must gaze reverentially into rooms of old, at the Hale Springs Inn one can actually stay in them (see below).

The privately owned **Krickbaum House,** at 324 W. Main St., was built around 1830 out of homemade brick and has an English boxwood hedge thought to be over 200 years old. The house is not open to the public.

Ebbing and Flowing Spring

The spring, just outside of town, begins with a barely discernible trickle and, two hours and 47 minutes later, reaches a flow of 500 gallons per minute. It has been doing this for more than 200 years, and no one knows exactly why. One theory holds that an underground basin is right under the spring. When the basin fills to the top, a siphon action works to empty it. Then the siphon is broken, and the spring has to wait until the basin is full again.

The second remarkable thing about this phenomenon is that it has not been commercialized. The people who own the spring charge no admission and sell no souvenirs. A lane to the side of the spring leads up the hill to Ebbing and Flowing United Methodist Church, a beautiful country church that stands beside an old school built before 1800. The cemetery contains a famous epitaph:

Remember me as you pass by
As you are now so once was I
As I am now, you soon shall be,
Prepare for death and follow me.

Some wag suggested the following lines:

To follow you I would not be content
Unless I knew which way you went.

To get to the spring, go east on Main St. 1.1 miles to Burem Rd., bearing right at the Amis House historical marker. Turn left on Ebbing and Flowing Spring Rd. at 2.3 miles. Go 1.4 miles to the spring, which is behind a little dairy house on the left. A lane on the right leads to the school and church. This spring is on private property, and visitors should keep that in mind as they come there.

Events

Rogersville holds **Heritage Days** on the second weekend in October. This harvest festival features agricultural demonstrations, open houses, and all manner of fun. For information on this and other Rogersville activities, go to the Rogersville Depot Museum, 415 S. Depot St., tel. (423) 272-1961. It's open Tues.-Thurs. 10 a.m.-4 p.m., weekends by appointment.

Spring Fling, a.k.a. "Heritage Days," is held on the fourth weekend in April.

Where to Stay

The nine rooms at the **Hale Springs Inn** are filled with period antiques, with no telephones to mar the experience. The Andrew Jackson Room on the third floor is the actual one in which he stayed. The corner table dates from 1824, and the sofa from 1835. Guests can set their glasses on the same mantel used by Ole Hickory. Rates begin at $45 per couple, most all rooms have private baths, and all guests receive a continental breakfast. Call (423) 272-5171, or write the inn at Rogersville, TN 37857. Inexpensive.

The **Cherokee Lake Campground,** 10 miles west of Rogersville on Hwy. 11 West, tel. (423) 272-3333, has 84 sites available year-round.

Food

Even if one doesn't have time to spend the night, one can partake of lunch and dinner at the **Carriage House Restaurant** inside the Hale Springs Inn. A typical dinner menu includes steak, seafood, buffalo, ostrich, and other high-end dishes. Prices run $16-19. The restaurant serves beer, but if patrons want wine, they have to bring it themselves.

Big John's Restaurant, 1212 E. Main St., tel. (423) 272-3999, boasts a table that no other eatery in town can claim: the Liar's Table. This round table is the headquarters for people with time on their hands and a willingness to talk about it. Anyone is invited to sit there and hold forth or just listen. An all-you-can-eat buffet of country cooking is the main attraction.

Pal's, Hwy. 66 in Rogersville, offers the finest in fast food of the burger and hot dog persuasion.

Shopping

Main Street Studio & Gallery, 116 E. Main St., sells functional pottery, while **Mountain Star Antique & Craft Mall,** 122 East Main St., offers all manner of antiques and collectible figures made of stone—bear stones, doll stones, and folk stones.

Information

The **Rogersville Depot Museum,** 415 S. Depot St., tel. (423) 272-1961, serves as the town's visitors center. It's open Tues.-Thurs. 10 a.m.-4 p.m., other days by appointment. The Hale Springs Inn also has brochures of walking tours and other local sites.

Pressmen's Home

The Hale Springs Inn's name comes from the springs in a resort area northwest of town. In the second half of the 1800s, it became fashionable to "take the waters" at various places. When the inn got its current name, the innkeepers would transport guests by carriage out of Rogersville for an all-day ride to the local watering hole on the other side of Stone Mountain. Here guests would quaff sulfurous water and hope it did them some good.

The appeal of the waters faded, as do most health fads, but in 1910 a most unlikely group entered the picture. The International Printing Pressmen and Assistants Union, hoping to help those of its members afflicted with tuberculosis, moved its headquarters to the old Hale Springs Resort. Medical thinking at that time held that mountain air was good for tubercular patients. Here, way back up in the hills, the visitor would come upon a hotel, a golf course, union headquarters, and a building containing the most modern presses available, where young printers could master useful skills. At its peak, Pressmen's Home, as it was called, also operated a dairy, a mill, and a cannery.

Tuberculosis was eventually brought under control with new drugs, and as the century wore on, Pressmen's Home seemed increasingly remote. The union began selling its holdings in the '50s, and in 1967 moved its headquarters to Washington, D.C. A real estate development bought some of the property and named it Camelot, but it could never quite come up with enough knights and damsels to make money. Now all that remains are gaping buildings, the new name on the map, and the 18-hole golf course, which is ardently played by locals. For information, call (423) 272-7499.

To get to Pressmen's Home/Camelot, go east on Main St. or Hwy. 11 West and turn left onto Hwy. 70. Drive 5.4 miles and fork left onto Hwy. 94. Drive four miles to get there.

SNEEDVILLE

Hancock is perhaps the most remote county in the state, yet it is an area of great beauty. Sneedville is the county seat, the birthplace of country singer Jimmy Martin, and the center of Melungeon culture. The Hancock County Historic Jail, which was built in 1860, is slated to become the Melungeon Cultural Heritage Museum, although at the time this book went to press there was still a long way to go.

Sneedville was also the home of Mahalia Mullins, a hearty eater who grew so fat that when she died in 1882 her coffin was constructed around the bed in which she lay. The chimney on one end of her cabin was being replaced, and to get the enormous coffin out a section of the wall was taken down.

The best way to approach Sneedville is on Hwy. 31. Route 66 winds up from Rogersville, but it is a long and winding road. **Elrod Falls** is a series of cascading falls just south of Sneedville on Hwy. 31. A small park has picnic tables and grills and a covered pavilion. The second waterfall contains an unusual flowstone formation, one seldom seen outside of caves.

In town a **Melungeon Cultural Heritage Museum** is located on Jail Street, one block south of the courthouse. This effort was just getting off the ground when this book was going to press.

North of Sneedville Hwy. 63 goes north over Newman Ridge, a longtime home to Melungeons. A right turn onto Vardy Rd. leads to the site of the Vardy Historic Community, where in

THE MELUNGEON MYSTERY

East Tennessee was settled primarily by people from the British Isles, and anyone who had a darker complexion was usually of Indian or African descent. In various parts of East Tennessee and Southwest Virginia, however—primarily Hancock and Hawkins counties—there lived communities of folks who had blue eyes, darker than usual skin, and straight blond or black hair. These people became known as "Melungeons," a term whose origin is not clear. Various theories claimed that the Melungeons were the descendants of Portuguese sailors, Spanish Moors, Indians, or Turks. A wilder theory holds that these are somehow the remants of the Lost Colony of Roanoke.

What did become clear, at any rate, was that being a Melungeon was something to hide. Like other racial minorities, they suffered all manner of abuse from their neighbors. Melungeons couldn't vote, own land, or go to public schools. Not surprisingly, this led to their distancing themselves from much of their culture, whatever it was and from wherever it came. Intermarriage with other people has almost entirely eliminated the distinctive Melungeon look nowadays, and to the casual visitor people walking around Sneedville look as good or as bad as anyone anywhere else.

In recent years, a growing number of Melungeon descendants have become curious about their hidden heritage and have brought what used to be a label of shame into a new and positive light. A Melungeon gathering in Wise, Virginia, has drawn crowds, and a Melungeon descendant named N. Brent Kennedy has written a book called *The Melungeons, The Resurrection of a Proud People: The Untold Story of Ethnic Cleansing in America*. Another book, by Mattie Ruth Johnson, is *My Melungeon Heritage*, from the Overmountain Press.

One observer in Sneedville, however, noted that most of the people who are celebrating Melungeon power have never lived in Hancock County, where the legacy of resentment and shame still exists. If out-of-towners see someone they think might be a Melungeon, it would not be a good idea to leap out of the car and ask.

1929 the Presbyterian Women's Mission Board built a school. Much like the Del Rio school depicted in the novel Catherine Marshall novel *Christy,* Vardy residents enjoyed a superb education, better health care than most of their neighbors, and encouragement to go to college.

THE WARRIOR'S PATH

In following Hwy. 11 West southwest from Rogersville, the traveler follows an ancient route. The Warrior's Path of the Cherokee came this way, and later Daniel Boone and 30 axmen cut a road from the Long Island of Kingsport to Cumberland Gap. They came through what is now Rogersville, following the Holston River, and then turned north to get to the Gap.

Mooresburg

This little community is a couple of miles south of Mooresburg Springs, which, according to the WPA Guide, were "highly impregnated with iron." The discoverers deeded the spring and about two acres of land "to the sick and afflicted of the State of Tennessee." According to the terms of the gift, any sick Tennessean could build a cabin there and stay as long as he or she wanted.

Modern-day visitors to Mooresburg can relax at the **Home Place Bed & Breakfast,** 132 Church Ln., tel. (423) 921-8424 or (800) 521-8424. The owner is descended from the founders of Mooresburg and Rogersville and offers four bedrooms and three baths. The first floor is handicapped accessible. Prices range from $45 to $100. Inexpensive-Expensive.

Bean Station

The place where Boone and his men turned north became known as Bean Station, which, as the population and commerce grew, became an important crossroads for travelers coming from as far as New Orleans and Baltimore. Travelers found an assortment of taverns and inns, the most famous of which was the Bean Station Tavern, a place that in its 1830s heyday could accommodate 200 people. Guests such as Andrew Jackson, James K. Polk, Andrew Johnson, and Henry Clay hobnobbed in parlors and had access to one of the finest wine cellars in the entire South.

Bean Station prospered even as horses and buggies gave way to railroads. In the late 1800s, Tate Springs became one of the better known resorts in the state. Six hundred guests could take the waters, play golf, or indulge in perhaps the laziest game ever invented—fly poker. The rules were simple: each player put down one card, and the first card on which a fly landed was the winner. As the new century rolled around, Tate Springs drew wealthy families, among them the Studebakers, Firestones, and Fords, but the advent of the automobile spelled the end for such resorts, and the Depression pushed them over the edge.

Tate Springs was bought in 1943 by a Methodist minister, Rev. A.E. Wachtel, who established the Kingswood School for neglected children. The students lived in the old hotel until 1963, when it burned down. New buildings were erected, however, and today the school continues serving children ages 5-18. Some are residents, while others are day students who are having behavioral or emotional problems in local schools. John Wachtel, son of the founder, presides over the school today. All that remains of the old resort is a gazebo that stands over the original spring. Kingswood School is not open to the public, but you can visit it on the Web at www.kidsurf.net/kingswood.

Rutledge

Farther down Hwy. 11 West lies the town of Rutledge, the seat of the only county in Tennessee named for a woman. Mary Grainger was the wife of John Sevier, the first governor of Tennessee.

On the grounds of the Grainger County Courthouse, in the middle of Rutledge, stands a brick building so small that it looks like a playhouse. This modest structure was once the tailor shop of Andrew Johnson. Here he stayed less than a year before returning to Greeneville to the woman who became his wife. Perhaps another reason for leaving Rutledge was that he had to share this building with the local sheriff.

Fish fanciers will appreciate the **Buffalo Springs Trout Hatchery** just south of Rutledge. This state-run hatchery has concrete raceways filled with thousands of trout. Admission is free, and someone is on hand every day 8 a.m.-4 p.m. to answer questions and give a brief tour. To get to the hatchery, take Hwy. 92 south of Rutledge to Owl Hole Gap Road. Turn right, and follow it to the hatchery.

The **Down Home Restaurant** on Hwy. 11 West, tel. (423) 828-3000, features country cooking, which is available Mon.-Sat. for all three meals.

A newcomer to the Rutledge culinary scene is Shine's Country Cookin' Hwy. 11 West, tel. (423) 828-8713, which serves all three meals every day and features catfish as well as other down-home delights.

Blaine

One of the only three known living Civil War widows in America makes her home in Blaine. For reasons known only to her, 18-year-old Gertrude Grubb married John Janeway in 1927. He was 81 years old and had fought for the Union in the last year of the Civil War as a 19-year-old soldier. He died in 1937, and she has received a pension check every month since then.

Indian Cave

Close to Knoxville on Hwy. 11 West from Rutledge sits Indian Cave, a venerable tourist attraction right on the Holston River. The cavern was used by the Cherokee for shelter and to hide from the army in the roundup preceding the Trail of Tears. Bat guano was mined in later years

---

THE TOMATO WAR

Almost every town in Tennessee has some sort of annual celebration with live music, crafts, beauty pageant, road race, etc. Rutledge's Grainger County Tomato Festival has all of these, but adds one very unusual event: the Tomato War. Here are a couple of the actual rules of this one-of-a-kind contest. "All participants will wear white T-shirts and will be provided with a fixed amount of tomato ammunition. A team member will be considered 'dead' when there is evidence of a direct hit on his shirt. Hits elsewhere will only be considered 'wounding.' To discourage excessive 'wounding,' the amount of ammunition will be strictly limited." The only possible improvement for this event would be speeches by politicians. The Tomato Festival is held every year on the last weekend in July. For further information, call (423) 828-8433.

for fertilizer. The visitor to Indian Cave has a choice of tours: the regular or the extended version. The former costs $5 and goes for a half mile; the latter costs $10 and goes 2.5 miles. Both are wheelchair accessible, and children under five get in free. Ardent cavers can take a Spelunking Tour by special arrangement.

Indian Cave is open all year. Summer hours run 10 a.m.-8 p.m., and all other times the cave is open by reservation only. To get there, go to the town of Blaine on Hwy. 11 West. Go south on Indian Ridge Rd. for approximately seven miles. Turn left at the sign and follow that road to the cave, about a half mile ahead.

Harrogate

Back at Bean Station, Hwy. 25 East heads northwest, climbing a series of ridges in the process. Just before coming to Cumberland Gap, the road leads through the town of Harrogate. A lot of English capital flowed into this part of Tennessee during the 1880s, and here it took the form of an enormous resort hotel, the Four Seasons, which contained seven hundred rooms. A mere three years later this structure was demolished to make room for the Harrow Academy, a private school.

O.O. Howard, a former general in the Union Army, spoke at a Harrow graduation and decided to champion the school. Recalling that President Lincoln had so appreciated the loyalty of East Tennesseans during the Civil War, the old general suggested dedicating the school to Lincoln and changing its name. The Harrow School evolved into Lincoln Memorial University, which was chartered in 1897 and has been educating locals since. The Internet address is www.lmunet.edu.

The university's **Abraham Lincoln Museum,** tel. (423) 869-6235, features a large collection of "Lincolniana," as some call it. The collection, which is housed in a building largely paid for by Colonel Sanders of chicken fame, contains the cane Lincoln used the night he was shot, various watches and his clothing, and a plaster model of the statue in the Lincoln Memorial in Washington, D.C. Other exhibits deal with Civil War medicine and documents from Lincoln's career.

The museum is open year-round. To get there, follow the signs from Hwy. 25 East. Admission is $2 for adults, $1.50 for seniors, $1 for children six to 12, with kids six and under getting in free. More information is available on the Internet at www.lmunet.edu/museum/musfront.html.

CUMBERLAND GAP

The town of Cumberland Gap was never a large place, and when passenger travel on railroads declined, it seemed to go into a long sleep. As a result, it largely escaped the ravages of modernization that were inflicted on so many Tennessee towns and has now become a very pleasant place to visit. To reflect its English heritage, the merchants have embraced the "Ye Olde Shoppe" school of retail nomenclature. They call their village "The Towne of Cumberland Gap," and someday may see the opening of "Ye Olde Software Shoppe." Visitors should just roll their eyes and enjoy this pleasant place.

TENNESSEE TOURIST DEVELOPMENT

Colleen Lester's Cookie Cabin and Cake Box lies near the Indian trail that Daniel Boone followed in 1775 as he hacked out the Wilderness Road.

Sights

The **Cumberland Gap Towne Hall,** which occupies a converted 1925 school building at the corner of N. Cumberland Dr. and Colwyn Ave., is a good place to start your tour. Here visitors can also obtain a map.

The oldest building in town houses the **Cumberland Gap Wedding Chapel,** on Colwyn Ave., tel. (800) 368-1890, a Victorian temple of matrimony complete with lace curtains, antique pews, and period furnishings. The owner points out two advantages of getting married in Tennessee: no blood test and no waiting period. It's shown by appointment only.

Where to Stay

Cumberland Gap Inn, 630 Brooklyn St., tel. (888) 408-0127, has rooms ranging from $49 to $65. You'll also find a wide choice of lodgings across the gap in Middlesboro, Kentucky. Inexpensive-Moderate.

Food

For hungry people passing through, the **Cookie Cabin and Cake Box** on Pennlyn Ave., tel. (423) 869-4487, offers pastries, fresh bread, pies, and candy.

"Food so good you'll think we stole your mom" is the motto at **Webb's Country Kitchen,** 602 Colwyn Ave., tel. (423) 869-5877, which offers country cooking such as biscuits and gravy, pinto beans, and hoecakes.

Perhaps the fanciest restaurant in Cumberland Gap is **Ye Olde Tea and Coffee Shoppe,** 527 Colwyn Ave., tel. (423) 869-4844, where the menu is far more extensive than the name might suggest. The restaurant is in an old brick building that once housed a bank, hardware store, and general store. In 1910 the bank was robbed, netting the crooks—caught shortly afterwards—the grand total of seven dollars. The vault from the bank is still there. Prime rib, steak, mesquite-grilled chicken, and seafood are available with the espresso and cappuccino.

A wide choice of fast food outlets and other restaurants lies across the gap in Middlesboro, Kentucky.

Shopping

The **Cumberland Gap General Store,** 503 Colwyn Ave., tel. (423) 869-2282, offers more than 6,000 giftware items—among them reproductions of antiques, Depression glass, and cast iron toys. They also have over 300 dolls.

Information

The Cumberland Gap Towne Hall, corner of Colwyn Ave. and Lynn, tel. (423) 869-3860, is open Mon.-Fri. 8 a.m.-4 p.m. or check out www.cumberlandgap.com.

CUMBERLAND GAP NATIONAL HISTORICAL PARK

Though only a small section of this park is in Tennessee, it deserves mention, both for its historical significance and natural beauty. Indeed, one can make the case that the visitor with a limited amount of time in Tennessee would get more out of this park than a trip to the much larger—and vastly more crowded—Great Smokies National Park.

While the Appalachian Mountains cannot compare in size to western ranges, they provide formidable obstacles. Anyone not believing this should try marching up the side of one of these mountains or ridges. Now imagine crossing them in muddy or snowy conditions, and doing so with a wagon.

HISTORY

A Gap in the Ridge

The earliest travelers through the Cumberland Gap were migrating herds of buffalo. As Indians moved into the region, they followed the buffalo and used the Gap to get to prime hunting grounds in Kentucky. The first settler to tell others of the passage was Dr. Thomas Walker, an English surveyor who came through in 1750. The French and Indian War and assorted problems with the Indians, not to mention the fact that the route over the Gap was basically a path, held down substantial migration for 25 years.

Daniel Boone first came through the Gap in 1769 and encountered hostile Indians. In 1773, while attempting to lead a group of settlers toward the Gap, Indians attacked Boone's party and killed his son James.

The Wilderness Road

After the 1775 land purchase consummated at Sycamore Shoals, however, Boone and 30 others hacked out the 208-mile-long Wilderness Road from King's Port to Boonesborough on the Kentucky River. This literally got things rolling. By the end of the Revolutionary War some 12,000 people had crossed the Gap, and traffic reached its peak during the 1790s. By 1800 an estimated 300,000 people had come through heading north and west, including Abraham Lincoln's parents. As people in the territory became settled and began producing more than they needed, the Gap served as a trade route back to the east.

In the 1820s and 1830s, when the Erie Canal and railroads pierced the mountains farther north, traffic through the Gap declined. The Civil War sparked interest in the Gap once more. Andrew Johnson, afraid to ride a train through hostile Confederate territory, used the Gap as a way to travel to Washington to take his place in the Senate. Thousands of Tennesseans who were loyal to the Union came the same way to join the Union Army.

CUSSING THE YANKEES

When the Confederates surrendered Cumberland Gap, one of their Fort Pitt officers refused to cease fire with his cannon and, in a final act of defiance, spiked and destroyed the piece. The Northern troops packed him off to a prison camp in Minnesota for the duration of the war.

After the war, he moved to Texas but never relented in his disgust with the Union. On his deathbed, he convinced his grandson to go to the site of Fort Pitt on the 100th anniversary of its fall, to face north, and to curse the Federal government for a full five minutes. On September 9, 1963, the grandson stepped up to the site of the former fort and fulfilled his grandfather's wish.

The Civil War

Realizing that these men and boys might come back through the Gap, this time wearing uniforms, the Confederacy built seven forts, all facing north, and cut down all the trees within a mile of each fort. Sitting atop this denuded landscape, they awaited an attack that never came, finally abandoning their positions in June of 1862 to fight elsewhere. Union forces numbering 20,000 then occupied the Gap and built their own set of forts, this time facing south. Their supply line was severed, forcing them to retreat, and the Gap was once more in the hands of Southerners. A Union force came and captured the main water supply, and the Confederates—among them the great-great grandfather of the author of this book—surrendered. The North held the Gap until the end of the war.

Wilderness Restored

During the 20th century a modern highway crossed the Gap, and in the 1940s and '50s another significant migration took place, this one involving black families moving north to take advantage of new economic opportunities.

Now Hwy. 25 East has been routed through a long tunnel under the Gap, and the Park Service plans to restore the Gap to the way it looked in the days of the Wilderness Road. When that project is finished, the Gap will have come almost full circle. Visitors can look at the road and ponder the words of Frederick Jackson Turner, who wrote in 1893: "Stand at Cumberland Gap and watch the procession of civilization, marching single file—the buffalo following the trail to the salt springs, the Indian, the fur-trader and hunter, the cattle-raiser, the pioneer farmer—and the frontier has passed by."

SIGHTS AND RECREATION

Historical Elements of the Park

Down in the town of Cumberland Gap, the remains of the **Iron Furnace** give a glimpse of how settlers supplied a basic need. Looking like a big, squat chimney, this furnace was heavy industry for the frontier; at its peak up to 300 men—some of them slaves—worked here. Their tasks consisted of assembling iron ore, limestone, and charcoal. The charcoal required 50

CUMBERLAND GAP TUNNEL

The 4,600-foot-long twin tunnels that now guide Highway 25E traffic under Cumberland Mountain are engineering marvels. Work was begun in 1991 with a 10-foot by 10-foot pilot tunnel that revealed several challenges hidden in the depths of Cumberland Mountain.

Several caves lay in the path, including one with an entrance 85 feet high and another with an underground lake 30 feet deep. In addition, pockets in the rock contained large amounts of clay. The company that insured the project estimated that four to six workers would die during the project.

Work commenced on the Tennessee and Kentucky sides, and workers met in the middle on July 9, 1992. The project was opened to traffic a little more than five years after work was begun, and no one lost his life in the effort. A sophisticated ventilation system and backup power source keeps the tunnel healthy for motorists, and the whole operation is controlled from a command center on the Kentucky side.

cords of wood each time the furnace was fired, resulting in a steady deforestation of the surrounding land. Oddly enough, the iron makers never used coal, which is abundant in the area. The molten iron was cast into Dutch ovens, skillets, and plows, but most of it wound up as "pig iron," which was sold to blacksmiths or shipped via river to Chattanooga. At peak production, the furnace daily produced about 43 "pigs" weighing 150 pounds each.

The limestone surface is smooth inside from the heat. It was last used in the 1880s, when cheaper steel from the East made this more home-grown variety uneconomical. To get there, follow the signs.

Fort McCook and **Fort Lyon,** remnants of Civil War earthworks with cannons, are visible near the Pinnacle and along the Pinnacle Road. Surrounded as they are now by a dense forest, they do not give an accurate view of the barren landscape over which Union and Confederate soldiers kept a boring watch. Sometimes historical inaccuracy is not a bad thing.

Hensley Settlement consists of some of the buildings left by a 20th-century group of pioneers who climbed Brush Mountain and lived

there for almost 50 years. Sherman Hensley and his family moved here in 1904, and at its 1925-35 peak the community had 12 scattered homesteads consisting of about 100 people. This was a largely self-sufficient place. If they didn't hunt it or grow it or make it—and that included about everything—they rode down off the mountain to get it. The last resident left in 1951, and since then the Park Service has restored about 25 buildings scattered over three farmsteads in a 70-acre area.

Getting there is not easy. Hikers can walk the 3.5-mile Chadwell Gap Trail up the side of Cumberland Mountain. To get there, take Hwy. 58 east along the route of the Wilderness Road. Turn left onto Virginia Rd. 690. Turn right onto Rd. 688 and park at the trailhead. Keep in mind that it can be much cooler on the top of the mountain and dress accordingly.

During summer the Park Service runs a van to Hensley Settlement once daily Friday through Monday. There's a small charge, and the holds just 10 people. Make reservations by calling park headquarters one week in advance.

Mountain bikers can come up the Kentucky side of the mountain to the park boundary, which is about a quarter mile from Hensley Settlement. To do this, take Sugar Run Rd., which after leaving the park becomes KY 988. Turn right onto KY 217 and drive to the Cubbage School, then go right on KY 987. Go right on the Brownies Creek Primitive Road.

Natural Sites

In addition to Cumberland Gap itself, the park runs northeast along the ridge top of Cumberland Mountain. That ridge alone, aside from having any historical significance, is worth a trip to the park. The **Ridge Trail** runs the length of the mountain—15.6 miles in all.

When Dr. Thomas Walker first came through the gap, he noted the presence of a large cave. During the Civil War, the cavern was used to store supplies, and was the setting of an 1864 novel called Cudjo's Cave. The coming of the highway and tourists brought about the commercialization of the cave, which somehow came into the possession of Lincoln Memorial University. The Park Service bought the cave and has opened it to the public once more as a "wild cave" experience. The sometimes-garish electrical lights have all been ripped out, and guides carry lanterns to show visitors the cave as Dr. Walker might have first seen it. Unlike Dr. Walker, however, modern-day cavers walk on manmade pathways.

A delightful natural feature of the park is **Sand Cave,** on the far eastern end of the park on the Kentucky side, though visitors must begin the hike in Virginia. The hike is about four miles one-way, but the cave is worth it. Sand Cave is technically a "rock house"—one enormous room almost an acre and a quarter in size. The 150-foot-wide entrance stands 40 feet high, and a waterfall streams down one side. The cave floor is a sloping surface of sand—tons and tons of it. Children of all ages love to climb to the top of the slope and run down. To get to the cave, take Hwy. 58 east to Ewing, Virginia. Turn left onto VA 724, and drive a short way to the Civitan Club parking lot.

Old-time travelers headed for Cumberland Gap on the Wilderness Road could look up and see white cliffs atop Cumberland Mountain. They viewed them with foreboding, as a symbol of the mountain barrier in their way. Today's travelers see **White Rocks** as a great hiking destination. Eons ago this area was under the sea, and the cliffs are made of conglomerate, a combination of light-colored quartz pebbles and sand. To get there, use the same directions for Sand Cave.

PRACTICALITIES

Camping
The park has a year-round, 160-site camping area on the Virginia side. Water and flush toilets are available, and 50 sites have electricity. Four primitive campsites lie along the Ridge Trail. These require permits from park headquarters.

Information
The **park headquarters** is off Hwy. 25 East in Kentucky. It's open daily 8 a.m.-5 p.m. year-round. Call (606) 248-2817, write the park at Box 1848, Middlesboro, KY 40965, or check the Internet at www.nps.gov/cuga.

The procession of civilization has passed through the Cumberland Gap.

ELIZABETHTON AND VICINITY

Jonesborough gets most of the attention from those seeking to explore Tennessee's colonial towns; it certainly has cornered the market on bed and breakfasts and cute shops. Elizabethton, however, with its Carter Mansion and the replica of Fort Watauga, offers a significant look at what was America's first frontier.

Elizabethton is noted for being the source of a genteel rivalry, the famous 1886 "War of the Roses" gubernatorial campaign between brothers Alf and Bob Taylor, respectively a Republican and a Democrat. In our age of attack ads and electronic mudslinging, the gentle race between these two seems as remote as high button shoes.

The Taylors supposedly pledged to their mother that they would confine their debates and speeches to the issues and would not lambaste each other. Both were accomplished humorists, and they entertained crowds with political speeches seasoned with fiddle music and jokes. A story dating from this time claims that the two spoke in a small town in which a makeshift wooden stage was erected atop a new manure spreader sitting outside a hardware store. After Republican Alf finished speaking, his Democrat brother climbed up and confessed that he "had never before stood on the Republican platform."

Elizabethton attracted industry throughout the 19th century, and in 1926, following the examples of Kingsport and other Southern towns, German firms began moving in and manufacturing rayon. Three years later Elizabethton was the site of a bitter strike by the rayon workers. The labor unrest involved 5,000 workers and led to a clash with 800 National Guardsmen. The strikes ultimately failed, but served as the first examples of Southern workers challenging exploitative conditions by Northern or foreign industrialists.

SIGHTS

Sycamore Shoals State Historical Area is the best place to begin sightseeing in Elizabethton.

The 50-acre park sits right beside the famous shoals, just west of town at 1651 W. Elk Ave., otherwise known as Hwy. 321. The fort and visitors center have good exhibits, and kids will love the opportunity to run inside the palisaded structure and peer out of the old doors and over the top. A trail leads down to the Watauga River, where one can see the famous shoals. The park is open daily 8 a.m.-4:30 p.m. and is closed on holidays.

Leaving the historical area, head downtown on Hwy. 321/Elk Avenue. As one crosses the Doe River, a look to the right reveals the **Doe River Covered Bridge.** Stretching 134 feet over the river, this 1882 structure can be crossed on foot or in a vehicle. There are few windows, supposedly so that horses or cattle driven across the bridge would not be scared by seeing the water below. This situation aided early courtships as well.

Elizabethton has several significant homes, which are discussed at great length in Carolyn Sakowski's excellent *Touring the East Tennessee Backroads.* Perhaps the best is the **John and Landon Carter Mansion.** To get there from the Historical Area, come into town on Elk Avenue/Hwy. 321 to the intersection where Hwy. 321 turns left and is joined by Hwy. 19. Go right on this four-lane road and proceed until the stoplight at Broad Street. Turn right, then turn right again on the Broad Street Extension. Go 0.3 miles; the house will be on the left.

The house may not look like a mansion now, but in the early 1770s this was high style. This house has been preserved, not restored, and the inside contains fancy woodwork—this in a time of rough log cabins—and oil paintings. An estimated 90% of what one sees is the original part of the house.

The Carter Mansion is administered by the Sycamore Shoals State Historic Area and is open from late May until late August. Hours are Wed.-Sat. 9 a.m.-5 p.m., and Sunday 1-5 p.m. During the off-season, visitors can see the house by appointment. Call (423) 543-5808. Admission is free. See it online at www.tnstateparks.com.

RECREATION

The following recreation areas are in the Cherokee National Forest. All offer picnicking, hiking, and various wilderness activities, and the Appalachian Trail (www.nps.gov/aptr/) runs through each one. For further information, write to the Watauga Ranger District Office at Rt. 9, Box 2235, or call (423) 735-1500.

The **Little Oak Recreation Site** is on Watauga Lake and stays open from late April until October or December, depending on the onset of winter. The site features a boat launching ramp, camping, and showers.

The **Big Laurel Branch Wilderness,** downstream from Elizabethton, is a 6,200-acre part of the Cherokee National Forest on Watauga and Wilbur Lakes. The latter is a small lake formed by damming the Watauga River before it flows into Watauga Lake. To get there, take Hwy. 91 East out of Elizabethton and turn right on the Wilbur Dam Road.

The **Pond Mountain Wilderness,** also a part of the Cherokee National Forest, contains several waterfalls and sits in the Laurel Forge Gorge Area. The area is noted as well for beautiful patches of mountain laurel and rhododendron. To get there, take Hwy. 19 East/321/37 south from Elizabethton to the town of Hampton. Highway 321/67 will fork off to the left. Stay on it until Dennis Cove Road.

The Appalachian Trail passes through this area, going through some wonderful scenery. There are many ways to get to the trail. **Laurel Fork Trail** is a good one that has a waterfall along the way.

Head out of Elizabethton toward Hampton on Hwy. 19 East/321/37. At Hampton, where the road splits, follow Hwy. 321/67. Go 1.1 miles from this intersection to the Dennis Cove Road. Turn right and follow this twisting road for 4.1 miles to Laurel Fork Fall trailhead on the left. This trail runs downhill with the Appalachian Trail along an old railroad bed for about a mile to the falls. Laurel Fork Falls are cascades, and beautiful ones at that.

Note: If a trailhead's parking lot is full, make sure you aren't parking on private property. Some locals take great umbrage at vehicles parked on their land.

ENTERTAINMENT AND EVENTS

Outdoor Entertainment
Sycamore Shoals State Historical Area is home to a two-act outdoor drama, *The Wataugans,* which is performed at 7:30 p.m. for several nights every year in mid-July. The cast of local people works hard to bring to life the stories of their forebears. For information, call (423) 543-5808.

Professional baseball takes the field in Elizabethton in the form of the **Elizabethton Twins,** part of the Minnesota Twins farm system. The

TENNESSEE TOURIST DEVELOPMENT

Modern mountain men gather at Sycamore Shoals State Historical Area to commemorate the Revolutionary War victory over the British at Kings Mountain.

Twins play at Joe O'Brien Field at Riverside Park. To get there, take Hwy. 321 to Holly Lane. Usual game time is 7 p.m. Call (423) 547-6443 for schedules.

Festivals

The **Peter's Hollow Egg Fight** is a one-of-a-kind event. Held on Easter weekend, the "fighting" consists of tapping hard-boiled eggs against each other to see which will crack first. This has been going on since 1823, and is free and open to anyone. There are a few rules: only chicken eggs can be used, adults fight adults and children fight children. To get to Peter's Hollow, take Hwy. 91 10 miles north of Elizabethton. And bring plenty of eggs. For further information, call (423) 474-3833.

Sycamore Shoals was a gathering area for Indians when white folks still thought the world was flat. The **Sycamore Shoals Indian Festival** recognizes these native Americans on the first weekend in June with an annual celebration at the Historical Area involving tomahawk throwing, Cherokee traditional dances, blowgun competitions, crafts, and storytelling. For more information, call (423) 543-5808.

Tennessee has lots of festivals, but this is perhaps the only one commemorating a bridge. The annual **Covered Bridge Celebration,** held on the second weekend in June, provides an occasion to display antique cars, hear down-home music, and much more. Call (423) 547-3852.

The third weekend in June marks the **Muster at Fort Watauga** at the Sycamore Shoals State Historical Area. Visitors can see actors and actresses wearing period clothing, firing muzzle-loading rifles, and bringing to life scenes from colonial days. For more information, call (423) 543-5808.

The **Overmountain Victory Trail March** takes place September 25. Marchers in period clothing arrive at the Historical Area around 1:30 p.m., spend the night and depart the next day at about 8 a.m. Usually 15-30 people walk all the way to Kings Mountain, South Carolina. For more information, call (423) 543-5808.

The second weekend in November features the **Christmas Craft Show** at the Historical Area, with 48 local craftspeople displaying and selling their wares. For more information, call (423) 543-5808.

Christmas at the Carter Mansion takes place on the third Saturday in December, when the historic house is decorated in 17th century style, lit by candles, and filled with period music. Refreshments are served, and admission is $1 per person or $2 per family. Visitors are sometimes surprised to see that there are no Christmas trees here, but that custom did not take root in this country until the 1800s. For information, call (423) 543-5808.

WHERE TO STAY

Motels

Visitors can choose from the **Comfort Inn,** 1515 Hwy. 19 East Bypass, tel. (800) 221-2222 or (423) 542-4466; or the **Days Inn,** 505 W. Elk Ave., tel. (423) 543-3344. Nearby in Hampton is the **Watauga Lakeshore Resort,** Rt. 2, Box 379, Hwy. 321, Hampton, tel. (423) 725-2201.

Camping

Camping at the following Cherokee National Forest campgrounds is strictly first-come first-served; no reservations are taken. Directions to each are listed above under "Recreation." For further information, call (423) 735-1500.

Dennis Cove on Laurel Creek has 18 sites, with drinking water and restrooms. It's open year-round.

Carden's Bluff has 43 campsites on Watauga Lake, with drinking water and restrooms. It's open mid-April to October.

FOOD AND INFORMATION

Food in Town

For a trip back to the '50s, check out the **Classic Malt Shop,** 630 Broad St., tel. (423) 543-7141. A 1958 Edsel is parked out front. Visitors can sit at a pink or green booth and have a blue plate special on a black table while listening to "Blue Suede Shoes." The food is Southern style, and the jukebox has 1,200 songs.

Dino's, 420 Elk Ave., tel. (423) 542-5541, presents lunches and dinners of very good Italian food—fresh sauces and pasta are made on the premises. Pictures of baseball greats adorn the walls.

Gregg's Pizza, in the Carter County Plaza, tel. (423) 543-3133, is one of the few nonfranchise pizzerias in this area.

Good Chinese food isn't common in East Tennessee, but the **Hunan Chinese Restaurant,** 361 W. Elk Ave., tel. (423) 542-6112, is an exception to the rule.

People with big appetites head for the **Mayflower** in the Betsytown Shopping Center on the Hwy. 19 East Bypass, tel. (423) 542-3667, where portions are so generous that almost every patron heads out with a doggie bag. This place offers seafood platters, steak, chicken, and daily specials.

The burgers and hot dogs at **Pal's,** 413 W. Elk Ave., tel. (423) 542-0550, go toe-to-toe and hold their own with the franchises.

Rustlers, 415 W. Elk Ave., tel. (423) 543-2727, serves barbecue, chicken, steak, and homemade fries every day.

Locals often go to **Odelly's Restaurant,** about two miles out of town on the Hwy. 19 East Bypass to Roan Mountain, tel. (423) 543-3354, just for the beans and cornbread. Others will like the country ham, tenderloin, chicken, seafood, sandwiches, and homemade ice cream.

The Southern Restaurant, 408 E. Elk Ave., tel. (423) 542-5132, is the kind of place Barney Fife and Andy Taylor would take Thelma Lou and Helen. It offers a full menu of—what else?—Southern food.

Food Nearby

It's often said that the **Ridgewood Restaurant,** tel. (423) 538-7543, serves the best barbecue in East Tennessee. It's on Hwy. 19 East between Elizabethton and Bluff City. On Friday and Saturday night, the place is packed with people eating beef or pork barbecue. However, it doesn't serve ribs.

The town of Hampton lies south of Elizabethton on the way to Roan Mountain. Here is **The Captain's Table,** tel. (423) 725-2201, a top-notch restaurant offering a full menu and specializing in fresh mountain trout. Try the crayfish for an appetizer. It's on Hwy. 321 in Hampton, overlooking Watauga Lake.

Information

The **Elizabethton/Carter County Chamber of Commerce** is located at 500 Hwy. 19 East Bypass, tel. (423) 547-3852.

BUTLER

By and large the Tennessee Valley Authority did some wonderful things for the state, but the downside of the dams and lakes was the forced relocation of dozens of towns. "Old Butler" rests on the bottom of Watauga Lake. The town that visitors see dates from the late '40s.

Doe Mountain Inn, 412 K & R Rd., tel. (423) 727-2726, offers two suites, each of which has a fireplace, television, microwave, and picturesque views of the mountains. Rates are $85 per night. Moderate.

Iron Mountain Inn, tel. (423) 768-2446, is a new log home with four bedrooms, each of which has a whirlpool bath and very nice views of the surrounding mountains. Rates are $120-150, which includes a gourmet breakfast. Write Box 30, 138 Moreland Dr., Butler, TN 37640. Premium.

Pappy's Marina, tel. (423) 768-2270, a 25-site campground on Watauga Lake, offers hookups, a store, boating, and fishing. Take the Sink Valley Rd. from Hwy. 67.

ROAN MOUNTAIN

Visitors who find themselves in East Tennessee during the last two weeks in June owe it to themselves to take in Roan Mountain's more than 600 acres of rhododendrons. These natural gardens contain Catawba rhododendrons, which blossom in reds and purples.

"Roan Mountain" refers to three things—a mountain, a state park, and a town. All are close together, and this entry will cover all three. The town is on Hwy. 19 East close to the North Carolina border. Turning right onto Hwy. 143, visitors follow the Doe River and will soon see **Roan Mountain State Park,** a 2,200-acre delight, on the left. Continuing up Hwy. 143 for about 10 miles, motorists will eventually come to Roan Mountain proper, which sits on the Tennessee-North Carolina border at a lofty altitude of 6,286 feet above sea level. Although the peak is technically in North Carolina, no one really cares, especially when the flowers are in bloom. The Appalachian Trail comes through here, and the views are stupendous. Keep in mind that the weather here can be a lot cooler than down below. Snow sometimes lingers into April.

Roan Mountain is one of a series of Appalachian peaks called "balds" for their lack of trees. No one has come up with a definitive reason for this condition. Mountains that are higher, such as Mt. Mitchell, have trees all the way to the top. A variety of Indian legends surround the balds, but these tales don't agree either.

However they came about, balds such as Roan Mountain are wonderful to climb. In the summer they are refreshingly cool. Here one can walk the famous Appalachian Trail as it wanders amid the rhododendrons toward the peak. At the top hikers can see the remnants of a turn-of-the-century hotel that had about 200 rooms and now, thankfully, is no more.

Back down the hill lies the state park, one of the finest in the entire Tennessee park system. This place has hiking, trout fishing, and even cross-country skiing (see below). Historic sights include the site of the Peg Leg iron ore mine, Native American artifacts, and, best of all, the Dave Miller Homestead. This old home sits in a hollow in the park, and here visitors can get a good sense of what life was like in the early part of this century. The first house was built in 1870, and the second in 1910. The interpreter at the house is Jackie Grindstaff, granddaughter of Dave Miller. Her depiction of farm life, its joys and sorrows, is about as authentic as one can find.

For those not staying in cabins or the campgrounds, the park is open 8 a.m.-10 p.m. The Miller Homestead is open May 30 through Labor Day, Wed.-Sun. 9 a.m.-5 p.m. and on weekends in October.

Recreation

Aside from hiking and trout fishing, this park is known for a sport seldom seen in the South—**cross-country skiing.** The park offers three trails totaling 8.5 miles. Skiers must provide their own equipment, or they can sometimes rent it from local outfitters. Ask the people at the park for tips on who offers skis.

Events

The first weekend in May signals the **Roan Mountain Wildflower Tour and Bird Walks.** Experts in both areas lead novices and col-

More than 600 acres of rhododendrons bloom on Roan Mountain.

leagues through the woods, pointing out specimens along the way.

Young trout anglers will like the Junior Trout Tournament, held on the second weekend in May. Kids 7-15 compete to catch tagged trout and win a variety of prizes.

The **Rhododendron Festival,** now a half-century old, takes place during the third week in June and features crafts, food, and entertainment.

For more than 30 years, the **Roan Mountain Naturalists Rally** has offered guided walks and presentations amid the splendor of fall colors. This event usually takes place on the first weekend after Labor Day. Note: In some circles, "naturalist" is a euphemism for nudist. Participants in nature walks are requested to stay dressed.

The third weekend in September brings the **Roan Mountain Fall Festival,** an autumn version of the Rhododendron Festival.

Where to Stay

The best place to stay is in the park, which has campgrounds and 30 **cabins,** basketball and tennis courts, a large swimming pool (heated!), and a playground for kids. The cabins rest against a hill close by the Doe River. They are furnished with linens and cooking necessities, have wood-burning stoves, and can sleep six. From the week of June 1 through the last Sunday in August cabins can be rented only by the week. Make reservations by calling (423) 772-3303. Cabins cost $102 per night and can be rented one year ahead of the desired date. Occasions such as Christmas, Thanksgiving, and the month of October are particularly in demand. Expensive.

Those seeking more luxurious accommodations should go to **General Wilder's Bed & Breakfast** in the town of Roan Mountain at 202 Main St., tel. (423) 772-3102. This 1880s house offers five rooms containing antiques and private baths. Rates are $69-99. Moderate to Expensive.

The park's **campground** offers a total of 107 sites, 87 with electric and water hookups. Tent campers have 20 sites apart from the motor homes and trailers. Bathrooms have flush toilets, hot showers, and a laundromat. A dumping station is on the premises. Camping sites cannot be reserved; first-come, first-served is the rule here. From November 15 until April 1, the campground is open only to self-contained RVs. The restrooms are closed, although electrical hookups are available.

Food and Information
The village of Roan Mountain has some restaurants open on a seasonal basis.

For information about the park, call **Roan Mountain State Park,** Rt. 1, Box 236, Roan Mountain, TN 37687, or call (423) 772-3303. See them online at www.tnstateparks.com.

JOHNSON CITY

Of the Tri-Cities—Kingsport, Bristol, and Johnson City—Johnson City is the youngest, getting its charter in 1869 and its name from David Johnson, a man for all seasons who was postmaster, depot agent, merchant, hotel keeper, magistrate, and first mayor of the town.

In 1911 the East Tennessee State Normal School came to Johnson City, and today East Tennessee State University (ETSU), with an enrollment of more than 12,000, is the center of education in the area. Johnson City enjoys the cultural, financial, and other aspects of being a college town. See them online at www.etsu.edu.

It also enjoys the reputation among the Tri-Cities as being the fun place to go. All those students and a plethora of restaurants in which one can drink something stronger than Dr. Enuf keeps Johnson City rolling long after Kingsport and Bristol have shut down for the night.

Johnson City is the setting of *My Own Country,* a 1994 book about the experiences of Abraham Verghese, a doctor from India who found himself treating AIDS patients in the city and surrounding area. His thoughts on East Tennessee culture and the poignant stories of his patients and their families make a fascinating book.

SIGHTS AND RECREATION

Historic Sights
Downtown Johnson City does not offer much of a historical nature, but significant places lie outside the city limits. The most significant is **Rocky Mount,** the oldest territorial capital in the country. When the United States came into being, the states ceded their westernmost lands to the federal government, which pronounced them territories. William Blount was named governor of the Southwest Territory, and he set up his capital at the home of William Cobb. Here Blount held forth for two years until he moved operations to Knoxville.

Today Rocky Mount is a living history museum, with individuals acting out the roles and doing the chores of the people who lived here 1790-92.

On the other side of town sits the **Tipton-Haynes Historic Site,** tel. (423) 926-3631. This place got its start as a watering hole for buffalo, then as a campsite for Indians and white hunters who stayed in a nearby cave. The home was built in the 1780s by Col. John Tipton, who was a member of the 1776 Constitutional Convention. In 1839 it was sold to the Haynes family and became the home of Landon Carter Haynes, a gentleman who bet on the wrong side in the Civil War. A Confederate senator, he was forced to skedaddle to Virginia at war's end.

The house has been restored to its 1860s glory and includes a museum, an herb garden, nature trails, and a gift shop. Children are intrigued by the cave. The historic site is open Mon.-Sat. 10 a.m.-5 p.m., Sunday 2-5 p.m. From November 1 until March 31, however, the site is open only on weekdays 10 a.m.-4 p.m. Admis-

DR. ENUF AND MOUNTAIN DEW

Much like cities and towns that used to have their own breweries, Johnson City was the birthplace of two carbonated soft drinks—one that made the big time, and one that has stayed local.

Mountain Dew, a phrase synonymous hereabouts for moonshine, was first bottled by Charles Gordon in Johnson City and marketed with a cornball campaign centered on the slogan "Yahoo! Mountain Dew!" The formula was sold to Pepsi and now Mountain Dew, minus any Appalachian connection, is sold coast to coast.

Dr. Enuf has stayed closer to home. Invented by a Chicago chemist, Dr. Enuf is a lemon-lime flavored concoction containing 260 percent of the daily vitamin B1 requirement, 90 percent of needed Vitamin B3, and 120 percent of a day's worth of potassium iodide. The drink was marketed beginning in 1949 as a tonic that contained a burst of energy, and to anyone with a vitamin deficiency, it probably did work wonders. (It was also said to be especially helpful for those with a hangover.) Whatever Dr. Enuf accomplished, it fit right in with folks who were accustomed to using Coca-Cola as a cure for an upset stomach.

Although the Food and Drug Administration prevents Dr. Enuf's makers from claiming any healthful benefits, the bottles are making their way from country store coolers to the shelves of health food stores alongside bottles of ginseng tea and other modern-day nostrums, and today can be found as far away as Birmingham, Atlanta, and Greensboro, NC.

sion is $3 for adults, $2.50 for seniors, $1.50 for children 12 and under, with children under three getting in free.

Museums

The **Carroll Reece Museum,** tel. (423) 929-4392, is ETSU's showplace for temporary exhibits, workshops, lectures, and films. Of its six galleries, three are usually devoted to items from the museum's collection. These include early settlement artifacts, musical instruments such as pianos and dulcimers, and antique toys. The other three galleries are filled with traveling exhibits, usually devoted to art or history.

To get to the museum, take Exit 31 off southbound I-181. Turn left at the traffic light and get on University Parkway. Proceed about one mile, when the university will appear on the left. Take the second entrance to the university—Stout Drive—and pull into the University Public Safety Building on the right to get a parking permit. The museum is straight ahead. Follow the signs. The museum is open Mon.-Sat. 9 a.m.-4 p.m., Sunday 1-4 p.m. Admission is free.

For the visitor with children who threaten to scream if taken to another historic site, the **Hands On! Regional Museum,** 315 E. Main St., tel. (423) 434-4263, is the place to go. Following the trend of science museums nationwide, this place offers hands-on exhibits ranging from an airplane cockpit to a coal mine. Best suited for children under age 12, the museum features demonstrations and exhibits. This is highly used by school groups, so if going during the school year, try to go in the afternoon. The museum is open Tues.- Fri. 9 a.m.-5 p.m., Saturday 10 a.m.-5 p.m., and Sunday 1-5 p.m. During the summer it is also open on Monday. Admission is $5 for adults, $4 for ages 3-17, and free for ages two and under. Its Internet address is www.handsonmuseum.org.

Mountain Home

Mountain Home, State of Franklin St., tel. (423) 926-1171, is the name most locals apply to the James H. Quillen Veterans Affairs Medical Center (www.qcom.etsu.edu) in Johnson City. Seldom listed in tourist promotions, it is both a beautiful place to visit as well as an interesting look at how medical treatment has changed over the years.

Founded in 1903 as an old soldiers' home for Union war veterans, Mountain Home was a self-contained community on 450 acres consisting of a large farm, dairy, power plant, and its own fire department. Most of the Beaux Arts buildings date from 1901-05. Andrew Carnegie gave $15,000 for a library, and a theater was built to provide entertainment. Here the veterans lived out their lives in "companies" complete with captains and sergeants. When they died, they were buried in a landscaped cemetery that now holds some 9,300 graves.

After World War I, Mountain Home changed from a soldiers' home to the National Sanitorium, a 1,000-bed hospital for disabled vets as well as those suffering from tuberculosis. The buildings were altered to provide "sleeping porches" in keeping with that era's treatments. When the Veterans Administration (VA) came into being in 1930, Mountain Home became a part of it, with patients filling 2,000 beds in the "doms," or domiciliaries, and 605 beds in the hospital.

After World War II, the VA began putting its hospitals near medical schools in urban centers. Mountain Home languished during those years, but in 1972 Congress passed a law enabling five VA medical centers to help establish medical schools, and Johnson City became one of the five sites. That made all the difference, and when ETSU's James H. Quillen College of

Rocky Mount is the country's oldest territorial capital.

Medicine came into existence, Mountain Home had a renewed life.

Instead of taking veterans in and keeping them for life, the goal of the center shifted to helping them live at their own homes while providing care for those who need it. Currently the Veterans Affairs Medical Center, as it is now called, has 202 hospital beds and 350 beds in the domiciliaries.

Visitors are welcome to the grounds at Mountain Home. The turn-of-the-century buildings are well maintained, and guests should look for the chapel and the theater. Veterans on the grounds are usually delighted to talk to visitors. To get to Mountain Home, find State of Franklin Street, where the entrance is clearly marked. The sign will say Veterans Affairs Medical Center.

As this book was going to press, efforts were getting underway to establish a museum at Mountain Home.

Buffalo Mountain Park

This outdoor playground lies just outside of Johnson City. The park offers picnicking and hiking, with some of the trails reaching the ridge top of Buffalo Mountain, 3,500 feet above sea level. Mountain bikers can enjoy a 1,500-foot-plus descent on Tower Rd., or, if they've had their grits that morning, they can ride up it.

To get to the park, take the University Parkway Exit off I-181. Go left onto the Parkway to Cherokee Road. Go left, then take an immediate left onto Buffalo Street. Follow it to Rolling Hills Road. Turn right on that road, which will merge with High Ridge Rd., which leads into the park. For more information, call (423) 283-5815.

ENTERTAINMENT

Down Home, 300 W. Main St., tel. (423) 929-9822, is the First Frontier's premier place for live music. Founded as a bluegrass picking parlor, it now bills itself as "the eclectic music room," a place one can hear bluegrass, blues, rock, and the inimitable Tennessee Swampadelic of Webb Wilder. John Lee Hooker and Koko Taylor have played Down Home, which seats 175 people. This place is open Wed.-Sat. nights. Doors open at 6 p.m. for dinner, and the music cranks up at 9 p.m. Call for information on upcoming concerts. Tickets are sold in person or by mail only. Check them out on the Web at www.downhome.com.

Generations Cafe 3101 Browns Mill Rd., tel. (423) 283-0912, has something to offer from morning to night. With 25 kinds of tea, 25 kinds of coffee, and the same number of desserts, this is a good place for breakfast, served daily. Lunch and dinner items include quiches, soups, sandwiches, and pizzas. Then there's the live music. Thursday through Sunday nights bring piano, jazz guitar, and the sorts of music whose lyrics seldom mention truck driving.

Highlander Theater is a dinner theater located not far from the Tri-Cities Airport. Look under Kingsport for a more complete listing.

The **Johnson City Cardinals** belong to the Short Season Rookie League and play professional baseball every summer at Howard Johnson Field. Fans can get information about this part of the St. Louis Cardinal farm system by calling (423) 283-5815. To get to the field, take Roan St., then turn left on Main Street. The park is visible from there. The usual starting time for games is 7 p.m. or, on Sunday, 3 p.m. Tickets cost $3 for adults, $2 for seniors, and $1 for kids under 12—a bargain.

WHERE TO STAY

Bed and Breakfasts
The Hart House Bed and Breakfast occupies a 1910 Dutch colonial house at 207 E. Holston Ave., tel. (423) 926-3147. Each of the three bedrooms has a private bath and comes with telephone and cable TV. Guests can enjoy two sitting rooms, an exercise room with various machines, and a large porch. Rates are $60 for two people or $50 for one. For reservations call (888) 915-7239. Inexpensive.

The Jam 'N' Jelly Inn, 1310 Indian Ridge Rd., tel. (423) 929-0039, is a new log structure with six rooms, all of which have reproduction antique furniture and private baths. Other amenities include a hot tub, volleyball court, and business equipment. Rates run $55 to 75. Inexpensive-Moderate.

Hotels and Motels
With 207 units, the **Holiday Inn,** 101 W. Springbrook Dr., tel. (423) 282-4611, is the big boy in Johnson City. Other good choices among the multitude of offerings include the **Red Roof Inn,** 210 Broyles Dr., tel. (423) 282-3040; **Days Inn,** 2312 Browns Mill Rd., tel. (423) 282-2211; **Fairfield Inn,** 207 E. Mountcastle Dr., tel. (800) 228-2800; **Garden Plaza Hotel,** 211 Mockingbird Ln., tel. (423) 929-2000; **Ramada Inn,** 2406 N. Roan St., tel. (423) 282-2161; and **Super 8 Motel,** 108 Wesley St., tel. (423) 282-8818.

FOOD

Johnson City has a large number of restaurants, particularly on the north side of town. Most of these are of the franchise persuasion. Here are a few of the many eateries.

Barbecue
The **Dixie Barbecue Company,** 3301 N. Roan St., tel. (423) 283-7447, seats 51 people, all of whom can partake of pork and beef barbecue, ribs, chicken, and other earthly delights. The Dixie serves lunch and dinner Monday through Saturday.

In an old firehouse, the **Firehouse Restaurant,** 627 W. Walnut St., tel. (423) 929-7377, offers hickory-smoked pork and beef barbecue, pork ribs, and chicken dishes. It's open for lunch and dinner every day.

The House of Ribs, 3100 Kingsport Hwy., tel. (423) 282-8077, is about the fanciest barbecue place one will find. It offers barbecue, steaks, and chicken lunches and dinners Monday through Saturday.

One hundred and ten barbecue fanciers can sit down every day for lunch and dinner at the **Red Pig Bar-B-Q,** 2201 Ferguson Rd., tel. (423) 282-6585.

Steak and Seafood
Local bed-and-breakfast owners almost always recommend the **Peerless Steak House,** 2531 N. Roan St., tel. (423) 282-2351, one of the finer restaurants in the Tri-Cities. Steak heads the menu, but is followed closely by fresh seafood. This place prides itself on making items such as salad dressings, desserts, and breads inhouse. The Peerless serves dinner only Monday through Saturday.

Ethnic
Makato's Japanese Steakhouse, 3021 Oakland Ave., tel. (423) 282-4441, offers steaks, chicken, and seafood as well as a sushi bar. It's open every day for lunch and dinner.

Misaki Seafood and Steak House of Japan, 3104-C Bristol Hwy., tel. (423) 282-5451, features hibachi-fired foods for lunch and dinner every day.

A little farther afield but worth the trip is the **Harmony Grocery,** tel. (423) 348-6183, which features Creole and Cajun cuisine. This is the place for shrimp Creole, sausage or seafood gumbo, and fresh seafood and steaks. Brown-bagging is permitted. The restaurant is open

Tues.-Sat. for dinner, and Sunday noon-2:30 p.m. Call for directions, or see "Top of the Heap" under "Food" in the Kingsport section.

Lighter Fare
Down Home, 300 W. Main St., tel. (423) 929-9822 (see "Entertainment" above), serves burgers and the like.

An outdoor gazebo bar makes **Galloway's Restaurant,** 807 N. Roan St., tel. (423) 926-1166, a pleasant place to go in warm weather. Lunches feature sandwiches, soup, and pasta, and dinners center on pasta, seafood, and chicken and beef dishes. It's open Monday-Saturday.

Pals, an East Tennessee burger and hot dog tradition, has three Johnson City locations: 1200 W. State of Franklin St., tel. (423) 926-0647; Johnson City Mall, tel. (423) 283-4514; and 3206 Bristol Hwy., tel. (423) 854-9536.

Poor Richard's Deli has two locations—one near ETSU and one downtown. Both are open Mon.-Sat. serving deli sandwiches, nacho plates, and salads. The former, at 825 W. Walnut St., tel. (423) 926-8611, has a bar and live music on Thursday night. Call the latter, located at 106 E. Mountcastle Dr., at (423) 282-8711.

SHOPPING AND INFORMATION

Shopping
Visitors will find one of the best craft shops in the area between Johnson City and Kingsport. **Boones Creek Potter's Gallery,** tel. (423) 282-2801, carries pottery, sculpture, and stained and blown glass, as well as works in wood and iron. To get there, take I-181 from Johnson City to the Boones Creek/Jonesborough exit. Go east on Boones Creek Rd. until it intersects with Hwy. 36. Turn left. The gallery is about a half-mile on the left.

Information
Write or call the **Johnson City Chamber of Commerce,** 603 E. Market St., tel. (800) 852-3392 or (423) 461-8000, or find them on the Internet at www.johnsoncitytn.com. Or come by weekdays 8 a.m.-5 p.m.

ERWIN AND VICINITY

Tucked between the Unaka Mountains and the Nolichucky River, the Erwin area was first known as Greasy Cove. This curious appellation came from the "long hunters" who would bring their game to this area, dress it, render the fat, and tan the hides.

Southern Potteries, Inc. used to operate up here. When it comes to pottery, the phrases "hand-decorated" and "mass-produced" don't seem to go together, but for thirty years they did in Erwin, where Southern Potteries, Inc. employed up to 1,200 people who rolled out as many as 324,000 pieces of dinnerware per week—the largest such operation in the country. The most popular pottery was called Blue Ridge, which sold nationwide. Many of the workers were women, who hand-painted designs on the dishes before glazing them. The company closed in 1957, a victim of imports and plastic dishes. Today Blue Ridge pottery is prized by collectors, and samples of it can be seen at the Unicoi County Heritage Museum.

HISTORY

A Day at the Races

Greasy Cove was the site of one of Tennessee's greatest sports events, a horse race involving Andrew Jackson and Col. Robert Love—two fiery men with fast horses. In 1788, Jackson sent a challenge to Love to race their mounts. Word went out all over the region, and sporting types placed bets and made plans to attend the race. Ten days before the race, Jackson's jockey got sick and the future president announced that he would ride in the man's place, further whetting interest. On the appointed day an enormous crowd (for those days) gathered and the horses were led out. The race began.

Riding his own horse was a mistake. Jackson stood six feet, one inch tall—hardly jockey size—and he and his horse were left in the dust. Never a good loser, he loudly and profanely denounced Colonel Love, his family, and the horse he rode in on. Love responded in kind, and friends intervened, no doubt preventing a duel.

What's in a Name?

In the later 1800s, when local boosters heard that George Vanderbilt was going to buy up vast amounts of mountain land, they hurriedly changed the town's name to Vanderbilt. The man with the money, obviously unimpressed, instead bought his land near Asheville, North Carolina. The name Vanderbilt was changed to Ervin in honor of a local doctor who donated land so that the town would become the county seat. The post office, however, transmogrified the name to Erwin. Erwin it stays.

Hanging an Elephant

In 1909 Erwin was selected as the headquarters of the Carolina, Clinchfield, and Ohio Railroad. The repair yards and offices gave the town an enormous economic shot in the arm and played a major role in perhaps the most bizarre event in Tennessee history.

Our story begins in 1916 in Kingsport, where a circus was parading through the town. The author's maternal grandmother, then just a teenager, was there. The headliner of the parade was Mary, billed as the largest elephant on earth. For some reason, still in dispute, she trampled her handler to death in front of a horrified crowd. The owners of the circus, in a move that would have made Col. Tom Parker proud, announced that at that night's performance the murderous elephant would be electrocuted. At the climax of the show, 44,000 volts were shot through Mary, who reportedly only "danced around a little bit."

That's when some bright soul thought of Erwin and the large railroad cranes available there. Mary was taken there and hanged in front of an estimated 5,000 gawkers. Grandmother was *not* one of them. The first chain placed around Mary's neck broke when she was five feet off the ground, but the second chain did the trick.

No one can remember what happened to poor Mary's body. Perhaps some future paleontologist will stumble on her bones and write academic papers for the rest of his life on the occurrence of elephants in East Tennessee. For a more complete rendering of Mary's lynching, see www.electriclabs.com/ghost/mary.

SIGHTS

Hatcheries and Museum

Just east of town on Hwy. 107 lies **Erwin National Fish Hatchery,** one of the oldest fish hatcheries in the country. Built in 1897, complete with a Victorian mansion for its superintendent, the hatchery now produces millions of fertilized fish eggs and about 50,000 fully grown trout per year.

All this takes place in 24 concrete tanks flowing with water from a large spring. Children particularly like seeing all the fish, and this is a good place to have a picnic. The entire hatchery is open Mon.-Fri. 7:30 a.m. -4 p.m. (closed holidays), but visitors can see a section of it on the weekends. Admission is free.

An added attraction at the hatchery is in what was the hatchery superintendent's home. The **Unicoi County Heritage Museum** is one of the finest volunteer-run museums in the state. Here visitors can see Blue Ridge Pottery—the settings are changed with the seasons—artifacts from Erwin's early railroad days, and a photograph of the infamous elephant hanging. This museum is open daily 1-5 p.m. May-September. During October, the last two weeks in November, and the first week in December, the museum is open weekends only, 1-5 p.m. Admission is $1 for adults and 50 cents for children. Call (423) 743-9449. If those times aren't convenient, call the curator at (423) 743-4335 for a private tour. Make arrangements as far in advance as possible.

Those who haven't seen enough fish should try the **Erwin State Fish Hatchery,** tel. (423) 743-4842, not as well known as its federal counterpart, but one that welcomes visitors nonetheless. This is a rearing hatchery, a place that takes fingerlings and raises them until they are large enough to release into mountain streams. Visitors can see as many as 150,000 fish on the 12-acre hatchery. It's open daily 7:30 a.m.-4 p.m. To find it, take the Jackson-Love Highway Exit off I-181. Go left, over the interstate and under the railroad tracks, and pass a fire department on the left and the Erwin Motel. The hatchery is behind J.D.'s Market and Car Wash.

Take a left on Banner Springs Road. The employees are sometimes out stocking fish, so it's a good idea to call ahead.

Arts and Crafts

Negatha Peterson bought some of the molds from the old Southern Pottery and carries on the tradition at **Erwin Pottery,** where visitors can see dishes and bowls take shape. Each piece is signed and available for sale. Erwin Pottery is across from McDonald's at 1219 N. Main Street. The hours are uncertain—the place is open longer in the summer and has shorter hours in the winter. Call (423) 743-8278.

Farmhouse Gallery and Gardens, tel. (423) 743-8799 or (800) 952-6043, is in Unicoi, a small town between Erwin and Johnson City, and there is no place in Tennessee quite like it. In essence, the story here is a couple who want to "live off the land" in a way that works with nature instead of exploits it or plows it under.

Johnny Lynch is an artist whose wildlife and wildflower prints are created in a 160-year-old cabin. His wife Pat grows and dries wildflowers and herbs, some of which make good teas. Visitors to the gardens find something new every year—waterfalls, nature trails—and can learn through seminars, lectures, and classes.

And you can get something to eat there as well, for the Farmhouse folks serve barbecue for lunch from early April until early October.

To see this enviable way of living, take the Unicoi Exit off I-181. Go south to the old 19/23 highway, then go left for three miles.

The prize for best name of a shop in Erwin goes to **The Hanging Elephant Antique Mall,** 219 South Main St., tel. (423) 743-9661. The goods here range from collectibles to furniture.

Rick Murray runs a one-man wood turning shop on the banks of the Nolichucky River. To get there, call (423) 743-6868 to make sure he is in and to obtain directions.

Stegall's Pottery and Crafts Gallery, 379 Chandler Cove Rd., tel. (423) 743-3227 or (800) 788-POTS, specializes in creative pottery that is meant to be used. Their work can be microwaved, put in a dishwasher, and baked in ovens. One of their lighter-hearted works is a ceramic dog biscuit container labeled "Bone Appétit." See them online at www.stegallpots.com.

RECREATION AND EVENTS

Cherokee National Forest
The following recreation areas all offer picnicking, hiking, and wilderness activities. The Appalachian Trail runs through Beauty Spot and the Unaka Mountain Wilderness. For further information, go to the Cherokee National Forest's Nolichucky/Unaka Ranger District at just east of Exit 23 of Highway 19/23. Or call (423) 735-1500. Fees of $2 per vehicle are now charged for any activity at National Forest sites. Camping fees range from $10 to $30.

Rock Creek Park lies a few miles out of town on Rock Creek Road (Hwy. 395). Here visitors can fish, swim, and camp.

Continue past Rock Creek Park on Hwy. 395 to the top of the mountain, then go left on an unimproved road for about two miles. The road forks here. Take the right fork to the top of the mountain. This is **Beauty Spot,** an aptly named bald that straddles the Tennessee/North Carolina border at an elevation of 4,437 feet. The Appalachian Trail crosses the bald, and, unfortunately, this area has a bad reputation with hikers. It seems that the road enables local louts to prey on hikers. Be careful up there.

Continue northeast along the ridge to the **Unaka Mountain Wilderness.** Home of the 60-foot-high Red Fork Falls, this is an excellent place for hiking.

Whitewater Rafting
The Nolichucky River offers the finest whitewater rafting in upper East Tennessee. The water, even in the summertime, is chilling, so rafters should at a minimum bring a change of clothing. In spring or fall, wool clothing is the best; wet cotton fibers can quickly wick body heat away. In comparing prices, see if the quoted rate includes everything—the raft trip, wetsuits, taxes, and river fees. Ask about group and off-season rates.

Three rafting companies offer trips ranging from three hours to overnight. **Cherokee Adventures,** off Exit 18 of Hwy. 19/23, runs the upper Nolichucky, the Watauga, and the Russell Rivers. From Erwin, go one mile north on TN 81N along the Nolichucky River. Call (423) 743-7733 for information or (800) 445-7238 for reser-

vations. The shortest rides cost $21 per person, depending on the day of the week.

The Nantahala Outdoor Center runs the Nolichucky March through mid-July. The trips last five to seven hours, with three to five hours on the water. The price ranges $63-70. Its outpost is about 20 minutes outside of town at its take-out point and is not always staffed. Call (800) 232-7238.

USA Raft, with trips ranging from two to seven hours on the Nolichucky, has another far-flung outpost. Costs range $32-63 per person. Call (800) 872-7238 for information and current rates.

Biking
If two-wheeled adventure is more to visitors' liking, **Cherokee Adventures** will haul riders and their bikes to the crest of Rich Mountain, from where it is almost all downhill. Rental bikes are available, and a snack is included. The cost is $26-31 per person. Call (423) 743-7733 for information, or (800) 445-7238 for reservations.

Festivals
The **Apple Festival** pulls together Erwin and Unicoi County during the first weekend in October for handmade crafts, a Blue Ridge Pottery show, food, music, dancing, a footrace, and other activities. More than 300 craftspeople and thousands of participants jam the town. For information, call the chamber of commerce at (423) 743-3000.

WHERE TO STAY

Bed and Breakfast
The **Tumbling Creek Bed and Breakfast,** tel. (423) 743-5308, lies eight miles south of Erwin, almost in North Carolina. The 10-year-old house is built into the side of a mountain, and a large deck surrounds three-fourths of the structure. Two rooms, both sharing a bath and whirlpool, are available—one with twin beds and one with double beds. The house is furnished in an English Garden style and sits on three acres of land. Rates are $65 per couple. Moderate.

Motels
Try the **Best Southern,** 1315 Asheville Hwy., tel. (423) 743-6438; or **Holiday Inn Express,**

2002 Temple Hill Rd., tel. (423) 743-4100. Closer to Johnson City is the **Buffalo Mountain Resort/Family Inns of America** in Unicoi, tel. (423) 743-9181.

If you want to learn about hiking, perhaps the best place in the state to stay is the **Nolichucky Hostel, Cabins, Camping, Etc.,** tel. (423) 735-0548, an establishment that caters to through-hikers on the Appalachian Trail by offering rooms, showers, shuttle services, and a camping store. Located 80 feet from the Trail and 80 feet from the Nolichucky River, it has a wood-fired hot tub that is enormously popular with hikers. Located 1.1 miles from Exit 15 on Hwy 181 near the Chestoa Bridge. Closed January and February.

Camping

Private campgrounds include **Nolichucky Campground,** open year-round and right on the Nolichucky River, tel. (423) 743-8876. Take Jones Branch Road. **Cherokee Adventures,** tel. (423) 743-7733 or (423) 743-4502, a rafting company, has a campground farther downstream on Hwy. 81. It is open March through mid-November.

The U.S. Forest Service operates two campgrounds in the Erwin area. **Limestone Cove Recreation Area** lies east of town on Hwy. 107. Closer in, **Rock Creek Park** lies east of Main St. on 10th Street. These are usually open from the first weekend in May though the first week-end in October, but sometimes open late or close early because of inclement weather. For further information, call (423) 743-4452.

Nearby Unicoi offers the **North Indian Creek Campground** on Limestone Cove Rd., tel. (423) 743-4502. It has 22 sites and is open year-round.

FOOD AND INFORMATION

Food

Most Erwin eateries describe their fare as "country cooking." Local dispensers of such include Unicoi's **Clarences Restaurant,** which is open for three meals every day. Local clubs in Erwin hold their gatherings at **The Blue Ridge Restaurant,** 202 S. Elm Ave., tel. (423) 735-7203. The restaurant is open for three meals every day.

The best place to eat in these parts, by general consent, is **Granny's Kitchen,** tel. (423) 735-0728, in the mountain community of Flag Pond, a good 10 miles south of Erwin on Hwy. 23/81. Offering plate dinners of country cooking, this establishment is open for all three meals every day.

Information

The offices of the **Unicoi County Chamber of Commerce,** 100 S. Main Ave., tel. (423) 743-3000, are open Mon.-Fri. 8 a.m.-5 p.m. Outside is a kiosk with information on local attractions. See the site online at www.valleybeautiful.org.

JONESBOROUGH TO GREENEVILLE

HISTORY

House builders on the First Frontier seldom had to worry about zoning laws; people built whatever and wherever they wanted. This was not the case in Jonesborough, a town that seemed destined to make sure its old buildings survived. The oldest incorporated town in the state, Jonesborough was laid out in 1780, and the town officials made sure things were done right. The land was divided into lots and sold, and owners were required within three years to build a brick, stone, or frame house of a certain size. Anyone who didn't do this lost the land.

Jonesborough, as the county seat of North Carolina's Washington County, had a built-in business: government. Deeds were registered, criminals prosecuted and defended, and cases argued. In 1788 a 21-year-old lawyer rode into town and was admitted to the bar. His name was Andrew Jackson.

The Lost State of Franklin

Four years before, in 1784, North Carolina ceded its western lands to the young federal government, which didn't immediately accept them. This ambiguous situation bothered people in the area, who felt that during this interim they were without a government. Accustomed to provid-

THE REVEREND SAMUEL DOAK

The area between Jonesborough and Greeneville was once the domain of a singular Presbyterian minister, the Rev. Samuel Doak, whose legacy is one of education. A Virginian who was educated at Princeton, he rode a horse to what is now Washington County in 1777 and, following the sound of axes, found some pioneers cutting trees.

On learning that the well-spoken stranger was a minister of the gospel, the woodcutters asked him if they could round up a congregation and hear a sermon. Rev. Doak agreed and, sitting on his horse, preached to those who came to hear. They convinced him to settle with them, and he bought a farm and began spreading the Gospel, most notably in a rousing send-off prayer for the Overmountain Men as they left Sycamore Shoals to go off and fight the British.

Rev. Doak founded the Salem Presbyterian Church on his farm in 1780, one of the first churches in what would become Tennessee. Four years later he erected the first schoolhouse west of the Appalachians, naming it "The Martin Academy" in honor of the governor of North Carolina. In 1795, Rev. Doak rode a horse to Philadelphia and came back laden with books; some say he walked back so the horse could carry more volumes. He eventually changed the name of his school to Washington College.

During the period of the Great Revival that swept the country in the early 1800s, Rev. Doak became one of the first educated ministers who delivered sermons accompanied by "the jerks," a very physical, emotional style of preaching. Anne Kebenow, in her wonderful *200 Years Through 200 Stories,* quotes a member of a congregation who saw Rev. Doak when he was feeling the Spirit: "Often it would seize him in the pulpit with so much severity that a spectator might feel it would dislocate his neck and joints. He would laugh, stand and halloo at the top of his voice, finally leap from the pulpit and run to the woods, screaming like a madman. When the exercise was over he would return to the church, calm and rational as ever."

When the Rev. Doak was 69 years old, he resigned the presidency of Washington College to join his son, also named Samuel, in founding Tusculum Academy just east of Greeneville. Doak's slaves built him a large house, and when the house was finished, he gave them their freedom. Rev. Doak lived out his days and, while president of the school, taught subjects as diverse as chemistry and Hebrew. In 1830, like Abraham, "he gave up the ghost and died in a good old age, an old man, and full of years." He was 81, and lies buried today in a cemetery near what is now Washington College Academy.

---

ing for themselves, they organized into a new state, which they called Frankland. Later, thinking more politically, they called it Franklin, after the famed kite-flyer, and applied for admission to the new country.

Hearing of this, North Carolina reconsidered its offer and repealed the law that gave away the western lands. This plunged the overmountain people into chaos. Who was in charge? The Franklinites or the mother state of North Carolina? Who could make deals with the Indians? Would marriages and wills made during this time stand up in court?

The controversy swirled around Jonesborough, leading to fist fights and sometimes more serious conflicts. The idea of Franklin slowly faded away, and Jonesborough found itself back in North Carolina again, at least until the U.S. formally deemed Tennessee part of the Southwest Territory. What would have been the 14th state is now drilled into Tennessee schoolchildren as "The Lost State of Franklin." Meanwhile, the town of Jonesborough underwent a spelling change. To show their distaste for the British after the War of 1812, a lot of American towns ending in "-ough" dropped the "ugh" from their names. Thus, Jonesborough became Jonesboro.

Abolition and Reconstruction

Jonesboro seemed to be a magnet for men bent on upsetting the status quo. In 1820 Elihu Embree began publishing the first newspaper in the country devoted entirely to antislavery. *The Emancipator* lasted for only seven issues—Embree's death ended it—but it was read all over the United States.

In the 1830s another newspaper began running a fiery series of political articles written by a young minister. The editor persuaded the writer, William G. Brownlow, to abandon the ministry for journalism, a career switch that was to have profound implications later on for Tennessee, when the rabid writer became Tennessee's Reconstruction governor, arguably the most hated elected official in the history of the state.

Jonesboro mercifully escaped the ravages of the Civil War—another plus for building preservation—and eased into the 20th century. New highways and discount stores began to erode the downtown, however, and by the late '60s Tennessee's first town began to look run-down.

Restoration

In the early 1970s, town officials decided to restore the buildings, preserve the town, and go after the many tourists who come to Tennessee. At last forgiving the British—particularly the traveling ones—Jonesboro reverted to Jonesborough. Officials got the entire downtown placed on the National Register of Historic Places. As in many other towns, to celebrate the place and its people, they launched a festival—the usual gathering of craftspeople, food vendors, musicians, etc.

the Chester Inn

In 1973, the big idea landed: the National Storytelling Festival. Naming it the *National* Storytelling Festival was a stroke of brilliance. As far as anyone in Jonesborough knew, there was no other storytelling festival at all, so they declared theirs the national one, and that has made all the difference. Jonesborough is now to storytelling what Nashville is to country music. The oldest incorporated town in Tennessee now contains the National Association for the Preservation and Perpetuation of Storytelling, complete with archives, publications, and tapes for sale.

With all its success in renovation and preservation, however, Jonesborough has all but succumbed to a Disneyan version of its colonial heritage. The shops, bed and breakfasts, and traffic-stopping festivals are wonderful for the droves of tourists, but the visitor has to scan faces a long time to detect a local—unless it is one who has found himself fresh out of lilac-scented oatmeal soap.

DOWNTOWN SIGHTS

Pulling in from Hwy. 11-E, travelers to Jonesborough should turn on Boone Street and stop at the **Jonesborough Visitors Center and Museum,** tel. (423) 753-1015. Behind the center lies Duncan's Meadow, where Andrew Jackson once fought a duel, and behind it is an 1880s schoolhouse that is slated to become a museum about education.

Boone St. eventually intersects Main St., along which most of Jonesborough's offerings lie. On a slow day, one can park on Main St., but during festivals and the like a good place to park is behind the Washington County Courthouse.

If someone could conjure Andrew Jackson back from the dead, Jonesborough's Main St. is one of the few places in Tennessee where he would recognize several buildings that were there when he was. Perhaps the most significant is the **Chester Inn,** now the headquarters and gift shop of the National Storytelling Festival. Built in 1797 as an inn and a tavern, it hosted Tennessee's three presidents—Andrew Jackson, James K. Polk, and Andrew Johnson—as well as other luminaries such as Charles Dickens.

Beside the inn stands the **Christopher Taylor House,** a 1778 log structure that may well be the oldest log house still standing in the state. It stood for about 200 years outside of town before being moved to its present location.

Farther down the other side of the street stands the **Blair-Moore House.** Now a bed and breakfast, the house was built around 1832 and provides a good example of stepped gables, an architectural feature in which a stepped wall provides what might be called a false side. Jonesborough's Main St. has several buildings with this feature.

EVENTS

National Storytelling Festival

The National Storytelling Festival is always held on the first full weekend in October. Lasting three days, it fills the town with tall tales, ghost stories, "sacred telling," and the "Swappin' Ground." Visitors are strongly urged to register by phone ahead of time, thus ensuring admission to popular events such as the open-air ghost storytelling—not recommended for children under six. Call (800) 525-4514 to register. A full weekend will cost $95 per adult, $70 per child 6-12, or a special family rate of $275. This festival is not cheap. Those who buy their tickets early can get discounts, and the festival also sells tickets good for one day only. In 1998, for example, a Saturday Only ticket was $60. See the festival's site online at www.storynet.org.

More Events

Other events include the **Spring Doll Show,** held in April, which offers collectors and fanciers the chance to marvel over dolls ranging from Madame Alexanders to Barbies.

The first weekend in June features an **Andrew Jackson Festival** to honor the town's most famous resident. An actor plays the lanky Jackson, who takes part in a duel (he wins), reenacts some of his more memorable court cases, and delivers his famous Farewell to the People of Jonesborough Address. All this and the obligatory food, crafts, and music.

The Fourth of July brings forth **Historic Jonesborough Days,** an old-fashioned, family-oriented bash complete with art, food, crafts, and fireworks.

August marks the three-day **Quilt Fest,** featuring 25 instructors offering 50 classes. Lectures, buffets, and oodles of quilts round out this gathering.

For more information on all of the above, call the **Jonesborough Visitors Center** at (423) 753-5961.

ENTERTAINMENT AND RECREATION

If you're this close on a Saturday night, don't miss the pickin' and grinnin' at the **Rheatown Food Market** southwest of Jonesborough. See the section following Jonesborough for more details.

The town of Jonesborough owns **Wetlands Water Park,** west of town on Hwy. 11 East, tel. (423) 753-1550. A decidedly non-historical complex, it is open from Memorial Day to Labor Day. Here one can take the waters on slides, a wave pool, or a simulated lazy river. Admission is $7 for adults, $5 for seniors and children four to 12, with ages three and under getting in free.

WHERE TO STAY

Bed and Breakfasts

Not surprisingly, Jonesborough has the greatest concentration of B&Bs in upper East Tennessee. **Hawley House,** 114 E. Woodrow Ave., tel. (423)

Quilt makers create works of art from scraps of cloth.

753-8869, must be considered first, for it occupies lot number one in the town. The 1793 building, the oldest one in Jonesborough, is made of dovetailed chestnut logs. Hawley House is filled with museum-quality antiques, the newest of which dates from 1840. The owner is an eighth-generation Jonesborough resident. Hawley House offers three bedrooms, each with a private bath. People with children should call ahead. Rates run $70-125. Moderate-Premium.

Aiken-Brow House, 104 3rd Ave., tel. (423) 753-9440, is an 1850s board-and-batten house with antique furniture throughout. Two rooms have private baths—one in the room and one across the hall from the room. A third room with twin beds can be rented in conjunction with one of the others. Rates range $75-100. Moderate-Expensive.

The **Blair Moore House Bed and Breakfast,** 201 West Main St, tel. (423) 753-0044 or (888) 453-0044, is about as downtown as you can get in Jonesborough. This place has three guest rooms, one of them a Western Room that comes with a bearskin rug, old guns, Indian artifacts, and—best of all—a second story porch overlooking Main Street. All of the rooms have private baths, and all come with a gourmet—not a country—breakfast. Rates are $85-115. Expensive-Premium.

Franklin House, 116 Franklin Ave., tel. (423)753-3819, has three rooms and an extended stay apartment, all with private baths, inside a reconstructed 1840 home just a few minutes' walk from Jonesborough's historic district. Rates range $45-80. Inexpensive-Moderate.

May Ledbetter House, 130 West Main St., tel. (423) 753-7568 or (423) 913-2205. This 1904 Victorian home has two rooms with private baths down the hall. The beds are covered with quilts and the wraparound porch has bentwood rockers. Rates are $80, which includes a full country breakfast. Moderate.

The Old Yellow Vic, 411 W. Main St., tel. (423) 753-9558 or (423) 753-2141, gets its name from the fact that the house is an 1887 yellow Victorian home. The proprietor offers one room with a private bath or two rooms with a shared bath. Smokers can smoke in the house, but not in the bedrooms. The entire house is furnished with antiques. The rate is $75. Moderate.

Farther from the crowded streets is the **Bugaboo Bed and Breakfast,** 211 Semore Dr., tel.

(423) 753-9345. This is a contemporary house with an old English flair. Sitting amid 15 acres of woods and meadow, the house is very open. Guests particularly like the hot tub on the deck under the stars. Two rooms each have a private bath. Rates are $70-80. One pet is permitted, if it occupies its own bed. Moderate.

Camping
Davy Crockett Birthplace State Park (see under "West of Jonesborough" below) is a popular place to camp near Jonesborough. Then there's **Home Federal Park,** the campground that sounds like a bank. The name comes from the fact that a bank donated the land to the town, which owns this 45-site, full-hookup campground, located at 1521 Persimmon Ridge Rd., right beside the Wetlands Water Park in Jonesborough. Sites cost $10 per night. Call (615) 753-1555. It's open all year.

MORE PRACTICALITIES

Food
Andrew Jackson probably would snort at the news that Washington County restaurants are dry. This is bring-your-own-bottle country.

The Parson's Table is the headliner of Jonesborough's restaurants. Inside an 1870 Gothic church, it offers lunch and dinner of continental cuisine. Typical dinner entrees include rack of lamb, roast duckling a l'orange, or fresh seafood and shellfish. Prices range $13-20. Sunday features the Seventh Day Feast, a misnamed but good buffet served 11:30 a.m.-2 p.m. Lunches involve hearty sandwiches, and entree salads. The Parson's Table is in downtown Jonesborough behind the courthouse off Main St. at 102 West Woodrow Avenue. Reservations are a very good idea; call (423) 753-8002.

The **Harmony Grocery,** tel. (423) 348-6183, is out in the country from Jonesborough, but well worth the drive. This great eatery serves shrimp Creole, Cajun sausage or seafood gumbo, and fresh seafood and steaks. Brown-bagging is permitted. The restaurant is open Tues.-Sat. for dinner, and Sunday noon-2:30 p.m. Call for directions.

The **Main Street Cafe and Catering,** 117 West Main St., tel. (423) 753-2460, is a great place to go for sandwiches and homemade soups, salads, and desserts. The cafe is open for lunch and an early dinner Mon.-Fri. and for lunch on Saturday.

Cornbread's Coffee House, 107 West Main St., no phone. This is the only place in Jonesborough that serves breakfast all day. Lunch is served as well. The back of Cornbread's contains a coffeehouse wherein all beans have been roasted on the premises.

Shopping

Jonesborough's shopping district is concentrated within a block of the Washington County Court House. The shops include the **Tennessee Quilts,** 123 E. Main St., tel. (423) 753-6644, where quilting aficionados can choose from more than 1,000 bolts of cloth.

The National Storytelling Festival has a gift shop in the festival headquarters in the Chester Inn. Here buyers can find tapes and compact discs of over 100 storytellers—perhaps the greatest collection of tales in the entire state.

Information

Write the **Historic Jonesborough Visitor Center,** 117 Boone St., mailing address P.O. Box 375-E, Jonesborough, TN 37659; or call (423) 753-5961 or (800) 400-4221.

WEST OF JONESBOROUGH

Highway 11-E leads southwest straight from Jonesborough to Greeneville, or the traveler can take a more meandering route to see some sights. A few side trips offer some diversions for the traveler. Leave Jonesborough heading south on Hwy. 81, then turn right on Hwy. 353 by Little Limestone Creek. Note: 353 and Old SR 34 are the same. Go past Davy Crockett High School to the community of Telford. Here is a classic country store, a good place to go in get a soft drink and have a chat.

Then it's on down the road to Washington College Academy. Founded by the Rev. Samuel Doak, who is buried in the cemetery just a couple of hundred yards past the school, this place has graduated 22 college presidents, 28 members of Congress, three governors, 63 physicians, 16 missionaries, and 162 ministers. It is the eighth

oldest American school or college still in existence. Now a prep school, it has an enrollment of 100. To inspect the Salem Baptist Church, which is on the campus, call the Academy at (423) 257-5151 a day or so ahead. See them online at www.wcatvt.com.

Stay on Old SR 34. After Westview Elementary School, take the second left, at Gravel Hill Rd., which leads to the community of **Broylesville.** People came here in the early 1800s to take advantage of the water power offered by Little Limestone Creek. In its heyday, Broylesville had 300 residents, who supported mills, tanneries, a shoe factory, smithies, saw mills, grist mills, a cooperage, a distillery, and a store. Nine buildings that date as far back to 1797 are all that is left, all of them in private hands and not open to the public.

All except two. The 1869 Bashor Mill, at 203 Gravel Hill Rd., is occupied by Margaret Gregg and her **Mill 'n Creek Studio Gallery,** where visitors will find works in textiles, silk-screen prints, sculpture, printings, collectibles, and mixed media. Those who wish to spend more time in Broylesville can rent a room at the mill or make arrangements to pitch a tent in the yard. The hours here are generally 9 to 5, but call (423) 257-3875 to make sure someone is in.

Ledford's Antiques, tel. (423) 257-3293, features "good country furniture"—made by hand and not primitives—from a brick, Greek Revival store building built between 1830 and 1840.

To get from Broylesville back to Hwy 11-E, follow Old State Rd. 34 to the west. To get to the Davy Crockett Birthplace State Historical Area, also take Old State Rd. 34 west, then turn left on Davy Crockett Road.

Flintlock Inn & Stables, 790 G'Fellers Rd., Chuckey, tel. (423) 257-2489, offers guests a chance to take to the saddle and ride through farms or into the mountains. Riders can bring their own horses or use the ones at the inn, including Ben, a Tennessee mule who starred with Tyne Daly in television's *Christy*. Non-riding guests are welcome as well to the inn, which was built by combining three log cabins. The price for one night is $96. Lunch and dinner are available as well, and other add-ons include driving a Jeep on mountain roads, hot air balloon rides, golf, or cruising in a 1929 Model A pickup truck. Expensive.

Davy Crockett Birthplace
State Historical Area

Follow the signs from Hwy 11-E to this park, which lies on the banks of the Nolichucky River. The first thing that people of a certain age notice on seeing Davy Crockett's birthplace is that it is not "on a mountaintop in Tennessee," as the theme song for the old television show used to assert every week.

The centerpiece of the park is a replica of the Crockett Cabin, where David—people in his day did not call him Davy—first saw the light of day. The cabin is a replica of a typical cabin of that time and has no items in it that belonged to the famed wearer of coonskin caps. Crockett cut quite a swath in his time, moving from east to west Tennessee and coming to a glorious end at the Alamo. In between, he was a scout, bear hunter, humorist, statesman, and even industrialist.

This 60-acre park on the banks of the Nolichucky River has picnic and camping areas—75 sites, a pool, and a visitors center with exhibits on Crockett. For information, contact them at tel. (423) 257-2167 or online at www.tnstateparks.com.

The famed defender of the Alamo was born here.

Just down the road is the **Snapp Inn**, 1990 Davy Crockett Park Rd., Limestone, TN 37681, tel. (423) 257-2482, which occupies an 1815 federal brick home furnished with antiques. Painted white, the house has two bedrooms, each with a private bath. Guests can walk to Davy Crockett Birthplace State Park and go swimming there during summer, or they can stay at the inn and play pool. The cost is $65 for a double, with a third person for $10. Moderate.

Back on Hwy. 11-E near Chuckey is some down home entertainment that shouldn't be missed. Once a week the **Rheatown Food Market** (RAY-town), tel. (423) 257-5784, is transformed into a picking parlor. Local string musicians such as the Horse Creek Mountain Boys gather, pull up chairs, and play. Sometimes two or three groups will play at once throughout the store. Unpretentious, unrehearsed, and, judging by the reception, unbeatable. Coming from Jonesborough, turn right off Hwy. 11-E onto Rt. 351. Go less than a mile to Rheatown, where the music kicks into gear between 7 and 8 on Saturday night. Admission is free, and sometimes the picking lasts past midnight. On the way back, visitors should tune their radios to 630 AM and listen to the Grand Ole Opry.

Tusculum

This little town east of Greeneville is home to Tusculum College and well worth a stop. Home to approximately 500 on-campus students, this Presbyterian-affiliated college serves as a cultural center for Greeneville and outlying areas. The name allegedly comes from that of Cicero's home outside Rome.

Tusculum College came into being because of a merger with Greeneville College, founded in 1794, and Tusculum Academy, a private school founded in 1818 by father and son ministers, Rev. Samuel Doak and Rev. Samuel Witherspoon Doak. The latter engineered the academic merger and saw that his institution's name won out over that of Greeneville College.

Andrew Johnson was a trustee of the college, which served as his official presidential library. The **Andrew Johnson Library** occupies an 1841 building that contains several exhibits pertaining to the president: most of the books from his home, some carpet from the White House, the bed in which he died, and personal items such as his collar box and various items belonging to his wife. The Library is open Monday-Friday 9 a.m.-5 p.m. Admission is free, and the building is handicapped accessible.

The elder Doak lived the last years of his life in a large house whose construction began in 1818. Academy classes were taught there until the next building, now called Old College, was erected. The other noteworthy building on campus is Virginia Hall, one of only three buildings in the South designed by Chicago architect Louis A. Sullivan.

To find out what plays, concerts, or other collegiate activities are taking place at Tusculum College, call (423) 636-7304. Or see the Web site at www.tusculum.edu.

A pleasant place to eat is **Ye Olde Tusculum Eatery,** tel. (423) 638-9210, across the road from the college. Lunch is mostly sandwiches—with specials such as portobello mushrooms—while dinner brings forth steak, chicken, seafood, and Italian dishes.

Next door the **Three Blind Mice** gift shop, tel. (423) 639-0180, has artworks and craft pieces from local as well as national artists. Closed on Sunday except in November and December.

GREENEVILLE

If Frankin is the lost state, then Greeneville is the lost capital, for it was in this pleasant town that the Franklinites located their government for the two-year existence of that would-be state.

Greeneville is most associated with Andrew Johnson, who moved here as a teenager in 1825. (See special topic "Andrew Johnson.") He found a town that occupied the center of a rich agricultural area, one that readily grew tobacco and other crops. The farmers and merchants here were what would later be called "self-made men," and their pride was exceeded only by their independence.

Just how independent they were was evidenced in 1861, when the state of Tennessee voted to leave the Union. This action, driven by interests in Middle and West Tennessee, found little support in the eastern part of the state. Nine days later, 26 East Tennessee counties sent delegates to Greeneville to discuss seceding from the secessionists, and they asked the state legislature to let them form a separate state. Permission was denied.

This did nothing to halt the division in East Tennessee and in Greeneville, a situation best exemplified by the murder of Confederate General John Morgan. Morgan had led a band of mounted troops on an unauthorized raid deep into Kentucky, Ohio, and Indiana. Depending on how one viewed it, the raid was either a daring feat that gave the Yankees a taste of their own war, or a bunch of thugs on a spree of terror.

After one of his forays, the general came to Greeneville for some needed rest and found hospitality at the spacious Dickson-Williams House, the home of a local doctor and his wife. Someone—no one ever found out just who—slipped off and informed a Union general a few miles off that Morgan was in town. The general led Union forces into town and surrounded the

house. According to one Southern account, Morgan leapt out of bed and ran into the back garden, where he was captured. As he stood there, a Union soldier ran up and shot him dead, snatched up his body, and rode off with it across his horse. After parading the late general around the Union camp, the soldier unceremoniously dumped the body in a ditch. This incident, probably magnified in the telling, further inflamed passions in this divided town.

The divisions that once split Greeneville still show in the Civil War monuments that stand in the courthouse yard. One is a rhapsodic paean to Morgan, while the other commemorates Union soldiers.

Today Greeneville is the county seat of Greene County and a center of the tobacco business. In recent years the town has acknowledged its heritage and abundance of historic buildings. Most conveniently for the visitor, the majority of Greeneville's historic sites lie along a route following Business 321 coming from Hwy. 11-E. Here stand the old homes, bed and breakfasts, the General Morgan Inn, and the Andrew Johnson National Historic Site. The best guide to the town is a brochure entitled "A Walk With the President," which is available at the General Morgan Inn, the Andrew Johnson National Historic Site, and the Greeneville/Greene County Area Chamber of Commerce at 115 Academy Street.

SIGHTS

The **Cumberland Presbyterian Church,** the Greek Revival church with the tall steeple on the right, was used as a hospital and a stable during the Civil War. The day that General Morgan was killed, the church was shelled, and you

ANDREW JOHNSON

Poor Andrew Johnson. For decades he was known primarily for the fact that he was impeached, and of late has had to suffer the indignity of being mentioned in the same paragraphs as Monica Lewinsky and Kenneth Starr. All this notoriety, plus the fact that he followed the greatest president of all time, siphons interest away from this remarkable man. And that is unfortunate, for Andrew Johnson was a complex individual. His rise from a poor, uneducated worker to the highest office in the land is an embodiment of the American dream. An excellent account of his life and times exists in *Andrew Johnson: A Biography*, by Hans L. Trefousse.

Even more so than Abraham Lincoln, Andrew Johnson came from humble beginnings. He was born in Raleigh, North Carolina, in 1808, and his childhood was one of poverty; he never spent a day in school, and by age 10 was apprenticed to a tailor. The young Johnson got in a dispute with his master about how long he should serve, and he fled to Greeneville, Tennessee, riding into town on a wagon at age 16.

Keenly aware of his lack of education, Johnson strove to improve his mind. He had once worked in a shop where a man read aloud to the tailors, and in Greeneville he hired people to read to him. He entered a local debating society and honed his public speaking, eventually becoming an orator who could hold a crowd for two or three hours and, typical of hard-knuckled Tennessee politics, sarcastically belittle an opponent as well as take care of any hecklers in the process.

Johnson was a good tailor who prospered in Greeneville, and in 1829 he consented to run for alderman in an election that pitted wealthier candidates against Johnson and a more working-class slate. Johnson's group won, and the victory launched his political climb. If anything can characterize Johnson's politics, it was a willingness to stand up for the common man and woman. His supporters, small farmers and shopkeepers typical of East Tennessee, distrusted the wealthy plantation owners who controlled politics in Middle and West Tennessee, and Johnson never forgot those who elected him. A Democrat, he served as mayor, state representative, state senator, and congressman. Always intent on educating himself, during his five terms in Congress he read for hours in the Library of Congress, possibly spending more time there than any representative before or since.

In 1853 he was elected governor of Tennessee, and for two terms he supported public education and the construction of railroads, and brought about the purchase of Andrew Jackson's home, the Hermitage. Johnson followed his gubernatorial terms with election to the U.S. Senate in 1857. In the critical 1860 election to select his fellow senator, he and his supporters backed a Democrat who favored secession—a so-called "war Democrat." Nonetheless, when the issue of secession arose in Tennessee, Johnson argued long and loudly against it. When the state left the Union, Johnson traveled to Washington and became the only Southern senator to keep his seat.

In reward for Johnson's loyalty, in March of 1862 President Lincoln appointed him military governor of Tennessee, the first Southern state to fall to Union

President Andrew Johnson achieved a series of firsts in his remarkable political career.

armies. Johnson proved a stern figure in this post, jailing ministers for preaching pro-Confederate sermons and earning the contempt of many Tennesseans from the Mississippi to the mountains. His two years as military governor ended when Lincoln picked Johnson as his running mate on the 1864 ticket. Lincoln, a Republican, and Johnson, a Democrat, ran together on the Union Party ticket.

Johnson had been vice president for 42 days when John Wilkes Booth fired his pistol into Abraham Lincoln. Lincoln and Johnson had held that, since secession was impossible, the southern states had never left the Union, and thus should not be treated as conquered territories. With the Great Emancipator gone, the radical Republicans in Congress showed no restraint in their attack on the man who was left to carry out Lincoln's reconciliatory policies. They began to look for reasons to remove him from office. (Sound familiar?)

Johnson had inherited Lincoln's secretary of war, Edwin Stanton, who proved extremely disloyal to his new boss. Knowing that Johnson wished to rid himself of Stanton, Congress passed the Tenure of Office Act, which stated that a president could not remove an officeholder who had been approved by the Senate without getting that body's consent. Johnson, wanting to let the courts decide this constitutional matter, and confident that he would win, ordered Stanton to resign anyway.

The House of Representatives now had what it considered a smoking gun. Not willing to let the courts settle the issue, it impeached Johnson on several charges based on his violation of the Tenure

of Office act. Put on trial before the U.S. Senate, he was saved from conviction by only one vote. He ended his term in bitterness, refusing to attend U.S. Grant's inauguration in 1869, but returned to Greeneville in triumph. The man who had been so detested as military governor was now considered a hero in Tennessee as well as in the rest of the South.

Out of office for the first time in 30 years, and in no way content to rest on his laurels, Johnson jumped right back into politics. Running for the U.S. Senate in 1869, he lost by a vote of 55-51—in those days the Tennessee Senate elected U.S. senators—and in 1872 he lost a three-way race for Congress. Still the old campaigner fought on. In 1875, the Tennessee Senate, after putting itself through 55 ballots in a period of days, elected Johnson once more to the U.S. Senate—the only ex-president to serve in that capacity. Johnson took enormous satisfaction in his election to the group that had tried him, and rose in a special Senate session on March 20 to attack President Grant in a speech. He ended his address, as he had done so many times over the years, with a ringing appeal to support the Constitution, and was heartily applauded by his colleagues. He has not been so lauded by historians; a 1996 poll rated him a "failure," a fate shared by his successor as well.

Back in Tennessee during a Senate recess, Johnson had a stroke while visiting his daughter and died three days later on August 1, 1875. Sixty-six years old, he was buried on Signal Hill in Greeneville after a funeral attended by thousands of people.

---

can still see a cannonball from the skirmish imbedded in the front wall.

The block across from the Cumberland Presbyterian Church contains **Bicentennial Park and Big Spring,** the source of water that caused Greeneville to be located here. The same block contains what might be called **The Lost Capitol Building of the Lost State of Franklin.** The real capitol stood for years beside Greene County's present courthouse on Main Street. During Tennessee's centennial celebration in 1896, however, the old log building was shipped off to Nashville, where it was displayed, dismantled, and promptly lost. A few years ago interest in the Lost Capitol of the Lost State was rekindled, and a suitable replacement building was found.

After Crossing Church St. and looking to the right, the **General Morgan Inn & Conference Center,** 111 North Main St., tel. (800) 223-2679 or (423) 787-1000, is worth a look even if you have no intention of staying here. (For info on spending the night, see "Where to Stay" below.) This complex came about when Greeneville, like so many towns in Tennessee, was trying to revitalize its downtown. Four buildings that had been "railroad hotels" stood close to each other. Chief among these was the Hotel Brumley, which had operated from 1920 until 1981. Using a combination of local and Federal money, the General Morgan Inn came into being and opened in 1996.

Just off the lobby, Brumleys restaurant retains the name of one of the old hotels. Above

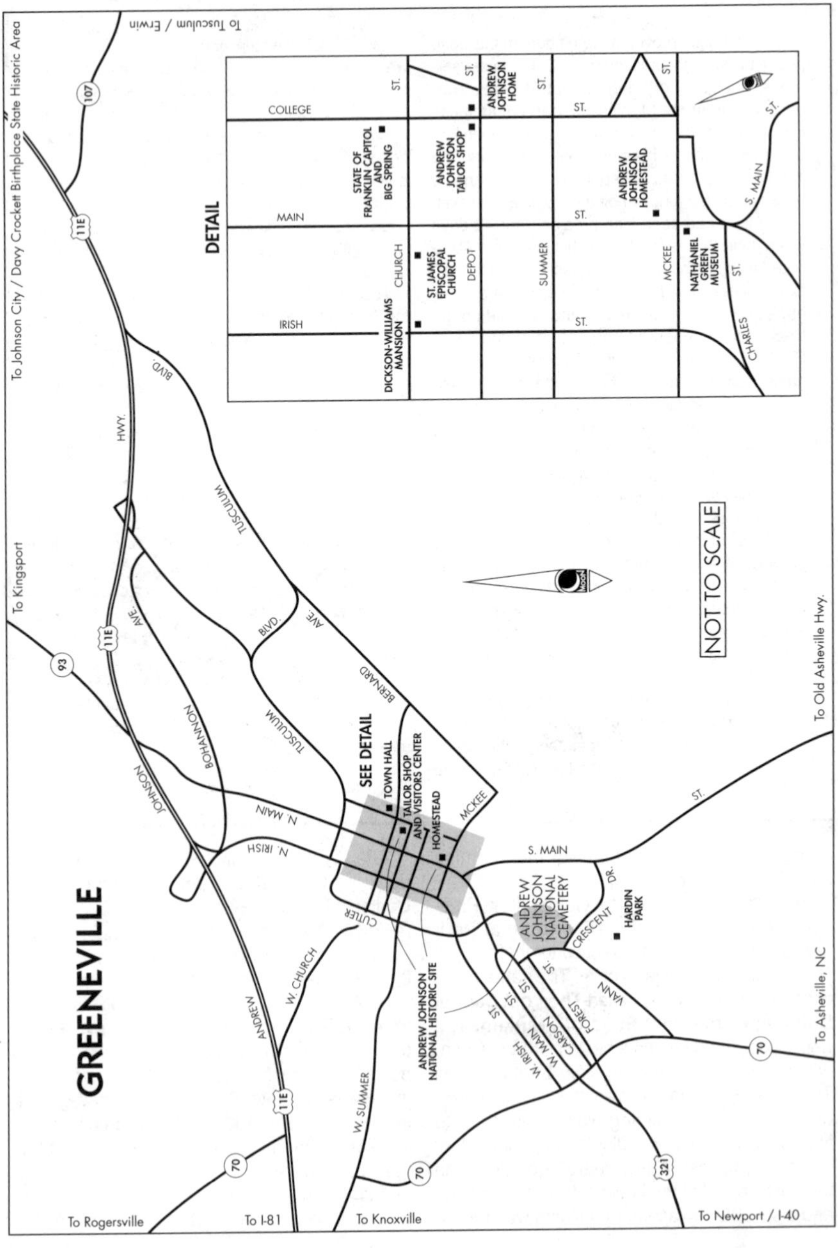

GREENEVILLE

DETAIL

NOT TO SCALE

To Tusculum / Erwin

To Johnson City / Davy Crockett Birthplace State Historic Area

To Kingsport

To Rogersville

To I-81

To Knoxville

To Newport / I-40

To Asheville, NC

To Old Asheville Hwy.

© MOON PUBLICATIONS, INC.

SEE DETAIL

TOWN HALL

TAILOR SHOP AND VISITORS CENTER

HOMESTEAD

ANDREW JOHNSON NATIONAL HISTORIC SITE

ANDREW JOHNSON NATIONAL CEMETERY

HARDIN PARK

STATE OF FRANKLIN CAPITOL AND BIG SPRING

ANDREW JOHNSON TAILOR SHOP

ANDREW JOHNSON HOME

ANDREW JOHNSON HOMESTEAD

DICKSON-WILLIAMS MANSION

ST. JAMES EPISCOPAL CHURCH

NATHANIEL GREEN MUSEUM

COLLEGE   MAIN   IRISH

the bar is an etched glass scene depicting nymphs cavorting on wine glasses. In the old days, this was considered so naughty that on Sundays curtains were drawn so as not to give offense. This accommodation to prudishness still prevails.

General John Hunt Morgan had his sleep, and shortly thereafter, his life interrupted while he was a guest at the **Dickson-Williams Mansion,** which stands behind the General Morgan Inn. Begun in 1815 as "the showplace of East Tennessee," this home and its extensive gardens once occupied an entire city block. Guests in the home included the Marquis de Lafayette, Andrew Jackson, James K. Polk, and Henry Clay. The house passed out of the family and began the decline that so often overtakes such mansions. After being a school, a tobacco factory, an inn, and a hospital, it was bought by the city. It's open Mon.-Fri. 10 a.m.-4 p.m., and closed on holidays. For further information, call (423) 638-4111.

Returning to Main St. and turning left onto Depot St. brings the visitor to Johnson Square and the **Andrew Johnson National Historic Site.** The log cabin replica of the president's birthplace is not a part of the park, which includes three separate units. Begin at the Visitor Center Complex, which contains Johnson's original tailor shop, a museum, and park headquarters. The museum displays a coat that Johnson stitched, as well as a poster from a disgruntled employer in North Carolina offering a reward for his runaway apprentice.

Across the street sits a two-story brick home where Johnson and his family lived from 1838 to 1851. Oddly enough, Johnson bought this property on which the house stands from the heirs of Abraham Lincoln's second cousin. Two rooms here are open to the public, and they contain a genealogy of the family as well as changing exhibits.

The Homestead on S. Main St., the second unit, was the home of Johnson from 1851 until his death in 1875. Due to astute real estate dealings, Johnson was at one time one of the wealthier people in Greeneville, and this house reflects his prosperity. It was vandalized by both Union and Confederate sympathizers during the Civil War. Now the house contains Johnson family furniture and items given to him while he was president.

The final unit is the Andrew Johnson National Cemetery, where the 17th president and his family are buried. To get there, follow the signs down W. Main St. from the Homestead.

There is no charge to visit the Visitor Center Complex or the cemetery. Tours of the Homestead, which are offered on the half hour, cost $2 for adults and are free for anyone under 18 or over 62. For more information, call (423) 638-3551, or see www.nps.gov/anjo.

The **Old Greene County Gaol,** which stands behind the current Greene County Detention Center on Main St., was built in 1804-05 beside a creek whose water was periodically channeled through a trough in the stone floor to flush out the contents. In 1838 it was moved to its present

Andrew Johnson's homestead

locale, and a half century later its brick second story was added.

Named for the man for whom the county and the town were named, the **Nathanael Greene Museum of Greene County History,** on W. McKee St. off Main St., tel. (423) 636-1558, contains an eclectic mixture of town memorabilia. Visitors can see a suit made by tailor-turned-president Andrew Johnson, tickets to Johnson's impeachment trial, and other relics of Greeneville and Greenevillians. The museum is open Tues.-Sat. 10 a.m.-4 p.m. Admission to the museum, which has limited accessibility, is free.

RECREATION

Parks
Kinser Park, tel. (423) 639-5912, along the No-lichucky River has a nine-hole golf course, driving range, tennis courts, water slide, and playground. To get there, take Hwy. 70 South about five miles. Turn left onto Old Allen's Bridge Rd., drive about three miles, then turn right at the fork in the road near the University of Tennessee Tobacco Experiment Station. After that turn, the entrance to the park is about a mile to the right. Kinser Park is open from March 15 to October 15, and possibly longer if weather permits.

Cherokee National Forest
The following recreation areas are in the Cherokee National Forest. All offer picnicking, hiking, and wilderness activities. For further information, go to the Nolichucky Ranger District Office at 120 Austin Ave. in Greeneville or call (423) 638-4109.

Paint Creek Recreation Area lies in a mountain cove beside a creek south of Greeneville in the Cherokee National Forest. Dudley Falls is a popular place for swimming and picnicking, and the area is fun to simply explore. To get there, take Hwy. 70 South for about 14 miles. Look for the Forest Service signs and follow them for three more miles.

Farther up the ridge lies **Horse Creek Recreation Area,** where one can swim in the creek free of charge. Nature trails are also available, including one paved for accessibility. To get to Horse Creek take Hwy. 107 north from Greeneville for six miles,

then turn right and follow the signs for two miles.

The **Old Forge Recreation Area** lies at the foot of Coldspring Mountain and is very popular with horse riders. Visitors can swim in the stream or hike on the nearby Appalachian Trail. Take Hwy. 107 north of Greeneville for six miles, then turn right and follow the signs to the Horse Creek Recreation Area. Once there, take a Forest Service road to Old Forge.

At the bottom of Meadow Creek Mountain lies the **Houston Valley Recreation Area,** where hikers can climb to the Meadow Creek fire tower. Farther down the road boaters can enjoy the French Broad River. From Greeneville take Hwy. 70 South to the intersection with Hwy. 170. Turn right, then go about eight miles. Look for the campground on the left, just before Burnett Gap.

Close by the Appalachian Trail, **Round Mountain Recreation Area** lies at an elevation of 3,400 feet and offers great views, particularly during the fall color season. Take Hwy. 70 South from Greeneville for about nine miles. Turn right on Hwy. 107 and continue for about 13 miles to the intersection with Hwy. 25/70 at the Del Rio post office. Remain on Hwy. 107 for about six miles until the pavement ends and the road becomes gravel; it will climb Round Mountain for about six miles. Look for the sign to the campground.

To get to **Round Knob Recreation Area,** take Hwy. 350, the Jones Bridge Road, south from Greeneville toward the Camp Creek community. Continue on a country road there for two miles, then turn right onto Forest Service Rd. 88 for five miles.

ENTERTAINMENT AND EVENTS

Music and Theater
The **General Morgan Inn & Conference Center,** 111 North Main St., tel. (800) 223-2679 or (423) 787-1000, periodically presents "Summer's End," a one-act dinner theater that tells the story of the demise of General Morgan, the inn's namesake, who met his maker less than 100 yards from where the play is performed. Tickets for dinner and the play cost $42 per person. The Inn offers out-of-towners a package including the play, dinner, a room, and breakfast. Call for details.

Every year the **Little Theatre of Greeneville** trots out musicals, dramas, and children's plays. Call (423) 638-3481 for information about theatrical events.

Events and Festivals

The **Battle of Blue Springs,** a Civil War re-enactment, takes place west of Greeneville in Mosheim (MOSS-hime) on the third weekend in October. Those who attend will get a chance to take a look at authentic military and civilian campsites, the firing of full-scale cannons, cavalry maneuvers, a battle with about 200 participants in period dress, a battlefield hospital, and a period church service. To get there, take Exit 23 from I-81 and follow Hwy. 11 East to Mosheim, where signs will guide you to the battlefield. Admission is $2 per person, free for children under 12. For further information, call Earl Fletcher at the Mosheim Town Hall, tel. (423) 422-4051.

The **Iris Arts and Crafts Festival** takes place in May. Traditional and contemporary crafts are available, plus food. Some crafts are demonstrated. For further information, call the Greene County Partnership at (423) 638-4111.

WHERE TO STAY

Bed and Breakfasts and Inns

The **Big Spring Inn,** 315 N. Main St., Greeneville, TN 37745, tel. (423) 638-2917, is a bed and breakfast in a turn-of-the century, three-story Greek revival house surrounded by 100-year-old trees and gardens in Greeneville's Historic District. The six rooms in the inn, most of which offer private baths, are named for prominent Greeneville women. The rate is $86 per night per couple. The inn is open April through October. Expensive.

General Morgan Inn & Conference Center, 111 North Main St., tel. (800) 223-2679 or (423) 787-1000, offers perhaps the most luxurious accommodations on this end of the state. The Presidential Suite, which goes for $235 a night, has a bathroom with heated floor tiles, a fireplace, and a Chippendale-style canopied bed. More modest rooms go for $89 per night. The Inn has 82 rooms in all. Expensive-Luxury.

Hilltop House, Box 180, Rt. 7, Greeneville, TN 37743. tel. (423) 639-8202, is a spacious old bed and breakfast sitting on a bluff that overlooks the Nolichucky River valley. Decorated with English antiques, the house features afternoon tea and lawn croquet, and the innkeeper—a former landscape architect for the U.S. Forest Service—likes to arrange weekends centered on quilting, fishing, hiking, or gardening. The rate is $70 for two people, with dinner available at $10-12 per person. Moderate.

Nolichucky Bluffs, 400 Kinser Park Ln., tel. (423) 787-7947 or (800) 842-4690, offers a B&B and cabins overlooking the Nolichucky River about seven miles south of Greeneville. The B&B has three rooms, all with private baths and one with a whirlpool bath, and the cabins have stoves or fireplaces. Rates are $75-95 per night. See the Bluffs online at www.usit.net.cabins. Moderate-Expensive.

Motels

Try the **Charray Inn,** 121 Seral Dr., tel. (423) 638-1331 or (800) 852-4682; or the **Holiday Inn,** 1790 E. Andrew Johnson Hwy., tel. (423) 639-4185 or (800) 465-4329.

Camping

Kinser Park has 108 campsites, some with full hookups, and is open from March 15 to October 15. See "Parks" under "Recreation" above.

Davy Crockett Birthplace State Historical Area offers 75 campsites open year-round along the Nolichucky River. See under "West of Jonesborough" above.

Camping at the following **Cherokee National Forest** campsites is strictly first-come, first-served; no reservations are taken. They are open, depending on the weather, from May through mid-November. Directions to each are listed under "Cherokee National Forest" under "Recreation," above. For further information, contact the Nolichucky/Unaka Ranger District Office at 120 Austin Ave. in Greeneville or call (423) 638-4109.

Paint Creek in the Cherokee National Forest offers 21 sites. **Horse Creek** has 10 campsites.

Old Forge's nine tent sites sit near a waterfall. **Houston Valley** has 10 campsites, and **Round Mountain** has 16.

FOOD AND INFORMATION

Food

Augustino's Restaurant, 3465 E. Andrew Johnson Hwy., tel. (423) 639-1231, specializes in Italian cuisine.

The **Brumleys** is the in-house restaurant of the General Morgan Inn & Conference Center, 111 North Main St., tel. (800) 223-2679 or (423) 787-1000. It offers Continental and Southern cuisine.

The **Butcher's Block,** 125 Serral Dr., tel. (423) 638-4485, not surprisingly, features beef—from eight-ounce to 32-ounce steaks. It also offers seafood, barbecue, and chicken.

Pal's, with burgers and hot dogs, operates out of 1357 Tusculum Blvd., tel. (423) 638-7555.

Stan's Bar-B-Q, 2620 E. Andrew Johnson Hwy., tel. (423) 787-0017, is one of the more upscale barbecue places on this end of the state. They have pork, ribs, chicken, and beef. Try the dry ribs with a Memphis rub.

Information

To learn more about Greeneville and Greene County, write or call the **Greeneville/Greene County Area Chamber of Commerce,** 115 Academy St., Suite 1, Greeneville, TN 37743, tel. (423) 638-4111. Or drop by during business hours. Find them on the Web at greene.xtn.net/~gcp or www.greeneville.com.

WEST OF GREENEVILLE

BULLS GAP

Highway 11 East rolls through a low place in Bays Mountain and emerges in the little town of Bulls Gap, which was named for John Bull, a frontier rifle maker. The town became a rail center in the 1800s and was greatly fought over during the Civil War. Union forces holding Bulls Gap were summoned to Greeneville to capture and kill Southern cavalry leader General Morgan. By 1912 as many as 14 passenger trains per day stopped there. Bulls Gap, however, is far more famous as the home of an entertainer who made a career out of claiming he was the town's mayor.

Archie Campbell is a name most familiar to the viewers of *Hee Haw,* the CBS television show for which he was a performer and writer. Among his talents was an ability to make ordinary stories funnier by interchanging the beginning consonants in words. Cinderella thus became Rindercella, and Sleeping Beauty transmogrified into Beeping Sleuty. He began his career in Knoxville as a radio performer, working with Chet Atkins, Roy Acuff, Bill Monroe, Flatt and Scruggs, and the Carter Family. In 1959 he joined the Grand Ole Opry, and 10 years later he helped launch *Hee Haw.* An accomplished painter, in later years he sold limited-edition prints of his works. Campbell died in 1987 at the age of 72.

To get to the center of town, turn southwest at the traffic light and go over a hill. If anyone wanted to establish another Jonesborough-type tourist operation, or an eastern version of Middle Tennessee's Bell Buckle, Bulls Gap lies waiting. Its railroad heritage, surplus of available buildings, and proximity to Interstate 81 would all contribute to success. As for now, the local tourism industry centers around the **Bulls Gap Tourism Complex,** a fancy name for a collection of historic buildings that don't seem to have much purpose in life. Archie Campbell's boyhood home has been moved into town and restored with period furniture. Downhill stands the Town Hall, which contains a museum with Archie Campbell's artwork, items from his career, and the usual odd items that town museums contain. This one has, among other things, a Samurai sword and a tommy gun. Admission to the complex is free, although donations are cheerfully accepted, and it is open May 1-October, Mon.-Sat. 10 a.m.-4 p.m., Sunday 2-4 p.m. or whenever the City Recorder is on duty.

Bulls Gap has a big celebration every Labor Day, with food and craft booths, games for children, and live music. For information call City Hall at (423) 235-5216.

Live gospel music is presented once a month April-June and August-October in a theater downtown. Call Robin Horner at (423) 235-2917 for details.

MORRISTOWN

In the 1960's many towns across Tennessee attempted to spruce up their downtowns and make them "modern." Often this resulted in beautiful 19th century storefronts being covered with hideous fabrications of aluminum and or plastic. Preferring to take the high road, Morristown chose to launch its sidewalks into the air.

That's right. On Main St., which runs parallel to and south of Hwy. 11-E, the sidewalks have been raised 20 or so feet off the ground. New doors were cut into the facades of buildings, and crosswalks high above the pavement enable shoppers to cross the street. There is nothing in Tennessee quite like this.

This fascination with elevated endeavors has a long history in Morristown. One interesting if obscure 19th-century Morristonian was Melville Milton Murrell, who patented the first flying machine in America while the Wright brothers were still in short pants. Others had patented "ornithopters," but Melville's 1876 model was the first one to take a human aloft. The wings flapped like a bird's, and the pilot attempted to control it with his hands and feet. The plane, aided by guide wires, flew for several hundred yards but could never manage sustained flight. In 1912 he tried again, this time using a motorcycle engine, but to no avail. Melville gave up trying to conquer the skies and turned his attention to heaven, becoming a Methodist circuit-rider.

Sights

The second stop on the David Crockett tour is the **David Crockett Tavern and Museum,** 2002 E. Morningside Dr., tel. (423) 587-9900. The building is a replica of his parents' tavern, and the contents are period pieces, but the visitor can get a sense here of the kind of world that made up Crockett's formative years. The Loom Room contains a very good collection of devices used to make cloth from flax fibers. It is open May-Oct. Tues.-Sat. 9 a.m.-5 p.m. Admission is $4 for adults and $1 for students.

Many Tennessee towns have museums, but few have them in as beautiful a building as Morristown's **Rose Center,** 442 W. 2nd North St., tel. (423) 581-4330. The brick 1892 former high school houses a regional museum, traveling exhibits, and gift shop. Here one can see plans and parts of Melville Murrell's ornithopter as well as other historic exhibits. The Rose Center is open Mon.-Fri. 9 a.m.-5 p.m. and Saturday 9 a.m.-1 p.m.

Events

Every year on the last weekend in October the **Mountain Makin's Festival** takes place in the Rose Center. More than 50 juried craftspeople display their goods, and artists demonstrate their work. Live entertainment, country cooking, and an old-time medicine show round out the festivities for the estimated 12,000 who attend. For further information, call (423) 586-6382.

Where to Stay

Visitors can rest at **Baneberry Golf and Resort,** 704 Harrison Ferry Rd., Baneberry, TN, tel. (800) 951-GOLF, which has accommodations for people passing through. Guests stay in a hotel or "golf villa" for $86-96 per couple. The price includes green fees as well. Expensive.

Victoria Rose Bed & Breakfast, 307 East 2nd North St., Morristown, TN 37814, tel. (423) 581-9687, occupies one of Tennessee's many Barber Houses. George Barber was an architect who sold mail-order houses; customers picked out a design, placed an order, and then picked up all the materials for the house at the depot. This one was built at the turn of the century and includes a wraparound porch and a third-floor cupola. Three guest rooms await the visitor inside; two of them have private baths. The house has central heat and air and is furnished with Victorian antiques. The host serves a full breakfast. Rates are $45-65. Inexpensive-Moderate.

Franchise options include **Comfort Suites,** 3660 W. Andrew Johnson Hwy., tel. (423) 585-4000; **Days Inn,** 2512 E. Andrew Johnson Hwy., tel. (423) 587-2200; **Holiday Inn of Morristown,** 3230 W. Andrew Johnson Hwy., tel. (423) 581-8700; **Ramada Inn,** Hwy. 25 and I-81 interchange, tel. (423) 587-2400; and **Super 8 Motel,** 2430 E. Andrew Johnson Pkwy., tel. (423) 586-8880.

Camping

Owned by Hamblen County and open year-round, **Cherokee Park** is a 178-acre recreation area containing 52 campsites with water and electricity hookups. There are also eight primitive sites. Showers and bathrooms are available from March through October. From I-81, take Exit 8—Hwy. 25-E—nine miles north to the park entrance. For information and reservations call (423) 586-5232 or (423) 586-0260.

Several miles southwest of Morristown on Hwy. 11 East, a sign points the way to **Panther Creek State Recreational Park.** These 1,435 acres sit on the banks of Cherokee Lake, a.k.a. the Holston River. This lake, one of the many that TVA uses for flood control, appears half empty during the fall and winter. Bird watchers like to post themselves atop a long ridge in the park and wait for migrating hawks and waterfowl. The park shelters some rare albino white-tailed deer as well. Panther Creek offers nature trails, picnic sites, a playground and swimming pool, plus camping on 50 sites, each with water and electricity. The campground is open year-round, but the water is not available from Thanksgiving through mid-March. For further information, write to 2010 Panther Creek Rd., Morristown, TN 37814, or call (423) 587-7046. Or see them online at www.tnstateparks.com.

Food

Angelo's Fine Dining, 3614 W. Andrew Johnson Hwy., tel. (423) 581-4882, is the fanciest restaurant in town. Patrons can enjoy fresh seafood, steaks, spaghetti, and Greek dishes such as moussaka. So it can serve drinks in a dry county, Angelo's is a "private club," with membership open to those who fill out an application and fork out $5. It's worth it, say regulars.

Buddy's Barbecue, 2275 W. Andrew Johnson Hwy., tel. (423) 587-5058, is one of a chain of barbecue places operating out of Knoxville.

The Little Dutch, 115 S. Cumberland St., tel. (423) 581-1441, is a longtime Morristown favorite. Amid decor inspired by a trip to Holland, this eatery serves lunch and dinner every day consisting of steaks, seafood, spaghetti, and Greek dishes. Whatever you order for dinner, you should finish off with the baklava.

The **Mexico Lindo Restaurant,** 3351 W. Andrew Johnson Hwy., tel. (423) 587-9754, has Mexican food. Try the chile rellenos.

Information

The **Morristown Chamber of Commerce** is at 825 W. 1st North St., tel. (423) 586-6382, and on the Internet at www.morristownchamber.com.

BETWEEN MORRISTOWN AND JEFFERSON CITY

Motorists heading west from Morristown will see a large antebellum house on the right. This is **Arrow Hill Bed and Breakfast,** 6622 W. Andrew Johnson Hwy., Talbott, TN 37877, tel. (423) 586-1523, which was once the centerpiece of a 2,200-acre plantation. The house features adjoining twin parlors which—when both doors were open—provided an excellent space in which to dance the Virginia Reel. The brick house changed hands seven times during the Civil War, and Confederate General James Longstreet spent the night there. By the turn of the century the plantation was gone and the house fell into disrepair. From 1910 through 1919 it was actually used as a barn.

Then came Margaret, a 19 year-old woman who agreed to marry a 46 year-old man if he would buy the house and restore it to the condition of its glory days. He agreed, and the two were wed. Unfortunately, in 1923 he went bankrupt and lost the house as well as Margaret, who died in 1998 at the age of 99. She is commemorated for guests with "Margaret's Room."

The house is filled with antiques and period reproductions. Guests can choose from three bedrooms, one of which has a private bath. The other two rooms share two baths that are down the hall. Rates are $55-65. Take a peak online at www.bbonline.com.tn.arrowhill. Inexpensive-Moderate.

JEFFERSON CITY

Travelers can go straight from Morristown to Jefferson City, but a better route turns northwest at a shoe store onto the Old Andrew Johnson Highway. When a Farmer's Co-op appears on the right, look up the hill to the left to see **Glenmore Mansion,** built in 1869 and described as "perhaps the grandest Second Empire country house remaining in Tennessee." Often rented for weddings and other frivolities, it is open to the public May-October. Admission is $2.50 for adults and $1 for kids. Call (423) 475-5014.

Jefferson County is a center for zinc mining, and from 1950 through 1995 this county produced more zinc ore than anywhere else in the country.

Jefferson City is chiefly known for **Carson-Newman College,** which came about by a 1889 marriage between the Carson College for Men, founded in 1851, with the Newman College for Women, founded in 1852. Affiliated with the Tennessee Baptist Convention, the college has just over 2,100 students, who for years were not permitted to dance. Finally the ban was lifted, and students cheerfully take part in what they term "Foot Functions." See the school website at www.cn.edu.

For those who wish to come back with something from Tennessee, one of the best places in the state to stop is **Made in Tennessee,** 1418 Russell Ave., tel. (800) 255-2613 or (423) 475-5944. Just off Hwy 11-E, this place stocks books, cheese, barbecue sauce and rub, candy, Dr. Enuf beverages, and all manner of Tennesseana. Or visit them at www.tntreasures.com.

For further info on this town, try the Jefferson City Chamber of Commerce, tel. (423) 397-9642, 532 Patriot Drive or online at www.jeffersontnchamber.org.

THE GREAT NEW MARKET WRECK

New Market briefly entered popular culture because of a dreadful train wreck. Two Southern railroad passenger trains carrying a total of 300 people crashed head-on here at 10:18 on the morning of September 4, 1904. Sixty-four passengers died and 152 were injured. A ballad about the wreck was written two years later by one of the survivors and was widely performed by a variety of singers. *The WPA Guide to Tennessee* contains the following verses:

One autumn morning in Tennessee
An awful wreck was heard;
East of Knoxville and New Market
Was where the crash occurred.

The east and west-bound passenger trains
Were running at highest speed;
They struck each other in the curve;
'Twas a horrible sight indeed.

The engine crew on the west-bound train
Their orders had misread;
About one hundred and fifty were hurt,
And nearly seventy were dead.

NEW MARKET

This town lay on the stage route between Knoxville and Abingdon, Virginia, and in those days Tucker's Tavern provided the accommodations for those coming or going. It was not a posh place; the 1939 WPA Guide to Tennessee tells the tale of one guest who was thrown out of the tavern because he objected to using a towel that had already been used by 15 people.

During the Civil War, East Tennessee was a center of support for the Union, and in 1862 some 450 young men gathered here to march off and join the Northern army. They had no guns, however, and were apprehended by Confederate troops and forced to spend the rest of the war in Tuscaloosa, Alabama.

In 1865, the year the Civil War ended, 15-year-old Frances Hodgson moved to New Market with her mother and three siblings from Manchester, England. Frances and her sister ran a school to which most of the students paid tuition with the products of their families' farms. In her free time, she wrote short stories and mailed them to editors, at one point picking blackberries to obtain money for postage.

Hodgson moved to Knoxville in 1869, married a surgeon, and then moved to Washington, D.C. She continued her writing, eventually writing over 40 novels, among them the children's classics *Little Lord Fauntleroy* and *The Secret Garden.* She often came back to visit in New Market, and locals like to think that her greatest books were written in part while she was here. A roadside marker commemorates her time here. Part of the house closest to the marker—a log cabin now covered with boards—is where she lived. It is not open to the public.

Tennessee has several places where people used to come to "take the waters"; Red Boiling Springs in Middle Tennessee is a good example of this. Most of the water alleged to have curative powers was discovered in the 1800s. New Market's **Houston Mineral Water,** however, was discovered in 1931. As Carolyn Sakowski tells the tale in *Touring the East Tennessee Backroads,* William Avery Houston had kidney disease so bad that he thought he was going to die. One night he had a dream that instructed him to dig a well in a particular place. He did so, drilling to a depth of 252 feet until he struck water. This was odd, for most people in New Market could hit water a mere 20 or 30 feet down. At any rate, he drank the water for several days and was cured. Later he began to bottle this natural elixir, which is available free to passersby. Look for a well house (close to the Frances Hodgson house) at 1005 Old Andrew Johnson Hwy., which runs parallel to Hwy. 11-E, and go inside. You can get a taste at a fountain or fill jugs from a spigot. A small box accepts contributions to defray the costs of making the water available.

Finally, New Market is well known in some circles as a center for social activism. The **Highlander Research and Education Center,** which occupies a 104-acre site north of Hwy 11-E, began as the controversial Highlander Folk School in Middle Tennessee. It was there that Martin Luther King, Rosa Parks, and other icons of the civil rights movement came to work together to forge the tactics that brought them victories.

Highlander School was more or less run off from Grundy County in 1962, then existed for a decade in Knoxville, and moved to New Market in 1972. Today Highlander works with community groups, primarily from Appalachia and the Deep South. "We bring people together to learn from each other," says the group's mission statement. This takes the form of residential workshops, training sessions, and other methods that develop leadership in issues such as fighting corporate pollution, bringing U.S. and immigrant workers together, and combating the increasing use of part-time, temporary, and contract workers. The Highlander Center is not open to the public, but you can visit its site online at www.hrec.org.

One of the best restaurants in East Tennessee, the **Great Barrington Inn,** has a New Market address, but is actually closer to Dandridge. Look under that town in the Gateways chapter for a listing.

KNOXVILLE

INTRODUCTION

"We are now talking of summer evenings in Knoxville, Tennessee in the time that I lived there so successfully disguised to myself as a child." Those words begin James Agee's novel, *A Death In The Family,* a wonderful evocation of 1915 life in the Fort Sanders neighborhood of this largest East Tennessee city, the third largest in the state.

Agee is part of a long line of creative people to emerge from or do significant work in Knoxville. Clarence Brown, the Metro-Goldwyn-Mayer stalwart who directed more Greta Garbo movies than anyone else, grew up in Knoxville. So did Quentin Tarantino. Radio stations WROL and WNOX were hotbeds of country music, with Roy Acuff, Chet Atkins, Archie Campbell, Homer and Jethro, and other luminaries making their mark before moving on to Nashville. Hank Williams stopped at the Andrew Johnson Hotel before taking his last ride in a Cadillac up Hwy. 11. The Everly Brothers

combed their pompadours in the mirrors of West High School, and a shy Sevier County girl first faced television cameras in Knoxville, where early morning viewers caught their first glimpse of Dolly Parton. Eva Barber, the country singer for Lawrence Welk, was born here, as was country singer Carl Butler. Actresses Patricia Neal and Polly Bergen and actor John Cullum also came from here. Novelist and National Book Award winner Cormac McCarthy spent many years in Knoxville and used it for the setting of some of his work. And the city is home to the Reverend J. Bazzel Mull, a gospel music disc jockey whose gravelly voice has pushed Chuck Wagon Gang records and tapes on clear channel stations from Alaska to Venezuela.

From its earliest days, East Tennessee's largest city has attracted wheeler-dealers, gospel music and otherwise, who weren't afraid to roll the dice—theirs or someone else's.

HISTORY

From Fort to Capital

Like so many of the early towns in Tennessee, Knoxville's location was determined by how easily it could be defended from the Indians. In 1786 James White built a fort on a hill a few miles downstream from where the Holston and French Broad Rivers combine to form the Tennessee River. When William Blount, a member of the Constitutional Convention whom George Washington appointed governor of the Southwest Territory, came from Rocky Mount to look for a permanent capital for the territory, White's Fort seemed just right. It just happened that Blount owned land nearby.

William Blount was the kind of man who insisted on wearing powdered wigs and silver buckles even on the frontier. Ever the politician, he renamed White's Fort Knoxville in 1791 in honor of Henry Knox, Washington's secretary of war, who doled out money to the Indians in hopes of keeping them in line. James White gracefully accepted the name change and began marking off and selling lots in the new town. Houses and other structures sprang up—most notably Governor Blount's extravagant house, which the locals immediately dubbed "Blount Mansion."

In short order Knoxville grew into a booming place with its own newspaper and a college, and it became a center for trade, most of it aimed downstream. Adventuresome merchants cut down trees, built flatboats, loaded them with goods such as flour, lime, and cotton, and shoved off. They drifted down the Tennessee, down the Ohio, and down the Mississippi to New Orleans, where they would sell everything, including the boats they floated in on.

As Tennesseans moved toward statehood, they wrangled and wrote their state constitution in Knoxville. Vermont and Kentucky were admitted as

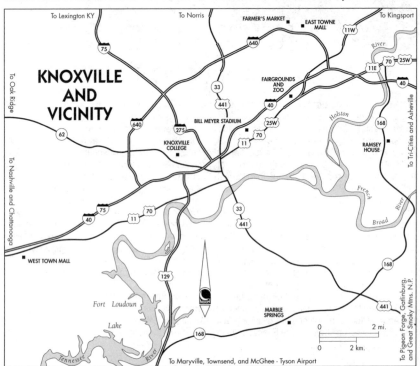

MUST-SEE HIGHLIGHTS

The **Knoxville Museum of Art,** perched above the site of the 1982 World's Fair, presents exhibits that stir the imagination.

Blount Mansion, the first frame house in a town of log cabins, is the most significant historical site in the entire city.

The **Tennessee Theater,** with its mighty Wurlitzer organ console rising through the floor, shows the glories of past movie palaces.

The **Old City** gives new life to 19th-century warehouses, offering an engaging mixture of shops, clubs, and restaurants.

The Knoxville Zoo is one of the better zoos in the entire South. Kids love this place, and adults will find it more interesting than they might think.

Davis-Kidd Booksellers is the best bookstore this side of Nashville.

Mull's Singing Convention is a Sunday morning television show—7-8 AM on WBIR—featuring one of the more colorful characters in East Tennessee and his perennial straightwoman, Mrs. Mull. "Ain't that right, Lady Mull?

The **Laurel Theatre and Jubilee Community Arts,** has wonderful acoustic music and occasional dancing.

states to join the original 13, but neither of these two had been territories first. Tennessee was the first state to go through this new constitutionally required process. On June 1, 1796, Tennessee became the 16th state, with Knoxville as its capital.

Although it was the state capital, Knoxville never had a capitol. The legislature met in taverns and other convivial buildings to work through its business. As the population in more western parts of the state grew, the pressure to move the seat of government closer to the center of the state led to Nashville's designation as the state capital in 1826. Fortunately for Knoxville, the college—by 1840 called Tennessee State University—stayed.

Civil War Siege

When the Civil War broke out, Knoxville was a Confederate lion in a den of Daniels; the city had many Southern sympathizers, but they were surrounded by staunch Unionists. Both sides

recognized, however, that East Tennessee's largest city was a strategic prize, and accordingly, a Confederate army under Gen. Felix Zollicoffer occupied the city for the first two years of the war.

In 1863, Union General Ambrose Burnside, the popularizer of sideburns, forced the Southerners to leave. When they returned in the form of Gen. James Longstreet, they found a well-fortified city awaiting them. Longstreet set up his headquarters west of the city in "Bleak House," built and named by an admirer of the Charles Dickens novel. The name proved prophetic. Longstreet set up a siege, planning to bombard and starve the city into submission. The loyal Unionist farmers, however, flummoxed these plans by floating rafts full of food down the river at night.

Longstreet finally attacked Fort Sanders, an earthen fort at the western edge of Knoxville, and was repulsed in a brief but bloody battle. When Union Gen. William Tecumseh Sherman forced Longstreet to give up the siege, the future torcher of Atlanta rode into town expecting to find a starving populace. Instead, he and his staff were served a turkey dinner with all the trimmings, delicious proof that Knoxville was the only city to withstand a prolonged Civil War siege.

Prosperity

In the years after the Civil War, railroads boomed and so did Knoxville. Its location as a gateway to the South led to a flow of people, goods, and money through the city. Tennessee State University received designation as a land grant college, rebuilt its bombarded buildings, and became the University of Tennessee (www.utk.edu). Knoxville College was founded in 1875 to prepare young black men for the Presbyterian ministry.

Rebuilt railroads and increased steamboat traffic made Knoxville's cash registers jangle, and by the turn of the century the city felt a need to show off. This took the form of the 1910 Knoxville Appalachian Exposition, and the populace had such a good time that two years later they did it again with a federally financed National Conservation Exposition. According to Betsy Creekmore, author of *Our Fair City,* one of the ideas that came from this exposition was the notion that a national park should be established in the East. The ideal place would be the Great Smoky Mountains.

THE DEATH OF HANK WILLIAMS

Hank Williams, who wrote so many great country songs, and who lived his life as if it were a country song, spent his last day in Knoxville. As recounted in Colin Escott's *Hank Williams, The Biography,* Williams had left Montgomery, Alabama, headed for a New Year's Eve show in Charleston, West Virginia. On December 31, 1951, he rode into Knoxville in a Cadillac driven by an 18-year-old Auburn University freshman, Charles Carr. Bad weather had delayed the two, and in an attempt to get to the show on time they caught a plane at Knoxville's airport, but a snowstorm forced the plane to turn back.

Realizing they couldn't make the Charleston show, William and his young driver checked into the Andrew Johnson Hotel on Gay Street. Williams had to be carried to his room. Long plagued by back pain that was exacerbated by long car trips,

Williams found relief in morphine shots, and that night, allegedly suffering from violent hiccups, he found a doctor who was willing to administer two shots of the opiate and pronounce him fit to travel.

Porters carried an inanimate Williams back out to his Cadillac, and he and Carr set off at 10:45 p.m. up Hwy. 11 West. Carr drove quickly and was pulled over for speeding near the town of Blaine. The arresting officer expressed concern about the comatose figure in the back of the car but was assured that Williams had been sedated.

Carr discovered that Williams was dead after pulling off the road in Oak Hill, West Virginia. Biographer Escott suggests that Williams died either in Knoxville or shortly after leaving town. His most recent single, "I'll Never Get Out of This World Alive," reached number one on the country charts. Williams was 29 years old when he died.

Arrival of the TVA

Knoxville suffered along with the rest of the nation in the Great Depression, but because of that economic calamity the city landed the headquarters of the Tennessee Valley Authority (TVA), a federal agency born of the New Deal. It was charged with reducing floods, producing abundant electrical power, and, in a grandiose mission statement, assisting in "the development of the natural resources of the Tennessee River drainage basin and its adjoining territory for the general social and economic welfare of the Nation." How successfully TVA did all that is still debated, but the impact on Knoxville was overwhelmingly positive. By the time TVA was finished damming Tennessee rivers, the lakes had almost as much shoreline as Florida has coastline. The once wild Tennessee River that had subjected so many of the old boatmen to harrowing rides became a safe waterway plied by stately barges and a host of pleasure craft.

World War II made Knoxville's factories hum, and much of the activity that went on at the secret city of Oak Ridge had benefits for Knoxville as well.

Knoxville Nowadays

The greatest 20th-century impact on Knoxville, however, came in the form of the 1982 World's

Fair, an energy-focused event that, apart from bringing 11 million visitors and a lot of excitement and controversy, delivered three big blessings: improved interstate highways, a renewal of downtown, and a host of new hotels and restaurants, all of which provide lasting value for the visitor.

One of the champions of Expo 82 was Jake Butcher, a high-rolling banker who with his brother put his own mark on the city with the construction of his headquarters' sparkling twin towers. His banking empire was built on a foundation of paper, however, and it came down with a crash. Jake wound up in prison, and a good many people lost money when his banks went under.

Across the street—local wags call the intersection of Main and Gay Sts. "Ego Intersection"—stands what looks for all the world like a college campus. Built at a cost of $55 million by Christopher Whittle, this lovely three-building complex was for a time the headquarters of Whittle Communications, the company that, among other things, brought commercials to a captive audience of high school students. Known irreverently as Whittlesburg, it occupies an entire city block in Knoxville, and for a brief shining moment was filled with media experts, writers, and designers of an intensity never before seen in these parts. The presence of these trendy souls contributed mightily to the transformation of an old warehouse and office area into Knoxville's fashionable Old City area.

Whittle, like Butcher before him, dazzled Knoxville with his visions and taste, but his multimedia reach far exceeded his financial grasp.

Whittlesburg went on the sales block and was turned into a collection of government offices.

Having survived a Civil War siege, a world's fair, and the latest incarnations of the hustlers who founded the city, Knoxville thrives and is eager to provide visitors a good time.

SIGHTS AND RECREATION

THE LAY OF THE LAND

Knoxville is a city on a hill, or a series of hills, and for visitors can be divided into four areas: downtown, the World's Fair Site, Old City, and the University of Tennessee (UT). Walkers can easily tour the first two from one parking place. Old City is a bit of a hike, and a walking tour to UT will wear your soles even farther. Many of the city's restaurants line Kingston Pike, a four-lane street that heads west from the UT area and extends for miles in parallel with I-40/75.

The following sections give an overview of each area. For specific information about the various sites and attractions, look under the appropriate category—Museums and Galleries, Shopping, Food, etc.

the Victorian Houses of the
11th Street artists' colony

WORLD'S FAIR PARK

The best place to get an overview of Knoxville is the observation deck at the **Sunsphere,** the most prominent remnant of the 1982 World's Fair. Resembling a water tower á la Las Vegas, this one-of-a-kind edifice stands 26 stories high. Visitors can ascend to the 22nd story, the lowest floor of the five-story ball, and gaze over the city.

World's Fair Park used to be Second Creek Valley, and the stream, now home to several schools of carp, still flows through it. The restored **L&N Station** anchors the upper end of the park. Built in 1904, the station now contains a restaurant and shops.

Farther down the valley stands **Fort Kid,** one

of those delightful wooden structures that kids can tear through at high speeds and easily elude any pursuing adults. Admission is free, and the fort is open during daylight hours.

The Candy Factory, tel. (423) 522-2049, will also please kids of all ages. This 1919 building was built to house a candy factory, and now is home to an unabashed firm named The South's Finest Chocolate Factory, which does all of its production here. Visitors can peer through windows to see machines and people busily cranking out the calories, and the shop sells more than 100 kinds of candy. Its hours are Mon.-Sat. 9:30 a.m.-6 p.m., Sunday 1-5 p.m.

Beside the Candy Factory stands the **Knoxville Museum of Art,** and if visiting the museum spurs visitors to add to their own collections, the artists in **Victorian Houses,** corner of 11th St. and Laurel Ave., will happily provide. This brightly colored row of houses boasts shops containing original arts and fine crafts. The shops are open Tues.-Sat. 10 a.m.-5 p.m., Sunday 1-5 p.m.

Farther down the valley lies the **Tennessee Amphitheater,** where performance events take place during warm weather. Check at the Sunsphere to see what's happening here.

DOWNTOWN

The hill that constitutes downtown Knoxville is bookended by the twin towers of the TVA's headquarters to the north and the City/County Building overlooking the river to the south.

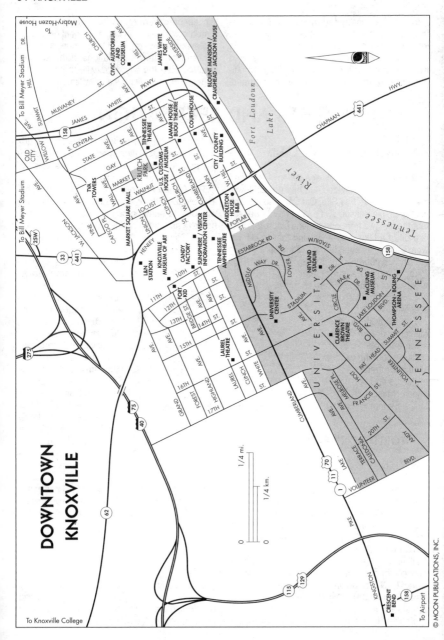

DOWNTOWN KNOXVILLE

To Knoxville College

© MOON PUBLICATIONS, INC.

Like other Tennessee cities, Knoxville is rediscovering its riverfront, and hereabouts this has taken the form of **Volunteer Landing,** a mile-long waterfront development beginning downtown and stretching downstream along the UT campus. At spots the walkway goes out over the river on piers. The **Women's Basketball Hall of Fame** is slated to open here.

A hundred yards inland, Knoxville's history begins with the replica of **James White's Fort** and the very real **Blount Mansion,** which was the seat of government for America's first territory. This and other facts can be gleaned from **The Museum of East Tennessee History** on Market St., which also contains several restaurants and spots to sit down.

Right beside the museum is the most delightful downtown park in the entire state. **Krutch Park** is an inspired blend of greenery and water that offers respite to the footsore tourist. Farther down Market St. is **Market Square Mall,** an open-air place where farmers once sold their produce.

Parallel to Market St. is Gay St., Knoxville's historic main drag. The principal hotel for a long time was the Andrew Johnson Hotel, 912 S. Gay St., and it was here that Hank Williams spent his last day on earth. Two wonderful old theaters hold court here, and both are worth a visit. The **Lamar House-Bijou Theatre,** 803 Gay St., is a former hotel with a theater behind it, while the **Tennessee Theater** is a 1928 movie palace. A stroll north on Gay St. leads to the edge of the Old City.

OLD CITY

The intrepid tourist can walk north on Gay Street, turn right on Jackson Ave., and march into Old City, a collection of turn-of-the-century brick buildings whose offices and warehouses made Knoxville the center of commerce for East Tennessee and much of the South. Left to slumber for years, these buildings became home in the '80s to an eclectic mixture of eateries, drinkeries, boutiques, antique shops, galleries, and nightclubs. Here you'll also find the greatest collection of live music in East Tennessee—dance music, jazz, rock, and blues. Simply walking around is exciting. On Sunday and other mornings, the Old City offers several places to drink very good coffee while leisurely reading the paper.

If visitors are driving, a good place to stop is the corner of Jackson and Central Streets. From I-40, take Exit 388A onto the James White Parkway, then go right on Jackson. During busy weekends, parking can be tight in these parts, so if at all possible try to hoof it.

THE UNIVERSITY OF TENNESSEE

Cumberland Ave. goes from Downtown to the University of Tennessee. The Knoxville campus of UT is the largest in the statewide system; approximately 19,000 undergraduates and 7,000 graduate students study here. The campus contains 229 buildings spread over 532 acres, and a driving tour is the best way to take in the sights.

The Law School is on the right as you drive or walk up from the World's Fair Site. On the left at the corner of Stadium Dr. and Cumberland Ave. is the **University Center,** which houses an art gallery, two restaurants, and the university's enormous bookstore. Here you can buy books as well as every imaginable item colored orange and white and bearing the UT logo. The center is a good place to find out what's happening on campus—speakers, plays, movies, etc.

The oldest and most architecturally unified part of the campus lies up a hill adjacent to the University Center. This "hallowed hill," as UT's alma mater puts it, has brick buildings in the collegiate Gothic style. Of these the most impressive is **Ayers Hall,** which crowns the hill.

UT has a wonderful theater program with the **Clarence Brown Theater** and **Carousel Theater.** The former shows 35mm foreign and art movies on Sunday nights. Museum-goers should check out the **Frank H. McClung Museum,** East Tennessee's main natural history collection, while art lovers should wander over to **Ewing Gallery of Art and Architecture.**

MUSEUMS AND GALLERIES

History
The **Beck Cultural Center,** at 1927 Dandridge Ave. east of town, tel. (423) 524-8461, houses collections relating to Knoxville's black citizens.

Old photographs depicting community events and church life are the bulk of the exhibits. Admission is free, and the center is open Tues.-Sat. 10 a.m.-6 p.m.

The Museum of East Tennessee History, 600 Market St., tel. (423) 544-5732, focuses on regional history from the mid-18th century up to 1982, the year of the World's Fair. Exhibits include the surveying equipment used by James White to lay out the original town; "Old Betsy," one of David Crockett's rifles; and early furniture made in East Tennessee. The Civil War section displays uniforms, rifles, pistols, and a regimental flag. The museum is open Mon.-Sat. 10 a.m.-4 p.m., Sunday 1-5 p.m. Admission is free. Visit online at www.korrnet.org/eths/museum.htm.

Every decent university has a museum, and UT's **Frank H. McClung Museum,** 1327 Circle Park Dr., tel. (423) 974-2144, has perhaps the best collection of natural history on the eastern end of the state. Portions of the permanent display include a collection of Indian artifacts, historical items, and the odd exhibits of art and geology. They also have some items from ancient Egypt. Admission is free, and the museum is open Mon.-Sat. 9 a.m.-5 p.m. and Sunday 2-5 p.m. See them online at www.mcclungmuseum.utk.edu.

The **Volunteer State Veterans Hall of Fame,** 4000 Chapman Hwy., tel. (423) 577-0757, contains more than 2,000 war-related artifacts from the Revolutionary War up to and including Operation Desert Storm. Admission is free, and the Hall of Fame is open Thurs.-Sat. 10 a.m.-4 p.m., Sunday 1-4 p.m.

Art

The **Ewing Gallery of Art and Architecture** in the Art and Architecture Building at 1715 Volunteer Blvd. on the UT campus, tel. (423) 974-3200, features traveling exhibits as well as those generated from within the university. Admission is free. May-August, it's open Mon.-Fri. 8 a.m.-4:30 p.m.; September-April, it's open Mon.-Thurs. 8 a.m.-4:30 p.m. and 7-9 p.m., Friday 8 a.m.-4:30 p.m., and Sunday 1-4:30 p.m.

The **Knoxville Museum of Art,** 1050 Worlds Fair Park Dr., tel. (423) 525-6101, occupies a beautiful building. Pink Tennessee marble graces the outside, while inside visitors will find traveling exhibits such as "From Blast to Pop, Aspects of Modern British Art 1915-1965." Call to find out the current exhibits. The museum also has a cafe and a shop and is open Tues.-Thurs. 10 a.m.-5 p.m., Friday 10 a.m.-9 p.m., Saturday 10 a.m.-5 p.m., and Sunday noon-5 p.m. Admission is free. Visit online at www.knoxart.org.

Specialty

The **East Tennessee Discovery Center,** tel. (423) 594-1494, is one of those children's museums where there are no "Don't Touch!" signs. Exhibits include, to list a few, *Rocks, Minerals, and Fossils,* an insect zoo, and a planetarium. To get there, take Exit 392 off I-40 east of downtown. Take Rutledge Pike southeast until it hits Magnolia Avenue. Go right, then turn right again onto Beaman Road. Follow the signs. Open Monday-Friday 9 a.m.-5 p.m. and on varying hours on Saturday. Admission is $3 for adults, $2 for seniors, $2 for children five and over, and $1 for kids ages three and four. See them on the Web at funnelweb.utcc.utk.edu/~loganj/etdc.

The only gallery in town, if not the state, that is devoted to athletics, the **Joseph B. Wolffe Gallery,** tel. (423) 974-0967, on the UT campus at 1914 Andy Holt Ave., features a collection of 130 bronze statues, medals, and bas-reliefs, and other items created by R. Tait McKenzie (1867-1938). Admission is free; hours are Mon.-Fri. 1-5 p.m.

In a town west of Knoxville, the **Farragut Folklife Museum** in the Farragut Town Hall at 11408 Municipal Center Dr., tel. (423) 966-7057, contains local items as well as those pertaining to Adm. David Farragut of "Damn the torpedoes, full steam ahead!" fame. Farragut was born here and spent his first five years in Tennessee. Admission is free, and the museum is open Mon.-Fri. 2-4:30 p.m.

PARKS AND ZOOS

The **Knoxville Zoo,** tel. (423) 637-5331, is the best zoo in Tennessee, if not the entire South. This zoo shelters more than 1,000 creatures representing 225 species, most of which live in re-creations of their natural surroundings. The zoo boasts an extensive large cat collection, and visitors can walk through habitats with names like Gorilla Valley, Cheetah Savannah, and Tortoise Territory. Kids particularly enjoy a petting zoo, a train, and the occasional opportunity to ride on the back of an elephant.

The zoo is open daily 9:30 a.m.-5 p.m. Admission is $6.95 for adults, $3.95 for children three to 12 and seniors, and free for anyone younger. To get there, take Exit 392 off I-40 east of downtown and follow the signs.

The wildlife at the **Ijams Nature Center,** 2915 Island Home Ave., tel. (423) 577-4717, is a bit less spectacular and a little harder to see. This 80-acre environmental education center consists of woods, meadows, and perennial gardens, all interlaced with trails. Admission is free. Open daily from 8:30 a.m. until dark.

THEATRICAL JEWELS

One street east of Market St. lies Gay St., Knoxville's historic main drag. The main hotel for a long time was the Andrew Johnson Hotel, 912 S. Gay St., and it was here that Hank Williams last saw the light of day. Two wonderful old theaters hold court here, and both are worth a visit. The **Lamar House-Bijou Theatre,** 803 Gay St., tel. (423) 522-0832, began in 1816 as a tavern, then saw service as a hotel. In 1909 the two-balconied Bijou Theatre was built onto the back of the hotel, and vaudeville and other live performances of all kinds entertained generations of Knoxvillians. This literal jewel of a theater is a wonderful place to see or hear anything. Musicians such as Michelle Shocked and Richard Thompson have played here, along with theater groups and classical and jazz artists.

For a period in the '60s and '70s, however, the Bijou hosted a pornographic movie theater, giving countless UT students another sort of education. In 1970, two intrepid freshmen carrying borrowed ID cards sat guilt-filled in the darkened theater as various pleasures of the flesh played over the silver screen. Hearing approaching sirens and assuming the theater was being raided by police, these two clawed their way over patrons and burst out the exit, only to see Knoxville's fire trucks roaring by to answer an alarm.

The theater lobby houses the **East Tennessee Hall of Fame for the Performing Arts,** a series of oil paintings of Dolly Parton, Chet Atkins, and others. Visitors can tour the Hall of Fame weekdays 10 a.m.-5 p.m., and perhaps

can sneak a peek of the theater itself. Admission is free.

Farther north sits the **Tennessee Theater,** 604 Gay St., tel. (423) 525-1840, a wonderful movie palace opened in 1928 in the waning days of silent films. Stage productions and concerts occasionally take place in this extravagantly decorated theater—among them Bob Dylan and Allison Krauss—but movies are the real reason to go. Most are preceded by a brief concert on "the mighty Wurlitzer," an organ console that rises from the floor and whose thunderous notes resonate in the chests of theatergoers. Occasionally silent films are shown with organ accompaniment. This is not to be missed. Call to see what's playing.

HISTORIC SITES

James White's Fort
Perhaps the best place to begin is just outside the downtown area at James White's Fort, 205 E. Hill Ave., tel. (423) 525-6514, not far from the Hyatt House Hotel. Had James White been more assertive, Knoxville might be Whitesville, for he was here first. White built a fort in 1786, and thus provided a place for William Blount to move the capital of the Southwest Territory. James White's fort no longer stands at its original location, but his house and the buildings that surround it give a vivid picture of Knoxville in its earliest days. The fort is open from March 1 through December 15 Mon.-Sat. 9:30 a.m.-4:30 p.m. Admission is $4 for adults, $3.50 for senior, $2 for children under 12, and free for those under six.

Blount Mansion
Blount Mansion, possibly the most significant historic building on this end of the state, introduces the visitor to downtown Knoxville. People who have seen grand houses in Middle and West Tennessee sometimes find Blount Mansion a bit disappointing. It's a nice house, to be sure, but a *mansion?*

To understand the importance of this house, one has to put it in context. George Washington appointed William Blount governor of the Southwest Territory, and for the first two years Blount operated out of someone else's house at Rocky

Mount, near Johnson City. When it was time to move his capital to Knoxville, he wanted to do it in style. With this aim, he ordered one of the first frame—i.e., not log—houses west of the mountains, a house with so many glass windows that the Indians who saw it called it the "house with many eyes." Knoxville was so raw at this time that it didn't even have a sawmill capable of producing the lumber; it all had to be shipped from points east.

In this house walked Andrew Jackson, and in an office behind the house Blount and others wrote the state constitution. The office served as the territorial capital from 1792 through 1796, when Tennessee became a state, with Blount as its first senator.

Today's guests can see original Blount family furnishings, a period garden, and occasional demonstrations of activities likely to have taken place here. Visitors to Blount Mansion also get a two-for-one deal. The visitors center for the mansion is the 1818 **Craighead-Jackson House,** an example of federal-style architecture. Both are open all year. March through December, the hours are Tues.-Sat. 9:30 a.m.-4:30 p.m. and Sunday from 12:30 -5 p.m. The one-hour tours begin on the hour, with the last tour at four. In January and February, the mansion is open Tues.-Fri only. Visitors may arrange a weekend tour by calling (423) 525-2375. Admission is $5 for adults, $4.50 for seniors, and $2.50 for children 6-12.

Other Historic Spots

Crescent Bend, 2728 Kingston Pike, tel. (423) 637-3163, is a relatively easy-to-find place that consists of a lovely house, formal gardens, and a collection of 18th- and 19th-century English silver and Federal furniture. The house, known as the **Armstrong-Lockett House,** was built in 1834 as the centerpiece of a 600-acre farm. The terraced gardens step down from the house to the Tennessee River. Crescent Bend is open March-Dec., Tues.-Sat. 10 a.m.-4 p.m. and Sunday 1-4 p.m.; there's a small admission fee. The gardens are frequently rented out for weddings, etc., so call ahead during wedding season. Admission, which includes a guided tour, costs $4.50 for adults, $2.50 for kids 12-18, and free for children under 12.

Farther west lies the **Confederate Memorial Hall,** 3148 Kingston Pike, tel. (423) 522-2371,

otherwise known as **Bleak House.** Confederate General James Longstreet used this 15-room house as his headquarters while laying his futile siege to Knoxville. Owned by Chapter 89 of the United Daughters of the Confederacy, the house contains period furniture and artifacts. It's open Tues.-Fri. 1-4 p.m. Admission is $5 for adults, $4 seniors, $3 for children 12-18, and $1.50 those under 12.

Fort Dickerson sits in a commanding position atop a hill across the Tennessee River from downtown Knoxville. Union General Ambrose Burnside set up earthworks here, and the remnants of these are about all there is to see today. To get there, take Henley Street across the bridge and turn right. The earthworks are at the top of the hill, for what is literally a commanding view of Knoxville.

Mabry-Hazen House, 1711 Dandridge Ave., tel. (423) 522-8661, built by Joseph A. Mabry in 1858, served as headquarters for both sides during the Civil War. The Hazen family lived here until 1987, and the house contains their original furnishings. Now on the National Register, the house is open Mon.-Fri. 10 a.m.-4 p.m., weekends 1-5 p.m. Admission is $4 for adults and $2 for children six to 12. To get there, go east on Hill Avenue to its intersection with Dandridge Avenue. Follow the signs.

A two-block walk from the Mabry-Hazen House leads to **Confederate Cemetery,** where 1,600 Southern troops rest.

Blount Mansion may have wowed the people in town, but outside of Knoxville, Francis Ramsey hired an English-born master carpenter and cabinetmaker to design and build a home appropriate for the owner of more than 2,000 acres of land. **Ramsey House,** tel. (423) 546-0745, was the result, a stately 1795 Georgian stone house—Knox County's first such structure. Knoxville's first elected mayor was born here, and the W.B.A. Ramsey family inhabited the house until 1866. The house is filled with period furniture, including two Chippendale chairs that are original to the mansion. The house is open April-Dec., Tues.-Sat. 10 a.m.-4 p.m., Sunday 1-4 p.m. Admission is $3.50 for adults and $1.50 for children. To get there, take Exit 394 off I-40, go east on Asheville Hwy., then right onto Hwy. 168. Cross Strawberry Plains Pike, then turn left onto Thorngrove Pike.

Ramsey House is on the left. It's on the Web at www.korrnet.org/ramhse.

John Sevier was the first governor of Tennessee, back in the days when Knoxville was its capital, and he lived at **Marble Springs,** tel. (423) 573-5508, during this time and until his death in 1815. The house is surrounded by seven period structures and contains Sevier family artifacts. Hours are year-round Tues.-Sat. 10 a.m.-5 p.m., Sunday 2-5 p.m. When a guide is present, admission is $5 for adults and $3 for children and seniors. When the guide isn't around, the admission price drops by half. To get there, take, appropriately enough, the John Sevier Hwy., either from Hwy. 129 near the airport, or from Hwy. 441.

CRUISES

Passengers on the **Star of Knoxville Riverboat,** tel. (423) 522-4630, can choose from a sightseeing cruise or a dinner cruise. The former lasts one and a half hours, while the latter takes a leisurely two hours. Seeing the sights costs $10.43 for adults, $6.95 for kids, and free for children under three. Dinner cruises cost $25.99 for adults and $14.74 for kids Sunday-Thursday. On weekend nights, the dinner cruise costs $33.80 and $16.90. The 325-passenger boat is hard to miss on the waterfront; it docks at 300 Neyland Drive. The boat runs from April through New Year's Eve.

ENTERTAINMENT AND EVENTS

ON THE STAGE

Venues
With 25,000 seats, the **Thompson-Boling Arena,** 1600 Stadium Dr. on the UT campus, is the big daddy of performing halls hereabouts. Call (423) 974-0953 for info and (423) 656-4444 for tickets.

Until the Thompson-Boling Arena appeared on the scene, the **Knoxville Civic Auditorium and Coliseum,** 500 E. Church St., was the venue for most big rock concerts, wrestling matches, and high-decibel events. It still gets a fair number of these. The auditorium hosts traveling road shows and smaller events. Call (423) 544-5388 for information or (423) 656-4444 for tickets

The **Bijou Theatre,** 803 Gay St., tel. (423) 522-0832, is the oldest stage in town and features concerts, dance, theater, and various other events.

A legacy from the 1982 World's Fair, the **Tennessee Amphitheater, World's Fair Park** hosts outdoor summertime concerts.

Tennessee Theatre, 604 Gay St., tel. (423) 525-1840, is a wonderfully restored old movie palace featuring classic films and the occasional concert.

The **Laurel Theatre and Jubilee Community Arts,** 1538 Laurel Ave., tel. (423) 522-5851, is located in the Fort Sanders area just off 17th Street near UT and is home to traditional folk music and dancing. This is the place to hear Irish, English, Bluegrass, Cajun, as well as other kinds of music. Call to find out what is happening or go on the Web to funnelweb.utcc.utk.edu/~tkoosman/jca/.

The **Clarence Brown Theater,** 1714 Andy Holt Blvd. on the UT Campus, tel. (423) 974-5161, is the flagship of the UT theaters and arguably the best equipped theater in the state. The plays and musicals here are put on by UT students and faculty, as well as professional actors and actresses. Also on campus is the **Carousel Theater,** 1714 Andy Holt Blvd., a theater-in-the-round that hosts various plays throughout the year.

Finally, the **UT Music Hall and Opera Theatre,** 1741 Volunteer Blvd. on the UT Campus, tel. (423) 974-3241, hosts recitals and concerts by UT students, faculty, and touring professional performers.

Music and Dance
City Ballet of Knoxville, 803 S. Gay St., tel. (423) 544-0495, is a professional company that performs throughout the year, especially before Christmas, when they roll out guess what.

Knoxville Opera Company, 612 E. Depot St., tel. (423) 524-0795, presents quarterly productions of professional artists. The Tennessee Theatre is their home turf, but the audiences for opera are so large in East Tennessee that they occasionally stage productions in the Knoxville Coliseum.

Knoxville Symphony Orchestra and Chamber Orchestra, 623 Market St., tel. (423) 523-1178. The various components of this talented group perform over 250 times per year.

Theater

Tennessee Children's Dance Ensemble, 4216 Sutherland Ave., tel. (423) 588-8842, is an amazing organization of 24 dancers ages 10-17 who are the official goodwill ambassadors of the state of Tennessee. They have performed their modern dance around the world, from Japan to London and Norway. They're on the Internet at www.korrnet.org/tcde.

West Side Dinner Theatre, 12801 Kingston Pike, tel. (423) 966-8768, offers one-stop dining and entertainment.

The University of Tennessee has a very strong theater department, and Knoxville enjoys excellent productions by professional thespians as well as students. The crown jewel of Knoxville's dramatic culture is the **Clarence Brown Theater,** built with funds provided by the alumnus and longtime MGM director. Not surprisingly, the theater contains a first-rate 35mm movie projection system, which often shows foreign or art films. For film titles and times only, call (423) 974-5455. Adjacent to the Clarence Brown is the in-the-round **Carousel Theater.** For information about plays and tickets at all UT theaters, go to 1714 Andy Holt Ave., call (423) 974-5161, or visit www.utk.edu/~cbt/.

Lively local theater takes place Thurs.-Sat. at **Theatre Central,** which presents light fare at 141 Gay St., tel. (423) 546-3926. Ticket prices are light on the wallet as well, and no reservations are required.

Shakespeare in the Park unfolds at the Tennessee Amphitheater at the World's Fair Park. Tickets cost $5 for adults, and anyone under 12 gets in free. For information on what's playing, call the Knoxville Convention and Visitor's Center at (423) 523-2316.

FESTIVALS AND EVENTS

If visitors somehow miss the Fourth of July, then **Boomsday,** held the night of Labor Day, will catch them up very quickly. Said to be the largest fireworks display in Tennessee, it's held on the waterfront. Call (423) 693-1020 for details.

The **Dogwood Arts Festival** gets its name from the many dogwood trees that grace Knoxville. Held in April, the festival offers all manner of performing arts, big-name concerts, athletic activities, and various events all over the city. Knoxville suburbanites position lights under their dogwood blossoms and show off their property at night to hordes of slow-driving admirers along "Dogwood Trails," whose intricacies are marked by pink arrows painted onto streets. For information, call (423) 637-4561.

The biggest fair on this end of the state is the **Tennessee Valley Fair,** held every year beginning on the first Friday after Labor Day. All the usual agricultural contests and exhibitions take place, along with live entertainment, usually of the country music persuasion. To find your way to the fairgrounds, take the Cherry Street Exit off I-40 east of downtown Knoxville, go south, then turn left onto Magnolia. Or just follow the crowd. Admission is $6, with children under 11 getting in free. For further information, call (423) 637-5840.

SPECTATOR SPORTS

Sports are a very big deal at UT. Neyland Stadium is one of the largest stadiums in the country, seating more than 102,000 people, and the Thompson-Boling basketball arena seats 24,535 for basketball games. UT is a member of the Southeastern Conference, and fans enjoy high-level performances in 17 NCAA sports. The women's basketball team has won several national championships.

Tickets, at least for the football games, are hard to come by. If fans show up the day of the game, however, all manner of helpful people will emerge from parking lots and dark alleys with tickets to sell. Smart consumers wait until five minutes before kick-off before forking over the cash.

GRIDIRON GRIDLOCK

Visitors to Knoxville and the surrounding area who have no interest in football should clear out of town during home games, when more than 102,000 fans fill the stadium, jam hotels, occupy restaurants, and—most of all—clog the roads. Here is UT's home schedule for the years 1999 and 2000:

1999	2000
Sept. 4	Sept. 2
Sept. 25	Sept. 16
Oct. 2	Sept. 23
Oct. 9	Oct. 21
Oct. 30	Nov. 11
Nov. 6	Nov. 18
Nov. 27	

Try www.utsports.com, and for great links to Vol sites, go to www.geocities.com/colosseum/track/4335/links.

To find out who's playing what, call the **UT Sports Information Office** at (423) 974-1212. To buy tickets, call (423) 656-1200. Out of town fans can call (800) 332-VOLS from anywhere in Tennessee. Or try www.utsports.com.

NIGHTLIFE

Not exactly renowned for its night life (it's the city that sleeps a lot), Knoxville nonetheless manages to offer something for just about everyone. If you're just looking for an alcohol-fueled night out, here's a handy short list, sorted by the tenor of the evening you can expect to experience. These reviews were compiled by "Bonnie Appetite," restaurant reviewer and indefatigable arbiter of taste for the *Metro Pulse,* whose weekly edition—available free all over town—contains the best source of what's happening on any given weekend.

The Unbearable Hipness of Being

To hang with the closest thing Knoxville has to club kids, hit **The Underground,** 214 W. Jackson Ave., tel. (423) 525-3675, an Old City staple inscrutably located in the second floor of an old

warehouse. Finding the place ain't easy (the entrance is located in a dark alley under a viaduct), and just getting in the door can feel like a trial by fire. But if crowd-watching is your bag, you couldn't ask for a better place to go—this is where Knoxville's urban primitives (replete with piercings and tattoos) go to gyrate until dawn. Don't forget to pack your psychedelics.

Bluesy + Boozy

Knoxville's blues aficionados gravitate toward **Sassy Ann's,** 820 N. 4th St. , tel. (423) 525-5839, an erstwhile Victorian home in the central 4th and Gill neighborhood that's experiencing a happy second go-round as a casual music bar. It's the best place in town to shed a tear in your beer.

Diver Down

Knoxville's favorite dive bar is a classic: **The Long Branch Saloon,** 1848 Cumberland Ave., tel. (423) 546-9914. Located on campus in a building rumored to have previously housed a brothel, it's for folks who like their beer straight up—no frills, no pretension, no one noticing that you're on your ninth. At the same time, there's no fear of imminent death (unless you elect to ingest a pickled egg from the giant jar behind the bar), which makes the Long Branch the perfect place to tie one on.

The Center of the Universe

Perhaps the most interesting club in Knoxville is **Neptune,** 125 W. Jackson Ave., tel. (423) 637-8634. Most of the college-oriented/punk bands passing through town play there, and on off nights you can catch anything from Alternative Dance to Swing to Gothic. But Wednesday's the day to be on hand for the now-infamous Secret Garden Fetish/Dance Night. Wear what turns you on.

Rainbow Rooms

The most fun to be had dancing in Knoxville is at one of its many gay bars: **The Electric Ballroom,** 1213 Western Ave., tel. (423) 525-6724. It's ambitious, this huge, no-holds-barred dance-a-teria, and the entertainment line-up features something for everyone, including live music, nightly drag shows, female-on-male oil wrestling

In Old City awaits the greatest collection of live music in East Tennessee—dance music, jazz, rock, and blues.

at midnight, and an array of DJs spinning the bootie-shaking best.

Adventure on the High Cheese

Let's say dancing the night away with the rhythmically challenged-yet-horny is more your style. Get thee straight to **Michael's,** 7049 Kingston Pike, tel. (423) 588-2455, where you can boogie-oogie-oogie 'til you just can't boogie no more to the hits of the '70s and '80s with a crowd of shiny happy people just looking to make a love connection. It's a cheeseball scene, a nightlife punch line. Still, it's the place to go if you're looking to get lucky.

Beer Bash

Like every other city in the country, Knoxville's seen a rash of microbreweries come and go and come again. The best of the lot is **Great South-**

ern Brewing Company, 424 Gay St., tel. (423) 523-0750, a downtown restaurant and bar where the taps flow freely and the menu features fine Southwestern fare. It's the happy hour of choice for the young downtown crowd.

If pizza and beer are more your style, there's the **Blackhorse Pub & Brewery,** 4429 Kingston Pike, tel. (423) 558-6161, which serves fine pies with tasty beer and boasts a biggish game room where you can babysit your inner child.

Calhoun's Bearden location, 6515 Kingston Pike, tel. (423) 673-3377, styles the buttoned-down rib restaurant as a microbrewery, as evidenced by the giant, shiny vats on display for all to see. The quaffable beer is most noted for its local-color names—try the Thunder Road Ale or Rocky Top Red.

The new entry is **Hops,** 338 N. Peters Rd., tel. (423) 692-1430, a chain brewery with drinkable beer that will do in a pinch if you find yourself intractably trapped in traffic-laden suburban hell that is West Knoxville.

Frat Party

For throw-back brewskis with the aging Preppie crowd, hit **Toddy's Back Door Tavern,** 4951 Kingston Pike, tel. (423) 584-6828. Conveniently located over a liquor store (*the* pre-game place to tank up), Toddy's sports a genuine ratty, dive-bar ambience, which seems wildly entertaining to its upscale clientele.

Closer to the heart of things is **BW3,** Old City, tel. (423) 522-4293, which has a killer patio and lots and lots of beer on tap. But beware—the guy on the barstool next to you is probably just about to puke. It's that kind of place. If all else fails, head to one of the many bars lining the UT "Strip" (Cumberland Ave.), and start your own personal pub crawl.

Smoke Gets in Your Eyes

Having an affair? With cigarettes? Then head straight to **Ivory's,** 4705 Olde Kingston Pike, tel. (423) 588-6023, a jazzy little piano joint that's perhaps the most smoker-friendly establishment in town. Even if you don't smoke, it's worth holding your breath and ducking in—it's a discreet place, but one in which there's never a dull moment. Go figure.

High-Brow Hi-Balls

Fulfill your Rat Pack fantasies while martinis, cigars, and jazz are still in, baby. You can play adult at the **Baker-Peters Jazz Club,** 9000 Kingston Pike, tel. (423) 690-8110, out west, or **Lucille's,** 100 N. Central St., tel. (423) 637-4255, in the Old City. They're both fitting venues for Knoxville's surprisingly diverse and accomplished jazz musicians (including Donald Brown, Marcus Shirley, Bill Scarlett, and Hector Qirko), as well as great places to be seen.

TELEVISION LIFE

The Nashville Network's *Club Dance* tapes shows at the Cinetel Production building on Sherill Lane. To dance on one of the shows, boot scooters must call (423) 690-7699 for reservations. Club Dance is open for dancing only during tapings, but visitors are welcome for a tour during business hours. Check it out on the Internet at www.country. com/tnn/program/program-clubdance-f.html

WHERE TO STAY

BED AND BREAKFASTS AND INNS

The **Maple Grove Inn,** on 16 acres west of Knoxville at 8800 Westland Dr., tel. (423) 690-9565 or (800) 645-0713, is a 1799 house whose eight rooms all offer private baths. Two master suites feature fireplaces and whirlpool baths. Guests have access to a swimming pool and tennis court. Rates run $125-200 on weekends or $95-150 during the week for two people. Dinner is available for guests on Thurs.-Sat. nights. Expensive-Luxury. To get there, take the Cedar Bluff Exit off I-40/75 and go south to the first traffic light. Go left on N. Peters Rd., then drive two miles to Westland Dr. Turn left and go 0.3 miles to the first driveway on the left.

Mimosa Bed and Breakfast, 512 Mimosa Ave., tel. (423) 577-1744, offers two guest rooms that share a bath. Mimosa Ave. is on the Smokies side of the Tennessee River. Rates are $95 per night. Expensive.

Mountain Vista, on the road to the airport yet close to UT at 3809 Vista Rd., Louisville, TN 37777, tel. (423) 970-3771, consists of a seven-acre estate and a big porch looking straight at the Smoky Mountains. Six full bedrooms have private baths, and the inn offers access to a heated pool—glassed in for all-year use—as well as a laundry. The rate is $120 for two people. Premium.

Wayside Manor Bed and Breakfast lies south of Knoxville in the little town of Rockford at 4009 Old Knoxville Hwy., Rockford, TN 37853, tel. (423) 970-4823 or (800) 675-4823. The 13 rooms here include a separate two-bedroom cottage, Dove's Nest, as well as a separate five-bedroom house, Eagles Lodge, which comes with fireplaces and in-room whirlpool baths. Outside are a tennis court, swimming pool, creek, shuffleboard, croquet, basketball, and volleyball. Rates range $89-225. Expensive-Luxury.

HOTELS AND MOTELS

Like most larger cities, Knoxville is blessed with the usual national-chain hotels—Hilton, Hyatt, and Radisson—downtown and the usual motels stretched along the interstates. (See "Where to Stay" under "Accommodations and Food" in the On the Road chapter for a list of franchise accommodations and their toll-free reservation numbers.)

CAMPING

North of Town

Open all year, the 98-site **Fox Inn Campground,** tel. (423) 494-9386, has all the amenities. To get there, get off at the Hwy. 61 Exit of I-75 and go about a quarter-mile east.

Jellystone Park Camp-Resorts, 9514 Diggs Gap Rd., Heiskell, tel. (423) 938-6600 or (800) BET-YOGI, offers 77 sites and everything from a pool to a restaurant. It's open year-round.

Escapees Raccoon Valley, 908 Raccoon Valley, Heiskell, tel. (423) 947-9776, has 76 sites open all year, plus a pool and laundry. Take Exit 117 off I-75, then go west on Raccoon Valley Road.

Knoxville sits amid TVA's "Great Lakes of the South."

East

The following campgrounds are quite a ways out of Knoxville, but strike a good compromise for those wanting to see K-town and the touristy areas of the Smokies.

Knoxville East KOA, 241 KOA Dr., tel. (423) 933-6393, offers 200 sites and is open all year; this place has all the amenities. Take Exit 407 off I-40 and go north.

Smoky Mountain Campground, tel. (423) 933-8312 or (800) 684-2267, weighs in with 246 sites and is open all year with all the amenities. It's off I-40 at Exit 407. Go south on Hwy. 66 for about 100 yards, then a half mile east on Fore-travel Drive.

South and West

Southlake RV Park, 3730 Old Maryville Pike, tel. (423) 573-1837, has 125 sites along a river and is open year-round. Take Exit 386B off I-40 and follow Hwy. 129 South for 5.5 miles. Turn east onto Hwy. 68, go about one mile, then go one mile south on Hwy. 33.

West Knoxville Campground, 118 Lovell Rd. (Exit 374 South), tel. (423) 966-2414, offers 133 sites, a swimming pool, and most amenities.

FOOD

Knoxville has more good places to eat than the rest of East Tennessee combined. The following lists only a sampling, and an idiosyncratic one at that, of the places available. Barbecue places warrant their own category. These were compiled by "Bonnie Appetit," the restaurant critic of *Metro Pulse,* Knoxville's weekly newspaper. For her latest culinary opinions, go to www.metropulse.com.

BARBECUE

While Knoxville has gone fancy with all manner of ethnic and vegetarian restaurants, barbecue still holds a place in the hearts—and the arteries—of Knoxville diners.

If most Knoxvillians were asked what word precedes "barbecue," chances are they would reply "Buddy's." **Buddy's Bar-be-que** is a hometown success story, a franchise that is spreading throughout East Tennessee. In Knoxville, Buddy's is at: 5806 Kingston Pike, tel. (423) 588-0528; 8402 Kingston Pike, tel. (423) 691-0088; 3700 Magnolia Ave., tel. (423) 523-3550; 4500 N. Broadway, tel. (423) 687-2959; 4401 Chapman Hwy., tel. (423) 579-1747; and 121 West End Ave., tel. (423) 675-4366.

Calhoun's serves a lot more food than barbecue, but it deserves mention here. Probably the most upscale barbecue source in town, it's open for lunch and dinner seven days a week at three locations: 400 Neyland Dr. on the river, tel. (423) 673-3355; 10020 Kingston Pike, tel. (423) 673-3444; and (the newest) 6515 Kingston Pike, tel. (423) 673-3377. The third one features an in-house brewery.

Corkey's Ribs and BBQ, 260 N. Peters Rd., tel. (423) 690-3137, is a branch of a famous Memphis barbecue place, and an excellent place to try dry ribs. Most folks, especially those with brushy mustaches, are familiar with "wet" ribs—those slathered with barbecue sauce. My friends, there is another way. Dry ribs are coated with a special rub—usually pepper, paprika, chili powder, and assorted secret ingredients. Like their wet brethren, dry ribs are slow-cooked for hours, and are wonderful. Corkey's fixes wet ribs, too. Way out west of town, but well worth the drive, it's open for lunch and dinner every day of the week.

Scruggs Real Pit Barbecue and Package Store, on the east side of town at 1920 Magnolia Ave., tel. (423) 524-4333, bears a classic name for a barbecue place. The catch is that patrons can't drink the beer on the premises, but the barbecue is worth the inconvenience. If anyone wants to re-enact the Hank Williams drive up Hwy. 11, this is the way to go. It's open for lunch and dinner seven days a week.

TOP OF THE HEAP

For years, the very definition of Knoxville cuisine has been provided by **Regas Restaurant,** 318 N. Gay St. at Magnolia Ave., tel. (423) 637-9805, an upscale institution situated in a very decidedly downscale part of town. Nevertheless, it's beloved by high-powered businessmen for its utter predictability (always good, uncomplicated food; always attentive, unobtrusive service), and it serves as the meet and greet spot for the town's politicos. With a menu that borders on the bland (think steak and potatoes) and an austere ambience (think dark woods and brass rails), it mirrors the political character of the town in which it has thrived—traditional, conservative, and circumspect. Plead for a lunch time seat in the hearth room (Monday through Friday only) to witness an orgy of handshaking, back-slapping, and gritted-toothed smiles—Southern politics at its best. Dinner is served seven nights a week.

For a more happening scene, check out **Harry's by Regas,** which carries the cache of the Regas name and the culinary stylings of Bruce Bogartz, a chef who earned his reputation at the Warner Brothers studios in California. Very of-the-moment, the place features a heavy em-phasis on martinis and cigars and boasts an inventive menu featuring dishes like sesame salmon with frizzled leeks and ginger-scented beurre blanc sauce and couscous-crusted chicken with apricot chutney. Don't miss the signature dessert—a homemade moon pie.

For a slick urbane ambience that would make anyone feel pretty, witty, and gay, the place to go is **Mango,** 5803 Kingston Pike, tel. (423) 584-5053. With its brushed steel tables, palm trees, and warm yellow walls, it's the perfect place to indulge in glib small talk while noshing on such ambitious fare as calamari tempura with ginger-apricot glaze and a green curry chutney; grilled pork tenderloin with potato pancakes in an espresso-chipolte barbecue sauce; and paella with saffron-jasmine rice, green-lip mussels, clams, roasted chicken, chorizo, lima beans, and grilled shrimp. Trés chic, but also trés chere.

For an intimate dinner à deux, **By the Tracks Bistro,** 130 Northshore Dr., tel. (423) 558-9500, is your best bet. The place is tiny, but somehow each table in the place seems a remote island unto itself. Expect terrific service, a small-but-impeccable wine list, and fantastic food. Local favorites include the mixed greens salad with strawberries, bleu cheese, and walnuts in a strawberry vinaigrette; roasted chicken pasta in a tarragon pesto sauce; and luscious sesame-encrusted shrimp. By the Tracks also has a masterful way with crème brûlée.

If you're in town celebrating a special occasion—a wedding, anniversary, Valentine's Day, whatever—and want something truly special, make your reservation to dine at the **Maple Grove Inn,** 8800 Westland Dr., tel. (423) 690-9565—a restaurant situated in an 18th century farm that's as special as they come. The limited selection of pricey three-course meals (salad or soup course, entree, and dessert) change from week to week, but might include such delectables as filet mignon in a bourbon demi-glacé, black-and-blue seafood (shrimp, scallops, and crab with a bleu cheese cream sauce served within a pastry crust), and pan-seared chicken over angel-hair pasta with oven-dried tomatoes in a basil sauce. Open Wednesday through Saturday nights by reservation only. BYOB.

Copper Cellar, 1807 Cumberland Ave., tel. (423) 673-3411, is an upscale, downstairs tradition on the UT campus. No fancy-schmancy culinary contortions here, just an emphasis on the very highest quality steak and seafood that can be had. The newer **West Knoxville Copper Cellar,** 7316 Kingston Pike, tel. (423) 673-3422, is equally good, if less atmospheric. It is, however, *the* place to go for Sunday brunch, featuring as it does a fantastic buffet with everything you could possibly want—and then some.

The best of the best is unquestionably **The Orangery,** 5412 Kingston Pike, tel. (423) 588-4964, Knoxville's only four-star restaurant and recipient of AAA's Four Diamond Award. It's the only place to go if your tastes are running to caviar, champagne, wild boar, escargot in puff pastry, or lobster flamed in cognac. Formal dress only, make reservations, and try your best to remember your table manners.

EASIER ON THE WALLET

Steaks

Located in an eponymous antebellum mansion in West Knoxville that—thanks to Knoxville's skillful zoning approach—sits nestled behind a self-serve gas station, the **Baker-Peters Jazz Club,** 9000 Kingston Pike, tel. (423) 690-8110, nonetheless manages to provide a swell time for all who seek its divine mix of martinis, jazz, and certified Angus steaks. Since it's decidedly upscale, you'll want to look your best and take lots of cash. Dinner is served Tuesday through Saturday.

If you're a control freak with very particular ideas about what should and should not happen to your steak, you can do it yourself at the **Butcher Shop,** 801 W. Jackson Ave., tel. (423) 637-0204, a holdover from the 1982 World's Fair. There, you can crowd in around the giant barbecue and scrabble with the masses for your favorite seasonings.

Steaks served with a Southwestern flair are a specialty of the **Great Southern Brewing Company,** 424 S. Gay St. tel. (423) 523-0750, a downtown brew pub. Delicious, marinated beef is available straight up, atop Knoxville's best Caesar salad, or as a featured player in fajitas and quesadillas. While you're there, grab a cold, handcrafted brew—guaranteed to make you hoppy.

Ye Olde Steak House 6838 Chapman Hwy., tel. (423) 577-9328, is a steak-purist's dream.

They'll flame broil your cut for you, perfectly done every time. And should you flip out and ask for, say, A-1 Sauce, they'll even save you from yourself. Bring your own bottle and see if you can hit the place on game day—it's the best party in town. Dinner seven nights a week.

Seafood

Chesapeake's, 500 Henley St., tel. (423) 673-3433, is a Knoxville original, since spun off into a successful chain. Featuring the finest in fresh seafood flown in daily, it's a no-fail place to indulge a craving for oysters Rockefeller. And the downtown location makes it perfect for doing business. Be sure to try the sherry-infused crab bisque, a specialty that will linger on your mind until you pass through town again. Dinner seven nights a week; lunch on weekdays.

If you'd like a more laid-back approach to seafood, one that will take you back to last year's beach vacation, try **The Shrimp Shack,** 8027 Kingston Pike, tel. (423) 539-1700. There's plenty to choose from on the menu—oysters, crab, and fish galore—but the shrimp reigns supreme. Try them barbecued or served swimming in a delicious garlic sauce. Dinner and lunch are served daily.

Asian

Canton, 8515 Kingston Pike, tel. (423) 693-6424, is a Knoxville favorite that features *dim sum* on the weekends. Can you guess what regional Chinese cuisine the place specializes in? That's right—Cantonese, which means lots of noodles, exotic vegetables, and multiple meats served in mostly mild sauces. Closed on Mondays.

Knoxville's had a long-running love affair with **China Inn,** 6450 Kingston Pike, tel. (423) 588-7815, an upscale restaurant serving sophisticated versions of all the usual suspects—moo goo gai pan, eight-treasure chicken, moo shu pork, and so on. However, vegetarians take note—many dishes are available made with seitan in lieu of meat, which makes a nice change from Buddha's delight. Lunch and dinner seven days a week.

Rich, decadent Indian fare—think lots of ghee and cream—can be attained at **Kashmir,** 711 17th St., tel. (423) 524-1982, a campus-based restaurant with a brunch buffet. You can have an exotic condiment tray with your choice of a baker's dozen of breads. Or create your own good karma by ingesting their terrific korma. Lunch and dinner weekdays plus Sunday; on Saturday, dinner only.

If you're looking for quality Korean, try **Kaya,** 149 Montvue Rd., tel. (423) 691-0237, an elegant restaurant that serves authentic Korean cuisine, which means hae mool pa jun (seafood pancake), bulkoki (barbecue), and jap chae (marinated noodles). Everything comes with an array of side dishes guaranteed to stimulate your tonsils. Hours tend to vary, so call ahead.

Don't know much about Korean food, but willing to learn? The place for you is **Korea House,** 1645 Downtown West Blvd., tel. (423) 693-3615, where the staff would like nothing better than to spend the next hour explaining everything you need to know and making sure you love everything—whether its the gulbi gui (marinated beef ribs grilled right at the table), the baked mushroom with fruit juice, or the bibim bab (a rice dish served with vegetables and eggs in a red-hot stone dish that continues to cook the rice as you eat). Lunch and dinner Tuesday through Sunday; dinner only on Monday.

Food as entertainment can be had nightly for dinner at **Kyoto** a.k.a. **Miyabi,** 8207 Kingston Pike, tel. (423) 691-3121, where hibachi chefs will entertain with the old salt shakers and spatulas as they cook your Japanese-style stir fries. The place is going by two names now, which is curious—but brave diners will plow forward. Their reward will be premium steak and seafood, and access to one of the best sushi bars in town.

If curries and noodles are your bag, head to **Malaysia,** 6761 Clinton Hwy. in the Wal-Mart Shopping Center, tel. (423) 947-3333. Similar to Thai, Malaysian food employs ingredients like peanuts, coconut, lime, and fish sauce. But it's milder and less complex—comfort food for the culinarily adventurous.

Located just a hop, skip, and jump from the airport, **The Ming Tree,** 2754 Alcoa Hwy., tel. (423) 984-3888, offers both traditional Chinese and Thai dishes. Their pad Thai is fantastic, as are the coconutty, lime-infused evil jungle prince stir-fries. As an appetizer, the crispy tofu with peanut dipping sauce simply cannot be beat. Lunch and dinner are served seven days a week.

Stir Fry Cafe, 7240 Kingston Pike, tel. (423) 588-2064, is a local favorite, consistently voted

Best Asian Restaurant by the readers of *Metro Pulse.* That's thanks to a hip but low-key atmosphere and a nice fusion menu featuring the best of Chinese and Thai cuisine. Vegetarians will love the fact that nearly all dishes include a vegetables-only or tofu option. Try the spicy noodles, the basil-curry fried rice, the prik king, or— if you want a real wake-up call—the green curry. Open for lunch and dinner seven days a week.

The best spring rolls in the world are to be had at **T. Ho,** 815 Merchants Dr., tel. (423) 688-5815, a hole-in-the wall Vietnamese place in North Knoxville. Chinese dishes are on the menu, too, but skip them and try the eggless crepe with shrimp and bean sprouts. Closed on Monday and no lunch on Saturday, but otherwise open for your dining pleasure.

For sushi, check out **Tomo,** 112 S. Central Ave., tel. (423) 546-3308, a funky little Old City spot that attracts East Tennessee's collection of expatriate Japanese businessmen (many of them working for Denso in nearby communities like Maryville and Sweetwater). Along with great sushi and sashimi, the restaurant offers Japanese noodles (the yakisoba is really top notch), teriyakis, and tempuras. Treat yourself to the red-bean cake for dessert—a delicious workout for your jaw. Dinner Tuesday through Sunday; closed Monday.

Burgers

Burgers and fries simply don't come any better than those served at **Litton's,** 2803 Essary Dr., tel. (423) 688-0429, a Fountain City institution. It's a great place to go with your family in tow, as there's something for every carnivore, big or small. Skip the trip to the more upscale Litton's Back Room, no matter how compelling those tablecloths look—the food is no better, despite much higher prices. Open for lunch and dinner Monday through Saturday. B.Y.O.B.

Coffee

Knoxville's cup runneth over with java joints. One of the best is **JFG Coffee House,** 132 Jackson Ave, tel. (423) 525-0012, serving the best of the hometown brew. It's an open, airy Old City spot, its walls lined with used books (for sale, naturally)—the perfect spot for brainstorming, schmoozing, or whiling away an hour by daydreaming. It's open most all the time, except Sunday.

But since what constitutes "good" in coffee-houses is entirely subjective, here's a list with notes to give some idea of the overall flavor of the city's java spots. Go forth and be caffeinated:

11th Street Expresso House, 1016 Laurel Ave., tel. (423) 546-3003: Bohemian

195 Degrees, 109 1/2 Central Ave., tel. (423) 546-0051: Catch-all

Casablanca Coffee House, 11831 Kingston Pike in Farragut, tel. (423) 675-1001: Exotic

CC Coffees, Western Plaza, tel. (423) 584-2902: Republican

Cup-A-Joe, 1911 Cumberland Ave., tel. (423) 673-3148: Beat

Daily Grind, 1823 Cumberland Ave, tel. (423) 971-5406: Wired

Golden Roast, 825 Melrose Place, tel. (423) 544-1004: Posh

Java, 5115 Homberg Dr., tel. (423) 558-9100: Original

Joe Muggs Cafe, 8513 Kingston Pike in Books-a-Million, tel. (423) 691-2665: Literary

Line's Sweets and Eats, 412 Clinch Ave., tel. (423) 523-2414: Blue-collar

Pete's Coffee Shop, 428 Union Ave., tel. (423) 523-2860: Dineresque

Ruby's Coffee Shop, 3920 Martin Luther King Ave., tel. (423) 522-0782: Family-style

The Varsity Inn, 1713 Cumberland Ave., tel. (423) 523-8903: Hangover helper

Italian

For fancy-schmancy, upscale Old World atmosphere and gourmet Northern Italian fare, hit **Cappuccino's,** 7316 Kingston Pike, tel. (423) 673-3422. Open for lunch and dinner Sunday through Friday; dinner only on Saturday.

City slickers in search of an escape from Knoxville's sprawling suburbia will love the **Italian Market & Grill,** 9648 Kingston Pike, tel. (423) 690-2600, for its fantastic food and cosmopolitan ambience. The food is sophisticated and complex, from the wood-fired pizzas to the epicurean salads to the penne Julia, an Italian Market signature dish featuring prosciutto ham, peas, and mushrooms in a rich cream sauce accented with pungent romano cheese. The Sunday brunch buffet will haunt you for years to come. Lunch and dinner daily.

Romance is in the air always at **Naples,** 5500 Kingston Pike, tel. (423) 584-5033, a place just right for the making of memories. Except for the imaginative daily specials, the food is fairly standard. Still, it's worth making the trip for the ambience and extensive wine list; lovers, you'll want to call ahead to request the special curtained-off booth so you can discover for yourself whatsa amore. Dinner seven nights a week; lunch on weekdays only.

Pizza

Exotic pizzas are the specialty of the house at the **Blackhorse Pub & Brewery,** 4429 Kingston Pike, tel. (423) 558-6161. There's a meat-lover's dream appropriately called the Heart Attack, a sauceless honey-curry chicken model called Tunisia, along with an array that includes Hawaiian, barbecue, Southwestern, Mexican, and even Buffalo pies. Best of all is the bleu cheese with spinach and bacon, rich nearly beyond human comprehension. The brews are quite quaffable as well.

The downtown **Tomato Head,** Market Square Mall, tel. (423) 637-4067, has a cult following, and for good reason. The pizzas are excellent, as are the sandwiches served on freshly baked breads. Try the roast beef gorgonzola, the smoked turkey with red onion, the goat cheese, or the aptly named vegetarian—a sammie featuring marinated tofu with sprouts, spinach, onions, Swiss cheese, and pesto. Take your breath mints along—garlic is the not-so-secret ingredient in just about everything. Diners can also take in local artists' works, always on display. Open for lunch and dinner Tuesday through Saturday; dinner only on Monday.

Etcetera

Do the Cuban thing at **Alex's Havana Cafe,** Homberg Pl., tel. (423) 588-8681, where the secret-recipe black beans are nothing short of terrific—fiber never tasted so good. Open for lunch and dinner Tuesday through Saturday.

Old City shoppers can take a well-deserved lunch break at **Blue Moon Bakery & Cafe,** 125 Jackson Ave., tel. (423) 546-0332, a European-style bakery and bistro. The bread is crusty and delicious, as are all the salads, desserts, quiches, and sandwiches ready for your perusal in the display cases (yes, they taste as good as they look). You'll love the turkey with Swiss and chutney, the roasted red pepper and goat cheese on foccacia, or the delightful Italian tuna salad with capers. Lunch is served Monday through Saturday.

Gumbo that will knock your socks off is the specialty at **Bayou Bay Seafood House,** 7112 Chapman Hwy., tel. (423) 573-7936, where Knoxville's own "ragin' Cajun" Andy Cantillo keeps it very, very real. Try the chargrilled amber jack po-boy, the spicy popcorn shrimp, one of several Louisiana seafood salads, or oysters served any way you like them. Or, if you feel like suckin' dem heads, order up a mess of crawfish. Lunch and dinner seven days a week.

Many downtowners swear by the **Crescent Moon Cafe,** 705 Market St., tel. (423) 637-9700, where lunch is served up with warm greetings and hugs. Oh yes, the food is great, too—especially the wrap sandwiches, the mashed potatoes du jour, and the tantalizing sweet corn chowder with roasted veggies. Good, and good for you. Breakfast and lunch on weekdays; fixed-price four-course meal on Fridays.

If you've got the time to spare, **The Melting Pot,** 111 N. Central Ave., tel. (423) 971-5400, is a fun throw-back fondue restaurant. No dining and dashing here; by ordering, you embark upon a unique and intimate two-hour experience. The salads and wine list are about as good as they get, but the fondue is the centerpiece of every meal. Meats, cheeses, vegetables, fruits and breads are prepared at your table, where you then cook them either in the traditional peanut oil or the lighter Court Bouillon. Open for dinner seven days a week.

Homestyle Hungarian is what's for dinner at **Budapest Cafe,** 270 Seven Oaks Dr. in Windsor Square, tel. (423) 694-8177. Try the house specialty, a whole chicken stuffed under the skin with a combination of pork, carrots, parsnips, and mushrooms, baked for 2-1/2 hours until tender and suffused with flavor. The paprikas and crepes are outstanding; the peas are canned.

No doubt you'll add your dining experience at **King Tut's,** 4123 Martin Mill Pike, tel. (423) 573-6021, to your personal strange-but-true file. That's because owner Mo Girgis is a showman as well as a restaurateur—during the meal you'll shoot Nerf baskets, enjoy any number of obnoxious toys, play along in a restaurant-wide rendition of "Rocky Top," and grind your pepper from a grinder that screams in Brooklynese, "You're breakin' my neck!" Located in a downscale neighborhood in what used to be a greasy spoon, King Tut's melds Egyptian cuisine with standard meat-n-three fare, often to enticing and amusing effect. Don't miss Egyptian night on Wednesdays. Open for breakfast, lunch, and dinner Monday through Saturday.

MORE PRACTICALITIES

SHOPPING

Like those in most Southern cities, Knoxville's big stores have fled to shopping malls. In their place, however, have sprung up interesting communities of shops. Try downtown, the Old City area, and Homberg Pl., near the corner of Kingston Pike and Homberg Place.

Malls

West Town, 7600 Kingston Pike, tel. (423) 693-0292, provides mall fans with their fix on the west side of town. It offers 140 stores, a food court, and full-serve restaurants. Take the West Hills Exit (380) off I-40/75.

Knoxville Center shopping mall, tel. (423) 544-1500, has 165 stores, a food court, and full-service restaurants. Take Exit 8 off I-640.

Assorted

Book Eddy, 2537 Chapman Hwy., tel. (423) 573-9959, is a book lover's dream come true—85,000+ used books on every subject imaginable. Check out their selection at www.bookeddy.com. For those who shop to live, the **Knox County Regional Farmer's Market** offers fresh produce, fish, meat, plants, crafts, and artwork. During the winter, the hours may be reduced. To get there, take Exit 8 off I-640. Follow the signs.

If you're looking for something old in the Old City, **Jackson Antique Marketplace,** 111 E. Jackson Ave., tel. (423) 521-6704, offers some 24,000 square feet of antiques.

Fine Arts and Crafts

Jim Gray is perhaps the best-known artist in this part of the state. His oils and drawings depict seascapes, Tennessee landscapes, people, wild-

A quilter practices her craft.

KNOXVILLE CONVENTION BUREAU

flowers, and birds. His bronze statues include Dolly Parton in Sevierville and Andrew Johnson in Greeneville. The **Jim Gray Gallery,** 5615 Kingston Pike, tel. (423) 588-7102, offers works in a variety of media from this talented artist.

In addition to sugary creations, **The Candy Factory,** in the World's Fair Park, contains several galleries, including **Beads & Feathers & Bones & Stones Gallery,** tel. (423) 525-2323, with jewelry, tribal art, and beads; **The Art Market,** tel. (423) 525-5265, offering work of 90 local artists; **Ashley-Elliott Gallery,** tel. (423) 523-4421, with traditional crafts and original folk art; and the **Cityside Gallery & Frame Shop,** tel. (423) 524-5312, selling original art and gifts.

The **Victorian Houses** at the corner of 11th Street and Laurel Avenue also have shops containing original arts and fine crafts. Given the changing tastes of the public and the vagaries of the artistic existence, shops come and go, but the quality remains high. Current residents include **Art & Antiques Gallery,** tel. (423) 525-7619, with work from more than 40 area artists; **The Toy Shelf,** tel. (423) 637-0858, offering wooden toys and collectible dolls; and **Onyx Gallery,** featuring watercolors.

West of downtown is **Hanson Gallery Fine Art and Craft,** 5706 Kingston Pike, tel. (423) 584-6097, offering oils, Thomas Pradzynski's Parisian street scenes serigraphs, lithographs, and gifts.

In Farragut, **Homespun Crafts and Antique Mall,** 11523 Kingston Pike, tel. (423) 671-3444, is a large assembly of artists and dealers selling antiques, jewelry, pottery, and all manner of creations. It's near Exit 373 off I-40/75.

SERVICES AND INFORMATION

Knoxville Convention and Tourist Bureau, 810 Clinch Ave., Knoxville, TN 37901, tel. (423) 523-7263, occupies Knoxville's Old City Hall just up the hill from the World's Fair site at 601 West Summit Hill Drive. The best place to go for info is the **Welcome Center** in the Candy Factory building on the World's Fair site at 1060 Worlds Fair Drive. Or go to www.Knoxville.org or www.goknox.com.

Metro Pulse is a free weekly that keeps close tabs on the entertainment scene. Find it on the Internet at www.metropulse.com.

GATEWAYS TO THE SMOKIES

On September 2, 1940, Pres. Franklin D. Roosevelt and thousands of other people rode in a caravan up the dirt road to Newfound Gap in the new Great Smoky Mountains National Park. The people in the villages they passed through, Sevierville, Pigeon Forge, and Gatlinburg, had no way of knowing the impact that the park would have on the places they lived.

Today the Smokies is the most visited of the national parks, and those three towns thrive on industrial-strength tourism. Millions of cars from all over the country converge here, disgorging people looking for a good time and carrying money in their pockets to pay for it.

They'll find a myriad of ways to spend it here.

Outlet shopping, country music shows, amusement parks, T-shirt shops, helicopter flights, and you-name-it await the charge card. H.L. Mencken once wrote that "no one ever went broke underestimating the taste of the American public," and there's proof plenty of that hereabouts.

Amid the hokum, however, visitors will find high-quality crafts, wonderful inns and bed and breakfasts, and places where Appalachian music rings out clearly. And kids who are weary of traveling will utterly love the Gateway area. Those parents intent on getting into the sanctity of the Smokies should stop and take in a few indulgences; they'll make the wilderness all that much sweeter.

SEVIERVILLE

The town and the county were named for John Sevier, Tennessee's first governor, who negotiated with the Cherokee to secure this area for settlers. Like many towns in those early days, Sevierville had no courthouse, so judicial proceedings were held in a local stable. According

to one account, this structure was so badly infested with fleas that the itching attorneys finally burned it to the ground. While it stood, however, perhaps nowhere else in Tennessee did the accused receive quicker versions of the speedy trials due them.

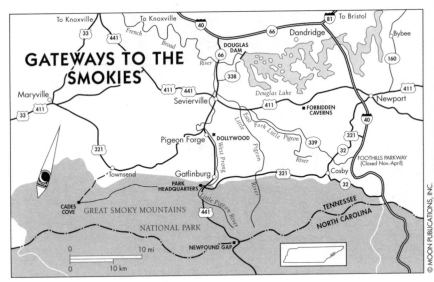

Sevier County has produced some great music makers. Dolly Parton grew up here, as did two great dobro players, both associated with Roy Acuff. Clell Summey, a.k.a. Cousin Jody, joined Acuff in 1933 and became the first person to play dobro on the Grand Ole Opry. He was replaced by Pete Kirby, a.k.a. Bashful Brother Oswald, who became the foremost dobro player in country music.

Close to 30% of Sevier County lies within the boundaries of the Great Smoky Mountains National Park, and the tourists lured by the park are the town's focus nowadays. Not so long ago, motorists whizzed through Sevierville on their way to Pigeon Forge, Gatlinburg, and, if they made it that far, to the park. About the only way Sevierville could get them to stop was to give them speeding tickets, which the local constabulary did with enthusiasm.

SIGHTS AND RECREATION

Nowadays Sevierville has come into its own and provides several reasons for visitors to slow down and spend a little time. The first is the **Sevier County Courthouse,** which stands against the mountains in the distance. This Victorian

structure was built in 1895-96, and its four-sided Seth Thomas clock still keeps time. Beside the courthouse is the **Dolly Parton Statue,** a bronze depiction of the young Dolly by Tennessee artist Jim Gray.

Between the Little Pigeon River and the intersection of the Forks of the River Parkway and Church Street lies the **McMahon Indian Mound,** all that is left of some Indians from the Mississippian period—long before the Cherokee. Excavations here revealed a village of about 75 people who lived in structures made of wood, thatch, and clay.

Outside of town, the **Harrisburg Covered Bridge** crosses the East Fork of the Little Pigeon River. Built in 1875, this bridge is still in use. Go east of Sevierville on Hwy. 411, turn right onto Hwy. 339, and follow the signs. Highway 441 East leads as well to **Forbidden Caverns,** tel. (423) 453-5972, a commercial cave whose name comes from an Indian legend involving the burial of a princess in a place that is forbidden. Later the cave was used for making moonshine. The caverns contain a large wall of cave onyx, a beautiful mineral, as well as unusual formations, all illuminated with special lighting and augmented with a sound system. It is open seven days a week from April 1 through

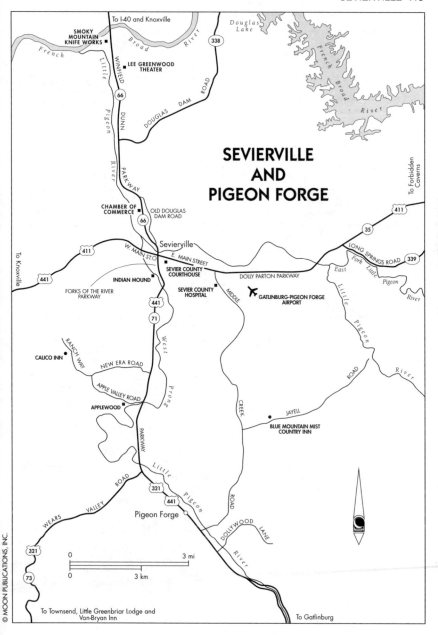

SMOKY MOUNTAIN KNIFE WORKS

LEE GREENWOOD THEATER

To I-40 and Knoxville

Douglas Lake

French Broad River

Broad River

338

Little Pigeon River

WINFIELD DUNN PARKWAY

DOUGLAS DAM ROAD

French Broad River

SEVIERVILLE AND PIGEON FORGE

To Forbidden Caverns

411

66

CHAMBER OF COMMERCE

OLD DOUGLAS DAM ROAD

Sevierville

35

411

W. MAIN ST.

E. MAIN STREET

LONG SPRINGS ROAD

339

To Knoxville

441

INDIAN MOUND

SEVIER COUNTY COURTHOUSE

SEVIER COUNTY HOSPITAL

DOLLY PARTON PARKWAY

GATLINBURG-PIGEON FORGE AIRPORT

East Fork Little Pigeon River

FORKS OF THE RIVER PARKWAY

441

71

WEST PRONG

MIDDLE CREEK ROAD

Little Pigeon River

CALICO INN

RANCH WAY

NEW ERA ROAD

APPLE VALLEY ROAD

APPLEWOOD

JAYELL

BLUE MOUNTAIN MIST COUNTRY INN

PARKWAY

Little Pigeon River

321

441

Pigeon Forge

WEARS VALLEY ROAD

DOLLYWOOD LANE

ROAD

River

321

73

0   3 mi

0   3 km

To Townsend, Little Greenbriar Lodge and Von-Bryan Inn

To Gatlinburg

© MOON PUBLICATIONS, INC.

MUST-SEE HIGHLIGHTS

For those who carry a knife except when wearing pajamas or bathing suits, Sevierville's **Smoky Mountain Knife Works** is heaven on earth.

The **Dixie Stampede,** in Pigeon Forge, epitomizes tourism run amok as more than 1,000 people eat whole chickens, ribs, and soup without silverware while horse-drawn chuck wagons tear around an earthen arena.

People come to **Dollywood** expecting an amusement park, but this place is true to its Appalachian roots.

The Great Smoky Arts and Crafts Community: Far from the madding crowd, here one can enjoy meeting artists and seeing their work.

Arrowmont Shop is a serene island of high-end crafts amid a sea of T-shirt shops.

The Buckhorn Inn offers classic hospitality in the area's oldest inn.

The Ramp Festival: Two days later, others will know you've been there.

MusiCrafts is a wellspring of books and music about the mountains.

Fort Marx, a make-no-pretenses joint up Dark Hollow Road outside of Cosby, offers a walk on the wild side of the Smokies. Don't get too friendly with someone else's wife.

The Front Porch restaurant on Hwy. 321 halfway between Cosby and Newport is perhaps the only place in the state where patrons can eat portobello mushroom steaks and listen to live bluegrass music.

November 1. Call about December hours. Admission is $8 for visitors 13 and older, $4 for children five to 12, free for younger kids.

Halfway between Sevierville and Pigeon Forge motorists will pass **Applewood,** a complex that began with an family-owned apple orchard, but now offers a cider mill, cider bar, bakery, candy factory, smokehouse, winery, gift shop, and two restaurants. The winery produces eight apple wines—some of them mixed with other fruit. Cider production begins in late August and runs through February, depending on the supply of apples. The complex is open Mon.-Thurs. 9 a.m.-7 p.m., Fri.-Sat. 9 a.m.-9 p.m., and Sunday 1-7 p.m. In October the hours are 9 a.m.-9 p.m. every day but Sunday, when it is open 9 a.m.-7

p.m. From January to March the hours are Mon.-Sat. 9 a.m.-5:30 p.m. and Sunday 1-5:30 p.m. For information about the restaurants, see below.

On Horseback
Cedar Ridge Riding Stables, on Hwy. 441, tel. (423) 428-5802, are open daily year-round.

Douglas Lake View Horse Riding, 1650 Providence Ave., tel. (423) 428-3587, offers short rides or the overnight variety.

Rafting
The closest river rafting in Tennessee to Sevierville is the Pigeon River, which flows along Interstate 40. Two companies offer trips along it, **USA Raft,** tel. (800) USA-RAFT, and **Rafting in the Smokies,** tel. (423) 436-5008. Trips last two to three hours and cost around $20-39.

Another option is to go to Bryson City on the North Carolina side of the Great Smokies National Park and run the Nantahala River, which flows into Fontana Lake.

A bust of NASCAR driver-turned-politician Richard Petty gazes over I-40 outside Sevierville.

Lee Greenwood, Sevierville theater crooner

ENTERTAINMENT AND EVENTS

Live Music

Show business, or "bidness," as they sometimes say around here, is never easy. Some of the headliners in the Smokies shows are getting rather long in the capped teeth, and they don't stick around from year to year. Others, like Jim Ed Brown and Helen Cornelius, each of whom had their own shows, combine forces. Some outfits like Southern Nights Theater or Music Mansion in Pigeon Forge go for hardworking but little-known entertainers who can be replaced if necessary while letting the show go on.

All this is a long-winded way of saying that the following may or may not be around when you come to the region—call first.

The **Lee Greenwood Theater,** on the north side of the French Broad River, tel. (800) 686-5471, features the singer who rose to fame in the 1980s with patriotic songs and who sports the most famous stubble since Yassar Arafat. The theater is open April-December. Tickets cost $24 for anyone over 12, and up to two people

under 12 get in free with each paying adult.

Southern Nights Theater, tel. (423) 908-0600 or (800) 988-7804, puts together a show with elements of country, rock, oldies, bluegrass, and comedy. Tickets cost $20 per adult, with up to two kids 12 and under getting in free.

Festivals

Sevierville, Pigeon Forge, and Gatlinburg all get together to promote **WinterFest,** a Nov.-Feb. celebration of the season that gives the shops and businesses a great opportunity to don thousands of lights. The events that make up WinterFest differ from year to year, but generally consist of concerts, storytelling, winetastings, and so on. For details, contact each town's chamber of commerce or tourist bureau. In Sevierville, the number is (423) 453-6411 or (800) 255-6411. Or hit the Web at www.seviervilletn.org/tourism/accomod/htm.

WHERE TO STAY

Sevierville, Pigeon Forge, and Gatlinburg contain one of the greatest inland concentrations of places to stay in the South. Inns and bed and breakfasts are covered in some detail, but many of the rest are of the franchise variety. "Chalet" is a term often used in these parts. Originally used to mean an A-frame or building along that line, it now usually means a detached structure. Often a "cabin" and "chalet" are virtually indistinguishable. Condominiums have become a big part of the lodging scene in the Smokies, and having a kitchen can help keep costs down.

When inquiring about views of the mountains, visitors should ask if they'll be able to see Mt. LeConte or Clingmans Dome from the place in which they are interested. Almost every hill around here is called a mountain, and a "mountain view" may not be what they had in mind.

Potential visitors can call the Sevierville Chamber of Commerce, tel. (423) 453-8574 or (800) 255-6411, for a list of lodging places that are members.

Bed and Breakfasts and Inns

Blue Mountain Mist Country Inn, mailing address 1811 Pullen Rd., Sevierville, TN 37862, tel. (423) 428-2335, consists of 12 guest rooms in a

Victorian-style house and five guest cottages set on a 60-acre farm with views of the mountains. Each room in the inn has a private bath, and cabins come with whirlpool baths, fireplace, porch swing, kitchenette, television set, and VCR. Outside await a picnic table and grill. The Sugarlands Bridal Room—the top of the line—contains a whirlpool bath with views out of a turreted window. A large country breakfast appears every morning. Rates range $90-130 in the inn and $140 for the cottages. Visit online at www.bbonline.com/tn/bluemtnmist. Expensive-Premium.

The **Calico Inn,** 757 Ranch Way, tel. (423) 428-3833 or (800) 235-1054, is a log house sitting amid 25 acres. The three rooms have private baths and are decorated with folk art and antiques. Guests get a full breakfast, complete with bread or muffins. Rates are $89-99. Expensive.

Grandma's House Bed and Breakfast, 734 Pollard Rd., Kodak, TN 37764, tel. (423) 933-3512 or (800) 676-3512, offers three rooms, all with private baths. The B&B sits on a country lane that leads to the French Broad River and offers a big front porch with rockers and a swing. Inside one will find a country decor with quilts such as Double Wedding Ring, Maple Leaf, and Snowball. Guests enjoy a big country breakfast. The rate is $75 for two. Moderate.

The **Little Greenbriar Lodge,** 3685 Lyon Springs Rd., tel. (423) 429-2500 or (800) 277-8100, overlooks Wears Valley and was built in the '30s as a hunting lodge. It has survived various incarnations since to become a very pleasant inn with 10 double rooms and one single, all decorated with Victorian antiques. Three of the rooms share two baths, but all the rest have their own. The lodge serves a full country breakfast. Rates are $75-110. Moderate-Expensive.

The **Von-Bryan Inn,** 2402 Hatcher Mountain Rd., Sevierville, TN 37862, tel. (423) 453-9832 or (800) 633-1459, has one of the best views guests can get—360° of mountain scenery from atop Hatcher Mountain. The inn contains seven guest rooms as well as a chalet. Each room has a private bath—some have a whirlpool or steam shower—and every guest can enjoy a large gathering room with cathedral ceiling and large fireplace. Rates run $100-145 for two people in the guest rooms, and $220 for four people in the chalets. Guests feast on a breakfast buffet. Guests can

smoke in the chalet but not in the inn. Extra guests can stay for $20. Expensive-Premium.

Cabins, Chalets, and Condos

The offices that rent cabins, condos, and chalets are usually not on-site; call these agents for complete listings.

Wildflower Mountain Rentals, tel. (800) 726-0989 or (423) 453-2000; **Echota Cabins,** tel. (800) 766-5437 or (423) 428-5151; **Great Smoky Mountain Real Estate and Rentals,** tel. (800) 642-5021 or (423) 429-3231; **Hidden Mountain Resorts,** tel. (800) 541-6837 or (423) 453-9850; **Cornerstone Chalets,** tel. (800) 205-6867 or (423) 453-4331; and **Hidden Mountain Resorts,** tel. (423) 453-9850.

Hotels and Motels

Prices for lodging hereabouts depend mightily on when you go, and in October can change dramatically from weekday to weekend. The best idea is to shop by phone.

A few good choices among moderately priced places include **Comfort Inn Interstate,** Dumplin Valley Rd. at Hwy. 66, tel. (800) 441-0311 or (423) 933-1719; and the **Mize Motel,** 804 Pkwy., tel. (800) 239-9117 or (423) 453-4684.

More expensive are **Best Western Dumplin Valley Inn,** 3426 Winfield Dunn Pkwy., tel. (423) 933-3467; **Comfort Inn Mountain Suites,** 806 Winfield Dunn Pkwy., tel. (800) 441-0311 or (423) 428-5519; and the **Hampton Inn,** 681 Winfield Dunn Pkwy., tel. (800) 426-7866 or (423) 429-2005.

Camping

It's heads or tails at the bare bones campgrounds at **Douglas Dam Headwater** or **Douglas Dam Tailwater,** above and below TVA's Douglas Dam. A total of 113 sites—20 with hookups—are open from early April through October.

Knoxville East KOA, 241 KOA Dr., tel. (423) 933-6393, with 200 sites, has all the amenities and is open all year. Take Exit 407 off I-40 and go north. You can't miss it.

River Plantation RV Park, 1004 Pkwy., tel. (800) 758-5267 or (423) 429-5267, features 166 large sites—40 by 60 feet. It offers rental cars, full hookups, outdoor pool, satellite TV, and camping cabins, and is open all year.

Riverside Campground, on the French

Broad River, tel. (423) 453-7299, has 165 sites, most of them with full hookups, along with planned group activities, swimming pool, pavilion, playground, and more. Take the Hwy. 66 exit off I-40, and go south four miles, then right a quarter-mile on Boyds Creek Road. It's open all year.

Smoky Mountain Campground, tel. (423) 933-8312 or (800) 684-2267, weighs in with 246 sites and is open all year. With all the amenities, it lies off I-40 at Exit 407. Go south on Hwy. 66 for about 100 yards, then a half mile east on Foretravel Drive.

FOOD

Sevierville is a dry town. There are no liquor stores; if visitors want a bottle of wine, they have to buy it at the winery or bring it with them. Restaurants do not serve alcoholic beverages, although some will allow diners to carry in their own. To be sure, call ahead.

The Applewood complex on Apple Valley Rd. off the Parkway between Sevierville and Pigeon Forge, tel. (423) 428-1222, includes two restaurants. The **Applewood Farmhouse Restaurant** and the **Farmhouse Grill** offer dishes such as chicken à la Orchard and other varieties of country cooking. Both places really shine, however, when it comes to desserts: apple cider pie, apple fritters, apple butter, you name it. Both are open for all three meals every day.

Josev's, in downtown Sevierville at 130 W. Bruce St., tel. (423) 428-0737, serves lunch Tues.-Sun. and dinner Tues.-Saturday. This place offers American food and homemade desserts.

Virgil's '50s Restaurant, just off the town square on 109 Bruce St., tel. (423) 453-2782, is a fun place to go. The black-and-white tiled floor, pink neon, and colorful booths seem just right for the fifties music that's always on tap here. The cuisine is burgers, sandwiches, and country cooking.

SHOPPING AND INFORMATION

Shopping

Visitors must see the **Smoky Mountain Knife Works,** 3.75 miles off I-40 on Hwy. 66, tel. (423) 453-5871, www.smkwknife.com, even if they have no interest in knives. This is the largest knife store in the world as well as a museum depicting factory collections, antique knives, and antique advertisements. There is nothing like it anywhere. Tennessee's largest collection of mounted trophy heads gazes down on a waterfall that flows into a trout stream right in the store. The store carries leather jackets, jewelry, and regional souvenirs. It's open daily.

If one gets inspired by all the picking hereabouts and wants to start making music, **Music Outlet,** close to the Super 8 Motel on Hwy. 66, tel. (423) 453-1031, is the place. Not an outlet in the usual sense of the word, this 20-plus-year-old establishment is a good place to buy instruments, sheet music, and recordings.

The **Robert A. Tino Gallery,** 812 Old Douglas Dam Rd., tel. (423) 453-6315, offers original paintings and limited-edition prints of mountain and country scenes by this native Tennessee artist. The shop is in an old house now on the National Register.

Information

Sevierville Chamber of Commerce, 806 Winfield Dunn Pkwy., tel. (423) 453-6411 or (800) 255-6411, is open Mon.-Sat. 8 a.m.-5 p.m., Sunday 1-5 p.m. You can find it on the Web at www.seviervilletn.org/tourism.

PIGEON FORGE

Pigeon Forge has been visited by millions for a long time. The first notable influx was enormous flocks of passenger pigeons attracted by the beech trees that lined the river. "Pigeon" became the name of the river, and in time it powered an ironworks built by Isaac Love and operated until the 1930s—thus the "Forge." In the years that followed, the Great Smoky Mountains National Park came into being, and an ever-growing number of tourists started coming through town.

For years Pigeon Forge struggled along as a Gatlinburg wannabe—a place that would do just about anything to snare passing tourists. In the last 10 years, however, Pigeon Forge has begun to shed its tacky image. Part of this has to do with geography—Pigeon Forge has room to expand, and Gatlinburg, all but surrounded by the Great Smoky Mountains National Park, doesn't. The second element fell into place when local girl Dolly Parton bought Silver Dollar City and transformed it into Dollywood. Then the town took a look at the success of Branson, Missouri, and went into the music business. Now a

handful of music halls hold forth nightly, with more on the way.

Just the same, when it's 90°, traffic is bumper to bumper, and radiators and tempers are boiling over, driving through here can seem anything but fun. Pigeon Forge and Gatlinburg have buses resembling trolleys that can get visitors from place to place. They are exceptionally useful for dispatching older children to their favorite destinations.

SIGHTS AND RECREATION

Dollywood
Let's take it from the top. Dollywood, tel. (423) 428-9488, combines live music—more than 40 performances daily—with more than 30 amusement park rides. Dollywood puts an Appalachian spin on all this, with 20 craftspeople working on traditional activities such as weaving, pottery, and woodcarving. The Dollywood Express, a steam-powered train, rides along a five-mile track, and Dolly Parton's Museum tells this extraordinary entertainer's life story. The Eagle Mountain Sanctuary displays bald eagles that for one reason or another cannot be released into the wild. Dollywood Boulevard focuses on the movies, offering a ride simulator and a restaurant with a Hollywood theme.

Dollywood opens in late April and closes at the end of December, staying open the latest during the heart of the summer. All-day admission for one adult is $28.99, for children 4-11 $18, for seniors (60 and older) $22, and for three and under free. The best deal is to enter the park after 3 p.m.; you can come back the next day free of charge. Preview the park online at www.dollywood.com.

Museums
Carbo's Smoky Mountain Police Museum, 3311 Pkwy. at the building with bars on the windows, tel. (423) 453-1358, takes a curatorial look at the constabulary with badges, guns—official as well as confiscated ones—uniforms, drug exhibits, etc. The centerpiece is the Buford Pusser

---

THE BACK DOOR TO DOLLYWOOD AND PIGEON FORGE

Highway 441 through Pigeon Forge and Gatlinburg is often just called "The Parkway," and when traffic clogs this artery on weekends and during the leaf season, the name is apt: it looks like all the cars are parked.

To avoid this mess, follow the instructions in the special topic The Back Doors to the Smokies to get onto Hwy. 411 east of Sevierville. Less than two miles east of Sevierville, turn south on Middle Creek Road. This goes past a hospital and, several miles later, sneaks into the back entrance to the Dollywood parking lot. Jump on a tram and try to keep from smiling as you listen to everyone else complain about the traffic.

To get to Pigeon Forge, stay on Middle Creek Rd., which comes out near The Old Mill on the Parkway.

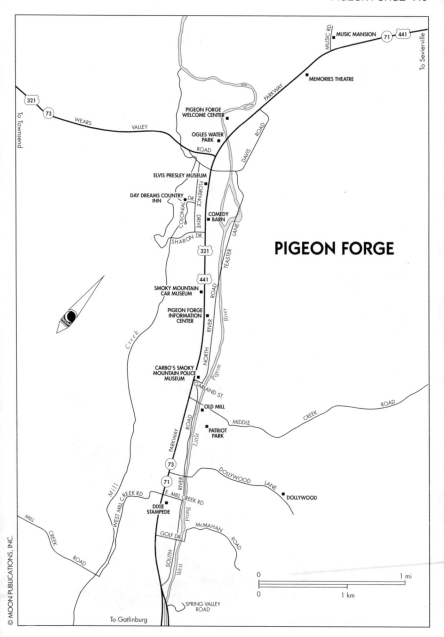

DOLLY PARTON

Sevier County's Dolly Parton possesses three aspects that make her perhaps the best-known female country performer in the world: her pure soprano voice, her songwriting, and her eye-popping appearance.

Dolly's life began on January 19, 1946. Eventually she had 11 siblings—she was number four—in a family of mountain people near the community of Pittman Center, north of Gatlinburg. The family was financially poor but musically very rich. Her grandfather was a songwriter/fiddler who once wrote a song recorded by Kitty Wells. Other members of her family played various stringed instruments and sang and composed songs.

Helped by her family, Dolly appeared on Knoxville radio stations and television shows. She made her Grand Old Opry debut at age 13, and her first record emerged a year later, but her career seemed stalled. Her big break came when she teamed up in 1967 with Porter Wagoner, who had his own television show. Wagoner was perfectly suited for TV—a pompadoured, gaudily dressed performer whose fiddler often danced while playing—and Dolly, with her extravagant blonde wigs and prominent figure, fit right in.

Dolly and Porter worked together for the next decade, churning out duets such as "We'll Get Ahead Someday" and "Two Sides to Every Story." Dolly continued to write her own songs, and gradually her career outgrew her musical relationship with Wagoner. In 1971, *Joshua* marked her first number-one single on the country charts, followed two years later by "Jolene," which appeared in pop charts as well. She was named country's Female Vocalist of the Year twice in a row, in 1975 and '76.

In 1976 she gained her own TV show, and the next year her "Here You Come Again" rolled up the country and pop charts. Dolly had hit the big time. She appeared in movies, had more song hits, and saw her picture on the cover of major magazines. She co-starred in the 1982 film version of *Best Little Whorehouse in Texas* and in 1984's *Rhinestone,* which proved conclusively that even Hollywood could not make a silk-purse singer out of Sylvester Stallone. The next year she inaugurated Dollywood in Pigeon Forge.

Trio, a 1987 album recorded with Linda Ronstadt and Emmylou Harris, marked an artistic peak for Dolly, showing off her many skills: her songwriting, her voice, and her willingness to collaborate with other recording artists. *Trio II,* released in 1999, continues this winning combination. Dolly's 1993 autobiography, *My Life and Other Unfinished Business,* reached the national best-seller list. The title was particularly apt for this tremendously talented Tennessean.

MATT BARNES/DECCA RECORDS

"death car." (Who is Buford P.? See "Adamsville" in the Western Plains chapter.) Admission is $6 for adults and $3 for children 10 and under.

For those who can't make it to Graceland, the **Elvis Museum,** one block south of Ogles Water Park on the Parkway, offers the King's last personal limousine, the first dollar bill he ever earned, guns, musical instruments, clothes, and the original $250,000 "TCB" ring. Admission is $9.75 for adults, $6.50 for kids over 12, and $4.50 for kids six to 12.

If Elvis's limo and Buford Pusser's death car only whet your appetite, the **Smoky Mountain Car Museum,** 2970 Pkwy., tel. (423) 453-3433, will prove delightful. See James Bond's cars from *Goldfinger* and *Thunderball* as well as vehicles once belonging to Elvis, the ubiquitous Buford Pusser, Al Capone, Stringbean, and Billy Carter. The museum is open varied hours from late spring through December. Call ahead. Admission is $5 for adults and $2 for children three to 10.

Patriot Park

Visitors who have never had the occasion to look at a Patriot missile should decamp to Patriot Park, where they'll find one of the four on display in the United States. This free public park in the Old Mill area, near traffic light no. 7, also contains flags of all the states displayed in the order in which they were admitted to the Union.

Liquid Refreshment

Mountain Valley Vineyards, 2174 Pkwy., tel. (423) 453-6334, produces 16 different kinds of wine—mostly sweet and medium sweet. Muscadine wine is the best-selling one, although berry wines run a close second. Visitors can watch wine being made in August and September. Mountain Valley is open for tastings all year seven days a week.

Ogles Water Park, on the Parkway, tel. (423) 453-8741, has an antidote for long hours spent in a car: 10 water slides, a wave pool, and a "lazy river." Open during the summer, it costs $17 for adults, $16 for kids four to 11, free for those under four.

Rafting

The closest river rafting in Tennessee to Pigeon Forge is the Pigeon River, which does not, as one might assume, flow through Pigeon Forge.

That's the *Little* Pigeon River. The *Pigeon* River parallels Interstate 40 from the North Carolina Border until it reaches Douglas Lake. Two companies offer trips along it, **USA Raft,** tel. (800) USA-RAFT and **Rafting in the Smokies,** tel. (423) 436-5008. Trips last two to three hours and cost around $19-33.

ENTERTAINMENT AND EVENTS

The shows in the Smokies emphasize family entertainment. Alcoholic beverages are not served in theaters, and patrons will never see any Dwight Yoakam lookalike making pelvic thrusts behind a guitar. Many shows include gospel music as a part of their presentations. All this is mildly ironic, for country music's staples through the years have been drinking, honky-tonking, and experiencing what might be termed the continuing difficulty of interpersonal relationships. The roadside tradition of "fightin' and dancin' clubs" gets no homage here.

Theaters generally open in April for weekends only, and then expand to six or seven nights a week when summer arrives. They cut back on the number of shows as the fall winds down. "There's no business like show business," as the song goes, and that's very true in Pigeon Forge. Acts change, theaters open, theaters close, and a new Elvis periodically comes to town. To get the most accurate information of who's playing where, check with the tourist bureaus or pick up a handful of brochures when hitting town.

Dollywood Venues

Dollywood, tel. (423) 656-9620, is the place for the biggest country music names in country music to be found: Stars such as Kathy Mattea, John Anderson, Patty Loveless, and the Statlers sing during the summertime. Dolly herself usually makes one appearance per year—usually at the opening of the season. Concerts begin in May and run through October—usually on weekends except during the last week of June through the first week in August, when every day is show time. The music plays at 2 and 7 p.m., and those who come to the later show do not have to pay to get into Dollywood. All seats are reserved. Call for information and tickets.

Dixie Stampede, at the intersection of Mill Creek Rd. and the Parkway, tel. (423) 453-4400 or (800) 356-1676, has to be the most unusual dinner show in the entire state. More than 1,000 patrons sit side by side on five tiers of seats facing a U-shaped, dirt arena. The meal consists of whole rotisserie chicken, ribs, soup, and accompanying dishes, all enjoyed without silverware. The show involves 30 horses, people riding ostriches, singing, trick riding, roping, and performers dressed as Union and Confederate soldiers. The price for all this is $32.69 for adults and $16.34 for kids four to 11. Children three and under get in free if they sit on an adult's lap and eat off that person's plate. Owned by Dollywood, Dixie Stampede runs March-December. Call for tickets. Visit online at www.dixiestampede.com.

Music Mansion, on the Sevierville side of Pigeon Forge on the Parkway, tel. (423) 428-7469, is another part of the Dollywood empire, presenting an exuberant group of 25 men and women amid scene and costume changes that pay homage to Big Bands, patriotic music, country, gospel, and oldies. The star of the show is James Rogers, a versatile entertainer who has been with the Dollywood organization for more than 10 years. Music Mansion stages shows from mid-April through mid-December. Tickets cost $25 for adults; two children ages 4-11 get in free with each paying adult. Call for reservations and information.

More Music
Memories Theatre, tel. (423) 428-7852, should be the first East Tennessee stop for Elvis fans—the home of first-class impersonators of the King. Memories Theatre seats 900 and is open every month except January. It's on the left coming into Pigeon Forge from Sevierville before traffic light no. 1. Admission is $18.50 for anyone over 12; two kids get in free for each paid adult.

Comedy
Comedy Barn, on the north side of the Parkway between traffic light nos. 3 and 4, tel. (423) 428-5222 or (800) 29LAUGH, packs them in with corny comedy perfected during years of work on cruise ships. A one-man band, live country music, and juggling round out the act. It's open late April through December; tickets cost $18.50 for adults, with kids under 11 getting in for free.

Festivals
Pigeon Forge joins Sevierville and Gatlinburg in **WinterFest** Nov.-Feb., a celebration of the season that gives the shops and businesses a great opportunity to don thousands of lights. WinterFest differs from year to year, but generally consists of concerts, storytelling, and so on. For details about Pigeon Forge events, call (423) 453-8574 or (800) 251-9100.

WHERE TO STAY

There are lots of lodging choices in Pigeon Forge. As in Sevierville, if visitors expect a true mountain view, they should ask specifically if they'll be able to see Mt. LeConte or Clingmans Dome from the room in question.

For the most up-to-date information, call (800) 251-9100 and ask for a copy of the Pigeon Forge Vacation Planner. Another good resource is the Pigeon Forge website, www.pigeon-forge.tn.us/lodging.html.

Bed and Breakfasts and Inns
Three blocks off the Parkway doesn't sound like a good place for a B&B, but **Day Dreams Country Inn,** 2720 Colonial Dr., tel. (423) 428-0370 or (800) 377-1469, offers a close-in oasis from the outlets and crowds of Pigeon Forge. On three wooded acres with rail fences along Mill Creek, this two-story, hand-hewn log home of 6,000 square feet contains six large rooms, each with private bath. The front and back porches have swings, and guests are served full country breakfasts. Rates are $79-119. Moderate-Premium.

Close to Dollywood, the **Evergreen Cottage Inn and Forge Mountain Honeymoon Village,** Old Mill Rd., tel. (423) 453-4000 or (800) 264-3331, offers two cabins and 11 honeymoon suites in a separate structure. Rooms in the inn go for $69-89, while to become one of the village people costs $105-120. Moderate-Premium.

The **Huckleberry Inn,** 1754 Sandstone Way, tel. (423) 428-2475, is a log house built by hand and containing three guest rooms decorated in country style. All rooms have private baths, and two have fireplaces and whirlpools. The inn serves a full country breakfast daily. It's 1.2 miles from Dollywood, yet just a half-mile off the busy Parkway. Rates are $79-89. It's online at www.bbonline.com/tn/huckleberry. Moderate-Expensive.

Cabins, Condos, and Chalets

"Chalet," a term often used in these parts, usually means a detached structure. "Cabin" and "chalet" usually mean the same thing. The offices listed below rent cabins, condos, and chalets.

County Oaks Cottages, tel. (423) 453-7640 or (800) 662-1022; **Eagles Ridge Resort & Cabin Rentals,** tel. (800) 807-4343; **Forge Mountain Honeymoon Village,** tel. (423) 453-4000 or (800) 264-3331; **Heritage House,** tel. (423) 453-8529; **Kimble Overnight Rentals,** tel. (423) 429-0090 or (800) 447-0911; **Little Creek Cabins,** tel. (423) 453-4625 or (800) 553-0496; and **Mill Creek Resort Club,** tel. (423) 428-3498 or (423) 428-4490.

Also try **Serenity Mountain Cabin Rentals,** tel. (423) 429-8514 or (800) 422-2246, and **Wildflower Mountain Rentals,** tel. (423) 453-2000 or (800) 726-0989.

Hotels and Motels

Pigeon Forge offers dozens of lodging options, franchise and otherwise, just a few of which are listed below. Prices vary greatly depending on when you visit, and in October can change dramatically from weekday to weekend, so check by phone. (See "Where to Stay" under "Accommodations and Food" in the On the Road chapter for a list of franchise accommodations and their toll-free reservation numbers.)

People who see a listing for **Wonderland Hotel,** 3889 Wonderland Way, tel. (423) 428-0779, sometimes think "Didn't that place close?" They're thinking of the original Wonderland Hotel, a 1912 vintage hotel that was grandfathered into becoming the only such place in the Great Smokies National Park. Time finally ran out for the old hotel, which closed in 1992. This edition of the hotel continues the traditions of its predecessor—no phones, no TVs, plain furnishings, and rocking chairs on the porch. Rates are $56-72 Although the hotel has a Sevierville address, it is located in Wears Valley between Pigeon Forge and Townsend. Check it out on the Internet at www.smoky.net/wonderland. Inexpensive-Moderate.

River Lodge South, 3251 Pkwy., tel. (423) 453-0783 or (800) 233-7581, is another Moderate-priced choice.

More expensive: **Bilmar Motor Inn,** 3786 Pkwy., tel. (423) 453-5593 or (800) 343-5610; **Smoky Mountain Resorts,** 4034 River Rd. S, tel. (423) 453-3557 or (800) 523-3919; **Heartland Country Resort,** 2385 Pkwy., tel. (423) 453-4106 or (800) 843-6686; **McAfee Motor Inn** 3756 Pkwy., tel. (423) 453-3490 or (800) 925-4443; **Parkview Motel,** 2806 Pkwy., tel. (423) 453-5051 or (800) 239-9116; **Vacation Lodge Motel** 3450 Pkwy., tel. (423) 453-2640 or (800) 468-1998; and **Willow Brook Lodge** 3035 Pkwy., tel. (423) 453-5334 or (800) 765-1380.

Those who don't mind spending more can try the **Shular Inn,** 2708 Pkwy., tel. (423) 453-2700 or (800) 451-2376.

Camping

Alpine Hideaway RV Park and Campground, 251 Spring Valley Rd., tel. (423) 428-3285, offers 96 sites, a pool and cable TV, and all the other roughing-it amenities. It's open mid-April through early November.

Clabough's Campground, a half mile off the Parkway on Wears Valley Rd., tel. (423) 453-0729, has 152 sites and all the amenities and is open all year.

Creekstone Outdoor Resort, on the Little Pigeon River, tel. (423) 453-8181 or (800) 848-9097, has 150 sites and full amenities. To get there, turn off the Parkway onto Golf Dr., then turn right on McMahan Road. It's open year-round.

Eagles Nest Campground, 111 Wears Valley Rd., 1.5 miles off the Parkway, tel. (423) 428-5841 or (800) 892-2714, has 200 sites with the works. It's open year-round.

Fort Wear Campground sits a half mile off the Parkway on Wears Valley Rd., tel. (423) 428-1951 or (800) 452-9835. Open all year, it has 150 sites and all the amenities.

KOA, tel. (423) 453-7903 or (800) 367-7903, offers 200 sites complete with Kamping Kabins, heated pool, whirlpool, and other amenities. Turn off the Parkway onto Dollywood Ln., then left on Cedar Top Road. It's open April 1 through December.

River Bend Campground, tel. (423) 453-1224, has 101 sites between Pigeon Forge and Sevierville. It's open April through November 15.

Park the Winnebago at one of the 175 sites at **Riveredge RV Park,** tel. (423) 453-5813 or (800) 477-1205. It offers all the amenities. To get there coming from Sevierville, turn right at traffic light no. 1, then turn west on Henderson Chapel Road. Open year-round.

Shady Oaks Campground, tel. (423) 453-3276, sits on the Gatlinburg side of Pigeon Forge. It offers 150 sites that are open all year and quite a few amenities. To get there from downtown Pigeon Forge, turn right at the first street past traffic light no. 8, Conner Heights Road.

The small **Foothills Campground**—only 46 sites—sits on the edge of town at 4235 Huskey St., tel. (423) 428-3818. Open April-November.

Z Buda's Smokies Campground, on the Parkway past traffic light no. 8, tel. (423) 453-4129, weighs in with 300 sites that are open April-October.

FOOD

Pigeon Forge does not permit the sale of alcoholic beverages in stores or restaurants. Diners can carry in their own to some restaurants, but it's a good idea to call ahead.

Bel Air Grill, 2785 Parkway (next to the Comedy Barn), tel. (423) 429-0101, has a '50s and '60s decor and claims to offer the best cheeseburger in the Smokies. Other dishes include steak, shrimp, and chicken.

Chef Jock's Tastebud Cafe, 1198 Wears Valley Rd., tel. (423) 428-9781, is far from the madding crowd on the Parkway. This very unassuming place offers a respite from country cooking in the form of sea scallops, pork tenderloin with herbs, and a great number of healthy yet tasty dishes. Open for lunch and dinner Tuesday through Saturday. Reservations are a good idea.

The Old Mill Restaurant, in the Old Mill complex, tel. (423) 429-3463, offers dining overlooking the Little Pigeon River. Breads are made from flour and meal from the nearby mill. It offers country cooking seven days a week for all three meals.

Santo's Italian Restaurant, 3270 Pkwy., tel. (423) 428-5840, offers fine fettucine with snow crab, linguine primavera, and other Italian dishes. It's open all year Monday through Saturday.

Smokies Breakfast House, 2751 Pkwy., tel. (423) 453-0624, is a good place to fuel up for a hike in the mountains. The place offers 45 different breakfasts April-December seven days a week 7 a.m.-1 p.m.

Trotter's Restaurant, 3716 S. Pkwy., tel. (423) 453-3347, offers family-style dining April-November. It serves all three meals daily.

SHOPPING

Pigeon River String Instruments, 3337 Old Mill St., tel. (423) 453-3789, awaits folk fanciers who need dulcimers, hammered dulcimers, or psalteries; it offers a few guitars and mandolins as well.

Stages West, 2765 Pkwy., tel. (423) 453-8086, offers fancy duds that are the closest thing to Nashville one will find in these parts.

Arts and Crafts

Jim Gray is perhaps the best-known artist in this part of the state. His oils and drawings depict seascapes, Tennessee landscapes, people, wildflowers, and birds. His bronze statues include Dolly Parton in Sevierville and Andrew Johnson in Greeneville. The **Jim Gray Gallery,** 3331 S. River Rd. across from the Old Mill, tel. (423) 428-2202, offers works in a variety of media from this talented artist.

When the founder of **Pigeon Forge Pottery,** across from the Old Mill on Middle Creek Rd. off the Parkway, tel. (423) 453-3883, came to town in 1937 looking for good clay, he fired the earthen nests made by mud dauber wasps. Convinced that the clay here was of high enough quality, Douglas Ferguson began the pottery, which now produces art objects inspired by Smoky Mountains subjects. Visitors can watch the artisans at work. The biggest sellers are bears and owls.

SERVICES AND INFORMATION

Bus Tours of the Smokies, 2756, no. 1, Middle Creek Rd., tel. (423) 428-3014, will come to one's door and then head to visit Cades Cove, the Cherokee Indian Reservation in North Carolina, and several other places.

The **Pigeon Forge Department of Tourism,** 2450 Pkwy., tel. (423) 453-8574 or (800) 251-9100, offers information Mon.-Sat. 9 a.m.-5:30 p.m., Sunday 1-5 p.m. and on the Internet at www.pigeon-forge.tn.us.

GATLINBURG

Longtime visitors to this mountain town often lament the passing of "the old Gatlinburg." While a certain amount of this longing for the past goes on everywhere (How many preservationists does it take to change a light bulb? Three: one to change it and two to talk about how good the old one was), in this case the old-timers have a point.

Gatlinburg used to have a laid-back ambience of hotels with rocking chairs on the porches and restaurants with simple yet hearty fare. The town enjoyed a family atmosphere largely free of the gimcrackery that characterizes places such as Myrtle Beach, Pigeon Forge, or Cherokee, North Carolina. Compared to these tourist pits, Gatlinburg had taste.

Not anymore. A walk down the Parkway, the main drag in town, reveals what seems like an endless row of T-shirt shops and assorted dopiness. The passerby occasionally has to step aside for a pack of 14-year-olds, who, rushing from Ripley's Believe it Or Not to the Guinness World Records Museum, appear to be in some sort of adolescent yahoo heaven. At a time when all four of Tennessee's major cities are reinventing their downtowns, one wonders how long it will be before the burghers of Gatlinburg abandon their we-don't-care-how-tacky it-is-if-it-makes-money-it's-fine-by-us philosophy and shape this town up.

Having said all that, however, Gatlinburg does offer some redeeming features for the visitor. Restaurants here are more upscale than those in outlying towns. The town is small enough to walk to just about everything. Gatlinburg allows its eateries to offer mixed drinks, wine, and beer, and the town has several liquor stores. And its lodges and cabins are as close to the National Park as one can get.

Perhaps the best thing about the whole place is the Great Smoky Arts and Crafts Community Loop, which lies east of downtown Gatlinburg off Hwy. 321. Driven out because of the high rents, artists and craftspeople moved to this outlying area, and those who appreciate this sort of thing have followed them, leaving downtown to the mob.

SIGHTS

During the busy season the best idea is to park the vehicle and leave it, seeing the sights on foot

---

THE BACK DOOR TO GATLINBURG

Coming from the east or west route mentioned in the special topic The Back Doors to the Smokies, savvy motorists will be on Hwy. 411 east of Sevierville. From either direction, turn south on TN Hwy. 416, a.k.a. the Pittman Center Road. Stay straight on this road when 416 turns off to the left. You should now be on Birds Creek Rd., which will eventually become Buckhorn Rd. and terminate onto Hwy. 321, on which a right turn will put you on the road to Gatlinburg.

Minimizing the Gatlinburg Traffic

Coming from Pigeon Forge, look for the Gatlinburg Bypass and take it. This will bring you into the Great Smoky Mountains National Park very close to the visitors center.

Again coming from Pigeon Forge, if you miss the bypass, or for some reason want to come through Gatlinburg, when you come into town take the River Road to the right. While a little longer than Hwy 441—The Parkway—it is mostly lined with motels and will not have any shops or hordes of pedestrians. The River Rd. rejoins the Parkway on the south end of town just in time to turn right and escape into the Park.

If you are coming into town on Hwy. 321, turn left onto Baskins Creek Bypass, which is just south of where the Roaring Fork Motor Nature Trail—a one-way road—exits. Turn left onto Cherokee Orchard Rd., and then right onto Airport Road. This road comes out on the Parkway at Traffic Light Number Eight, from which a left turn and two more traffic lights will put you in the Park.

If you have rented a cabin or condo on the mountain overlooking Gatlinburg, you can often get to it from the Gatlinburg Bypass instead of coming through town. Ask your rental agent if this is possible.

or taking the trolley that makes frequent stops all over town. Rides cost 25 cents per person.

Christus Gardens
Countless church youth groups have taken advantage of the gardens on River Rd., tel. (423) 436-5155, to nag their elders into permitting a trip to Gatlinburg. The focus of the gardens is 81 wax figures in dioramas depicting scenes from the life of Jesus. The culmination of this is a 40-foot-long depiction of Leonardo da Vinci's *Last Supper.* Visitors can also see collections of Bibles and other religious texts, 168 coins dating from the 6th century B.C., and oil paintings that interpret nine of the parables. It's open every day year-round; admission is $8 for adults, $3.25 for kids seven to 11, and free for those under six.

Frippery
Considerably more secular items hold court at **Guinness World Records Museum,** 631

Pkwy., tel. (423) 436-9100, where 12 galleries depict such wonders as the world's most tattooed lady, the heaviest man, and the obligatory Elvis. It's open daily. Admission is $7.95 for adults, $5.95 for seniors and teenagers, and $3.95 for kids 6-12.

Devotees of shrunken heads and the like will enjoy **Ripley's Believe It or Not,** at traffic light no. 7, tel. (423) 436-5096, a museum based on an illustrated newspaper feature that those of a certain age may recall. Admission is $8.75 for adults, $5.75 for first graders through high schoolers, and free for pre-school kids.

Delectables
Longtime visitors to Gatlinburg remember the candy kitchens. These heavenly-smelling places have intricate machines that stretch taffy, measure it out into little finger-sized pieces, whack them off, and wrap them in paper. Fudge and other decadent delights can be had at **Aunt Mahalia's Candies** (three locations on the Park-

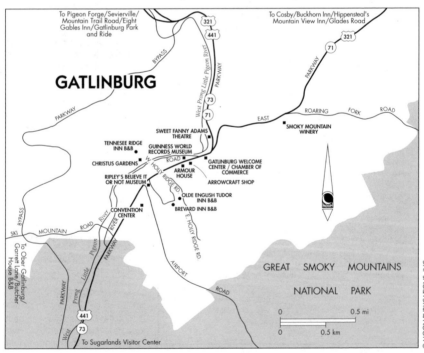

bunnies on the loose

way), **Mountaineer Kandy Kitchen,** and **Ola Kate's Candy Kitchen.** Kids love these places.

The Smoky Mountain Winery is up Hwy. 321 a half mile from Parkway traffic light no. 3, tel. (423) 436-7551. Here visitors can observe the winemaking process and sample the products. Seventy-five percent of the grapes used come from Tennessee. Among the wines offered are cabernet sauvignon and American riesling. It's open year-round, 10 a.m.-6 p.m. in good weather, shorter hours in the winter.

RECREATION

Ober Gatlinburg
This park, tel. (423) 436-5423, is Gatlinburg's ski resort and summertime amusement park. Visitors can either drive up or take the aerial tramway, which departs from downtown and goes 2.5 miles up the mountain. Tram rides cost $7 for adults and $4 for kids seven to 11. The skiing, while puny by New England or Western standards, nonetheless enthralls the locals, as does the indoor ice-skating, which operates year-round. The latter is a great idea for rainy days.

Summertime activities include bungee jumping, batting cages, go-carts, water slides, and an alpine slide. The chairlift that carries skiers in the wintertime carries sightseers to the top of a mountain.

There is no charge to enter Ober Gatlinburg. All activities are individually priced. Meals are available at Ober Gatlinburg, but their prices are considerably ober what visitors might pay at lower elevations. See what you're getting into ahead of time at www.obergatlinburg.com.

Arrowmont School of Arts and Crafts
The school, P.O. Box 567, Gatlinburg, TN 37738, brings 1,500 students and 150 instructors together each summer to a 70-acre campus to work on carving, weaving, pottery, and more than 15 other media. The school originated in 1912 when Pi Beta Phi opened a settlement school in what was then the economically depressed Appalachian town of Gatlinburg. Noting the high value people put on local crafts, the school added crafts instruction along with the other subjects. When improved public schools eliminated the need for the settlement school, the emphasis was shifted entirely to crafts. Those seeking information on the crafts programs should write the school.

Stables
One can be back in the saddle here for trips ranging from one to four hours at **McCarter's Riding Stables,** tel. (423) 436-5354, 1.5 miles south of Gatlinburg close to the Sugarlands Visitors Center. Lead horses are available for children. It's open daily 8 a.m.-6 p.m. from early spring through late fall.

Smoky Mountain Stables, four miles east of Gatlinburg on Hwy. 321, tel. (423) 436-5634, offers guided trail rides lasting one or two hours. It's open from March through Thanksgiving.

Outfitters

Old Smoky Outfitters, 511 Pkwy. in the Riverbend Mall, tel. (423) 430-1936, offers fishing, hunting, and historical and nature tours. A half-day trout fishing trip for novices begins at $135 and goes up from there. Overnight backcountry hikes, including all equipment, are available. See it on the Web: www.oldsmoky.com.

Smoky Mountain Angler, at 376 E. Parkway, tel. (423) 436-8746, offers access to a six-mile-long private stream where the big fish live. Full-day guided trips with lunch begin at $150 per person or $100 for a half day. The shop contains a good selection of flies and some great advice.

Or try **Smoky Mountain Guide Service,** tel. (423) 436-2108 or (800) 782-1061.

The Happy Hiker, tel. (423) 436-5632 or (800) HIKER-01, offers gear rentals, shuttles, and lockers. Located behind the Burning Bush Restaurant on the Parkway. See them on the Web at www.happyhiker.com.

Rafting

The closest river rafting in Tennessee to Gatlinburg is the Pigeon River, which parallels Interstate 40 from the North Carolina Border until it reaches Douglas Lake. The good news is that the river is very accessible; the bad news is that it flows alongside an interstate highway—not exactly a wilderness experience. At least two companies offer trips on the Pigeon, **USA Raft,** tel. (800) USA-RAFT, and **The Whitewater Company,** tel. (800) 723-8462. Trips last two to three hours and cost around $19-40 per person.

ENTERTAINMENT AND EVENTS

Music

Compared to the music halls of Pigeon Forge, the 200-seat **Sweet Fanny Adams Theatre,** 461 Pkwy., tel. (423) 436-4038, is tiny. The entertainment consists of musical comedy, a singalong, and a vaudeville-type review six nights a week. A five-member cast performs one show Monday, Wednesday, and Friday, and a seven-member cast presents a completely different show Tuesday, Thursday, and Saturday. Curtain time is 8 p.m. Mon.-Sat. May-Dec., with shows only on the weekends in November and December. Admission is $15.50 for adults and

$5.50 for kids up to age 12. Any small child who sits on a lap gets in free. Call for reservations.

Fairs and Festivals

Held in July and October in the Gatlinburg Convention Center, the very popular **Craftsmen's Fairs** bring in about 150 craftspeople from all over the United States. The dates fluctuate every year—usually one week in July and one in October—so call (423) 436-7479 for information.

Gatlinburg joins Sevierville and Pigeon Forge in **WinterFest,** a Nov.-Feb. celebration of the season for which shops and businesses decorate with thousands of lights. WinterFest differs from year to year, but generally consists of concerts, storytelling, and winetastings. For details about Gatlinburg events, call (423) 430-4148 or (800) 568-4748.

WHERE TO STAY

The visitor to Gatlinburg will find a massive concentration of places to stay. Listed below are inns and bed and breakfasts of note, along with a sampling of hotels and motels. Visitors interested in a mountain view should ask exactly what they will be able to see from the room in question, as almost every hill around here is called a mountain.

Long a honeymoon destination—an estimated 10,000 couples tie the knot here annually—Gatlinburg features an enormous number of "chalets" with bathtubs that rival those in the Poconos of Pennsylvania. Indeed, an anthropologist from afar studying the ads for these plumbing extravaganzas might conclude that the marital bath has surpassed the marital bed for connubial pleasures.

Smoky Mountain Accommodations, tel. (423) 436-9700 or (800) 231-2230, can help find the lodging—motel, condo, cabin, or chalet—that meets visitors' needs. There is no charge for this service, which represents approximately 40% of the lodging available. Call 9 a.m.-5 p.m. on weekdays and 9 a.m.-3 p.m. on Saturday.

Bed and Breakfasts and Inns

The **Brevard Inn Bed and Breakfast,** 225 W. Holly Ridge Rd., mailing address P.O. Box 326, Gatlinburg, TN 37738, tel. (423) 436-7233, consists of the inn and two authentic log cabins.

The three rooms in the inn have private entrances, their own bathrooms, cable TV, and fireplaces. The cabins have kitchens. The rate is $75. Moderate.

The **Buckhorn Inn,** 2140 Tudor Mountain Rd., tel. (423) 436-4668, is the grande dame of inns in the Gatlinburg area, serving guests since 1938. The inn contains six rooms and has four cottages, all situated on 32 wooded acres six miles from downtown Gatlinburg. The inn centers on a large living room with views of Mt. LeConte. The room contains a grand piano, and in the hour preceding dinner or in the evening a guest will often sit down and tickle the ivories. The Buckhorn strives to maintain an atmosphere of informal elegance; tables are set with linen, and guests should not show up for meals in jeans and T-shirts. Rooms in the inn offer neither telephones nor televisions. The cottages have TVs, as well as limited cooking facilities.

Children must be at least six years old to come to the Buckhorn, and even then they must occupy the cottages. Rates range $105-275 and include breakfast. Sack lunches can be arranged, and guests must make reservations for dinner. Weekends and holidays require a two-night minimum stay. Expensive-Luxury.

Guests at the **Butcher House Bed & Breakfast,** 1520 Garrett Ln., tel. (423) 436-9457, rest above it all at 2,800 feet above downtown Gatlinburg. The four rooms each have a private bath. The house contains Victorian, French, Queen Anne, and American Country furniture, and outside is a deck with a wonderful view of Mt. LeConte. Rates are $79-109. Moderate-Expensive.

The **Cornerstone Inn,** 3956 Regal Way, tel. (423) 430-5064, is filled with angels. The owner collects them, and they appear in the three guest rooms, each of which is named for a painting it contains. Each room has its own bath. Guests get a full country breakfast. Rates range $85-95. Expensive.

Eight Gables Inn, 219 N. Mountain Trail, tel. (423) 430-3344 or (800) 279-5716, is a large building with wraparound porches. It has 12 guest rooms, all with private baths. Two suites feature whirlpool baths, and each room has its own theme—perhaps centered on a sleigh or four-poster bed. Breakfast comes in four courses. Rates are $109-165. See the Inn online at www.bbonline.com/tn/eightgables. Premium-Luxury.

Vern Hippensteal is an artist who produces scenes of the Smokies in watercolors, limited-edition prints, and pen and ink sketches. His biggest creation, however, is **Hippensteal's Mountain View Inn,** tel. (423) 436-5761 or (800) 527-8110, an eleven-room inn in the Gatlinburg Arts and Crafts Community. Each room has a fireplace, comfortable reading chairs, television, and private bath with whirlpool tub. A large common room enables guests to mingle, and many delight in taking in the view from rocking chairs on the wide porches that wrap around the inn. Rate is $135 per night. See www.hippensteal.com for more information. Premium.

The **Olde English Tudor Inn Bed & Breakfast,** 135 W. Holly Ridge Rd., tel. (423) 436-7760 or (800) 541-3798, is close enough to downtown Gatlinburg to walk to most of the attractions. The three-story building has an English garden and a waterfall out front. The eight guest rooms plus a cottage all have private baths and cable TV. The common room contains a TV and a woodstove, and a large breakfast is served. Rates are $79-150. See their Web site at www.oldenglishtudorinn.com. Moderate-Premium.

7th Heaven Log Inn, 3944 Castle Rd., tel. (423) 430-5000 or (800) 248-2923, sits beside the seventh green of the Bent Creek Golf Club outside Gatlinburg. The log structure contains five guest rooms, all with private baths. All have access to a big deck with a hot tub and a large recreation room with pool table, television, and various games. Unlike some B&Bs, in which guests feel as if they are in someone else's house, this place was built from the start as an inn. Guests have their own entrance and access to a full kitchen. Breakfast is a five-course affair with homemade bread. Rates run $87-137. Find out more at www.7heaven.com. Expensive-Premium.

Sitting a thousand feet above the town of Gatlinburg, the **Tennessee Ridge Inn Bed and Breakfast,** 507 Campbell Lead, tel. (423) 436-4068, has stunning views of the Great Smokies. The 8,500-square-foot, three-story house has a dining room with glass on three sides. Guests can choose from seven rooms, five of them with whirlpool baths. Breakfast is a full-service, sit-down affair that changes daily, from a full country meal to individual casseroles. Rates range $75-135. See the place online at www.tn-ridge.com. Moderate-Premium.

Cabins, Condos, and Chalets

The offices that rent cabins, condos, and chalets are usually not on-site; call the agents for full details on their listings.

The cabins at **Heritage Hollow,** tel. (800) 359-6117, are 100-year-old genuine cabins furnished with antiques and country collectible furniture. Equipped with modern kitchens and baths, they have an authenticity that is hard to find in these parts.

Find other places through **Alan's Mountain Rentals,** tel. (423) 436-2512 or (800) 843-0457; **Edelweiss Condominiums,** tel. (423) 436-7846 or (800) 824-4077; **High Chalet Condominium Rentals,** tel. (423) 430-2193 or (800) 225-3834; **Log Cabins of Gatlinburg,** tel. (423) 436-7686 or (800) 666-7686; **Masons Mountain Manors,** tel. (800) 645-4911; and **Smoky Top Rentals,** tel. (800) 468-6813.

Motels

The following are just a few of the motels in Gatlinburg. Call (800) 568-4748 for a more complete list and ask for the Vacation Guide.

A good choice among Moderate-priced motels is **Brookside Resort,** East Parkway, tel. (423) 436-5611 or (800) 251-9597.

The places that will set you back more include: **Edgewater Hotel,** 402 River Rd., tel. (423) 436-4151, in Tennessee tel. (800) 423-4532, outside of Tennessee tel. (800) 423-9582; **River Terrace Resort & Convention Center,** 240 River Rd., tel. (423) 436-5161 or (800) 251-2040; and **Rocky Waters Motor Inn,** Parkway, tel. (423) 436-7861 or (800) 824-1111.

Camping

Crazy Horse Campground, 12.5 miles up Hwy. 321 from Gatlinburg, tel. (423) 436-4434 or (800) 528-9003, has 207 sites and full amenities. It's open April-October.

Dudley Creek Travel Trailer Park and Log Cabins, just a half-mile from downtown G-burg on the Pigeon Forge end of the Parkway, tel. (423) 436-5053, has 105 sites with the works and is open all year.

Great Smoky Jellystone Park Camp Resort, 14 miles east of town on Hwy. 321, tel. (423) 487-5534 or (800) 210-2119, offers 110 sites. Open April-Nov., it has all the amenities.

LeConte Vista RV Resort and Campground sits four miles east of town on Hwy. 321, tel. (423) 436-5437. Open March-Dec., it has all the works spread over 85 sites.

Outdoor Resort, 10 miles out on Hwy. 321, tel. (423) 436-5861 or (800) 677-5861, has 150 sites and a wide range of amenities. It's open all year. No tents are permitted.

Trout Creek Campground, three miles out of Gatlinburg on Hwy. 321, tel. (423) 436-5905, has 75 sites. Open April-Nov., it offers the works.

Twin Creek RV Resort offers 75 sites within the city limits of Gatlinburg on Hwy. 321, tel. (423) 436-7081 or (800) 252-8077, and has all the amenities. It's open April-October. No tents.

FOOD

The **Buckhorn Inn,** 2140 Tudor Mountain Rd., tel. (423) 436-4668, outside of Gatlinburg offers perhaps the finest and most luxurious meals in the area. Typical entrees include poached fillets of salmon and red snapper with champagne dill sauce, or grilled lamb chops with rosemary butter. One of the appetizers frequently served is cappellini with prosciutto and fontina cheese in basil sauce. Bring your own bottle. Seating at the inn is limited; guests have first choice, and everyone else must make reservations no later than 10 a.m. on the day they wish to dine. Dinner is served at 7 p.m. and has a fixed price, usually about $30 and worth every penny. To get to the inn, take Hwy. 321 North out of Gatlinburg. Pass Glades Rd. on the left. Take Buckhorn Rd. to the left, then go right on Tudor Mountain Road. See them online at www.buckhorninn.com.

The **Burning Bush Restaurant** lies about 30 feet from the park boundary at 1151 Pkwy., tel. (423) 436-4669, and patrons can gaze out the windows and watch squirrels cavorting. The food is basic American fare, several notches up from country cooking. Breakfasts come with a glass of LeConte Sunrise, a mixture of fruit juices. It's open 365 days a year.

Calhoun's, 1004 Pkwy., tel. (423) 436-4100, is a chain offering ribs, prime rib, seafood, and chicken. It serves lunch and dinner seven days a week.

The Greenbriar, 370 Newman Rd., tel. (423)

436-6318, lies east of Gatlinburg off Hwy. 321 in a log structure built by George Dempster, who was the mayor of Knoxville and of the Dempster Dumpster family. This place serves dinner only, year-round, and diners can choose from entrees such as slow-cooked prime rib or Smoky Mountains strip steak, marinated in olive oil and garlic for several days.

The Little Italian Restaurant, 463 Pkwy., tel. (423) 436-7880, makes its own sausage, meatballs, bread, and sauces. It serves lunch and dinner every day.

Maxwells Beef & Seafood, 1103 Pkwy., tel. (423) 436-3738, features fresh seafood and steaks, prime rib, and lamb. Begin with wine or cocktails, and finish off with a flambé dessert. It's open for dinner seven days a week.

Open Hearth, on the Parkway at the entrance to the Smokies, tel. (423) 436-5648, offers fresh trout or salmon, barbecued ribs, and steak along with an extensive wine list. It's open every day all year for dinner only.

The Park Grill, 1110 Parkway, tel. (423) 436-2300, has a wonderful log building that pays homage to the sorts of lodges one might see in the Adirondacks or in Yellowstone National Park. The logs came from Idaho, and it took seven trucks to bring them to Gatlinburg. The food—all with Smoky-oriented names—ranges from "Moonshine Chicken" to Franklin Delano Rib Eye. This place takes no reservations, so get on the list and then go for a stroll. See them online at www.peddlerparkgrill.com.

Smoky Mountain Brewery and Restaurant located behind 1004 Parkway, is a wonderful place to come back to after a long hard hike through the mountains. Away from the Parkway, there are always at least eight microbrews on hand for the tasting. Some nights bring live music, with karaoke on other nights. The food is pizza, sandwiches, and burgers for lunch and steaks, trout, and ribs for dinner.

On the Great Smoky Arts and Crafts Trail

For those whose eyes have glazed over after seeing too much pottery and need a light lunch, this is the place. **The Wild Plum Tearoom,** 555 Buckhorn Rd., tel. (423) 436-3808, is open for lunch only from March through mid-December. Try one of their combo plates of pasta salad, chicken salad, and fruit, and don't forget the wild plum tea.

SHOPPING

Unlike Pigeon Forge, Gatlinburg has no large outlet malls. Instead, dozens of small shops sell just about anything a visitor could want. Here is a highly idiosyncratic list of favorites.

Armour House, in the Marketplace at 651 Pkwy., tel. (423) 430-2101 or (800) 886-1862, sells Civil War paintings, books, and artifacts.

The Happy Hiker, tel. (423) 436-5632 or (800) HIKER-01, caters to outdoor enthusiasts by offering all manner of outdoor clothing and camping gear. Here's the place to rent backpacks, sleeping bags, tents, and stoves. Returning hikers can take showers and do laundry. This useful place lies between the Parkway and River Rd. behind the Burning Bush Restaurant, very close to the entrance to the park. It's on the Web at www.happyhiker.com.

Arts and Crafts

The Gatlinburg area has long been known for its arts and crafts. The self-sufficient mountaineers produced quilts, pottery, and other day-to-day items, and through the years the presence of tourists lured other artists to town. When rents for shop space in town became oppressive, a few artists started selling things out of their houses. Thus evolved the Gatlinburg **Great Smoky Arts and Crafts Community** on two roads east of town—Buckhorn and Glades—that lie off Hwy. 321. The trolley goes there as well.

Shops offer leather goods, baskets, quilts and rugs, woodcarvings, brooms, candles, pottery, and stained glass. Others sell wooden toys and puzzles, dulcimers, photographs, and oil paintings. Here visitors can escape the crowds and drive from shop to shop in the woods. Many craftspeople make their items in studios beside their shops and sometimes take time to talk to visitors.

Highlights along the way include **Ogle's Broom Shop,** which produces fireplace brooms, traditional mountain brooms, and walking sticks on Glades Road. **Alewine Pottery,** on the same road, sells very attractive pieces. Those who want to go home with a great photograph of the Smokies should stop at **A Frame of Mind,** also on Glades Road. Most of these stores are open daily, but during the winter many reduce hours or open only on weekends.

The **Arrowcraft Shop,** tel. (423) 436-4604, occupies one of the oldest and most beautiful buildings in town. Built in 1939, it features native hand-split slate. The rooms inside are paneled in chestnut, which gives the visitor a glimpse of this hardwood that once dominated nearby forests. The shop sells the work of local and regional artists—not the students at Arrowmont—and is operated by the Southern Highland Craft Guild.

The **Jim Gray Gallery,** at The Carousel Mall (traffic light no. 3), tel. (423) 436-5262, and at 670 Glades Rd., tel. (423) 436-8988, sells works in a variety of media, including oils, drawings, and statues, from one of the state's most talented and famous artists.

The **Vern Hippensteal Gallery,** 452 Pkwy., tel. (423) 436-4328 or (800) 537-8110, features the work of this Gatlinburg resident—watercolors, limited-edition prints, and pen and ink sketches of the Smokies. Open seven days a week all year long.

More than 300 locally made quilts await shoppers at **Quilts by Wilma,** which is 3.5 miles up Hwy. 321 from traffic light no. 3, tel. (423) 436-5664. None are imported and none are machine-quilted. Some have pieces no larger than postage stamps. Call ahead.

INFORMATION

The **Gatlinburg Welcome Center,** on the Parkway at the Pigeon Forge side of town, tel. (423) 436-0519 or (800) 568-4748, is open Mon.-Sat. 8 a.m.-6 p.m. and Sunday 9 a.m.-5 p.m. Find them online at www.gatlinburgtennessee.com.

a gnarled-handle broom

EASTERN GATEWAYS

COSBY

This little town has escaped the industrial-strength tourism of this side of the Smokies, and is home to several celebrations of East Tennessee life. The first stop, particularly for music lovers, should be the **Musicrafts,** a.k.a. The Folklife Center of the Smokies, tel. (423) 487-5543. To get there from Gatlinburg, take Hwy. 321 until it intersects with Hwy. 32. Go right on Hwy. 32 for less than a mile and turn right. Founded almost 30 years ago, the center publishes books, releases recordings of folk music, and distributes the work of others. It also sells dulcimers (a cherrywood one goes for $750), hammered dulcimers, and other instruments. The center is open daily from 10 a.m. until "5 or so" and may close during cold winter weekends.

Perhaps the best time to visit the Folk Life Center is during one of the festivals. The **Dulcimer and Harp Festival** begins on the second Friday in June, and other, smaller gatherings are held Memorial Day, the Fourth of July, and Labor Day weekends. Each takes place on Saturday and is characterized by traditional mountain music, covered-dish meals, old-time dancing, and other events.

The longest-running gathering in Cosby is the **Ramp Festival,** a celebration of ramps, a pungent, onionlike plant that has been described as "the gift that keeps giving"—in one's breath and through one's pores. Ramps are eaten in omelets, straight, or as side dishes along with barbecue and chicken. The festival, held the first Sunday in May, is a one-day affair consisting of music, crafts, the selection of the "Maid Of Ramps," and plenty of hand-picked bluegrass music. Admission is $5 for adults and $3 for kids. Call (423) 487-3492 or (423) 623-5410.

Food

Cosby Barbecue Pit, Hwy. 321 near the Cosby Post Office, tel. (423) 487-5438, offers ribs, pork barbecue, hamburgers, and steaks. It's open seven days a week except Dec.-March, when it is open only on weekends.

The Front Porch, on Hwy. 321 halfway between Cosby and Newport, tel. (423) 487-2875, itself is worth coming to Cosby. This restaurant features a trained culinarian as chef—a rarity in these parts—and this evidences itself in portobello mushroom steaks, rib-eye steak, and dry ribs. Patrons can also enjoy live bluegrass and occasionally blues. Open only Fri.-Sun, this place serves lunch and dinner consisting of enchiladas, chimichangas, and other Mexican dishes,

the genuine articles: Gene and Lee Schilling, owners of Musicrafts

as well as vegetarian versions thereof. American food is available, too, especially ribs, as well as Italian dishes. The experience of eating ribs while listening to someone playing blues harp is about as down-home as one can get.

Get seats early for dinner; the music takes off at 8:30 p.m. and soars until 10:30 or 11. There is no cover charge, although diners are expected to order at least $4 worth of food, and the band is very likely to pass the hat. Brown-bagging is permitted. Sunday night's atmosphere is more akin to that of a coffeehouse.

One of a Kind Place
Halfway between Cosby and Newport stands **Fort Marx,** tel. (423) 487-2112, a singular establishment up Dark Hollow Road, an address that sounds right out of a bluegrass song. Octagenarian Fred Marx is the owner of this extremely distinctive drinking establishment, although a younger couple runs the place, which is alleged to occasionally serve a liquid derivative from locally grown corn. Guests have included Dale Ernhardt and Tanya Tucker, and if the visitor has no clue as to who those two are, then he or she had best not come to Fort Marx. It is open every day except Sunday from 4 p.m. "until everyone goes home."

To get there from Cosby, go north on Hwy. 321 to Wilton Springs Road. Turn right and drive one mile to Dark Hollow Rd. which goes off to the right just before a bridge. Go one mile and look up on the hill on the right. And don't get in any arguments inside.

Shopping
Cosby is also home to several apple orchards. **Carver's Orchard,** on Hwy. 321 about 3.5 miles beyond the Cosby post office, tel. (423) 487-2419, grows more than 100 varieties of apples, old favorites as well as exotics such as Ginger Gold, Jena Gold, and Fuji. Apple harvesting begins in June and extends well into the fall. Visitors are welcome to watch cider being pressed, taste it, and buy apples, honey, molasses, pumpkins, and Indian corn. Carver's is open seven days a week year-round.

Holloways Country Home, in a log building at 3892 Hwy. 321, tel. (423) 487-3866, offers high-quality quilts—usually 80 to 100 in the store at any given time—clothing, and quilting supplies.

NEWPORT

Anyone who has eaten canned vegetables or made pasta sauce from canned tomatoes has probably had an inadvertent brush with Newport. About the turn of the century the Stokely family began canning tomatoes and shipping them downstream to the growing cities of Knoxville and Chattanooga. The company headquarters was in Newport, and the company grew so strong that it bought Van Camp, an Indiana food producer. Even though the headquarters then moved to Indianapolis, Stokely remained a big name in Newport until the operations merged with Quaker Products.

Although the Stokelys produced comestibles, one branch of the family has turned to food for the mind. James Stokely, son of the first president of the family firm, married Wilma Dykeman of Asheville, North Carolina, and together they wrote books on the causes of racism and about the lives of people who worked to overcome it. On her own, Dykeman has published a series of novels, all listed in the back of this book, as well as a history of the state. Her writings on Tennessee, fiction as well as nonfiction, have illuminated the state in a manner that few writers can match. Jim Stokely, their son, continued the literary tradition with his co-editorship of *An Encyclopedia of East Tennessee.*

Newport and surrounding Cocke County used to be home to entrepreneurs who became skilled at transforming corn into a much more portable and potable product. At one time it was said that more Mason jars were sold in Newport than anywhere in the country.

Motorists in Newport, and in Pigeon Forge and Gatlinburg, notice right off that all the traffic lights on Main Street are numbered. Someone giving directions will say, "Go to light no. 4 and turn right" or something to that effect. This is an idea that ought to be followed elsewhere.

While driving along Main St., take a look at the building to the right at traffic light no. 9. The stone building is the **Rhea-Mims Hotel,** at one time one of the more famous hostelries in these parts. The round stones prominent in the walls are said to be Indian mill wheels.

At the corner marked by traffic light no. 3, turn onto Hwy. 321 to see the **Cocke County Mu-**

seum, tel. (423) 623-7201, and Newport Chamber of Commerce. Here one can get information about the past and the present. The former includes artifacts from Ben Hooper, a local boy who became governor of the state, and from Grace Moore, a singer from the nearby community of Del Rio who sang in New York's Metropolitan Opera. The museum is open Mon.-Fri. by appointment only. Admission is free.

A far different music was played and sung by "Pappy Gube" Beaver, a Newport native who appeared on Knoxville radio stations and released several records. According to an article in Barry McCloud's *Definitive Country,* Beaver gave up "singing for the devil" and became a minister noted for his tent revivals, wherein he would get so enthusiastic he would stand on his head or climb poles, truly an example of that old-time religion.

The nearby community of Bybee is the birthplace of the late Buster Moore, half of the husband-and-wife team of Bonnie Lou and Buster, whose homegrown bluegrass and country music graced local television in Appalachia for decades.

Where to Stay

Most of Newport's lodging lies along I-40. Here the weary will find: **Best Western Motel,** tel. (423) 623-8713 or (800) 528-1234; **Family Inns,** tel. (423) 623-6033 and (423) 623-2626; and **Holiday Inn,** tel. (423) 623-8622.

Just off I-40 and open all year, **Newport KOA,** tel. (423) 623-9004, offers 75 sites, hookups, laundry, swimming pool, fishing, and recreation hall.

TMC Campground, 112 Carson Springs Rd., tel. (423) 625-0433, is also open all year and has 210 sites, hookups, a store, a pool, and pretty much the works.

Food

A visit to **The Grease Rack,** tel. (423) 623-9279, gave one diner a sense of what it must have been like to go to a speakeasy. The parking lot of the former garage—thus the name—was full of cars and pickup trucks, yet the door was locked. After a tentative knock, then the door opened, revealing a honky-tonk bar with country music blaring away. All the patrons turned to inspect the visitor. "Is this a restaurant?" "Sure," came the reply, "just follow me." In the back was a large, windowless room

filled with all manner of folks—couples, families, and singles. Steak and seafood is the fare here, in generous portions. It's open for dinner Wednesday-Saturday. To get there from the interstate, go to traffic light no. 12, then right for 0.7 miles on Lincoln Avenue. At a blinking yellow light go 0.3 miles on Morrell Springs Road. To see a lively side of Cocke County, secure a table when a University of Tennessee football game is being televised on a Saturday night.

The **Fox and Hounds,** on Fox and Hounds Ln., tel. (423) 623-9161, is a bit more sedate and considered Newport's premier restaurant. Steaks, prime rib, and seafood make up the menu, served for lunch and dinner Monday-Saturday. To get there, get off I-40 at Exit 432B and go north on Hwy. 25/70 for about a mile and a half. The driveway to the restaurant is between Slammer's and Knight's Auto.

The **Log Cabin Inn,** 2477 Elkway, tel. (423) 623-5959, features a buffet of country cooking for dinner Thurs.-Sat. and for lunch on Sunday.

Newport is also the home of one of the best Thai restaurants in East Tennessee. The **Thai Kitchen,** at 323 Village Shopping Center, tel. (423) 623-2752, serves traditional Thai food for lunch Mon.-Fri. and dinner Monday-Saturday.

Just outside of town, Greek-American food is the order of the day at **C.J. Papadops,** 551 Briar Thicket Rd., tel. (423) 623-0933. Located down Hwy. 160 between Morristown and Newport, here one can have lamb and Greek salads as well as steak, lasagna, and spaghetti. This place is open for dinner Thursday-Sunday.

Information

Visit the **Newport/Cocke County Chamber of Commerce,** 803 Prospect St., tel. (423) 623-7201, or the tourism office at (423) 625-9675. Or see them online at www.cockecounty.com.

DANDRIDGE

Here is a town whose historic buildings, though on the National Register, are still inhabited, where cute little shops have not invaded, and where the drugstore still has a lunch counter.

Dandridge, as far as anyone knows, is the nation's only town named for Martha Dandridge Custis Washington, wife of George. Created in

RAFTING COMPANIES

Rafting and kayaking are becoming big business in the Smokies. Generally speaking, the boating on the Tennessee side of the Smokies is considerably milder than that on the Nantahala River in North Carolina. Both are listed here.

Big Pigeon Rafting, tel. (423) 487-2080 or (800) 438-9938, offers trips on the Big Pigeon River.

Blue Ridge Outing, tel. (800) 572-3510.

Carolina Outfitters Whitewater Rafting, 12121 Hwy. 19 West, Bryson City, tel. (800) 468-7238.

Cherokee Adventures, tel. (800) 445-7235, runs the Nolichucky and Pigeon Rivers.

Endless River Adventures, tel. (800) 224-RAFT, runs the Nantahala.

Family Adventure, on Hwy. 321 about six miles out of Gatlinburg, tel. (423) 436-5008, offers whitewater rafting on the Big Pigeon and Nantahala Rivers from late March through October. The Big Pigeon trip is for ages four and up in Class I water. It lasts about one hour and costs $16.28 per person. The Nantahala trip lasts three to three and one-half hours on Class II and III water. Rafters must weigh 60 pounds to make this trip, which costs $25.06 per person.

The **Nantahala Outdoor Center,** tel. (800) 232-RAFT, takes rafters on the Nolichucky, Nantahala, and French Broad Rivers.

Rafting in the Smokies, tel. (800) PRO-RAFT, goes down the Pigeon, Nantahala, and French Broad Rivers.

Wahoos, tel. (800) 444-RAFT, offers trips on the Pigeon, Nolichucky, and French Broad Rivers.

Whitewater Rafting, based in Hot Springs, North Carolina, tel. (800) 872-7437, runs the Nolichucky and French Broad Rivers.

1793, Dandridge became the county seat of Jefferson County. Troops moved back and forth through the town during the Civil War. One night a Union general stayed in a local house. Events the next day caused him to depart in haste, leaving a bottle of very good brandy. That night Confederates stayed in the same house and made humorous toasts with the brandy until it was gone.

Dandridge may have been named after Mrs. Washington, but another president's wife once saved the town. When TVA was planning Douglas Dam on the French Broad River, it looked like curtains for Dandridge—the town would soon be under water. A local grande dame bombarded senators with letters, to no avail, but finally she sent her poems and pleas to Eleanor Roosevelt, who prevailed on Franklin to issue a presidential decree ordering that a dike be built to save the town. Newcomers still get a surprise when they climb what looks like a big hill behind the town and top it to see a great expanse of water.

The **Jefferson County Courthouse** contains one of those wonderfully eclectic museums that fill Tennessee. Here, in corridors that lead to offices of assorted bureaucrats, one can gaze (free) on a hornet's nest, a World War II German helmet, Vietnamese sandals, the remnants of a moonshine still, Civil War bullets, and the marriage license issued to one David Crockett. The courthouse is generally open Mon.-Fri. 8 a.m.-4 p.m., and Saturday 8-11 a.m.

Across the street lies **Tinsley-Bible Drugs,** tel. (423) 397-3444, a store with old furnishings and new merchandise. The action, however, takes place at the six-seat lunch counter, where a cheeseburger is inexpensive but the accompanying dose of small-town life is priceless. Here one will see county officials—one dignified-looking gent addressed as "Judge"—giggling high school girls, and assorted others.

Birds of an entirely different feather live out of town on an ostrich farm that one can see from Hwy. 25/70. Go almost two miles past the bridge over the French Broad River. The farm has no provisions for visitors, but people can pull off and gawk through the fence.

Where to Stay

The Barrington Inn, 1174 McGuire Rd., New Market, tel. (888) 205-8482 or (423) 397-3368, is actually out in the country between Dandridge and New Market, but a mere 2.5 miles off I-40. The Inn offers four rooms in a restored farmhouse and three more in a Dairy House. All rooms have some sort of sitting area as well as private baths. Rates range from $75 to $125. Perhaps the best reason to stay here is for the food, which is described below. Dinner is available to guests every night by prior arrangement. See them online at www.bbonline.com/TN/Barrington. Moderate-Premium.

Take Hwy. 139 West out of Dandridge for a pleasant drive to the **Mountain Harbor Inn,** 1199 Hwy. 139, Dandridge, TN 37725, tel. (423) 397-3345, a more modern place right on Douglas Lake where one can look across the water and see the Smoky Mountains. All 12 rooms have quilts hanging on the walls and come with microwave ovens, coffeemakers, refrigerators, and private baths. Rates are $85-135. Expensive-Premium.

Douglas Lake Campground is the closest to Dandridge, offering 100 sites with full hookups available, a laundromat, boating, fishing, and swimming. To get there, go east on Hwy. 9 out of town. Turn right on Oak Grove Road.

Fancher's Willow Branch Campground lies on the French Broad River (Douglas Lake) upstream from Dandridge. It has 150 sites with hookups, boating, swimming, and fishing. It also has a lot of noise from the traffic on I-40. Take Hwy. 9 east out of town, cross the river, and look for the sign.

Food

The Barrington Inn, 1174 McGuire Rd., New Market, tel. (888) 205-8482 or (423) 397-3368, is one of the better restaurants on this end of the state. Dinner is offered to non-guests Thursday through Saturday nights by a couple who used to run a restaurant in Key West. The menu constantly changes due to the availability of the food, but typical entrees include New Zealand grilled lamb chops, beef Wellington, ground ostrich wrapped in veal, and lobster and shrimp croustade. These cost less than $25 per person. It doesn't get much better than this.

Cowboys on the Water, 1435 Hwy. 139, tel. (423) 397-2529, has a name that doesn't make sense until diners understand that "Cowboy" was the founder of this very informal and very fun place. There's fishing and western gear on the walls, sawdust and peanut shells on the floor, but it's what's on the plates that keeps people coming back: shrimp, clams, flounder, catfish, crab legs, as well as steak and burgers. Open every day for dinner only.

Dandridge Seafood Restaurant, on Meeting St., tel. (423) 397-2315, offers catfish, flounder, shrimp, and orange roughy, as well as steaks.

Or try the restaurant at **Mountain Harbor Inn,** 1199 Hwy. 139, tel. (423) 397-3345. The restaurant is open Wednesday-Saturday. Reservations are a good idea. Prime rib is the specialty of the house—10 ounces for $18—while grilled chicken breast and chargrilled fish are available as well. Lunch is served Tues.-Sat. and includes a wide choice of sandwiches, salads, and pastas.

If you want a burger, and the Tinsley-Bible Drugs lunch counter doesn't satisfy, go to the Dandridge Exit of I-40, Exit 417, for a selection of franchise restaurants.

TOWNSEND

Townsend bills itself as "the peaceful side of the Smokies," and, compared to Gatlinburg and Pigeon Forge, that's certainly the truth. Townsend lies in a cove—a flat area in mountain parlance—called Tuckaleechee Cove. Tourists have been coming to this area since 1904, when the railroad came through.

Millions of people across the country have seen Townsend without realizing it as they watched CBS's (later the Family Channel's) *Christy,* the saga of a young teacher who comes to a remote mountain area to teach school. The story comes from the novel of the same name by Catherine Marshall.

Townsend is home to **Earthtide School of Folk Art,** in a yellow house next to the Townsend Post Office, 7645 E. Lamar Alexander Pkwy., tel. (423) 448-1106, which offers people a chance to take classes that last an afternoon, three or four days, or longer. The subjects include basketry, drawing, pottery, spinning, weaving, and the study of wild foods and medicinal plants. A gallery on the premises features the work of the school's instructors as well as other local craftspeople. Passersby are welcome to watch various artists at work.

SIGHTS

People who want to see the greatest concentration of wildflowers in this region—400+ species—should beat a path to **Hedgewood Gardens,** Bethel Church Rd. off Hwy. 321, tel. (423) 984-2052. A woman named Hedy Wood designed the six acres of gardens to look as natural as possible, nurturing them for 23 years. She died in 1993 and her daughter, Hope Woodard, has opened the gardens to the public by appointment only.

View Townsend's nonfictional history at the **Little River Railroad & Lumber Company Museum** on Hwy. 321, tel. (423) 448-2211. Most people who look at the verdant forests hereabouts can't imagine that most of it was at one time cut down. This free museum gives a sense of what those times were like with a restored Shay locomotive, depot, and steam-powered sawmill. It is open every day in the summer and in October, and weekends only in May and September.

Tuckaleechee Caverns, 825 Caverns Dr., tel. (423) 448-2274, also cools off visitors, but only to 58°. With the usual colorfully named geological features, a visit to this cave is a great rainy day excursion. Home to a huge room approximately 400 feet by 150 feet, it is open March 15 through November 15. Admission is $8 for adults, $4 for children 5 to 11, and free for children under five.

RECREATION

The Townsend "Y" has nothing to do with the YMCA, but it is perhaps the best swimming hole in these parts. Just inside the park, two streams come together in a pool deep enough to entice brave (and exceedingly warm-blooded) souls to jump off rocks into it. The only bad news is that this attracts a great many people of the yahoo persuasion, who can get very tiresome.

Farther downstream is **River Romp Tubes,** 8203 Hwy. 73, tel. (423) 448-1522. Located in the Bodywear Outlet store at the junction of Hwy. 321 and Hwy. 73, this place rents high quality inner tubes and life jackets for the float down the Little River.

On Horseback
Cades Cove Riding Stables, in the Walland area between Townsend and Maryville at 4035 E. Lamar Alexander Pkwy., tel. (423) 448-6286, offers horseback rides, carriage rides, and hayrides through Cades Cove in the park. It's open April-October.

Davy Crockett Riding Stables, 232 Stables Dr. near the park boundary, tel. (423) 448-6411, does not require customers to wear coonskin hats on its guided rides. It's open every day except Christmas.

Double M Ranch, 4033 Miser Station Rd., tel. (423) 995-9421, has horse rides, hiking, and a paved road for bicycling.

On Foot

Little River Outfitters, 7807 E. Lamar Alexander Pkwy., tel. (423) 448-9459, is both a fly shop and a guide service, backpacking store and clothing shop.

ENTERTAINMENT AND EVENTS

The **Townsend in the Smokies Spring Festival** takes place during one week in April, and the **Autumn Leaves Arts & Crafts Fair** is held for a week in September. Contact the **Townsend Visitors Center,** 7906 E. Lamar Alexander Pkwy., a.k.a. Hwy. 321/73, tel. (423) 448-6134 or (800) 525-6834, for more information.

WHERE TO STAY

Bed and Breakfasts and Inns

Staying at the **Richmont Inn,** 220 Winterberry Ln., tel. (423) 448-6751, is reason enough to visit this side of the Smokies. The inn was built to resemble the cantilevered Appalachian barns found only in East Tennessee and western North Carolina. Inside, however, the traveler finds 18th-century English antiques, French paintings, and Swiss cooking. The 10 rooms are named for prominent Appalachian folks and contain whirlpool baths, king-sized beds, fireplaces, and balconies. Rates range $100-150 per night. The rooms are among the best to be found in these parts, but the food is icing on the cake—literally. Room rates include a candlelit dessert prepared by a chef who once won the grand prize in *Gourmet* magazine's dessert recipe contest. Breakfast consists of dishes such as French baked eggs or French toast à l'orange. Find the Inn online at www.thesmokies.com/richmont_inn. Expensive-Premium.

The **Blackberry,** 1471 W. Millers Cove Rd., tel. (423) 984-8166, hearkens to the grand hotels of old, where guests went to one place, paid one price, and spent all their time there. This elegant inn sits on 1,100 acres and has 44 guest rooms, all furnished with English and American antiques and priced at $395-695 per night. The price includes three gourmet meals per day and fully stocked pantries. Once guests stagger from

the table, they can work off the calories at a fitness center, four tennis courts, a swimming pool, a trout pond, a three-acre bass and bream lake, and two off-site golf courses. Equipment available for use includes mountain bikes, fly-fishing gear, golf carts, binoculars, and tennis rackets. See them online at www.blackberryhotel.com. Luxury.

Terrapin Point Retreat, 426 Cameron Rd., tel. (423) 448-6010, has a suite with mountain views, whirlpool bath, and private bath. Rates are $110 per night. Expensive.

At the **Twin Valley Bed and Breakfast Horse Ranch,** 2848 Old Chilhowee Rd. in Walland, tel. (423) 984-0980, energetic guests can pitch in with taking care of the horses, while the rest can just relax. This is not one of those B&Bs filled with antique English furniture, but it is a comfortable place where guests can walk around. This bed and breakfast is housed in a hand-hewn log building decorated in country style. The two rooms share a bath, and cabins are also available, as are backwoods wilderness shelters. The ranch serves a full country breakfast. Rates range $75-95. See them online at www.bbonline.com/ten/twinvalley. Moderate-Expensive.

Cabins, Condos, and Chalets

The following is a short list of what is available in Townsend. For a more complete list, call (800) 525-6834.

Gilbertson's Lazy Horse Retreat, tel. (423) 448-6647; **Laurel Valley/White Oak Realty-Cabin Rentals,** tel. (423) 448-6697; **Mountain Laurel Cabins,** tel. (423) 448-9657; **Pioneer Cabins and Guest Farm,** tel. (423) 448-6100 or (800) 621-9751; **Goode Night Vacation Rentals,** tel. (423) 448-6842; and the **Timberwinds Log Cabin Rentals,** tel. (800) 359-1507.

Motels

Among the options are the **Best Western Valley View Lodge,** Hwy. 321, tel. (423) 448-2237 or (800) 292-4844; **Big Valley Motel,** 7052 E. Lamar Alexander Pkwy., tel. (423) 448-6639; **Hampton Inn,** 7824 E. Lamar Alexander Pkwy., tel. (423) 448-9000 or (800) HAMPTON; **Highland Manor Motel,** Hwy. 321, tel. (800) 213-9462; and **Talley-Ho Inn,** 8314 Hwy. 73, tel. (423) 448-2465 or (800) 448-2465.

Camping

All of the campgrounds in the Townsend area lie between Wears Valley Rd. and the entrance to the park along the Little River.

The 75 sites at **Lazy Daze Campground,** 8429 Hwy. 73, tel. (423) 448-6061, some of them along the Little River and all with cable TV, await campers here. It's open all year.

Little River Village Campground, tel. (423) 448-2241, also lies along the Little River, with 136 sites and all the amenities. It's open March-November.

Mountaineer Campground, on the Little River, tel. (423) 448-6421, offers 49 sites and is open all year.

The 144 sites at **Tremont Hill's Campground,** tel. (423) 448-6363, are open from March 1 to the Sunday after Thanksgiving.

Ye-Olde-Mill Anderson's Campground, tel. (423) 448-6681, offers 26 sites and fewer of the amenities than the larger places. It's open April-November.

MORE PRACTICALITIES

Food

The **Carriage House,** 8310 Hwy. 73, tel. (423) 448-2263, serves three daily meals of country cooking April-November 15.

The **Creekside Inn,** 7016 E. Lamar Alexander Pkwy., tel. (423) 448-1215, has steaks, seafood, pasta, and dishes such as teriyaki chicken.

Laurel Valley Country Club, tel. (423) 448-9534, serves dinner on Friday and Saturday, brunch on Sunday, and lunch Monday-Friday. Meals include shrimp marinara, wild boar tenderloin, and grilled chicken. To get to the club, take Old Tuckaleechee Rd. off Hwy. 321, go two miles, and follow the signs.

Mill House Restaurant, 4737 Old Walland Hwy., tel. (423) 982-5726, occupies what used to be the home of a mill owner on the Little River. The mill is no more, but the house has been transformed into what is perhaps the best place to eat on this side of the Smokies. The Mill House is a prix fixe restaurant—one in which all meals cost the same, in this case around $20. Seven courses make up the meal, with entrees of steak, seafood, chicken, or pork. The ambience is very relaxed; diners linger for a long time over the delicious meals. Reservations are a very good idea. To get there, leave Townsend and drive toward Maryville. Watch for the sign 1.5 miles past the Walland turnoff. Open weekends only.

T.J.'s Smoky Mountain Bar-B-Q, 7305 E. Lamar Alexander Pkwy., tel. (423) 448-9420, offers beef, pork, ribs, and chicken—takeout or eat in.

Shopping

Lee Roberson's Studio/Gallery, 758 Wears Valley Rd., tel. (423) 448-2365, presents idealized scenes of the Smokies past and present. The artist's prints and other work are available at this gallery, which is just two miles outside Townsend.

Nancy's Art & Frame Shop, 7249 E. Lamar Alexander Pkwy., tel. (423) 448-6377, sells prints of local scenes by a variety of artists.

Information

Beside the Hampton Inn one will find the **Townsend Visitors Center** at 7906 E. Lamar Alexander Pkwy., a.k.a. Hwy. 321/73, tel. (423) 448-6134 or (800) 525-6834. It's open daily 9 a.m.-6 p.m., except in January and February, when it is open only Friday-Sunday. You'll find more Smokies information online at www.smokymountains.org.

MARYVILLE

This town is the county seat of Blount County and was named for the wife of Governor Blount. This part of Tennessee saw a lot of conflict between the Indians and the settlers as the latter moved closer to the strongholds of the former. When the edge of the frontier was pushed west and south, Maryville lay on the route back east, and it prospered from travelers and trade.

Sam Houston (see special topic) moved to the area from Virginia when he was 14 years old, and when he was 19 taught school for one term in a log schoolhouse that still stands. In 1819 a Presbyterian minister founded a seminary that eventually became Maryville College. The college broke ground in many ways: it was the first seminary in the South, one of the first colleges to offer co-education, and one of the few colleges open to black and Indian students.

Maryville is the birthplace of Lamar Alexander, Republican governor of Tennessee from 1979-87, the first governor to be elected to consecutive four-year terms. He campaigned by wearing a plaid shirt and jeans and walking across the state. He has yet to get a leg up in his perennial presidential races, however, and threatens to become the Harold Stassen of our time.

SIGHTS

The **Sam Houston Schoolhouse,** tel. (423) 983-1550, where the future president of the Republic of Texas served as a 19-year-old teacher, is a small structure built of poplar logs. It includes a visitors center with a museum containing artifacts and pedagogical implements used by Houston and other teachers of that time. To get there, go three miles north out of Maryville on Rt. 33 to the intersection of Sam Houston Schoolhouse Road. Go right for two miles. The schoolhouse is open daily 10 a.m.-5 p.m., and Sunday 1-5 p.m. Admission is 50 cents for adults, and children get in free.

The **Peregrine International Museum of Scouting,** 15 miles south of Maryville at 6588 Hwy. 441 in the community of Greenback, tel.

(423) 856-0244, was founded by Guy Singer, a former Scout and Scout leader who has collected Scouting memorabilia for decades. The museum includes exhibits of Scout handbooks, badges, and patches, as well as hands-on activities such as animal tracking, signaling with Morse code and semaphore, and various outdoor skills. The museum is open year-round, 10 a.m.-9 p.m. April-Oct., and 10 a.m.-6 p.m. Nov.-March. Admission is $4 for adults and $2 for kids.

PRACTICALITIES

Where to Stay
The **High Court Inn,** 212 High St., tel. (423) 981-2966, occupies a 1911 house just down the street from the Blount County Courthouse. The house, which has been completely restored, has three guest rooms, all with private baths, four-poster beds, and claw-foot bathtubs. Rates range $59-69. Moderate.

Also try the **Executive Lodge,** 215 Hall Rd., tel. (423) 984-9958; or the **Princess Motel,** 2614 Hwy. 411/129, tel. (423) 982-2490.

Food
Buddy's Bar-be-que, 518 Foothills Plaza, tel. (423) 984-4475, is a Knoxville-based chain with good food. It's open daily for lunch and dinner.

Order in the Court Cafe, 212 High St., tel. (423) 984-3861, presides Mon.-Fri. over lunches consisting of soups, sandwiches, and salads. Brunch is served on Sunday 10 a.m.-1 p.m.

The Southern Skillet, 1311 E. Lamar Alexander Pkwy., tel. (423) 984-9680, offers country cooking and homemade desserts. It serves all three meals seven days a week.

Shopping
Halls Furniture and Auction, 3501 E. Lamar Alexander Pkwy., tel. (423) 983-1598, offers a down-home sort of entertainment every Friday evening with an auction of junk and valuable treasures. The trick is knowing which is which.

SAM HOUSTON

Linguists often note that present-day Texans sound like Tennesseans, and that's not at all surprising; much of the Lone Star State was settled by people from The Volunteer State. Among these was one of the foremost Texans, Sam Houston. Houston was born in Virginia in 1793, and his father died in 1807, leaving his wife with nine children. When Sam was 14 years old, the family moved to the Maryville area, and Sam went to work as a clerk in a store shortly thereafter.

He ran away when he was about 15 years old and went to live with the Cherokee for three years on an island where the Hiawasee River meets the Tennessee. He lived with Chief Jolly, known to Indians as Olooteca, who presided over a group of about 300 Indians. They gave young Houston the name Colonneh, or The Raven.

Houston was no lost boy. It is said that he took with him a six-volume set of *The Iliad,* much of which he committed to memory before returning to his own people. While living with the Indians he had incurred some debts to traders, and, to pay them off, he agreed on returning to Maryville in 1812 to teach school for one term.

"The Raven" lived with the Cherokee, but he was willing to fight other Indians. During the War of 1812, he resigned his teaching post and fought under Gen. Andrew Jackson against the Creek in Alabama. In 1819 he assisted the federal government as a subagent in removing some Cherokee from East Tennessee to a reservation in Arkansas. With Jackson's political backing, Houston was elected to two terms in Congress and became Tennessee's governor in 1826. While running for a second two-year term, he astonished Tennesseans by relinquishing his office and going off to live with the Cherokee once more.

A friend to the Indians, he came to Washington more than once to protest their treatment, but, unlike David Crockett, who also opposed the Indian removal, he did not break his ties with Jackson. Sent by President Jackson to Texas in 1832 to negotiate with the Mexicans for the protection of American traders, Houston decided to stay.

Houston achieved most of his historic accomplishments in Texas. He helped draw up the Texas Constitution, commanded its army, and, after David Crockett and his companions were killed at the Alamo, led a greenhorn army into battle against Mexican general Santa Anna, who commanded a vastly superior force. Houston and his troops defeated the Mexicans, captured Santa Anna, and avenged the Alamo.

Houston became the president of the Republic of Texas and one of its first senators to Washington after statehood. In the Senate he spoke up for the rights of Indians—views that did not sit well with his constituency. He served only one term and came back to Texas to be elected governor in 1859, just in time for the Civil War. Houston argued strenuously against secession, to no avail. When he refused to take an oath of loyalty to the Confederacy, he was removed from office. "The Raven" died in Huntsville on July 26, 1863.

The Cherokee knew Sam Houston as "The Raven."

BARKER TEXAS HISTORY CENTER

ALCOA

Several Tennessee towns have been founded by or controlled by industries that located themselves to profit from the natural resources of the state. Alcoa was perhaps the only company town whose raw materials did not come from Tennessee. Alcoa is an acronym for the Aluminum Company of America, which in 1910 began buying land along the Little Tennessee River so as to create a series of lakes whose water power could produce cheap electricity—a big part of the cost of making aluminum.

The company located its factory outside of Maryville in 1913 and incorporated the town of Alcoa to house workers. The town was built into four living areas—segregated into black and white—that included parks, commercial areas, and schools. Although labor strife plagued the town in the 1930s, the town and its industry boomed during World War II, when the workforce hit 12,000 people. Alcoans had a high standard of living compared to the rest of the state, and that prosperity influenced Maryville and Blount County as well.

The company no longer owns the town, which is virtually indistinguishable from Maryville, but still gets electricity from the four dams on the Little Tennessee River. And the company continues to prosper, with a workforce of 2,000 that makes aluminum for beverage cans.

The bidding gets rolling at 7 p.m. and can continue past midnight.

Jazzberry General Boutique and Gallery, 205 Court St., tel. (423) 984-0391, offers an eclectic collection of art and clothes. Visitors can find original paintings, pottery, metalwork, blown glass, and handcrafted jewelry as well as clothing for men and women.

Lee's World of Crafts, 370 Gill St. in Alcoa, tel. (423) 984-7674, sells prints, quilts, baskets, furniture, and other items.

Information
Visit the **Blount County Chamber of Commerce,** 309 S. Washington St., Maryville, tel. (423) 983-2241; it's open Mon.-Fri. 8 a.m.-5 p.m. On the Internet, you'll find more information at www.smokymountains.org.

GREAT SMOKY MOUNTAINS NATIONAL PARK

INTRODUCTION

More people come to the Great Smoky Mountains National Park than to any other national park in the country; the Park Service counts over nine million "visits" every year. One visitor can make several visits, so the number of actual people who come and go is hard to determine, but it is a lot.

As visitors stand on the ridge of the mountains that makes up the Tennessee-North Carolina border, it is easy to see why the hordes come. The mountains, all covered with trees, seem to go on and on and on. Visitors can see whole square miles where the only evidence of humans is an overhead jet trail, and at times even that does not mar the view. These views are the same ones the Cherokee enjoyed before the arrival of the Europeans.

An ancient mountain range once stood here, and over the millennia it was worn to the point

that an ocean covered the old rocks. As oceans are wont to do, this one deposited thousands of feet of sediment over the mountain remnants, and the resulting pressure transformed the lower layers into metamorphic rock.

Then the African tectonic plate bumped up against its North American counterpart, and the old, compressed rock layers slid up and over the more recent ocean deposits. Thus came the Smokies, which in those days looked more like the Rockies. Erosion has worn them down to the gentle shapes that people enjoy today.

The Smokies constitute the largest wilderness area in the East, one that is home to more species of plants than any comparable area in the country. As motorists drive from outlying towns up the mountains, the vegetation changes as much as if they were driving from Tennessee to Canada.

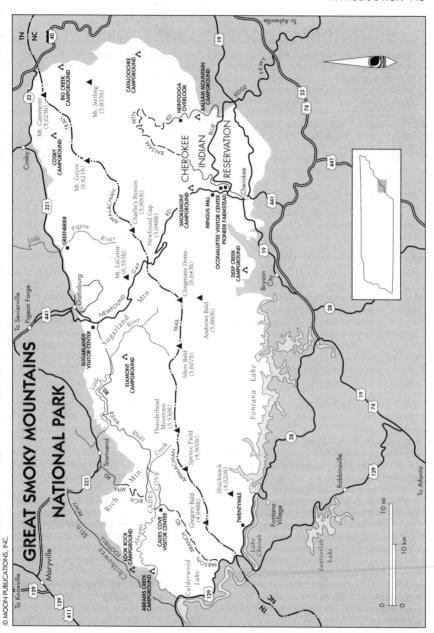

© MOON PUBLICATIONS, INC.

GREAT SMOKY MOUNTAINS NATIONAL PARK

THE BACK DOORS TO THE SMOKIES

It looks simple: to get to the Smokies, take I-40 to Hwy. 66 and cruise straight down to Gatlinburg and the Great Smokies. It's so simple that millions of people do so every year, and traffic sometimes gets so backed up that lines of traffic extend back onto the interstate. For anyone with small children or little tolerance for congestion, this is a horrible introduction to a Smokies vacation. Here are some ways to avoid the hassle:

Coming from the East, you have two options. The first goes through Cosby, an interesting place in and of itself, while the other takes back roads to Gatlinburg or Pigeon Forge.

To come through Cosby, get off I-40 east of Newport at the Wilton Springs/Hwy. 321 Exit, then follow Hwy. 321/32 to Cosby, turn right, and take Hwy. 321/73 all the way into Gatlinburg.

For the second option, take Exit 432 off I-40 near Newport and head southwest on Hwy. 411/35 toward Sevierville.

Coming from the West, motorists can get on a four-lane highway that parallels I-40 and carries only a fraction of the interstate traffic. While on I-40 in Knoxville, take the exit for Hwy. 441 South, which goes through a tunnel and passes the Sunsphere, a relic of the 1982 World's Fair. The highway crosses the Tennessee River and, a few miles later, merges with Hwy. 411. Before long Sevierville comes into sight, and with it all the lost souls who came off I-40 on Hwy. 66.

Those who crave outlet stores, T-shirt shops, and the like should stay on Hwy. 441 and join the mob. Those who want a less commercial and much less-crowded route should continue on Hwy 411.

The fact that this 800-square-mile park appeals to so many people means that those who want to go there have to think about how to avoid other members of their species. For the most part, the answer is simple: get out of the car. Something like 95% of all visitors to the Smokies never get more than 100 yards from their vehicles. That cuts the nine million visits down to a much more manageable size.

THE LAND

Climate

The weather in the Smokies is generally wetter and colder than in the surrounding parts of Tennessee. The big difference is in the high country, particularly in the winter and spring. The higher elevations get much more snow than anywhere else; snowfall at Newfound Gap averages almost six feet per year, and temperatures can drop to 20° below zero. During the winter the Newfound Gap road is often closed.

The Smokies are at their most treacherous in the spring, when hikers might set off in balmy weather only to encounter snowstorms or freezing rain just a few hours later. This particularly affects college students from northern climes who come south on spring break for backpacking trips.

Summertime brings heat and humidity. The Smokies get a lot of rainfall, and this tends to take place in the afternoons or whenever someone sets off without a poncho or other raingear.

Fall is perhaps the best time to come. The rains of summer subside, replaced by cool days and chilly evenings. Keep in mind that the first snowfall of the year in Tennessee will likely take place in the Smokies' higher elevations.

Flora

Designated an International Biosphere Reserve, the park contains more than 1,500 species of flowering plants, including 125 species of trees—more species of trees than in all of northern Europe combined. Part of this is due to the variety of elevations, but much of the park's biodiversity can be attributed to lush soil and 40 inches of rainfall a year.

Springtime brings the wildflowers, and some visitors take advantage of special programs and walks led by botanists who identify the plants and describe their uses. Mushrooms and fungi grow abundantly in this moist environment, and, it must be pointed out, so do plants such as stinging nettle and poison ivy.

Although the park is almost entirely wooded, botanists note five different types of forest in the park. One of the first ones that visitors encounter is a **Cove Hardwood Forest.** Deciduous trees such as sugar maples, yellow birches, and yellow poplars dominate, and these are the ones whose fall colors attract the multitudes. Three other forest groups, named for the trees that occur there, are **Pine and Oak, Hemlock,** and **Northern Hardwood.**

The trees at the tops of the mountains make up **Spruce-Fir Forests,** coniferous collections of red spruce and Fraser fir. More than 95% of the latter have been wiped out by the balsam woolly adelgid, which has left hundreds of acres of dead trees. Oddly enough, blackberries that grow at this altitude have few thorns.

Vegetation in the Smokies can be so thick that a person can stand within four feet of a hiking trail and not be seen. Mountain laurel and rhododendron grow so thickly that mountain people referred to them as "hells."

Perhaps the most intriguing botanical phenomenon of the Smokies is the **balds**—areas on mountaintops or ridges that have no trees. These occur as grass balds or heath balds—ones covered with shrubs. Either is a delight for hikers, for high in the mountains the balds open onto wide vistas with ample area for picnics or other frolics. No one knows for sure what caused these balds. Lightning fires, fires set by Indians, or overgrazing have all been suggested as reasons for Gregory Bald, Andrews Bald, Spence Field, Silers Bald, Little Bald, and Parson Bald. Mountain residents used to use grass balds as summertime pastures for cattle and sheep, for this was land that didn't have to be cleared of trees, and taking livestock up in the mountains kept them from eating important crops such as corn. However the balds came about, they are superb hiking destinations.

Fauna

Black bears are the best-known animals in the park, and whenever a member of *Ursus americanus* emerges from the woods along a road, traffic grinds to a halt and hundreds of pictures are taken. Unfortunately, and despite all manner of warnings against the practice, some people persist in feeding bears. Doing so threatens a bear's life, for when bears lose their natural fear of humans they are much more likely to cause problems and have to be moved or even killed. Furthermore, feeding bears—or any wild animals—can subject the feeder to a fine of $5000 and six months in jail.

The park shelters an estimated 500 bears. They spend the winters in dens or high in trees, and during this time their young are born. Bears eat berries, acorns, other nuts, seeds, and insects—and whatever human food they can scrounge.

No grizzlies live in the Smokies—or anywhere else in the East—and black bears usually leave people alone, but visitors should treat them with caution. They are strong, intelligent animals. Bears can peel open car doors to extract food within and have been known to outsmart backcountry hikers who thought their backpacks were securely tied high off the ground. Mother bears with cubs are particularly dangerous. Visitors who pester bears often wind up paying the consequences—usually involving a trip to the emergency room.

More than one visitor, on looking carefully at a herd of cattle grazing in Cades Cove, has said, "Hey! That's not a cow!" What they are usually seeing is a **white-tailed deer,** *Odocoileus virginianus.* These deer are never hunted, so they sometimes seem as tame as cows, but if people approach too close these fleet animals will bolt, leaping tall fences in a single bound.

Several national parks are plagued by non-native species—animals that somehow invaded an area where they never occurred naturally. These critters tend to upset the ecological balance and make nuisances of themselves. The Smokies' chief non-native is the **European wild hog,** *Sus scrofa,* a prolific pig that can top 200 pounds and stand three feet high. These fierce hogs come equipped with sharp tusks, and, if

---

MUST-SEE HIGHLIGHTS

Cades Cove offers a combination of nature and the remnants of the community who lived there.

Spence Field, one of the tree-free mountaintop "balds," offers a great hike and a wonderful view at the end.

Mount LeConte Lodge, a hike-in lodge atop one of the loveliest mountains in the park, is the absolute best place to stay in the Smokies.

Abrams Falls drains Cades Cove and offers a wonderful hike.

cornered, they don't hesitate to attack humans or eviscerate pursuing dogs. That's the bad news. The good news is that they are largely nocturnal and tend to avoid people.

The hogs probably escaped from a North Carolina game preserve stocked by 1912 "sportsmen." Since then the animals have interbred with domestic porkers and slowly moved into the park, where they root up wildflowers, foul streams, and compete with bears for berries, acorns, and other food. The Park Service is actively trapping the estimated 500 beasts and removing them to far-off wildlife management areas. Visitors who come across any pig traps in the wild should leave them alone in hopes they will catch more of these pests.

One animal that might offer some natural help for the pig problem is the **red wolf,** *Canus rufus.* Wolves once roamed the Smokies but were wiped out by farmers and a loss of habitat. First reintroduced in 1991, 17 wolves live in the park, but right now it is too early to say if they will make it. People in Cades Cove have seen wolves and heard them howl, but generally these newest residents of the park avoid people.

During the last 10 years, about 140 **river otters,** *Lutra canadensis,* were reintroduced to the Little River, Middle and West Prongs of the Little Pigeon River, Cosby Creek, and Abrams Creek.

Most people think of **turkeys,** *Meleagris gallopavo,* as the fat, stupid birds that appear on Thanksgiving tables. The ones that live in the park, however, are lean, smart, and incredibly fast—once aloft they can hit 50 miles per hour. The most likely place to see them is in the fields of Cades Cove.

Challenges Facing the Park

The surge of visitors is just one of the challenges facing the park. The Smokies also suffer from various forms of air pollution, among them acid rain. The topography of the mountains causes pollutants to linger longer here than in cities. Burning coal at power plants in Tennessee and as far away as Illinois leads to haze that reduces visibility in the summertime as much as 80%. Rainfall in the park has a pH of 4.4—five times the natural acidity.

Ground-level ozone results when sunlight breaks down pollutants from vehicles and power plants. Unlike the ozone layer high in the at-

mosphere that shields the earth from ultraviolet rays, ground-level ozone damages plants and people. Monitoring stations in the Smokies give off the highest readings of ground-level ozone of any place in the East.

Another challenge facing the park is a tiny insect called the balsam woolly adelgid, which attacks Fraser fir trees. This non-native pest has killed off most of these firs, which make up the bulk of the high-country forests in the Smokies. Park workers have saved some trees by spraying on a soap-and-water mixture that wipes out the bugs, but this is impractical for trees far from roads.

Perhaps the greatest challenge to the Smokies—and all parks—is federal budget-cutting. Despite nefarious politicians and hordes of visitors, it is possible to find solitude in the Smokies, and every season of the year the visitor can come into this wonderful wilderness and return refreshed and with a profound admiration of this very special place.

HISTORY

The Cherokee

Anthropologists suggest that the first humans to see the Smokies were the Cherokee, offshoots of the Iroquois tribes who lived in the Northeast. These first residents found a rich land from which they could easily gather their necessities, so they settled in villages and did not have to roam. The Smokies provided abundant fresh water and game, and the rich soil grew a variety of crops such as corn, beans, and tobacco. Herbs for medicine, dyes, and other uses were abundant.

As in other parts of Tennessee, white settlers crossed the mountains and pushed farther and farther west. At first, almost none of them wanted to live in the mountains per se, for life there was simply too hard. They might graze their cattle in high mountain pastures in the summer, but that was about it.

The Cherokee who lived in the Smokies fell subject to Pres. Andrew Jackson's 1830 Removal Act and with their fellow tribes were rounded up and ordered to walk to Oklahoma in the winter of 1838-39. A small number of them, displaying great courage, escaped to the mountains and managed to elude the roundup parties sent after them. By 1889—almost 60 years after the Removal Act—the Qualla Indian Reservation was organized to provide these remaining Cherokee with a place to live. They became known as the Eastern Band of the Cherokee, and they live just outside the park in North Carolina.

Settlers, Loggers, and Tourists

As more white people came to the area, they found the good land gone, and they moved into "hollers" and onto hillsides that earlier arrivals had disdained. These folks lived hard lives, but they were very proud of their self-sufficiency and independence. Many of them traded and bartered for the things they needed and never dealt with cash.

The biggest change on the land came from a situation far beyond the mountains—an incessant demand for wood. From the 1880s on, as immigration swelled the population of the United States, many of the trees up and down the Eastern Seaboard had been cut, so timber companies began eyeing far-flung sources of lumber. What made it all possible was the railroad, and by the 1920s the sound of sawmills filled the valleys. Within 10 years most of the land that makes up the park had been logged. The loggers spared only the most remote areas.

The trains that hauled out the lumber began to haul in tourists, and a few enterprising souls began opening restaurants and motels. Several of those early names—Ogles, Reagans, and Maples—appear on modern-day Gatlinburg eateries and places to bed down. Those early visitors to the Smokies were so impressed with what they saw—despite the devastation from logging—that they joined Knoxvillians in suggesting a national park. Prominent among the group was Horace Kephart, who had moved to the Smokies to restore his health and was so captivated that he devoted his life to founding the park.

Fortunately, the federal government of those days was willing to listen. The large national parks in the West had proved very popular, and the government was looking to replicate that success in the East. It created the National Park Service in 1916 to reflect the growing interest in parks. Creating parks in the East was far more complicated than in the West, however. To begin with, the federal government owned most of the

This couple once lived in the area that is now the national park.

GREAT SMOKY MOUNTAINS NATIONAL PARK

land in the West, and setting up a park was inexpensive. Since few people lived in or near western parks, there were few if any howls of protest. All this would change back East.

Birth of the Park

The federal government didn't want to spend any money acquiring land, so Tennessee and North Carolina's state governments contributed, each hoping to land the park within its borders. Private citizens and companies gave land and money, and eventually John D. Rockefeller Jr. donated $5 million, which put the drive over the top.

Not everyone was in favor of the park. The lumber companies led the opposition, but they could be and were bought out. More intense and more personal opposition came from the people whose small farms sat within the proposed boundaries of the park. By the year 1930, about 7,300 people lived on 1,200 farms in this area. These people, who had had little if any contact with the federal government all their lives, found it outrageous that someone was going to take their land. A few managed to get lifetime leases on their property—the Wonderland Hotel, several dozen vacation cabins, and Mount LeConte Lodge—but everyone else had to go.

On June 15, 1934, the Great Smoky Mountains National Park came into existence, but it was a while before the park was ready to receive visitors. The Civilian Conservation Corps built trails and roads, and on September 2, 1940, Pres. Franklin D. Roosevelt bumped along in a caravan up the dirt road to Newfound Gap, where thousands of individuals in hundreds of cars attended the dedication. Thus came the Smokies National Park, and from the beginning came its tradition of traffic.

The park in those days would shock current-day visitors. Whole sections had been clear-cut, large gullies ran down the hillsides, and streams were in some cases filled with silt and almost devoid of life. Left alone, however, nature quietly reclaimed the land. Now towering trees grow along roads that were once railbeds, and the vegetation is so lush that most of the people who blissfully drive along probably think they are seeing virgin forest.

Visitation has steadily increased in the Smokies over time. The interstate highway system put the Smokies within a day's drive of an estimated 70% of the U.S. population, and a great many of those people have made the trip. While the number of visitors has doubled and doubled and redoubled again, the roads in the park have largely stayed the same, causing intense congestion during the summer and even worse traffic during the fall foliage season. The Park Service has wisely resisted efforts to widen the roads and ignored other schemes raised over the years, among them a hare-brained suggestion to run a chairlift from Gatlinburg to Clingmans Dome. In doing so, the Park Service has preserved a wonderful wilderness area, one that continues to provide inspiration and joy to those who come to see it.

SIGHTS AND RECREATION

THE PEOPLE OF THE SMOKIES

There is little left to mark the presence of the Cherokee who lived in the Smokies, although the Qualla Reservation adjacent to the park in North Carolina has a museum and "living village" that sheds light on the way they lived.

Cades Cove

Although most of the buildings on the 1,200 farms that were in the park were demolished, a few remain to show what life was like. The biggest collection of these lies in Cades Cove, a large, relatively flat area first settled in 1821. Eventually the 15,000+ farmed acres supported a peak population of 685, which kept several churches and mills in operation. The park permits cattle to graze in order to keep the pastures from returning to for-

Cades Cove mill

est, and it also maintains the farm building, churches, and a mill.

A narrow, 11-mile one-way road goes around the cove, with 19 stops that explain the way of life that once took place here. This is the best place in the park to ride bicycles, for two reasons. First, it is a mostly level road. Second, traffic along Cades Cove's one-lane road can be frustratingly slow, particularly if visitors get stuck behind someone who wants to gaze reverently at every fence post. Bikes can easily pass them by.

The Tipton Place features a cantilevered barn, an example of mountain ingenuity whereby a building spreads out at its second story to provide shelter for work or for animals. The best part of the Cove, however, centers on the Cable Mill, a working mill alongside a frame house and several farm buildings. During the visiting season crafts and farming

OUTSMARTING THE CROWDS IN THE SMOKIES

Seeing the most crowded park in the country can go more smoothly if visitors take a little time to plan their trips. Here are a few tips.

Go when school is in session. If you have no school-age kids, try to get to the Smokies before June or after the last week in August.

Know when the University of Tennessee plays home football games. Check the list of home dates listed under Knoxville. UT's stadium seats more than 102,000 people, and guess where a lot of them come after the game.

Get up with the chickens. Do your driving before most of the mob has eaten breakfast. Try to enter the park before 9 a.m. If you plan on hiking, you'll get to your trailhead, find plenty of parking places, and have the trail to yourself.

Stay in Gatlinburg. It may cost a little more than outlying areas, but what you are paying for is time. You'll get to the park more quickly and when you come out later in the day you won't have far to go to get to your room.

Use the Gatlinburg bypass. If you are coming from Pigeon Forge, drive around the town of Gatlinburg, not through it.

Come in the back way. On October weekends or during crowded peak weekends, don't approach the park by way of I-40 Exit 407. This puts you in line with all the outlet shoppers and horrendous hordes of traffic in Sevierville and Pigeon Forge. Drive to Exit 443 and come to Gatlinburg and the park via Hwy. 321.

Tailgate. Don't put yourself in the position of having to drive out of the park and back into town to eat lunch. Carry food with you. If you are taking a hike, have a gourmet dinner waiting for you in the car when you emerge from the woods. You can eat there in leisure until the traffic thins out.

Drive the Newfound Gap Road early in the day. Almost everyone makes the drive from Gatlinburg to Clingmans Dome. Do it early and then take your hike.

---

demonstrations take place. Sorghum molasses is made the old-fashioned way one weekend in October.

In North Carolina

Across the border, **Cataloochee Valley** contains a school, churches, houses, and barns. While this area does not compare to the sights and sites of Cades Cove, neither does its traffic. **Oconaluftee Mountain Farm Museum,** right beside the visitors center on Newfound Gap Road, offers periodic demonstrations. Nearby **Mingus Mill** is also worth a stop. Most mills in Tennessee have a large vertical wheel on the side of the building. This one is a "tub" mill, or turbine mill, in which the wheel lies flat while it's spun by the water. Mingus Mill grinds corn and wheat, and cornmeal and flour are on sale at the gift shop.

LEARNING IN THE SMOKIES

During the peak visiting season—roughly June through August—the Park Service provides daily walks, strolls, or talks involving various aspects

of the Smokies. Some are geared for children, while others can be enjoyed by all ages. Check the visitors centers for information on what is happening on specific dates.

Two groups provide educational experiences in the Smokies for teachers, children, families, or individuals who wish to immerse themselves in some aspect of this park.

The **Smoky Mountain Field School,** tel. (800) 284-8885, offers courses ranging from two days to one week involving topics such as geology, stream life, waterfalls, hiking, birds, insects, mammals, bears, and mushrooms. Classes are run in conjunction with the park and the University of Tennessee, and tuition is $36-295. Participants are responsible for arranging their own lodging and meals.

By contrast, the **Great Smoky Mountains Institute at Tremont,** 9275 Tremont Rd., Townsend, TN 37882, tel. (423) 448-6709, offers a package deal—program, lodging, and food all in one price. The institute, on the Middle Prong of the Little River in Walker Valley, offers days filled with geology, wildflowers, forest ecology, or cultural history. Evenings include Appalachian music, guest speakers, night hikes, and other activities.

The institute has a dormitory with 125 beds, and participants sleep Shaker style—males on one side and females on the other. It serves hearty meals family style. Typical programs include a summer adult backpack trip, $110; a naturalist-led LeConte trip, $230; and a women's backpack trip, $110. Other programs include photography workshops, grandparent-grandchild weeks, and teacher escape weekends.

HIKING

Whether a stroll in the woods or a multiday trek in the backcountry, hiking ranks high on the list of things to do in the Smokies, where more than 800 miles of trail await the walker. Below is a selection of good **day-hikes** in the park. Most are on well-marked trails, but it's never a bad idea to carry a good map. An excellent guidebook for hiking is *Hiking Trails of the Smokies,* which covers 149 trails with a detailed narrative, full-color map, and trail profile charts for 165 trails. Printed on lightweight paper, it's easy for hikers to carry. It costs $16.95 and is available at visitors centers' gift shops.

Anyone wanting to hike for longer than a day and to camp along any trail in the Smokies needs a permit, available from ranger stations. See "Camping" under "Practicalities" below for details.

Appalachian Trail Hikes
The most famous trail in America runs along the 68-mile mountain crest that makes up the Tennessee-North Carolina border. Here Maine-to-Georgia hikers tramp alongside weekend hikers who mingle with day-trippers who want to experience the famous trail. As a result, the section of the trail near Newfound Gap can be very crowded.

Leave the Newfound Gap parking lot and head east for four miles to **Charlies Bunion,** a sheer drop of 1,000 feet. A spectacular view awaits. The trail climbs 980 feet in the first three miles.

Newfound Gap to Clingmans Dome, a 7.5-mile section of the Appalachian Trail, is the highest in the park and offers superb views. The elevation rises 1,600 feet. An easier route begins at Clingmans Dome and goes downhill to Newfound Gap.

Cades Cove Hikes
The five-mile roundtrip **Abrams Falls** hike is a good one for people with kids; they love to play in the water at Abrams Creek, which drains Cades Cove. Begin along the Cades Cove Loop Road and hike down to the falls, or go to the Abrams Creek Ranger Station off the Foothills Parkway on the west side of the park and hike upstream to the falls. The latter is the more appealing route, although a bit out of the way.

Two trails lead to **Gregory Bald,** a former summer pasture. The Gregory Ridge Trail, 11 miles roundtrip, begins at the turnaround at the start of Parson Branch Road and climbs 2,600 feet up Gregory Ridge. The Gregory Bald Trail, nine miles roundtrip, begins farther down the Parson Branch Road and climbs 2,100 feet. Keep in mind that Parson Branch Road is a one-way road leading out of the park. If hikers are camping in Cades Cove, they are in for a long drive to get back to the sleeping bag.

The **Rich Mountain** trail begins on another of those one-way roads out of Cades Cove. Once motorists get to the boundary of the park—Rich Mountain Gap—traffic runs in both directions. Walk east from here along a fire road until the trail takes off to the left. Follow it to the top of the mountain and the intersection with the Indian Grave Gap Road. A good view of the mountains and Cades Cove awaits.

Hikers can reach the beautiful mountain bald of **Spence Field** by two trails. The first is the Bote Mountain Trail, a jeep road that begins on Laurel Creek Road, which is the road that leads into Cades Cove. Spence Field lies 13 miles ahead, a climb of 2,900 feet. The shortest trail is also the steepest. Begin at the Cades Cove Picnic Area and follow the Anthony Creek Trail to its intersection with the Bote Mountain Trail. Prepare to walk nine miles and gain 3,200 feet in elevation.

IT'S A JUNGLE OUT THERE

Here are a few points to keep in mind as you hike through the Smokies:

The higher one goes, the colder it gets. This may come as a relief during the heat of the summer, but hikers should carry enough clothing to keep warm when venturing to the higher elevations. Getting chilled is no fun and in bad weather can prove life-threatening.

Never drink water from streams or creeks! Contamination from wild boars and other critters can lead to digestive tract disorders that will stay for a long time. Carry enough water or take a filtering device with you.

Watch children. Because of the dense foliage, it is very easy for kids to run ahead and get lost. It's not a bad idea to equip kids with a whistle, provided they use it only if necessary.

Unless hikers want to walk along doing a Leonard Bernstein-at-the-podium impersonation, bug repellent during warm months is a good idea.

The Smoky Mountains gets an average of 40 inches of rain per year. Carry a poncho.

Mount LeConte Hikes

Mount LeConte is a very popular mountain in the Smokies, perhaps because of the presence of LeConte Lodge at the top. Five trails lead up, so a common practice is to hike up one trail and down another. Depending on which trails hikers choose, they may need two vehicles. The Boulevard Trail begins at Newfound Gap, thus eliminating a good deal of the climb, so this is a good one to go up. The Alum Cave Trail has more things to see than the others, so it is a good one to come down.

The shortest and steepest way up Mt. LeConte, the **Alum Cave Trail** is 5.5 miles one way and a 2,800-foot climb. This trail is misnamed; there is no cave. It does offer a rock arch along the way, some bluffs from which saltpeter was mined during the Civil War, and some great scenery. The trail begins at the Alum Cave Bluffs parking lot off the Newfound Gap Road.

Park at Newfound Gap and head east on the Appalachian Trail. The **Boulevard Trail** will turn off to the left. The total distance is eight miles one way, with an actual elevation gain of 1,545 feet. Since the trail follows a ridge top, the actual up and down may seem like more climbing than that.

The next three trails leave from the Gatlinburg area and are particularly recommended when the park is jammed with cars that make it difficult to get to the other trails.

So named because the mountain it crosses resembles the head of a bull, **Bullhead Trail** begins in the Cherokee Orchard parking lot near Gatlinburg. The elevation gain is 4,017 feet, and the hike is 7.25 miles one way.

Rainbow Falls Trail, another trail setting off from the Cherokee Orchard parking lot, is a 6.75-mile one-way hike that passes an 80-foot waterfall and gains 4,017 feet. Some hikers avoid this trail because of its condition—rocky and steep with lots of gullies.

Hikers from the Gatlinburg area can save 700 feet of elevation gain by taking the **Trillium Gap** trail, which begins along the Roaring Fork Motor Nature Trail at the Grotto Falls parking lot. The elevation gain is 3,473 feet over seven miles one way.

More Trails on the Tennessee Side

Right outside of Gatlinburg on the Newfound Gap Road and one of the more popular trails in the park, **Chimney Tops** is only two miles one-way, with an elevation gain of 1,335 feet. By the steep end most people are using hands and feet, but the view is worth it.

The 1.5-mile one-way **Grotto Falls** hike is cool on the hottest days. Leave the Roaring Fork Motor Nature Trail at the Grotto Falls parking area and walk upstream to this waterfall. Hikers gain only 500 feet in elevation and can look for salamanders on the way. The park shelters 23 species of them.

The **Hen Wallow Falls** hike leaves from a less crowded area. Drive to the Cosby Picnic Area on the northeast end of the park for a two-mile one-way hike. The elevation gain is 600 feet through a forest with magnificent poplars and hemlocks. The falls are two feet wide at the top and 20 feet wide at the bottom.

The **Ramsay Cascades** trail is one of the few dead-end trails in the Smokies, but what a finale! The 100-foot Ramsay Cascades, while not a straight drop, is the highest waterfall in the park. The trail begins in Greenbrier Cove, about six miles due east of Gatlinburg on Hwy. 321. Four miles one way, the trail gains 1,600 feet in elevation, and hikers should be careful at the falls; several people have fallen to their deaths.

MORE RECREATION

Bicycling

Riding a bike in the most crowded park in the country is not easy. Inhaling the exhaust is bad enough, but getting clipped in the back of the head by a wide mirror on an RV driven by a flatlander can ruin one's day. If bikers are going to brave the roads, they should get out there early.

The best place to ride bikes in the park is Cades Cove. A concessionaire at the campground store rents bikes, or bikers can bring their own. From spring through September the Cades Cove Loop Rd. is closed to motor traffic on Saturday and Wednesday mornings until 10 a.m., and that is the very best time to go.

Mountain bikes are prohibited on all Smokies trails—as are all vehicles—but a few unimproved roads make good riding. Try the Cataloochee Valley on the eastern end of the park, or the Parson Branch Road out of Cades Cove, but keep in mind that it is one-way out of the cove.

Fishing

Approximately 730 miles of streams thread through the park, and Fontana Lake lies on the southern border. Except for Fontana, which harbors smallmouth and rock bass, trout is the name of the game here. The park is one of the last refuges of the brook trout, the only species native to these parts; if anglers catch one, they must release it. Efforts to restore brook trout populations have led to the closing of some streams, and rangers at visitors centers can advise which ones to avoid. The rainbow trout, however, are fair game.

Trout season never stops in the Smokies; visitors can fish all year. A Tennessee or North Carolina fishing license enables the angler to fish all over the park, and licenses are available in various gateway towns. Trout stamps are not required, but anglers can use one-hook artificial lures only—no bait is allowed.

Visitors can fish right beside the road or backpack into the most remote streams in the park. (See "Camping" under "Practicalities" below.) Or they can hire guides who will take them to the best places. For lists of guides, see "Services and Information" under "Gatlinburg." A good book for anglers is Don Kirk's *Smoky Mountains Trout Fishing Guide,* which costs $8.95.

Horseback Riding

Horse owners can ride in the park and go on overnight trips with permission from the Park Service. Because of the damage that horses do to trails, their numbers are limited, and riders must bring horse feed with them. The park will provide a complete set of guidelines for horse riding. Call (423) 436-1200 or write to: Superintendent, Great

The mountains have since recovered from the devastating effects of logging.

WHAT TO DO WITH KIDS IN THE SMOKIES

The Great Smoky Mountains National Park is a wonderful place for children. Here are a few suggestions for making their trip more enjoyable.

Keep the time in the vehicle to a minimum. Children who are not used to spending long hours in a vehicle—particularly if they have ridden a long way to get to the Smokies—will not relish the notion of riding 22 more miles to get to Clingmans Dome. Get out of that vehicle as soon as possible.

Don't worry about the destination on hikes. Adults tend to be goal-oriented—"We're going to climb Mt. LeConte!" Kids tend to enjoy the experience along the way. If a child is having a good time playing on a fallen log or climbing on a rock, don't repeatedly insist on moving on. You don't want their memory of the Smokies to resemble the Bataan Death March.

Take advantage of special programs for kids. The visitors centers can provide information about storytelling, ranger walks, and other programs designed for kids. The Junior Ranger program is an especially good one.

Get in the water. Children love playing in streams. Take their shoes off and let them pick up the smooth stones and look for crawfish. One of the very best things you can do is take a picnic lunch out of Gatlinburg to the Chimneys Picnic Area and play in the water. Don't let them drink it, however, no matter how clear it looks. Older kids may want to jump from boulder to boulder. Caution them not to jump from a dry rock to a wet rock. Have a towel, a change of clothes, and dry shoes on hand.

Use horse sense. Cades Cove offers hayrides, and stables around the park have horseback riding. Most kids love this.

Spend time in town. No matter how much the heathen pleasures of Gatlinburg and Pigeon Forge may make adults grit their teeth, kids love to do those sorts of things. Don't be a stick in the environmental mud.

Smoky Mountains National Park, 107 Park Headquarters Rd., Gatlinburg, TN 37738.

Rental horses are available from several places in the park. All rides are guided, usually at a most sedate pace, and children under six have to ride with an adult. On the Tennessee side, visitors can rent horses at stables near Park Headquarters, tel. (423) 436-5354; Cades Cove Riding Stables, tel. (423) 448-6286; and east of Gatlinburg on Hwy. 321, tel. (423) 436-5634. On the North Carolina side, try Smokemont, tel. (704) 497-2373; or Deep Creek, tel. (704) 488-8504.

Whitewater

Except in the spring and after torrential downpours, the rivers and streams in the park are not big enough to canoe, raft, or kayak. Some intrepid kayakers who know what they are doing will run some sections of the river, but most visitors who want to experience whitewater should go elsewhere, perhaps the French Broad or Nantahala Rivers.

Those who want a milder experience and who don't mind taking a cool dip can ride inner tubes down the Sinks area of the Little River Road. Rocks—those underwater as well as the boulders around which the water flows—can make this hazardous.

Skiing

The park offers no downhill skiing, but during the winter cross-country skiers practice various forms of their sport on roads and trails. Clingmans Dome Road, the Cherokee Orchard Road, and the Roaring Fork Motor Nature Trail provide excellent skiing when the weather cooperates.

PRACTICALITIES

WHERE TO STAY

When it comes to a place to stay in the most visited national park in the country, **Mt. LeConte Lodge** is the only game in town—and it's 5.5 miles from the nearest road. Jack Huff built LeConte Lodge in the 1920s, and when the park came into existence the lodge was allowed to remain. Various environmental hard-liners have argued for the demise of the venerable lodge, but public sentiment has overwhelmed them every time.

LeConte Lodge holds about 50 guests, either in cabins or private rooms within cabins. Accommodations are extremely rustic; there is no electricity, indoor plumbing, telephones, television, or fax service. Most of dinner and breakfast comes out of cans that llamas carry up the mountain. Guests are seated around tables with total strangers and served family style. There is no evening entertainment, and guests retire to beds with wool blankets and cabins with kerosene heaters. All this costs $73 for adults and $64 plus tax for kids. Premium.

Most of the guests wouldn't have it any other way.

LeConte Lodge probably has more demand for its rooms than any other hostelry in Tennessee. Open from late March through November, the lodge accepts reservations for the following year on October 1 (if this falls on a weekend, then the following business day) by phone at (423) 429-5704. Reservations go quickly, although it is possible to call up at the last minute and still get a bunk. People do cancel.

An alternate way to get a bunk at the lodge is to sign up for a Smoky Mountain Field School hike. The lodge reserves three Saturdays a year for Field School hikes—one each in the spring, summer, and fall. Call (800) 284-8885 for Field School dates.

CAMPING

The National Park Service takes a rather puritanical stance toward those who stay in its campgrounds: Campers are going to rough it, like it or not. Thus there are no showers, flush toilets only when the numbers overwhelm pit toilets, and no electrical or water umbilicals for RVs. The larger campgrounds offer campfire programs at night. Call (423) 436-1200 for information.

Campers can reserve sites up to five months in advance at Cades Cove, Smokemont, and Elkmont from May 15 through October 31 by calling (800) 365-2267. (The park code is GREA.) Any

The Smokies are named for the mist that usually hovers in the mountains.

GREAT SMOKY MOUNTAINS NATIONAL PARK

campsites not reserved are available on a first-come, first-served basis, which is the policy for all of the other campgrounds. No more than six people can occupy one site, either in two tents or one RV and one tent. During the summer and fall campers can stay only seven days; the rest of the year they can stay 14 days. Pets are permitted in campgrounds but must be restrained. (Note to dog owners: The wildlife that occasionally wanders through campsites—raccoons, skunks, and bears—tends to make dogs bark like maniacs, especially in the wee hours of the morning, thus earning massive detestation from fellow campers. If at all possible, leave Fido at home.)

The park offers 1,008 campsites at 10 developed campgrounds, five in Tennessee and five in North Carolina.

Tennessee Campgrounds

Cades Cove, with 161 sites, lies in a part of the Smokies rich in things to do. Besides the cabins and the Cable Mill, trails lead to a bald and a waterfall. This is the only campground with a store, and the Cades Cove Loop Road is the best place in the park to ride a bike. The campground can handle 35-foot RVs, is handicapped accessible, and is open year-round.

Cosby, with 175 sites, is a less crowded place and a good one for seeing the Greenbrier area and hiking to Ramsay Cascade. "Tubing" Cosby Creek is a favorite activity here. Cosby can handle 25-foot RVs and is open late March through October.

Elkmont, with 220 sites, is the biggest campground in the entire park and close to the Metcalf Bottoms Historic Area and the delightful Little River. Laurel Falls is nearby, and Elkmont is the campground closest to the worldly pleasures of Gatlinburg. It can handle all size RVs, is handicapped accessible, and is open year-round.

Look Rock, with 92 sites, often has space when the others do not, perhaps because of its location on the extreme western edge of the park. It offers access to Abrams Creek. It can handle 25-foot RVs and is open late March through October.

Abrams Creek, with 16 sites, is the smallest park campground in Tennessee. This gem lies in a forest of huge conifers that lend it a cathedral effect. It is the trailhead for a hike up to Abrams Falls and is handicapped accessible. It can handle 16-foot RVs and is open late March through October.

North Carolina Campgrounds

Balsam Mountain, with 46 sites, is a good base for exploring the Cherokee Indian Reservation; Mingo Falls is a good trip. It can handle 30-foot RVs and is open mid-May through October 18.

Deep Creek, with 108 sites, lies near Bryson City and within two miles' walk of three waterfalls: Juneywhank Falls, Indian Creek Falls, and Toms Branch Falls. It can handle 25-foot RVs and is open mid-April through October.

Smokemont, with 140 sites, is the largest campground on the North Carolina side and a good place to take in the Pioneer Homestead at Oconoluftee and Mingus Mill. It is the park campground closest to Cherokee, North Carolina. Open year-round and handicapped accessible, it can take all RV sizes.

Big Creek, with nine sites, is the smallest campground in the park and lies on the far eastern end of the Smokies. It's open May 1 to November 2 and can take 26-foot RVs.

Cataloochee, with 27 sites, also on the eastern end of the park, lies at the end of a rough, unpaved road that will guarantee campers freedom from crowds. The Cataloochee area contains several old buildings remaining from a community of 1,200 settlers. It's open late March through October.

Trail Shelters

These shelters, most of them on the Appalachian Trail, offer accommodations for hikers who do not want to carry tents. Each shelter has three walls and a chain-link fence across the front, and inside are eight to 14 beds made of wire mesh strung between logs. Outside somewhere in the vicinity is a pit toilet. The good news is that shelters are dry and bear-proof, with beds up off the ground. The bad news is that campers may find themselves spending time in close quarters with anywhere from seven to 14 total strangers, any of whom may be champion snorers, late-night talkers, or otherwise obnoxious.

There is no charge for shelter use, but they are in great demand and must be reserved. Call Park Headquarters at (423) 436-1231 up to one month in advance.

Backcountry Camping

Despite all the talk of crowding in the park, it offers close to 100 backcountry sites where, some contend, the ultimate camping experience takes place. Backcountry sites lie all over the park; their locations are shifted from time to time to minimize the wear and tear on the land. The sites can accommodate from eight to 20 campers, who can stay up to three days at each site. Reservations are required for some sites, but there is no charge. Write to Backcountry Permits, Great Smoky Mountains National Park, Gatlinburg, TN, 37738 or call (423) 436-1231.

What makes backcountry camping attractive is getting away from it all. To keep things as pristine as possible, campers must pack out all garbage. It cannot be buried or thrown into pit toilets. Tents should not be trenched, and any hand-dug toilets must lie well away from the campsite and any sources of water. Campers can build fires if fire rings are present, but park officials prefer that visitors use portable stoves to lessen the impact on the land.

A final note about camping: Park rangers are very strict about camping in unauthorized places. This means campers cannot spend the night in a parking area or picnic area or on the side of the road, even if all the campgrounds are full and it is 10 p.m. on Saturday night. The same holds true for the backcountry. Campers should allow enough time to get to their destinations.

SERVICES AND INFORMATION

Emergencies

In case of trouble, call **Park Headquarters,** tel. (423) 436-1230; **Gatlinburg police,** tel. (423) 436-5181; or **Cherokee, NC, police,** tel. (704) 497-4131.

If visitors need a **hospital,** the closest one to Gatlinburg is 15 miles away, Sevier County Hospital, Middle Creek Road, Sevierville, TN, tel. (423) 453-7111. The closest to the Cades Cove area is 25 miles away at Blount Memorial Hospital, Hwy. 321, Maryville, TN, tel. (423) 983-7211. In North Carolina, go to Swain County Hospital, Bryson City, NC, tel. (704) 488-2155—16 miles from Smokemont.

Information

The best place to get oriented to the park and to find out the latest information on what's happening is the **Sugarlands Visitor Center** just outside Gatlinburg. It contains a small natural history museum, a slide show, free maps, and people who can answer questions. A bookstore offers helpful volumes and film. The **Oconaluftee Visitor Center** sits on the North Carolina side. Both are open daily 8 a.m.-7 p.m.

Rangers at stations scattered throughout the park will do their best to answer questions or help deal with problems.

CYBERSMOKIES: THE SMOKIES ON THE WEB

The official Web site for the Park is www.nps.gov/grsm/. The *Knoxville News Sentinel* offers www.gosmokies.com, while an outfit called American Park Network provides information at www.americanparknetwork.com/parkinfo/sm.

HILLS AND PLATEAUS
INTRODUCTION

Northwest of Knoxville

The area northwest of Knoxville is the most remote in Tennessee, so remote that when the convicted killer of Martin Luther King Jr. escaped from Brushy Mountain Prison, he had nowhere to go. Though the terrain is not as rugged as in places farther east, the thin soil never did support farming on a level that attracted a great many people. Most of the value lay under the ground in the form of coal or on top in the form of timber.

Nonetheless, the land attracted visionaries. England's Thomas Hughes came here in 1880 with a colony of "second sons" who sought to earn a living in a place not bound by Victorian notions of what constituted acceptable work. The Tennessee Valley Authority built its first dam in these parts, constructing beside it a town to serve as an example of a very livable place. And military leaders and scientists came here in the 1940s in a desperate effort to defeat the forces of Germany and Japan with uranium processed in the secret city of Oak Ridge.

This area might not be known for great crops, but it produced some remarkable individuals. Samuel Clemens was conceived here. Alvin York was a Fentress County conscientious objector who became World War I's greatest hero, a man who renounced fame to come home and run a mill. Cordell Hull, born not too many miles from York, won the 1945 Nobel Peace Prize. And John Rice Irwin single-handedly created the greatest collection of Appalachian items and artifacts in the world.

As Tennesseans and tourists explore the state, this area will delight them. Here stand enormous state parks filled with clear lakes and steep canyons. The Big South Fork National River and Recreation Area, with its rock formations and whitewater thrills, stacks up well against the Great Smoky Mountains National Park, with only a tiny fraction of the larger park's visitors. The oldest winery in the state, historic Rugby, and a place where grown men play a unique kind of marbles are just three of the things that await the traveler.

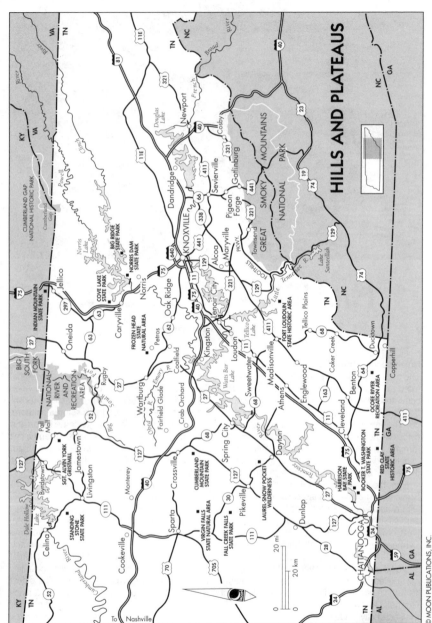

HILLS AND PLATEAUS

MUST-SEE HIGHLIGHTS

Museum of Appalachia, outside of Norris, is the best museum in the country devoted to the people of Appalachia. Most of the collection is not behind glass and is housed in log buildings.

Fall Creek Falls, near Pikeville, is the highest waterfall in the eastern United States. This park has a hotel, camping, and swinging bridges.

Rugby, sometimes called "the last colony," is a village founded by Victorians who had high hopes of providing a new way of life for aristocratic young men. The architecture and events held here are a delight.

The Oak Ridge **Museum of Science and Energy** at once looks back to the Manhattan Project and ahead to energy problems and solutions.

Fort Loudoun State Historical Area and the nearby **Sequoyah Birthplace Museum** reflect the interaction of two sets of people, one who prevailed and the other who were exiled from their ancestral home.

Benton's Smoky Mountain Country Ham, outside of Madisonville, sells the finest country hams and smoked bacon in the entire state.

Dayton's **Rhea County Courthouse,** whose courtroom has been restored to its appearance at the 1925 Scopes Trial, offers a place to reflect on a small-town booster stunt that spectacularly backfired.

The **Ocoee River Drive** along Hwy. 64 is one of the prettiest drives in the state. Look for the whitewater rafters.

Fields of the Woods, just across the North Carolina border from Ducktown, is perhaps the largest piece of folk art in the region.

The Cumberland Plateau

Sojourners heading west from Knoxville find themselves climbing the Cumberland Plateau, an obstacle once so formidable to Nashville-bound travelers that they would go through Kentucky to get around it. The Plateau is 1,000 feet higher than the Knoxville area, and its soil is thin and not much given to raising crops. For that reason, the area is one of the less populated ones in the state, yet it's an area with some wonderful things to see.

Heading the list is Fall Creek Falls State Park, home to the highest waterfall in the eastern United States. Crossville's Homestead Tower Museum recalls a Depression-era attempt at an ideal community.

The route south down the Sequatchie Valley certainly marks one of the more pleasing drives or bike rides in the state. The river offers canoeists a gentle drift ideally suited for families or those who like to take their rivers easy.

Southwest of Knoxville

Most of this part of the state, stretching between Knoxville and Chattanooga, lies in Tennessee's Great Valley. The land is much flatter than in upper East Tennessee and is ideally suited for farming. Held back by TVA's dams, the Tennessee River follows the valley to the southwest, slowly flowing and gathering the waters of the fast-rushing streams that pour out of the mountains to the east. The whitewater rafting in these rivers is unsurpassed in the state.

This area was the center of activity for the Cherokee. Their principal towns were here, and it was from this area that the infamous Trail of Tears began. Towns in the southeast part of Tennessee have banded together to promote themselves as "the Tennessee Overhill," the old name given to the Cherokee strongholds.

The coming of the railroad created many towns in this section, bringing industry and jobs. Towns dreamed of businesses or schemes that would "put them on the map," and one of them—Dayton—did so with a "monkey trial" that is still argued about and discussed today.

NORTH OF KNOXVILLE

NORRIS

For students of urban design, this town is a great stop. Norris, named after Sen. George Norris of Nebraska, began as housing for the workers who built TVA's first dam. In those vision-filled early days of the agency, however, the town took on greater import. This was to be a model community, a place to try out ideas and to set up an example from which others could learn.

These innovations took several forms: all-electric houses, because TVA wanted to demonstrate the uses of its chief product; roads that were adapted to the existing contours instead of forcing the land to conform to a plan; and houses clustered around common areas of land. The road leading to Norris was designated the "Norris Parkway," and billboards were banned, a radical concept in the 1930s. The people in the various houses—there were 12 designs from which to choose—loved their town, but there

THE TENNESSEE FALL HOMECOMING AT THE MUSEUM OF APPALACHIA

If a visitor to Tennessee can go to only one event in the state, this is the one.

Held every October, the Homecoming brings together musicians, craftspeople, writers, and plain old folks for a lively celebration of Appalachia. College presidents rub shoulders with retired farmers, all tapping their feet to bluegrass music that pours forth from two stages.

Musically, it doesn't get much better than this. Here is a partial list of the participants who have appeared in recent years: Bill Monroe, Jimmy Driftwood, Grandpa Jones and Ramona, Ava Barber, Roy Book Binder, Joe and Janette Carter, Bashful Brother Oswald, Mike Seeger, and Mac Wiseman. Bands such as the Dismembered Tennesseans, the Bottom of the Barrel Bunch, and the New River Boys serve up hand-picked bluegrass.

Visitors can watch demonstrations of many old-time crafts and activities, such as apple butter- and molasses-making, pottery, quilting, woodcarving, spinning and dyeing, rifle firing, and white-oak basket-making.

Country cooking is dished up from wood-burning stoves and open pots, and washed down with fresh-squeezed cider and sassafras tea.

Admission for this four-day event is $35 for adults and $15 for children. Daily admission begins on weekdays at $10 for adults and $5 for children. Saturday rates go to $20 for adults and $5 for children, and Sunday's admission is $15 for adults and $5 for

Sherman Wooten, chairmaker

MUSEUM OF APPALACHIA

children. Advance tickets are a very good idea. Write to the Museum at P.O. Box 0318, Norris, TN 37828. For further information, call (423) 494-0514.

FRANK HOFFMAN

Sisters Grace Rutherford and Alverta Stooksbury snap string beans on the porch of the Homestead House at the Museum of Appalachia.

was one big catch: TVA owned everything.

In 1947, TVA announced it would sell the entire town to any buyer who could come up with $1.8 million. A Philadelphia company bought the town, then began selling the houses to their owners. By 1953, the parks and town buildings had been sold as well, and Norris could govern itself much as any other town. Today the town stands as an example of good planning and the willingness of the residents to adhere to high standards.

Museum of Appalachia

Norris is renowned for two museums of Appalachian culture. The Museum of Appalachia, tel. (423) 494-0514, is a nationally known collection of some 250,000 items brought together by John Rice Irwin, a remarkable individual who was awarded a "genius" grant by the MacArthur Foundation. The items are displayed in 20 buildings on a 65-acre farm just off I-75 at Exit 122.

Irwin started out collecting odd items as a boy, and as he grew up he realized that the tools and other objects that marked Tennessee mountain life were slowly slipping away, as was the knowledge of what they were and how to use them. Using his own money, he assembled his collection of musical instruments, traps, bits, hand tools, and axes. He has millstones, stagecoach horns, blacksmith tools, sheep shears, and on and on and on. The visitor is simultaneously impressed with how hard life was in "the old days" as well as with the ingenuity and imagination of the people who lived in those times and confronted basic problems without the benefits of hardware stores. Irwin believes that museum objects "should be tied in some way to the people who used them." This philosophy has produced a museum with a warm personality—not a sterile place where visitors walk around with their hands clasped behind them.

An important part of the museum is the Appalachian Hall of Fame, which recognizes, among others, Sgt. Alvin York, the Carter Family, and Cordell Hull, with artifacts from each person. A relatively new exhibit is a Jamestown cabin that once belonged to the parents of Samuel Clemens. His parents moved down to Hannibal, Missouri, before Samuel was born, but the calendar suggests America's foremost humorist was conceived while they lived in Jamestown. The museum periodically sponsors demonstrations of crafts, tool use, music, quilting, and a once-a-year "shooting of the anvil." This earth-shaking event involves two anvils, black powder, and a long fuse.

Admission to the museum is $7 for adults, $4 for children ages six to 15. Families get in for $17, and seniors receive a discount. It is open during daylight hours year-round.

The Lenoir Museum is a part of the Norris Dam State Park (see below).

Practicalities

The **Fox Inn Campground,** tel. (423) 494-9386, is right off I-75's Exit 122 on Hwy. 61. Ninety-eight sites are open all year, with a swimming pool and other amenities.

The Museum of Appalachia has a restaurant that is open daily. Diners do not have to pay admission to the museum to eat cornbread, soup, beans, and chicken pot pie, as well as burgers and hot dogs.

NORRIS AREA PARKS

Norris Dam State Resort Park

Although TVA took over several dams when the agency came into existence, this was the first one it built. Work began in 1933 and ended three years later. The result is a 265-foot-high dam that stretches across the valley for 1,860 feet, holding back a lake that covers 34,000 acres of land. Visitors may tour the powerhouse below the dam free of charge Mon.-Fri. 8 a.m.-3 p.m. To arrange a tour, call (423) 632-3631.

The park that commemorates Norris Dam covers 4,038 acres and also contains the **Rice Gristmill,** a 1798 mill that was once operated by the kinfolks of John Rice Irwin. During the summers this mill still grinds corn, and the meal is available in a gift shop.

The **Hill Cave Tour,** offered twice a week during the summers, enables the intrepid to walk and crawl through this local cavern. Reservations for the trip, which costs $2 per person, can be made at (423) 426-7461.

The **Lenoir Museum,** tel. (423) 494-9688, in the park is the work of the late Will Lenoir, another of those individuals who was driven to collect odd items—Appalachian and otherwise. Among the latter is a German barrel organ dating from 1826 with 44 moveable figures. Another is a Ming dynasty vase. This museum is open seven days a week in the summer, with reduced days the rest of the year. Every Sunday afternoon features live traditional music. Admission is free.

The park maintains 29 cabins and 85 campsites for use by visitors. Amenities include boat rentals, swimming pool, and hiking trails. The campground is open all year. For information or reservations, call (423) 426-7461 or (800) 543-9335.

Big Ridge State Rustic Park

Norris was TVA's demonstration town, and Big Ridge was the agency's demonstration park. The heavily wooded 3,642 acres overlook Norris Lake and feature 52 campsites, cabins, hiking trails, swimming, boat rentals, and a visitors center with nature exhibits. To get there, take Hwy. 61 northwest from I-75. For information, call (423) 992-5523.

NORTH TO KENTUCKY

Cove Lake State Recreational Park

Right outside the town of Caryville on Hwy. 25 West sits Cove Lake State Recreational Park, a 673-acre park with nature trails and bike paths from which visitors can see Cumberland Mountain. The lake is home to hundreds of Canada geese in the winter, and other visitors will find tennis courts, 97 camping sites open all year, swimming, fishing, and boat rentals. For more information, call (423) 566-9701.

Jellico

This little town on the Kentucky border was the scene of a terrible explosion on September 21, 1906, when a railroad car full of 10 tons of dynamite blew up. Nine people died, 200 were injured, and almost one-fourth of the town was left homeless. The explosion broke every pane of glass in a one-mile radius and could be heard for 20 miles. The crater left by the blast was 20 feet in diameter and 20 feet deep.

That same year a little girl named Grace Moore and her family moved to Jellico from Del Rio, Tennessee. She sang in the local Baptist choir and went on to become Tennessee's most famous opera singer, making her debut at the New York Metropolitan Grand Opera Company in 1927 and appearing in *La Bohème, Tosca,* and *Romeo and Juliet,* to name a few. She went on to star in a series of movies, of which *One Night of Love* is the most famous. "The Tennessee Nightingale" died in a plane crash outside Copenhagen in 1947.

Motels include the **Best Western Holiday Plaza Motel,** Exit 160 of I-75, tel. (423) 784-7241; **Billy's Motel,** Exit 160, tel. (423) 784-4362; **Days Inn,** Exit 160, tel. (423) 784-7281; and **The Jellico Motel,** Exit 160, tel. (423) 784-7211 or (800) 251-9498.

The small **Indian Mountain State Camping Park**—only 213 acres—was developed on land that had been strip-mined for coal. It offers 49 campsites, hiking trails, fishing, and boating, and it is open all year. For information, call (423) 784-7958.

ONEIDA

As the biggest town on the eastern end of the Big South Fork National River and Recreation Area, this is the place to rest one's head, get something to eat, and find other necessities of life.

It is also the birthplace of the Smith Brothers, not the cough lozenge duo, but two brothers whose career ran from the '30s to the '60s. "Tennessee" and "Smitty" played country, western swing, and other varieties of music, eventually winding up with gospel.

The **Sorghum Festival** marks the annual arrival of members of the Muddy Pond Mennonite Community, who set up a horse-powered mill that grinds cane to extract the sap, which is then boiled down to produce sorghum, a.k.a. molasses. The festival, usually held on the second weekend in September, includes live music, arts and crafts sales, and lots of food. For more information, call (423) 569-6900 or (800) 645-6905.

Where to Stay
Try the **Williams Creek Wilderness Resort,** tel. (423) 569-9847; **Galloway Inn,** S. Hwy. 27, tel. (423) 569-8835; or **Holiday Inn Big South Fork,** Lakeside Drive in Huntsville, tel. (423) 663-4100 or (800) HOLIDAY.

Food
Flonnie's Drive-In, south of town at the intersection of Hwy. 27 and Hwy. 63, tel. (423) 663-2851, is a good example of the kind of restaurant that preceded McDonald's, Hardee's, and others of the franchise ilk. Patrons can sit in their cars or inside. The food includes the popular "Flonnieburger" as well as other dishes such as chicken and chili. Milk shakes are made one at a time. It's open for lunch and dinner every day.

Milt's Chicago Restaurant on South Alberta Ave., tel. (423) 569-8178, serves lunch and dinner Monday-Saturday.

Phillip's Drive-In, 212 Alberta Ave., tel. (423) 569-4002, offers "Jerryburgers," pizza, fried chicken, and fish seven days a week. It opens at 8 a.m. and does not close until after dinner.

Preston's Loft Steak and Pizza, 1047 N. Alberta Ave., tel. (423) 569-4158, opens for lunch and dinner seven days a week.

Tobe's Restaurant, on North Alberta Ave., tel. (423) 569-4689, dishes up country cooking for all three meals seven days a week.

Tray's 5, 110 Oneida Pl., tel. (423) 569-9888, offers Chinese food.

Uncle Roy's, on Industrial Ln., tel. (423) 569-4633, features country cooking three meals a day Monday-Saturday.

Information
Scott County Chamber of Commerce, 410 N. Alberta St. in Oneida, tel. (423) 569-6900 or (800) 645-6905, dispenses information Mon.-Fri. 8 a.m.-4 p.m.

BIG SOUTH FORK NATIONAL RIVER AND RECREATION AREA

If the millions of people who whiz south on I-75 or east on I-40 heading for the Great Smoky Mountains National Park knew what they could see and do in the Big South Fork National River and Recreation Area, the people in the outlet stores of Pigeon Forge and parking lots of Gatlinburg might have a little more room. The Smokies can't be beat for sheer size and grandeur, but when it comes to hikes with fascinating natural features, the Big South Fork wins hands down. And it's just 65 miles from Knoxville and less than 30 miles from I-75. As one Big South Fork ranger admitted, "This is where people who work in the Smokies come for their vacations."

The name comes from the south fork of the Cumberland River, and the park looks like a gerrymandered political district as it snakes upstream from Tennessee into Kentucky. Like the Smokies, the land that makes up this park was once exploited for timber. Coal was mined in some areas. Underlying it all is a geology that, combined with running water, created some of the most fascinating landscapes in the entire state, but this is not apparent on first entering the area. In this part of Tennessee visitors initially look down to see the scenery, not up.

The Cumberland Plateau on which this area lies is covered with a hard layer of sandstone. Underneath this surface layer, however, sits much softer sandstone. When a stream breaks through the hard capstone, it readily cuts through the underlying material. Thus Big South Fork has 500-foot-deep gorges, dramatic cliffs, arches, and "rock houses" where present-day visitors can see the same stones that sheltered Indian hunters and settlers. Whitewater aficionados will find water varying from family float trips all the way to Class V expert-only runs. Unlike the Smokies, Big South Fork permits mountain biking on several designated trails.

All this is relatively new. The Army Corps of Engineers long had its eye on damming the river, at one time proposing what would have been the highest dam in the East, but, luckily, could never get funding from Congress. Local con-servationists began making noises about pre-serving the land and rivers in the 1960s, but it took the political push of then-Senator Howard Baker to bring the efforts to fruition. The area has an unwieldy name, but nothing a handy acronym—BSFNRRA—can't solve. The park, which extends into Kentucky as well as Tennessee, totals more than 113,000 acres, not counting the adjacent Pickett State Rustic Park and Forest, which adds 11,700 acres, or the Daniel Boone National Forest, with 500,000 acres.

The newness of Big South Fork cuts both ways. The positive side is that the facilities—campgrounds, visitors centers, bridges, and trail steps—are all relatively new. The down side is that towns around the park have not quite caught up with visitor services, and the traveler to these parts has to do some careful planning, on the trail and off. On the trail, hikers and boaters are very often totally by themselves. This is the best way to enjoy the wilderness, to be sure, but not so great if one gets hurt or somehow needs help. Outside of the park, many of the access points to Big South Fork are in remote areas, with no nearby restaurants, stores, or gas stations.

RECREATION

Hiking

Almost 150 miles of hiking trails range through Big South Fork. They vary from less-than-one-mile jaunts to trips lasting for days. Here are a couple of examples, one on the east side and one from the west.

From the east, the **O&W Bridge Trail** goes 4.6 miles roundtrip to an old railroad trestle for trains on the Oneida and Western Line that once connected Oneida and Jamestown. To get to the trailhead, go 2.2 miles from the park's east entrance on Hwy. 297 to the Leatherwood Ford River Access and Leatherwood Ford Trailhead.

Begin walking south under the Leatherwood Ford Bridge to a trail junction sign. Don't climb the steps leading to the bridge. Instead, follow the John Muir Trail straight into the woods. Hike along the river on the right until you see another junction with a trail going to the left up the bluff. Don't take the trail to the left, but follow the John Muir Trail about 1,200 feet, where it begins to climb the bluff.

At the top the trail joins an old roadbed that descends to cross a creek. The trail then goes downstream, and soon the bridge comes into sight. According to Russ Manning and Sondra Jamieson, authors of *Tennessee's South Cumberland,* the bridge is of Whipple Truss design, used from 1847 to 1900. This particular bridge was moved here from another site in 1915, and it was used until 1954. The park has built a pedestrian walkway across the bridge.

From the west, **Twin Arches Trail** leads 1.4 miles roundtrip to one of the more amazing geological wonders in these parts, two big sequential arches in which one begins where the other ends. One reaches a length of 135 feet and a height of 70 feet, while the other extends 93 feet with an opening 51 feet high. To get to the trailhead, turn right out of the Bandy Creek Visitors Center onto the Bandy Creek Road and follow it for two miles to the intersection with Hwy. 297. Go right and continue to Hwy. 154. Turn right and continue on Hwy. 154 for 1.8 miles. Turn right onto Divide Road. In 1.3 miles the road will fork, but drivers should remain to the left on Divide Rd. for another 2.7 miles. Turn right onto the Twin Arches Rd., and the trailhead is 2.4 miles ahead.

The trail begins at the parking area. Hike out a narrow ridge and go to the left, where two steep sets of stairs lead to the base of the bluff. Turning right, walk along the bluff line to North Arch. An exhibit here explains how the arches are formed, and then the trail leads up and over South Arch. While exploring South Arch, look for the "fat man's squeeze," a narrow tunnel leading out to the end of the ridge where one can go left or right to come back to the arch. The stairway between the two arches leads up to the top of the bluff and back across the top of North Arch to form a small loop. Hikers will return to the trailhead by the same route they came down.

Hikers should keep in mind that hunting is permitted in Big South Fork. The prudent hiker will either wear blaze orange or avoid the woods entirely during deer and boar hunting season, which generally runs for two weeks beginning in the middle of November. Rangers can explain when and where hunters might be lurking.

Bicycling

Bikers can ride on any road within the park. Mountain bikes can go on any trail designated by "Bike" signs as well as any horse trails, which are marked with yellow horse heads on trees along the trail. Bikers must yield the right of way to horses and, given the skittishness of some equines, it's not a bad idea to dismount the bike and move to the side of the trail.

The 5.3-mile **Duncan Hollow Loop** bicycle trail leaves from and returns to the Bandy Creek Visitor Center. The trail crosses a creek and includes several sections of single track riding.

Visitors can rent bikes from Backwoods Adventures in Oneida, listed under "Whitewater" below.

Fishing

Everyone fishing in Big South Fork must have either a Tennessee or Kentucky fishing license—depending on where they are fishing—which are available at stores in surrounding towns. The area is noted for smallmouth bass, rock bass, and bream. Any rafters or kayakers hooked come under catch-and-release rules.

Horseback Riding

With more than 130 miles of trails on which to ride, Big South Fork is a horse fancier's dream. Visitors with their own horses can board them at stables at Bandy Creek and take advantage of two horse camps in the park. The **Station Camp Horse Camp** is on the east side of the park, with 25 sites, each of which has four tie stalls. In Kentucky, the **Bear Creek Horse Camp** also has 25 sites.

One place in the park rents horses. **Bandy Creek Stables,** tel. (931) 879-4013, offers rides varying from a few hours to several days. Guided one-hour rides, which are offered May-Oct., cost $15 per person. Two-day and three-day overnight rides include food, lodging, and everything else; riders need only bring personal items. These cost, respectively, $175 and $265 per person, and require a four-person minimum group. These rides take place year-round.

Riders can also choose from other stables that are listed at visitors centers.

Hunting

Hunting is permitted in sections of Big South Fork, and hunters are governed by the laws and rules of the state in which they hunt. For information, contact the Tennessee Wildlife Resources Agency at tel. (931) 484-9571 or (800) 262-6704 in Tennessee, or Fish and Wildlife Information in Kentucky at tel. (502) 564-4336.

Whitewater

Big South Fork has water varying from stretches that are ideal for beginners to sections that will challenge experts. As with all whitewater areas, a key piece of information is the flow rate. Rivers that are easy to raft at 2,500 cubic feet per second (CFS) will become monsters at 10,000 or 20,000 CFS. Boaters should also understand that once they head down certain areas of Big South Fork, they cannot come back. A free paddler's guide is available at visitors centers, and rangers are always willing to advise those who would head downstream.

Canoe and kayak rentals and guided trips are available from several places.

Backwoods Adventure, 327 Industrial Ln. (Hwy. 297) in Oneida, tel. (931) 569-9573, rents canoes and inflatable kayaks and can provide shuttle service for boaters. This is a one-person operation, so call ahead.

Cumberland Rapid Transit, on Hwy. 297 between Oneida and Big South Fork, tel. (931) 879-4818, rents canoes, kayaks, and wetsuits and takes customers on flat trips ranging from a half day to five days. Half-day trips cost $40 per person and go on Class III and IV water. Full-day trips cost $70 per person. Longer trips cost $110 per person per day and include tents and gourmet food such as stuffed trout amandine.

Although based in Kentucky, **Sheltowee Trace Outfitters** in Whitley City, tel. (606) 376-5567 or (800) 541-RAFT, offers raft trips and canoe rentals in Tennessee. From mid-March through June it offers full-day Class IV raft trips that last approximately five to six hours. These cost $70 per person, and children must be at least 12 years old. Class III raft trips last three hours and cost $40 per person. Kids must be five years old.

The outfitters also rent canoes for specific sections of the river, for trips ranging from several hours to several days. Its practice is to meet parties at the anticipated take-out point and then shuttle canoes and canoers to the put-in point.

WHERE TO STAY

Oneida, the largest town on the eastern end of the park, offers various accommodations for travelers. Within the park, visitors have the choice of staying in a lodge or camping.

Charit Creek Lodge

Sitting at the confluence of Charit Creek and Station Camp Creek on the west side of the park, Charit Creek Lodge, tel. (931) 429-5704, is accessible only by foot or horseback. The shortest trail is 0.8 miles long, yet the ambitious visitor can use a network of connecting trails to take all day to get to the lodge, if desired.

Once there, by horse or foot, the weary traveler finds a big log building, a bathhouse, and outlying cabins. Accommodations consist of a lodge with two rooms each sleeping up to 12 people, and two freestanding cabins, each of which can hold up to 12. Guests sleep in bunk beds—most of them double bunk beds—that come with linens. On weekend nights the cabins have a six-person minimum, and unless guests arrive in a large group, they will share their bedroom with strangers—not recommended for honeymooners.

A cabin that makes up part of the lodge was built here in 1817. There is no electricity, but cabins come with kerosene lamps and woodstoves and access to a solar-heated shower and flush toilets. The lodge maintains libraries of books and board games inside as well as horseshoe pitching and volleyball outside. A hearty dinner and country breakfast are included in the price, which is $52 for adults and $41 for children ages four to 10.

Reservations for weekdays are relatively easy to get. Weekends are another matter. The lodge begins accepting phone reservations in August for the next calendar year. Expensive.

Camping

Big South Fork has two developed campgrounds. **Bandy Creek** has 150 sites—100 with

EMERGENCY NUMBERS IN BIG SOUTH FORK

Bandy Creek Visitor Center, tel. (423) 879-3625, 8 a.m.-4:30 p.m. EST (8 a.m.-6 p.m. during daylight saving time)

For the East Side of Big South Fork

Scott County Hospital, Hwy. 27, Oneida, TN, tel. (423) 569-8521
Scott County Ambulance, tel. (423) 569-6000
Scott County Sheriff, Huntsville, TN, tel. (423) 663-2245

For the West Side of Big South Fork

Fentress County General Hospital,
    W. Central Ave., Jamestown, TN
    tel. (615) 879-8171
Fentress County Ambulance,
    tel. (615) 879-8147
Fentress County Sheriff, Jamestown, TN
    tel. (615) 879-8142

In Kentucky

Blue Heron Interpretive Center,
    tel. (606) 376-3787
McCreary County Ambulance Service,
    tel. (606) 376-5062
McCreary County Sheriff, tel. (606) 376-2322

---

hookups—all available year-round on a first-come, first-served basis. **Blue Heron,** in Kentucky, has 20 sites open April-October. **Alum Ford,** farther north in Kentucky, has primitive camping with 10 sites. There is no charge for using it.

Backcountry campers can generally stay wherever they want in Big South Fork, with the following exceptions: no one should camp within 25 feet of a cave, cemetery, grave site, historic site or structure, rock shelter, rim of the gorge (that makes sense!), trail, road, or any area designated with a No Camping sign. Camping is not permitted within 100 feet of the center line of the major roads running through the park.

Big South Fork shows some evidence of overuse. Campers should work to minimize their impact on the land; for example, pitch tents on existing sites rather than create new ones. Fires are allowed, except under arches, rock shelters, or near historic structures. Only trees that are both dead and down can be used for wood.

Permits are not required for backcountry camping, but they are a good idea. If campers should have an emergency, the permits give the park personnel a place to start looking. Permits cost nothing and are available from visitors centers or by calling (931) 879-3625.

Wildwood Lodge

Just 12 miles west of the Bandy Creek portion of Big South Fork is one of the better places to stay on the entire Cumberland Plateau. The Wildwood Lodge's 12 rooms have private baths, televisions, private entrances from the parking lot, and comfortable furniture. A big country breakfast is served, and guests—with advance reservations—can have a dinner prepared by the proprietor, a European-trained chef. Reg and Julie Johnson are from England and have a wonderful attitude toward hospitality: "We cater to activity people," says Reg. "We don't do dainty things for breakfast—we give them a bloody country breakfast 'cause they're going to be out burning energy all day." Rates are $65-75. Call (931) 879-9454. Moderate.

INFORMATION AND GUIDEBOOKS

Big South Fork has a large number of pamphlets covering various aspects of the park. These are available at the Bandy Creek Visitors Center, tel. (931) 879-3625. The visitors center is on the west side of the river to the north of Hwy. 297.

Two good books cover this area in great detail. *Hiking the Big South Fork,* by Brenda D. Coleman and Jo Anna Smith, contains topographical maps of the trails. *Trails of the Big South Fork,* by Russ Manning and Sondra Jamieson, provides a thorough guide to hiking trails. Both are available at visitors centers.

Although the Park Service provides free maps, a much better map of the area is available from Trails Illustrated. These excellent topographical maps are available at the visitors center or by calling (800) 962-1643. Or find them online at www.npps.gov/biso/.

OAK RIDGE

John Hendrix had it all figured out. This 19th-century prophet predicted that the area around Black Oak Ridge would be "filled with great buildings and factories. . . . Thousands of people will be running to and fro. They will be building things and there will be a great noise and confusion and the world will shake." People at the time thought he was a crackpot, but his visions came to pass when Oak Ridge played its role in the race to build an atomic weapon.

Oak Ridge is no longer a secret city, giving visitors, whatever their thoughts on the A-bomb, a look at wartime city planning and logistical accomplishment in a town that has turned out to be a very pleasant place to spend some time. This is one place where the predominance of cuisine is not "country cooking," and where museums and culture play a prominent role in the lives of the residents.

The Atomic City is not exactly a hotbed of country music, and at this writing has yet to pro-duce any famed figures. The nearby hamlet of Oliver Springs, however, is the birthplace of Hugh Cross, an early country musician best known for his 1928 recording of "You're As Welcome as the Flowers in May."

SIGHTS

Museums

The **American Museum of Science and Energy,** 300 S. Tulane Ave., tel. (423) 576-3200, is one of the better science museums in the state. Taking visitors at first back to the days of World War II, it gives a vivid sense of "life behind the fences" with rationing, government housing, and the intensity of the war effort. Visitors can see models of eight nuclear weapons, among them Hiroshima's "Little Boy." Live demonstrations of scientific principles take place from time to time, among them a static electricity device that

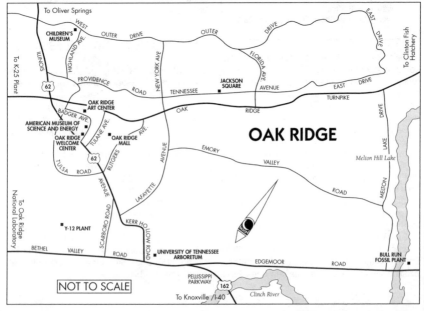

THE OAK RIDGE STORY

In a very real sense, Oak Ridge is the most extraordinary city in all of Tennessee. Other towns have been built from scratch by industry or government—Alcoa, Norris, Homestead—but nothing on the level of Oak Ridge.

It all began with the 1939 realization that a weapon of hitherto unimaginable power could be made from splitting the atom. The Manhattan Project, a top-secret effort, swung into action to bring this bomb into existence as fast as possible. Planners needed a place that was out of reach of enemy bombers, had plenty of available electricity, a good workforce, and rail and highway connections. They also needed, it must be said, a remote site far from population centers in case something went dreadfully wrong.

Government officials came in and bought up approximately 60,000 acres—about 10 miles by two miles—forcing 3,000 people living in 1,000 homes to move. Fences went up around the compound, which was dubbed Oak Ridge after the nearby Black Oak Ridge.

Scientists determined that three methods showed the most promise of producing fissionable material from natural uranium; the government decided to go with all three. The electromagnetic process emerged as the Y-12 plant, about 170 buildings spread over a factory covering 500 acres. The gaseous diffusion method was given its chance in a 44-acre building called K-25. The final method, thermal diffusion, was tested in the S-50 complex of 160 buildings occupying 150 acres. A graphite reactor, code-named X-10, served as a pilot plant for a larger plutonium-producing plant in Hanford, Washington.

In each of these buildings, men and women worked round the clock at labor whose goal was a mystery to them. They could see trains full of ore go into the buildings, but nothing seemed to come out. A worker might spend an entire shift watching one gauge and using knobs to control some unknown force to keep the needle in the appropriate zone.

The various uranium plants represented only one aspect of the enormous logistical operations going on in the city. People and materials poured into the town, making it within three years the fifth-largest city in the state—75,000 people in all. Planners had to lay out an entire city in a matter of weeks and months. Architects furiously designed buildings that could be raised in a hurry. None of them were designed to last a long time—one kind of housing had canvas roofs. As things got a little less frantic, single-family homes called "cemestos" appeared in a variety of plans, schools were built, and shopping centers sprang up.

The dropping of the first atomic bomb on Hiroshima meant that the curtain of secrecy at Oak Ridge could be partially lifted. At last the workers and their families found out what they had been doing, and a surge of pride roared through the town. Oak Ridgers called and wrote to relatives all over the country telling what they had been doing for all those months.

The end of World War II, however, did not mean that Oak Ridge was entirely open. Production of fissionable material increased as the Cold War set in, as did efforts to prevent loss of atomic secrets. Children who repeated at school something their parents said over the dinner table about work could expect a visit from security personnel and a lecture on the need to keep quiet. The town was opened to the public in 1949, and six years later the government permitted residents to buy their homes and land. The city was incorporated in 1959.

Now Oak Ridge has a population of 28,000. While production of fissionable material has largely halted, the focus of the town is Oak Ridge National Laboratory, which works on deciphering the human genetic code and coming up with ways to deal with nuclear and other toxic waste. Some of the nuclear waste is in Oak Ridge itself; weapons producers during World War II and the subsequent Cold War did not always properly dispose of their hazardous materials.

The high education level of Oak Ridge residents expresses itself in many ways. The town supports the oldest performing symphony orchestra in the state, a ballet association, contemporary dance, an art center, and the Oak Ridge Playhouse, whose productions began during the war. A final benefit of all those Ph.D.s is a lively craving for Chinese food, which fuels a hearty competition among the restaurants hereabouts.

makes volunteers' hair stand straight out. The museum isn't entirely about atomic energy. Exhibits also cover "Earth's Natural Resources," "The Age of the Automobile," and "The American Experience." Admission is free. See their site online at www.korrnet.org/amse.

The **Oak Ridge Art Center,** 201 Badger Ave., tel. (423) 482-1441, displays permanent collections of modern and contemporary art, as well as changing exhibitions. It's open Tues.-Fri. 9 a.m.-5 p.m., Sat.-Mon. 1-4 p.m. Admission is free.

It's no surprise that a town this devoted to science would have a first-rate **Children's Museum,** 461 W. Outer Dr., tel. (423) 482-1074. This hands-on place enables kids to learn in 12 exhibit areas, among them "Pioneer Living," "Coal in Appalachia," and "Waterworks." The museum is open Mon.-Fri. 9 a.m.-5 p.m. year-round. September through June, the museum is also open weekends 11 a.m.-3 p.m. In July and August the museum is open Saturday 11 a.m.-3 p.m. Admission is $4 for adults, $3.50 for seniors, and $2.50 for children over three.

Oak Ridge National Laboratory

This laboratory once focused solely on producing plutonium from uranium. Visitors to Oak Ridge can tour present-day Oak Ridge National Laboratory or the landmarks of the past. With advance notice, Oak Ridge National Laboratory will provide guided group tours of the lab. Call the Office of Public Affairs at (423) 574-4160, or

check out www.ornl.gov. For those who provide their own vehicles, the tour is free. If the Lab provides transportation, there is a charge.

The past is easy to see. A self-guiding tour begins at the New Bethel Church, a house of worship that was transformed during the war to a meeting room for scientists bent on producing a device that would bring about almost Biblical destruction. A visitor overlook gives some background to the Manhattan Project. The most interesting sight is the graphite reactor, the world's first operational reactor. Graphite is the material used to regulate the rate of fission of the reactor's fuel. The K-25 overlook displays the enormous—and at one time top-secret—facility used to produce fissionable uranium.

The University of Tennessee Arboretum

The arboretum, tel. (423) 483-3571, consists of 250 acres of former farmland whose timber was harvested before World War II. The land was acquired by the Manhattan Project and in 1961 given to the University of Tennessee, which uses it to study the effectiveness of plants in reclaiming strip mines, test-breed late-blooming and frost-resistant magnolias, and determine which plants can attract wildlife to urban settings.

For visitors, however, the arboretum is a great place to walk in the woods. Admission is free, and trails of less than a mile take visitors through various habitats. The arboretum visitors center is

In the days of the Manhattan Project, Oak Ridge was heavily guarded and surrounded by security gates and fences.

open Mon.-Fri. 8 a.m.-4:30 p.m.; the grounds stay open until sunset. Visitors cannot take pets, have picnics, jog, ride bikes, cross-country ski, or collect any plants.

Sights outside Town

TVA's **Bull Run Fossil Plant,** tel. (423) 945-7200, sits right outside of town, one very visible example of how electricity in the region is produced. Powered by coal, the steam turbines turn generators that send electricity into TVA's power grid. Unfortunately, the combustion process also sends pollutants into the atmosphere—pollutants that contribute to the reduction of visibility in the Smokies and elsewhere. TVA has installed "scrubbers" on the smokestacks to remove some of the pollution, and how that is accomplished is explained here. Visitors can see exhibits on power production in the lobby, which is open Mon.-Fri. 7 a.m. to 3:30 p.m. Admission is free.

The **Eagle Bend Fish Hatchery,** tel. (423) 457-5135, provides lake fish for Tennessee: striped bass, walleyes, bluegills, and largemouth bass. The fish are raised in ponds, and if employees have time they will give brief tours to visitors Mon.-Fri. 8 a.m.-4:30 p.m. To get to the hatchery, take Hwy. 61 northeast from Oak Ridge through Clinton. The hatchery lies along the Clinch River just outside of town. Sometimes no one is there; they are all out stocking fish.

WHERE TO STAY

Among the options are **Comfort Inn,** 433 S. Rutgers Ave., tel. (423) 481-8200 or (800) 553-7830; **Days Inn,** 206 S. Illinois Ave., tel. (423) 483-5615 or (800) 325-2525; **Garden Plaza Hotel,** 215 S. Illinois Ave, tel. (423) 481-2468 or (800) 3GARDEN; and **Ramada Inn,** 420 S. Illinois Ave., tel. (423) 483-4371.

FOOD

For those whose palates and arteries have grown weary of country cooking, Oak Ridge provides a culinary oasis, and it probably has more

Asian restaurants per capita than any place in Tennessee.

Bleu Hound, 80 E. Tennessee Ave., tel. (423) 481-6101, features dishes such as grilled quail, roast duckling, and fresh fish every evening. It's open Mon.-Fri. for lunch and Mon.-Sat. for dinner.

Buddy's Bar-be-que, 328 S. Illinois Ave., tel. (423) 481-8102, is a local franchise offering very good pork barbecue and ribs. It's open for lunch and dinner daily.

The Daily Grind, downtown at Jackson Square, tel. (423) 483-9200, makes the best muffins in town. Diners also enjoy deli sandwiches, pastries, and salads served Mon.-Sat. 7 a.m.-4 p.m.

The Mustard Seed Grill, at the Ramada Inn, tel. (423) 482-9952, serves down-home food for lunch and dinner every day.

Asian

Kim Son Restaurant, 171 Robertson St., tel. (423) 482-4958, serves Vietnamese and Chinese food Mon.-Sat. for lunch and dinner.

Lichee Garden, 1150 Oak Ridge Turnpike, tel. (423) 483-9944, is open for lunch and dinner every day.

BIG ED'S PIZZA

Tennessee, unlike northeastern America, never had much of a tradition of mom and pop pizza places. For that reason, alas, Tennessee has been fertile ground for various franchise operations—20th-century versions of the carpetbaggers that descended on the South after the Civil War.

Big Ed's, 101 Broadway in historic Jackson Square in Oak Ridge, tel. (423) 482-4885, offers the best pizza in the state. The dough is spun high into the air, the ingredients are of the highest quality, and the beer somehow tastes better than it does at other establishments.

The late Big Ed, who for years presided over the place, was a bear of a man who looked like a former Marine drill instructor on Parris Island. The darkened restaurant's display cases contain game balls from UT football games and trophies won by military shooting teams.

Big Ed's serves lunch and dinner, hot pizza and cold beer, Monday-Saturday.

Magic Wok Restaurant, 202 Tyler Rd., tel. (423) 482-6628, is open Mon.-Fri. for lunch and dinner.

New China Palace, Melton Lake Dr., tel. (423) 482-3323, is perhaps the fanciest of the Chinese restaurants in these parts. It overlooks the lake and is open nightly, serving dinner only.

Wok 'N' Roll, 1169 Oak Ridge Turnpike, tel.

(423) 481-8300, dishes up lunch and dinner Monday-Saturday.

INFORMATION

Oak Ridge Welcome Center is located at 302 S. Tulane Ave., tel. (423) 482-7821. See its site online at www.ci.oakridge.tn.us.com.

NORTHWEST OF OAK RIDGE

THE ROAD TO RUGBY

Leaving Oak Ridge, the traveler goes to Oliver Springs and ascends Walden Ridge, the eastern edge of the Cumberland Plateau. The rich farmland and wide rivers of the Ridge and Valley are gone, replaced by mountains of sandstone. Here is Tennessee's only wild and scenic river, along with more waterfalls than anywhere else in the state. It's an area of exceptional beauty.

This is also a place with a lot of what are termed "extractive industries," mostly coal and timber. Strip mines slice off the tops of mountains, and clear cuts remove hundreds of acres of trees seemingly at once. Although most of the coal hereabouts is now extracted by strip mining, a great many people here can testify from experience that Merle Travis was right when he sang, "It's dark as a dungeon way down in the mines." Oliver Springs hosts an annual **Coal Miners Convention** on the first Saturday in October. The "convention" features bluegrass or country music, food booths, and a 100-foot long board of mining memorabilia. To get there, turn east just before Oliver Springs' sole traffic light and follow the signs to the Union Valley Baptist Church. For further information call (423) 435-2307.

Farther up Hwy. 62 the visitor can take Hwy. 116 to see a place where people do not have fond memories of mining. **Brushy Mountain Prison** lies off Hwy. 62 along Hwy. 116 in the town of Petros. Tennessee used to believe that prison inmates should earn their keep, and in the 1890s the state bought coal lands and erected the prison, using convict labor to build it. Prisoner/miners worked two 12-hour shifts, while others labored on the farm or worked at

various other duties. Mining by prisoners continued until 1966.

In 1977, the late James Earl Ray, convicted killer of Martin Luther King, Jr., escaped from here into the surrounding forest. The prison is so remote that the warden, on hearing that certain roads had been closed, said, "We've got him. It's just a matter of time." The guards released bloodhounds, and in 54 hours the escapee was back in custody.

Frozen Head State Natural Area

This is wonderful place to take children. To get to it, visitors must drive though the Morgan County site of the Brushy Mountain prison complex, and kids can press their noses to the glass for a look at a place where bad things happen to bad people. The Natural Area is named for Frozen Head Mountain, elevation 3,324 feet, a peak that stays frozen longer than anything else in these parts. Comprising almost 12,000 acres, the area offers great hiking—more than 50 miles of trails—and little crowding. Activities include camping, fishing, mountain biking, and horseback riding. The campground has 20 spaces, flush toilets, and hot showers and is open April 1 through November 1. Backcountry camping is also available. The visitors center, tel. (423) 346-3318, is open every day 8 a.m.-4:30 p.m.

Obed Wild and Scenic River

Over the millennia this river has cut through the sandstone of the Cumberland Plateau to a depth of 400 feet—sometimes straight down. Virgin forests exist in some places along the river and its tributaries. The Obed was added to the national park system in 1976 as a wild and scenic river—the only one with this designation in the state. The federal government owns only the land right along the river, yet much of it flows through Tennessee's Catoosa Wildlife Management Area. The federal government has yet to acquire land necessary to fully protect the streams from pollution and the surrounding land from development.

For these reasons, not much has been done to date to develop hiking trails and campgrounds—the one campground there has only five spaces. This ensures that the visitor will find the river uncrowded, but it also limits access to the area. Camping is permitted along the river all year, and no permits are required. To get a good look at the river, go to the Lilly Overlook, which lies off Hwy. 62 on Ridge Rd. about 12 miles from Wartburg.

The whitewater on the Obed, during late winter and early spring, is superb. The rapids range from Class II to Class IV. The visitors center for the Obed is in Wartburg on Hwy. 62 just west of its intersection with Hwy. 27, tel. (423) 346-6294. Or find information online at www.nps.gov/obed/.

RUGBY

In this most backwoods portion of Tennessee, it seems astonishing to come upon a town full of anglophiles drinking tea and paying homage to a place often called "the last English colony in America." Yet it is this remote land that caused Rugby to be established here, contributed to its demise, and yet preserved it. Today Rugby pulls in a lot of visitors and is well worth the trip.

The best place to get one's bearings, as the British might put it, is the **Schoolhouse Visitor Center,** where exhibits tell the story of Rugby with photos, artifacts, and displays. After collecting an admission of $4.25 for adults, $3.75 for seniors, and $2.25 for children—of a per-family price of $10—a guide takes visitors to the first stop, **Kingston Lisle,** Rugby founder Thomas Hughes's home when he summered in Rugby. The **Thomas Hughes Free Public Library** attests to the literate colonists who founded Rugby. Inside is a wonderful collection of Victorian books. On the other side of the road is the Gothic **Christ Church, Episcopal,** which was built in 1887. The little church contains a rosewood organ made in London in 1849.

Farther west on Central Avenue—Hwy. 52—is the **Harrow Road Cafe,** and beside it is the **Board of Aid Book Shop,** both described below. Visitors can walk or drive the old streets of Rugby, whose names—Donnington Road, Farringdon Road—sound very British indeed. Many of the original houses are private homes, and visitors should not intrude.

The visitors center has maps showing trails that lead down to the "Gentlemen's Swimming Hole" and the "Meeting of the Waters." Go west on Hwy. 52 and turn right onto Donnington Road. This leads to the Rugby cemetery, where Margaret Hughes and other colonists are buried. Nearby are a parking lot and trailhead for a 0.4-mile jaunt to the swimming hole on the Clear Fork River. Continuing for 1.7 miles brings the hiker to the "Meeting of the Waters"—where White Oak Creek and the Clear Fork River meet.

Some people have become so enthralled with Rugby that the old street plans have been dusted off and used to create Beacon Hill, a residential neighborhood in Rugby comprised of houses that replicate Victorian cottages. Almost 30 lots have been sold, and a growing number of new Rugbyans have moved into "The New Jerusalem."

Entertainment and Events

The **Spring Music & Crafts Festival,** held in May, brings British Isles and Appalachian music and dancing, puppet theater, and more than 80 craftspeople demonstrating and selling their work. Tours of buildings and horse and buggy rides round out the offerings; there's a small admission fee.

Crafts workshops, held throughout the year, allow participants to make something under the instruction of an expert. Typical subjects from the past include honeysuckle basketry, Nantucket basketry, bark basketry, and handbuilding with clay. For details call (423) 628-5166.

Every year during the **Rugby Pilgrimage,** private homes built in the colony's heyday are open to the public—the only time of year that this happens. The pilgrimage takes place the first weekend in September, and a small admission fee is charged. The Pilgrimage also includes music, food, dancing, and crafts.

The **Halloween Ghostly Gathering** begins with a fireside buffet dinner, then ghost stories

THE NEW JERUSALEM

One of the more frustrating notions in Victorian England was primogeniture—the practice whereby aristocratic parents would leave all their worldly goods to their oldest son. Daughters, if they were lucky, married into other wealthy families, but the younger sons were out of luck. Social pressures of the day permitted them to enter only the professions of law, medicine, clergy, or the military. If these did not work out, they were expected to "starve like gentlemen." Any sort of manual labor was considered scandalous.

Thomas Hughes thought this situation was outrageous and determined to do something for these "younger sons." Having written *Tom Brown's School Days,* a best-seller, he funded a group that bought 75,000 acres in the Cumberland Mountains of Tennessee and set about founding a place where these unfortunate lads could toil with dignity, far from a disapproving society.

In 1880 the colony opened, and approximately 200 people moved there and began putting Hughes's ideas into action. The colonists erected buildings, planted crops, and built a cannery. The also built a library, a church, and an inn. Hughes's 83-year-old mother, Margaret Hughes, settled in Rugby in 1881 and became the center of a burgeoning social life.

The younger sons might have been short on cash, but they all knew how to have a good time, and in short order they also built cricket fields, tennis courts, rugby fields, and croquet grounds. They organized themselves into literary societies, music and drama clubs, and a cornet band. Every day at tea time all activities, whether productive or recreative, came to a halt for tea. The proverbial good time was had by all.

Especially visitors. Rugby's experiment was followed with great interest by the British and American press, and a good many people, British and American, came calling on Rugby. The Tabard Inn was built to accommodate these guests. When it burned in 1884, another was built to take its place.

Although everyone had a marvelous time, Rugby was doomed. Its agricultural production never came close to meeting the costs of the place. A typhoid epidemic hit in 1881, thus preventing Rugby from cashing in on the health resort boom of the time. Hughes poured as much money as he could into the effort, but even he had to say "enough" at last, and the colony came to an end.

Rugby slumbered through most of the 20th century. Too remote to be threatened with development, its Victorian architecture bore silent witness to the dreams of Thomas Hughes and the others. In the 1970s, however, a young man named Brian Stagg took on the task of restoring Rugby and spreading the word of its glory days.

Now the town is on the National Register, and more than 20 of the original buildings remain and are open to the public. Rugby's various festivals draw increasing crowds, and bed and breakfasts and the like are opening in the area. Several of the original streets have been opened for new housing construction, with all of the houses to be built in the Rugby style. While it's not exactly the New Jerusalem that Hughes envisioned, his efforts to make a better life have been given new life themselves.

Thomas Hughes, founder of Rugby

HISTORIC RUGBY, INC.

with area tellers, a "calling of the spirits of Rugby past" in the library, and a candlelight walk to the cemetery for more stories. Reservations are required for this event and there's a small admission fee.

Thanksgiving Marketplace consists of a regional art show and sale, an early look at Christmas decorations, hot cider, and tours of historic buildings. It's usually held the weekend after Thanksgiving.

Christmas at Rugby, held the first two Saturdays in December, brings classical musicians, carolers, and Rugbyans of the past portrayed by professional actors. A sumptuous Victorian dinner is available at the Harrow Road Cafe, and buildings are decorated and lit with candles. There's a small admission fee.

Where to Stay

Visitors can capture a bit of Rugby experience with a stay at **Newbury House Bed and Breakfast,** tel. (423) 628-2441, a restored house that contains some of the original Rugby furniture. The house has a two-bedroom suite and six single bedrooms, three of which have private baths. After a day of seeing the local sights, guests can relax in the Victorian parlor and enjoy coffee or tea. Included in the $63-80 price is a full breakfast at the Harrow Road Cafe. Moderate.

Guests can rent two Rugby houses in their entirety as housekeeping cottages. **Pioneer Cottage,** tel. (423) 628-2441, was the first house built in Rugby in 1879. Thomas Hughes stayed there while awaiting construction of Kingston Lisle. The cottage costs $68 per night per couple; additional guests are charged $10. **Percy Cottage,** tel. (423) 628-2430, is a reconstructed Victorian Gothic cottage offering a two-room suite and is rented under the same policies as Pioneer House. It costs $62 per couple. Both are Moderate.

Not a part of historic Rugby, but very much in the spirit of the town, **Grey Gables Bed 'n Breakfast Inn,** tel. (423) 628-5252 or (800) 347-5252, was built to be an inn. Each of the eight bedrooms is decorated with country and Victorian antiques. Four rooms have private baths. Rates begin at $115, which includes lodging, a gourmet evening meal, and breakfast. Breakfasts at Grey Gables are full country ones, and reasonably priced lunches and dinners are avail-

able as well for guests and others. A typical dinner might include grilled pork tenderloin with hickory nuts, bananas Foster, and homemade rolls. Madame Hughes' Afternoon Tea, served 2-4 p.m. during the annual Rugby Pilgrimage, includes fresh-baked scones and crumpets and assorted tea sandwiches. Reservations are required for all meals.

Grey Gables also sponsors events throughout the year, such as an Herb Luncheon and Workshop, Valentine High Tea Dinner, and other holiday events. To get to Grey Gables, go west of Rugby on Hwy. 52. Premium.

Clear Fork Farm, on Brewstertown Rd., tel. (423) 628-2967, was also built to be a bed and breakfast, and its three bedrooms all have private baths, each with skylights. Quilts cover the beds, and each room offers a view of the Cumberland Mountains. A recreation room includes a large-screen television. Breakfast is served on antique china, and rates are $65 per night. The farm sits on 200 acres, and guests with horses can board them in the four-stall barn. Mountain stream fishing, mountain biking, and hiking trails are available, and when guests come back they can soak in the hot tub or sit on the screened-in porch. To get to the farm, go south of Hwy. 52 for 0.8 miles on Shirley Ford Rd., and then follow the signs on Brewstertown Road. Moderate.

The **Central Avenue Motor Lodge,** just west of downtown Rugby, tel. (423) 628-2038, is the least expensive place to stay hereabouts. Rooms cost $42. Inexpensive.

Food

In the town of Rugby, the **Harrow Road Cafe,** tel. (423) 628-2350, is the only place to eat. This inviting place is open March-Dec. for three meals a day. In January and February it is open 9 a.m.-4 p.m. Among the items on the menu are Welsh rarebit, grilled leg of lamb, and bangers and mash.

Just east of Rugby, the **Cumberland Safari Club,** tel. (423) 627-4444, offers great barbecue and imported beer. Sometimes it also offers acoustic country or bluegrass music on Saturday night. It's open all year for lunch and dinner every day except Monday.

The **Grey Gables Bed 'n Breakfast Inn,** (see above) serves lunch and dinner.

Shopping

The **Rugby Commissary** offers a selection of fine crafts by more than 100 area artists as well as English goods. The **Board of Aid Bookshop** stocks *Tom Brown's School Days* and books about Rugby and the region.

Information

Rugby's **Schoolhouse Visitor Center,** tel. (423) 628-2430, is open March-Dec. daily 9:30 a.m.-5:30 p.m. EST, and Jan.-Feb. daily 10 a.m.-4:30 p.m. Tours take place Mon.-Sat. 9 a.m.-5 p.m. EST, Sunday noon-5 p.m. Find them online at www.oars.utk.edu/volweb/schools/morgan/central/rugby.htm.

Between Rugby and Jamestown

Just west of Rugby on Hwy. 52, the **R.M. Brooks General Store,** tel. (423) 628-2533, gives a look at time before Wal-Marts and shopping malls. Filled with antiques, the store still sells staples and serves simple lunches. Ask for a bologna and hook cheese sandwich.

Crossing into Fentress County, travelers move from Eastern to Central Time. About 10 miles from Rugby is a sign for **Colditz Cove State Natural Area.** Erosion combined with the geology of this area has led to the creation of many "rock houses," or cavelike overhangs. These were used by Indians and whites alike as shelters and still provide comfort to hikers caught in a storm. Colditz Cove, between Allardt and Rugby, contains both a rock house and a 60-foot waterfall. Depending on the local rainfall, the falls can be a roaring torrent or a much smaller stream of falling water. The natural area totals 75 acres, which include some large hemlock trees. To get there, look for the sign on Hwy. 52 at Crooked Creek Lodge Road. It's a 1.5-mile hike to see the falls and a rock house.

ALLARDT

A group of Germans settled this area about the same time the English came to Rugby. Unclouded by any particular mission other than making money—and taking no time off for afternoon tea—they prospered, making a living out of timber, coal, and farming. Their architecture was never as distinctive as that in Rugby, which in part explains why people usually blitz through here en route to the better-known colony to the east.

The first weekend in October brings the **Allardt Pumpkin Weigh-Off and Festival,** which includes a parade, food, music, and costume contests.

There are some good places to stay here. The **Old Allardt Schoolhouse,** at the junction of Hwy. 52 and Hwy. 296, tel. (931) 879-8056 or (800) 771-8940, is just that—a small schoolhouse that has been transformed into two rooms furnished with antiques, private baths, and fully equipped kitchens. Rates begin at $55. Inexpensive-Moderate.

Bruno Gernt House, on Baseline Rd., tel. (931) 879-1176 or (800) 978-7245, is a farmhouse built in 1845 and restored to its original appearance. It has four bedrooms and can be rented for $75-85. **Scott House,** at $85 per night, and various log cabins scattered thoughout the woods, available for $60-75, are available from the owners of the Gernt House. These properties come with linens and fully furnished kitchens. All are Moderate.

JAMESTOWN AND VICINITY

This town can boast one incontrovertible fact: Samuel Clemens was conceived here. He was born in Hannibal, Missouri, but that in no way diminishes his Tennessee roots. Clemens's father owned 75,000 acres of land here, and to his dying day he believed it would make his family's fortune, telling his wife to hold onto it at all costs. The land never did pay off, but it provided material from which the younger Clemens spun *The Gilded Age,* whose "Obedstown" closely resembles Jamestown. The **Mark Twain Spring** in a downtown park commemorates the town's embryonic connection to the author; fortunately, his output was greater than the spring's is today.

About the time the Clemens family headed for points west, a Jamestown resident, one Joseph Stout, was hauled in on charges of witchcraft. A suspicious character, he frequently sat up late reading, had little to say, and few friends to whom to speak. Locals whispered that he could enter houses through keyholes, and a posse armed with silver bullets was dispatched to bring him to court. Wiser heads prevailed, however, and the man's persecutors were themselves arrested.

Jamestown is home to one of the best high schools in the state. While Sgt. Alvin York steadfastly refused to cash in on his worldwide reputation, he was instrumental in helping Fentress County by establishing the **York Institute,** a school for local children. He personally ran the school from 1926 until 1937, when it was taken over by the state. Now it remains the only high school administered directly by the state of Tennessee, and occupies a campus of 400 acres.

SIGHTS AND RECREATION

Despite a long and honorable tradition of drinking, it took Tennessee decades to get over the thinking that led to Prohibition, but finally the state legislature saw the light. **Highland Manor Winery,** on Hwy. 127 South, tel. (931) 879-9519, sprang into being in 1980 and thus became the oldest winery in the state. Housed in an English Tudor building, the vintner produces a variety of wine—and not all of it the sweet varieties so favored in this state. Visitors can choose from, among others, chardonnay, cabernet sauvignon, white riesling, and rosé. The best-sellers, however, are rosé and muscadine, the latter so popular that the winery maintains a two-year waiting list for bottles. It also makes a muscadine champagne that flies off the shelves. It offers free tours and tastings.

East Fork Stables, tel. (931) 879-1176 or (800) 978-7245, lies on 12,000 acres five miles south of Jamestown on Hwy. 127. It offers more than 100 miles of marked trails and two rustic cabins for riders. It's open all year.

WHERE TO STAY

The **Big South Fork Lodge,** 13 miles west of Jamestown on East Port Rd. off Hwy. 52, tel. (931) 879-7511, has 20 cabins with rates $50-325 per night. They also rent houseboats, with daily rates of $130-535.

Northwest of town and close to Pickett State Rustic Park is **Wildwood Lodge,** tel. (423) 879-9454. For details, look under "Where to Stay" in the Big South Fork Park section.

East Port Marina and Resort lies halfway between Jamestown and Livingston; go driving north on East Port Rd., tel. (931) 879-7511.

Camping
Laurel Creek Travel Park, tel. (931) 879-7696, lies northeast of Jamestown and contains 48

CENTRAL TIME

Travelers in this part of Tennessee should be mindful of the time. To the east, the state runs on eastern time, while parts northwest of Knoxville operate on central time. Scott and Morgan Counties are in eastern time, while Pickett and Fentress Counties are in central. The "time line" runs right through the Big South Fork National River and Recreation Area.

ALVIN YORK

In a time when anyone with an iota of fame immediately wrings every drop of value from it, a man such as Alvin York seems absolutely unreal. Born in 1887, he lived an unimpressive early life, working as a laborer on a farm that belonged to a minister. Under his employer's influence, York became a Christian and gave up his drinking and card-playing, but he continued squirrel hunting, becoming known as a crack shot.

So devout was young York that when he was drafted for World War I, he tried to obtain conscientious objector status. Draft officials in The Volunteer State turned him down flat, so he entered the Army and was sent to the European front. On October 8, 1918, his platoon came under withering fire from the Germans. When his commanding officers were killed, Corporal York took charge, leading seven men in a charge on the machine gun nest responsible for the deaths of so many of his comrades.

The machine guns were silenced, and York and his men captured four German officers and 128 men and marched them back across the lines. York himself marched into instant fame and was awarded more than 40 decorations. He came home to a media blitz hitherto unseen for a common soldier. He was offered almost everything: movie roles, advertisements, and all manner of product endorsements.

Turning it all down, he returned to Pall Mall, married his childhood sweetheart, and operated a gristmill north of town. He did accept a farm paid for by admirers' donations and lived there the rest of his life. He also headed the York Institute, a Jamestown school he established to benefit the mountain children of the area.

Right before World War II, York was persuaded to allow Hollywood to tell his story. He hoped it would encourage patriotism and wanted the money to build an interdenominational Bible school. Gary Cooper won an Oscar for his starring role, and *Sergeant York* introduced a new generation to the story of the brave mountain soldier.

Not used to large sums of money, York ran into tax troubles. A 1954 stroke left him bedridden and owing $172,723 to the government. The IRS settled for much less, and U.S. Speaker of the House Sam Rayburn led a drive to collect the money. An industrialist set up a trust fund enabling York to live comfortably for the rest of his life. Alvin York died on September 2, 1964, and is buried in Pall Mall.

The famous hero of WW I operated this century-old gristmill when he returned to Tennessee.

sites. Open May-Nov., it has a swimming pool, fishing, and recreation facilities. Take Hwy. 154 north out of town for nine miles.

FOOD

The **Mark Twain Motel,** on Main St., tel. (931) 879-2811, serves three meals a day except on Sunday, when it offers breakfast and lunch only. Country cooking is the fare.

PICKETT STATE RUSTIC PARK

If this park weren't in such a remote area on the Tennessee/Kentucky border, it would no doubt be one of the most-visited places in the state.

Created from 12,000 acres donated to the state in 1933 by the Stearns Coal and Lumber Company, the park contains 15-acre Pickett Lake, rock houses, caves, and natural bridges.

Activities include more than 58 miles of hiking trails, fishing, swimming at a cliff-lined beach, rowing, and canoeing. During the summer naturalists lead walks, demonstrate various activities, and conduct campfire talks.

The accommodations at the park include five chalets, five stone cabins, five wooden cabins, and five new "villas" with three bedrooms each; all come with fully equipped kitchens and linens. Open year-round, they cost $65-115. Moderate-Premium.

The park has 40 campsites, 31 of which have hookups. The campground has a bathhouse with hot showers. It accepts no reservations; campers are accommodated on a first-come, first-served basis and can stay for two weeks maximum.

The park is open in the summer 8 a.m.-6 p.m., and in the winter 8 a.m.-4:30 p.m. For further information, or to make reservations, call (931) 879-5821 or (888) TNPARKS. See them online at www.tnstateparks.com.

SERGEANT ALVIN YORK GRISTMILL AND PARK

The steep descent from Jamestown to Pall Mall reminds motorists that they are leaving the Cumberland Plateau. The park contains Alvin York's home, a country store, a Bible School founded by York, and his family's gristmill.

The house has been restored and contains original furniture, a telephone, and household items owned by the York family. Best of all is the park ranger, Andrew Jackson York, who is the son of Sergeant York and a wonderful source of information and stories about his famous father. The mill is open daily 8 a.m.-5 p.m., and the house is open daily 9 a.m.-5 p.m. No admission is charged.

For information about the park, call (931) 879-6456 or see www.tnstateparks.com.

The **Valley of the Three Forks Antique and Gift Shop,** tel. (931) 879-1262, lies across the street from Sgt. York's grist mill in an old building and sells quilts, books, and local crafts—among them covers that can make one's upright vacuum cleaner look like Aunt Jemima.

WEST TO CELINA

BYRDSTOWN

What Alvin York was to war, another native of these parts was to peace. Byrdstown, west of Pall Mall, is the birthplace of Cordell Hull, congressman, senator, secretary of state under Franklin Roosevelt, winner of the 1945 Nobel Prize for Peace, and widely regarded as the "father of the United Nations." Hull was not always peaceably inclined. He is said to have delivered "a thorough Tennessee tongue-lashing" to the Japanese diplomats who were in his office in 1941 when word came that Pearl Harbor had been attacked.

A reconstruction of the log cabin in which Hull was born is the centerpiece of the **Cordell Hull Birthplace and Museum,** tel. (931) 864-3247. The museum contains his Nobel Peace Prize, library, chair and desk, photos of Hull with world leaders, and other items and documents from his long and productive life in politics. No admission is charged, and the site is open Monday 8 a.m.-12 p.m., Wed.-Sat. 8 a.m.-4:30 p.m., and Sunday noon-4:30 p.m. It is closed on Tuesday.

The **Cordell Hull Folk Festival,** usually held on the Saturday closest to his October 2nd birthday, brings together local music makers, craftspeople, and townsfolk for a friendly festival in honor of their native son. For information, call (931) 864-3247.

LIVINGSTON

This little town became the seat of Overton County through some inspired chicanery. The original county seat was in Monroe, and by the 1830s residents clamored to have it moved to Livingston, which was closer to the center of the county and much more convenient. The matter was put to a vote in 1833, and a group of six to eight men, among them one "Ranter" Eldridge, set forth to cast their votes. The journey required the men to spend the night in an inn. When Eldridge learned that his companions intended to vote to keep the county seat in Monroe—which he opposed—he rose earlier than his neighbors and turned their horses loose. The proponents of Livingston won the referendum by four votes.

Holly Ridge Winery and Vineyard, tel. (931) 823-8375, is the newest one in the state, although the vintners here have been coaxing wine out of grapes for over 10 years. Twenty-three kinds of wine are bottled here, including the sweet wines that Tennesseans love so well, along with drier wines such as a good vidal blanc and a merlot. To find the winery, take Hwy. 85 three miles out of Livingston toward Hilham and follow the signs.

Where to Stay

Cornucopia Bed & Breakfast, 303 Mofield St., tel. (931) 823-7522, is just two blocks from the town square. It features three rooms, all with private baths. Rates are $75. See them online at www.bbonline.com/tn/cornucopia. Moderate.

The Overton Motel, East Main St., tel. (931) 823-2075, isn't a bad place if it is minus 20° or the tent leaks or the driver can't stay awake long enough to get back to the interstate.

Deep Valley Park & Trout Farm, north of town off Hwy. 52, tel. (931) 823-6053, has 30 sites and is open from mid-March through October.

Food

The Apple Dish Tea Room, 114 North Court Square, tel. (931) 823-3222, serves lunches featuring a different casserole and soup each day, along with homemade bread and desserts.

The Overton Motel Restaurant, East Main St., tel. (931) 823-2075, features country cooking 4 a.m.-10 p.m.

Shopping

Court Square Emporium, on East Court Square, tel. (931) 823-6741, sells quilts, baskets, pottery, books, and many more items from 40 area and regional craftspeople.

STANDING STONE STATE RUSTIC PARK

This 2,555-acre park was named for a stone that is no longer standing and that was never in the park. According to a Cherokee legend related in Russ Manning's *The Historic Cumberland Plateau,* a god told a man to build a raft, for a flood would soon come and destroy everything. The man finished the raft as the water was rising, and just as he was about to shove off a dog spoke to him from the bank and asked to go with him, telling the man, "When you are in danger of losing your life, let me be the sacrifice." The man agreed, and the two drifted for 40 days. Sound familiar? The man was dying of hunger, and the dog reminded him of its earlier pledge. The man threw the dog into the water, and seven days later it came back with mud—evidence that land lay nearby. This land was North America. In appreciation to the dog, the Indians carved a statue of him out of sandstone as a reminder of the god who had helped them find their home.

That's the story. Settlers came upon the stone, which stood outside the town of Monterey, and over the years chipped away at it. Blasting for a railroad line demolished what was left of the stone, and later its largest piece was put at the top of a park monument in Monterey. The second Thursday in October is always **Standing Stone Day,** and Cherokee groups come to the park to commemorate their ancestors.

The park, no matter how it got its name, offers a lot to do. It adjoins the 8,445-acre Standing Stone State Forest. An X-shaped lake surrounded by forested cliffs marks the center of the park. In addition to fishing and boating, the park offers hiking trails, nature trails, a playground, a swimming pool, tennis courts, and a recreation building. Overnight accommodations include 24 cabins, which cost $50-90. Thirty-five campsites are available on a first-come, first-served basis, and a group camp and lodge is available by reservation. Call (931) 823-6347.

Standing Stone State Park is the site of the annual **Rolley** (rhymes with holy) **Hole National Championship,** a game involving two-person teams who endeavor to shoot stone marbles in a hole. The action, so fierce that mere glass marbles cannot withstand the impact, has been played for decades in these parts, and of late has been featured by network television. The championship usually takes place two weeks after Labor Day weekend (mid-September) and features pancake breakfasts, demonstrations of marble-making, and other amusements. Call (931) 823-6347. See the park online at www. state.tn.us/environment/parks/standstn.

CELINA

This little Cumberland River town used to be a center for rafting, but not the whitewater variety. Beginning about 1870, lumberjacks would cut down trees and drag the logs to the river, then send them downstream to Nashville's lumberyards in huge rafts—sometimes as long as 300 feet and three logs thick. This practice continued through the 1930s.

Sights and Recreation
In recent years, recreation on the water has become important around Celina. The **Dale Hollow Dam,** which was finished in 1943, backs up the Obey River into a lake with 620 miles of shoreline. Unlike most Tennessee lakes, the water here is very clear, making it popular with scuba divers as well as the usual boaters and anglers. The fishing here is very good; the record-holding smallmouth bass—11 pounds, 15 ounces— came from these waters. Fifteen marinas are scattered around the lake. Many have boats, including houseboats, available for rent. Interested parties can obtain a complete list of marinas by calling the Army Corps of Engineers, which administers the lake, at (931) 243-3136.

The **Dale Hollow National Fish Trout Hatchery,** two miles north of town on Hwy. 53, tel. (931) 243-2443, raises thousands of rainbow, brown, and lake trout for federal waters in several states. Visitors can view the operations seven days a week 7:30 a.m.-4 p.m. Admission is free.

In the years before the Civil War, a North Carolina slaveholder named Virginia Hill bought 2,000 acres here and gave them to her slaves along with their freedom to create the community of **Free Hills,** just north of Celina. After the war, former slaves also moved here, and the community continues today.

The **Clay County Museum,** 805 Brown St., tel. (931) 243-4220, contains artifacts from the county's old days, photographs, and information about the town.

Where to Stay
Try **Cedar Hill Resort,** 2371 Cedar Hill Rd., tel. (931) 243-3201; **Dale Hollow Marina,** tel. (931) 243-2211 or (800) 321-1669; **Horse Creek Resort,** tel. (931) 243-2125 or (800) 545-2595; **Holly Creek Resort,** Rt. 1, tel. (800) 331-1780; or **Valley View Motel,** tel. (931) 243-2641.

Dale Hollow Lake has several public campgrounds on its shores. Developed ones usually have amenities such as bathhouses, boat rentals, restaurants, and playgrounds. Visitors can make reservations by phone at these campgrounds. **Dale Hollow Dam,** with 81 sites, tel. (931) 243-3554, is open April through mid-November. **Willow Grove,** also with 81 sites, tel. (931) 823-4285, is open May 15 through mid-September. **Lillydale,** with 115 sites, tel. (931) 823-4155, and **Obey River,** with 132 sites, tel. (931) 864-6388, are both open mid-April through mid-October.

There are 40 primitive campsites around the lake. These may have pit toilets but no picnic tables or anything else. They require use permits, which are free and available by calling or visiting the resource manager's office below the Dale Hollow Dam, tel. (931) 243-3136.

Food
On the square you'll find **Gone Country Cafe,** tel. (931) 243-9302. The name says it all.

New Day Subs, 201 Westlake Ave., tel. (931) 243-4001, is a sandwich shop where a clerk, in asking about putting lettuce and the like on a sandwich, offered to "run it through the garden." The shop offers quiche as well. It's open Mon.-Sat. for lunch and dinner.

Twin Rivers Restaurant, 820 E. Lake Ave., tel. (931) 243-3333, offers a buffet lunch and menu service for lunch and dinner every day. It serves breakfast April through Labor Day.

Information
The **Clay County Chamber of Commerce,** 427 South Brown St., tel. (931) 243-3338, has brochures and other information about the surrounding area.

DOWN THE TENNESSEE RIVER

Southeast Tennessee does a great job of regional tourism promotion. See them online at www.setenn.org.

KINGSTON

By 1800 the seat of Roane County, built on an easily defensible hill above the Clinch River, lay on the eastern end of the first road to Nashville and was an important trading town. The state legislature met here once in 1807, making Kingston the state capital for a day. The **Roane County Museum of History and Art,** tel. (423) 376-9211, occupies one of the seven antebellum courthouses left in the state and contains displays on each town in the county as well as prehistoric artifacts from Indian mounds. It's open Tues.-Fri. 9 a.m.-4 p.m. Admission is free.

In 1979, **Fort Southwest Point** was built where the Clinch River joins the Tennessee River. This was the frontier between United States and Indian lands, and the structure was built there to help keep the peace between the settlers and the Cherokee. It served as the headquarters for Jonathan Meigs, the Indian Agent for these parts. The town of Kingston owns the site and has erected structures and walls in the same locations as the original. There are a good many reconstructed forts in the state, but this claims to be the only one reconstructed on its original foundations. It is open April-Dec., and a donation is requested. To get there, take Exit 352 off I-40 and go south. Call the visitors bureau or look at www.teamparish.com/kingston/fsw.html for more information.

Visitors who call ahead can tour TVA's **Kingston Fossil Plant,** tel. (423) 717-2120, which burns coal and oil to produce electricity. To find it, look for the 1,003-foot-high smokestacks, which were built to disperse the pollutants produced by the plant. Guides lead 40-minute tours Monday through Friday. Guests will see boilers, the turbine floor, and the enormous stacks.

For more information about Kingston, call the **Roane County Visitors Bureau** at (800) 386-4686 or look at www.teamparish.com/kingston.

THE TENNESSEE VALLEY AUTHORITY

During the depths of the Great Depression, the administration of Franklin D. Roosevelt took a look at the area surrounding the Tennessee River—all of Tennessee and parts of Alabama, Georgia, Kentucky, Mississippi, North Carolina, and Virginia. They saw that a large number of people lived in abject poverty, only one of 30 farms had electricity, and that there were few industries, even in the cities. The Tennessee River was a capricious stream that periodically caused massive flooding, yet at other times ran so shallow that using it for shipping was all but impossible.

The solution to a lot of these problems was the Tennessee Valley Authority, which came about through the efforts of George Norris, a progressive senator from Nebraska. TVA was set up as an independent corporate agency of the federal government, run by three directors appointed by the president and confirmed by the Senate. Relatively free of governmental meddling, TVA was able to move decisively and, backed with federal dollars, effectively. It was charged with a list of tasks, among them to improve the region's "general social and economic welfare."

In the early years, it took over Wilson Dam and other properties from other federal agencies, but TVA soon began building its own dams. Norris Dam was the first, and now the agency operates 51 dams on the Tennessee River and its tributaries. This has all but eliminated the flooding, and a system of locks provides a channel for year-round navigation all the way to Knoxville.

Other benefits of the agency included efforts to curb malaria, education about soil conservation techniques, and examples of city planning such as the town of Norris. TVA built roads, constructed water purification and sewage treatment plants, and helped develop fertilizers.

It took thousands of people to accomplish all this, and the jobs provided to Tennesseans and others boosted economies, local and statewide. The downside of TVA's aggressive flood control

Where to Stay

Options include **Bayside Marina,** 134 Bayside Dr., tel. (423) 376-7031; **Days Inn-Kingston,** 495 Gallaher Rd., tel. (423) 376-2069 or (800) 325-2525; **Family Inns of America-Kingston,** I-40 and Gallaher Rd., tel. (423) 376-5573 or (800) 472-8383; and **Knight's Inn,** 1200 N. Kentucky St., tel. (423) 376-3477.

The **Four Seasons Campground,** tel. (800) 990-CAMP, not surprisingly, is open all year. Campers will find 45 sites complete with swimming pool, playground, and games. Take Exit 356 off I-40 and go one block north on Hwy. 58.

Food

Mama Mia's, 705 W. Race St., tel. (423) 376-5050, offers homemade pizza, ravioli, and other Italian dishes as well as sandwiches made with homemade bread. It's open Tues.-Sat. for lunch and dinner.

HARRIMAN

Like Rugby to the north, Harriman was founded as an ideal community, one centered on the Prohibition movement of the late 1800s. A group of investors—one of them Clinton B. Fisk, the founder of Nashville's Fisk College—set out to build a model city of culture, sobriety, and industry. They also hoped to make money in the process.

The East Tennessee Land Company was chartered in 1889, bought 10,000 acres of countryside, and began selling lots. Three years later 3,672 people lived and worked in 29 manufacturing companies in Harriman, which was named for Walter C. Harriman, former governor of New Hampshire. Every deed contained a provision "forbidding the use of the property, or any building thereon, for the purposes of manufacturing, storing, or selling intoxicating liquors or beverages as such." This was to be a "Utopia of Temperance," complete with American Temperance University, a somewhat ambitiously named prep school.

Prohibition was very much a women's issue, and the Prohibition Party strongly supported women's suffrage. Women voted in Harriman's first election in 1891, possibly the first time in Tennessee they did so.

The town prospered until the Panic of 1893, which bankrupted the East Tennessee Land Company. Harriman continued to grow, however, until hit later on with a double whammy—a 1929

and dam building was that thousands of families were forced to move from places where, in some cases, their families had lived for generations. Whole towns were flooded, and residents had to remove their dead to higher cemeteries.

One of TVA's missions was to provide electricity to the valley, and in doing so it literally brightened the lives of thousands of people. The relatively cheap electricity lured industries, thus providing jobs. At first the electricity was produced by falling water at the dams, but later the demand became so great that other sources were needed. Gradually the production of electricity became the prime focus of TVA, and today the agency operates 38 hydroelectric sites, 12 coal-fired generators, and two nuclear power plants.

The abundance of electricity was one of the reasons that the Manhattan Project leaders chose to build their complex at Oak Ridge, yet it was the emphasis on power production that got TVA in trouble later on in the 1970s. By then the agency, the largest utility in the Western Hemisphere, had embarked on the most ambitious nuclear power plant-building effort in the world. At the same time, coal-fired plants were belching out pollutants and creating a demand for strip-mined coal, playing unprecedented environmental havoc in mountain communities in Tennessee and Kentucky. Electricity that had once been some of the cheapest in the nation soared in price, leading to complaints from the very people TVA had been designed to serve.

It must be said that TVA has worked hard on its pollution problems and tried to help consumers save electricity through special programs, such as one aimed at better insulating houses. And it scrapped most of its nuclear power plants.

In recent years TVA has downsized, and, feeling pressure from Congress, has cut back on many programs. Its legacy for Tennessee, however, remains in the form of lakes on which millions of people play, a strong industrial base, and a better life for its people. TVA was perhaps the best thing ever to come from the federal government to this state.

flood and the Great Depression. The flood took out the entire industrial area, and hard times did the rest. Not until nearby Oak Ridge came into existence did Harriman make a comeback. The Utopia of Temperance now has four liquor stores.

Today's visitor should head for the **Harriman Heritage Museum,** 330 Roane St., tel. (423) 882-8570. This 1891 building served as the offices of the East Tennessee Land Company, then American Temperance University, and later on as City Hall. The restored building, known to locals as the Temperance Building, contains beautiful woodwork, the original vault, and the usual small-town collection of memorabilia—Masonic items, photos, and a communion set from a Universalist church. Admission is free. For info, call (423) 882-0335.

Victorian houses can be found in the Corn Stalk Heights Historic District on the hill above town. Coming out of the museum, turn right on Walden Street and left on Trenton Street. The district covers 10 blocks and includes 135 buildings.

Harriman celebrates itself on Labor Day weekend with **Hooray for Harriman,** a street fair complete with music, food, crafts, etc. For info, call (423) 882-8570.

Where to Stay
Bushrod Hall, 422 Cumberland St, tel. (423) 882-8406 or (888) 880-8406, has a massive oak staircase from Sweden, and guests can use it to climb to three rooms, all with private baths. Rates are Moderate-Expensive. See it online at www.bbonline.com/tn/bushrod.

SPRING CITY

Travelers who follow Walden Ridge to the southwest come to Spring City, named for the many sources of water here. One of them, Rhea Springs, was said by the Indians to possess healing properties. Slave traders apparently believed in the power of the waters, for they would bring work-wearied slaves here before selling them so they would become rejuvenated and thus worth more money.

Spring City is the only place to examine all three sources of TVA electricity. **Watts Bar Dam,** southeast of town, was built in 1939-42 and supplies hydropower. As demand grew, a steam plant (now mothballed) was added during World War II, and in the '70s the agency began building the Watts Bar nuclear power plant, which loaded fuel for the first time in 1995. Visitors can view the dam from an overlook on its west end and see the locks from an east end overlook. Highway 68 passes right over the top of the dam.

Spring City is the birthplace of Hargus "Pig" Robbins, whose piano playing has graced many Nashville recording sessions.

Parks and Recreation
Bowater, Inc., which has extensive timber holdings in the South, has opened certain areas to the public. These "Pocket Wildernesses" contain scenic trails, waterfalls, and occasional places to camp. Brochures with topographic maps are available at chambers of commerce. Several of these lie close to Spring City:

A waterfall that drops 30 feet highlights the 104-acre **Stinging Fork Pocket Wilderness.** The roundtrip hike to it is three miles. To get to the trailhead, go out of Spring City on the Shut-In Gap Rd. for five miles.

Twin Rocks Nature Trail, 2.5 miles roundtrip, leads to a Walden Ridge overlook. To get there, go out of Spring City on the Shut-In Gap Rd. for one mile.

The **Piney River Trail** follows the Piney River and connects a picnic area and the Newby Branch Forest Camp near Dayton. The trailhead is the same as the Twin Rocks Nature Trail above.

Where to Stay
Motels include the **Southern Style Motel,** 22320 Hwy. 27, tel. (423) 365-6548; and the **Spring City Motel,** Hwy. 27 South, tel. (423) 365-6764.

Toestring Cottages , 2296 Toestring Valley Rd., tel. (423) 365-5712 or (800) 851-1656, rents four cabins.

Arrowhead Resort, tel. (423) 365-6484, has 31 campsites open April-October. Go 4.5 miles north on Hwy. 27 and follow signs to the right.

Newby Branch Forest Camp, seven miles west of town, tel. (423) 336-7424, has primitive sites open all year. To get there, go out of Spring City on the Shut-In Gap Rd. for 6.3 miles, then turn left on Branch Rd. and go 0.7 miles.

Food
Friend John's Catfish House, 831 Stump Hollow Rd., tel. (423) 365-4880, offers dinner only Thurs.-Sat. April-October.

Terrace View, tel. (423) 365-5238, offers American cuisine overlooking the Tennessee River for lunch and dinner every day in the summer. In the spring and fall, it's open Thursday-Saturday. To get there, go 4.5 miles north from Spring City and right on Rocky Springs Rd. and follow the signs.

The Front Porch Restaurant at Arrowhead Resort, tel. (423) 365-6484, offers all three meals seven days a week. Seafood, chicken, steaks, and chops round out the menu. Go 4.5 miles north on Hwy. 27 and follow signs to the right.

Information

Spring City Chamber of Commerce is in a caboose that sits at 384 Front St., tel. (423) 365-5210.

DAYTON

Most people who come to Dayton head for the **Rhea** (pronounced "RAY") **County Courthouse** at 1475 Market St., tel. (423) 775-7801, where the famous Scopes Trial of 1925 took place amid great hoopla. During court recesses or when court is not in session, visitors can tour the third-floor courtroom, which has been restored to its 1925 appearance. Downstairs is the **Scopes Museum,** where documents and memorabilia tell the story of the most famous trial in Tennessee. Admission is free.

Just outside of town lies Bryan College, founded to honor the proponent of the Biblical version of creation. Find the school online at www. bryan.edu.

Parks and Recreation

Bowater, Inc., has opened certain sections of its extensive timber holdings to the public. These "Pocket Wildernesses" contain scenic trails, views of waterfalls, and occasional campsites. Brochures with topographic maps are available at chambers of commerce or by calling (423) 336-7424.

Laurel-Snow Pocket Wilderness totals 710 acres and includes two waterfalls. Laurel Falls drops 50 feet and Snow Falls drops 30 feet. The roundtrip hikes to each are, respectively, five and six miles. One can reach the trailhead for both by going north on Hwy. 27, left for 1.5 miles on Walnut Grove Rd., left on Black Valley Rd., then right on Richland Creek Road.

Entertainment and Events

Dayton's **Strawberry Festival** takes place in early May when the berries get ripe. Along with fresh strawberries, visitors can partake of carnival rides, crafts shows, a country music concert, a parade, and a beauty pageant. Call (423) 775-0361 for information.

The Scopes Trial Play and Festival, held the third weekend in July, is a reenactment of the trial in the historic courtroom using dialogue from 1925 court transcripts. Unlike *Inherit The Wind,* the play and film that left local hero William Jennings Bryan looking rather bad, this theatrical production leaves it to up the audience to interpret the result of Tennessee's most famous trial. Other events include a crafts festival, traditional Appalachian and gospel music, an antique car show, and an occasional academic colloquium on the events of 1925. For information, call (423) 775-0361.

Where to Stay

Try the **Best Western Dayton,** 7835 Hwy. 27 N., tel. (423) 775-6560 or (800) 437-9604; or the **Days Inn,** 3914 Rhea Co. Hwy., tel. (423) 775-9718 or (800) DAYS-INN.

Food

The best breakfast in town is at the **Dayton Coffeeshop,** 280 Main St., tel. (423) 775-6156, which opens its door Sun.-Fri. at 5 a.m.

Offering country cooking, the **Frontier House,** north of town on Hwy. 27, tel. (423) 775-6353, never closes.

Diners at **Rafaels,** 7835 Hwy. 27 N. in the Best Western, tel. (423) 775-0707, can enjoy Italian cuisine Mon.-Sat. amid memorabilia of the Scopes Trial.

Prime Steak Out, 8748 Hwy. 27 N., tel. (423) 775-0598, is as the name says, along with seafood, chicken, and sandwiches. It offers dinner Tuesday-Saturday.

Shopping

Smiths Crossroads, 1356 Market St, tel. (423) 775-8007, offers a coffee bar and Italian sodas in the middle of a large space selling antiques, collectibles, and art.

Information

Dayton Chamber of Commerce, 107 Main St., tel. (423) 775-0361, is open Mon.-Fri. 8:30 a.m.-5 p.m.

THE SCOPES "MONKEY TRIAL"

If there were a hall of fame for public relations stunts that backfired, the Scopes trial would be one of the first entries. It all began in 1925 with a group of Daytonians sitting in Robinson's Drug Store, discussing, as people in small towns did and still do, what it would take to "put them on the map." The newspaper had recently carried an article on a new Tennessee law that forbade the teaching of evolution.

In walked John Scopes, an amiable young man who had recently substituted for the high school biology teacher, and he admitted that he had taught the illegal subject. The drugstore publicists convinced him to take part in a test case of the law, and he agreed. A call was placed to the Chattanooga newspaper that a teacher had been arrested and would be tried for breaking the anti-evolution law. The news went out on the telegraph to the nation and the world, and the show got under way.

More than 200 newspaper writers flooded the town, a Chicago radio station set up the first nationwide radio hookup, and newsreel photographers hand-cranked their movie cameras. An estimated 10,000 people showed up in town, which quickly took on a carnival atmosphere. There was even talk of moving the trial to a local ballpark to accommodate the masses.

William Jennings Bryan, three-time Democratic nominee for president, was invited to lead the prosecution team. This inspired Clarence Darrow, a famed trial lawyer and noted agnostic, to defend young Scopes. The trial culminated when Bryan agreed to take the stand as an expert witness, and Darrow baited "The Great Commoner" into testifying, among other things, that humans were not mammals.

The Dayton boosters succeeded beyond their wildest dreams in publicizing the town, but the stories that flowed through the fingers of the 22 Western Union telegraph operators weren't quite what the drugstore planners had in mind. Perhaps the most acerbic commentary came from H.L. Mencken of the *Baltimore Sun,* who wrote about Bryan that "his one yearning was to keep his yokels heated up—to lead his forlorn mob of imbeciles against the foe." The locals responded as best they could. A still-quoted line has a Dayton waitress denying food service to Mencken and then saying, "And furthermore, I have mistletoe tied to my apron strings!"

Both sides claimed victory. Scopes was duly convicted, but the conviction was overturned on appeal because of a mistake by the judge. Bryan died in Dayton five days after the trial, and in his honor Bryan College was established nearby. The law stayed on the books, an embarrassment that was largely ignored until an enlightened legislature repealed it in 1967.

CHATTANOOGA AREA CONVENTION AND VISITORS BUREAU

Rhea County Courthouse, site of the trial

CROSSVILLE AND VICINITY

For 19th-century travelers this town on the Cumberland Plateau was an important crossroads. It still is, serving as a jumping-off point from which to explore the area.

Many of the buildings here are constructed of sandstone known as Crab Orchard stone. The Palace Theatre on Main St. is a good example of this.

During World War II, Crossville was the site of one of the 11 prisoner-of-war camps established in Tennessee. Writing in *The Tennessee Encyclopedia of History and Culture,* Jeff Roberts relates the following: "Three German submariners who escaped from Crossville came upon a mountain cabin. Out came a 'granny,' who told them to 'git.' When they did not leave, she shot one of them dead. When a local deputy arrived and told her of the circumstances, the woman sobbed, claiming she would have never fired if she had known they were Germans. 'I thought they wuz Yankees,' she said."

SIGHTS

The **Homesteads Tower Museum** sits south of town at the junction of Hwy. 127/28 and Hwy. 68, tel. (931) 456-9663. Here one can see documents and photographs of the Depression-era Homesteads Project as well as furniture made by the residents. It's open March-Dec., Mon.-Sat. 10 a.m.-5 p.m., Sunday noon-5 p.m. Admission is $1.

Grassy Cove

Motorists who leave the Homestead Community and follow Hwy. 68 will find themselves descending into a lovely valley called Grassy Cove. This 3,000-acre valley is full of caves, into which most of the water here flows only to emerge in the Sequatchie River to the south. All of the caves are on private property, and none have been commercially developed. Visitors can see one, the **Old Mill Cave,** behind the **J.A. Kem-**

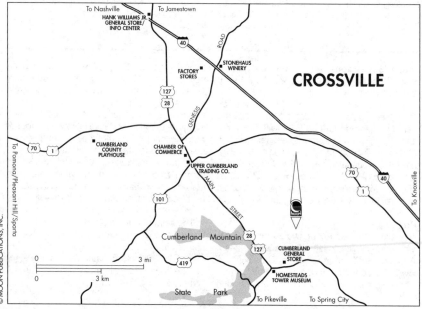

THE SHOWPLACE OF THE NEW DEAL

Among the social experiments generated as the United States endeavored to escape the Depression, the Cumberland Homesteads project stands as an interesting chapter. The idea was simple: Take people of good character who would work hard, put them in good housing with enough land to raise a garden, and then lure industry that would gainfully employ them. That's what the federal government set out to do.

It bought 10,000 acres of land south of Crossville from a timber company and in 1934 began work on the community. More than 4,000 people applied for the 250 homesteads, each of which consisted of approximately 20 acres. Cottages of Crab Orchard sandstone and wood interiors were built, and people moved in. By and large, the inhabitants were delighted to do so; the houses were wired for electricity and had indoor plumbing—luxuries that were new to many locals.

Cooperatives were set up so that women could make their family's mattresses, can their own food, and make cloth on looms. Men were taught construction trades and put to work building more houses and administrative buildings. A cooperative store, sorghum mill, and coal mine were among the enterprises that sprang up under the guidance of social planners. The most striking presence of the Homesteads was an 80-foot-high tower erected over an administrative building. Eleanor Roosevelt visited the Homesteads twice and pronounced it good.

Like many things in the New Deal, the idea was a decent one, but problems arose in keeping it on track. The community was shifted from agency to agency, and residents grew frustrated as their goals were repeatedly changed. Furthermore, the independent-minded people of the Cumberland Plateau did not mesh well with the socialist dreams of the planners and the ineptitude frequently displayed by the managers.

In 1939 the government offered the residents an opportunity to buy their land and houses. Virtually all of them did so, and the social experiment came to an end. While it lasted, however, it drastically improved the standard of living for the fortunate people who became residents, pumped a lot of needed funds into the economy, and left the area with houses of a type found nowhere else in the state.

Visitors can pick out the distinctive cottages by looking for stone houses with chimneys on each end. Some have additions, but others look just as they did when Eleanor Roosevelt came to call. All of the houses are privately owned, so a close inspection is not a good idea.

mer & Sons Store on Hwy. 68. Ask permission at the store, which is open Mon.-Sat. 6 a.m.-6 p.m.

The store, one of two in the cove, is owned by the descendants of one Conrad Kemmer, who came to these parts from Pennsylvania in the early 1800s. The J.C. Kemmer General Store, tel. (931) 484-4075, on the southern end of the valley, has been in operation since 1886. Visitors will find a selection of hardware, boots, work clothes, and staples such as Vienna sausage and Moon Pies. It's open Mon.-Sat. 6:30 a.m.-6 p.m.

Pomona

Homestead and Rugby are two examples of idealistic communities on the Cumberland Plateau. Another was Pomona, west of Crossville on Hwy. 70. John M. Dodge, a portrait painter whose subjects included Andrew Jackson and Daniel Webster, bought 5,000 acres, moved here in the mid-1800s, and planted 82,000 apple trees. Others in his artistic circle joined him, and the resulting community was named Pomona for the Roman goddess of fruit. A poet named Margaret Bloodgood Peake hit town and founded a philosophical cult whose young female devotees began their summer days by rolling without any clothing in dew-drenched fields of clover. This came to an end when members looked up from their gamboling to see the woods full of local boys, all grinning, as the expression goes, like a mule eating briars.

The spirit of Pomona lives on at Timberline Lodge and Cherokee Lodge, where visitors can roll in the dew-drenched clover with likeminded enthusiasts in "naturalist," i.e. nude, resort settings. (See "Naturalist Resorts" under "Where to Stay," below.)

Pleasant Hill

Farther west on Hwy. 70/1 in the Pleasant Hill community is the **Pioneer Hall Museum,** on Main St., tel. (931) 277-3872. It was the first dormitory of the Pleasant Hill Academy, a school operated 1884-1947 by the American Missionary Society of the Congregational Church when the public schools in these parts were almost nonexistent. Later it became a boarding school with students from a much wider area.

Through the efforts of the principal's wife, a physician named May Wharton, Pleasant Hill gained a hospital that was later transformed into a sanitarium for tuberculosis patients. When new drugs eliminated the need for this sort of treatment, the hospital became a retirement center. Dr. Wharton also founded the Crossville Medical Center.

This 10-room museum is open May-Oct., Wednesday 10 a.m.-4 p.m. and Sunday 2-5 p.m. or by appointment. Visitors can see exhibits pertaining to the academy—a girl's room and a boy's room—as well as medical artifacts from Dr. Wharton's time. Other exhibits include an early kitchen, country store, and antique tools. Admission is free.

Just down the street from the museum is **Polly Page's Mountain Crafts** on Main St., tel. (931) 277-3402, which is worth a stop just to talk to the gregarious Ms. Page. She carves dolls from red cedar and has been doing so since 1922, when a crafts teacher came to her school.

ENTERTAINMENT AND EVENTS

The **Cumberland County Playhouse,** tel. (931) 484-5000, came about when Paul and Mary Crabtree drew on their New York theatrical experience to create one of the best regional theaters in the South. Operating since 1965, the playhouse has delighted audiences with Shakespeare, musicals, and original plays with Tennessee themes. The season runs year-round, and more than 100,000 people per year attend. The playhouse lies six miles off I-40 Exit 317. Follow the signs. See them online at www.ccph.org.

WHERE TO STAY

Bed and Breakfasts and Inns

Betty's Bed and Breakfast, across from Fairfield Glade's entrance on Peavine Rd. four miles north of I-40, mailing address Rt. 7, Box 359-E, Crossville, TN 38555-9807, tel. (931) 484-8827, occupies one acre with a pond. Guests can choose from five bedrooms, all but one of which have private baths. The rate is $65 per night. Moderate.

Resorts

The Cumberland Plateau of old served as a magnet for idealistic communities. Now it is home to a variety of resorts, most filled with vacation homes and condos and offering golf, tennis, and swimming. The following also offer accommodations to the traveler.

Mountain Ridge, on Hwy. 70 North in Monterey, tel. (931) 839-3313, offers six two-bedroom villas. Take Exit 301 off I-40.

Cumberland Gardens Resort, in Crab Orchard—Exit 329 off I-40, tel. (931) 484-5285—offers overnight accommodations in one- or two-bedroom condos.

CRAB ORCHARD STONE

Many of the buildings in Crossville and surrounding areas feature a distinctive kind of stone. This is Crab Orchard Stone, a sandstone with a lot of silica that is common on the Cumberland Plateau. Early settlers used the stone in their fireplaces, the first commercial use was in 1903, and locals built houses with the tan, buff, gray, or blue-gray stone.

Crab Orchard Stone got a big boost when Scaritt College in Nashville hauled in the stone to construct a chapel and other buildings. Most of the New Deal's Homestead Houses were built with the stone, which can also be seen in Rockefeller Center, the headquarters of the United Auto Workers Union in Detroit, at Graceland, the Nintendo office building in Honolulu, and at the vice presidential residence in Washington, D.C.

Local companies find Crab Orchard Stone by strip-mining—digging down until they hit a layer of acceptable stone. These layers might be 18 to 36 inches or as thick as four feet. Find out more at www.opup.org/~sces/stone.

Fairfield Glade, Exit 322 off I-40, tel. (931) 484-7521, has 12,251 acres on which visitors can go horseback riding, rent boats, and play miniature golf, among other activities. More than 200 overnight accommodations are available, from hotel rooms to two-bedroom condos. The price range is $70-100 per couple per night in the summer, less in the off-season. See them online at www.fairfieldglade.com. Moderate-Expensive.

Lake Tansi Village, south of Crossville to the west of Hwy. 127/28, tel. (931) 788-6724, covers 5,000 acres, including a 550-acre lake with 14 miles of shoreline. Visitors can choose from cabins or time-share rentals ranging $80-100 per night. Moderate-Expensive.

Holiday Hills Inn, west of Crossville on Hwy. 70/1 on Holiday Lake, next door to the playhouse, tel. (931) 484-9566, offers a 48-unit inn, where one night costs $50 for two. Inexpensive.

Naturalist Resorts

Timberline Lodge, Exit 311 off I-40, south one mile to a stop sign, then left for a half-mile, tel. (931) 277-3522 or (800) TAN-NUDE, has been in operation for more than 30 years. This family-oriented resort features a swimming pool, private lake and beach, dancing, and indoor and outdoor hot tubs. When it's time to turn in, guests have a choice of a lodge with 12 rooms, a campground, cabins, or mobile homes. The season begins on Valentine's Day and rolls on until December's Christmas Party. During the summer the house band plays beach music on Friday nights, and dancers take to the floor in the 4,000-square-foot clubhouse.

Approximately 25% of the clientele comes from Tennessee and Kentucky, and the most of the rest hail from the Midwest. Timberline also gets a lot of European visitors, according to a spokesperson. Timberline has a relaxed policy toward clothes. If shy visitors want to wear them, that's perfectly fine.

Another nudist option is the 350-acre **Cherokee Lodge,** at the corner of I-40 and Exit 311, tel. (931) 277-5140. Cherokee Lodge is a private club and has room for travelers on a space-available basis April-Oct. only. Accommodations include rooms in a lodge, cabins, and a campground. Guests can enjoy a swimming pool, hot tub, volleyball, tennis court, game room, and clubhouse.

Dances are held on Saturday nights. Find more information online at www.cherokeelodge.com.

Motels

Try the **Best Western,** Exit 317 off I-40, tel. (931) 484-1551 or (800) 528-1234; or the **Hampton Inn,** I-40 Exit 317, tel. (800) 426-7866.

Camping—Buck Naked and Otherwise

Shier types can park their tents and RVs at the following: **Bean Pot Holiday Trav-L-Park,** off I-40 at Exit 322, tel. (931) 484-7671 or (800) 323-8899, has 61 sites and is open all year. **Crossville KOA,** off I-40 at Exit 322, tel. (931) 484-0860, is open mid-April through October and has 74 sites.

For the less inhibited, **Cherokee Lodge & Campground,** off I-40 at Exit 311, tel. (931) 277-5140, has 25 sites and is open April-October. **Timberline Lodge Naturalist Resort,** tel. (931) 277-3522 or (800) TAN-NUDE, offers nude camping at 60 sites. It's open March 1-Oct. 31. Take Exit 311 off I-40, go south one mile to a stop sign, and then turn left and proceed for a half-mile.

FOOD

The **Bean Pot,** on Peavine Rd. at Exit 322, tel. (931) 484-4633, is open 24 hours a day and serves country cooking.

China One, 1601 West Ave. N, tel. (931) 484-3178, is open for lunch and dinner seven days a week.

"HOLD THE SIZZLING FAJITAS"

The **Restaurant at Cherokee Lodge,** at the corner of I-40 and Exit 311, tel. (931) 277-5140, is the place to go if you don't have a thing to wear. Cherokee Lodge is one of Crossville's two clothing-optional resorts, and this is perhaps Tennessee's only fine dining restaurant that does not require patrons to wear shirts and shoes. This establishment grows its own herbs, prepares its own sauces, and offers steaks, fresh fish, and pasta. Open to the public every day for all three meals, April through October.

The Donut Shop, 777 West End Ave., tel. (931) 484-4312, makes the best omelets in town—so large they almost cover the plate. Lunch brings forth Reuben, club, and BLT sandwiches.

Lefty's Bar-B-Que dishes up pork barbecue, chicken, and ribs on Peavine Rd., tel. (931) 484-4205. It's open for lunch and dinner seven days a week.

Halcyon Days, in the same building as Stonehaus Winery, tel. (931) 456-3663, serves continental cuisine Mon.-Sat. for dinner. Typical entrees include stuffed quail, chicken Wellington, and lobster.

SERVICES AND INFORMATION

Shopping

South of town on Hwy. 127/28, the **Cumberland General Store,** tel. (931) 484-8481, offers an eclectic mixture of books, cast-iron cookware, veterinary supplies, crocks, honey, and quirky items that appeal to travelers. See them online at www.cumberlandgeneral.com.

Made By Hand, tel. (931) 484-8827, carries local and regional weavings, pottery, toys, and woodwork. Travelers will find it at Betty's Bed and Breakfast across from Fairfield Glade's entrance on Peavine Rd., four miles north of I-40.

Fine-food fanciers should stop at **Stonehaus Winery,** north of I-40 at Exit 320, tel. (931) 484-WINE, which offers red, white, rosé, and blush wines plus a gift shop featuring 40 kinds of cheeses. The winery also has a deli and kitchenware shop.

The next stop for picnic assemblers is **Simonton's Cheese House,** 1226 Industrial Blvd., tel. (931) 484-5193. This place makes some of its own cheese and ships it all over the country.

The **Merrimack Canoe Company,** 170 Harper Ave., tel. (931) 484-4556, cranks out fiberglass and Kevlar canoes with wooden ribs. Visitors can see samples of its work at the Stonehaus Winery by the interstate, and visitors who call ahead can get a tour of the manufacturing operations.

Factory Stores of America Outlet Center, at Genesis Rd. and I-40, tel. (931) 484-7165, is open daily.

The **Hank Williams Jr. General Store and Tourist Information Center** occupies a series of Old West-style buildings north of I-40 Exit 317, tel. (931) 484-4914. Hank Williams Jr. has no particular historical connection to this area, but a room devoted to Hank "Bocephus" Jr. paraphernalia is the centerpiece of this offering of fireworks, T-shirts, and other tourist-oriented souvenirs.

In mid-August, one can hunt for bargains at the **World's Longest Yard Sale,** which stretches along Hwy. 127 from Covington, Kentucky, to Chattanooga.

Information

The **Greater Cumberland County Chamber of Commerce,** 34 South Main St., tel. (931) 484-8444, is open Mon.-Fri. 8 a.m.-4:30 p.m. See them online at www.crossville.com.

A wooden Indian stands guard at the Cumberland General Store.

CUMBERLAND MOUNTAIN STATE RUSTIC PARK

Originally part of the Cumberland Homesteads, this 1,562-acre park was built for the pleasure of the inhabitants. The seven-arch dam was built of Crab Orchard stone by Civilian Conservation Corps workers and is said to be the largest steel-free structure built by that agency. The road goes right over the dam.

The park has 37 cabins, some of them open year-round. Prices range $57-102. In the summer they must be rented for one week and can be reserved up to one year ahead. The group lodge is a lovely stone building originally intended to serve as a mill below the dam. The park has 147 campsites, 28 of which are open over the winter. For reservations, call (931) 484-6138.

The park has a restaurant overlooking the lake, where iron skillet-fried chicken is the most popular dish in the buffet. It's open for lunch and dinner every day from March to mid-December. It closes mid-December to mid-January and is open only on weekends until March. Call (617) 484-7186 or see the park online at www.tnstateparks.com.

MONTEREY

This little town holds the only existing remnant of the "standing stone" for which Standing Stone State Park was named. The stone allegedly resembled a gray dog and had significance to the Cherokee Indians. Chunks of the stone were chipped away, however, and all that is left sits atop a monument on E. Commercial Avenue.

An amazing collection of animals stands stone-still at **Wilson's North American Wildlife Museum**, 914 Chestnut, tel. (931) 839-3230. Described as "a taxidermist's dream," this deceptively small-looking place holds 60 exhibits—grizzlies, caribou, wolverines, minks, foxes, coyotes, and wolves, just to name a few—all mounted in museum-quality displays. The place is laid out as if it were a long cave, with views into grottoes that cluster together animals that live in the same habitats. Definitely worth a stop, particularly for kids. Admission is $5.41 for adults and $3 for kids 3-12.

Nearby

TN 164 leads east out of Monterey toward the **Muddy Pond Mennonite Community**. After driving about seven miles, turn right on Union B Road and follow the signs. These folks sells a variety of home-grown and homemade products at a local store. They raise cane all summer and make sorghum, a.k.a. molasses, on October weekends.

Where to Stay

The Garden Inn, 1400 Bee Rock Rd., tel. (931) 839-140 or (888) 293-1444, is for people who like to live on the edge. The inn sits on 15 acres that lead to the edge of a 100-foot cliff with a great view into Stamps Hollow. The 10 rooms in this new structure feature have private baths. Visit online at www.bbonline.com/tn/gardeninn. Premium.

COOKEVILLE AND VICINITY

Cookeville is unusual in that it possesses two downtowns—one where the town was founded and another surrounding the train station. It is the home of Tennessee Technological University, ostensibly an engineering college, but one that wields a considerable liberal arts influence in the area. You can visit the college online at www.tntech.edu.

The town was also the home of Bryan Looper, a perennial office-seeking Republican who had his name legally changed to Byron Low Tax Looper. In October 1998, Cooper was charged with murdering state Sen. Tommy Burks, whose seat Looper was contesting.

The best place to start here is the town square, which contains a wonderful bookstore right beside a coffee shop.

SIGHTS AND RECREATION

The **Depot Museum**, 116 W. Broad St., tel. (931) 528-8570, is in the old Tennessee Central Railroad Station, which was built in 1909. Permanent exhibits include railroad artifacts, photographs, and a caboose, and temporary exhibits focus on topics such as World War II. Admission is free, and the museum is open Tues.-Sat. 10 a.m.-4 p.m.

Existing as they do so close to the country-side, most towns hereabouts do not have extensive parks. Cookeville, however, boasts 260-acre **Cane Creek Park,** which has bike and hiking trails, fishing, paddleboats, and plenty of places to picnic. To get there, go three miles off I-40 Exit 286.

City Lake Natural Area at Bridgeway Rd. is a 40-acre park with hiking, a waterfall, and a boat-launching ramp. It's open all year.

Hidden Hollow Park, off Hwy. 70 at I-40 Exit 290, tel. (931) 526-4038, offers outdoor activities for the whole family. A mill, covered bridges, and waterfalls sit among a petting zoo and places to swim and fish.

ENTERTAINMENT AND EVENTS

The Tennessee Tech **Backdoor Playhouse,** tel. (931) 372-3478, presents a variety of plays throughout the year.

WHERE TO STAY

Among the franchise offerings are the **Best Western Thunderbird Motel,** I-40 Exit 287, tel. (931) 526-7115; **Days Inn,** I-40 Exit 287, tel. (931) 528-1511; **EconoLodge,** I-40 Exit 287, tel. (931) 528-1040; **Executive Inn,** I-40 Exit 287, tel. (931) 526-9521; and the **Super 8 Motel,** I-40 Exit 287, tel. (931) 528-2020.

A little pricier are the **Hampton Inn,** I-40 Exit 287, tel. (800) 426-7866 or (931) 520-1117; and **Holiday Inn,** Exit 287 off I-40, tel. (931) 526-7125 or (800) HOLIDAY.

MORE PRACTICALITIES

Food
Mamma Rosa's Restaurant, 1405 N. Washington St., tel. (931) 372-8694, offers good Italian food Mon.-Sat. for lunch and dinner. It serves pizza, pasta dishes, lasagna, and manicotti.

Poets, sitting beside Bookworks on the square at E. Broad St., offers a good selection of coffees, bagels in the morning, and desserts after lunch.

The **Scarecrow Country Inn,** 644 Whitson Chapel Rd., tel. (931) 526-3431, offers "country gourmet" food for dinner only.

Spankies, 203 East Ninth St., tel. (931) 528-1050, has good food and drinks that seem that much better when served on an outdoor patio. The food here includes salads, sandwiches, chicken, steak, and shrimp.

Shopping
The Attic, 1281 Bunker Hill Rd., tel. (931) 528-7273 is one of the better antique stores hereabouts.

The best bookstore outside of Tennessee's four large cities is **Bookworks,** on the square at 230 E. Broad St., tel. (615) 372-8026. One room leads to another here, with chairs for sitting and browsing.

Chocolate lovers should pull over at the **Russell-Stover Candy** factory's outlet store, 1976 Chocolate Dr., tel. (931) 526-8424, for great prices on seconds and bulk candy. To get there, take I-40 Exit 288.

Information
The **Cookeville Chamber of Commerce,** 302 S. Jefferson Ave., tel. (931) 526-2211 or (800) 264-5541, is open weekdays. See them online at www.cookeville.com.

BURGESS FALLS
STATE NATURAL AREA

Water from the Cumberland Plateau flows to its western edge and falls 130 feet over three falls in this delightful park south of Cookeville. Early settlers, appropriately enough, named this the Falling Water River and used it to power grist- and sawmills. In the days before TVA, the city of Cookeville built a dam and used the water power to generate electricity. TVA's power made the dam obsolete, but Cookeville held onto the dam and land around it nonetheless.

This wise decision resulted in this beautiful 155-acre park, which is great for hiking and picnicking. There's no restaurants, lodging, or camping, and the park is closed Dec.-February. For information, call (931) 432-5312 or go online at www.tnstateparks.com.

SOUTH OF COOKEVILLE

SPARTA

Coming to Sparta from the east, motorists descend approximately 1,000 feet from the Cumberland Plateau to Tennessee's Highland Rim. **Sunset Rock** on Hwy. 70 offers a great view to the west. Nineteenth-century travelers passing this way were on a toll road and would have no doubt stopped at the **Rock House Shrine,** 3.7 miles east of town on Hwy. 70, tel. (931) 836-3552. Built of sandstone sometime between 1835 and 1839, it served as a toll house and stagecoach inn. The house is open Saturday 2-4 p.m.; call to arrange visits at other times.

Nearby Overton County is the birthplace of Lester Flatt, the country flat-picker whose 21-year partnership with banjo player Earl Scruggs constituted the most famous bluegrass duo ever. Flatt sang "The Ballad of Jed Clampett," the theme song for TV's "Beverly Hillbillies." Flatt died in 1979 and is buried in Sparta.

One of the many people to play with Flatt & Scruggs was Sparta native Benny Martin, who for a time was managed by Col. Tom Parker and opened for the young Elvis Presley.

Parks and Recreation
Golden Mountain Park, east of O'Connor Crossroads off Hwy. 111, tel. (931) 526-5253, is a 300-acre private park offering bumper boats, sports fields, arcade games, and pavilions for picnics and gatherings. It's open daily March-October.

Bowater, Inc., has extensive timber holdings in the South and has opened certain areas to the public. These "Pocket Wildernesses," as they are called, contain scenic trails, waterfalls, and occasional places to camp. Brochures with topographic maps are available at chambers of commerce or by calling (423) 336-7424. One of these is close to Sparta.

Virgin Falls Pocket Wilderness centers on a waterfall that emerges from a cave, drops 110 feet, and enters another cave. The roundtrip hike is eight miles. To get to the trailhead, drive 11 miles west of Sparta on Hwy. 70 to the community of De Rossett. Turn right and go 5.9 miles on Mourberry Rd. to a sign for Chestnut Mountain Wilderness. Go right on the Scott Gulf Rd. for two miles to the parking area for the trail.

Entertainment and Events
The **Midway Music Barn,** tel. (931) 657-2336 or (931) 761-3741, offers live country music every Saturday night in a family setting. No alcoholic beverages are permitted, and admission is $3 for adults and children over 10. It's five miles south of Sparta off Hwy. 70 South. Look for the sign. Turn left on John Henry Demps road and go a half mile.

On the first weekend in May **Benny Martin Day** takes place at the Midway Music Barn. Well-known bluegrass groups and parking lot jams make this a great festival. Call (931) 761-3741 for info.

Where to Stay
Cookeville has a host of franchise motels along the interstate. Or try the **Royal Inn,** 803 Valley View Rd., tel. (931) 738-8585.

Food
The Beechwood, 673 Charles Golden Rd., tel. (931) 738-4488, offers an elegant dining experience in an 1820 plantation mansion. Entrees include quail, steak, duckling, and seafood. Everything served here is made here, including bread, dressing, and desserts. Dinners and lunches by reservation only.

The Buckboard, 115 Mayberry St., tel. (931) 836-2659, is open seven days a week, serving all meals except dinner on Sunday. The cuisine includes steak, catfish, and plate lunches.

What's Cooking? is at 279 N. Spring St., tel. (931) 836-2535. The answer is country cooking.

Shopping
Country Treasures and Gifts, 447 W. Bockman Way, tel. (931) 836-3572, occupies a two-story log house with a 14-foot wooden Indian out front. Inside are folk art, quilts, and antiques.

The falls at Fall Creek drop 90 feet farther than Niagara's.

Information
Sparta/White County Chamber of Commerce, 16 W. Bockman Way, tel. (931) 836-3552, is open Mon.-Fri. 9 a.m.-5 p.m. See them online at www.shoponthenet. com/SpartaChamber/.

FALL CREEK FALLS STATE RESORT PARK

If visitors can go to only one Tennessee state park, this should be the one. Its almost 20,000 acres make it one of the largest state parks, but its waterfalls are the main attraction. The highest, Fall Creek Falls, drops 256 feet, the highest waterfall east of the Rocky Mountains—90 feet higher than Niagara Falls. The amount of water varies with the season, but it's an impressive drop anytime. Scenes from Disney's recent live-action version of *The Jungle Book* were filmed here.

Cane Creek Cascades has a swinging bridge that crosses the creek, and just downstream is Cane Creek Falls, an 85-foot drop. Nearby is 110-foot Rockhouse Falls, and the park also houses 85-foot Piney Creek Falls.

The state of Tennessee has extensively developed this park, building an 18-hole golf course and a lodge with 144 rooms. Thirty cabins sit by the 345-acre lake, which offers fishing and boat rentals. These lodgings are enormously popular and should be booked as far ahead as possible. Rates range from $48 in the off-season to $66 in the summer. For information, call (423) 881-5241. Moderate.

Campers will find 227 developed sites as well as backcountry sites, and all visitors can avail themselves of a swimming pool, an archery range, bike rentals, tennis courts, a Frisbee golf course, and a restaurant.

For further information about the park, call (423) 881-3297. To make reservations at the inn, call (800) 250-8610. For campground reservations, call (800) 250-8610. See the park online at www. tnstateparks.com.

THE SEQUATCHIE VALLEY

PIKEVILLE

This friendly town lies in the Sequatchie Valley, a 70-mile valley in the Cumberland Plateau. Unlike the thin-soiled Plateau, the valley is great for farming, and the visitor will see beautiful farms here. Downtown, there are still residences on the square surrounding the 1909 courthouse. Many Middle Tennessee towns used to be this way, but in most the houses have been supplanted by shops or businesses.

Just north of the Bledsoe County Courthouse stands the **John Bridgman House,** tel. (423) 447-2931, a federal-style home built between 1810 and 1830, constructed of handmade brick. Its walls are one foot thick and in some places are brick on the inside as well. Owned by the First National Bank of Pikeville, the house is furnished in period antiques and shown by appointment during banking hours. Admission is free.

Theron Hale and his daughters, an early group on the Grand Ole Opry, hailed from Pikeville. Their most popular song was "Listen to the Mockingbird."

Where to Stay
Colonial Bed & Breakfast, 303 S. Main St., tel. (423) 447-7183, occupies a two-story, 100-year-old house. It has four rooms, all with private baths. Handmade quilts cover each bed, and guests can enjoy two sitting rooms. Alcoholic beverages are not permitted. Rates range $45-50. Inexpensive.

Fall Creek Falls Bed and Breakfast, tel. (423) 881-5494, is a manor home on 40 acres one mile from Fall Creek Falls State Park. The eight rooms are air-conditioned, and each has a private bath and is decorated in country or Victorian style. To get there from the Fall Creek Falls State Park entrance, visitors should go one mile up Hwy. 284 until they see the sign. Rates range $75-140. Preview it online at www.bbonline.com/ten/fallcreek. Moderate-Premium.

The **Coachmen's Inn** is on Main St., tel. (423) 447-2424.

Food
The Vaughn House, 233 Main St., tel. (423) 447-2678, serves elegant lunches and dinners Mon.-Fri. in a 100-year-old house—all by reservation only. Typical lunch entrees include quiche or baked chicken, while dinner brings forth stuffed flounder or prime rib.

Shopping
The Fabric House, in a 100-plus-year-old building at 100 Main St., tel. (423) 447-6195, offers one of the largest collections of quilts that visitors will find in this part of the state—hundreds at any given time. Pillows, crocheted items, and 2,000-3,000 bolts of cloth are available as well.

The Vaughn House, 233 Main St., tel. (423) 447-2678, features antique furniture, Depression glass, and collectibles. Run by the same people and just up the street is **Yesterday & Today,** selling similar goods.

Drive along Hwy. 127 from Covington, Kentucky, to Chattanooga in mid-August for the **World's Longest Yard Sale.**

Information
Bledsoe County Chamber of Commerce, 203 Cumberland Ave., tel. (423) 447-2791, is open Mon.-Fri. 8 a.m.-4:30 p.m. See them online at www.bledsoe.net.

DUNLAP

An old Tennessee joke centers on the definition of Dunlaps Disease: a man so portly that his stomach done laps over his belt. The affliction has nothing to do with this town, although a few individuals hereabouts appear to suffer from it.

The Cumberland Plateau above the Sequatchie Valley contains coal, and at the **Dunlap Coke Ovens Historic Site** visitors can see how coal was converted to coke, a concentrated form of fuel used in iron foundries and steel mills in Chattanooga. The operation ran from 1902 until 1927, and at one time employed 350 men who ran 268 stone ovens. Now in a leafy forest, the site has a visitors center that is open on weekends between Memorial Day and Labor Day, and perhaps other times. Call (423) 949-3483 to find out. To get there, go west on Cherry Street in the middle of town off Hwy. 127 and follow the signs. Admission is free.

Scott's Choo Choos, across from Canoe the Sequatchie, tel. (423) 949-4400, is a display of Lionel "O" and "O-27" gauge railroad trains, open to the public on summer mornings and around the second Sunday in December. No admission is charged.

Recreation

The aptly named **Canoe the Sequatchie,** south of town on Hwy. 127 at the river, tel. (423) 949-4400, enables visitors to do just that. The Sequatchie River is a gentle stream ideally suited for families or for those who wish to take it easy. It's open weekends only from April until Memorial Day, daily during the summer, and week-

ends after Labor Day until the first snow. Trips range from the three- to four-mile variety to overnight excursions.

Where to Stay

Try the **Dunlap Inn,** Hwy. 127 N., tel. (423) 949-2184.

Food

The **Dunlap Restaurant,** on Hwy. 127 N, tel. (423) 949-2595, offers great country breakfasts, lunches, and dinners seven days a week.

The Hickory Pit, 108 New Hwy. 8, tel. (423) 949-4222, serves pork, beef, ribs, and chicken daily for lunch and dinner.

Shopping

The **World's Longest Yard Sale** opens for business in mid-August along Hwy. 127 from Covington, Kentucky, to Chattanooga.

FROM KNOXVILLE TO CHATTANOOGA

This area poses problems for books such as this one that adhere to the "lay out a route and they will follow" school of travel writing. There are two main highways that roughly parallel the Tennessee River, each with a string of interesting towns and villages along the way, so it behooves the visitor to read this entire section before choosing which route to take. The resulting itinerary may turn out to resemble "Drunkard's Path," a classic Appalachian quilt pattern, but the side trips will be well worth the effort.

The first tour heads down US 11 from Knoxville toward Chattanooga, a road that runs alongside Interstate 75. The second tour begins where US 411 crosses the Little Tennessee River, a route that runs alongside the railroad tracks. And the final tour abandons both highways, turns east, and heads for the hills.

HIGHWAY 11

This highway follows the Tennessee River Valley, an area of rich farmland. The mountains to the right are the edge of the Cumberland Plateau, while the ones to the left are the Appalachians. Getting away from the thundering

trucks on nearby I-75, it is hard to believe that this road, still two-lane in some stretches, once carried most of the motor traffic from the northeastern United States to Alabama, Mississippi, and points west.

LENOIR CITY

Ambitiously named a city by a man who built the area's first cotton mill, this town benefitted from its location at the confluence of the Tennessee and the Little Tennessee Rivers, and from the railroads that passed through. About the turn of the century, northern capital established industries in Lenoir City, among them factories making chairs and hosiery. Chief among these was the Lenoir Car Works, which built railroad cars.

The famed Lee Hwy., connecting Virginia to points south, rolls through Lenoir City. For years most of the traffic across Tennessee came to Dixie Lee Junction east of town, where Hwy. 11 heading southeast split off from Hwy. 70 headed west.

Dixie Lee Junction is the birthplace of Richard Marius, whose 1969 novel, *The Coming of Rain,* was set in East Tennessee after the Civil War. In his 1994 *After the War,* he transformed the story of his father, a Greek immigrant who rose to head the Southern Railroad's Lenoir City Car Works, into a powerful work of the imagination.

Where to Stay
Motel options include the **Crossroads Inn,** 110 Hwy. 321 N, tel. (423) 986-2011 or (800) 526-4685; **Econo Lodge,** 1211 Hwy. 321 N, tel. (423) 986-0295 or (800) 424-4777; and **King's Inn,** 1031 Hwy. 321 N, tel. (423) 986-9091.

For campers, **The Cross-Eyed Cricket,** tel. (423) 986-5435, is open all year with 47 sites. It has a swimming pool, laundry, and boat rentals. Get off I-40 at Exit 364 and go north on Hwy. 95, then follow the signs.

Lotterdale Cove, south of town off Hwy. 95 on Tellico Lake, tel. (423) 856-3832, has 90 campsites open April-October.

Food
Calhouns at the Marina, 4550 City Park Dr. on the water, tel. (423) 673-3366, is a chain offering ribs, prime rib, seafood, and chicken.

The Cross-Eyed Cricket, tel. (423) 986-4367, features fresh trout and channel catfish as well as burgers and chicken. It's closed November 1 to March 1. Get off I-40 on Hwy. 95 and follow the signs.

Gerald's Smokehouse, 501 Hwy. 321 N, tel. (423) 986-6159, offers barbecue—pork, beef, chicken, and ribs—along with other American entrees.

Information
Loudon County Tourist Information Center, near I-75 Exit 81 at 1075 Hwy. 321, tel. (423) 986-6822, is open Mon.-Sat. 9 a.m.-5 p.m. See them online at www.loudoncountry.org.

A TALE OF TWO DAMS

L enoir City offers the visitor a chance to compare two dams, one built in TVA's heyday, the other erected when many in the valley reviled the agency. **Fort Loudoun Dam** spans the Tennessee River east of town on Hwy. 321. The dam has the highest set of locks in TVA's system, and its completion in 1943 created Fort Loudoun Lake and played an important role in flood control and navigation.

Visitors can go to a deck and watch the locks. You can arrange free tours of the dam and power plant by calling (423) 986-3737.

By contrast, many people opposed construction of the **Tellico Dam.** It wasn't necessary, they argued, and would flood the Little Tennessee River, a wonderful trout-filled river that flowed past significant archeological sites. TVA countered that the dam would send more water through Fort Loudoun's Dam generators, would aid in flood control, and would create more recreation opportunities.

Construction on the dam proceeded until a University of Tennessee researcher identified a new species of fish—the snail darter—that seemed to exist only in the Little Tennessee River. Under the provisions of the Endangered Species Act, work on the dam had to stop. Eventually the snail darter was found to inhabit other streams, the dam was finished, the floodgates closed, and Tellico Dam became TVA's 51st dam. It has no visitors center.

LOUDON

Loudon was settled in 1790 and grew up around a ferry across the Tennessee River. Farmers in the area got accustomed to trading in the town, and steamboats did a lively trade out of this port. At particularly busy times, the docks were so full that boats had to wait several days to unload. Until a bridge over the river was built, trains coming from the south were turned around on a turntable here. The 1855 opening of a railroad bridge over the river ended the heyday of the town. It became the seat of Loudon County in 1872 and remains a pleasant place to visit.

Sights
The **Historic Loudon Walking Tour** offers a chance to see Loudon's historic buildings up close. Among them are Victorian houses, a home that was lost in a bet on a presidential election, and the Mason Place, where after the Civil War an unrepentant Southerner built the balusters of his upper porch to resemble the Confederate battle flag. The 1883 Cumberland Presbyterian Church is a fine example of the

carpenter Gothic style, and the 1810 Carmichael Coach House serves as the **Loudon County Museum,** tel. (423) 458-1442. For a map, go to the museum, which houses local artifacts, furniture, and documents, and is staffed by enthusiastic locals who sometimes wear period dress. It's open Mon.-Fri. 10 a.m.-4:30 p.m.

Loudon is blessed with two wineries. The first, **Loudon Valley Winery,** on the banks of the Tennessee River, tel. (423) 986-8736, produces dry, semi-dry, and sweet wines from 15 kinds of grapes. The tasting room overlooks the river. To get there, take Exit 76 off I-75, go east on Sugar Limb Road, and follow the signs.

The **Tennessee Valley Winery,** also at Exit 76 of I-75, tel. (423) 986-5147, offers tastings Mon.-Sat. 10 a.m.-6 p.m. and Sunday 1-5 p.m. and gives tours during the winemaking season. This place produces a variety of wines, including classic red, muscadine, and a Lambrusco-like Cherokee Red.

Entertainment and Events

Musicians gather in a big tent for the **Smoky Mountain Fiddler's Convention** late in August in Loudon. The competition features bluegrass bands, banjo, mandolin, and other instruments, as well as gospel music, clogging, and antique cars. Vendors sell crafts, antiques, and food. For information, call (423) 986-6822.

Where to Stay

The Mason Place, 600 Commerce St., tel. (423) 458-3921, is a bed and breakfast occupying an 1865 Greek revival home on the Tennessee River and is listed on the National Register. Both sides in the Civil War camped here, and when General Longstreet advanced on Knoxville, he and 30,000 troops crossed the Tennessee River at this point. A swimming pool, gazebo, and wisteria-covered arbor await visitors outside amid the three-acre grounds, from which Civil War artifacts are still unearthed. The five guest rooms have private baths, period antiques, fireplaces, and feather beds. A gourmet breakfast of items such as stuffed French toast is served daily. Rates range $108-120. Premium.

Also in town are the **Holiday Inn Express,** 12452 Hwy. 72 N, tel. (423) 458-5668 or (800) HOLIDAY; and the **Knight's Inn,** 15100 Hwy. 72 N, tel. (423) 458-5855 or (800) 843-5644.

Knight's Inn also has 16 **campsites** open all year.

Shopping and Information

Loudon boasts a good number of antique stores. Among them is the **General Store,** 411 Mulberry St., tel. (423) 458-6433 or (423) 458-5989, which has antiques, contemporary folk art, textiles, and advertising spread over three floors.

Loudon County Tourist Information Center is located near I-75 Exit 81 at 1075 Hwy. 321, tel. (423) 986-6822.

SWEETWATER

As scores of billboards will remind the traveler, Sweetwater is the home of the **Lost Sea,** tel. (423) 337-6616, an underground lake approximately 4.5 acres in size, the largest such underwater pool on the planet. It occupies a section of the Craighead Cavern System, in which divers have found 13 acres of flooded rooms so far.

The drier parts of the cave have been put to various uses. Cherokee artifacts have been found here, and during the Civil War the South mined saltpeter, an ingredient of gunpowder, from the cave. Moonshiners and cockfighters drank and gambled in the large rooms, and when the cave was commercially opened in 1915 it was used for a dance hall.

The Lost Sea is open daily 9 a.m.-dusk. Visitors cruise the sea in glass-bottom boats and walk though other areas. Admission is $9 for adults and $4 for children six to 12. To get there, take Exit 60 off I-75 and follow Hwy. 68 southeast to the cave.

Where to Stay

Among Sweetwater's motel options are the **Best Western Inn,** I-75 Exit 60, tel. (423) 337-3541; **Comfort Inn,** 803 Main St., tel. (423) 337-6646 or (800) 228-5150; **Comfort Inn West,** I-75 and Hwy. 68, tel. (423) 337-3353 or (800) 228-5150; and **Days Inn,** 229 Hwy. 68, tel. (423) 337-4200 or (800) 325-2525.

For a non-franchise place, the **Sweetwater Motel and Convention Center,** I-75 Exit 60, tel. (423) 337-3511 or (800) 523-5727, offers a good place to lay one's head, as well as a pool and hot tub.

Sweetwater Valley KOA, Murray's Chapel Rd.—Exit 62 off I-75—tel. (423) 213-3900, is open all year with 50 sites.

Food

China East, 793 Hwy. 68, tel. (423) 337-2800, offers country cooking—but from another country entirely. Not at all bad for a place away from the city lights.

Davis' Restaurant, 310 E. North St., tel. (423) 337-5651, serves up country cooking, sandwiches, and hot plate lunches.

Usually hotel food is to be avoided like the plague, but the **Sweetwater Motel and Convention Center,** I-75 Exit 60, tel. (423) 337-3511 or (800) 523-5727, does a good job. Their rolls, said to be made by a little old lady back in the kitchen, are divine.

Shopping

The World's Largest Flea Market has its charms, no doubt, but right next door stands a little house containing **Amish 1,** 121 County Road 308, tel. (423) 337-2919, which sells hand-crafted goods, some of which are made by Amish folks. Next door is **Country Store,** tel. (423) 337-6540, which has an eclectic bunch of antiques and collectibles.

NEARBY TOWNS

Niota

Niota, south of Sweetwater on Hwy. 11, boasts the **Niota Depot,** an 1853 structure said to be the oldest train station in the state. One of the passengers who caught the train here was Henry Thomas Burn, who in 1920 at age 23 was the youngest state legislator in Tennessee. On August 18 of that year he cast the most significant vote of his life: His "Aye" gave American women the right to vote. He put Tennessee's ratification of the 19th Amendment over the top, with Tennessee as the 36th state to ratify. Burn had previously voted against the Amendment but got a letter from his mother encouraging him to support it. "Hurray and vote for suffrage," his mother penned. An excellent book on the fight for women's suffrage in Tennessee is *The Perfect 36—Tennessee Delivers Woman Suffrage,* published by Serviceberry Press.

Englewood

This town was built on textile manufacturing and at one time had 25 mills. Women and children as young as 10 years old worked here. The **Englewood Textile Museum,** on the square in Englewood, tel. (423) 887-5455, commemorates this time with exhibits on mill workers, mill life, and the history of Englewood. Exhibits include pre-industrial items—a flax wheel and a hand loom—and actual mill machinery. Hard times are depicted by a feed sack dress. The saddest exhibit is a complete trousseau sewn by a bride whose parents would not allow her to marry her chosen. Miss Ellie, as she was known for the rest of her life, lived to be 81 years old. The museum is open Tues.-Sat. noon-5 p.m. all year. Admission is free.

ATHENS AND VICINITY

ATHENS

This pleasant town, like many between Knoxville and Chattanooga, saw its fortunes rise with the coming of the railroad. Billing itself as "The Friendly City," it is home to **Tennessee Wesleyan College,** a four-year, 600-student institution owned by the United Methodist Church. The college occupies 40 acres in downtown Athens and provides concerts and cultural and sports events for the edification of local residents. For information about college events, call (423) 745-9522 or check out www.tnwc.edu.

Sights

Housed in a former high school building, the **McMinn County Living Heritage Museum,** 512 W. Madison, tel. (423) 745-0329, offers more than 7,000 items arranged into 30 exhibit areas covering Cherokee times through 1940. Visitors can see displays on rural doctors, a print shop, and military uniforms, to name a few. It's open Mon.-Fri. 10 a.m.-5 p.m., weekends 2-5 p.m.

The **Mayfield Dairy Farms Visitor Center,** 4 Mayfield Lane, tel. (423) 745-2151, is a great place to take kids. A film history of the dairy precedes a plant tour that shows milk bottling and ice cream production. Admission is free, and the dairy is open year-round Mon.-Fri. 9 a.m.-5 p.m. From Nov.-April, it's also open Saturday 9 a.m.-2 p.m. and the rest of the year on Saturday from 9 a.m.-5 p.m.

The **Strikers' Premium Winery,** 480 County Rd. 172, tel. (423) 507-8816, is one of the newer sources of wine in the state. Twelve out of the 17 wines offered are sweet or semi-sweet, and this place is open Mon.-Sat. 10 a.m.-8 p.m. and Sunday 12 a.m.-6 p.m. To get there, take Exit 49 off I-75, go east on Hwy. 30, then left on Lee Irwin Road. Follow the signs.

Outside of town at the McMinn County Airport is the **Swift Museum,** tel. (423) 745-9547, which is devoted to Globe and Temco Swift airplanes—aluminum-bodied, two-seat aircraft first made in the 1940s. Fully restored planes and related items are displayed Mon.-Fri. 9 a.m.-5 p.m. The museum sponsors several annual events, among them the Annual Swift National Fly-In on the week preceding Memorial Day, to which up to 100 planes arrive. Admission is free.

Where to Stay

One popular bed and breakfast spot in town is the **Woodlawn Bed and Breakfast,** 110 Keith Ln., tel. (423) 745-8211 or (800) 745-8213, which is in a National Register 1858 Greek revival house built of bricks made on the site. The four guest rooms all have private baths and tall ceilings—13.5 feet high. The dining room is very traditional, with Chippendale chairs. Rates are $95-115. See them online at www.woodlawn.com. Expensive-Premium.

Majestic Mansion Bed and Breakfast, 201 E. Washington St., tel. (423) 746-9041, occupies a 1909 home that now has four guest rooms, three of which have private baths.

A bit farther afield is **Cross Creek Farm,** Hwy. 30 E, tel. (423) 334-9172, which has a restored early 1800s two-bedroom cabin for guests. From the porch visitors can watch alpacas and Shetland sheep safely graze. Guests can participate in farm chores if so inclined. Rates are $85. Moderate.

Motel options include the **Days Inn of Athens,** 2541 Decatur Pike, tel. (423) 745-5800 or (800) 325-2525; **Homestead Inn East,** 1827 Holiday Dr., tel. (423) 744-9002; **Homestead Inn West,** 2808 Decatur Pike, tel. (423) 745-9002; **Ramada Limited,** I-75 and Mt. Verd Rd., tel. (423) 745-1212; and the **Super 8,** I-75 Exit 49, tel. (423) 745-4500.

The place to camp locally is **Athens I-75 Campground,** 2509 Decatur Pike—Exit 49 off I-75—tel. (423) 745-9199, which has 59 sites and is open all year.

Food

Burkett's Pit Bar-B-Q, 117 E. Madison, tel. (423) 745-9791, serves barbecued pork, beef, chicken, and ribs as well as a full breakfast. It serves all three meals Mon.-Fri., and breakfast and lunch on Saturday.

Ming Dynasty, 1635 Decatur Pike, tel. (423) 744-9341, offers Chinese food for lunch and dinner seven days a week.

Monterrey Mexican Restaurant, 319 S. Congress St., tel. (423) 744-8644, has fajitas, chiles rellenos, steaks, and 30 combination dishes for lunch and dinner seven days a week.

Riddle and Wallace Drugstore, on the Square, has what can only be called "drugstore food"—chicken salad, cherry cokes, and grilled cheese sandwiches. Open Mon.-Sat. for breakfast and lunch.

Temptations, 330 S. White St., tel. (423) 745-8060, is a great stop anytime. They have a complete soda fountain plus a menu that runs the range from burgers and sandwiches to shrimp dinners.

Shopping

Artist's Alcove, on the square in Athens at 6 S. White St., tel. (423) 745-7312, features handmade pottery, jewelry, wood items, glass, and weavings. Some are locally produced, but most items come from different places all over the country.

Information

Try the **Athens Area Chamber of Commerce,** 13 N. Jackson St., tel. (423) 745-0334, or find information online at www.athenschamber.org.

RICEVILLE

Mouse Creek Nursery, located on County Rd. 67 between Riceville and I-75, tel. (423) 462-2666, is one of the largest perennial nurseries in the state with over 600 species. It has a restored 1855 church on site.

Sunshine Hollow, located on County Rd. 52, tel. (423) 745-4289, has such extensive daylilly plantings that busloads of perennial fanciers come to visit. It also offers hosta perennials—shade-loving plants said to be the most favored herbaceous perennial in the United States. The bakery specializes in pecan fruitcakes and other delights.

CLEVELAND

Of the towns along the railroad between Chattanooga and Knoxville, Cleveland prospered the most. Relatively untouched by Civil War hostili-

ties, the town was poised to take advantage of the industrial boom that came to the South in the 1870s and '80s. Locals are justifiably proud of the Victorian homes built during that period and around the turn of the century.

Cleveland is also the headquarters of the Church of God denominations—at least two of them—and therein lies a tale. As explained by Charles A. Sherrill in the *Tennessee Encyclopedia,* The Church of God sect came into existence in 1906, a group whose services contained "fervent prayer, weeping, shouting, and speaking in tongues." The next year Cleveland minister Ambrose Tomlinson was appointed to head the organization.

Tomlinson helped increase church membership by 20-fold, but in 1922 he was accused of mismanaging the money and forced out. Refusing to go gentle into that charismatic night, he stayed in Cleveland, formed his own church, and called it the Tomlinson Church of God. This prompted the original Church of God to take the splinter group to court to resolve who could use the name they shared. A court ruling held that the newer sect had to append the words "of Prophecy" to their "Church of God." (You'll find its Web site at www.cogop.org.)

Tomlinson died in 1943, and his two sons, Milton and Homer, each sought the leadership role. Milton won out, leaving Homer to move to New York City, where he abandoned the church, pronounced himself "King of the World," traveled with a throne, and ran for president four times on the Theocratic ticket.

Approximately 75 percent of the Church of God of Prophecy members live outside the United States, although the Church reports 2,000 congregations in this country, and 133 in Tennessee.

Meanwhile, the original Church of God, which has its own website at www.chofgod.org, managed to thrive without the Tomlinsons. It founded Lee University (www.leeuniversity.edu) and the adjoining Church of God Theological Seminary, which currently enroll, respectively, 2,850 and 262 students. The denomination claims over 51,000 members in Tennessee, 792,000 in North America, and 3.2 million in the world.

Now that the feuding factions have largely gone on to their respective heavens, the two denominations with their shared heritage have come much closer together. In the meantime, they both have to sometimes deal with confusion caused by the existence of another denomination, the Church of God in Christ, the second largest black denomination in the country, headquartered in Memphis. (You'll find this third group online at www.cogic.com.)

Thus endeth the lesson.

Sights

Apple Valley Orchards, 351 Weese Rd., tel. (423) 472-3044, has 50 acres growing 23 kinds of apples. From August to December, the orchard is open to the public Mon.-Sat. 9 a.m.-6 p.m. and Sunday noon-6 p.m. People can buy apples, watch cider being pressed, and go through the gift shop and bakery, from which all manner of apple-related goods flow forth.

The **Morris Vineyard** offers visitors an opportunity to pick scuppernong, muscadine, and other grapes as well as blueberries—the largest such enterprise in the state.

OOH Ostrich Ranch , 3270 Tonia Dr., tel. (423) 472-9785, gives visitors a chance to see ostriches, emu, and rheas up close before they are processed into burgers, roasts, and kabobs. Usually about 200 ostriches are on the ranch at any given time. A gift shop sells plain and decorated eggs, ostrich leather, and other goods. Call ahead to schedule a tour, which costs $3 per person. See the ranch online at www.oohranch@aol.com.

Reconstructed log cabins, furnished with authentic farm and household items, make up **Primitive Settlement,** which lies six miles east of Cleveland off Hwy. 64 on Kinser Rd., tel. (423) 476-5096. Each cabin is full of antiques, some of them dating to the age of their structure. It's open daily April-October. Admission is $5 for adults and $2 for children six to 12. A dance is held every Saturday night at Primitive Settlement, where a live band gets toes tapping and people clogging and line dancing. Admission is $3 per person.

The **Tennessee Mountain View Winery,** 352 Union Grove Rd. in Charleston, a community eight miles north of Cleveland on Hwy. 11, tel. (423) 479-7311, sells muscadine, Concord, Niagara, Catawba, and white riesling wines. The vineyard is open July 4-October, Tues.-Sun. 8 a.m.-8 p.m. The winery is open then, too, as well as November-July 3, Mon.-Fri. 4-8 p.m., Saturday 10 a.m.-6 p.m.

Where to Stay

Brown Manor Bed and Breakfast sits in downtown Cleveland at 215 20th St. NE, tel. (423) 476-8029. The large, French-style brick house offers a 20-foot by 40-foot pool and four guest rooms, three of which have private baths. It serves a full breakfast daily. The rate is $75 per night. Moderate.

Rose Hill Inn, 367 Horton Rd. SE, tel. (423) 614-0700 or (888) 813-ROSE, is one of the more elegant B&Bs in these parts. Located on nine acres out in the country, this New England saltbox-style house has four guest rooms, all of which feature private baths. Outside is a pool, whirlpool, and well-stocked fishing pond. Rates are $95-140 and include a full country breakfast and evening dessert. You can find the inn online at http://.earth.vol.com/~rosehill. Expensive-Premium.

A little farther out is **Chestnut Inn Bed & Breakfast,** Box 124 Delta Dr., Conasauga, tel. (423) 338-7873 or (800) 993-7873. This inn was built in 1940 of native chestnut and has three bedrooms, all with private baths. Rates are $75. Moderate. See the Web site at www.bbonline.com/tn/chestnut.

Good choices among Moderate-priced motels include the **Budgetel Inn,** 107 Interstate Dr., tel. (423) 339-1000 or (800) 428-3438; **Hospitality Inn,** I-75 and Hwy. 64, tel. (423) 479-4531; **Quality Inn-Chalet,** 2595 Georgetown Rd., tel. (423) 476-8511 or (800) 221-2222; and **Travel Inn,** 3000 Valley Hills Trail, tel. (423) 472-2185.

Cleveland-area motels in the Expensive category include **Best Western Cleveland Inn,** 156 James Asbury Dr., tel. (423) 472-5566 or (800) 528-1234; **Hampton Inn,** 185 James Asbury Dr., tel. (423) 559-1001 or (800) HAMP-TON; and **Holiday Inn Cleveland,** I-75 and Hwy. 60, tel. (423) 472-1504 or (800) HOLIDAY.

For visitors who prefer camping out, there is the **Cleveland KOA,** at I-75 Exit 20, tel. (423) 472-8928, with 83 sites; **Exit 33 Campground,** at I-75 Exit 33, tel. (423) 336-5277, with 26 sites; and **Golden Chain Village,** I-75 and Hwy. 411, tel. (423) 336-3170, with 12 sites, are all open year-round.

Food

Angelo's Rib House, 720 S. Lee Hwy., tel. (423) 476-2727, barbecues beef, pork, chicken, and ribs and also serves steak and other dishes. Angelo's is open Tues.-Sat. for lunch and dinner.

Catie's Kitchen, 1301 S. Lee Hwy., tel. (423) 479-4530, features hot plate lunches and is open Mon.-Sat. for breakfast, lunch, and dinner.

Visitors to the OOH Ostrich Ranch who would like to try an ostrich burger should head for **Deat's Restaurant & Deli,** tel. (423) 559-8838, which sells two to six Ostrich burgers every day at lunch. Other offerings include hamburgers, "deli food," homemade chili, and country cooking.

The Gondolier, 3300 Keith St., tel. (423) 472-4998, serves homemade lasagna, spaghetti, and manicotti as well as American dishes. It's open all week for lunch and dinner.

Jenkin's Deli, 88 Mouse Creek Rd., tel. (423) 478-1648, has sandwiches and burgers. It's open Mon.-Sat. for lunch and dinner.

Jordan's BBQ, 910 Stuart Rd., tel. (423) 478-2171, serves pork, beef, and ribs, and is famous for stuffed potatoes—potatoes filled with barbecue and topped with cheese or various sauces. Follow this with homemade desserts, including Key lime pie. It's open Mon.-Sat. for lunch and dinner.

Roblyn's Steak House, 1422 25th St., tel. (423) 476-8808, serves dinner Mon.-Sat. and lunch on Sunday. Diners can expect steak, seafood, poultry, and a salad bar.

Rose Hill Inn, 367 Horton Rd. SE, tel. (423) 614-0700 or (888) 813-ROSE, offers wonderfully prepared gourmet dinners at a bed and breakfast. Four people minimum, and 24-hour notice is requested.

Stadfields, 1430 25th St., tel. (423) 479-3123, offers a buffet as well as a full menu. It's open for all three meals Mon.-Sat. and breakfast and lunch on Sunday.

Witherspoons Deli, 124 Stuart Rd., tel. (423) 472-7242, has sandwiches and burgers. It's open Mon.-Sat. for lunch and dinner.

Information
The **Cleveland/Bradley Chamber of Commerce, Convention & Visitors Bureau,** 2145 Keith St., tel. (423) 472-6587, is also online at www.clevelandchamber.com.

RED CLAY STATE HISTORIC AREA

The 260 acres that make up this historical area served as the last seat of the Cherokee Nation's government before the Trail of Tears. The visitors center shows a film about the Cherokee and displays artifacts and documents from the 1832-38 period. Outside are replicas of a council house, a farm, and the sleeping quarters that tribe members would use when they gathered for a council. The Great Council Spring, also known as the Blue Hole, is about 15 feet deep and still produces more than a half million gallons of water daily. The Eternal Flame of the Cherokee burns here as well.

Cherokee Days of Recognition take place on the first weekend in August, when 18,000 people come for authentic Cherokee food and crafts, storytelling, dancing, and a blowgun competition.

The visitors center is open Mon.-Sat. 8 a.m.-4:30 p.m. and Sunday 1-4:30 p.m. The park is open daily 8 a.m.-sunset. From December to February the visitors center is open Mon.-Fri. 8 a.m.-4:15 p.m., weekends 1-4:15 p.m. The park is open daily 8 a.m.-4:30 p.m. Admission is free. To get here from Cleveland take either Blue Springs Rd. or Dalton Pike south from Hwy. 64/40 Bypass. Follow the signs for 12 miles to the park. For more information, call (423) 478-0339 or visit www.tnstateparks.com.

THE RAILROAD ROUTE

Highway 411 roughly follows the path of the railroad from Knoxville to Chattanooga. The rails were first laid in 1855 and had a profound effect on the towns along the way. Etowah first came into being as a railroad town, and the others benefited from their proximity to the rails.

FORT LOUDOUN STATE HISTORICAL AREA AND SEQUOYAH BIRTHPLACE MUSEUM

The land along the Little Tennessee River was the stronghold of the Cherokee. Here were their chief towns, and from here came the leaders of their people. Three sites just off Hwy. 411 shed light on the troubled relations between the Cherokee and the whites.

This reconstructed fort commemorates the first British fort built west of the mountains; it served as the empire's southwesternmost outpost. Unlike most forts in Tennessee, this one was built at the request of the Cherokee, who had allied themselves with the British during the French and Indian War and wanted protection for their families while their warriors were fighting French-allied Indians to the north.

Fort Loudoun was built in 1756, just as relations between the colonists and the Cherokee entered uncertain times. Various outrages and misinterpretations led to bloodshed, and the Cherokee laid siege to the fort. An agreement permitted the besieged colonists to leave in August of 1760, but the Cherokee attacked the departing group one day later and then burned the fort to the ground. This provoked retaliatory attacks on the Cherokee towns in the area and led to further bloodshed.

Today the reconstructed Fort Loudoun gives a good look at the old enclosure, although the visitor must keep in mind that nearby Tellico Lake was just the Little Tennessee River in the 1700s. The walls are made of upright logs sharpened to a point at the top. Inside are several buildings and gun platforms. The visitors center, a separate building, contains a good museum. Children will like this place, which is open daily 8 a.m.-sunset. The visitors center is open daily 8 a.m.-4:30 p.m. Admission is free. For more information, call (423) 884-6217, or see www.tnstateparks.com.

Events

The **Memorial Day Encampment** brings forth a re-creation of the South Carolina Independent Company, the British soldiers who were garrisoned at Fort Loudoun. As many as 170 actors in period dress take part, some of them as British soldiers, some of them as "provincials," and some Cherokee. Admission is free for this event.

During the year 10-20 people in period dress participate in **Garrison Weekends.** These are held approximately once a month, February-December. Call the fort for exact dates.

September brings the **18th Century Trade Fair** to Fort Loudoun, with craftspeople selling replicas of period textiles, pewter, jewelry, blown glass, and other products. All are for sale, as are food and drink. Call the fort for dates and details.

Christmas at Fort Loudoun brings period decoration, a candle-lined trail, carols and games germane to the 18th century, and often a buffet of traditional foods. For information and dates, call the fort.

Blockhouse and Birthplace

In three decades after the 1760 fall of Fort Loudoun, several things changed. The British were gone, the United States government was in place, and the Cherokee knew they could no longer dream of pushing back the whites. The old Fort Loudoun site marked the boundary between the Cherokee lands and those of the United States. Once again, the Indians requested that the Americans build an outpost in which to regulate trade, conduct negotiations, and prevent the more rapacious settlers from violating Indian lands. William Blount, governor of the Southwest Territory, was happy to do this, for it gave him an excuse to station troops there who could readily and quickly deal with any Indian uprisings.

In 1794, Blount had the Tellico Blockhouse erected within sight of the Fort Loudoun site. People traveling downstream to New Orleans

SEQUOYAH

In 1871 a Cherokee woman and a colonial soldier produced a boy named George Gist, or, to his Cherokee relatives, Sequoyah. He grew up in Tennessee and Alabama, never attended school, and fought for Gen. Andrew Jackson at the War of 1812 Battle of Horseshoe Bend against the Creek.

One of Sequoyah's legs was disabled during the war, and about that time he and many other Cherokee willingly moved to the Arkansas Territory. It was there that he began to work on an alphabet for the Cherokee language. The story goes that Sequoyah came up with the idea when a relative came home from an American school and Sequoyah saw him writing letters.

Withdrawing to a cabin outside his house, he labored on the alphabet, suffering ridicule from his neighbors in the process. By 1821 he had devised a syllabary—so named because its letters stand for syllables—of 86 letters, some of them English ones, that captured the language of the Cherokee. He taught it to his daughter, Atoya, and together they demonstrated it to a council of tribal leaders. First Sequoyah wrote down a message from the elders. Then Atoya came in, picked up the paper, and, to the astonishment of the council, read their words back to them. Sequoyah's

creation was an immediate success; it was so simple that people could teach it to each other and could then send letters back to their relatives in the East.

Sequoyah achieved much-deserved renown, among his own people and the nation at large; Congress passed a bill to give him $500 for his accomplishment. The Cherokee people gained access to a printing press and by 1828 were publishing their own newspaper in New Echota, Georgia.

Just ten years later came the Trail of Tears, when the Cherokee were moved forcibly to Oklahoma. Those in Arkansas were moved first, and the county in which Sequoyah lived was named in his honor, as were the enormous redwood trees in California. He lived until 1843, a leader who helped his people in Oklahoma and elsewhere. He died while on a trip to New Mexico.

Cherokee alphabet

often made a side trip up the Little Tennessee River to see the blockhouse. The most prominent of these early tourists was the Duke of Orleans, who later became King Louis Philippe of France. Carolyn Sakowski, in her book *Touring the East Tennessee Backroads,* tells how the duke was ill and, following the medical practices of the day,

bled himself. This mightily impressed the Cherokee, who asked him to do the same to an elderly chief. The duke obliged, and the old gentleman improved so quickly that his tribe members were astonished. For his services, the duke was thanked by getting to sleep in the chief's house on the family mat in the place of honor—between the grandmother and the great-aunt. It is not recorded whether or not the duke was inspired to continue his medical practice.

The Tellico Blockhouse site has not been restored, and there isn't a great deal to see there. Visitors can drive off the island, go right on Hwy. 411, then turn right onto Old Hwy. 72 and follow signs to the blockhouse site.

A mere half-mile away is the Sequoyah Birthplace Museum, tel. (423) 884-6246, which is owned and operated by the Eastern band of the Cherokee, who live in a reservation on the North Carolina side of the Great Smoky Mountains National Park. The museum commemorates the inventor of the Cherokee alphabet and includes artifacts from villages, Cherokee crafts, and explanations of various myths and legends. Outside the museum is a memorial to 191 Cherokee whose remains were unearthed during the frantic archaeological efforts that preceded the damming of the river and the creation of Tellico Lake. The museum is open Mon.-Sat. 9 a.m.-5 p.m., and Sunday noon-5 p.m. Admission is $2.50 for adults and $1.50 for children six to 10.

MADISONVILLE

Madisonville is the birthplace of Estes Kefauver (1903-1963), who served in the House and the Senate and was the Democratic vice-presidential nominee on the Adlai Stevenson ticket in 1956. He achieved national fame when in the early '50s he conducted nationally televised hearings investigating organized crime. He and Senator Albert Gore Sr. were the only Southern senators who refused to sign the 1956 Southern Manifesto, a document opposing racial integration in schools.

Country crooner Eddy Arnold was born near here in 1918. Early in his career he was dubbed "The Tennessee Plowboy," but his singing reached a level of smooth sophistication far beyond any rural nickname. His country hits were played from the 1940s through the '80s, and he survived both rock 'n' roll and being managed by Col. Tom Parker, who many think mismanaged the career of Elvis Presley.

Madisonville is now home to **Orr Mountain Winery,** tel. (423) 442-5340, which offers tours

and tastings of its six wines—blush, sweet red and white, and dry red, rosé, and white—Wed.-Sat. 10 a.m.-6 p.m. and Sunday 2-6 p.m. It's open seven days a week in July and August, and irregular hours in January and February. To get there, go west on Hwy. 68 from Madisonville toward Sweetwater. Turn left onto County Rd. 117 at the sign between Mileposts 8 and 9. Go one mile and turn right onto County Rd. 121, then 0.3 miles and turn right again.

Entertainment
Bluegrass and country fanciers head out to the **Magic Mart** at the corner of Hwy. 411 and Hwy. 68 every Thursday evening for a wonderful jam session. Admission is free, and the pickers keep going until 10:30 or 11 p.m. Call (423) 442-6563.

Where to Stay
Motels include the **Holiday Motor Lodge,** 4930 Hwy. 411, tel. (423) 442-4982; **Motor Inns of America,** 4740 Hwy. 68, tel. (423) 442-9045; and **Town and Country Motel,** Hwy. 411 S, tel. (423) 442-2084.

Food
The **Countryside Restaurant,** at the junction of Hwy. 411 and Hwy. 72, tel. (423) 884-6673, offers smoked prime rib, ribs, and barbecue as well as steaks and seafood daily for lunch and dinner.

Donna's Ole Towne Cafe, 100 College St., tel. (423) 442-3304, specializes in buffets for all three meals. Depending on the night, one can enjoy a Mexican, seafood, or Italian buffet.

Stefano's Chicago Style Pizza, 1004 Hwy. 441 N, tel. (423) 442-2222, offers pizza, steamed sandwiches, a salad bar, lasagna, and spaghetti daily for lunch and dinner.

Information
Monroe County Chamber of Commerce, at the intersection of Hwy. 68 and Hwy. 411, tel. (423) 442-9147 or (800) 245-5428, is open weekdays 8:30 a.m.-5 p.m.

ETOWAH

This is a town where almost everyone could sing "I've been workin' on the railroad. . . ." The L&N

Railroad picked this site in 1902 as their Atlanta division administrative headquarters and also set up a facility to manufacture wooden boxcars. The town was built in 1906 virtually from scratch—a two-story station was built first—and by 1927 the people working for the railroad numbered over 2,250. This was a young man's town; a newly established funeral home almost went broke during its first 10 years, and a music store in Knoxville claimed that it sold more instruments and sheet music in Etowah than anywhere else in East Tennessee. All this changed in 1928, however, when the railroad switched to steel boxcars and moved its offices to Knoxville, a two-punch combination that reduced the number of employees here to 80.

The centerpiece of town today is the wonderfully restored 1906 **L&N Depot and Railroad Museum,** tel. (423) 263-7840. Inside, amid wonderful wooden floors and wainscoting, is the museum and art gallery; outside sits a caboose. The museum gives an excellent picture of Etowah's railroad days. Admission is free. The museum is open Mon.-Fri. 9 a.m.-4:30 p.m., Sunday 1-4 p.m.

The depot is also the home of the Tennessee Overhill Heritage Association, a source of excellent information about the sites and events in McMinn, Monroe, and Polk Counties. Etowah is still a rail town and a magnet for rail buffs; the CSX Railroad's main line from Cincinnati to Atlanta passes right by the station, and just across the tracks the railroad maintains a yard office where crew changes are made.

Events
Across and a little way up the street is the 540-seat Gem Theater, a 1927 moviehouse that now features live events such as the **Gospel Explosion,** tel. (423) 263-7232, and the **Cousin Jake Tullock Bluegrass Convention,** tel. (423) 263-7608, which take place, respectively, in the middle of March and the third Saturday in February. The gospel music is of the exuberant Black variety, and Cousin Jake was the bass player for the Flatt and Scruggs bluegrass band for 20 years.

Other local events of note include the **Starr Mountain Street Rodders Annual Rod Run,** tel. (423) 263-7909, which takes place on the first weekend in June, and the **Delano Blue-** **grass Festival,** tel. (423) 263-7498, south of Etowah on the second weekend in September.

Food
The Cafe Etowah, 328 N. Tennessee Ave., tel. (423) 263-7762, is alone worth making a trip to this town. The chef has worked in New York and produces dishes such as blackened chicken Cordon Bleu baked in puff pastry—not exactly country cooking.

COUNTRY HAM

In the days before refrigerators, Tennesseans preserved hams by rubbing them with a mixture of salt and sugar and hanging them in smokehouses for months to cure. The result is country ham, a down-home version of prosciutto that can be served as hors d'oeuvres, as a main dish, or as flavoring for beans and other foods. One favorite way of serving country ham is frying it for breakfast, then pouring water and a little bit of coffee into the frying pan to whip up what is called "red eye gravy," best served over biscuits or grits. Country ham is very salty and is an acquired taste. Novices should cut off a little piece and eat it with a big biscuit.

When it comes to hams, Allen Benton, the proprietor of **Benton's Smoky Mountain Country Hams,** 2603 Hwy. 411 N, tel. (423) 442-5003, is the product of a mixed marriage. "My father's family sugar-cured hams," he explains, "and my mother's people salt-cured them." He uses a mixture of brown sugar and salt, which he and his crew apply to approximately 14,000 hams per year. They begin with a 20- to 26-pound ham, then apply the sugar and salt and store it for 75-80 days. "Hams lose a lot of their moisture during this part of the process," he explains. Then the hams are hung for 60-80 days in a room kept at 50 degrees. "At the end of that time, they've lost 16-18 percent of their weight." Finally, some of the hams are smoked for three and half days and all of them are hung to cure for 90 or 100 days. The result is the best country ham in Tennessee, if not the entire South.

One can get Benton hams plain or smoked—whole or by the slice—and country bacon, all available by mail order as well. Benton's is open Mon.-Sat. 8:30 a.m.-5 p.m.

Nearby

On Hwy. 163 between Delano and Calhoun is **Trew's Store,** a country store that's more than 100 years old. Here visitors can get a sandwich made with hoop cheese and fresh-sliced bologna. It's open until mid-afternoon every weekday but Tuesday.

For information, go to the **Tennessee Overhill Heritage Association,** L&N Depot, tel. (423) 263-7232 or visit www.toda.dst.tn.us/ovhill.htm.

BENTON

Deep in Cherokee country, the grave of **Nancy Ward,** perhaps the most famous Cherokee woman, lies west of the Ocoee River on Hwy. 411/33 between Benton and Ocoee. She held the position of "Beloved Woman," which entitled her to sit on the tribal council. She could decide the fate of captives and vote on whether or not to wage war. Ward befriended the settlers many times, once sending word that an attack was imminent. She readily assimilated and introduced her people to many practices of the whites, such as raising cattle, to her people, but she adopted their worst practices as well; later in life she owned slaves.

Sights and Recreation

The **Old Fort Marr Blockhouse** sits east of the Ocoee. This "fort" is actually one blockhouse from a larger stockade that was first used to supply Andrew Jackson in his war against the Creek. Later it served to protect the Cherokee whose warriors were off fighting the Creek. Its final and most shameful use was that of holding the Cherokee before the Trail of Tears march to Oklahoma.

Where to Stay

Southern Memories Country Inn is five miles north of town on Hwy. 411 North, tel. (423) 338-4351. The house was built in 1916 as a plantation house from hardwood grown on the farm. The four bedrooms all have private baths and queen-sized beds. The inn also has two Victori-

an housekeeping cottages and a carriage house with a whirlpool bath in the silo. Rates are $65-180. Moderate-Luxury.

Or try **Lake Ocoee Inn,** Hwy. 64, 4.5 miles from Reliance, tel. (423) 338-2064.

Camping

The **Ocoee Ranger District,** in Benton, tel. (423) 338-5201, of the **Cherokee National Forest** administers the following local campsites: **Chilhowee,** with 88 sites, open April-October; and **Sylco,** with 12 sites; **Parksville Lake,** with 17 sites; **Thunder Rock,** with 42 sites; and **Tumbling Creek,** with eight sites. The latter four are open all year.

The **Hiwassee Ranger District,** headquartered in Etowah, tel. (423) 263-5486, administers the following campsites: **Quinn Springs Campground,** with 24 sites, and **Lost Creek Campground,** with 15 sites, both open all year.

Outdoor Adventures of Tennessee in Benton, tel. (423) 338-8914, has 30 sites and is open April-October.

Parksville Lake Campground, east of town on Hwy. 64 and one mile up Hwy. 30, tel. (423) 338-5201, has 36 sites, open mid-March to early November.

Food

Lake Ocoee Inn Restaurant, on Lake Ocoee 12 miles west of Cleveland on Hwy. 64, tel. (423) 338-2064, has country cooking three meals a day, seven days a week from Memorial Day until Labor Day. Thereafter it serves lunch and dinner daily, with breakfast added only on weekends.

Tinsley's Restaurant and Barbecue, half a mile north of Benton on Hwy. 411, tel. (423) 338-9118, offers big breakfasts and lunches Monday through Saturday. The barbecue is pork, chicken, and ribs; it's available for takeout dinners on Friday and Saturday.

Information

The **Polk County Chamber of Commerce,** in Town Plaza in downtown Benton, tel. (423) 338-5040, www.polkcotn.com, is open Mon.-Fri. 8:30 a.m.-5:30 p.m. and Saturday 9 a.m.-2 p.m.

WHITE WATER AND GREEN MOUNTAINS

Highway 64 crosses Hwy. 411 and follows the Ocoee River upstream. The first body of water is Lake Ocoee, home to jet-skis and bass boats. Further upstream the river emerges once more, and the craft become decidedly less motorized—canoes, kayaks, and rafts predominate. The highway follows "The Old Copper Road," the road by which copper was brought from the mines at Ducktown and Copperhill.

This is a beautiful drive, but motorists should be mindful that there are very few gas stations or eateries along the way until getting to the Ducktown/Copperhill area.

OCOEE

Head east on Hwy. 64 to the Ocoee Whitewater Center, a log structure built for the whitewater events at the 1996 Olympics and slated to host a World Cup event in 2000. This is an excellent place to stop for a picnic, pick up some information about the area, and take a look at the man-made kayaking course. About 2.4 miles of the original Copper Rd. awaits the hiker or mountain biker, and a 44-mile trail system is under development.

RAFTING ON THE OCOEE

Whitewater enthusiasts have long known of the Ocoee River, but the 1996 Olympics vividly showed the whole world the thrills available on this Tennessee stream.

Outfitters offer guided raft trips on weekends April-Oct. and on weekdays June-August. As a general rule, rafters have to be at least 12 years old and should plan to get wet; wear sneakers and shorts or a bathing suit. On cold days, put on wool clothing and raingear. Some rafting companies make wetsuits available to customers. In any case, an extra set of dry clothes is a good idea.

The locations of the following rafting companies are given only in general terms. Very often the offices are nowhere near where the rafts are put in and taken out. A company with headquarters in North Carolina, for example, might conduct some of its operations in Tennessee.

Adventures Unlimited, Ocoee, tel. (423) 662-0661
Cherokee Adventures, Erwin, tel. (423) 743-7733
High Country, Ocoee, tel. (800) 233-8594
Nantahala Outdoor Center, Bryson City, North Carolina, tel. (800) 232-7238

Ocoee Inn Rafting, Benton, tel. (800) 272-7238
Ocoee Outdoors, Ocoee, tel. (423) 338-2438 or (800) 533-PROS
Quest Expeditions, Benton, tel. (800) 277-4537
Southeastern Expeditions, Ocoee, tel. (800) 868-7238
Sunburst Adventures, Benton, tel. (800) 247-8388
Wildwater Limited, Longcreek, South Carolina, tel. (800) 451-9972

CHATTANOOGA AREA CONVENTION AND VISITORS BUREAU

RELIANCE

The center of everything in the village of Reliance is **Webb Brothers Store**, located along the Hiwassee River at the intersection of Hwy. 30 and TN 315. This is a good place to, as locals might put it, "come in and sit a spell."

Harold Webb serves as proprietor, ardent preservationist, and provider of "Duckies"—in-

THE "BELOVED SCAR"

Tennessee gets a lot of mileage out of its striking landscapes, but perhaps the most eye-popping one for decades was an area of bare rock, deep gullies through red dirt, and so little vegetation that it looked like the Badlands. Coming out of lush forests, visitors to the Copper Basin were in for a shock.

This 56-square-mile, desertlike appearance resulted from the processing of copper ore. It all began in 1843, when a prospector found a rich vein of what at first looked like gold. Eight years later three mines opened. To separate the copper from the ore, huge fires built to "roast" out the copper burned 24 hours a day. This created devastation in three stages: loggers seeking timber to fuel the roasters denuded 30,000 acres of surrounding hillsides; sulfur dioxide fumes from the roasting process killed off any remaining vegetation; and the over 50-inch annual rainfall did the rest, carrying the soil into streams and rivers and turning the land into a moonscape.

Old-timers recall that it wasn't all bad. The pollution that eliminated the vegetation also drove off flies, mosquitoes, ticks, rats, and snakes. Residents took stubborn pride in where they lived and in the way it shocked outsiders.

Technological improvements at the turn of the century led to the end of the open roasting. By 1907 the sulfur dioxide was captured and processed into sulfuric acid, a valuable by-product, and by the 1930s, the company made more money from sulfuric acid than it did from copper. But the damage was done.

Reforestation efforts mark a partnership between government and the copper company. The Tennessee Valley Authority, charged with fighting erosion throughout the Tennessee Valley, conducted extensive studies to determine what flora would best work here. The copper company once ordered 5,000 chestnut trees to plant on its land. As trees and other vegetation began to grow back, however, some longtime residents of the area claimed they wanted to keep the Copper Basin's distinctive appearance, referring to it as "our beloved scar." For that reason, a couple of hundred acres of land in Ducktown have been left alone. Overall, approximately 800 acres are still denuded, while less than 6,000 acres are in various stages of restoration.

Mineshafts, ruins of mining structures, and piles of slag still mark the area. The Ducktown Basin Museum, on the site of the Burra Burra Mine, contains photographs, artifacts, and people who can tell the story of their beloved scar.

TENNESSEE TOURIST DEVELOPMENT

Copper mining created a moonscape in the mountains.

flatable canoes with kayak paddles that are just perfect for descending the Hiwassee River, a gentle stream very suitable for families. He hauls people up the river and they drift back down to the store. When things are slow, get him to talk about the historic structures hereabouts.

DUCKTOWN

This town derives its name from that of the Cherokee chief Cowanneh, whose name translates as "Duck." The town, which is situated almost in the middle of the Copper Basin, was dominated for decades by the copper mines whose ore processing denuded the landscape. The National Register of Historic Places lists more than 200 area buildings as part of the Copper Basin Historic District.

"BIBLICAL WONDERS" OF THE UNCONVENTIONAL KIND

Visitors to Ducktown are a mere nine miles from something over which future civilizations will ponder. The Church of God of Prophecy (COGOP), whose ecclesiastical carryings-on have made Cleveland, Tennessee, a spirited place to live, erected a collection of religious monuments in 1941 that they bill as one of the "Biblical Wonders of the Twentieth Century."

It certainly is that. Here on 216 acres stands the world's largest cross—150 feet tall and 115 feet wide; the world's largest representation of the Ten Commandments on tablets 300 feet square, with letters five feet high and four feet wide; and a replica of the tomb in which Jesus was laid to rest. Capping it all is a 24-foot-high, 32-foot-wide version of an open New Testament, complete with a platform on top, to which visitors are invited to climb. The purpose for all this, according to COGOP's website, is to "provide a powerful Gospel witness to multitudes who are unsaved and/or unchurched and who are not being reached by conventional evangelistic methods."

No admission is charged to this unconventional place, which is open every day of the year from sunrise to sunset. Call (828) 494-7855 for more information or take a peek online at www.cogop.org/~cbl/heritage3.html.

The **Ducktown Basin Museum,** Burra Burra Street/Hwy. 68, one mile from Hwy. 64, tel. (423) 496-5778, recounts the fascinating story of the Copper Basin and those who lived in it. The museum occupies a building on the site of the Burra Burra mine. It's open April-Sept., Mon.-Sat. 10 a.m.-4:30 p.m.; and from October to the beginning of April 9:30 a.m.-4 p.m. Admission is $3 for adults, $2 for seniors and students 12-18, and 50 cents for children.

One of the southernmost native cranberry bogs sits amid the **Ducktown Green-Gold Conservancy,** 100 acres with trails and a garden of plants used by the Cherokee. The rather ornate building, now used for an elementary school, was built to be a junior college.

Where to Stay

The White House Bed and Breakfast, 104 Main St., tel. (423) 496-4166 or (800) 775-4166, occupies a two-story Victorian house, circa 1900, listed on the National Register. It features a wraparound porch with rocking chairs. Inside three bedrooms await, one of them with a private bath. The host serves a full country breakfast daily. Rates are $65-75. Preview the White House online at www.bbonline.com/tn/whitehouse. Moderate.

The Company House, 125 Main St., tel. (423) 496-5634 or (800) 343-2909, is an 1850 house with a rocking-chair porch. The six rooms all have private baths and are filled with antiques or reproductions. Rates are $69-75 and include a full country breakfast. Visit online at bbonline.com/tn/companyhouse. Moderate.

Also try the **Best Western Copper Inn,** Hwy. 64, tel. (423) 496-5541 or (800) 528-1234.

COPPERHILL

Many houses were built on the sides of steep hills in this long-time mining town. Residents would park their cars at the bottom of the hills and climb long staircases, some of which survive. Just north of town is a huge pile of slag, the impurities removed in processing copper. Just one mine produced an estimated 15.6 million tons of ore.

Where to Stay

The Lodge at Copperhill, 12 Grande Ave., tel. (423) 496-9020, once the home of Copperhill's

THE TRAIL OF TEARS

The Southeastern part of Tennessee was the setting for one of the United States's most shameful actions: the forced removal of the Cherokee from their homelands to a reservation in Oklahoma. The Indians still refer to it as the Trail of Tears. Today we might call it ethnic cleansing.

Unlike their counterparts in the West, the Cherokee never waged war on a large scale against the settlers. As early as 1730, some of them traveled to England and came home with the realization that they could never overcome white men in battle. And so, for the most part, they tried to accommodate the newcomers, entering into a series of treaties and sales of their land as they retreated from the growing number of settlers. On a personal basis, they intermarried with settlers and began adopting many of the new ways of living.

By the late 1820s, the Cherokee governed their nation in eight districts, each having a bicameral legislature. The nation as a whole had a constitution that outlined courts and other parts of government. They even had a bureaucracy that took care of tax collections, licenses, education, and maintaining an infrastructure of bridges and roads. All this was centered in the Georgia town of New Echota.

In 1828, Andrew Jackson was elected president. Although he had cheerfully accepted the Cherokee's help in his battle against the British and their Indian allies, the Creek, he was an Indian-hater at heart. The same year, gold was discovered in Dahlonega, Georgia—less than 70 miles away from New Echota.

The Georgia legislature moved to strip the Cherokee of all their rights. Among other things, the Georgians prevented the Indians from assembling for any public purpose. To escape this ban, the Cherokee moved their capital to Red Clay, Tennessee, the site of a huge spring that gave forth a half million gallons of water daily. Here the Cherokee decided to fight the Georgians on legal grounds—with lawsuits and lobbying efforts in Washington. After all, that was the "civilized" thing to do.

The United States government should have protected the Cherokee from the rapacious Georgians, and, indeed, the Supreme Court ruled that the Cherokee were not subject to the laws of Georgia. But President Jackson, despite his oath to uphold the Constitution, refused to enforce the court's de-cision and allowed all manner of Georgian riff-raff to brazenly steal Cherokee houses and property.

The Cherokee split over what to do. One faction wanted to give up and try to get the best deal possible as they moved West. Others wanted to continue the legal and political struggle. While the latter faction was traveling to Washington in 1836, a group of 20 of the former signed the infamous Treaty of New Echota, which allowed the federal government to move the Cherokee to the Oklahoma Territory.

Those who opposed this treaty, headed by John Ross, presented petitions bearing the names of 16,000 Cherokee who did not want to leave. By one vote, the Senate ratified the treaty, and the fate of the Cherokee was sealed. Jackson was succeeded by Martin Van Buren, who put the Cherokee removal into effect.

The task of evacuation fell to Gen. Winfield Scott, whose 7,000 troops fanned out and rounded up the Cherokee. Many had little time to gather belongings, which fell into the hands of whites who followed the soldiers. The Cherokee were crammed together in various stockades—forerunners of concentration camps—until it was time to move out.

The first group of Cherokee went by boat to Oklahoma, but John Ross and other leaders secured permission to take the remainder—about 13,000 men, women, children, and old people—overland. The Cherokee paid private contractors to supply them with food and other necessities, and they set out in 1838 in September—arguably the worst possible time to go.

It took six months to walk the 1,200 miles to Oklahoma. During the winter, food ran short, bad weather hit, and the Cherokee suffered shortages of warm clothing and blankets. They walked through Dayton, McMinnville, Murfreesboro, and Nashville before crossing into Kentucky and out of Tennessee forever. An estimated 10-25% of the Cherokee died along the route and were mostly buried in unmarked graves.

As quoted in Carolyn Sakowski's *Touring the East Tennessee Backroads,* a Georgian colonel in the Confederate Army later admitted, "I fought through the Civil War and have seen men shot to pieces and slaughtered by thousands, but the Cherokee removal was the cruelest work I ever knew." For more information on this cruelest work visit http://rosecity.net/tears.

famous Dr. Hicks, bills itself as "the only European-style inn in Appalachia." This means that they charge by the person—$25 per head—not the room. Unlike the inns of old, they do not put guests in with strangers. Inexpensive.

Maloof's Bed and Breakfast Suites, 41 Ocoee St., tel. (706) 492-2016 or (800) 475-2016, is housed in a building originally constructed in 1921 as a department store. The state line runs through the building. The five guest rooms have private baths and come with televisions, kitchenettes, and, in some cases, sitting rooms. For breakfast, guests can choose from one of three local restaurants. Rates range $85-135. See them online at www.mtnescape.com. Expensive-Premium.

Food
New York Restaurant, 95 Ocoee St., tel. (423) 496-3855, has country cooking Mon.-Sat. for all three meals.

Just across the border in McCaysville, Georgia, is a rarity—a Japanese restaurant in a small town. **Michiko's Restaurant** at the corner of Blue Ridge Dr. and Toccoa, tel. (706) 492-5093, has California rolls, tempura, gyoza, and other traditional dishes.

COKER CREEK

According to an old tale, one day a settler asked a Cherokee lass where she got the gold nugget she wore on a necklace. She told him Coqua Creek, and, for the Indians, things went downhill from there. This was the second gold strike in the U.S.—the first was south of here in Dahlonega, Georgia—and fortune seekers poured into the area, even though it was on Cherokee land. Operations reached a peak before the Civil War but slowed because the gold was too difficult to separate from the surrounding material.

Coker Creek Village is a collection of working craftspeople, gold panning, horseback riding, and a country store. **The Old Country Store,** tel. (423) 261-2310, sells crafts, antiques, and things to eat. It's open Mon.-Sat. 9 a.m.-5 p.m. and Sunday noon-5 p.m.

Where to Stay
The **Mountain Garden Inn,** on Hwy. 68, Coker Creek Village, tel. (423) 261-2689, specializes in family reunions of up to 17 adults, although other guests are welcome. The log inn was built in 1993 and features a wraparound porch from which one can gaze into three states. The two suites and two "cozy bedrooms" all have private baths. It serves a full country breakfast. Rates run $55-80. Inexpensive-Moderate.

Coker Creek Village, on Hwy. 68, tel. (423) 261-2310 or (800) 448-9580, offers cabins and has 100 camping sites open March-November.

THE CURIOUS LEGACY OF DOCTOR HICKS

In the 1950s and '60s, a quiet stream of upper-class women with unwanted pregnancies came from Chattanooga and Atlanta to Copperhill or across the river to McCaysville, Ga., where a discreet country doctor either performed their abortions or delivered their children. At the same time, a couple seeking a baby to adopt drove south from the Midwest, returned home with a newborn infant and, a few weeks later by mail, received a false birth certificate attesting they were the child's real parents. For this they were charged anywhere from $250-1,000.

The man at the center of this enterprise was Dr. Thomas Hicks, who practiced medicine in Copperhill for decades and who died in 1972 at the age of 83. His medical sideline was revealed in 1997 when an adopted Ohio woman, curious to learn about her birth parents, found out that she was "a Hicks baby." Her research revealed the existence of as many as 200 children who came into the world in the hands of Dr. Hicks. In 1997 his picture was featured in *The New York Times, USA Today,* and on network television. Although the stories were datelined McCaysville, Dr. Hicks, the great-uncle of the author of this book, lived in Copperhill in what is now the Lodge bed and breakfast.

Dr. Hicks leaves a curious legacy. He lost his Tennessee medical license in the 1940s after being convicted of illegally selling narcotics. He served time in prison, and on his release he moved his clinic a few blocks across the state line into Georgia and resumed business as usual. Some of the residents, however, recall him as a generous man who provided free medical care to more poor people than any other local doctor.

CHEROHALA SKYWAY

"Cherohala" sounds like one of the many Indian words that mark Tennessee's landscape and provided the name of the state itself. However, this new road owes more to what might be called the Delmar school of nomenclature, also frequently seen in the state, in which two names—Delbert and Margaret, for instance—are joined together to create the name of a trailer park or restaurant. This 52-mile road crosses from the Cherokee National Forest into the Nantahala National Forest, so there you have it—Cherohala.

However it got named, this is one beautiful drive. It begins at Tellico Plains—look for Highway 156—and crosses into North Carolina, where it inexplicably becomes Hwy. 143. The drive features overlooks, campgrounds, a swimming beach, and hiking and biking trails.

The road ends in Robbinsville, a lovely little burg, where one can turn left on Hwy. 129 and come back to Tennessee along Lake Santeetlah. Another option is staying on Hwy. 43 and turning left on Hwy. 28, which will take the motorist along Fontana Lake, with a possible stop at the 480-foot-high Fontana Dam, the highest such structure east of the Mississippi. This route should be avoided by those who dislike curvy roads. Either route will eventually put the traveler back on Hwy. 129, which leads to Maryville and civilization.

Food
The Village Inn Restaurant in Coker Creek Village, tel. (423) 261-2310, offers country cooking buffets Saturday for breakfast and lunch, Sunday dinnner, and lunch on weekdays. Closed November-March.

Shopping
Coker Creek Gallery, on Hot Water Road off Hwy. 68, tel. (423) 261-2157, offers the works of more than 30 area and regional artists in pottery, candles, dolls, metal, woodcarving, weavings, watercolors, and oak baskets. It's open Tues.-Sat. 10 a.m.-5 p.m.

At **H&W Frontier Willowcraft,** 4.9 miles up the mountain from Tellico Plains and 1.5 miles north of Coker Creek, craftspeople make furniture from willow wood. Operators couldn't agree on who would pay for the phone, so they took it

out. Nonetheless, visitors can watch the production of chairs, loveseats, tables, and baskets. It's open Mon.-Sat. 9 a.m.-7 p.m. and Sunday 9 a.m.-6 p.m., though furniture is not made on Sunday.

TELLICO PLAINS

It was from one of the Cherokee's main towns, Talequah, that a group of Indians departed in 1730 to visit England. They met the king, and were feted all over London. One of this party was Chief Attakullakulla, whose friendship with the British proved invaluable in keeping the Cherokee from joining the French in the French and Indian War and in subsequent dealings with settlers.

Bald River Falls drops 100 feet to the Tellico River, and visitors can see it by driving 4.2 miles out of town on Hwy. 165 and turning right on Forest Service Rd. 210 for another six miles. The waterfall is easy to see from the car, and a foot trail leads to the top.

To get to the **Tellico Trout Hatchery,** tel. (423) 253-2661, continue up Forest Service Rd. 210. Follow it to Sycamore Road, where one can see the hatchery. Someone is almost always there 8 a.m.-4 p.m., but call ahead.

Where to Stay
Near Tellico are the **Green Cove Motel,** Tellico River Rd., tel. (423) 253-2069; and the **Tellico Riverside Motel,** 222 Rafter Rd. Box 759, tel. (423) 253-7360.

Camping
The Tellico Ranger District office, tel. (423) 253-2520, of the **Cherokee National Forest** is on the Tellico River Road just outside of town. It administers these year-round campgrounds: **Indian Boundary,** 26 sites; **North River,** 11 sites; **Holly Flats,** 17 sites; **Davis Branch,** four sites; **State Line,** seven sites; and **Jake Best,** seven sites; along with **Spivey Cove,** 17 sites, and **Big Oak Cove,** six sites, both open April-October.

Cherokee Campground, located on Ballplay Rd., tel. (423) 253-3094, offers 24 sites; open all year.

Food
The **Tellicafe,** 228 Bank St., tel. (423) 253-2880, serves seafood, steaks, pasta, and other dishes in a casual atmosphere.

CHATTANOOGA
INTRODUCTION

Until country music staked out Nashville and Elvis laid claim to Memphis, Chattanooga was the town many people thought of when they connected music with Tennessee. "Pardon me, boy, is that the Chattanooga Choo-Choo?" actually used the name of the city only because it fit the needed number of syllables, but the song, recorded dozens of times by a variety of artists, put Chattanooga on the musical map.

The city produced Adolph Ochs, who made *The New York Times* into the nation's best newspaper, and Bessie Smith, a blues singer famous around the world.

Chattanooga got its name from a Creek Indian word for Lookout Mountain, which dominates the city's skyline. The mountain was the scene of a bloody Civil War battle, and in this century it became the site of legendary tourist attractions. Rock City and Ruby Falls still manage to compete with modern-day Oprylands and the frenetic activity around the Smoky Mountains.

HISTORY

The fourth-largest city in Tennessee sits just upstream from what used to be the wildest section of the Tennessee River. After flowing peacefully down the Great Valley, the river turns west, confronting two prongs of the Cumberland Plateau that point to the south, and cuts through them in gorges so deep that they are called "The Grand Canyon of the Tennessee River." Though the nickname is an exaggeration, the terror that flatboaters faced in these waters was not. The worst of the obstacles to navigation was a whirlpool called "The Suck."

Dragging Canoe

Flatboaters faced other hazards as well. Dragging Canoe, the Cherokee who was so opposed to the Sycamore Shoals sale of his people's land, in 1777 led more than 1,000 renegade followers to this part of Tennessee, where they called themselves the Chickamauga and continued to wage war on settlers. They allied themselves with British forces and did whatever they could to make life difficult for the colonists.

When the women and children of the Donelson Party came floating down from Long Island in 1779 on their way to the site of Nashville, the wild waters caused a boat in their flotilla to wreck. While trying to save it, the group came under fire from the Chickamauga. One of the travelers was 15-year-old Rachel Donelson, the future wife of Andrew Jackson.

John Sevier's militia led a raid in 1782 on Dragging Canoe's villages and destroyed them. Since Dragging Canoe was allied with the British, local boosters have seized upon this attack as "The Last Battle of the Revolutionary War," occurring as it did after Yorktown and before the U.S. and England signed a peace treaty. Knowing that they were a part of this larger effort would no doubt have been news to Dragging Canoe and John Sevier, whose mutual detestation would probably have led to the battle, war or no war. Dragging Canoe, after more raids, died in 1792 after an all-night party. He was 60 years old, a ripe old age for someone in his line of work.

Steam and Rail
Once the Chickamauga were defeated, relations between the settlers and Indians improved. The Cherokee owned the south side of the Tennessee River, and about 1815 Chief John Ross built Ross's Landing, a place to which traders came by ferry. After the Cherokee were rounded up and removed to Oklahoma, whites poured across the river and named the town Chattanooga. Increasing steamboat traffic helped the town grow, but the railroad put Chattanooga on the map. Tracks from Atlanta and Nashville and Knoxville converged here, and when the Civil War broke out, the city became an immediate prize.

The war (covered in Special Topics throughout this chapter) was bad enough, but in 1867 a severe flood, followed by another eight years later, crippled the city. The 1870s marked a

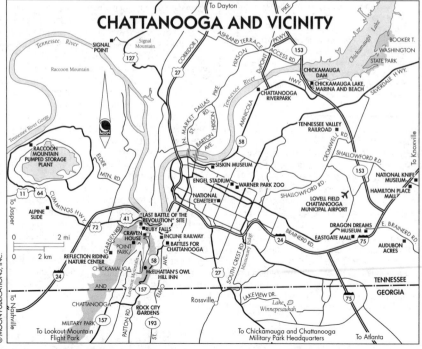

CHATTANOOGA AND VICINITY

MUST-SEE HIGHLIGHTS

Often lost in the rush to get to the Tennessee Aquarium, **Ross's Landing** is a superb piece of landscape art that deserves a visitor's full attention.

The **Chattanooga Choo-Choo** gives a glimpse of railroading's importance in this town, celebrated wherever big bands still play.

Rock City, heralded for decades by barns and birdhouses, remains much the same as in the days when people traveled on blue highways to see its wonders.

Point Park, at the tip of Lookout Mountain, provides a vista of Chattanooga and admiration for the brave troops who fought their way up the mountain slopes.

Raccoon Mountain Pumped-Storage Project shows TVA's ingenuity in producing electric power with a lake that fills by night and empties by day.

The **Mountain Opry,** up on Signal Mountain outside of town, offers live acoustic music that can't be beat.

The **Tennessee Aquarium,** although sometimes dreadfully crowded, is worth working into the traveler's schedule.

Visitors will delight in the cultural and culinary offerings at the **Bluff View Art District.**

One of the best depictions of an aspect of Tennessee history is the **Chattanooga African-American Museum.** The exhibits on Bessie Smith are a must for music lovers.

mauga and Chattanooga battlefields became the first national military parks. They ate Moon Pies, which were invented in Chattanooga, and happily drank Coca-Cola (KO-ko-la) from the first bottler franchised by the Atlanta company. It had bought the rights to bottle the new soft drink for only $2.

Arrival of the TVA

The Depression brought the Tennessee Valley Authority to town and an increasing number of tourists who took the advice painted on scores of barns to "See Rock City." One reason for the founding of the Tennessee Valley Authority was flood control, and Chattanooga was perhaps the chief beneficiary of this aspect of the agency. TVA took over an existing utility, established a presence in the city, and controls its immense power-producing plants from here. Find more information online at www.tva.gov.

Like the other main Tennessee cities, Chattanooga saw its downtown deteriorate after World War II and the decline of the railroads. The interstate highway system came through, following the paths of the railroads, and funneled lots of traffic through the city. But most of that traffic was not going downtown. And no wonder—in 1969 the Federal government pronounced Chattanooga "the dirtiest city in America." This galvanized the city, which put teeth in pollution controls, and by 1989 Chattanooga was one of the few cities in the East that fully complied with air quality standards. But this came with a price. For a variety of reasons, downtown lost 18,000 manufacturing jobs between 1973 and 1984. The city looked to its two strong points—the river and the stream of people passing through—and decided to do something that would get those people to stop and spend money.

Chattanooga Nowadays

The 1980s and 1990s have brought a dramatic revitalization of downtown Chattanooga. The Tennessee Aquarium and Ross's Landing Park and Plaza have breathed new life into this interesting place. The city has embraced the river, and, in return, visitors have embraced this most interesting city.

turnaround in Chattanooga, however, as money from the North flowed in to exploit the area's coal and iron resources. Soon iron and steel mills multiplied to the extent that Chattanooga was called "The Pittsburgh of the South." These mills brought a lot of money and good jobs to the town, but they also belched forth clouds of pollution, which the surrounding hills tended to pool in Chattanooga. Anyone with enough money built a house on one of the the surrounding ridges—Lookout Mountain, Signal Mountain, and Missionary Ridge.

From their lofty perches, the citizens of Chattanooga took great pride in their city. The Chicka-

THE BATTLE FOR CHATTANOOGA: CHICKAMAUGA

By 1863 things were not looking good for the South. In July, Ulysses S. Grant took Vicksburg on the Mississippi River, and the Battle of Gettysburg marked an end to any chance of the Confederacy's attacking the North. The Union turned its attention toward Georgia, and to get there it had to come through the rail center of Chattanooga.

Braxton Bragg was commander of Southern forces numbering 43,000 in Chattanooga when a Union army of 60,000 commanded by William Rosecrans approached. Chattanooga, beside the looping Tennessee River and next to high mountain ridges, was a very good place to get penned, so the Confederates retreated into Georgia. Sensing the chance to catch and defeat Bragg, Rosecrans pursued him into the heavily wooded plains near Chickamauga Creek. He did not know that Confederate troops from Gettysburg and other places had come by train to reinforce Bragg, bringing his forces to 66,000. The armies skirmished on the night of September 18, and at dawn the next day clashed in one of the bloodiest battles of the war.

Unlike Gettysburg or other places where battles were fought out in the open, the land here was covered with trees and thick underbrush. Much of the fighting was hand-to-hand, and officers had no clear idea of what was happening. This situation—and a huge piece of luck—determined the outcome of the battle.

One of the Union officers erroneously reported to General Rosecrans that there was a gap in the lines, and the general ordered a division to shift over and fill it. It did so, thus creating a real gap at the exact place where Gen. James Longstreet—who had roomed with Rosecrans at West Point—poured 11,000 soldiers, who broke through the Union lines.

Rosecrans took the advice of his chief of staff, future president James A. Garfield, and retreated toward Chattanooga. One Union commander was not so willing to go. George Thomas took a stand on Snodgrass Hill and held off the Southerners long enough for the Union to make an effective retreat. For this he became known as "The Rock of Chickamauga," while Rosecrans in his retreat was labeled a coward.

Despite the victory, Bragg didn't fare well either. He refused to pursue the fleeing Northerners, to the disgust of Nathan Bedford Forrest and other Confederates. The cost of the battle was appalling. Bragg lost an estimated 30% of his men, and Union and Confederate losses totaled 4,000 men dead—among them 10 Southern generals—and 35,000 wounded.

The Union forces stumbled into Chattanooga, and Bragg, following them at last, took up positions high above the city on Lookout Mountain and Missionary Ridge. His guns commanded the rail and river approaches, and other troops were so placed that no one could supply the vanquished troops. Bragg meant to starve them into submission, and the situation for the Union got so bad that a newly promoted general was summoned to help. His name was U.S. Grant, and his arrival set the scene for the battle of Lookout Mountain and Missionary Ridge.

LAY OF THE LAND

Downtown

More than any of the other four main cities in Tennessee, Chattanooga's downtown seems custom-made for visitors. There's plenty of parking, not a great deal of traffic, and many of the attractions are clustered close together. The Chattanooga Visitors Center is a great place to get oriented and perhaps dispatch segments of the traveling group in different directions.

The Tennessee Aquarium and IMAX Theater and Ross's Landing Place surge with tourists. An option is to head down Broad St., which contains lots of shops such as Allbooks and a great barbecue place called Hog Wild. A walk in the opposite direction across the Walnut St. Bridge leads to a collection of shops and restaurants.

Bluff View Art District

For a totally different experience, hike up Third St. and turn left onto High St.t—or follow the Riverwalk from Ross's Landing Park under the Walnut Street Bridge to the **Bluff View Art Dis-**

THE BATTLE FOR CHATTANOOGA:
LOOKOUT MOUNTAIN AND MISSIONARY RIDGE

After the defeat at Chickamauga, Abraham Lincoln's administration ordered Generals U.S. Grant, William T. Sherman, and Joseph Hooker to relieve the siege of Chattanooga. Grant was in charge, and by November 1, 1863, he established a supply line that was out of reach of Confederate troops and artillery. The next step was to drive the Southerners from the heights that overlooked the city.

While the Union was beefing up its forces, Confederate generals argued about Braxton Bragg's competence, their squabble reaching such intensity that Pres. Jefferson Davis came to personally work out an agreement. The upshot was that Nathan Bedford Forrest left, James Longstreet was dispatched with one-fourth of the troops to attack Knoxville, and Bragg remained in charge.

On November 24, Grant sent Hooker's troops up the side of Lookout Mountain—a 1,716-foot gain in elevation—to take out the artillery. A fog covered the mountain that day, and under its cover Union infantry fought their way with surprising ease over boulders and around trees to the top, suffering only 500 casualties. Later on this became known as "The Battle Above the Clouds," "Battle in the Fog" not quite having the right ring to it.

With a big American flag planted at the top of Lookout Mountain, the Union forces turned their attention the next day to Missionary Ridge. Fought six days after Lincoln's Gettysburg Address and involving Southerners who had fought at that battle, in many ways this engagement looked to be a mirror image of Gettysburg, with the Southerners waiting at the top of a ridge for the Union troops to charge. Unlike the Northerners at Gettysburg, however, the Confederates had been digging in on Missionary Ridge for two months, and the hill was wooded and much steeper—453 feet higher than downtown Chattanooga.

Grant thought that a direct assault would be suicidal, so he ordered attacks on each side. Neither was very effective, so to keep the Confederates from shifting troops to reinforce the ends he commanded men under Gen. George Thomas (a.k.a. "The Rock of Chickamauga") to attack the first row of defenders straight on.

The word to go was all these troops needed. Stung by their defeat five weeks before at Chickamauga, they overran the first row of trenches and kept going. From his headquarters Grant could see regimental colors climbing higher and higher on the ridge. Fearing for the men, he asked who had ordered the charge. Reportedly, he was told, "No one. They started up without orders. When those fellows get started, all hell can't stop them."

The Confederates certainly couldn't. The Union troops took the rifle pits, captured the artillery, and chased the Rebels down the back of Missionary Ridge yelling, "Chickamauga! Chickamauga!" One of the victors was an 18-year-old lieutenant who carried his Wisconsin regiment's colors up the hill after three men had died doing the same thing. He won the Medal of Honor for this deed and went on to sire Douglas MacArthur.

Chattanooga was never again in Southern hands. Grant was named lieutenant general, a rank last held by George Washington, and moved east to act as general-in-chief. Sherman set his sights for Atlanta and the march to the sea that would bring the South to its knees.

COURTESY OF THE STATE HISTORICAL SOCIETY OF WISCONSIN

Lieutenant Arthur MacArthur of the 24th Wisconsin was 18 when he led a Union charge up the slopes of Missionary Ridge to end the Confederate siege of Chattanooga.

trict, a small enclave with galleries, restaurants, and an overall European feel.

North Chattanooga
If things seem a little hectic around the Tennessee Aquarium, walk across the Walnut Street Bridge to this neighborhood. Be sure to check out the **Mudpie Coffeehouse and Newsstand.**

Lookout Mountain
Coming from Downtown and heading south, Broad Street becomes Hwy. 58, which leads to Lookout Mountain, home of the Incline Railway, Rock City, Ruby Falls, and the site of the "Battle Above the Clouds."

Signal Mountain and Raccoon Mountain
Signal Mountain and Raccoon Mountain and the Tennessee River running between them make up "The Grand Canyon of the Tennessee River." To get to the former, take the Hwy. 127 exit off Hwy. 27 N, and to get to the latter, take the Cummings Hwy. exit off I-24 heading toward Nashville.

SIGHTS AND RECREATION

DOWNTOWN CHATTANOOGA

A good place to begin is the **Shuttle Park South,** adjacent to the Chattanooga Choo-Choo on Market Street. A 500-space parking garage offers a safe place to leave the vehicle before setting out to explore downtown. The electric shuttle buses—free to all—run from here to the Tennessee Aquarium and all points in between. The schedule is as follows: Mon.-Fri. 6 a.m.-10 p.m., Saturday 9 a.m.-10 p.m., and Sunday 9 a.m.-8:30 p.m.

Ross's Landing Park and Plaza
Visitors sometimes think that Ross's Landing is part of the Tennessee Aquarium, which is the focal point of what is sometimes called "Chattanooga's Front Porch." Ross's Landing at once provides open space and pays homage to Chattanooga's history. It accomplishes this with landscaped bands that use public art and native plantings to tell Chattanooga's story. With surfaces that are alternately paved, grassed, or covered with running water, the bands begin with the year 1992, the dedication date, and work back in time as they move toward the river. Commemorated subjects include Sequoyah and his Cherokee language syllabary, Chattanooga's railroad heritage, and Bessie Smith.

The **Chattanooga Visitors Center,** just off Ross's Landing at 2 Broad St., tel. (423) 756-8687 or (800) 322-3344, is a great place for visitors to orient themselves and plan their sightseeing. In addition to a huge collection of brochures, the center offers a slide show about the city, a reservation service for local hosteleries, and information about events soon to take place. The slide show costs $2 for adults and $1 for children six to 12.

Tennessee Aquarium
The $45 million aquarium, tel. (800) 262-0695, smack in the middle of Ross's Landing Park and Plaza, was the first of its kind devoted to freshwater aquatic life. The displays replicate the habitats that water falling in an Appalachian mountain forest would go through as it made its way to the sea. Visitors can see plantlife and animals—some 7,000 species of mammals, fish, reptiles, and amphibians—as different in distance and evolution as mountain salamanders and Gulf Coast sharks. Life from rivers around the world is included—South America's Amazon, Africa's Zaire, Japan's Shimanto, and Siberia's Yenisey.

The aquarium's **IMAX Theater** shows educational and entertaining films on a six-story-high screen backed with a state-of-the-art sound system. Anyone subject to motion sickness should sit near the aisle. The admission price changes depending on the length of the film, but runs about $7 for adults and $5 for kids three to 12. A combination ticket to the IMAX and the aquarium costs $14 for adults and $9 for kids.

The aquarium has proven enormously popular and at times gets very crowded. Ordering tickets ahead of time by phone is a very good idea. Admission is $10.25 for adults, $5.55 for kids three to 12, and free for kids under three. The gift shop

DOWNTOWN CHATTANOOGA

is free and open to the public. To get there, take I-24 to downtown Chattanooga to Exit 1-C, Hwy. 27 North. Take a right onto 4th St., then turn left at the second stoplight onto Broad Street. Go two blocks and the aquarium will be in sight.

River Sights

The 2,370-foot-long **Walnut Street Bridge** was built over the Tennessee River in 1891 and carried pedestrians, trolley cars, and motor traffic. It served the locals for 87 years before it was closed. Unlike similar situations, in which such bridges are typically demolished or left to decay in public, Chattanoogans had the vision to renovate the bridge and dedicate it to human-powered traffic. Thus the visitor will see walkers, runners, bi-

cyclists, and in-line skaters crossing what is billed as the longest pedestrian walkway bridge in the world. No fee is charged to use it.

Bluff Furnace Historical Park, on the Riverwalk between the Walnut Street Bridge and the Hunter Museum, marks the site of the city's first heavy industrial plant. Completed in 1854, Bluff Furnace produced bars of pig iron. In 1859, the plant was leased by Northern industrialists and began burning coke, a fuel used nowhere else in the South. Today the park features a stainless steel outline of the original furnace stack, a scale model of the complex, explanatory signs, and a multimedia, interactive computer program highlighting the history of the riverfront. Admission is free.

Chattanooga Choo-Choo

The Chattanooga Choo-Choo, 1400 Market St., tel. (800) TRACK 29 or (423) 266-5000, is the latest incarnation of Chattanooga's 1909 Southern Railway Terminal, where in its heyday 68 trains arrived and departed daily on 14 tracks. The 85-foot dome is the highest freestanding such structure in the world. The last regularly scheduled train pulled out of Chattanooga in 1971, and the 61-year-old terminal was boarded up and all but abandoned. Twenty-four investors had other ideas, however, and after a year of renovation the station opened once more. It's been going strong ever since.

The 30-acre complex includes four restaurants (see below), a Holiday Inn, and shops. Guests can stay in railroad coaches that each contain two complete rooms. Visitors can ride around the grounds in a 1930s New Orleans trolley, shop in 14 stores, and view an enormous 174-foot by 33-foot H.O. gauge model train display that contains more than 3,000 feet of track, 1,000 freight cars, and model cities.

MUSEUMS

History

Chattanooga African-American Museum, 200 E. Martin Luther King Blvd., tel. (423) 267-1076, houses cultural and historical documents and artifacts pertaining to the city's black community. Admission is $5 for adults, $4 for seniors, $3 for students, free for children under 12. The museum is in **Bessie Smith Hall,** tel. (423) 757-0020, which contains a 264-seat performance hall and exhibits relating to the great blues singer. Blues and jazz concerts of national, regional, and local artists are presented here, and visitors can use a listening room to hear tapes of Bessie Smith and others. The exhibits here are first class.

Two blocks from the Tennessee Aquarium, the **Chattanooga Regional History Museum,** 400 Chestnut St., tel. (423) 265-3247, interprets area history for all ages. "Chattanooga Country: Its Lands, Rivers, and Peoples," the museum's permanent exhibit, offers hands-on activities for kids. Other displays pertain to the Civil War, historic clothing, sports history, and other themes. Admission is $2.50 for adults, $1.75 for seniors, $1.50 for children five to 18.

The **National Medal of Honor Museum of Military History,** 400 Georgia Ave., tel. (423) 267-1737, has been put together by an all-volunteer staff. Here visitors will see collections of guns, knives, and sabers; uniforms from a variety of wars; enemy memorabilia; and displays that commemorate wars from the Revolution to Operation Desert Storm. Admission is free.

Art and Antiques

THE EMPRESS OF THE BLUES

Bessie Smith was born on April 15, 1894. As a little girl, she sang and danced as a street performer on Chattanooga street corners. As a teenager, she joined the Moses Stokes group of performers and was heavily influenced by Gertrude "Ma" Rainey, a great blues singer.

Smith stayed less than a year with the group before setting out on her own to tour Southern theaters. Though renowned as a blues singer, she branched into jazz, and during the 1920s she was the highest-paid black performer in the country. In 1923 Columbia Records released her "Down Hearted Blues," which sold 750,000 copies in one month—an unprecedented number of sales. She was billed as the "Greatest and Highest Paid Race Star in the World" and the "190-Pound Favorite of Negroes Everywhere."

Smith succeeded because she was a brilliant lyricist, a captivating performer, and one of the wildest women of her era. She penned such classics as "Black Water Blues," "Preachin' the Blues," and "Wasted Life Blues," which singers still perform today. Critics regard her as the first important jazz singer. She recorded "St. Louis Blues" and "Careless Love" with a young trumpet player named Louis Armstrong, who recalled, "Bessie used to thrill me at all times. It's the way she could phrase a note in her blues, a certain something in her voice that no other singer could get. She had real music in her soul and felt everything she did."

En route to a concert in Mississippi in 1937, she was injured in a car accident and bled to death. A famous myth contends that she died after being turned away from a whites-only hospital. This is not true. Bessie Smith was only 43 years old when she died.

The **George Ayer Kress Gallery,** at the corner of Vine and Palmetto Streets, tel. (423) 755-4371, is part of the University Fine Arts Center and features exhibits of contemporary art in two galleries. Admission is free.

The **Houston Antique Museum,** 201 High St., tel. (423) 267-7176, is the legacy of one Anna Safely Houston, who had 10 siblings and who managed to get married nine times. She opened an antique shop in 1920 and built up a collection that consisted of more than 10,000 pieces of art glass, pressed glass, and furniture. She was partial to pitchers, and the collection contains several thousand of them. Hard times in the Depression caused her to close the shop, sell her house, and move into an old barn that had glassware from floor to ceiling, with pitchers hanging on ropes. For years she would let no one see this collection but willed it to the city of Chattanooga in 1951. In 1957 a group of citizens established a museum to house it. However eccentric its founder, the collection is world class, containing Peachblow, Tiffany, and Steuben pieces as well as cruets and miniature lamps. Now the collection is at home in a turn-of-the-century house; admission is $5.

The **Hunter Museum of Art,** 10 Bluff St., tel. (423) 267-0968, sits on a 90-foot-high limestone cliff overlooking the city and the Tennessee River. It consists of two buildings: a 1904 mansion and a contemporary building erected in 1975. Inside resides a collection of 1,500 works, only a small part of which can be displayed at any one time. Here the visitor will have the opportunity to view works by Mary Cassatt, Thomas Hart Benton, Ansel Adams, Albert Bierestadt, Willem de Kooning, and Alexander Calder, to name a few. The pieces are rotated every two to four years, although some favorites remain on display all the time. The museum hosts touring shows as well.

The museum takes a leading role in Chattanooga's cultural community and offers all manner of programs and activities. Admission is $5 for adults, $4 for seniors, $3 for students, $2.50 for children three to 12.

Religious
The Messianic Museum, just north of Chattanooga off Hwy. 153 at 1928 Hamill Rd., Hixson, tel. (423) 876-8150, is housed in the headquarters of the International Board of Jewish Missions (IBJM), whose purpose is to convert Jews to Christianity. The two-story museum focuses on Jews and Israel and the founder of the IBJM. Exhibits include dioramas depicting events such as Moses on Mt. Sinai, large photos of Israel, lamps, scrolls, and works of art. Admission is free.

The **Siskin Museum of Religious Artifacts,** One Siskin Plaza, tel. (423) 634-1700, resulted from a promise to God. In 1942, Garrison Siskin was badly injured in a train accident and promised to God that if his life and injured leg were saved he would spend the rest of his life helping others. Siskin lived, and he and his family became prominent philanthropists in Chattanooga. The family dispatched its rabbi to Europe in the 1950s to find and buy significant Jewish religious artifacts. Over time the family acquired items from other faiths, and now visitors can see the collection at this museum.

Specialty
The **Creative Discovery Museum,** 321 Chestnut St., tel. (423) 756-2738, is a wonderful $16.5 million hands-on place with four exhibit areas: an artist's studio, an inventor's workshop, a field scientist's lab, and a musician's studio. In the inventor's workshop, for example, kids can sit in the driver's seat and program a full-size electric car, experiment with mechanical devices on a discovery table, and make their own inventions. Admission is $7.75 for adults and $4.75 for kids three to 12. See them online at www.cdmfun.org.

Dragon Dreams Museum, 6724-A East Brainerd Rd., tel. (423) 892-2384, occupies a house with eight rooms containing more than 2,000 assorted dragons. The curator says the museum sprang from a personal collection "that was making the house a little strange." Each room of the museum has a theme—Fun Room, Fantasy Room, Japanese Room, and so on. Admission is $5 for adults and $2 for children 13 and under.

Patrons of the **International Towing and Recovery Hall of Fame and Museum,** at 4th and Broad Streets, tel. (423) 238-4171, should be careful where they park. Housed in a former car dealership, the museum is across the street from the site of the nation's first commercial tow truck business, established in 1916. The goal of the organization is to improve the towing industry's negative image. Exhibits include antique wreckers and other vehicles and a 1930s filling station. Admission is $3.50 for adults, $1.50 for children five to 18 and for seniors.

Knife devotees shouldn't miss **The National Knife Museum,** 7201 Shallowford Rd., east off I-75 at Exit 5, tel. (423) 892-5007, the showplace for the Chattanooga-based National Knife Collectors Association. One will see all manner of knives here, from gargantuan Bowie knives to miniature models with blades as thin as a fingernail. Other exhibits include a bronze dagger dated at 212 B.C. and a five-foot-long pocketknife made as a promotion by the Ka-Bar company. Admission is $2 for adults; children under 12 are free.

PARKS, ZOOS, AND SANCTUARIES

Chattanooga's **Riverpark** stretches for 20 miles from Chickamauga Dam downstream past the city to Moccasin Bend. This greenbelt includes walkways, playgrounds, a rowing center, fishing piers, and boat docks. Riverpark celebrates the Tennessee River.

Audubon Acres, tel. (423) 892-1499, is a 120-acre wildlife sanctuary east of Chattanooga at which visitors can see a cabin built by the Cherokee, cross a swinging bridge, and take hikes on 10 miles of trails. To get there, take Exit 3A off I-75, then go right on Gunbarrel Road. From November to March the closing time is 5 p.m. Admission is $2 for adults and $1 for children five to 12.

In the middle of the river near downtown lies **MacLellan Island,** an 18.8-acre wooded area also owned by the Audubon Society and operated as a wildlife sanctuary. Trips to the island are scheduled from time to time, or interested people can catch a ride with a visiting school group. For info, call (423) 892-1499 or see www.audubon.net.

Warner Park Zoo, downtown at 1254 E. 3rd St., tel. (423) 697-9722, is a small city-owned collection of animals. Highlights include a pair of jaguars in a natural habitat, one chimp and various monkeys, and a petting zoo. It charges a small fee for admission.

Booker T. Washington State Park, 5801 Champion Rd., tel. (423) 894-4955, comprising 353 acres on Chickamauga Lake created from TVA land, offers a swimming pool, boating and fishing, and a group camp for 40 people, but no individual campsites.

Don't show up at **Reflection Riding** expecting to get back in the saddle. The 375-acre botanical garden, which snugs up against the west side of Lookout Mountain, has nothing to do with horses. The "riding" in the name is an affectation involving an English usage of the word to mean "path of pleasure." A three-mile drive goes through the park and connects to more than 12 miles of trails. Here one can see more than 1,000 species of plants, Civil War skirmish sites, and more than 300 kinds of wildflowers. The Great Indian Warpath goes through here and is maintained in its original condition. Hernando de Soto is alleged to have come this way as well. Joint admission for Reflection Riding and the Nature Center, below, is $2.50 for adults, $1.50 for kids four to 12 and for seniors. Call (423) 821-1160 for more information.

The **Chattanooga Nature Center,** tel. (423) 821-1160, serves as an educational center complete with exhibits and a 1,200-foot Wetland Walkway. The red wolf exhibit is a good one to see. Feeding time—when the wolves come out of their dens—takes place at 2 p.m. on weekdays and 3 p.m. on weekends. To get there, take I-24 Exit 175 S on Lookout Mountain Road. Turn left on Hwy. 41, go 0.7 miles, then turn right on Hwy. 318 S, then turn right again on Garden Road. Go one mile.

The 1,199-acre **Harrison Bay State Park** sits off Hwy. 58 on the Chickamauga Reservoir, a.k.a. the Tennessee River, just northeast of Chattanooga. With 39 miles of shoreline, the water is the chief focus here, and the park has one of the most complete marinas on any of the TVA lakes. It also has a restaurant (open March-Oct.), camping, hiking trails, and stables. For more information, call (423) 344-6214.

LOOKOUT MOUNTAIN

Lookout Mountain rises just outside of Chattanooga's city limits and extends southwest more than 50 miles into Georgia and Alabama. If the

SEEING THE CIVIL WAR IN CHATTANOOGA

Chattanooga is perhaps the best place in Tennessee to take in the Civil War. Significant battles were fought here and, because of the lay of the land, what happened here is relatively easy to follow.

In the decades after the war, Union and Confederate veterans held reunions at the battlefields and saw a need to protect them from encroaching development. *Chattanooga Times* publisher Adolph Ochs lent his support, and in 1890 Congress passed a bill creating Chickamauga and Chattanooga as the nation's first national military parks. The **Chickamauga and Chattanooga National Military Park** was dedicated September 18-20, 1895. Veterans carefully placed about 1,400 monuments and historical markers indicating which brigade fought where. Ochs, even after he moved to New York to run *The New York Times,* was instrumental in buying land on Lookout Mountain and donating it to the public.

The best place to begin is the headquarters of the park, across the state line in Georgia. To get there, take Hwy. 27 south or get off I-75 on Battlefield Parkway and follow the signs west. The visitors center holds various artifacts, a collection of 355 weapons, and an excellent bookstore. A multimedia production gives an overview of the battle. During warm weather, the museum often demonstrates activities related to the Civil War. Visitors can drive a seven-mile tour of the battlefield. If the weather is nice, bicycles are the best way to get around.

The Chickamauga battle was fought in a forested area with visibility of about 100-150 yards, one of the reasons that commanders were confused and the casualties were so high. The present-day forest, which has much more underbrush, may prove frustrating to those expecting a wide vista where one can clearly see who fought where. If visitors are pressed for time, they should see the visitors center and depart for Lookout Mountain.

Adolph Ochs, publisher of The Chattanooga Times *and later of* The New York Times, *was instrumental in creating the national military park.*

The visitors center, tel. (706) 866-9241, is open 8 a.m.-4:30 p.m., although the battlefield stays open from dawn to dusk. The Battle of Chickamauga slide show costs $2.25 for adults, $1 for children six to 16, and $1 for seniors. Admission is free to the visitors center or the park.

The **Gordon-Lee Mansion,** tel. (706) 375-4728, south of the Chickamauga Battlefield site, served as headquarters for Union General Rosecrans before the battle and as a hospital afterward. The mansion is now a bed and breakfast. To get there, drive south of the battlefield on Hwy. 27. Turn right on Lee/Gordon Mill Rd. and go 2.5 miles to the town of Chickamauga. The mansion is on the right. Visitors can tour it in the afternoon in groups of 15 or more for $4.50 per person if they call ahead.

Known for years as "Confederama," the **Battles for Chattanooga Museum,** 3742 Tennessee Ave. in the St. Elmo neighborhood, tel. (423) 821-2812, another private enterprise, now has a name likely to appeal to Yankees as well. The museum's centerpiece is a three-dimensional, 480-square-foot layout consisting of 5,000 miniature soldiers, 650 lights, and sound effects that illustrate the battles of Lookout Mountain and Missionary Ridge. The museum also features dioramas and Civil War artifacts. During the summer, Sgt. "Fox Jim" McKinney holds forth and answers questions about the war. At other times he can be summoned by advance phone call at no additional cost. Admission is $5 for adults, $3 for children three to 12, with discounts for seniors. The museum is open daily except Christmas.

Closer in, **Point Park** occupies the end of **Lookout Mountain.** The Park Service maintains a small visitors center here. During summer rangers offer walks, talks, and demonstrations of Civil War-related activities. Parking is limited here, so if there's no room in the Park Service parking lot, visitors should keep an eye on the meters.

The entrance gate to the park is the world's largest replica of the Corps of Engineers insignia. It was erected in 1905, not surprisingly, by the Corps. Various batteries contain different kinds of cannons used in the battle, and the Ochs Museum and Overlook offers a very good view of Chattanooga. The hike down to it descends 500 feet and may tax those not up to a good climb back.

Craven House, the Confederate headquarters during the early parts of the battle, lies off Hwy. 148, the Scenic Highway. The original house was pretty much shot up during the battle and demolished for firewood afterward, so what visitors see is rebuilt and furnished to reflect the life of the Craven family. Admission is $2 for those ages 16-62, or $4 for an entire family. Hours vary, according to the park budget, but usually Craven House is open weekends April-May, daily June-Aug., and weekends Sept.-October.

The **National Cemetery,** 1200 Bailey Ave., tel. (423) 855-6590, was established in December 1883 by Union General George Thomas, the famous "Rock of Chickamauga." Soldiers tended to be buried haphazardly after battles, and this was an effort to give them a final resting place with honor and dignity. More than 12,000 Union soldiers—half of them unknown—from various battles, as well as veterans from all of this country's wars, including the Revolution, make up the largest national cemetery in the state. No Confederates are buried here.

Oddly enough, Germans are buried here as well, some 186 prisoners of war from World War I and II. Chattanooga is the only national cemetery containing prisoners of war from both world wars.

The most famous marker is that of James Andrews' Raiders, a group of Union spies who slipped into Georgia, stole a locomotive named The General, and headed north. The daring Raiders were eventually caught by the Confederates and hanged for their activities. Eight of them rest beneath a marker topped by a replica of The General. Four of them were the first recipients of the newly created Medal of Honor. Andrews himself is not buried here, for he was not in the military.

Keep in mind that this cemetery still has funerals and behave accordingly. Admission is free.

The **Orchard Knob Reservation,** in downtown Chattanooga, marks the hill from which Grant directed the assault on Missionary Ridge. It contains a tall marker but little else to see.

For the Civil War buff, **Missionary Ridge** did not fare so well as Lookout Mountain. During the various real estate booms in the late 1800s, homeowners snapped up property along the ridge, and now most of it is in private hands. When the veterans came back in the 1890s, they found houses on many of the places they had fought. Several significant sites lie along Crest Road, among them the **Bragg Reservation, Ohio Reservation, De Long Reservation,** and **Sherman Reservation.** From the south, you can get to Crest Rd. from Hwy. 27 in Rossville, Georgia. Several streets in Chattanooga, such as Shallowford Rd., run up to the ridge.

Signal Mountain faces Lookout Mountain and was, as its name implies, a place for Union communications after the Confederates had cut telegraph lines. **Signal Point Reservation** commemorates the the U.S. Signal Corps and offers an imposing view of "The Grand Canyon of the Tennessee River."

Note: Visitors may note a lively trade in Civil War artifacts—bullets, buttons, and the like—in local shops. These are supposed to have come from private lands. It is strictly against the law to dig for artifacts, remove them from national park property, or damage them in any way. Visitors who observe ny suspicious activity should notify park officials.

National Register had a category for "Historic Tourism Destinations," then surely Lookout Mountain would be on this list. Ruby Falls and Rock City have survived the days of tourist homes and blue highways, and the Incline Railway still goes up and down what's called the steepest track in the world. Because of the fancy neighborhoods at the top, however, there are not many places to eat, particularly of the fast-food persuasion. Visitors are advised to pack a picnic lunch or order takeout from restaurants in Chattanooga.

Lookout Mountain Incline Railway

The railway, 827 E. Brow Rd., tel. (423) 821-4224, was built back in the 1890s, when Lookout Mountain had large hotels where people came and stayed for weeks at a time. The cars operate like San Francisco's cable cars by grasping a moving cable that stretches from top to bottom between the tracks. At their steepest, the mile-long tracks climb a 72.7% grade, perhaps the steepest tracks in the world.

Once at the top, visitors who wish to see Ruby Falls or Rock City can take a shuttle bus during

The Incline Railway has been climbing some of the steepest tracks in the world since 1895. The grade reaches 72.7%.

summer and can walk the three blocks to Point Park. The Incline Railway is open every day but Christmas, and cars leave three or four times per hour. A roundtrip ride takes 30 minutes. Admission is $7 for adults and $4 for children three to 12.

Ruby Falls

Ruby Falls, on the Lookout Mountain Scenic Hwy., tel. (423) 821-2544, is the latest incarnation of a cave with a long history. Local Indians long knew of a cavern extending under the north end of Lookout Mountain. During the Civil War it was used as a hospital; later, a railroad tunnel cut off the original entrance. In 1928, a man named Leo Lambert hired a crew to drill a shaft down to the cave so he could commercialize it. On the way down, the crew hit a hitherto unknown cave, and when Leo and his wife, Ruby, explored it, they discovered a 145-foot-high waterfall. Leo named it after his wife.

Visitors descend to the cave in an elevator, then stroll approximately 2,200 feet back to the waterfall. The walk is very flat, almost like walking along a mine. At the falls visitors are greeted with a light show and music only slightly less portentous than that planned for the Second Coming. Back on top kids can enjoy a "Fun Forest" consisting of various climbing structures. Admission is $9 for adults and $4.50 for children 3 to 12.

Rock City Gardens

Those who choose to see Rock City, tel. (706) 820-2531, find paths that wind among large rocks. Steps lead over rocks, bridges span chasms, and visitors walk through tight places with names such as "Fat Man's Squeeze." The culmination is the highly promoted view of seven states. Given today's pollution, this probably is not possible anymore, but it's an impressive view nonetheless. Perhaps the oddest thing about Rock City are the "Fairyland Caverns" and other places filled with figures seemingly designed in the '30s. These

peering through the Needle's Eye at Rock City

SEE ROCK CITY

Those of a certain age who traveled through the South can recall the "See Rock City" barns and birdhouses. Though long associated with Chattanooga, **Rock City Gardens** is actually on the part of Lookout Mountain that extends into Georgia. No matter where it is, this is perhaps the South's most famous attraction.

Rock City began with Garnet and Frieda Carter, who owned 10 acres on the top of Lookout Mountain. The property was filled with enormous pieces of rock in odd shapes. In the depths of the Depression, the couple got the notion to charge admission to their "rock city." The problem was that it lay quite off the beaten path—not the kind of place that people would see while driving along.

The Carters had the inspiration to hire a paint crew and put them on the road painting enormous signs on barn roofs. The farmers got a few dollars and a new paint job, and Rock City gained invaluable publicity. As if this weren't enough, the Carters designed birdhouses whose roofs read "See Rock City" and scattered them far and wide. At one time approximately 900 barns as far as Michigan, Texas, and Florida lured tourists and unforgettably brightened America's blue highways.

Garnet Carter further contributed to popular culture by inventing miniature golf. The story goes that a guest at Carter's Fairyland Inn, wishing that the golf course was open, jokingly suggested putting a putting green in front of the inn. Using the odd piece of pipe and other materials, Carter built the first miniature golf course. This archetype was such a hit that Carter franchised the idea all over the country.

seem designed to elicit exclamations of "Isn't that cute!" from people who spend inordinate amounts of time in Christmas shops.

To get there, get on Hwy. 58 heading south up Lookout Mountain and follow the signs into Georgia. Admission is $9.95 for adults and $5.50 for children three to 12. Food and, needless to say, souvenirs are available here.

Lookout Mountain Natural Bridge
Not too far from Rock City is a rock arch that is 85 feet long and, at its highest, 15 feet off the ground.

This little-publicized arch rises in a ravine between the Good Shepherd Episcopal Church and Bragg Ave., which turns off Hwy. 148. A sign indicates the presence of the arch, but visitors must park several hundred feet south of the sign.

Lively times used to take place here. The Southern Association of Spiritualists bought this property and an adjacent hotel in 1883 and conducted seances and pseudo-Indian ceremonies on the arch, some of them lasting well into the night and complete with Indian chants. This is a good place for a picnic. Don't forget the Ouija board.

Lookout Mountain Flight Park
For those not content to just look off the mountain, the flight park, below Covenant College on Hwy. 189 in Georgia, tel. (706) 398-3541 or (800) 688-5637, offers the opportunity to fly off it. Claiming to be the number one hang-gliding school in the U.S., it provides a variety of training/flight packages. The simplest is a tandem flight, in which visitors are buckled into a two-person hang glider with an experienced pilot, towed by an airplane to a height of 1,000 feet, and released. The flight down is about 20 minutes long and costs $129. For $30 more the airplane will cut riders loose at 2,000 feet. If wind conditions are right, the school offers flights off the side of the mountain. Visitors can watch free of charge.

RACCOON MOUNTAIN AND SIGNAL MOUNTAIN

Downstream from the city of Chattanooga the Tennessee River cuts through the Cumberland Plateau, and the mountains that face each other across the gorge are Signal Mountain on the north bank and Raccoon Mountain on the south side.

Signal Mountain got its name from the belief that Indians used it for signal fires, but it truly lived up to its name when the Union Army was under siege in Chattanooga. The Confederates had cut the telegraph wires, forcing the brand new U.S. Signal Corps to send coded messages by flags or torches. The town of Signal Mountain was developed in the years after 1910. Signal Point is an excellent place from which to gaze at "the Grand Canyon of the Tennessee River."

Raccoon Mountain is home to TVA's most unusual source of electric power: the **Raccoon Mountain Pumped-Storage Project,** tel. (423) 825-3100. Since it is impossible to store large amounts of electricity, utilities have to have the capability to produce or buy enough power to meet peak needs. Power plants that run flat out from 6 a.m.-11 p.m., however, sit largely idle during the hours when most power users are asleep—the "off-peak" time.

The Pumped-Storage Project uses off-peak power to pump water from the Tennessee River 1,204 feet up tunnels to a 528-acre reservoir. When TVA needs power, the water flows down a passageway to the same pumps, only this time turning them to generate electricity. It takes 27 hours to fill the reservoir and 20 hours to release the amount used to generate power.

TVA provides escorted tours from a visitors center at the top of the reservoir to the underground power plant. The tour begins with a 1,200-foot descent in an elevator—the equivalent of a 106-story building. Tours are given daily, and the last one begins at 4 p.m. Admission is free. This is a good place for picnics and other recreation. Because of the ups and downs of the reservoir, however, no boating or fishing is allowed.

Raccoon Mountain Caverns, one mile off I-24 Exit 174, tel. (423) 821-9403 or (800) 823-CAMP, offers a 45-minute tour through a cave full of formations. Visitors can choose from a 45-minute walk in the cave—$8 for adults and $4 for kids 5-12—or various "wild cave" tours, which go off the beaten path. These can run from two hours to overnight, costing $25 to $40 per person. Call ahead for reservations.

AMUSEMENT PARKS

For youngsters who say, "The heck with all this history," Raccoon Mountain's **Alpine Slide** and **Grand Prix,** tel. (423) 825-5666, are just the ticket. Riders get on a low-slung cart with wheels—not a water slide—and roll down a half-mile-long track. Or they can race around a track in go-carts or scaled-down Formula One cars. The race cars usually charge by the lap. To get there, take Exit 124 off I-24 and go north on Hwy. 41.

The **Lake Winnepesaukah Amusement Park** is six miles from downtown Chattanooga at 1730 Lakeview Dr. in Rossville, Georgia, tel. (706) 866-5681 or toll-free (877) 525-3946, but the kids won't mind crossing the state line for the more than 30 rides and attractions. During the season this place offers concerts by big-name country and oldies entertainers. Admission to the park is $3 for adults and $2 for children under 12. Rides cost extra. Preview the park online at www.lakewinnie.com.

EXCURSIONS AND CRUISES

By Rail
Chattanooga has more of a railroad legacy than any other Tennessee city, and here is the place to get on board. The largest operating historic railroad in the South, the **Tennessee Valley Railroad,** 4119 Cromwell Rd. and North Chamberlain St., tel. (423) 894-8028, operates steam- and diesel-powered trains. The 1911 steam locomotive 4501 is the gem of the collection, which among other rolling stock includes a 1917 office car, a 1926 dining car, and a 1929 caboose. The railroad owns 40 acres that includes four bridges and the 986-foot Missionary Ridge Tunnel. Grand Junction Depot is a 1900-vintage station containing an orientation center, a deli, and a large gift shop. On the other end of the line is a replica of a small-town station.

The ride lasts about half an hour between stations. On weekends during the summer the trains go to the Chattanooga Choo-Choo. Rides cost $8.50 for adults and $4.50 for kids three to 12. See the railroad online at www.tnrail.com.

Another option for train lovers is **Dixie Land Excursions,** tel. (423) 894-8028, a ride on a restored train along the old Central Georgia main line. Trains leave April-Oct. from the Tennessee Valley Railroad's Grand Junction Station at 4119 Cromwell Rd., and then chug along to one of several locations in northwest Georgia. The day-long excursions include lunch either on the train or at a depot. The fare is $35-65, depending on itinerary. Not recommended for patrons in wheelchairs or anyone with difficulty walking or climbing stairs. Seats are limited, so reservations are essential. Find the TVR online at www.tnrail.com.

Southern Belle

On the Water

The 500-passenger *Southern Belle,* tel. (423) 266-4488 or (800) 766-2784, offers visitors a variety of cruises departing from Ross's Landing at the foot of Chestnut Street. Trips include rides through the "Grand Canyon of the Tennessee River," dinner cruises, and even a gospel dinner cruise. Call for schedule information.

ENTERTAINMENT AND EVENTS

Chattanooga boasts more than 60 art, cultural, and historic groups that put on a wide variety of events. The **Allied Arts** line, tel. (423) 756-2787, supplies information on what is happening.

ON THE STAGE

The **Chattanooga Theatre Centre,** 400 River St., tel. (423) 267-8534, offers 16 productions a season with community players. Plays have included *Peter Pan, Cat on a Hot Tin Roof,* and *A Christmas Carol,* as well as special youth productions. Tickets cost $6-18 and are available by phone or at the box office. Find them online at www.theatrecentre.com.

Built in 1921, the **Tivoli Theatre,** 709 Broad St., tel. (423) 757-5042, was known as "The Jewel of the South," and no wonder. With a high domed ceiling, crystal chandeliers, and grand lobby, it was a wonderful movie palace wherein the likes of Buster Keaton and Mary Pickford appeared on the silver screen. It was the first theater in the South to have air conditioning,

but times changed and the theater almost slipped into oblivion. In the 1980s, fortunately, it underwent a $7 million renovation and expansion to its current 1,762 seats, not to mention the hydraulic orchestra pit, dressing rooms for 70 performers, and state-of-the-art theatrical equipment. Here one can enjoy an eclectic mixture of blues, classical, country, opera, theatrical productions, and dance. Call to find out what is playing.

Bessie Smith Hall, 200 E. Martin Luther King Blvd., tel. (423) 757-0020, named for the blues singer, offers a performance hall with 264 seats, along with Bessie Smith exhibits and a listening room featuring tapes of her and other artists. National, regional, and local performers present blues and jazz concerts here.

Soldiers and Sailors Memorial Auditorium, 399 McCallie Ave., tel. (423) 757-5042, locally known as Memorial Auditorium, opened in 1924 to honor Hamilton County veterans. It underwent a complete renovation in 1990 and reopened in January 1991 as a mid-sized performance hall. Throughout the year numerous theatrical and musical productions, mostly touring shows, are presented here.

The **University of Tennessee Fine Arts Center,** on the campus at Vine and Palmetto Streets, tel. (423) 755-4371, offers a full season of dance, music, and theatrical performances by students as well as professional touring groups. See the Web site online at www.utc.org.

FESTIVALS AND EVENTS

In May, barbecue lovers should come to the **River Roast,** a barbecue cooking competition, volleyball tournament, and rowing regatta. Held at Ross's Landing, the event concludes with a Saturday night fireworks display. Call (423) 265-4397 for information.

The **Nightfall** series of concerts plays on summer Fridays at Miller Place, at the corner of Market St. and Martin Luther King Boulevard. Lasting 7-10 p.m., Nightfall consists of blues, jazz, zydeco, country, or bluegrass music, along with various concession stands. Call (423) 756-2787 for information.

Mid-June brings the **Riverbend Festival,** a nine-day salute to music. Each day a different kind of music takes center stage—classical, country, blues, rock, etc. Local, regional, and up-and-coming national performers hit the stages along with a daily headliner—always a big-name star. One of the events is the *Bessie Smith Strut.* For scheduling information and tickets, call (423) 265-4112.

The **Hamilton County Fair** takes place in September at Chester Frost Park on the west side of Chickamauga Lake. Call (423) 842-6748 for details.

The **Bluff View Art District Oktoberfest,** tel. (423) 265-5033, ext. 4, kicks off on the second weekend in October with guided walking tours of the neighborhood, polka dancing, Bavarian food, music, and children's events.

The **Fall Color Cruise and Folk Festival** takes place at the height of the fall season, downstream from Chattanooga at the Shellmound Recreation Area. Participants travel by riverboat, bus, or car. Music, dance, other entertainment, and food await. Call (423) 892-0223 or (800) 322-3344.

Christmas on the River, held on the first Saturday in December, centers on a fleet of lit-up boats that cruise past Ross's Landing and also includes a parade of lighted floats. Local groups sing carols, and the event ends with a fireworks display. Call (423) 265-0771 for information.

The Southern Brewers Association Beer Festival presents a sudsy salute to the rapidly growing craft of beer-making. Live music, barbecue, and beer samples from the various brewers round out the festival, which is held in August. For further information, call (423) 267-BREW.

SPECTATOR SPORTS

The **University of Tennessee Arena,** 4th St. at Mabel, tel. (423) 755-4618, known hereabouts as the Roundhouse because of its shape, presents UT-Chattanooga's men's and women's basketball teams as well as concerts, the circus, and other big events. Call for schedules and ticket information. To buy tickets, call (423) 266-6627.

The **Chattanooga Lookouts** play AA minor league baseball every summer in the Southern League. A part of the Cincinnati Reds organization, the Lookouts play at historic Engel Stadium, although there were plans to build a new ballpark downtown. To get to Engle Stadium, take I-24 to I-27 North to the 4th St. Exit. Follow the signs a half-mile to the park. Usual game times are 7 p.m. for night games, 12:30 p.m. Wednesday, and 2 p.m. Sunday. For tickets, call (423) 267-2208 or (800) 852-7572.

NIGHTLIFE

Chattanoogans have been tapping their toes to country music for years. But they like jazz, rock, and just about every other kind of music, too. Many restaurants feature live entertainment regularly. The Friday edition of the local newspaper offers a pretty good listing.

Blue Angel Cafe, 224 Frazier Ave., tel. (423) 266-6535, provides music and dining on the water in North Chattanooga, Monday-Thursday. The music varies. The menu includes sandwiches, pasta, and vegetarian dishes.

Brass Register, 618 Georgia Ave., tel. (423) 265-2175, especially popular with local college students, has live contemporary music Wednesday-Saturday.

Nationally known comedians entertain at **Comedy Catch,** 3224 Brainerd Rd., tel. (423) 622- 2233 (info line) or (423) 629-2233 (reservations), Wednesday-Saturday nights. Sunday is open mike night.

Dino's, 2100 S. Market St. in the Ramada Inn, tel. (423) 265-9605, features a mix of oldies, pop and country music for dancing Friday and Saturday nights.

Dancers can do the two-step, the 10-step, or any step they want Wednesday-Sunday at **Governor's Lounge & Restaurant,** 4251 Bonny Oaks Dr., tel. (423) 624-2239. The music is live. The dance floor is usually crowded. Occasionally a top-of- the-chart group headlines or stops in to do a late set.

North of Signal Mountain, the **Mountain Opry** is a bit out of town but well worth the trip. Every Friday night 8-11 p.m. local musicians gather for bluegrass picking sessions. To get there, take I-124 across the Tennessee River. Exit onto Signal Mountain Blvd., which becomes the Taft Hwy. 127. Go to the top of Signal Mountain and through town past the shopping center. Go 1.6 miles from the shopping center to Fairmont Road and turn right at Fairmont Orchard sign. The Civic Center that houses the Opry is 0.4 miles ahead on the left. The Opry has no phone.

Boot scooters wanting to rock-a-billy their babies around the floor should head for the **Rock and Country Club,** 6175 Airways Blvd., tel. (423) 894-9921. The music is live Wednesday-Sunday.

At the **Rhode House,** 2819 Cummings Hwy., tel. (423) 825-6962, it's a mix of country and Southern rock Thursday-Saturday.

Sing Sing, 221 Market St., tel. (423) 267-4644, rocks with dueling pianos Wednesday-Saturday. The club also brings in out-of-town talent. Reservations are suggested.

Southside's Jazz Junction 114 W. Main St., tel. (423) 267-9003, provides live jazz and an extensive tapas menu Wednesday-Saturday.

WHERE TO STAY

BED AND BREAKFASTS AND INNS

The **Adams Hilborne,** 801 Vine St., tel. (423) 265-5000, www.bbonline.com/tn/hilbourne, occupies an 1886 home designed for a man who was mayor of Chattanooga. The stone house is adorned with porches, balconies, gables, and balustrades built in a Victorian Romanesque style. Inside are hand-carved coffer ceilings, arched doorways, and Tiffany glass. Guests in the 15 rooms can lie in bed and gaze at 16-foot ceilings surrounded by fine antiques and original artwork. All rooms have private baths, televisions, and telephones; some have fireplaces. Rates range $95-275. Expensive-Luxury.

Alford House, 5515 Alford Hill Dr., tel. (423) 821-7625, sits on the lower side of Lookout Mountain between I-24 and Ruby Falls. Adjacent to National Park land, the house was built in the 1940s and features two decks and a hot tub. The four rooms—one of them a three-room suite—have private baths, and the breakfast here is "light and healthy." Rates run $75-165. Moderate-Luxury.

Housed in a 1928 colonial revival mansion overlooking the Tennessee River and the city, the **Bluff View Inn,** 412 E. 2nd St., tel. (423) 265-5033, contains antiques and fine art throughout. The nine rooms all have private baths, and the inn serves a full gourmet breakfast consisting of items such as lobster hash with poached eggs. Rates are $95-225. Expensive-Luxury.

Charlet House Bed & Breakfast, 111 River Point Rd., tel. (423) 886-4880, sits in the Olde Towne section of Signal Mountain. A quiet place where the property backs up to woods, the house was built in the 1930s and has a heated pool. The large rooms inside are decorated with antiques. All three suites have private baths, and one has a whirlpool bath. "The Retreat" comes with a full-sized kitchen, fireplace, and screened porch. Smokers are welcome. Breakfast is "homemade continental." Rates run $80-110. Moderate-Expensive.

McElhattan's Owl Hill Bed & Breakfast, at 617 Scenic Hwy., tel. (423) 821-2040, sits on four secluded acres near the top of Lookout Mountain. Decorated with antiques and oriental rugs, the house has two guest rooms, each with a private bath. Guest amenities include a pool table, fireplace, and cable TV, as well as games and books. Breakfast is cooked to order. Rates run $95-125. Expensive-Premium.

HOTELS AND MOTELS

Chattanooga is loaded with accommodations of the franchise persuasion. (See "Where to Stay" under "Accommodations and Food" in the On the Road chapter for a list of franchise accommodations and their toll-free reservation numbers.) Among other options:

The Radisson Read House, 827 Broad St., tel. (423) 266-4121 or (800) 333-3333, is to Chattanooga as the Peabody is to Memphis, serving as Chattanooga's grande dame since 1872. Five U.S. presidents as well as British Prime Minister Winston Churchill have stayed here. The hotel fell on hard times as Chattanooga's downtown declined, but new owners have brought the old girl back with a complete renovation. In an inspired touch, each of the 13 floors will feature a different battle of the Civil War through framed illustrations. Rates are $66-112. Moderate-Expensive.

The more budget-minded can try the **Cascades Motel,** 3625 Ringgold Rd., tel. (423) 698-1571, rates $22-50; or **Kings Lodge,** I-24 Exit 181, 2400 Westside Dr., tel. (423) 698-8944 or (800) 251-7702, rates $38-55. Budget-Inexpensive.

Chanticleer Inn, 1300 Mockingbird Ln. on Lookout Mountain, tel. (706) 820-2015, occupies a series of stone cottages, and a pool is open seasonally. The 16 rooms have individual entrances and private baths. The inn serves a Southern-style breakfast. Rates run $40-86. Inexpensive-Moderate.

The Chattanooga Choo Choo offers some of the more unusual accommodations in the state. Guests can stay in 48 suites on board sleeping cars or stay in a Holiday Inn on the premises. There's a lot to see and do on the Choo Choo grounds—especially for kids. Rates are $99 for rooms in the hotel and $125 for a room on the rails. Call (800) TRACK-29 or (423) 266-5000. See the Choo Choo online at www.choochoo.com. Expensive to Premium.

CAMPING

Best Holiday Trav-L-Park of Chattanooga, tel. (706) 891-9766, has 171 sites with full amenities. It's open year-round. Take East Ridge Exit 1 and follow signs.

Chester Frost Park (Hamilton County Park), tel. (423) 842-0177, has 188 sites. It's open all year, offering lake swimming, boating, and fishing. From I-75 take Hwy. 153, exit at Hixson Park and follow signs.

Harrison Bay State Park, 11 miles northeast on Hwy. 58, tel. (423) 344-6214, has 164 sites. It's open all year and offers a pool, canoeing, and hiking trails.

Raccoon Mountain Campground, one mile north of I-24 at Exit 174, tel. (423) 821-9403, has 104 sites. It's open all year and features lots of amenities, including the Raccoon Mountain Caverns' Crystal Palace Tour.

Shipp's Yogi Bear Jellystone Park Camp-Resort, 100 yards east off I-75 Exit 1, tel. (423) 892-8275, offers 351 sites with full amenities. It's open all year, and reservations are recommended.

FOOD

Visitors to Chattanooga have no problem finding something good to eat. In the major tourist areas around the Tennessee Aquarium and near the Chattanooga Choo-Choo and in the North Chattanooga shopping district, there are dozens of places for a quick lunch. Menus range from submarine sandwiches and burgers to soups, salads and complete meals.

When it comes time for dinner, the options are a little less numerous but equally varied. Long known as a steak-and-baked-potato town, Chattanooga today offers a much wider selection of dinner options, created by imaginative chefs specializing in contemporary dishes from across the country and around the world. Of course, you can still get a steak or some down-home country cooking. Those with a hankering for a truly Southern dish can pay a visit to one of the city's many barbecue joints. (The following restaurants—as well as the preceding nightclubs—were reviewed by Suzanne Hall, the premier food writer in Southeast Tennessee.)

BARBECUE

Looking for a great place for barbecue in Chattanooga? Ask 10 people and you'll get 10 different recommendations. Everyone has their favorite—that's because there's plenty of good barbecue in town. This list below is just the beginning. If one doesn't suit your fancy, just go a mile or two down the road and try another. The main event at each is pork, but most serve chicken and some beef as well. All are open daily for lunch and dinner.

Buck's Pit Barbeque, 3147 Broad St., tel. (423) 267-1390, and Hwy. 153 at Hamill Rd., tel. (423) 870-8006.

Hot Sauce Charlies Bar-B-Q, 3625 Tennessee Ave., tel. (423) 265-2827.

Rib & Loin, 5946 Brainerd Rd., tel. (423) 499-6465.

Shuford's Smokehouse, 924 Signal Mountain Rd., tel. (423) 267-0080.

Smokey's Barbecue, 3850 Brainerd Rd., tel. (423) 622-8996.

Sportsman's Bar-B-Q, 231 Signal Mountain Rd., tel. (423) 265-1680.

Sweeney's Pit Bar-B-Q, 4818 Hwy. 58, tel. (423) 894-4674.

TOP OF THE HEAP

Reservations are strongly suggested for diners who want to eat in the authentic Victorian railway car at **Dinner on the Diner,** 1400 Market St., tel. (423) 265-5000. Lobster bisque is a specialty and precedes dishes such as filet mignon with bernaise sauce, salmon en croute or sautéed veal chops. The setting is elegant but the atmosphere relaxed at the **Chattanooga Choo-Choo** complex restaurant, which serves dinner Monday-Saturday. The complex also includes the less expensive **Station House,** where singing waiters and waitresses serve chicken, steaks, and ribs Mon.-Sat. for dinner only. The well-stocked salad bar includes all-you-can-eat boiled shrimp. The Choo-Choo's **Gardens** restaurant offers Southern specialties like fried chicken, catfish, and rainbow trout. New Orleans-style bread pudding is a highlight on the dessert menu. Open seven days a week for breakfast, lunch and dinner, the Gardens is a great place for families.

Chattanoogans have been marking special occasions in **Steaks at the Green Room,** 827 Broad St., tel. (423) 266-4121, for decades. Housed in the historic Radisson Read House, the room is formal but not stuffy. The menu's focus is steak, but it also includes pasta, seafood, and other dishes. Dinner is served Mon.-Saturday. Reservations are suggested. The **Read House** also has a great scotch and cigar bar.

In the Bluff View Inn, a bed and breakfast overlooking the Tennessee River, **Back Inn Cafe** is an Italian Bistro offering upscale Italian cuisine, gourmet pizzas and other fare. Lunch and dinner are served seven days a week either in the mansion or on an outdoor terrace. Reservations are a good idea on Friday and Saturday. The inn is the centerpiece of the Bluff View Art District, a collection of museums, galleries, shops and an outdoor sculpture garden. For less expensive din-

MOON PIES

The scene: In Cambridge, Massachusetts, two Southerners and someone else are planning where to eat lunch. Amid the various options, one Southerner suggests "a Moon Pie and an R.C. Cola." The second Southerner bursts out laughing, but the other person, not recognizing a longtime favorite lunch for working class Southerners, doesn't get it.

Moon Pies were invented at the Chattanooga Bakery in 1919. The originals consisted of a marshmallow-type filling between two four-inch-diameter cookies. The whole thing—at least the classic version—is covered with a chocolate coating. These "pies" became enormously popular throughout the South, and for some people a Moon Pie and a Royal Crown Cola was as good a snack as one could get.

Because of vending machine requirements, today's Moon Pies are smaller and thicker than the original, but now they have *three* cookies separated by filling. They also now come in a low-fat version and, seasonally, with vanilla, banana, strawberry, and other flavors.

The Chattanooga Bakery turns out about 300,000 Moon Pies a day and sells them as far away as Japan, where they are known as Massi Pie. The epicenter of Moon Piedom, however, is the annual Moon Pie festival held in the Middle Tennessee village of Bell Buckle in June.

in European breads, pastries, and fine coffee. Both offer indoor and outdoor dining and are open for lunch and dinner seven days a week. Sunday brunch is served at Renaissance Commons. Bluff View Art District restaurants are on High Street across from the Hunter Museum of American Art, tel. (423) 265-5033.

Many Chattanooga shakers and movers are regulars at **Southside Grill,** 1400 Cowart St., tel. (423) 266-6511. The talented kitchen staff specializes in dishes of the New South, giving traditional ingredients like pork, chicken, fish and vegetables an upscale, contemporary flair. The kitchen does wonderful things with portobello mushrooms. In a restored historic building near the Chattanooga Choo-Choo, Southside serves dinner seven nights a week and lunch Monday-Saturday. The restaurant is totally nonsmoking except for the patio.

A consistently imaginative kitchen staff, led by a chef-owner, makes **212 Market Restaurant,** 212 Market St., tel. (423) 265-1212, one of the most popular spots in town. The menu features pork, poultry, beef, fish and lamb served with a flair. The appetizers and pasta dishes are excellent. There's live music every Friday night and a great Sunday brunch, enhanced once a month by live jazz. Across from the Tennessee Aquarium, it's open for lunch and dinner seven days a week.

EASIER ON THE WALLET

The Greek, Italian, and American dishes are ample and well prepared at **Acropolis,** 2213 Hamilton Place Blvd., tel. (423) 899-5341. It's adjacent to Hamilton Place, one of Tennessee's largest shopping malls, and open for lunch and dinner seven days a week.

Big River Grille & Brewing Works, 22 Broad St., tel. (423) 267-2739, near the Tennessee Aquarium, serves good food, presented in a casual atmosphere, and their beer, root beer, ginger ale, and cream soda are made on the premises. The menu includes sandwiches, salads, and full meals. It serves lunch and dinner seven days a week.

The menu changes nightly and includes Caribbean, French, and American dishes at **Chef's Underground Cafe,** 720 Walnut St., tel. (423) 266-3142. Down a flight of stairs from the street,

ing, the complex includes **Tony's Pasta Shop,** offering a menu of freshly made pastas and sauces, and **Rembrandt's Coffee House,** specializing

this restaurant is owned by its chef, who serves lunch weekdays and dinner Tuesday-Saturday. Tuesday night's special is prime rib. On Wednesday, the featured item is a rib sampler. Thursday is Jamaican night. The chef will gladly prepare vegetarian dishes. The cafe serves beer, and diners are welcome to bring their own wine. Reservations are advisable.

One of Chattanooga's most popular restaurants, **The Loft,** 328 Cherokee Blvd., tel. (423) 266-3601, specializes in steaks, prime rib, seafood dishes, and indulgent desserts. Just north of downtown, it serves dinner seven nights a week. Lunch is available Monday-Friday, and brunch is served on Sunday.

Don't pass up the amaretto creme pie at **Mount Vernon,** 3509 Broad St., tel. (423) 266-6591. A favorite with Chattanoogans for more than 40 years, Mount Vernon serves top quality Southern dishes in an attractive and friendly setting. Salad dressings are a specialty and available for purchase. Mount Vernon is open for lunch and dinner Mon.-Fri. and for dinner on Saturday.

Ocean Avenue Seafood Grill and Bar, 6925 Shallowford Rd., tel. (423) 899-7858, is just across I-75 from Hamilton Place Mall and open at 3 p.m. seven days a week. The specialty is fresh seafood, but the menu also includes pasta, chicken and beef.

Town and Country, 110 N. Market St., tel. (423) 267-1643, has been dishing up steaks, prime rib, fish, and Southern-style entrees and vegetables since the 1940s. Located across the river from downtown in North Chattanooga, it's a good place for families. Dinner is served nightly Monday-Saturday and at midday on Sunday. Lunch is available Monday-Friday.

Coffeehouses

Chattanooga boasts a fair number of coffeehouses serving good espresso-based beverages and light food. The one cited below is especially worth visiting if caffeine fans want some entertainment while sipping.

Cafe Tazza Espresso Bar, 1010$^1/_2$ Market St., tel. (423) 265-3032, newspapers from around the world free on the Internet. It's open daily.

MORE PRACTICALITIES

SHOPPING

Across the street from the Hunter Museum, the **River Gallery,** 400 East 2nd St., tel. (423) 267-7353, offers original fine arts and high-end crafts. Visitors can peruse woodcarvings, jewelry, sculpture, basketry, studio art glass, handmade books, art furniture, and textiles. The gallery has a sculpture garden outside.

Tafachady Gallery, 3908 Tennessee Ave., tel. (423) 821-7080, features Native American art, clothing, jewelry, and pottery, most of it from Southeastern artists.

Eight of Chattanooga's old railroad warehouses make up **Warehouse Row,** 1110 Market St., tel. (423) 267-1111, outlet shopping in downtown Chattanooga. More than 40 shops of high-end merchandise, including Tommy Hilfiger, J. Peterman, and Danskin, are open daily.

North of town

The area north of the river, i.e., across the Tennessee River from downtown, offers a collection of interesting shops. **Turner and Carver** offers art objects made from wood. **New Moon Gallery** sells New Age sorts of things. **Rock Creek Down Under** is a great outfitter. Nearby one will find **The Clay Pot, Loafer's Glory, The Garden Gallery,** and **Rising Fawn Folk Art Gallery.**

Hundreds of contemporary crafts workers sell their goods at **Plum Nelly,** 1101 Hixson Pike, tel. (423) 266-0585. Shoppers can find functional pottery made by more than 150 potters and jewelry from more than 100 artists.

Mole Hill Pottery, 1210 Taft Hwy. on Signal Mountain, tel. (423) 886-5636, sells a wide variety of pottery goods—dishes, *objets d'art,* and kitchen items.

Malls

Hamilton Place, tel. (423) 894-7177, will keep shopping mall addicts happy in Chattanooga. Go north on I-75 to Exit 4-A or Exit 5 and follow the crowd.

Northgate Mall, tel. (423) 870-9521, offers more than 100 stores. Take I-75 N to Hwy. 153 N and the intersection of Hixson Pike.

Eastgate Mall, tel. (423) 894-9199, was Chattanooga's first mall. To get there, take Exit 184 from I-24 W and go on Moore Rd. N to Brainerd Rd. East.

TRANSPORTATION

Shuttle Express, tel. (800) 896-9928 or (423) 954-1400, offers van service between the Chattanooga Airport to the Nashville and Atlanta airports. Vans leave from 6:30 a.m. until 5 p.m., and cost $29 one-way to Nashville. Vans leave from the back of the Eastgate Mall at 5600 Brainerd Rd. or, for an extra $5, from the Chattanooga Airport itself.

SERVICES AND INFORMATION

Chattanooga Area Convention & Visitor's Bureau, 1001 Market St., tel. (423) 756-8687 or (800) 322-3344, is open daily 8:30 a.m.-5:30 p.m. A larger visitors center at 2 Broad St. is just down from the Tennessee Aquarium. Access them online at www.chattanooga.net/cvb.

NASHVILLE
INTRODUCTION

For better or worse, many people think Nashville *is* Tennessee. The image of country music and the city with which it is most associated has spread around the world. Tourists from Japan and Europe unload at Nashville's airport and join the throngs riding buses, clapping at the Grand Ole Opry, riding buses, dancing at the Wildhorse Saloon, riding buses, and touring the Hermitage. This is a city that is imminently ready to accommodate one and all.

From the beginning, Nashville has attracted people who like to make money. The first settlers here carved out a place on the river and traded upstream and down. They quickly adapted to steamboats, the railroad, and the electronic waves of radio. Printing and other businesses thrived here because of Nashville's location between North and South. So did music.

Nashville and the rest of the South kept its music pretty much to itself until the '50s. Even then, country stars moved in a small but ever-expanding universe. Now, country performers such as Garth Brooks are going around the country breaking arena records formerly held by rock groups, and country music has established a strong presence in almost every American radio market.

The city that spawned it all, however, retains a laid-back approach that travelers will appreciate. The courtesy extended by people who have the toughest jobs—those who deal with thousands of tourists a day—makes Tennessee's capital seem like a much smaller place. Even the celebrities, unlike most other famous people, keep in touch with their supporters through events such as Fan Fair.

Nashville, more than any city in Tennessee, is geared for visitors. The welcome extended, whether a helping hand off the General Jackson riverboat, or the smile of a server who submerges turkey and dressing in gravy, makes this a most pleasant place to visit.

MUST-SEE HIGHLIGHTS

Fisk University's **Van Vechten Gallery** exhibits a great collection of Picassos and other works of modern art.

Gruhn Guitars, though a very successful store, has guitars, banjos, fiddles, and other instruments so valuable and beautiful that they could be in a museum.

The **Country Music Hall of Fame and Museum,** though not without its faults, has to be on any music-lover's short list.

The Parthenon, a monument to the Athens of the South as well as the original center of learning, continues to inspire its beholders.

People who talk during the music at **Bluebird Cafe** will be hushed while songwriters strum and sing their way though their creations.

The **Hillsboro Village** has great shops, fresh-baked bread, and fire-brewed beer.

The adjoining campuses of **Fisk University** and **Meharry Medical College** give a look at two of the pillars of black higher education.

HISTORY

It all began with salt. Deer and other grazing animals crave sodium in their diets and will return again and again to places where naturally occurring salts appear on the surface of the ground. For thousands of years, buffalo, deer, bears, and other animals came in great numbers to the salt licks. Their presence attracted Indians, who hunted them and built mounds, but these first Americans never established as firm a presence in this part of Tennessee as they did in other places. The Shawnee lived here for a time but were forced out by other Indians in the early 1700s. Although the Cherokee did not live in Middle Tennessee in great numbers, they regarded the land as their hunting grounds and did not take kindly to interlopers.

The first of these interlopers were the "long hunters," so named because they would leave home and be gone a long time killing game and collecting furs. Once they had enough, they would either bring them back east on pack horses or drift down the rivers to New Orleans.

During the time of the long hunters, the French established a trading post known as French Lick about 1710. The 1763 Treaty of Paris put the land under English control, but a French-Canadian long hunter, one Timothy Demonbreun, established residence in a cave and stayed long enough to be considered the first resident of Middle Tennessee.

As settlers pushed into what is now East Tennessee, they heard tantalizing tales of rich land to the west, a place where buffalo were so thick that travelers were afraid to get off their horses and where a hunter could kill 19 deer in one day. The land was rich and much flatter than that in the East, and every long hunter who came back from the land around the Cumberland River found ready listeners for his tales.

Fort Nashborough

Richard Henderson, a land speculator, gained control of this desirable acreage, and in the spring of 1779 dispatched James Robertson and a crew of men to investigate the land about which everyone had heard so much. To get around the barrier of the Cumberland Plateau, which separates East and Middle Tennessee, Robertson and his party traveled through the Cumberland Gap into what is now Kentucky and then descended into Tennessee's Central Basin.

There they built a few cabins, planted corn, and came back to ready a group of settlers. By the fall of 1779 they were ready to move to their new home. Robertson split his party into two groups. About 200 men and boys would walk with Robertson to the banks of the Cumberland River, driving their livestock with them. John Donelson, a few men, and all the women and children would float downstream in flatboats and canoes—down the Holston, down the Tennessee—and then laboriously pole the fleet up the Ohio and up the Cumberland.

The parties had the misfortune to pick a brutal winter in which to travel. The men and boys made the 400-mile walk to French Lick by December, suffering no Indian attacks and losing none of their party. The Cumberland River was frozen so thick that the livestock could walk across. They settled in to await the others, who arrived in April after a harrowing, 1,000-mile trip by water.

The settlers built a stockade, which they named Fort Nashborough in honor of a Revolutionary War general. Far from any kind of established government, the residents drew up the Cumberland Compact, which outlined the duties of judges and other points of law.

The fort was soon put to use, as the Indians quickly attacked the settlements in the area. Indeed, residents abandoned several smaller settlements and moved closer to the protection of Fort Nashborough. The Chickamauga who had fired on John Donelson's flotilla attacked the fort in the spring of 1781, cutting off James Robertson and about 20 men from safety. His quick-thinking wife opened the gates and released a pack of dogs, which fell upon the surprised Indians with much barking and biting. Between avoiding the dogs and trying to catch the settlers' horses, the attackers were distracted and their would-be victims escaped.

Growth in Trade

Through treaties and retaliatory raids the settlers gradually lessened the Indian problem, and Fort Nashborough began attracting more residents. The area came under the control of the state of North Carolina, whose legislature in 1784 named the town Nashville—Nashborough sounded too English, and the colonies wanted nothing that recalled their colonial oppressors. By 1787 the town had a newspaper, and the next year a young attorney came to town and hung up his shingle. His name was Andrew Jackson.

Jackson came to a town that was booming. The Cumberland River location was ideal for trade, and Nashville produced iron, guns, cloth, and other goods and sold them upstream and downstream. Tennessee became a state in 1796, and in 1806 Nashville was granted a city charter.

Andrew Jackson's fortunes rose with Nashville's, and he came to national attention with his Battle of New Orleans victory over the British in 1815. In 1829, Jackson was elected president, the first from west of the Appalachians.

The first steamboat came to town in 1818, and this new form of shipping enhanced the city's growing commerce, as did a series of roads and turnpikes that radiated outward like spokes from the city.

The Tennessee legislature first met in Nashville in 1812 for one year and returned for good in 1826. Work was begun on a capitol building in 1845.

Along with the rest of Middle Tennessee, Nashville achieved great prosperity in the 1850s, which witnessed the construction of the Belmont and Belle Meade plantation houses. The rail-

BY BOAT TO FORT NASHBOROUGH

The river voyage of Capt. John Donelson and the rest of his party would make a great adventure movie. A flotilla of 30 boats shoved off from the Long Island of the Holston—present-day Kingsport—on December 22, 1779. The largest flatboat measured 100 feet long by 20 feet wide. The weather was so cold that the would-be settlers had to stop after going only a few miles, and they resumed their journey in mid-February. Other settlers farther downstream learned of the journey and joined the group along the way.

Almost everything that could go wrong did so on this trip. The dreaded smallpox broke out during the voyage, forcing the travelers to quarantine diseased people in separate vessels. Boats ran aground and got stuck. The food supply ran low. Then there were the Indians and the river itself.

As the boats descended the Tennessee, they floated past the Chickamauga, a breakaway group of Cherokee who had vowed to kill off settlers. One of the boats ran aground at the worst possible time—while Indians were firing on it—and men and women dodged bullets to get the boat moving again. One of these women had borne a child the night before, and during the battle the baby was killed.

Two sections of Tennessee River whitewater terrified the travelers. "The Suck" was a formidable whirlpool below what is now Chattanooga, and farther along in Alabama lay Muscle Shoals, where the currents ran the boats aground. Some of the party, weary of this journey, bailed out here. Others, when it came time to push the boats upstream along the Ohio and Cumberland Rivers, decided to drift down the Mississippi to Natchez.

Donelson and his party were reunited with James Robertson and the others on April 24, 1780. Their journey had covered more than 1,000 miles, taken four months, and suffered 33 casualties.

One of the survivors of this epic trip was Rachel Donelson, the 15-year-old daughter of the captain. Rachel later married Andrew Jackson.

road came to town in 1854, which further cemented Nashville's commercial success.

The Civil War Years

When the Civil War broke out, Nashville became a prime target. Its role as a transportation center was critical to help the North invade the Confederacy, and for the South it was an important manufacturing center—one of the few it had. The city's fate was sealed in February 1862, when Union General U.S. Grant captured Fort Donelson, which guarded the downstream approach to the city. The Confederates burned the bridges across the Cumberland River but did not have the manpower to defend Nashville, and they were forced to surrender it to Northern troops.

Abraham Lincoln appointed Andrew Johnson, the Tennessee senator who had kept his seat despite Tennessee's secession, military governor of the state. Johnson had twice been elected governor in the 1850s, so he was a good man for the job and went about his duties with enthusiasm. The new state capitol building was surrounded with enough artillery to make it look like a fort. Johnson infuriated Nashvillians by arresting preachers who delivered pro-South sermons, closing hostile newspapers, and summarily dismissing the mayor and city council and appointing Northern sympathizers in their places.

The South tried twice to get Nashville back. In January of 1863 Union General Rosecrans defeated Confederate General Braxton Bragg at Murfreesboro's Battle of Stones River, forcing the Southerners to retreat. Late in the war, when Union General Sherman was marching toward the sea, John Bell Hood moved his Confederates toward Nashville in a desperate move. He was crushed at the Battle of Franklin in 1864 by Gen. George Schofield, but he persisted in following the Union troops as they retreated into Nashville. On December 15 and 16, Union forces marched out of the city and further devastated Hood's army, and Nashville stayed in Union hands until the war was over.

Return to Prosperity

Tennessee was the first state to return to the Union, and once again Nashville's location in the middle of the nation provided it a means to regain its prosperity. A cholera epidemic in 1866 was followed by another in 1873. City officials traced the disease to contaminated springs and wells and moved to improve the city's infrastructure.

Nashville had enjoyed a university since 1828, but in the post-Civil War years education flowered. The Fisk School, later called Fisk University, was founded in 1866 to provide higher education for recently freed blacks. To raise money for the fledgling college, a group of students called the Fisk Jubilee Singers toured the nation and Europe. The same year another black college, Central Tennessee College, was chartered. In 1876 it gained a medical school, which was named Meharry Medical College. It became

Nashville's Parthenon is the world's only full-scale reproduction of the original in Greece.

DAVID WRIGHT

a separate institution in 1915. See it online at www.mmc.edu.

Vanderbilt College got its charter in 1873, and, in an effort to improve the education of school-teachers, the Peabody State Normal School of the University of Nashville was founded in 1875. Their online site is www.vanderbilt.edu.

The presence of these and other colleges led Nashville to adopt the name "the Athens of the South," and in 1897 the city hosted the Centennial Exposition. This fair featured a life-sized, plaster replica of the Parthenon, and residents so admired it that they would not let it be torn down after the event was over. It was eventually replaced with a more permanent concrete replica, which still stands.

Along with education, religious organizations played an increasingly important role in the city, a role that continues today. The Southern Baptist Convention's Sunday School Board produces more Sunday school literature here than is published anywhere else in the world. The United Methodist Publishing House prints hymnals and other religious material, as does the Sunday School Publishing Board of the National Baptist Convention USA, the largest black church group. The largest Bible producer in the country, Thomas Nelson Publishers, is in Nashville.

The Rise of Country Music

Nashville is best known to the world, however, as the Mecca of country music. The city had a long musical tradition, and as a Southern crossroads it was visited by musicians of every stripe. Radio came to Nashville in 1922, and three years later the National Life and Accident Insurance Company built a station it called WSM, an acronym of the company's motto, "We Shield Millions." WSM hired George D. Hay, a young announcer from WLS, a big Chicago station, but a man with Tennessee roots. A one-time writer for the Memphis *Commercial Appeal,* he achieved success with a column called "Howdy, Judge" that consisted of conversations between a white judge and assorted black defendants. Hay picked up the nickname "the solemn old judge" although he was neither old nor particularly solemn and had nothing to do with the judiciary.

Looking to duplicate the success of Chicago's *National Barn Dance* radio show, Hay first called Nashville's version the *Barn Dance.* The first

band to play country music on the radio in Nashville was led by Dr. Humphrey Bate, a Vanderbilt-educated physician whose string band wore business suits while on stage. Hay pushed things in a cornball direction, however, and Bate's band became "The Possum Hunters." Other groups were given similar names such as "The Fruit Jar Drinkers" and "The Dixie Clodhoppers," and the die was cast: country equaled corny. Another much-loved entertainer was Uncle Dave Macon, whose renditions of songs such as "Keep My Skillet Good and Greasy" delighted rural listeners.

The audiences loved it, although proper Nashvillians were appalled at the image of their city that was broadcast by one of the more powerful radio signals in the country. In 1927, Hay started calling his show *The Grand Ole Opry,* a not-so-sly dig at the Grand Opera that was a favorite of the Athens of the South set.

As the Opry grew in popularity, the management allowed its musicians to tour but insisted that they be available every Saturday night for the show. This meant they couldn't go far, and they would return to town almost every week to pick up new songs, work out deals, and form new bands. A growing group of songwriters and publishers took up residence in Nashville, and the industry slowly but surely grew.

World War II helped country music, dispersing Southerners all over the country and the world, where they demanded the music they loved and exposed others to it as well. The Opry moved into Nashville's Ryman Auditorium in the middle of the war, and more and more people clamored to see the country stars. As a measure of country music's growing audience, mainstream entertainers such as Bing Crosby and Tony Bennett began recording songs that were first heard in Tennessee.

Though the music industry grew, it still wasn't accepted in Nashville. Hank Williams's biographer Colin Escott tells how Roy Acuff threw a party at the Ryman Auditorium in 1943 to celebrate his radio show's being carried coast-to-coast on 129 stations. He invited Gov. Prentice Cooper to attend the festivities. The governor declined, in Escott's words, "saying he would have no part of a 'circus,' adding that Acuff was bringing disgrace to the state by making Tennessee the hillbilly capital of the United States."

Thoroughly miffed, Acuff ran for governor himself in 1948, but voters decided to keep him the king of country music.

All this time country music was called "folk music." *Billboard* magazine finally replaced its "American folk tunes" with a new name: "country & western." Whatever it was, Nashville was the place from which it came. Entertainers such as Elvis Presley and Buddy Holly recorded in Nashville, although neither made it as a country star. Nashville lost ground as rock 'n' roll ascended and young people began asserting their musical tastes.

In an effort to make country music more mainstream, producers such as Chet Atkins created the "Nashville sound." Singers were backed with soft choruses or even violins—not fiddles anymore. Uncle Dave Macon probably spun in his grave, but country music was heading uptown. The Grand Ole Opry moved to Opryland in 1974, and television shows began to feature country music. One of the more successful of these was CBS's *Hee Haw,* whose cornball comedy and down-home music were direct descendants of the vision of George Hay. *Hee Haw* no doubt had Governor Cooper spinning in *his* grave.

The recording expertise of Nashville did not go unnoticed by other musicians. Ex-Beatle Paul McCartney and other musicians came to record in Nashville to take advantage of the supply of excellent sidemen and the relaxed recording atmosphere. In 1975 Robert Altman filmed *Nashville,* a complex film that puzzled residents of the city; they were honored to be noticed by Hollywood, but somewhat suspicious that they were being mocked. Some of Altman's allegedly fictional characters seemed very similar to icons of country music.

Nashville remains the center of the country music empire. Busloads of fans come to the Opry, spend money at the various "museums" of the stars, and prowl Music Row for a glimpse of someone famous. Would-be stars come here as well, playing in the parking lot at Shoney's or hoping for a slot at the Bluebird, with the ghosts of Andrew Jackson and Hank Williams walking the streets, welcoming them all.

Big City?

Nashville now has a professional hockey team and a National Football League franchise. Does this make it a city big enough to rub shoulders with the Chicagos and Bostons of the country? While in some areas—music is the obvious choice—Nashville is right up there, the town is full of people from small towns who are incapable of shedding the inherent politeness and religion with which they grew up. This leads to some unexpected juxtapositions sometimes—a Mercedes with a bumper sticker that says, "I am an organ donor. I gave my ♥ to Jesus." It also leads to a city by and large full of nice folks—far more pleasant people than any big city you can mention.

SIGHTS AND RECREATION

THE LAY OF THE LAND

Nashville is a city on a hill, the state capitol at the top and the rest of the downtown area flowing down to the Cumberland River. Visitors to **Downtown** and **The District** should park their cars and get out. All those in decent shape should be able to walk to wherever they want to go. A particularly good route to follow is **Citywalk,** a two-mile walking tour that follows a blue line painted through Downtown and The District. It begins and ends at Fort Nashborough, although walkers can pick up brochures at various places along the route. For more information, call (615) 862-7970 Mon.-Friday.

The rest of town requires some wheels. **Music Row** is on one of the many spokes heading out of town, and the **West End** is farther out. **Music Valley,** beside the Opryland Hotel and the Grand Ole Opry, is upstream on the Cumberland River, and travelers can get there by boat. Call Opryland USA River Taxis at (615) 889-6611. One-way adult fare is $13.

Another way to get around town are trolleys. These buslike vehicles roll through downtown and Music Row, and during the summer they go out to Music Valley. They leave every 15 minutes from Riverfront Park, and the fare is 90 cents—exact change required. Call (615) 862-5969. Beginning October 15 every year, trolleys shift to a winter schedule, running only on Saturday to Music Row. On April 14, they begin full-time service again.

City buses are run by the Metropolitan Transit Authority. Fare is $1.30 for adults; call (615) 862-5950 for information about routes and schedules.

And then there are taxis. Call Allied Taxi at (615) 244-7433 or Music City Taxi at (615) 262-0451.

Downtown

Bob Dylan once recorded an album here called *Nashville Skyline,* and, viewed from afar, the city has a good collection of modern skyscrapers, including the corporate offices of BellSouth, whose science-fiction-inspired design looks as if the building could serve as headquarters of Flash Gordon's nemesis, Ming the Merciless. The **Tennessee State Capitol** sits at the top of a cluster of state buildings, among them the **Tennessee State Museum** and the **Performing Arts Center.**

Downtown Nashville—the area near the State Capitol—feels almost like an archaeological site because of the different historical layers that exist, if not vertically, then side by side. Some exist only in memory. The Maxwell House hotel served coffee so good that no less than Teddy Roosevelt said it "was good to the last drop." The hotel housed its last guest in 1961.

As in a lot of inner cities elsewhere, a lot of the businesses are still of the Woolworth's/Dollar Store/Discount Furniture type. This is the world that the shrines of country music—**Ryman Auditorium, Tootsie's Orchid Lounge, Ernest Tubb Record Shop**—inhabit; tourist sites from a different era, most of them still look like it. The more recent, squeaky-clean, anesthetic tourist stuff—whether of the Opry Mills variety or the Hard Rock Cafe type—is sprinkled uneasily amidst all this.

Nashville is a hodgepodge of architectural styles, and one of the more interesting downtown places is the **Arcade,** an ancestor of today's shopping mall. Built in 1903 and said to be one of only four such structures left in the country, its two floors of shops are sheltered by metal-girdered glass skylights. Some of the shops have seemingly been here forever and couldn't care less about tourists—shoe repair, tobacco. Some are tourist shops of long-ago vintage that remain unchanged—The Peanut Shop, "Serving Nashville Nuts Since 1927"; some are recent tourist/yuppie places—Tennessee Coffee Company, Starving Artist Deli; some are surprises—Hastee McTastee Fast Food, which despite the Chuck E. Cheese-ish name is old, selling inexpensive lunches and the small hamburgers once pushed by chains such as Krystal, Dairy Queen, or White Castle.

The Hermitage Hotel, 231 6th Ave. N, tel. (615) 244-3121 or (800) 251-1908, is the last

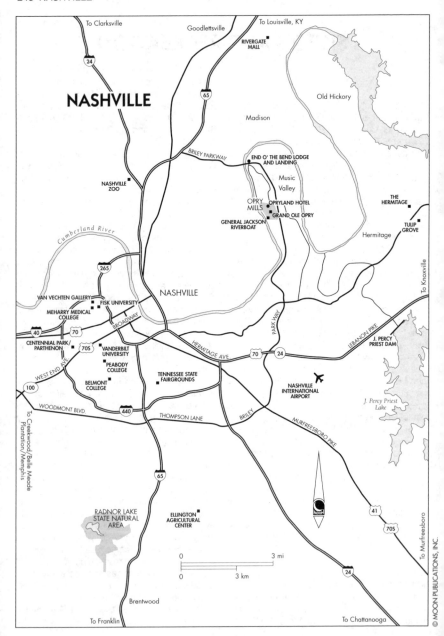

To Clarksville
To Louisville, KY
Goodlettsville
RIVERGATE MALL
24
65
NASHVILLE
Old Hickory
Madison
BRILEY PARKWAY
END O' THE BEND LODGE AND LANDING
Music Valley
NASHVILLE ZOO
OPRY MILLS
OPRYLAND HOTEL
GRAND OLE OPRY
THE HERMITAGE
GENERAL JACKSON RIVERBOAT
TULIP GROVE
Cumberland River
Hermitage
To Knoxville
265
VAN VECHTEN GALLERY
FISK UNIVERSITY
NASHVILLE
PARK WAY
MEHARRY MEDICAL COLLEGE
BROADWAY
40
70
CENTENNIAL PARK/ PARTHENON
70S
VANDERBILT UNIVERSITY
HERMITAGE AVE.
70
24
LEBANON PIKE
J. PERCY PRIEST DAM
WEST END AVE.
PEABODY COLLEGE
100
BELMONT COLLEGE
TENNESSEE STATE FAIRGROUNDS
NASHVILLE INTERNATIONAL AIRPORT
J. Percy Priest Lake
WOODMONT BLVD.
440
THOMPSON LANE
BRILEY
To Creekwood/Belle Meade Plantation/Memphis
MURFREESBORO PIKE
65
RADNOR LAKE STATE NATURAL AREA
ELLINGTON AGRICULTURAL CENTER
MooN
41
70S
To Murfreesboro
0   3 mi
0   3 km
24
Brentwood
To Franklin
To Chattanooga

© MOON PUBLICATIONS, INC.

RUMINATIONS ON DRIVING IN NASHVILLE

Many guidebooks and individuals talk about how confusing it is to drive in Nashville, and it's all true: major avenues radiate, sort of, like spokes of a wheel rather than follow any kind of grid pattern; the city can seem like a forest of one-way streets, with no sense of order about direction. Truly major intersections—chief of all being where Broadway heading west from downtown forks into Broadway and West End—may be marked only by tiny signs above (and beyond) the intersection itself, with no earlier warning, and maybe not even the tiny signs. Streets may intersect and one go on across the intersection under a different name, possibly picking up the previous name later; sometimes the previous name shows up somewhere out of the strict line of the original street; and (my most particular favorite) the same stretch of asphalt may be known as, for example, Franklin Pike on all your maps, Franklin Road on all advertising of businesses thereon, and 8th Ave. S on the actual street signs *in situ*.

All of this, everyone says, is difficult and strange, but it occurred to me (as I was looking for something that was supposed to be on 12th Avenue North, which I had innocently followed until I noticed that it was no longer called that, but had vanished) that the truth is that the streets are strange and odd only because they're so much different from those in other cities in the South. If you come from the Northeast (or, for all I know, out West), you see this kind of stuff all the time. If the Northeast is your point of origin, think about it this way: driving in Nashville is like driving and finding your way at home, only here you don't really know where anything is; you just know that the rules can include anything—there are no rules. It's not like driving in Memphis or Atlanta.

That leads to the inevitable: *you will get lost.* You just will, and you may as well accept it. The trick is not to freak out when you do, because there's very little that you can't remedy very easily once you're actually in the city itself, i.e., off the interstate. I made several hideous rookie mistakes and by dead reckoning and a little patience managed to find my way to my destination in every case. Nashville isn't Cairo; even things that are at opposite ends of town aren't terribly far apart in real distances. Stay calm. Ask directions. People in the places I went were almost invariably helpful and willing to talk and give information of whatever kind, and not in a condescending way or with the phony cheer of which Southerners get accused.

The interstate/beltway system here will also remind you of every other one you've ever seen, with the somewhat unusual added feature (see Paragraph 1) that the name of the exit—where the sign says it goes—may or often may not be what the map says, or even what you might obviously choose as the most important road once you exit.

In addition, at every entrance onto the I-440 beltway that I used, just as I was about to pull out into the slipstream, there stood a sign saying "Now Entering Forty-Four Parkway." If you get on I-440—almost anytime, but particularly at rush hour, late enough at night to hit the river of double-semis, or on a holiday, or, worse, any combination of these—you may conclude that the beltway was named for the Howlin' Wolf song, "Forty-four Blues." You will get no argument from me.

—Franklin Jones

of the old grand hotels in Nashville (another, the Andrew Jackson, is famous for being explosively razed in place without harming surrounding buildings about 20 years ago). Although not "renovated" to the never-was grandeur of, say, the Peabody in Memphis, it's a relatively small matron surrounded by huge moderns. Delicate bas-reliefs decorate the outside walls; inside are a two- or three-story lobby, stained glass and marble, and a brass "cashier" window. The hotel looks as if it were kept up rather than restored after falling to ruin.

To the southwest lies the **Union Station Grand Hotel,** once the flagship station of the Louisville and Nashville Railroad and elegant in ways that airports can never be. This is worth a detour. The gray stone exterior is castlelike; inside, vaulted ceilings shelter lots of stained glass, a big fireplace, and a marble fountain. In a nice touch, behind the check-in desk hangs an old schedule board with names of trains—Pan American, Azalean, and Dixieland.

Right beside Union Station is the High Victorian Gothic **Christ Church Episcopal** on the left.

Across from the church stands the 1876 **Customs House,** and one block east is **Hume-Fogg High School,** built in 1912. The next block to the left is the massive **Nashville Convention Center** and **Nashville Arena.** By now foot traffic has increased, and the visitor has come to The District.

The District

Like Knoxville's Old City and Memphis's Beale St., The District is the old made new. In this case it's a bunch of 19th-century warehouses that once serviced steamboats on the Cumberland River. A very downsized replica of **Fort Nashborough** sits in a park along the river, but the real action begins across the street to the west. Here is a collection of shops, restaurants, and clubs. The biggest is the **Wildhorse Saloon,** which is just a side-slide away from the **Market Street Brewery.** Here too are **Hard Rock Cafe** and **Planet Hollywood.** Across Broadway from the Hard Rock Cafe is **Acme Seed and Feed,** an establishment that reminds visitors of Nashville's rural roots. Plans were in the works for B.B. King's Blues Club and Restaurant to open soon.

A good place to begin sightseeing is the **Metropolitan Historical Commission,** 209 10th Ave. S, Suite 414, Nashville, TN 37203, tel. (615) 862-7970, a government office that dispenses information on Nashville's rich history. Its brochures include a Civil War driving tour and African-American historical sites. The staff is happy to mail brochures to out-of-towners.

It's hard to know what to say about **Printers Alley,** which is in the alley between 3rd and 4th Avenues, Union and Commerce Streets. The bars and clubs here seem to exist on a risqué/naughty reputation from the leering burlesque tassel-twirling G-string age that was utterly outdated 20 years ago.

The western boundary of The District is more vaguely defined, but includes several icons of country music. West on Broadway, as if to herald the wonders ahead, are **Hatch Show Print,** then **Gruhn Guitars,** then **Tootsie's Orchid Lounge.** Just up 5th Ave., like a wide-hipped matron at a concert, sits **Ryman Auditorium,** the longtime home of the Grand Ole Opry.

North Nashville

Many of the landmarks in Nashville's black history can be found in North Nashville, located north-

NASHVILLE'S JUGGS

The ability to laugh at itself has never been one of Nashville's strengths, but two sisters who call themselves "The Juggs" are finding plenty of people willing to pay for a wildly funny "Nash Trash Tour" on a lurid pink bus through Music City.

Sheri Lynn and Brenda Kay—perfect Nashville names—pick up passengers at the Farmer's Market in their pink bus and the show begins. There's singing, make-up tips, tacky hors d'oeuvres, and "celebrity" sightings. Any man wearing a cowboy hat and walking down the street is likely to hear a "There's Garth Brooks!" booming from the bus. It's all in great fun. Tours run year round and leave from the north end of the Farmers Market beside the Bicentennial Mall. They cost $20 and up per person. For info, call (800) 342-2132 or (615) 226-7300.

west of downtown. The area is bounded by Charlotte Avenue to the South and Jefferson St. to the North. Here are the campuses of **Fisk University** and **Meharry Medical College,** two of the most historically significant colleges in the country. Jefferson St. contains a variety of African-American shops, among them **Old Negro League Sports Shop, Alkebu-Lan Images,** and other galleries.

Music Row

This highly publicized place is neither a row nor a place of much music for visitors. Record companies have their offices here, and limousines glide in and out, but once the Country Music Hall of Fame and Museum move downtown, there will be little reason for music fans to come here at all.

Sited on land once owned by the inhabitants of **Belmont Mansion,** 16th and 17th Avenues between Demonbreun St. and Grand Ave. mark the center of the entertainment business in Nashville, a collection of studios and offices for the music companies and assorted hangers-on. The **Country Music Hall of Fame and Museum** is here, as are "museum" gift shops aimed at fleecing the faithful. Perhaps the best place to go is **Studio B,** which is run by the Hall of Fame.

This is the studio where Elvis, Roy Orbison, Dolly Parton, and a variety of people actually made the music. One place unrelated to music is **The Upper Room Chapel and Museum** One place unrelated to music is **The Upper Room Chapel and Museum,** a religious museum whose centerpiece is a carved version of the Last Supper.

Hillsboro Village

For those who weary of country music and anything to do with it, the sophistication of Hillsboro Village awaits. This is the closest thing in Tennessee to Harvard Square. Following 21st St. from Music Row leads into an enclave of book and coffee shops, Bosco's microbrewery, and Provence Breads & Cafe, the home of the best bread in the state. You can buy a *New York Times* here and not feel self-conscious carrying it around.

West End

If there's anything left of the Athens of the South, it hides out here in the shadow of **Vanderbilt University** and occasionally receives company in **Centennial Park.** Here are the **Parthenon** and a host of record stores and boutiques whose clerks couldn't name a Hank Snow song if a customer held a gun on them. **Elliston Place,** a collection of bars, restaurants, and shops in a strip a couple of blocks long, includes several where actual musicians, who are spending their own money, and music industry types, who are spending somebody else's, hang out. These places tend to be funkier and not as gussied up as those closer to Music Row/Division Street, in many cases because they've been here much longer.

Belle Meade

"Belle Meade" sometimes confuses visitors, for it is at once a plantation, a town, and, some would argue, a state of mind. The plantation from which it sprang is still considered one of the finest in Tennessee. The town, consisting of a mere 3,000 souls, is almost completely surrounded by Nashville.

The people who live here permit no commercial establishments to sully their world. The Belle Meade Country Club is perhaps the most exclusive in Nashville. The riff-raff come in to see the plantation and Cheekwood, or to ride bikes, jog, or glide along on in-line skates.

Music Valley

The centerpiece of this part of Nashville should be called the Grand New Opry. Here are **The Grand Ole Opry,** the **Opryland Hotel,** and a host of country-music-related tourist attractions. **The Nashville Network** beams programs from here and invites fans to sit in the audience. This is the home wharf of the *General Jackson Riverboat.*

It is also an area in transition. When the Gaylord Corporation pulled the plug on Opryland, the fount of motorized blessings that streamed into this area suddenly ceased to flow. Replacing the rides and the music will be **Opry Mills,** a glorified shopping mall in the works whose impact on the area is the subject of much speculation. Anyone planning to see the "museums," etc., in the area should call ahead to make sure they are still there.

MUSICAL SIGHTS

Many of the following aren't so much museums as stores, some entirely so. All sell frippery—T-shirts, caps, jackets, and glasses, plus, of course, CDs and (by far outnumbering compact

The renovated Ryman was once the home of the Grand Ole Opry.

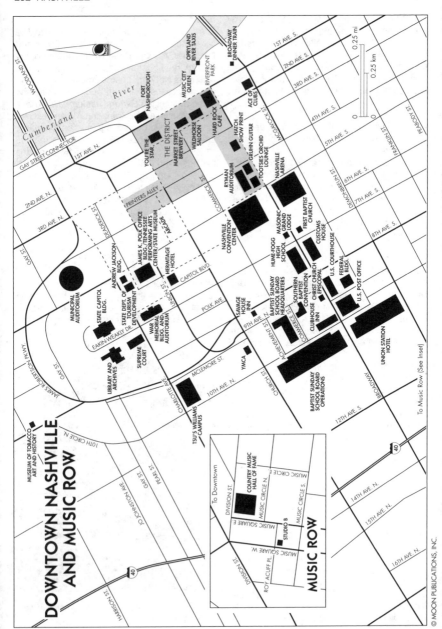

DOWNTOWN NASHVILLE AND MUSIC ROW

MUSEUM OF TOBACCO ART AND HISTORY

Cumberland River

GAY STREET CONNECTOR

FORT NASHBOROUGH

MUSIC CITY QUEEN

OPRYLAND RIVER TAXIS

BROADWAY DINNER TRAIN

RIVERFRONT PARK

THE DISTRICT

YOU'RE THE STAR

WILDHORSE SALOON

HARD ROCK CAFE

ACE OF CLUBS

MARKET STREET BREWERY

HATCH SHOW PRINT

GRUHN GUITAR

TOOTSIES ORCHID LOUNGE

RYMAN AUDITORIUM

NASHVILLE ARENA

PRINTERS ALLEY

JAMES K. POLK OFFICE BLDG.

TENNESSEE PERFORMING ARTS CENTER/STATE MUSEUM

HERITAGE ARCADE

HERMITAGE HOTEL

ANDREW JACKSON BLDG.

NASHVILLE CONVENTION CENTER

HUME-FOGG HIGH SCHOOL

MASONIC GRAND LODGE

FIRST BAPTIST CHURCH

CUSTOMS HOUSE

MUNICIPAL AUDITORIUM

STATE CAPITOL BLDG.

STATE DEPT. OF TOURISM DEVELOPMENT

CAPITOL BLVD.

POLK AVE.

SAVAGE HOUSE INN

BAPTIST SUNDAY SCHOOL BOARD HEADQUARTERS

SOUTHERN BAPTIST CONVENTION

CHRIST CHURCH EPISCOPAL

CLUBHOUSE INN

U.S. COURTHOUSE

FEDERAL BLDG.

U.S. POST OFFICE

WAR MEMORIAL BLDG. AND AUDITORIUM

LIBRARY AND ARCHIVES

SUPREME COURT

EAKIN-WEAKLY DR

MCLEMORE ST.

YMCA

BAPTIST SUNDAY SCHOOL BOARD OPERATIONS

UNION STATION HOTEL

TSU'S WILLIAMS CAMPUS

To Music Row (See Inset)

MUSIC ROW

To Downtown

DIVISION ST.

COUNTRY MUSIC HALL OF FAME

MUSIC CIRCLE N

MUSIC CIRCLE E

STUDIO B

MUSIC SQUARE E

MUSIC CIRCLE S

MUSIC SQUARE W

ROY ACUFF PL

DIVISION ST.

0 0.25 mi

0 0.25 km

© MOON PUBLICATIONS, INC.

discs) tapes—for fans of the singer for which each is named; souvenirs of Nashville itself; and a lot of the peculiarly Southern embarrassments of Mammy/Buckwheat depictions of black people mostly centered on watermelon in little figurines, pot holders, and trivets. These things disappeared or went underground for a long time, but now they're back in absolutely mainstream tourist spots.

Some of these places have been here for quite a while, 10-15 years or so. Like so much else in Nashville, the people who visit these places are easy to make fun of, but they are absolutely devoted longtime fans who come here from all over the country. On a typical day you'll find cars from 11 states lined up in just one block.

Ryman Auditorium and Museum

The Ryman, 116 5th Ave. N, tel. (615) 254-1445, was built because a steamboat captain got religion, and now it is the mother church of country music. Tom Ryman was a rough-and-tumble operator of a fleet of packet boats on the Cumberland River. He converted to Christianity in 1881 and provided much of the money that built what was originally called—and still bears the name—the Union Gospel Tabernacle. Its wooden interior proved to be a dandy concert hall, and it began to host traveling shows starring Caruso, Charlie Chaplin, Mae West, W.C. Fields, and the Ziegfield Follies. People in Nashville called it the Ryman Auditorium, and in 1943 it got its most famous tenant: The "Grand Ole Opry" radio show. Virtually everyone who was anyone in country music trod the boards there until the Opry moved to newer quarters in 1974. The Ryman was restored in 1993 and the next year reopened with another popular radio show, *A Prairie Home Companion*.

For such a storied place, and one that the industry decided officially to turn into a holy of holies, the Ryman nevertheless has the feel of a shrine

from which the god has flown, or maybe even been extinguished. For fans, it's worth seeing, but there's not a lot to see, and it unremarkably resembles any other theater of its era; what may be remarkable is that it wasn't torn down.

Visitors here can sit in the pews, walk up on the stage, and imagine how a packed house must have looked to Hank Williams, Patsy Cline, and the many others who sang here. A small museum displays memorabilia of performers,

---

COUNTRY MUSIC HALL OF FAME
by Margaret Britton Vaughn

I was in the Country Music Hall of Fame
down on Music Row,
they had collected everything,
even Roy's old yo-yo.
There were guitar straps
and cowboy hats
all down the hall,
cowboy suits and cowgirl boots
and posters on the wall.
They had Patsy Cline's pretty dress
and old papers with Opry news,
there were old hand fans
and past programs
and sheet music with the blues.
There were matching guitars of the Wilburns
and costumes around the bend,
there were old Ryman pews
Ralph Sloan's dancing shoes
a road atlas of Loretta Lynn.
There was a tux of Charley Pride's
and Pop Stoneman's autoharp,
there was Carl Smith's belt
and old hat of felt
and one of the girls' scarfs.
I left the memories all teared up
and heart so proud it swelled,
and as I left the museum room
an old Wurlitzer played Kitty Wells.

Maggi Vaughn of Bell Buckle is the poet laureate of Tennessee and a longtime Opry fan. "Country Music Hall of Fame" is reprinted with permission.

and there is a gift shop. Admission is $6 for adults and $2.25 for children 4-11. Performances still take place in the hall; visitors can find out what is on tap by calling (615) 889-6611.

Country Music Hall of Fame and Museum

This place, 4 Music Square, tel. (615) 256-1639, is truly holy for country fans. The displays contain a host of material varying from scraps of paper on which famous songs were written to a white Cadillac once owned by Elvis. The Hall of Fame itself is a series of plaques on a wall.

The museum is open daily 9 a.m.-5 p.m., with expanded hours during the summer. Admission is $9.95 for adults and $4.50 for kids 6-11. Pay attention to the guides; you might one day see them on a stage. Country singer Kathy Mattea once conducted tours here. Visit online at www.halloffame.org.

At press time, plans were under way for the Hall of Fame to move downtown in the vicinity of the Ryman Auditorium. This will put the museum more in the path of tourists and give it an opportunity to quadruple its exhibits.

After seeing the museum, for no extra charge visitors can take a trolley or walk a couple of blocks down the street to **RCA's Historic Studio B,** a recording studio used from 1957 through 1977.

More on Music Row

George Jones Records, 1530 Demonbreun St., tel. (615) 242-2466, takes "Possum's" reputation for alcohol problems and runs with it: Visitors can buy shot glasses with his picture and caps that say "No Show," and they can view a bottle of red wine sitting on a stool in a glass case at the back. They also can look at guitars, stage clothes, and sheet music. Nothing here about one-time wife and singing partner Tammy Wynette, standing by her man or otherwise. A postcard of George and current wife at home makes them look like Jim Bakker and Tammy Faye. Admission is free.

Show Business

Hatch Show Print, 316 Broadway, tel. (615) 256-2805, is the oldest poster print shop in the country. It produces the kind of posters visitors may recall from every concert/revue/fair/rodeo/wrestling match/circus in the dim recesses of memory—

the famous Hank Williams poster, Patsy Cline, minstrel shows, and Tojo Yamamoto wrestling. The shop contains an interesting and large display of wood and metal blocks used to print Hatch's distinctive and vivid prints. The gift shop offers prints produced on site, costing $3-50. Admission is free.

For those of a certain age who ever made a scratchy 45 record in one of those sweaty little recording booths, **You're the Star,** 172 2nd Ave. N, Suite 110, tel. (615) 742-9942, will come as a welcome opportunity. Here visitors can make their own audio recording or even a video. More than 550 songs await from which to choose: country, rock, and ballads. "Heartbreak Hotel" is a frequent choice, as is "Strawberry Wine." Audiotapes cost $18, videos $27.

One of a Kind

The **Tennessee Foxtrot Carousel,** at Riverfront Park near Broadway, is a wonderful combination of art, Tennessee history, and sheer fun. Red Grooms, a New York artist who was born in Nashville, has created a merry-go-round whose 36 whimsically fabricated figures include Andrew Jackson, The Bell Witch, Chet Atkins, Kitty Wells, and Rabbi Isadore Lewinthal. Rides cost between $1 and $2. Visit online at www.newschannel5.com/carousel.

Music Valley

Fans coming to **Bobby Bare Trap,** 2416 Music Valley Dr., tel. (615) 872-8440, to see memorabilia belonging to this artist, who has been described as "the Springsteen of country music," will find his tapes and CDs, but little else other than carloads of stuffed bears. Admission is free.

Grand Ole Opry Museum, Roy Acuff's Museum, and **Minnie Pearl's Museum** are all at the Opryland complex, 2802 Opryland Dr., tel. (615) 889-6611. Exhibits at the Grand Ole Opry Museum honor legendary performers such as Patsy Cline, George Jones, and Little Jimmy Dickens as well as more current stars along the lines of Reba and Garth. This place offers artifacts, interactive devices, and many opportunities to hear music. The Roy Acuff and Minnie Pearl Museums center on the late "King of Country Music" and the Opry's longtime comedienne, who died in 1996. Admission is free to both museums.

Music Valley Wax Museum, across from Opryland Hotel at 2515 McGavock Pike, tel. (615) 883-3612, presents more than 50 allegedly lifelike country music stars clothed in the entertainers' stage costumes. Outside is Nashville's nod to Hollywood with more than 250 stars' handprints, footprints, and signatures in concrete. Admission is $3.50 for adults, $3 for seniors, and $1.50 for children six to 12.

Willie Nelson & Friends Showcase Museum, in the Music Valley Gift Emporium at 2613A McGavock Pike, tel. (615) 885-1515, pays tribute to Willie Nelson, Elvis, J.D. Sumner, Patsy Cline, and others. It includes Nelson's gold and platinum albums and guitars and has a gift shop. Admission is $3 for adults, $1.50 for children six to 12, free for those under six.

Farther Afield

The **Jim Reeves Museum,** tel. (615) 776-3005, was moving at press time for this book, but the phone number should stay the same. Reeves, who died in a plane crash in 1964, had hits with songs such as "Four Walls" and "He'll Have to Go." Displays include "Gentleman Jim's" furniture and personal belongings, awards, gold records, guitars, photos, memorabilia, and even his touring bus and his 1960 Cadillac. The gift shop includes CDs, tapes, and records.

Outside Town

Enjoy the working models of the Tennessee Central and Hummingbird locomotives, and the 1957 Cadillac from the movie *Coal Miner's Daughter* at the **Kitty Wells/Johnny Wright Family Country Junction,** 240 Old Hickory Blvd. E, Madison, tel. (615) 865-6543. After 55 years in show business, these two country music greats left their memorabilia to the Junction. Admission is free. Find the Junction online at www.kittywells.com.

HISTORIC SITES

Tennessee State Capitol

The state capitol, on Charlotte Ave. between 6th and 7th Avenues, tel. (615) 741-1621, was finished just in time for the Civil War. Architect William Strickland considered it his crowning achievement and went so far as to work into the plans a tomb for himself. He died in 1854, while the building was still under construction, and he rests today above the cornerstone in the northeast corner.

Nashville fell quickly and relatively painlessly to Union troops, and the new capitol building, high on a hill overlooking the city, was barricaded and surrounded by cannons and was used as a fortress. Abraham Lincoln installed Andrew Johnson as military governor, and from here he ruled the captive state until he was nominated as vice president in 1864.

The capitol was built of local limestone, which was largely replaced in the 1950s. The interior walls consist of East Tennessee marble. In the late 1980s several sections of the capitol were restored to their 19th-century appearance, and visitors are invited to take a brochure and walk the old halls.

One of the more interesting of the restored rooms is the **State Library.** Building planners had a catalog of cast-iron figures of famous people, and it is interesting to see the choices they made. Among the more curious choices are Joseph Addison, Washington Irving, and John Milton.

The capitol grounds contain statues of famous Tennesseans. The one of Andrew Jackson riding a horse is said to be the first equestrian statue in America. President and Mrs. James K. Polk are buried on the capitol grounds, and statues of Sgt. Alvin York, Sam Davis, and Edward Ward Carmack surround the building.

Edward who?

Edward Ward Carmack was an 1890s newspaper editor who was elected to the U.S. House and then the Senate. While running for re-election in 1906, he championed the cause of Temperance but lost the race and a later primary in which he ran for governor. He returned to the press, becoming the editor of the Nashville *Tennessean,* a position that enabled him to rain abuse on his enemies, political and otherwise. One of his targets was his former employer, one Duncan B. Cooper, who took to carrying a pistol with him at all times. On November 9, 1909, Cooper and his son ran into Carmack rounding the corner of Union St. and 7th Avenue. In a scene more fitting for the Wild West, Carmack and the younger Cooper drew and fired at each other. Carmack was killed on the spot, his assailant was wounded, and later testimony revealed that the elder Cooper did no shooting at all. Carmack's killing was the talk of the state, and today he stands guard beside the capitol. The old Temperance man isn't too far from the Motlow Tunnel, a pedestrian walkway named in honor of the Jack Daniel family.

There is no charge to visit the Tennessee State Capitol, which is uphill from virtually anywhere in downtown Nashville.

Black Colleges

Fisk University was established in 1866 as Fisk Free Colored School, and since then has educated thousands of young men and women. The 40-acre Fisk campus is on the National Register, and many people come to see Jubilee Hall, a building paid for by a triumphal tour of Europe by the Fisk Singers. Today, in proportion to their enrollment, more Fisk graduates receive Ph.D.s than African-American graduates of any other college or university. See the school online at www.edu.fisk.

The Fisk campus can be found at 1000 17th Ave. North. Visitors are invited to stroll on the campus, which contains **Van Vechten Gallery.** For escorted tours, call (615) 329-8666, ext. 225.

Right beside Fisk is **Meharry Medical College.** Indeed, many Fisk graduates crossed the street to begin their medical education. From its beginnings in 1876, Meharry has graduated many of the African-American doctors and dentists in this country. Even now, when medical schools are no longer segregated, Meharry can claim as alumni 15% of all the black doctors and dentists in America and over 10% of the Ph.D.s in biomedical sciences given to black recipients. See Meharry online at www.mmc.edu.

Plantation Houses

Belle Meade Plantation, 5025 Harding Rd., tel. (615) 356-0501, is a tribute to the kind of lifestyle possible when one doesn't have to pay one's workers. Most Tennessee plantation owners started out with log houses, but in most cases these were demolished when the "big house" was built. Belle Meade, known as "The Queen of Tennessee Plantations," still has the original house, but the showpiece is the 1853 Greek revival mansion, which once commanded a 5,300-acre plan-

tation. Now down to a more manageable 30 acres, it includes the mansion, the old house, a carriage house, and various outbuildings.

One of Belle Meade's claims to fame is that it was the place where President William Taft, a portly gentleman, got stuck in one of the mansion's bathtubs. His hosts were so mortified that they installed a "stand up tub" in which the water came out of "a multitude of tubes." This was Nashville's first shower, and Taft—who came back to Belle Meade again—liked it so much he had one put into the White House.

Tour guides dress in period outfits. Admission is $8 for adults, $7.50 for seniors, and $3 for children six to 12. Preview the plantation online at www.citysearch.com/nash/plantation.

Belmont Mansion, 1900 Belmont Blvd., tel. (615) 460-5459, now the centerpiece of Belmont College, is an Italianate mansion built in 1850 by Adelicia Acklen, a woman who charmed Confederate and Union troops into letting her sell close to a million dollars' worth of cotton during the Civil War. Her grand salon was considered the most elaborate room in Tennessee, if not the entire South. Admission is $6 for adults and $2 for kids six to 12.

The Hermitage, Andrew Jackson's celebrated home, is in the town of Hermitage, which is covered under "Along I-40 East of Nashville" in the Heartland chapter.

Traveller's Rest, 636 Farrell Parkway, tel. (615) 832-2962, has a name expressing the hospitality often extended by homeowners in a time before bed and breakfasts. John Overton established a plantation here in 1796 and built the house in stages. Closely aligned with Andrew Jackson, Overton was Old Hickory's law partner, presidential campaign manager, and fellow land speculator. He was one of the founders of Memphis. The house has been restored and contains a variety of exhibits, some of them pertaining to the Civil War, when Confederate forces occupied the house during the ill-fated Battle of Nashville. It's open Mon.-Sat. 9 a.m.-4 p.m., and Sunday 1-4 p.m. Admission is $6 for adults and $3 for children six to 12.

The Parthenon

This structure in Centennial Park, tel. (615) 862-8431, is a legacy of the days when American cities hosted large exhibitions and built extravagant structures meant to last only for those celebrations. This duplicate of the quintessential Greek building in Athens is actually the second such replica. The first, hastily constructed of wood and plaster for the 1896 exposition, was so popular that citizens didn't want it torn down. The "temporary" building stood for 24 years, then was demolished in preparation for a permanent Parthenon, which opened in 1931.

The new and improved Parthenon—the only full-sized replica in the world—was built of concrete, with floors of Tennessee marble and a ceiling of Florida cypress. The building is impressive: 46 Doric columns encircle it, and the largest bronze doors in the world, some 7.5 tons each, stand at the east and west entrances. The sculptures and friezes are modeled on the Elgin Marbles in London, which the British stole from Greece.

Inside stands a statue of Athena, the Greek goddess from whom came the name of Greece's capital city. The 42-foot-high goddess stands here in her concrete Parthenon, Barnumly billed as "the largest indoor sculpture in the Western World," solemnly reflecting on the days when Nashville strove to be known as the Athens of the South.

The Parthenon's basement contains an art museum with four galleries. One holds the Cowan Collection, 63 works by 19th- and 20th-century American painters. Another exhibit is plaster casts of the Elgin Marbles. Admission is $2.50 for adults and $1.25 for seniors and kids four to 17.

More Historic Sights

City Cemetery, 1001 Fourth Ave. at Oak St., tel. (615) 862-7970, opened in 1822 and was Nashville's first public cemetery. Among the notables laid to rest here is James Robertson, the "Father of Middle Tennessee." The cemetery has about 23,000 graves and still accepts burials of anyone whose family plot has room. Others must go elsewhere.

Fort Nashborough, in Riverfront Park at 170 1st Ave. N, tel. (615) 862-8400, is a reconstructed miniature version of the settlement that started it all. Admission is free.

The **Governor's Residence,** 882 S. Curtiswood Ln., tel. (615) 383-5401, offers tours of the house Tuesday and Thursday mornings, 10 a.m.-noon. Admission is free, but parties larger than four should call for an appointment.

One of the more colorful occupants of this house was the late Ray Blanton, whose involvement in illegal efforts to sell state liquor licenses landed him in prison. In his heyday, however, he hosted dinner parties at which inmates of the nearby state prison prepared and served the food. At some point after the meal Governor Blanton would call for the servers to line up against the wall and recount their crimes for the edification of the guests. One observer recalled that these individuals were almost always murderers who had dispatched one or more people and who had subsequently found Jesus. No one in the room, least of all Blanton, ever dreamed the host would one day be a prisoner, too.

MUSEUMS AND GALLERIES

History

The **Tennessee State Museum,** 5th Ave. between Union and Deaderick Streets, tel. (615) 741-2692, offers an excellent look at the state's history. Combining permanent exhibitions with changing ones, it covers individuals such as Andrew Jackson, Davy Crockett, and Sam Houston as well as specific periods such as the Civil War and Reconstruction.

Walk one block west on Union St. to the **Military History Branch** in the War Memorial Building. The collection here focuses on the willingness of Tennesseans to involve themselves in wars, both foreign and domestic. Here are old uniforms—American as well as enemy—weapons, and other combat-related items. Admission is free to both museums.

Art

Aaron Douglas Gallery of African Art, 3rd floor of Main Library, Fisk University, tel. (615) 329-8720, houses the university's collection of African ceremonial items, masks, musical instruments, games, and other items. Admission is free, but donations are requested. (While you are at Fisk, see the Van Vechten Galley, described below.) Read more about the gallery online at www.fisk.edu.

American Pop Culture Gallery, 2055 Scaritt Pl., tel. (615) 327-1977, sells items such as romance novel covers, pin-ups, and other materials a clerk described as "low-brow art."

The Georgian mansion of **Cheekwood,** 1200 Forrest Park Dr., tel. (615) 356-8000, houses the **Museum of Art** and sits amid the 55-acre **Tennessee Botanical Gardens.** Built by the Cheek family 1929-32, the three-story mansion now houses a collection of 18th- and 19th-century American art, antique silver, Oriental snuff bottles, and period furniture. Outside, the grounds contain a boxwood garden, flowering trees, perennial borders, and display gardens. The Pineapple Room Restaurant serves lunch daily, for which reservations are not a bad idea. Call (615) 352-4859. Admission is $6 for adults, $5 for seniors and students, and $3 for children six to 17.

Leu Gallery at Belmont University, 1900 Belmont Blvd., tel. (615) 460-5578, hosts traveling exhibits, with occasional student and faculty shows. Admission is free.

The Parthenon Gallery, Centennial Park, tel. (615) 862-8431, presents several permanent collections, such as The Cowan Collection of late 19th- and early 20th-century American paintings. Two rotating galleries change exhibits about every six weeks; these generally display contemporary local or regional work in all media, including photographs, sculpture, paintings, mixed media, graphics, textiles, and ceramics. Some of these works are available for purchase. Every other year on the even-numbered years (in May), this gallery hosts the TACA Biennial Crafts Exhibition.

Sankofa-African Heritage Cultural Museum, in the Winston-Derek Center at MetroCenter, tel. (615) 321-0535 or (800) 826-1888, offers artifacts and artworks from the continent of Africa. Admission is $10 for adults, $5 for students and seniors, and free for those under 12.

The focal point of **The Upper Room Chapel and Museum,** 1908 Grand Ave., tel. (615) 340-7207, is an eight- by 17-foot wooden carving of da Vinci's "The Last Supper." The chapel also contains an eight- by 20-foot stained-glass window. The museum exhibits religious paintings, books by John Wesley, and English porcelains. At Christmas the museum brings out 100 nativity scenes, and at Easter it displays 73 Ukrainian eggs. Admission is free, but donations are encouraged.

Sarratt Gallery, on the fourth floor of the Sarratt Student Center at Vanderbilt Pl., tel. (615) 322-2471, is run by students—they select the shows and present an annual student art show every year. Admission is free.

Although primarily a history museum, **Tennessee State Museum,** 505 Deaderick St., tel. (615) 741-2692, also displays antique portraits of Tennesseans, work by local artists, and traveling exhibits. Admission is free.

Van Vechten Gallery, corner of Jackson St. and D.B. Todd Blvd., tel. (615) 329-8720, is a treat. Carl Van Vechten was a critic and supporter of the Harlem Renaissance, and he talked artist Georgia O'Keeffe, she of the cow skull paintings, into donating the 100-item art collection of her late husband, photographer Alfred Stieglitz, to Fisk University. When O'Keeffe did so, Fisk found itself in possession of the best collection of modern art in the state, if not the entire South. The paintings include works by Picasso, Cézanne, O'Keeffe, and Renoir. Admission is free, but donations are encouraged. (Visitors to the Van Vechten Gallery should also consider seeing the nearby Aaron Douglas Gallery of African Art.)

Vanderbilt University Fine Arts Gallery, 23rd and West End Avenues, tel. (615) 322-0605, features about five exhibitions per year, some of which are traveling shows. The other exhibitions are pulled together from the university's 7,000-piece collection, which represents more than 40 countries and cultures. Admission is free.

Specialty

Nashville's hands-on educational center is the **Cumberland Science Museum,** 800 Fort Negley Blvd. (from I-40 take Exit 310), tel. (615) 862-5160. This place has great science demonstrations, particularly on weekends. A host of interactive devices, a "Curiosity Corner" for ages 10 and under, and the Sudekum Planetarium round out the offerings. Admission is $6 for adults and $4.50 for kids four to 12. Planetarium shows cost $3, or $1 with admission to museum. See the museum online at www.csmisfun.com.

Music Valley Car Museum, 2611 McGavock Pike, tel. (615) 885-7400, sits across from the Opryland Hotel and contains about 50 cars, about half of which belonged to stars. The obligatory Elvis model is the limousine in which his family rode to his funeral. Admission is $3.50 for adults, $3 for seniors, and $1.50 for kids six to 12. Visitors can buy a combination ticket that admits them to Shotgun Red's Collections, right next door.

Nashville Toy Museum is at 2613 McGavock Pike, tel. (615) 883-8870. Kids may be bored with the items here, but adults will find these antique and not-so-old toys fascinating. One thousand tin soldiers stand steadfast, and old trains run tiny routes. Best of all, none of the miniature cars in this place were owned by Elvis. Displays include antique dolls, bears, model ships, and comic figures. Admission is $3.50 for adults and $1.50 for kids.

The **Oscar Ferris Agricultural Museum** is at the 207-acre Ellington Agricultural Center, about six miles below Nashville off I-65 at the Harding Pl. Exit, tel. (615) 837-5197. A large barn here houses a collection of household and farm implements that date from the 1800s up to the 1940s, when electricity came to Tennessee farms. Among the items are a massive steam engine by which threshing machines or sawmills could be powered, a rural mail buggy used into the 1940s, and a very early wooden plow. The Tennessee Agriculture Hall of Fame is here as well. Admission is free.

PARKS AND ZOOS

Bicentennial Mall

With statewide events and much hoopla, Tennessee celebrated its 200th birthday in 1996. One legacy of that year is the Bicentennial Mall, which stretches forth from the back side of the state capitol at 600 James Robertson Pkwy., tel. (615) 741-5800. This is the site of French Lick, the salt lick that attracted the deer and other game which in turn attracted the people who founded Nashville. This 19-acre site features a 250-foot granite map of the state, a Walk of Counties containing information about all 95 of them, A Walk of History, and a 31-fountain extravaganza called the Rivers of Tennessee. The 2,000-seat amphitheater is a good place for concerts. No admission is charged.

One of the more imaginative aspects of the Mall is the World War II Memorial, a nine-ton granite globe that depicts the world as it was from 1939-1945. The huge ball rests on a constantly flowing stream of water, and visitors can rotate it to view various parts of the world.

Farmer's Market, at 900 8th Avenue right beside the Bicentennial Mall, has some 200 vendor stalls spread over an 11-acre site.

Nashville Zoo

This Cheatham County facility is in the process of moving to Grassmere Wildlife Park in Nashville. The move will be done in four phases at a cost of $10 million, with the official grand opening planned for spring 2001.

For now, living at the zoo, northwest of the city off I-24 Exit 31 W, tel. (615) 833-1534, are more than 600 animals, among them lions, white tigers, snakes, giraffes, pandas, and monkeys. The settings in which the animals live resemble their natural habitats. Admission is $5.50 for adults and $3.50 for seniors and kids three to 12.

Radnor Lake State Natural Area

Radnor Lake, in southern Nashville, tel. (615) 373-3467, calls to those who have had too much of the city. The 85-acre lake was created by the L&N Railroad as a source of water for steam engines. Bought by the state in 1973, the lake's 1,000 acres offer wildlife refuge and nature trails. Here one can see deer, foxes, beavers, and all manner of birds. Wildflowers flourish in spring and fall.

To get there, take I-65 South's Harding Place Exit, go west on Granny White Pike, and then go south on Otter Creek Road. Follow the signs to the area. Admission is free, and the lake is open daily from sunrise to sunset. Visit online at www.tnstateparks.com.

OPRY MILLS AND THE OPRYLAND HOTEL

Opryland, the one-time amusement park beside the Opryland Hotel, bit the dust because it could only stay open about 100 days per year. While this was acceptable in the early years of the park, the more valuable the land became, the more Opryland movers and shakers decided that something more profitable should go there.

Noting that the most popular tourist attractions in 12 states such as Minnesota are shopping malls, the choice seemed clear, and so **Opry Mills** is in the works. Slated to open in spring 2000, the mall will have about 200 stores, movie theaters, and other entertainment such as Steven Spielberg's Gameworks. It is being developed by the Mills Corporation and Gaylord, who owns the Grand Ole Opry.

AMUSEMENT PARKS

Wave Country

This place offers the proverbial good, clean fun during the summertime. Operated by the city, Wave Country can be found off Exit 10 of the Briley Parkway on Two Rivers Parkway. The kids will love the water slides and wave pool. Admission is very reasonable for this sort of place: $5 for adults and $4 for children four to 12. Call (615) 885-1092 for hours and information.

CRUISES AND TOURS

On the Water

The **Music City Queen,** 106 1st Ave. S, tel. (615) 889-6611, is a riverboat with cruises that leave from Riverfront Park in downtown Nashville and from the Opryland Hotel. Cruises vary from sightseeing only to music and dining extravaganzas.

Many Tennessee cities and towns have riverboats, usually small, box-like affairs that seem rather puny. The **General Jackson Riverboat,** 2802 Opryland Dr., however, is enormous—300 feet long and four stories high—and looks appropriately majestic as it steams up and down the Cumberland River. A variety of cruises are offered morning, noon, and night, all with live entertainment and all departing from the dock near the Opryland Hotel.

Prices for cruises on either boat begin at $19 for daytime excursions. At night the price for the cruise and a meal approaches $55 per head. Call (615) 889-6611 for schedule and exact fare.

The Opryland organization also offers **Water Taxi** service from the Opryland Hotel to downtown Nashville. The price for this is $13 for adults and $10 for kids.

Riding the Rails

Broadway Dinner Train, 108 1st Ave. S, tel. (615) 254-8000 or (800) 274-8010, is for those who heed all those references to trains in country songs. On Thurs.-Sat. nights the train—powered by a 1952 diesel engine—pulls out for a two-and-a-half-hour ride to the town of Old Hickory. Riders eat dinner in two restored dining cars as the scenery rolls by. This costs $60 per adult. Those who want to go just for the ride can do so for $25 in the lounge car. The train runs year-round. See it online at www.broadwaydinnertrain.com.

Sightseeing Tours

Nashville has Tennessee's greatest concentration of tour operators. The ones listed below, unless otherwise noted, offer general tours—tourist spots, homes of country music stars, and historical sites. Prices are generally not listed, for the variations and permutations boggle the mind.

Country & Western/Gray Line Tours, 2416 Music Valley Dr., Suite 102, tel. (615) 883-5555 or (800) 251-1864, offers a variety of tours. It picks up passengers at hotels or campgrounds.

Cumberland Tours, P.O. Box 50590, Nashville, TN 37205, tel. (615) 352-4169, maintains a stable of knowledgeable guides who are experts on the history and personalities of this region. This company's forte is tailoring a tour to the needs of the visitor. Cumberland Tours can provide a guide who will ride in the visitor's vehicle, drive a van, or step onto the bus of a tour group. Tours typically run four to five hours, and prices begin at $60.

Grand Ole Opry Tours, at The Inn at Opryland, tel. (615) 889-9490, also offers a variety of tours of varying length. Tours depart from the Magnolia Canopy of the Opryland Hotel.

Johnny Walker Tours, 2416 Music Valley Dr., tel. (615) 834-8585 or (800) 722-1524, will pick up passengers at various hotels and offers a wide variety of tours.

Bill Daniel of **Nashville Black Heritage Tours,** 5188 Almaville Rd., Smyrna, tel. (615) 890-8173, gives a two-and-a-half- to three-hour escorted tour of significant sites pertaining to black heritage. He can make arrangements for any size group and prefers a three-day notice.

ENTERTAINMENT AND EVENTS

STAGE AND SCREEN

Grand Ole Opry

The Opry, 2804 Opryland Dr., tel. (615) 889-6611, the legendary country music show, is a must-see in Nashville. Old-timers such as Porter Wagoner and Little Jimmy Dickens share the stage with newer performers such as Allison Krauss and Alan Jackson. Shows take place on Friday and Saturday nights, usually at 6:30 and 9:30 p.m. During the winter the 9:30 Friday show is omitted, and during the summer matinees take place on Tuesday and Thursday at 3 p.m. Tickets cost approximately $16-19, and most of them are sold by phone. Get information online at www.opryhotel.com/grand.

The Nashville Network

TNN, 2806 Opryland Dr., tel. (615) 883-7000, produces a variety of television shows destined to flow through cables into the homes of millions of subscribers. TNN is always looking for enthusiastic people to make up the audiences for these shows, which are produced at the back of the Grand Ole Opryhouse. Shows require reservations, which can be had by calling (615) 457-PTC4 for *Prime Time Country*. Get information online at www.country.com/tnn/tapings/tapings-f.html.

The Crook and Chase Show, a long-running TNN talk show hosted by Lorianne Crook and Charlie Chase, consists of interviews with a wide range of people, not necessarily country music stars, at tapings held at the Jim Owens Studios off Music Row at 1525 McGavock Street. Audiences are admitted at 10:15 a.m. on weekdays; taping begins at 11 a.m. and ends at noon. Admission is free, but reservations are a good idea. Call (615) 242-8000. Find out more online at www.crookandchase.com.

Ernest Tubb Record Shop's Midnight Jamboree

If it just happens to be Saturday night about midnight, check out the jamboree. This free live radio show, much like the Grand Ole Opry, features Opry stars as well as some new faces. It all takes place after the Saturday night Opry at the **Texas Troubadour Theatre,** 2416 Music Valley Dr. near the Opryland Hotel, tel. (615) 889-2474. Get there by 11:30 p.m. Admission is free. For those who can't stay up that late but who can buy tickets, there's "A Closer Walk with Patsy Cline" show at 7 p.m. Visit the Record Shop online at www.etrs.net.

The LeGarde Twins Country Music Theatre

The country music shows of Branson, Missouri, caught Nashville napping, and the capital of country music has been playing catch-up ball ever since. The LeGarde twins' theater on Music Row inside the Quality Inn at 1407 Division St., tel. (800) 861-7007 or (615) 251-7007, was the first Branson-style place in Nashville offering dinner and a show. The Aussie-born LeGardes are very popular with the tour bus set, who come for traditional country music—songs by Johnny Cash, Slim Whitman, Jim Reeves, and the like. The LeGardes emphasize the western in country-western music.

This twosome may not have the name of other entertainers, but no one outdoes them in hospitality. Their theater is an intimate 136-seater, and after the show the performers come into a greeting area and talk to everyone who shows up. They pose for pictures and, in marked contrast to a great many grab-your-money-and thank-you-very-much places, make the audience feel most welcome. Dinner acts cost $27.50 for adults, and lunch matinees go for $20. The shows run Monday through Saturday. While there, check out the shop featuring Australian gifts.

Zanies Comedy Showplace

Zanies, 2025 8th Ave. S, tel. (615) 269-0221, pulls in some of the biggest names in stand-up comedy for two or more shows Wed.-Sunday. Doors open two hours before the show starts. Prices typically range $9-15 with a two-drink minimum.

MOVIES

In addition to the usual multiplexes, Nashville has two movie theaters that show classics, art films, and imports. Both of them are close to Vanderbilt:

Surratt Cinema, 24th Ave. S and Vanderbilt Pl., tel. (615) 322-2425 or (615) 343-6666.

Watkins Belcourt Theatre, 2102 Belcourt Ave., tel. (615) 383-9140.

THEATER

Nashville has a lively theatrical scene, with new companies bubbling up all the time. What follows is a partial list of what's out there. Check the local newspapers for more up-to-date listings.

The **American Negro Playwright Theater,** tel. (615) 871-4283, stages plays in various theaters around town.

The **Circle Players,** 505 Deaderick St., tel. (615) 254-0113, began in 1949 and are Nashville's oldest community theater group. They present six productions per year, from musicals to straight plays.

Chaffin's Barn Dinner Theatre, at 8204 Hwy. 100, tel. (615) 646-9977 or (800) 282-BARN, offers professional theater-in-the-round, some pretty darn good food, and a wonderfully comfortable country atmosphere. Prices are $30 per person for Sunday and weekday shows, and $32 for Friday and Saturday.

Mockingbird Public Theatre, P.O. Box 24002, Nashville, TN 37202, tel. (615) 463-0071, is a nonprofit, professional company that performs new plays and classic works, as well as plays with Southern themes. Most of the plays are presented in the Darkhorse Theatre at 4610 Charlotte Avenue.

Nashville Children's Theatre, 724 2nd Ave. S, tel. (615) 254-9103, dates to 1931, when it first began presenting plays for Nashville youngsters, and the group is the oldest such company in the country. Typical productions include *Goldilocks and the Three Bears.* Many school groups come to the theater, but individuals and families are welcome as well. Visit the theater online at www.nct-dragonsite.org.

Tennessee Repertory Theatre, 427 Chestnut St., tel. (615) 244-4878, is the largest professional group of thespians in the state. It puts on six plays per year—including dramas and musicals.

MUSIC AND CULTURE

The **Nashville Ballet,** 2976 Sidco Dr., tel. (615) 244-7233, puts on three productions per year in addition to the obligatory *Nutcracker.*

The **Nashville Opera,** 719 Thompson Lane, Suite 401, tel. (615) 292-5710, presents four productions per year, all in the Tennessee Arts Center.

The **Nashville Symphony Orchestra,** 208 23rd Ave. N, tel. (615) 329-3033, offers two series—classical and pops. In the summer it performs at Cheekwood and in local parks.

The **Tennessee Dance Theatre,** 625A 7th Ave. S, tel. (615) 248-3262, is the state's only professional modern dance troupe. It performs works from Southern heritage, such as the critically acclaimed *Quilts.* The troupe tours nationally and internationally.

FESTIVALS AND EVENTS

February
Americana Spring Sampler Craft, Folk Art, & Antique Show takes place at the Tennessee State Fairgrounds and brings more than 200 artists and antique dealers from a 30-state area. Call (615) 227-2080.

The second weekend of February brings the **Bobby Jones Gospel Explosion,** a three-day television taping from the Black Entertainment Television Network. Among the artists are John T. Kee and Stephanie Mills. For information, call (615) 665-1009.

April
The **Dove Awards,** gospel music's version of the Academy Awards, are given out during the third week in April. For information about the show and tickets, call (615) 242-0303 or look online at www.gospelmusic.org.

Tin Pan South brings more than 300 songwriters to town as an event of the Nashville Songwriters Association. Tunesmiths play various clubs around town, and the whole thing culminates with a wonderful acoustic concert at the Ryman Auditorium. For information, call (615)

251-3472 or check online at www.songs.org/nsai.

May

The **Annual Running of the Iroquois Steeplechase** brings Nashville's horsey set to Percy Warner Park to watch a steeplechase that benefits Vanderbilt's Children's Hospital. The tailgate picnics have to be seen to be believed. Call (615) 322-7284.

Tennessee Crafts Fair, held at Centennial Park, claims to be the largest market of Tennessee-made crafts. More than 165 artists take part, and the event includes live music and food. Call (615) 665-0502.

The Tennessee Jazz & Blues Society Concert Series takes place at Belle Meade and The Hermitage, offering music under the stars. Call the society at (615) 386-7500.

Summer Lights in Music City Festival takes place in late May (sometimes into early June) and brings more than 300 musical groups to six downtown stages. Dance, theater, and other arts are offered as well. Call (615) 259-0900.

June

The American Artisan Festival invites craftspeople from all over to Centennial Park. Call (615) 298-4691 for dates and information.

The International Country Music Fan Fair, usually just called Fan Fair by Nashvillians, brings thousands of country music fans to town to rub shoulders, get autographs, take photos of their favorite stars, and listen to hours of concerts. Unlike stars in any other entertainment genre, country music kings and queens are expected to make themselves available during these sweltering days. Why do they do it? One fan explained it like this: "These guys are smart. They know that if they take care of their fans while on top, those fans will stick with them later on when that performer may no longer be a headliner." Makes sense.

Held at the Tennessee State Fairgrounds, this weeklong event features concerts and a variety of events. For those not particularly interested in country music, this week might be a good time to avoid Nashville. Call (615) 889-7503. Tickets usually sell out in advance.

Chet Atkins Musical Days, held in the last week in June, is a more eclectic and much smaller musical gathering than Fan Fair. Some

of the outdoor concerts are free, as are master's classes and shows for kids. For info, call (615) 256-9596.

Dancin' in the District takes place every Thursday night June–Aug. at Riverfront Park at the corner of Broadway and First Avenue. This event features live music and good times.

July

Nashville's Independence Day Celebration takes place along the Cumberland River at Riverfront Park. Music kicks off the event at 5 p.m., with a massive fireworks show after it gets dark. This is a no-alcohol event. Call (615) 862-8400.

July brings another taping of the **Bobby Jones Gospel Explosion.** See February for details.

August

This month, there's another **Americana Summer Sampler Craft, Folk Art, & Antique Show**—see February for details.

The Athens of the South holds the Nashville Shakespeare Festival at the Centennial Park band shell, where each year a free play by the bard is presented on Friday, Saturday, and Sunday evenings in August. Call (615) 862-8400 for details.

The Music City Blues Festival is a one-day event that takes place in August or September. B.B. King is always the headliner, with various blues luminaries rounding out the bill. For information, call TicketMaster at (615) 737-4849.

September

The Country Fair, held at Nashville's historic Traveller's Rest, offers period food, clothing, and activities. Call (615) 832-8197.

The **Tennessee State Fair,** tel. (615) 862-8980, takes place at the state fairgrounds and includes all manner of agricultural displays, rides, livestock, and the usual offerings of corn dogs and other health food.

The African Street Festival, held at Tennessee State University's Main Campus, celebrates black culture with music, food, storytelling, fashion show, and lectures. Call (615) 299-0412 for information.

Belle Meade Plantation Fall Fest, tel. (615) 356-0501, takes place over two days at the plantation and includes food, antiques, crafts, and other items for sale.

Longhorn World Championship Rodeo, tel. (615) 876-1016 or (800) 357-6336, bucks into town at the Nashville Municipal Auditorium. The professional bull and bronco riders, calf ropers, and barrel racers bring a touch of the West to Music City.

Tennessee Association of Craft Artists Fall Crafts Fair is a juried crafts fair at Centennial Park. Crafts demonstrations highlight the event. Call (615) 665-0502 for details.

October

Southern Festival of Books, held in the War Memorial Plaza, brings together Southern and national writers for panel discussions, readings, and book-signings. Ninety to 100 exhibitors take part, and two stages provide storytelling and music. Call (615) 320-7001 or see them online at www.tn-humanities.org/sfob.

Oktoberfest, tel. (615) 256-2729, takes place—where else?—in Germantown at the corner of 7th Ave. N and Monroe Street. More than 80 booths offer German foods, tapes of polka bands, and American and European crafts. Live music and dancing are also on tap the second Saturday in October.

Pow Wow and Fall Festival, sponsored by the Native American Indian Association, brings Indian dance contests, demonstrations, traditional foods, and storytelling from a variety of tribes. It's held at Hermitage Landing on J. Percy Priest Lake. Call (615) 726-0806.

The annual **Storytelling Festival,** tel. (615) 889-2941, takes place on the third weekend in October at The Hermitage, whose original occupant no doubt listened to many a yarn.

November

Still another **Americana Christmas Sampler Craft, Folk Art, & Antique Show** occurs this month—see February for details.

Sinking Creek Film/Video Festival takes place at Vanderbilt's Sarratt Cinema, and country videos are shown at the Wildhorse Saloon. Panel members hold discussions, and individuals analyze various films and directors. Call (615) 322-4234.

Christmas at Belmont, at Belmont University, tel. (615) 460-5459, shows off one of Tennessee's fanciest houses with Victorian decorations.

Opryland Hotel stages **A Country Christmas** from November 1 until Christmas. Tennessee's largest hotel is decorated for the season, and a variety of events, musical and otherwise, take place there. Call (615) 872-0600.

December

Christmas at Belmont, A Country Christmas, and **Christmas at Opryland** all continue into December.

The Tribute to African Americans in the Battle of Nashville commemorates the Civil War defenders of Nashville with tours and lectures. Call (615) 227-7258.

SPECTATOR SPORTS

Professional

There is a school of thought that an American city cannot be a real city unless it is home to

the Nashville Arena, home of the Nashville Predators

all manner of professional sports teams. Nashville has gone for this hook, line, and sinker, pouring barrels of cash into the $145 million Arena and the $292 million Coliseum. The former Houston Oilers are now the **Tennessee Titans**. The Titans will begin the 1999 season in a new, 67,000-seat coliseum across the Cumberland River east of downtown. Tickets in 1998 cost $36-48. For info, find the team online at www.titansonline.com.

The **Nashville Sounds,** part of the Pittsburgh Pirates baseball organization, play 72 home games at Herschel Greer Stadium. To get there, take the Wedgewood Exit off I-65 and follow the signs. Usual game times are 7 p.m. for night games and 2 p.m. on Sunday. For tickets, call (615) 242-4371, or see them online at www.nashvillesounds.com.

The **Nashville Kats,** tel. (615) 254-KATS, play arena football, an indoor version of the game, at the Nashville Arena. The season runs from April through August. Tickets cost $9-30. Their website is www.katsfan.com.

The **Nashville Predators,** tel. (615) 770-PUCK, is a National Hockey League team that also plays in the Nashville Arena. Tickets go from $10 to $95. See their site online at www.nashnhl.com.

The **Nashville Metros,** tel. (615) 771-8200, play professional soccer at Columbia Soccer Stadium at 5135 Harding Place. The season goes from April through October, and tickets cost $7-10. The team is online at www.nashville/metros.com.

College

Vanderbilt University fields 13 intercollegiate teams in the Southeastern Conference. It is particularly noted for its women's basketball prowess—except when playing the University of Tennessee. For information on upcoming games, call (615) 322-4636. Order tickets by calling (615) 322-3544 or by going to the ticket office at 2601 Jess Neely Drive. Get more info online at www.vanderbilt.edu/athletics.

Tennessee State University plays in the Ohio Valley Conference. Teams include football and men's and women's basketball. The late Wilma Rudolph, track star and Olympic medalist, went to school here. For ticket information, call (615) 963-5841. TSU plays at the 10,500-seat Howard C. Gentry Center, 3500 John Merritt Boulevard. Get more information at www.tnstate.edu/athlete/athlete.

David Lipscomb University fields men's and women's basketball and nine other sports, primarily against other small colleges. Games are played at the McQuiddy Gymnasium at 3901 Granny White Pike. For tickets and information call (615) 269-1795 or see www.dlu.edu/athletics.

NIGHTLIFE

They don't call it "Music City" for nothing. And despite the reputation as a country music haven, you can hear a little bit of everything here. What follows is a listing of entertainment-only venues. There may be a few that serve food, but rarely of a caliber you'd accept if the place was only a restaurant. On the other hand, many—if not most—of the restaurants in Music City also include live music. Among the best are: Bongo Java, F. Scott's, Manhattan's, and Seanachie Irish Pub. Check their information under the restaurant section.

Barbara's, 207 Printer's Alley, tel. (615) 259-2272, is known as the place where the stars hang out—and more than one has been known to get in trouble late at night there. Live music nightly with a foot-stomping dance floor and a $5 cover on weekend if Barbara feels like charging it.

Blue, 207 Printer's Alley, tel. (615) 259-2272, offers swing dancing to live and recorded music, as well as dance lessons. Hit a vintage store first because this is the place to dress up and go dancing.

The Bluebird Cafe, 4104 Hillsboro Rd., tel. (615) 383-1461, *is* Nashville. With the finest writer's nights in the city, it's the kind of club where talkers will be shushed so others can hear the music. Though it is no longer *the* place to be booked, the Bluebird still draws many celebrities—most of who will jump onstage for a song or two. Featured shows are at 9:30 p.m. every Tuesday-Saturday, and earlier ones are usually free. Cover charge varies, and there's a food and drink minimum per table, but you can stand without incurring the minimum wrath.

Boardwalk Cafe, 4114 Nolensville Rd., tel. (615) 832-5104, sits inside a shopping center, but great music of all styles comes from within.

Bourbon Street Blues Boogie Bar, 207 Printer's Alley, tel. (615) 259-2272, draws in major R&B stars like Koko Taylor for shows.

Denim & Diamonds, 950 Madison Square Shopping Center in Madison, tel. (615) 868-1557 or (615) 868-1168, is another boot-scooter. The music's hot and the crowd is hotter. Get yourself out on the horseshoe shaped dance floor to dance to the DJ's music. Cover varies depending on the night's special.

Douglas Corner Cafe, 2106 8th Ave. S, tel. (615) 298-1688, may be a hole in the wall, but you'll always find top-notch entertainment there. Look for writers' showcases, open-mikes, and featured artists most nights. Hours and cover charges vary.

Ernest Tubb Record Shop's Midnight Jamboree is the place to be Saturdays 'round midnight. This free live radio show, much like the Grand Ole Opry, features Opry stars as well as some new faces. You'll think you've gone back in time. It all takes place in the Texas Troubadour Theatre, 2414 Music Valley Dr. near Opryland, tel. (615) 885-0028. You should plan to get there by 11:30 p.m.

Exit/In, 2208 Elliston Pl., tel. (615) 321-4400, is another venue that offers a little bit of every music style in an intimate setting. Billy Joel used to play piano there before he hit the big time. Entertainment is Tuesday-Saturday 10 p.m.-2:30 a.m. with a varying cover.

Gibson's Caffe Milano, 176 3rd Ave. N, tel. (615) 255-0073, burst onto the scene a few years ago as one of Nashville's premier clubs. Known for its intimate setting and its catering to stars, celebs love to play there. It brings in major acts of all types of music and tries to have a big-name artist in residence every Monday. The Italian food's not bad either. Reservations for most acts are required. Since the Gibson Guitar Co. bought the club in 1998, it has been in transition and may become the prototype for a chain of similar clubs around the country.

Gibson's Cafe and Guitar Gallery, 318 Broadway, tel. (615) 742-6343, also owned by the Gibson Guitar Co., is a quiet coffeehouse with singer/songwriters performing. It's nowhere near the level of entertainment that Gibson's Caffe Milano offers, but it is a nice place to stop, grab a cup of coffee, and hear some music.

Graham Central Station, 128 2nd Ave. N, tel. (615) 251-3545, is a multi-level manufactured music joint featuring dancing of all types. It is bigger than most dance places, but it's a chain and feels like it. There's nothing that smacks of Music City here.

Guido's, 416 21st Ave. S, tel. (615) 329-4428, is a hole-in-the-wall (or is it hole-in-the-basement?) beneath San Antonio Taco Company. It is an incredibly small club with great rock music.

Havana Lounge, 154 2nd Ave. N, tel. (615) 313-7665, features live music, a Swing Night once a week, and a connecting cigar bar. Currently the hottest flavor in town.

Have a Nice Day Cafe, 217 2nd Ave. S, tel. (615) 726-2233.is a '60s and '70s club down to the Partridge Family bus out front and the yellow smiley face logo. The drinks and appetizers go all the way, too. (John Ritter fritters, anyone?) The music consists mostly of a DJ playing hits from decades past. But have one of those spiked Kool-Aid drinks and it won't matter.

Johny Jackson's Soul Satisfaction, 328 4th Ave. S, tel. (615) 259-3288, isn't a club unto itself, really. But on Saturday nights from 9 p.m.-2:45 a.m., Johny Jackson turns 328 Performance Hall into the ultimate soul and disco pit. Jackson doesn't just spin the discs, he creates the mood.

Mulligan's Pub, 117 2nd Ave. N, tel. (615) 242-8010, is an authentic "Dublin-style" pub, with dart boards, international beers and acts from all over—including the Old Country.

Music City Mix Factory, 300 2nd Ave. S, tel. (615) 251-8899, has it all. This four-story dance and music venue has something to please everyone in the crowd, whether it's a place to have a quiet drink or boogie the night away. Late at night, though, the crowd—both inside and outside—can get a little rough. Cover varies.

Nashville Nightlife, 2620 Music Valley Dr., tel. (615) 885-5201, is the place for bus groups to stop. There's live country music and a dance floor, but the floor's often covered with tables. Dinner shows are offered Thursday-Sunday.

Nashville Palace, 2400 Music Valley Dr., tel. (615) 885-1540, is where Randy Travis used to work in the kitchen and occasionally get on stage. They may push the prime rib and lobster, but it's really a place for good country music and dancing.

NASHVILLE NIGHTLIFE ON THE WEB

Nightclubs in Nashville change quite a bit; some of the ones listed here may be gone by the time this book gets in your hands. For the most up-to-the-minute information, try www.onnashville.com/nightclubs.

The mammoth **Opryland Hotel,** 2800 Opryland Dr., tel. (615) 889-1000, has its share of entertainment venues. **Jack Daniel's Saloon** features live country entertainment and memorabilia from Tennessee's sippin' whiskey. **The Pickin' Parlor** is just around the corner and also features country entertainment in a small club. If you'd rather dance instead of sit, the **Stage-door Lounge** includes country entertainment and a dance floor, but it's open only on occasion. If you'd rather get away from country music, the **Cascades Terrace** revolves in the middle of the water-themed portion of the hotel. Pianist Vince Cardell performs a nightly show on a special stage high above. There's also the **Delta Lounge,** tel. (615) 889-1000, offering pop and jazz. Hours and cover charges for all five vary depending on the season.

At **Pennington's,** 2401 Music Valley Dr., tel. (615) 889-0800, located at the Ramada Inn across from the Opryland Hotel, country acts compete with the big-screen TV and the happy hour buffet.

Robert's Western Wear, 416 Broadway, tel. (615) 256-7937, may look like a typical western clothes store, but the boots are pushed aside for such bands as BR5-49 every night. And heck—if you stay for the music, they might even sell you some boots.

Rodeos Dance Club, 2265 Murfreesboro Pike, tel. (615) 361-9777, is another country dance place with music spun by a DJ. Keep your eye out for specials like penny beer.

The Starlite Dinner & Dance Club, 3976 Dickerson Pike, tel. (615) 868-2147, is a traditional country getaway, somewhat of a redneck heaven. Check out the large hardwood dance floor and live music nightly, as well as karaoke on Monday, Tuesday and Wednesday. Cover charge is $4 Friday and Saturday, and free the rest of the week.

Station Inn, 402 12th Ave. S, tel. (615) 255-3307, may look like a dive, but it's a hallowed place in these parts. Just inside those four nondescript walls is born some of the best pickin' around. Acts vary and so do cover charges, but Sunday night's the real bargain—a bluegrass jam session that's absolutely free.

The Sutler, 2608 Franklin Rd., tel. (615) 297-9195, offers national and regional acts playing blues, jazz, folk, and country, as well as an easy-access bar. The music's live Mon.-Sat., and the cover is $3-5.

328 Performance Hall, 328 4th Ave. S, tel. (615) 259-3288, is one of the best small performance venues in town. Acts vary widely, from rock to alternative and country to rap, and cover charges range widely as well.

3rd & Lindsley 818 3rd Ave. S (at the corner of Lindsley), tel. (615) 259-9891, offers live R&B from local acts nightly.

Tootsie's Orchid Lounge, 422 Broadway, tel. (615) 726-0463, is another Nashville legend. Sharing a back alley with the Ryman Auditorium, the bar was once the hangout where struggling songwriters like Willie Nelson hung out with Opry stars like Dottie West. More recently, people like Terri Clark have gotten their starts there.

The **12th & Porter Playroom,** tel. (615) 254-7236, with an entrance through 12th & Porter restaurant, has some of the best eclectic bands around. It's dark, it's hip and it's usually a just few bucks to get in, depending on who's playing.

Windows on the Cumberland, at 112 2nd Ave. S, tel. (615) 251-0097, is your best bet for jazz if you want to enjoy looking out over the Cumberland River as you listen to the music.

Zanies Comedy Showplace, 2025 8th Ave. S, tel. (615) 269-0221, pulls in some of the biggest names in stand-up comedy for side-splitting shows Wednesday-Sunday. Prices typically range $7-10 with a two-drink minimum.

MORNING LIFE

Nashville Nightlife, 2620 Music Valley Dr., tel. (615) 885-5201, serves up a breakfast buffet complete with a side dish of live country music for $15.95 per person. Get there by 8 a.m.; the show is over at 10:30 a.m. Call ahead to see who is playing.

DANCE CLUBS

Dancers can scoot their boots at **Denim & Diamonds,** 950 Madison Square Shopping Center in Madison, tel. (615) 868-1557 or (615) 868-1168. The music's hot, and the crowd is hotter. Dancers take their places on the horseshoe-shaped floor to DJ music Wed.-Sat. 6 p.m.-3 a.m. and Sunday 7 p.m.-3 a.m. Cover is $3 for women and $4 for men.

One more hot country spot is **Rodeos Dance Club,** 1031 Murfreesboro Rd., tel. (615) 399-2666. It's open Wed.-Sun. 6 p.m.-3 a.m. and occasionally offers specials such as penny beer.

Southfork Saloon, 2265 Murfreesboro Rd., tel. (615) 361-9777, offers free dance lessons Sunday, Monday, and Tuesday nights 7-9 p.m. The club, with a state-of-the-art sound system and DJ, is open daily 6 p.m.-3 a.m.

The **Wildhorse Saloon,** 120 2nd Ave., tel. (615) 251-1000, features a 3,300-square-foot dance floor and a restaurant; it's also used for taping numerous TV specials. It's open daily 11 a.m.-2 a.m. After 6 p.m., the cover is $3 on weekdays and $6 on weekends.

GAY AND LESBIAN HANGOUTS

Chez Colette, 300 Hermitage Ave., tel. (615) 256-9134, attracts a lesbian clientele, but other folks are welcome. The place features karaoke on Thursday night and four television sets, which are always on when the Vandy women's teams take to the court.

The Chute Complex, 2535 Franklin Rd., tel. (615) 297-4571, one of the older gay bars in Nashville, is actually five bars—one piano, one country, one leather, and two disco. When the place is rolling, 400-800 people fill it up.

Connection Nashville, 901 Cowan St., tel. (615) 742-1166, offers drag shows every Friday and Saturday night amid the largest gay club in the entire state. This is the place for pop music dancing and country music line dancing, for gay or straight guests.

Jungle, 306 4th Ave. S, tel. (615) 256-9411, offers drag shows on Friday and Saturday nights.

World's End, 1713 Church St., tel. (615) 329-3480, attracts a mixed crowd with a bar and restaurant offering pizzas, seafood, and burgers.

Your Way Cafe, 515 Second Ave. S, tel. (615) 256-9682, attracts a lot of women with live music.

Another popular club is the **Gas Lite,** $167^1/_2$ Eighth Ave. N, tel. (615) 254-1278.

For the latest on the ever-changing scene in Nashville, go to www.nashvillegayweb.com.

WHERE TO STAY

BED AND BREAKFASTS AND INNS

Reservation Services
Bed and Breakfast About Tennessee, P.O. Box 110227, Nashville, TN 37222, tel. (615) 331-5244 or (800) 458-2421, is the oldest and the largest reservation service in the state. It represents B&Bs across the state. Call for information or reservations.

In Nashville
End O' the Bend Lodge & Landing, 2517 Miami Ave., Nashville, TN 37214, tel. (615) 883-0997, is a five-room rustic log cabin on a bluff overlooking the Cumberland River about one

mile from the Opryland Hotel. The *General Jackson Showboat* steams majestically by twice a day. Guests rent the entire cabin, which comes with fully equipped kitchen, an outdoor grill, and a great room with a fireplace. No host is on site, and no breakfast is served, but the privacy is hard to beat. Rates are $135-250. Premium-Luxury.

The Hillsboro House, 1933 20th Ave. S, tel. (615) 292-5501 or (800) 228-7851, is a gingerbread cottage built in 1904 and located between Music Row and Vanderbilt. Its three guest rooms have feather beds and private baths. The rate is $85, which includes a full breakfast. Moderate.

Savage House Inn, 167 8th Ave. N, tel. (615) 244-2229, occupies one of the very few townhouses left in the central part of Nashville. This one, built in 1852 and home to a physician whose last name was Savage, is two blocks from the Convention Center and a short walk to many downtown attractions. The six guest rooms are all decorated with antiques, some with fireplaces, and some with private baths. Rates run $65-85 and include a full breakfast. Moderate.

Nearby

Apple Brook Bed, Breakfast & Barn, 9127 Hwy. 100, Nashville, TN 37221, tel. (615) 646-5082, is a farmhouse (circa 1896) complete with pool and horse barns. It has four nonsmoking rooms, all with private baths. It's 2.5 miles from the Natchez Trace. Rates are $95-115 and include a full breakfast. Expensive-Premium.

English Manor Bed & Breakfast Inn, 6304 Murray Ln., Nashville, TN 37027, tel. (800) 332-4640 or (615) 373-4627, has two horses, which, as the innkeeper said, "If you can get a saddle on them, you can ride them." This inn occupies a 1960s brick colonial home with seven guest rooms, all with private baths. The host serves a full breakfast. Rates are $75-125. Moderate-Premium.

HOTELS AND MOTELS

Nashville, as befits the city in Tennessee most geared toward visitors, offers dozens of motel and hotel rooms, most of them belonging to the major national chains and most in the Moderate to Expensive categories. (See "Where to Stay" under "Accommodations and Food" in the On the Road chapter for a list of the franchise places and their toll-free reservation numbers.) Among the other options:

Opryland Hotel

This hotel, 2800 Opryland Dr., tel. (615) 889-1000, consists of a series of jaw-dropping lobbies fronting 2,870 rooms and suites. One of the lobbies is the Cascades, a two-and-a-half-acre greenhouse containing tropical plants and a four-story-high waterfall. These places have themselves become tourist attractions, luring all manner of gawkers. The newest such area is the dome-topped Delta, more than four acres of tropical plants, a river, and a 560-foot-long moving sidewalk.

The rooms attached to these extravagances are not as impressive, but nonetheless make up *the* place to stay in Music City. Doubles go for $209-249, plus tax. Luxury.

All the Rest

Moderate to Expensive hotels include the **Nashville MedCenter Inn,** 1909 Hayes, tel. (615) 329-1000 or (800) 777-4904; **AmeriSuites,** 220 Rudy's Circle, tel. (615) 872-0422 or (800) 833-1516; and **Drury Inn Nashville Airport,** 837 Briley Pkwy., tel. (615) 361-6999 or (800) 444-4421.

The lobbies in the gigantic Opryland Hotel have become tourist attractions themselves.

GAYLORD ENTERTAINMENT

In the Expensive to Premium range, try the **ClubHouse Inn and Conference Center Hotel,** 920 Broadway, tel. (615) 244-0150 or (800) CLUB-INN; or the **Embassy Suites Hotel,** 10 Century Blvd., tel. (615) 871-0033 or (800) EMBASSY.

The Hermitage Hotel, 231 6th Ave. N, tel. (615) 244-3121 or (800) 251-1908, is Nashville's last grand old hotel. Rates are $129-159. Also in the Premium to Luxury range are the **Guest Quarters Suite Hotel,** 2424 Atrium Way, tel. (615) 889-8889 or (800) 424-2900; **Loews Vanderbilt Plaza Hotel,** 2100 West End Ave., tel. (615) 320-1700; **Regal Maxwell House Hotel,** 2025 MetroCenter Blvd., tel. (615) 259-4343 or (800) 457-4460; **Stouffer Nashville Hotel,** 611 Commerce, tel. (615) 255-8400 or (800) HOTELS-1; **Union Station Hotel,** 1001 Broadway, tel. (615) 726-1001 or (800) 331-2123; and the **Wyndham Garden Hotel-Nashville/Airport,** 1112 Airport Center Dr., tel. (615) 889-9090 or (800) WYNDHAM.

CAMPING

Holiday Nashville Travel Park, 2572 Music Valley Dr., tel. (615) 889-4225, has 438 sites with full amenities and features tours of Music City and transportation to the Grand Ole Opry. Reservations are recommended. It's open all year.

Nashville North Camground, tel. (615) 859-0075, has 200 sites. From I-65 take Exit 98, then go a half mile south on Hwy. 31 West. It's open all year.

Music City Campground, three miles south on Hwy. 40/70, tel. (615) 793-6254, offers 152 sites, phone hookups, cable TV, and fishing. It's open all year.

Nashville/Opryland KOA, 2626 Music Valley Dr., tel. (615) 889-0282 or (800) 562-7789, has 460 sites with full campground amenities. It features reserved seats to the Grand Ole Opry and free country music shows nightly; open all year.

FOOD

Seems like Nashville has as many restaurants as it does country music stars. You can find it all within the city limits, and chances are, your worst problem will be trying to choose the right one for you—or finding a place to park if you decide to head downtown. These eateries change like traffic lights, however, so consider calling ahead.

The following was compiled by two local residents for whom eating out is a joy of life.

BARBECUE

Bar-B-Cutie, at 5221 Nolensville Rd., tel. (615) 834-6556, and 501 Donelson Pike, tel. (615) 872-0207, is cheap and easy. They even have a drive-thru, so you can get their famous pork sandwiches to go.

Corky's Bar-B-Que, 100 Franklin Rd. in Brentwood, tel. (615) 373-1020, is a bit of a drive, but it's well worth the trip. Part of a Memphis chain, this is where you'll find ribs, pork, chicken, and beef. It's open 11 a.m.-9:30 p.m. daily, and until 10:30 on Friday and Saturday nights.

Whitt's, with nine locations, is known for its old-fashioned pit barbecue cooked over hickory

coals. It's also cheap. Hours are Monday-Saturday 10:30 a.m.-8 p.m.

Mary's Old Fashion Bar-B-Q, 1108 Jefferson, tel. (615) 256-7696, is one of the oldest and best barbecue joints in town. It's open 24 hours a day, and there's no dine in, just drive-thru.

Hog Heaven is located at 115 27th Ave. N, tel. (615) 329-1234. Of course, all hogs go to heaven, and this is where their smoked butts go. They'll even deliver if your order's more than $15.

Jack's Bar-B-Que with locations at 416 Broadway, tel. (615) 254-5715, and 334 W. Trinity Lane, tel. (615) 228-9888, is one of the best places for ribs.

Tennessee's Best Barbecue, 2016 West End Ave., tel. (615) 321-3766, makes a mighty big claim, but it's one they've earned in many a contest. Especially good is the oh-so-moist turkey. Like most area barbecue restaurants, however, the side dishes are hardly worth a mention.

TOP OF THE HEAP

Arthur's, 1001 Broadway., tel. (615) 255-1494, offers elegant dining in an incredible atmosphere. Inside the beautiful Union Station Hotel, once an actual train station, you'll find fine continental dishes. Many natives consider it Nashville's most luxurious restaurant. Average price of an entree is $28.

F. Scott's, 2210 Crestmoor, tel. (615) 269-5861, is a step back in time. You can enjoy contemporary American cuisine in this 1920s art deco setting. The bar, usually abop with live jazz, is a great place to hang out while you're waiting on a table.

The Mad Platter, 1239 6th Ave. N, tel. (615) 242-2563, offers quirky but creative five-course dinners in a casually elegant atmosphere.

The Wild Boar, 2014 Broadway, tel. (615) 329-1313, is considered world-class, with awards all over the place and a 15,000-bottle wine cellar. The atmosphere can be a tad stuffy and the waitstaff too attentive, but the food is always bound to be great.

GOO GOO CLUSTERS

Hershey supposedly produced the first candy bar in 1894, and just two years later Howell H. Campbell of Nashville rolled out the first combination bar—chocolate, marshmallow, caramel, and peanuts. Allegedly dubbed the Goo Goo Cluster after the only words that Campbell's baby boy could say, the concoction has sold ever since.

Goo Goo fans can tour the Standard Candy Factory at 715 Massman Drive. Call (615) 889-6360 or (800) 231-3402 for tour information.

Those who can't wait to get to Tennessee can order Goo Goos by calling (800) 231-3402. They cannot be shipped during summer months. Go Goo Goo on the Internet at www.googoo.com.

Sperry's, 5109 Harding Rd., tel. (615) 353-0809, is intent on being what it is: a nice restaurant serving fresh seafood and steaks in a very nice part of town.

Mere Bulles, 152 2nd Ave. N, tel. (615) 256-1946, offers a piano bar, elegant atmosphere, and food that sometimes tries too hard. Ask for a seat near the back where windows overlook the Cumberland River. Many of the sauces can drown out the taste of the food, but the appetizers and desserts really shine though, as does the Sunday brunch. Reservations recommended.

The Merchants, 401 Broadway, tel. (615) 254-1892, is reasonably priced at lunch but takes on a more elegant atmosphere at dinner. Watch out for the daily specials, which usually do live up to the name "special." There's also a less formal—and less expensive—grill at the restaurant. The waitstaff may not be as attentive at the grill, but the food's just as good. The five-pepper chicken is a must.

Ruth's Chris Steakhouse, 2100 West End Ave., tel. (615) 320-0163, may be a chain, but it's a favorite among Nashville big spenders. The big hunk of butter on top of the flavorful steaks must be the reason. Dress to impress.

Jimmy Kelly's, 217 Louise Ave., tel. (615) 329-4349, is steeped in tradition, serving Nashville for almost 60 years. Set in an old Victorian home, it offers steak, veal, lamb chops and fish served in an old Southern-plantation style. The corncakes are legendary 'round here. A great place to go if you're on an expense account.

Hermitage Steak House, 4342 Lebanon Rd., tel. (615) 872-9535, is a must-do for the true steak lover, featuring wonderfully aged beef, brought to your table before cooking so you can see just how lean it is. Other than the smoked oysters on the salad bar, there's nothing fancy about this place: plain atmosphere, plain decor, and an incredibly limited menu, but man, do they know how to cook a steak. Chicken and seafood are available too. Hard as it is, try to save room for the fudge pie.

The gigantic **Opryland Hotel,** tel. (615) 889-1000, boasts a number of upscale dining establishments. **Rachel's Kitchen,** the most moderately priced restaurant there, features a buffet breakfast and soups, sandwiches and burgers at lunch and dinner. Prices range $7-15. **The Cascades** restaurant is carved out of the water-themed area. Tables are seated between plants and waterfalls on several small islands. Seafood, veal and prime rib are among the highlights. Prices run $18-30 for dinner and $9-14 for lunch. **The Old Hickory Restaurant** is the hotel's most upscale, featuring fish, chicken, salmon, and 24-ounce steaks. Only dinner is served here—prices range $18-40. Reservations recommended. **Beauregard's,** a two-story, 400-seat restaurant, serves American/Cajun-style meals, with prices at $9-15 for lunch and $18-30 for dinner. There's also **Ristorante Volare,** an Italian restaurant with prices at $15-30. Virtually all the restaurants are overpriced, as you'd expect at a bloated hotel catering to conventioneers. However, the Sunday brunch at Volare, which features miles of breakfast and lunch foods and a pound-packing table loaded with incredible desserts, is worth the $22.95 price tag. Ages 6-12 pay half price. The buffet is available Sunday 9:30 a.m.-2 p.m. Hours for all other restaurants vary depending on the season.

Despite its chronic hipness, **Sunset Grill,** 2001 Belcourt Ave., tel. (615) 386-3663, offers very moderate prices at lunch, and still fairly reasonable ones at dinner. In recent years, the Grill has become a favorite for music business movers and shakers; you can usually spot a star or two. The downside of this is that if you're a nobody, you'll be made to feel like it, especially on Friday and Saturday nights. The creative pasta dishes and desserts, however, almost make the ego blows worth enduring.

The Stock-Yard, 901 2nd Ave. N, tel. (615) 255-6464, has long lived on its slogan as the place for "sizzling steaks and sizzling stars." The food is average and a tad pricey, especially for lunch. However, the reputation and aura of this restaurant somehow live on, partly because of the older country music stars who still frequent the place.

Manhattan's, 901 2nd Ave. N, tel. (615) 255-2899, is just downstairs from the Stock-Yard and bills itself as a supper club. The club part, with big band, swing and pop music, works just fine. The supper part includes spotty service and pricey, so-so food. Go to drink, dance and—if you're feeling brave—have an appetizer. This is one of the few restaurants in town with a dress code—jackets and collared shirts are recommended.

Mario's Ristorante, 2005 Broadway, tel. (615) 327-3232, another upscale favorite, features Northern Italian cuisine. The pasta is generally reliable if you don't mind a little pretense with your pasta.

New Orleans Manor, 1400 Murfreesboro Rd., tel. (615) 367-2777, offers all-you-can-eat in grand style. The $31 buffet features seafood and prime rib, served up in an elegant Southern mansion. You can dress comfortably, though, and you might need to, given all you'll be eating.

The Bound'ry, 911 20th Ave. S, tel. (615) 321-3043, boasts the unusual. In addition to creative presentation, you can order creative foods like plank trout and grilled ostrich. It's the place to be, and the bar has become the ultimate after-work place for the Singles set.

The Melting Pot, 166 2nd Ave. N, tel. (615) 742-4970, serves fondues upon fondues. Included are cheeses, filet mignon, chicken, seafood, and chocolate. It's a nice, relaxing atmosphere, and being relaxed here is a good thing, since it takes a little time to cook your own food. It can get expensive—in the $30-40 range without drinks. But you'll have so much fun with the fondue pot that it can count as dinner and a show.

Casablanca's, 1911 Broadway, tel. (615) 327-8001, is the newest of these upscale dining joints, featuring both French and Moroccan influences. They play up the name, complete with ceiling fans spinning from the ceiling and a piano bar that beckons someone to "play it again." The food is excellent, if pricey. Good food, great wines and a little atmosphere make this place a special treat.

Shogun, 1638 Westgate Circle, Brentwood, tel. (615) 377-7977, offers dinner and the show one comes to expect at such Japanese steakhouses. But unlike some, at Shogun there is a separate dining room where you can eat if you'd rather just be served than watch someone else work. Sushi is fresh and flavorful for those who are brave enough. And the barbecue eel, tuna, and miso soup beckon the truly adventurous. Even those who play it safe won't find a bland meal. One of the best items on the menu is a plain old teriyaki chicken. Shogun earns its place on the "expensive" list by virtue of the fact that some dinners exceed $25, but if one is on a budget, it's easy to eat well for under $15, too.

EASIER ON THE WALLET

American/Southern

Hermitage House Smorgasbord, 3131 Lebanon Rd., tel. (615) 883-9525, requires a loose belt. It may be more than you're accustomed to paying for comfort food, but it's worth every penny. The buffet is light on healthy and heavy on hearty: all-you-can-eat and then some.

Monell's, 1235 6th Ave. N, tel. (615) 248-4747, is the place to go if you'd like to visit with real Nashvillians. You'll find yourself sitting at a table with people you don't know and passing bowls around. Good food in those bowls, too.

The Loveless Motel & Restaurant, a bit of a drive at 8400 Hwy. 100, tel. (615) 646-9700, is simply a Nashville tradition. Expect a Southern breakfast like you've never seen, along with some of the best fried chicken ever to hit below the Mason-Dixon. The biscuits are world-famous.

Granite Falls, 2000 Broadway, tel. (615) 327-9250, offers year-round patio dining. Expect pasta, steaks, seafood, sandwiches and the house specialty—Rattlesnake Chicken with a real bite.

Green Hills Grille, 2122 Hillsboro Dr., tel. (615) 383-6444, offers the best in traditional foods as well as some items with a creative flair. You simply *must* have the Green Hills Greens. Spinach and artichoke dip, tortilla soup and barbecue shrimp quesadillas also are at the top of this comfort-food-with-a-twist list. Lunchtime is crowded with lots of large groups of women, for whatever reason, which is not to say groups of large women.

J. Alexander's, 73 White Bridge Rd., tel. (615) 352-0981, offers nice, straightforward renditions of plain ol' American food. The house soup, a wonderfully chunky, creamy chicken, is worth the trip.

Hard Rock Cafe, 100 Broadway, tel. (615) 742-9900, single-handedly shakes Nashville out of the too-much-twang groove. The hot spot, chock full of rock memorabilia and perky waitstaff, offers all the traditional American favorites. Hard Rocks around the world can be hit or miss. This one is one of the better ones, with food fresh from the grill instead of tasting like it's been sitting waiting for a waiter to get off the phone and bring it to you.

Planet Hollywood, 322 Broadway, tel. (615) 313-7827, sits just a few blocks down from Hard Rock, but its food doesn't get quite the rave reviews. Its service runs between overbearing and nonexistent. The food is only OK, though sometimes it'll surprise you with a really outstanding special, and the memorabilia isn't much to talk about either. Go in, walk around, buy the T-shirt, say you saw the car from *The Beverly Hillbillies* movie, and eat elsewhere.

NASCAR Cafe, 305 Broadway, tel. (615) 313-7223, sits about halfway between Hard Rock and Planet Hollywood and the food likewise ends up between the two. The food is decent and fresh, if a tad pricey. The atmosphere is only for race fans, what with the racing stripes and sounds of revving engines everywhere. The small arcade, though, is worth checking out.

Pancake Pantry, 1796 21st Ave. S, tel. (615) 383-9333, lovingly referred to as the "Russian Tearoom of Nashville," is the modest eatery where major music business is done. Besides, the waitresses call you "Hon." They have great pancakes, too, served anytime. They serve lunch, but it consists mostly of greasy sandwiches. "Pancake" is in the name for a reason.

South Street, 907 20th Ave. S, tel. (615) 320-5555, is a sure-fire winner for its original pastas, Memphis-style ribs, and creative sandwiches. Don't let all the Harleys out front scare you—these are mainly Yuppies on wheels.

Jody's Dining Hall and Barcar, 209 10th Ave. S, tel. (615) 259-4875, is in the recently renovated, ultra-happening Cummins Station. Its food is an eclectic mix, and its crowd, even more so. Like a few other places in town, Jody's daily specials are usually spectacular. The "barcar" includes a couple of pool tables in the back. Most nights, it becomes a swinging supper club with dinner and dancing.

Princeton's Grille, 3821 Green Hills Village Dr., tel. (615) 385-3636, is fairly new on the restaurant scene and includes fairly standard fare. Folks cheered its arrival to Green Hills, since the area has few medium-priced places to eat. If you're hungry in Green Hills, it's passable fare, but it's not worth making a trip out here.

12th & Porter, 114 12th Ave. N, tel. (615) 254-7236, blends atmosphere and food, and both are equally interesting. With revolving funky artwork, a waitstaff that would rather be any-

where than working, and a menu including items like the spicy Pasta Yaya, it's a fun place to visit. If the signature spicy dish isn't for you, check out the creative daily calzone or a burger.

Zola, 3001 West End Ave., tel. (615) 320-7778, is more eclectic than the average Nashville eatery. It's American cuisine with a definite European influence, and the results are wonderful. The desserts are especially worth saving room for. At dinner, it's casual chic.

Laurell's, 123 2nd Ave. N, tel. (615) 244-1230, is worth a visit just for its famous crab dip. The restaurant, popular long before its historic Second Avenue location was, is a tried and true favorite. The bar and grill is known for its oysters, especially the po' boy, as well as dishes like barbecue shrimp and seafood hot brown. If you don't like seafood, though, the menu's pretty limited.

The Capitol Grille, 231 Sixth Ave. N, tel. (615) 244-3121, in the lovely old Hermitage Hotel, is not at all new—unless you count the menu, chef, and spruced-up interior. *Esquire* magazine recently listed it as one of the top 25 new restaurants in the country, and you'll find things there like grilled eggplant sandwiches, spicy crawfish tail salads, and fresh smoked salmon arranged around a potato cake. Fair warning, though: prices rise substantially at dinner.

Cafe OneTwoThree, 123 12th Ave. N, tel. (615) 255-2233, serves exotic fare like peanut-coated pork chops, Black Angus ribeyes, and mashed sweet potatoes, and you simply *must* save room for dessert. How about gingerbread cake with lemon curd, brandy-laced pot de crème, or hazelnut cheesecake? Of course, the menu here changes rapidly so all of these items may be replaced by the time you get there.

Cock of the Walk, 2624 Music Valley Dr., tel. (615) 889-1930, has plenty of swagger. The casual atmosphere mixes good eats with reasonable prices, and its proximity to the Opryland Hotel makes it a haven for tourists.

The Pineapple Room, at Cheekwood Botanical Gardens, 1200 Forrest Park Dr., tel. (615) 352-4859, offers a lovely, light menu and a beautiful, peaceful view. The gardens and museum are spectacular, and this is a fine place to get sustenance while exploring them.

Belle Meade Brasserie, 101 Page Rd., tel. (615) 356-5450, offers a little romance, along with American favorites like pasta and chicken done in contemporary style. Dimly lit at night, it's the perfect place for grown-ups but probably too quiet for the kids.

Italian

Caesar's Ristorante Italiano, 88 White Bridge Rd., tel. (615) 352-3661, is impossible to leave without hearing a little Sinatra—or having some really good, very reasonably priced Italian food. The lunch buffet is the best bargain.

Valentino's Ristorante, 1907 West End Ave., tel. (615) 327-0148, featuring Northern Italian cuisine, has been voted Nashville's favorite place for Italian. It's another place that's reasonably priced at lunch and outrageously expensive at dinner.

Basante's, 1800 West End Ave., tel. (615) 320-0534, burst onto a very crowded Italian scene with flair, more than holding its own against the two other fine Italian restaurants only a meatball's throw away. From the bread brought to the table with a balsamic vinaigrette dip to the cinnamon banana fritters, you can't go wrong here. Potato dumplings, antipasto salads and anything with pesto are highly recommended. It is next to, but not part of, the Days Inn, which makes its atmosphere only slightly better than that of a motel restaurant, but the food more than makes up for the lack of ambience.

Finezza Trattoria, 5404 Harding Rd., tel. (615) 356-9398, offers Italian with a little American thrown in. Check out the family-style cafe.

Angelo's, a tiny hole-in-the-wall in Green Hills, 4109 Hillsboro Rd., tel. (615) 383-2779, shouldn't be overlooked. There may be a few ups and downs in the side dishes from time to time, and the service may be slow, but when it comes to pastas, tortellini and the like, you won't go wrong.

Antonio's in Bellevue, 7097 Old Harding Pike, tel. (615) 646-9166, may be a drive for many visitors, but it may just offer the best pasta in town. Everything is fresh, the waitstaff excellent, and families with children are more than welcome. No wonder, then, that reservations are virtually a requirement.

Demos' Steak and Spaghetti Restaurant , 300 Commerce St., tel. (615) 256-4655, is family owned and family run. It's name says it all—pastas and steaks. There are no middle-of-the-road fans here—you either love it or hate it.

DaVinci's, 1812 Hayes, tel. (615) 329-8098, offers pizza that's a work of art. The quaint joint is known for specialties like spinach and bleu cheese pizza, oysters Rockefeller pizza, and plain old faves like pepperoni—as well as a special crust made with pasta dough.

Asian

Kobe Steaks Japanese Restaurant, 210 25th Ave. N, tel. (615) 327-9081, is the place to see it prepared before your eyes. The restaurant offers steak, chicken, and seafood. And if your party is small enough, your table might just get rounded out with some locals.

The differences between rival sushi bars may seem minor enough to the non-sushi eater, but they are the kind of things that bring devoted sushi lovers to fisticuffs. Some Music City sushiites claim **Shintomi,** 2184 Bandywood, tel. (615) 386-3022, is the best bar in town, but that may just be for its atmosphere. Others prefer **Benkay,** 40 White Bridge Rd., tel. (615) 356-6600, perhaps for its teriyaki as much as its sushi. Others will go nowhere but **Goten,** 110 21st Ave. S, tel. (615) 321-4537, and **Goten2,** 209 10th Ave. S, tel. (615) 251-4855. This may be the best place for those who love sushi to take non-sushi eaters. It offers a split personality: one side sushi, the other side Hibachi grills. And **Ichiban,** 109 2nd Ave. N, tel. (615) 254-7185, can't be overlooked, either. It scores points for its location and ultra-hip post-work crowd.

Golden Dragon, with four locations, offers the best Chinese value in town. Its lunch buffet stretches for miles, and dinner includes fresh seafood as well. Everything is kept fresh and filled. Dinner, though, for the non-seafood lover can get a tad pricey. If you don't want the crab legs and fresh shrimp that swell the buffet price at night, order off the menu.

August Moon is a perennial Nashville favorite, consistently voted the best Chinese restaurant in town. The fresh, spicy food earned the distinction. You'll find three locations, at 116 Wilson Pike, tel. (615) 371-1999; 4000 Hillsboro Pike, tel. (615) 298-9999; and 7075 Highway 70 S, tel. (615) 646-5333.

Royal Thai isn't to be ignored, either. A true value at lunch and an elegant setting for dinner, Royal Thai runs the gamut. Of course, all Thai food is spicy, but Royal Thai's mild won't set you on fire, quite. The Tom Ka Kai soup is excellent, as is the Pad Kra Pao, stir-fried with basil and onions. There are two locations, at 204 Commerce downtown, tel. (615) 255-0821, and 210 Franklin Pike, tel. (615) 376-9695.

Arirang Korean Restaurant, 1719 West End Ave., tel. (615) 327-3010, shines with its lunchtime specials, featuring as many as nine courses for mere pennies. At night, things get fancier with open-flame cooking.

Middle Eastern

Baraka Bakery, 5596 Nolensville Rd., tel. (615) 333-9285, serves Nashville's best Middle Eastern food. Check out the fresh tabouli, the fabulous stuffed grape leaves, and the desserts.

Mexican/Southwestern

La Paz, 3808 Cleghorn Ave., tel. (615) 383-5200, offers a Southwestern twist to Mexican food. You could easily fill up on the chips and green salsa alone, but save room for the meal, usually a lively twist on typical Tex-Mex.

La Fiesta, 436 Murfreesboro Rd., tel. (615) 255-0539, offers more authentic Mexican food. Though not located in the best part of Nashville, it's worth the risk just for the hot sauce. Still, lunch is a safer option than dinner.

Chez Jose, 2323 Elliston Pl., tel. (615) 320-0107, offers Mexican with a healthy twist. Everything is fresh and grilled. Many dishes are cheeseless and the beans are cooked without lard. It gets very crowded at lunch, but hang in there: The salsa bar awaits at the end of the self-service line.

La Hacienda Taqueria, 2615 Nolensville Rd., tel. (615) 256-6142, and 1019 Gallatin Rd., tel. (615) 868-8327, may not be known for the most extensive menu or the most helpful waitstaff, but the burritos have chunks of avocado and fresh cilantro. They dominate the menu, and rightly so.

San Antonio Taco Co., 416 21st Ave. S, tel. (615) 327-4322, and 208 Commerce St., tel. (615) 259-4413, is a local favorite. Featuring cheap but hearty Southwestern food, its Vandy-area location draws college students with its buckets of beer, while its downtown location features an expanded dining menu.

Texana Grill, 847 Bell Rd., tel. (615) 731-5610, offers pure Texas food. Betcha didn't even know it was a cuisine unto itself. Texas fa-vorites—including Shiner Bock beer, authentic smoked brisket, and Blue Bell ice cream—make it yippy-yi-good. Be brave and try the armadillo eggs. Smoked meats and Southwestern food make up most of the rest of the menu. A fun place to kick up your bootheels.

Irish

When **Irelands,** 204 21st Ave. S, tel. (615) 327-2967, closed in the mid-'80s, Nashvillians wept. But it was happy days again when it reopened in late 1997. Happily, the famed stake-n-biskits were back on the menu, as was the to-die-for Killarney fudge pie. Go Celtic all the way with shepherd's pie or the Irish stew—complete with lamb. Skip the bread pudding, though.

Seanachie (Shawn-uh-key), 327 Broadway, tel. (615) 726-2006, offers Irish specialties like boxty and corned beef and cabbage in a setting reminiscent of an Irish street. The waitstaff is known to get lost from time to time, but the lively music and good food makes up for it.

Pub Food

Nashville got invaded by brew pubs a few years back, and the menu is largely the same at all of them. Pizzas, burgers, soups, salads, steaks and, of course, beers of all stripes. Your choice largely depends on what's closest. **Market Street Brewery and Public House,** 134 2nd Ave. N, tel. (615) 259-9611; and **Big River Grille & Brewing Works,** 111 Broadway, tel. (615) 251-4677, are both downtown. **Bosco's,** 1805 21st Ave. S, tel. (615) 385-0050, is in Hillsboro Village; and **Blackstone Restaurant & Brewery** is at 1918 West End Ave., tel. (615) 327-9969. If location doesn't make the choice for you, a slight edge goes to Bosco's.

A more established spot is **McCabe Pub,** 4410 Murphy Rd., tel. (615) 269-9406, which offers the hands-down best burger in town, along with a homey atmosphere. Everything on the menu is better than good.

Now that Nashville has two professional sports teams, it's only fair that sports bars would follow. Among the best places to see a game while grabbing a good burger and beer are **Box Seat,** 2221 Bandywood Dr., tel. (615) 383-8018; **End Zone,** 2227 Bandywood, tel. (615) 383-4969; and **Rivalry's,** 1038 Murfreesboro Rd., tel. (615) 361-5266.

Sportsman's Grille is a small local chain that offers a mean burger—but you really ought to try the open-faced chicken sandwich or any of the creative salads. The insides of the various locations hardly deliver the woodsy atmosphere that the name implies, but you can still expect a better-than-average sports bar. You'll find the Grilles at 5405 Harding Pike, tel. (615) 356-6206; 1601 21st Ave. S—as the **Sportsman's Grille In the Village**—tel. (615) 320-1633; and 1640 Westgate Circle—as **Sportsman's Lodge**—tel. (615) 373-1070.

Jonathan's Village Cafe, 1803 21st Ave. S, tel. (615) 385-9301, in the trendy Hillsboro Village, is another good burger and sandwich joint. Good stuff, indeed. Load up on those big sandwiches and buffalo wings. You'll need your strength for hailing a waiter.

Health Food/Vegetarian

Dancing Bear, 1805 Church St., tel. (615) 963-9900, may have a childlike name, but few children would appreciate this healthy menu. Health and vegetarian foods make up much of the offerings, but there's enough diversity to keep the Bear from being called an out-and-out health food joint. That's where the Mediterranean influences show up. Look for hummus, yogurt-marinated chicken, and Greek scampi.

Peaceful Planet Vegetarian Buffet, 1811 Division St., tel. (615) 327-0661—what better description than the name itself? It's a definite must for health-food nuts, but meat-and-potato types should steer clear. It offers a nice buffet, with fresh herbs providing mild seasoning for everything. The breads are worth filling up on, too. But a warning—unlike typical buffets here on Earth, which assess a one-size-fits-all price for a run down the buffet line, the Peaceful Planet weighs the food you gather and charges by the pound.

Deli

Noshville, 1918 Broadway, tel. (615) 329-6674, is one of the hippest places for breakfast and lunch, and, though it's open for dinner, nighttime finds the place virtually empty. Fine, mile-high kosher deli sandwiches, crispy potato latkes, outstanding pickles, and fabulous knishes are highlights.

Kiddie Chow

Cafe Bambino, 734 Thompson Ln., tel. (615) 383-4383, caters to children and those who love them. Mickey Mouse-shaped grilled cheese sandwiches and an atmosphere that begs to be romped in make this a great place for families. The food is good enough to draw those without children, but if noisy kids bug you, stay far, far away.

DOWNRIGHT REASONABLE

American/Southern

At **Ham 'N Goodys,** 825 West End Ave., tel. (615) 329-0193, a ham sandwich is not just a ham sandwich. You'll find wonderful sandwiches, soups, salads, and more—including Bible verses on the menu.

Satsuma Tea Room, 417 Union, tel. (615) 256-5211, like so many places in Nashville, does meat-n-threes well, especially when accompanied by the outstanding spoonbread.

THE BEST BREAD IN TENNESSEE

Tennessee is famous for biscuits and cornbread and variations such as hushpuppies. Nashvillians, however, now have access to "artisan" bread—a stylized form of baking that originated in France. The founder of **Provence Breads & Cafe,** 1705 21st Ave. S in Hillsboro Village, tel. (615)386-0363, apprenticed himself to French bread bakers and then came to Nashville with French ovens to see if he could make it in the land of Martha White Self-Rising Flour.

This bakery produces breads that are a treat for the eye as well as the palate. Choices include classic French baguettes, rustic sourdough, challah, *fougasse* brushed with olive oil, and more. One can literally make an entire meal of one of these loaves. The bakery opens at 7 a.m. on weekdays, so travelers heading out of town can stop by and load up before they go.

The cafe does a booming lunch business with sandwiches and soup. As one customer put it, "The Good Book says that man shall not live by bread alone, but if the bread is from this place, I'm willing to give it a shot."

BONGO JAVA
AND THE NUN BUN

This coffeehouse had its 15 minutes of fame when a cinnamon bun came out of the oven bearing a remarkable resemblance to the late Mother Teresa. The "nun bun," as it was dubbed, made television appearances and was widely covered by newspapers. The Bongo Java folks, knowing a marketing miracle when they saw one, began selling Nun Bun T-shirts and other goods.

Word eventually reached Calcutta, where the real Mother Teresa was not amused. Her organization asked Bongo Java to knock it off, and the coffeehouse respectfully obeyed. The Nun Bun is still there, however, where it still draws the faithful.

Don't venture far from the daily specials, though, or you'll likely be disappointed. And fair warning: It gets very crowded at lunch and the tables are spaced elbow-length apart. Lunch only Monday- Friday.

Mack's Cafe, 2009 Broadway, tel. (615) 327-0700, is another fine place for lunch. Originally a meat-and-three greasy spoon, it saw the light and got relatively healthy. Instead of cornbread, you'll find focaccia. Black beans have replaced pinto, and shrimp tacos have replaced fish sticks. Sandwiches are a highlight, and the 1920s style building offers a nice vibe.

Sub Stop, 1701 Broadway, tel. (615) 255-6482, is worth a pit stop. You can order half or whole subs any way you like 'em, and get some good, fresh soup of the day, too. The atmosphere is merely functional, so if the weather's nice, pick up the sandwiches and head for a nearby park.

At the **Belle Meade Buffet Cafeteria,** 4534 Harding Rd., tel. (615) 298-5571, you'll find all the fresh Southern foods you can possibly eat. The place has been around since 1961, and with good reason.

Swett's, is another of Nashville's favorite cafeterias, with entrees like beef tips and veggies like sweet potatoes to fill your tummy and warm your soul. Maybe that's why they call it soul food. A big hit among the movers-and-shakers in the state capitol. Check it out at 2725 Clifton Ave., tel. (615) 329-4418, and at 900 8th Ave. N, tel. (615) 742-0699.

Sylvan Park Restaurant, 4502 Murphy Rd., tel. (615) 292-9275, and 2201 Bandywood Dr., tel. (615) 292-6449, is a longtime favorite for meats and veggies. Hours vary from site to site. The food's cheap, the calories are high, and the pies are cut in large slices.

Rotier's, 2413 Elliston Pl., tel. (615) 327-9892, is among the best eateries here, especially if you want a cheeseburger on French bread.

Elliston Place Soda Shop, 2111 Elliston Pl., tel. (615) 327-1090, serves good burgers and homey daily specials. The milkshakes are the best in town.

Brown's Diner, 2102 Blair Blvd., tel. (615) 269-5509, is a great place to have a burger and a beer. Another music biz power place.

Asian
International Market and Restaurant, 2010B Belmont Blvd., tel. (615) 297-4453, is a favorite of college students who like cheap eats. It features various types of Asian foods—you never know what you'll get one day to the next. The cleanliness can be spotty, but the food is good for what it is: cheap Asian food served in a functional market.

Mexican
Casa Fiesta, offers good, authentic Mexican food and incredible fajitas at two locations: 2615 Elm Hill Pike, tel. (615) 871-9490, and 1111 Bell Rd., tel. (615) 731-3918. Truly, some of the best fajitas in town.

Varallo's, 817 Church, tel. (615) 256-9109, or 239 4th Ave. N, tel. (615) 256-1907, is a Nashville tradition, most notably for its chili. It's served straight-up, with macaroni or tamales (or both). The chili is the best thing on the menu, though breakfast is decent, too.

Caribbean
Calypso Cafe, offers a taste of the Caribbean without the plane fare. Specialties include rotisserie chicken and a black bean salad. Hours vary depending on location, but the one at the Arcade downtown, tel. (615) 259-9631, is open only for weekday lunch. Other locations are at 2424 Elliston Pl., tel. (615) 321-3878, and 722 Thompson Ln., tel. (615) 297-6530.

Deli
Goldie's Deli, 4520 Harding Pike, tel. (615) 292-3589, is one of only two kosher delis in town. It's authentic and its sandwiches are straight up (even the hard-to-find-in-Nashville corned beef).

Coffeehouses
Bongo Java, 2007 Belmont Blvd., tel. (615) 385-5282, is about as far from a cafeteria as you can get. With a definite student/funky at-mosphere, the place offers a wonderful coffee selection and interesting sandwich combina-tions—including peanut butter and jelly on white bread.

Fido, 1812 21st Ave. S, tel. (615) 777-FIDO, is connected with Bongo Java but offers a more up-scale atmosphere. On the menu: veggie burgers, pita pizza and cornbread with sweet potato com-pote. It also offers its own coffee roasting com-pany, which services both Fido and Bongo Java.

MORE PRACTICALITIES

SHOPPING

Fine Arts and Crafts
The American Artisan, 4231 Harding Rd., tel. (615) 298-4691, offers contemporary and tradi-tional handmade crafts in a variety of media, in-cluding pottery, wood, glass, leather, metal, and small furniture.

Auld Alliance Gallery, Westgate Center, 6019 Hwy. 100, tel. (615) 352-5522, carries con-temporary landscapes and still lifes from 25 to 30 local Tennessee artists along with more far-flung folks, as well as prints and antique prints.

Collector's Gallery, 6602 Hwy. 100, tel. (615) 356-0699, in business for about 30 years, is one of the oldest in Nashville. It features 19th- and 20th-century American art in all media, but the focus is oils on canvas and watercolors. It also carries sculpture (some bronze) and features nationally known Tennessee artists, the most popular being Carl Sublett.

Cumberland Gallery, 4107 Hillsboro Circle, tel. (615) 297-0296, features contemporary art in a variety of media, including paintings, works on paper, sculpture, photography, and limited-edition prints. It specializes in emerging artists, approximately 50% of whom are from the South-eastern United States.

In the Gallery, 624A Jefferson St., tel. (615) 255-0705, across from the Bicentennial Mall, features contemporary pieces, African-Ameri-can art photography, special collections, and African antiquities.

Local Color Gallery, 1912 Broadway near Music Row, tel. (615) 321-3141, represents Ten-nessee artists with contemporary painting, sculp-ture, pottery, jewelry, and furniture. The price range for these pieces is wide, $16-3500.

Midtown Gallery and Framers, 1912 Broad-way near Music Row, tel. (615) 322-9966, carries a variety of works from local, national, and in-ternational artists in the form of ceramics, mixed media, oil paintings, acrylics, and others.

Tennessee Art League, 3011 Poston Ave. near Centennial Park, tel. (615) 298-4072, has three galleries and features original art by Ten-nesseans. A small gallery presents small works, such as eight- by 10-inch pieces on canvas, var-ious media, and sculpture.

Woodcuts, 1613 Jefferson St., tel. (615) 321-5357, offers fine art prints, figurines, cards, and other items by African-American artists.

Zeitgeist Gallery, 209 10th Ave. S, Suite

Gruhn Guitars in downtown Nashville is the place to go for a vintage guitar.

ROBIN HOOD

223, Cummins Station Building, tel. (615) 256-4805, features paintings, sculpture, and photos from emerging artists. Most are regional, with the occasional interloper from St. Louis or New York.

Music

The **Ernest Tubb Record Shops** are the place to find the newest hits and those golden oldies. The original location, 417 Broadway across from Ryman Auditorium, tel. (615) 255-7503, used to host a radio show that took to the airwaves as soon as the Grand Ole Opry ended. Newer ones are at 1516 Demonbreun, tel. (615) 244-2845, and at 2416 Music Valley Dr., tel. (615) 889-2474. Find them online at www.etrs.net.

Gruhn Guitars, 400 Broadway, tel. (615) 256-2033, is perhaps the best source of vintage guitars in the world. This store, within yodeling distance of the Ryman Auditorium, carries all manner of guitars, mandolins, banjos, fiddles, National Steel guitars, dobros, and you name it. One can spend $10,000 here on one instrument—and have several to choose from. Gruhn has a strong website with great links at www.gruhn.com.

S. Friedman Loan Office, 420 Broadway, tel. (615) 256-0909, just a few steps from Gruhn, reflects the hard-luck stories of many would-be musicians. One person's troubles can be someone else's opportunity, however. This long-time pawn shop has a good selection of used guitars and other instruments.

Lawrence Brothers, 409 Broadway, tel. (615) 256-9240, is much more of a collector's place, with lots of old stuff, vinyl, thousands of 45s, old junky music souvenirs—none of it cheap. These people are the record equivalent of an antique store as opposed to a used furniture store. The store looks as if the decoration, or lack thereof, hasn't changed in ages.

Tower Records/Video, 2400 West End Blvd., tel. (615) 327-3722, is the largest music store in town, if not the entire state.

The Great Escape, 1925 Broadway, tel. (615) 327-0646, sells used and new recorded objects of all kinds, all the way back to 78s. On sale one day were a 78 of T. Texas Tyler's "You Turned a Good Man Down" ($2) and an LP of "Kitty Wells Country Hit Parade" ($5). This place also sells all kinds of comic books, music magazines, collector cards, Star Trek stuff, used paperbacks, etc.

It's great for browsing but not for something music fans want to be certain to find.

Book Shops

The bibliophile should head for Hillsboro Village, where most of these bookstores hold court. Farther south on Hillsboro Road is Davis-Kidd, one of the biggest bookstores in the state.

Bookman Rare and Used Books, 1713 21st Ave., tel. (615) 383-6555, is the place for first editions and signed books from the famous and the obscure.

Dad's Old Book Store, 4004 Hillsboro Rd., tel. (615) 298-5880, sells autographs as well as the odd volume.

Elder's Book Store, 2115 Elliston Pl., tel. (615) 327-1867, specializes in rare books on the Civil War, Tennessee history, and first editions. It also carries Tiffany-style lamps and fine children's books.

Nearby—across the street, actually—is **Mosko's,** 2204 Elliston Pl., tel. (615) 327-2658, the place for magazine and newspaper addicts. This place has one of Nashville's largest selections of cigars, all in a humidor so big that customers can walk in it.

Davis-Kidd Booksellers, Inc., 4007 Hillsboro Rd., tel. (615) 385-2645 or (615) 292-1404 (event hotline), is the largest independent bookstore in Middle Tennessee and home to a great many literary events. They have an in-store cafe and some sort of event for kids almost every Saturday morning.

Outloud! Books & Gifts, 1805-C Church St., tel. (615) 340-0034, offers gay and lesbian titles, fiction and nonfiction, as well as music and gift items.

Tower Books, 2404 West End Ave., tel. (615) 327-8085, right beside Tower Records, is the place for books on music and various aspects of popular culture.

Specialty Shops

A.J. Martin, 2817 West End Ave., tel. (615) 321-4600, offers some of the finest estate jewelry in Middle Tennessee. It also carries African art, modern glassware, pottery, and pillowcases. Jewelry customers appreciate the fact that this place can fix antique pieces as well as sell them.

Alkebu-Lan Images, corner of 28th and Jefferson, tel. (615) 321-4111, has African -American books, art, and gifts. It carries figurines, masks, tapestries, statues, and music boxes. See the shop online at www.alkebulan.com.

Maud's Junk Store, which at press time was moving, tel. (615) 383-3411, sells American items made prior to 1960, but the real attraction here is the proprietress, one Maud Gold Kiser, author of *The Treasure Hunter's Guide,* a wonderful guidebook to Middle Tennessee's antique and junk stores. Kiser is also an expert on cleaning and restoring almost anything. See her site online at www.goldkiser.com.

The Southern Historical Showcase, 1907 Division St., tel. (615) 321-0639, offers paper items from the Civil War and antebellum times—autographs, prints, and books. Join them on the Web at www.southernhistorical.com.

The **Phillips Toy Mart,** 5207 Harding Rd. in Belle Meade, tel. (615) 352-5363, was founded in 1946 and has supplied toys to generations of Nashvillians. This family-owned place is crammed with toys, hobby items—four gauges of model trains—and all kinds of dolls.

The **Old Negro League Sports Shop,** 1213 Jefferson St., tel. (615) 321-3186, is one of the very few shops in the country devoted to the Negro National Baseball League, in which blacks played ball from 1920 through 1950. The shop sells authentic replica clothing—caps, shirts, and jackets—posters, books, pennants, and, more importantly, memorabilia from those days. A typical example of the latter is an autographed baseball from Henry Kimbro, the 1939 Negro League batting champion. Surfers can find it on the Web through www.nashville.citysearch.com.

Nashville Clothing

Nashville's performers, more than any others, are known for fancy duds. One of the good things about the surge in country music is that the performers, particularly those of the male persuasion, no longer look as if they are the eighth runners-up in a used-car-salesman look-alike contest.

Fans often cannot resist going home without a pair of boots or at least a cowboy hat. Both are items that people should buy with time and care; a great many boots bought in haste wind up in the front yard at a garage sale. The best time to buy is afternoon, when one's feet have swelled to as large as they will get.

Dangerous Threads, downtown at 105 2nd Ave., tel. (615) 256-1033, is the place for that leather-fringed dress or rhinestone-studded belt.

Flemings, 2922B West End Ave., tel. (615) 327-1252, got its start making alligator belts. American alligator products are the specialty here—boots, handbags, watchbands, etc. One can get gold and sterling silver belt buckles, as well as contemporary clothing and men's shirts. About half of the customers are music industry types.

Manuel Exclusive Clothier, 1922 Broadway, tel. (615) 321-5444, is the clothier of choice these days for country performers. The prices reflect these elevated tastes, but there's no charge to look around.

Window to the Southwest, 208 Broadway, tel. (615) 259-3362, sells authentic Native American arts and crafts, silver belt buckles, drums, flutes, artworks, and "rain sticks"—delightful sticks that when turned on end make a sound like falling rain.

Malls, Etc.

Shoppers will find about 100 stores at **Bellevue Center,** at the Bellevue Exit of I-40, tel. (615) 646-8690.

Coolsprings Galleria, south of Nashville off I-65 at Moore's Ln. in Franklin/Brentwood, tel. (615) 771-2128, has more than 115 stores.

Factory Stores of America offers outlet shopping across from the Opryland Hotel. Seventy-plus stores await just off Briley Parkway Exit 12B. Call (615) 885-5140.

Harding Mall, Harding Pl. and Nolensville Pike, tel. (615) 833-6327, contains 60 stores.

Hickory Hollow Mall, Exit 60 off I-24E, tel. (615) 731-6255, is one of Nashville's biggest shopping places. Four department stores anchor a collection of almost 200 places to spend money.

The Mall at Green Hills sits at Hillsboro and Abbott Martin Roads, tel. (615) 298-5478. It's one of the more upscale places in the area.

100 Oaks Mall, off I-65 at the Armory Dr. Exit, has about 40 stores.

Rivergate Mall, Exit 96 off I-65 N, tel. (615) 859-3456, has 150 stores.

Opry Mills is scheduled to open in the spring of 2000 with over 200 shops.

The Farmer's Market
This is a good place to get food, even if visitors don't plan to cook dinner that night. Open year-round, the market features two restaurants, fresh fruits and vegetables in season, a meat market, a seafood market, and—every weekend—a flea market. It's beside the Bicentennial Mall at 900 8th Ave. N, tel. (615) 880-2001. Admission is free.

Impossible to Categorize
On the fourth weekend of every month—and the third weekend in December—hordes of people flock to the **Flea Market** at the Tennessee State Fairgrounds, tel. (615) 862-5016. Over 2,000 vendors sell everything from junk to high-end antiques. This place can get really crowded—as many as a quarter of a million people have come here on a Saturday and Sunday. The trick, as with all mob scenes, is to get there early. The Flea Market is open Saturday 6 a.m.-6 p.m. and Sunday 7 a.m.-5 p.m.

INFORMATION

Tourist Information
The Nashville Convention and Visitors Bureau has two drop-in centers. One is downtown at 161 4th Ave. N, 37219, tel. (615) 259-4700, but a much better place to go is the one in the Arena, 541 Broadway across from the Convention Center on Broadway, tel. (615) 259-4747. Both are open during daylight hours. Another source of brochures is the rest area off I-40 east of the city.

At the airport, the **Welcome Center** in the terminal is staffed during business hours.

Disabled visitors to Nashville need only call the **Disability Information Office** at (615) 862-6492 to get information on transportation and accessible attractions, restaurants, and clubs, as well as other issues. Furthermore, the Conven-tion and Visitors Bureau puts out a publication describing the accessibility of various Nashville locations.

On the Internet, go to www.citycentral.net/nashbest/htm or www.nashscene.com. Another great site is www.nashville.citysearch.com, with maps and suggestions for restaurants near various attractions.

Local Publications
Nashville's two newspapers, the *Tennessean* and the *Banner,* have weekly entertainment sections that list events and activities. Two alternative publications are distributed free all over town. *The Nashville Scene* is the larger of the two and has more listings. *Bone* focuses on the music scene and emphasizes rock, especially "alternative" music, but also weird jazz, experimental, hip stuff, and music referred to by one listener as "lawnmower music."

GETTING AROUND

Opryland USA River Taxis, tel. (615) 889-6611, take travelers to Music Valley by way of the Cumberland River. One-way adult fare is $13.

Trolleys, tel. (615) 862-5950, roll through downtown and Music Row, and during the summer they go out to Music Valley. They leave every 15 minutes from Riverfront Park, and the fare is one dollar. Call for information. Beginning October 15, trolleys run to Music Row on Saturday only. On April 14, they resume full-time service.

The Metropolitan Transit Authority runs **city buses,** tel. (615) 862-5950. Fare is $1.40 for adults. Call for information about routes and schedules.

Call **Allied Taxi** at (615) 244-7433 or **Music City Taxi** at (615) 262-0451.

See also "Excursions and Cruises" under "Sights and Recreation," above.

HEARTLAND

INTRODUCTION

In the Heartland of Tennessee, or Middle Tennessee, as locals call it, all roads seemingly lead to, or from, Nashville and divide the region, like a pizza, into slices.

THE OLD SOUTH

As in so much of Tennessee, the geology of this area has determined its destiny. This part of Middle Tennessee lies in the Central Basin, a depression in the state's Highland Rim with such rich farmland that it grows more bluegrass than all of Kentucky combined.

Combining the rich earth with a willingness to work hard enabled antebellum plantation owners to become extremely prosperous. Their wealth expressed itself in a tradition of taste and hospitality that extends to current times. The mansions here, headed by Rattle & Snap, give a glimpse into a way of life that hardly

seems believable today. And there is no question that the families here suffered greatly during the Civil War.

The other side of that coin is that much of this prosperity came about on the backs of slaves. This part of Tennessee strongly supported secession in 1860 and even today is a strong supporter of "our Southern heritage." The Sons of Confederate Veterans has its headquarters in Franklin, and the Ku Klux Klan was founded farther south in Pulaski.

This should not suggest to the visitor that this part of Middle Tennessee is populated solely by unrepentant Confederates. Indeed, this is a most welcoming part of the state with a great concentration of bed and breakfasts, restaurants, and places to see. General Motors, which had almost every state in the country standing on its head to land the Saturn assembly plant, chose this place. Visitors, even if they aren't looking to place a car factory, will like it, too.

MUST-SEE HIGHLIGHTS

Bell Buckle has turned itself into a crafts center and a good example of how small towns can revitalize themselves.

The Hermitage, outside of Nashville, offers a good look at the life of Andrew Jackson, one of the more complex and controversial men to come from Tennessee.

Manuel's Cajun Country Store, in Milton, combines Cajun food and music in a fashion that cannot be found anywhere else in Tennessee.

Wynnewood, east of Nashville, is the largest log structure in the state and a glimpse of Middle Tennessee before the antebellum splendor.

The Carter House, in Franklin, puts a human face on the Civil War by telling how a soldier finally came home to die in his family's house.

Jack Daniel Distillery, in Lynchburg, produces Tennessee's most famous product and successfully retains that small-town feel.

Rattle & Snap, south of Columbia, is the grandest antebellum home in the state. Restored to its splendor, it sheds light on a way of life that is gone with the wind.

University of the South, in Sewanee, is the prettiest campus in the state, if not the entire South.

At **The Farm,** outside Summertown, the communal living proved not so easy.

The **Natchez Trace Bridge** over Hwy. 96 stands as a monument to design and engineering.

Savannah's **Tennessee River Museum** offers a first-class look at the area's natural history, Civil War experiences, and river way of life.

Lumpy's Malt Shop in Mount Pleasant is a fun place to eat, for kids as well as nostalgia-minded adults.

The **Monteage Assembly** is a delightful Victorian village and proof that a good idea can last for a long time.

Red Boiling Springs, a vestige of the time when people went "to take the waters," is a most restful place to stay.

Rippaville, an antebellum home in Spring Hill, is a good place to begin the exploration of the Antebellum Trail.

Aviation fans should make a beeline for the **Walter H. Beech Staggerwing Museum** in Tullahoma.

The town square of **Fayetteville,** just a few miles past Jack Daniel's, offers a great diversion.

The Route

Beginning due south of Nashville in Franklin, this route takes in the section between I-65 and the Natchez Trace Parkway.

THE WHISKEY AND WALKING HORSE TRAIL

The intersection of Sam Davis Rd. and Nissan Dr. in Smyrna says a lot about this part of Middle Tennessee. Sam Davis is one of the larger figures in The Lost Cause view of the Civil War. The young soldier was hanged as a Confederate spy because he would not tell who gave him stolen information. Nissan Drive was named in honor of the huge Japanese auto and truck manufacturer that came to this part of Tennessee in the mid-1980s.

This intersection calls to mind this area's contrasting reaction to two sets of conquerors—the Union Army and Japanese car makers. The former is still vilified in some circles, while the latter,

who came here to lay economic siege to American auto producers, were greeted with open arms.

This part of Middle Tennessee encompasses some of the state's more famous traditional products—Jack Daniel's and George Dickel whiskeys, Tennessee Walking Horses, and Gallagher guitars. It is a region where little towns have picked themselves up by their bootstraps and dusted off their history and lifestyle, making them available to a growing number of visitors, no matter what they are driving.

The Route

This route begins in Smyrna, follows I-24 southeast toward Chattanooga, then veers off to the west and confines itself to the land between I-24 and I-65.

EDGE OF THE PLATEAU

In the days before air-conditioning, Southerners who had the money and the time would escape

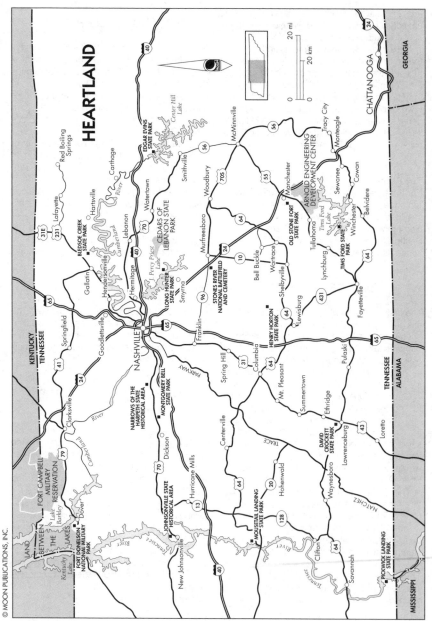

© MOON PUBLICATIONS, INC.

from the heat by coming here. High on the western edge of the Cumberland Plateau, this section of Middle Tennessee offered a variety of resorts.

It still does. Beersheba Springs and the Monteagle Sunday School Assembly still lure visitors, and walking the grounds of the University of the South in Sewanee can make visitors think they are in Oxford, England. The little railroad town of Cowan contains a house that was ordered from a Sears catalog, and Falls Mill, with its operating machinery and museum of old machinery, is perhaps the most interesting mill in the entire state.

The Route

For the most part, this route follows the western edge of the Cumberland Plateau, the high, longtime barrier to east/west travel in the state. Beginning with Edgar Evins State Park and Smithville, most of the towns and parks mentioned here lie south of I-40 and west of I-24.

EAST OF NASHVILLE

The first settlers of Middle Tennessee came to this area. Lured by tales of fertile land, the "long hunters" came first, followed by Revolutionary War veterans seeking to claim land that the state of North Carolina had paid them for their wartime service. They encountered fierce resistance from the Indians, who were not at all happy about finding these interlopers on traditional hunting grounds.

Andrew Jackson built his Hermitage here, and at one time or another visited almost all of the historic houses in the area. The area did not see a lot of action during the Civil War, and afterward Union and Confederate veterans alike would come to resorts such as Red Boiling Springs.

The Cumberland River remained an important means of transportation long after other parts of Tennessee had shifted to railroads. The Captain Ryman who found religion and then built Ryman Auditorium in Nashville ran his steamboats on this section of the river.

The Route

This route heads east along I-40 before turning north to circle back to Nashville.

THE CLARKSVILLE REGION

This region, which lies north of I-40 and west of I-24, offers some charming places and a lot of history. It is home to Tennessee's most famous ghost, one that Andrew Jackson tried in vain to exorcise. Its parks commemorate the state's fledgling iron industry, which produced the cannonballs that drove back the British at the Battle of New Orleans.

Here Union armies began their invasion of the South, taking Forts Henry and Donelson on their way to Nashville and Shiloh. Northern General Ulysses S. Grant and Southern General Nathan Bedford Forrest—warriors whose names reappear throughout the war—saw their first action in this region.

Finally, the Clarksville region contains the largest military installation in the state and the only town owned entirely by a country music diva.

The Route

The first part of this route leads the traveler northwest to Clarksville and the Land between the Lakes. The second part heads due west of Nashville to the Tennessee River and New Johnsonville, where Forrest destroyed General Sherman's supply lines.

NATCHEZ TRACE AND THE TENNESSEE RIVER

"Trace" is an old word for road. This section follows the historic Natchez Trace, taking in along the way the hometown of a Tennessee woman whose, "Howdeeee! I'm just so proud to be here!" brightened the hearts of generations of Grand Ole Opry listeners.

The route crosses over to the northward-flowing section of the Tennessee River; here is Savannah, the place where Gen. U.S. Grant was eating breakfast when he first heard the guns of Shiloh. Downstream is the town of Clifton, where people still talk about a mysterious German visitor who came on a motorcycle following the campaigns of the Civil War's greatest cavalryman.

FRANKLIN AND VICINITY

This charming town has been described as "15 miles and 100 years down the road from Nashville," a remark meant as a compliment. And it is. Franklin, unlike so many towns that let "progress" tear down their old buildings and replace them with unmitigated ugliness, took heed of the growth of Nashville and malls and interstates and then worked to protect itself.

Franklin has done a wonderful job of preserving its 19th- and early 20th-century heritage.

The entire 15-block original downtown area is listed on the National Register of Historic Places, offering the visitor a great place to shop, walk, and soak up history.

For those who like to see antebellum homes, this is the place. Franklin lies along the **Tennessee Antebellum Trail,** which runs from Nashville to Mount Pleasant. Brochures available at visitors centers or historic sites along the way point out the houses, many of which are

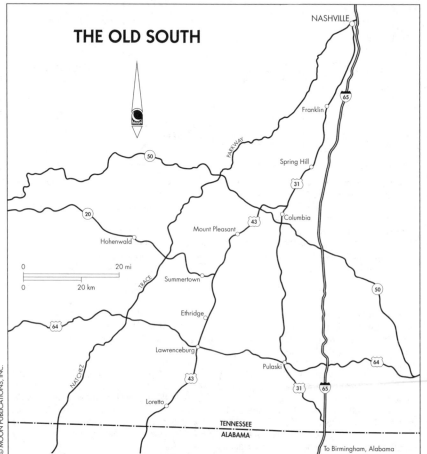

THE OLD SOUTH

NASHVILLE

Franklin

Spring Hill

Columbia

Mount Pleasant

Hohenwald

Summertown

Ethridge

Lawrenceburg

Pulaski

Loretto

0   20 mi
0   20 km

TENNESSEE
ALABAMA

To Birmingham, Alabama

© MOON PUBLICATIONS, INC.

DOWNTOWN FRANKLIN

1ST AVENUE NORTH · 1ST AVENUE SOUTH

REBEL'S REST CIVIL WAR MUSEUM AND ARTIFACT SHOP

HIRAM MASONIC LODGE

2ND AVENUE NORTH · 2ND AVENUE SOUTH

CHAMBER OF COMMERCE AND TOURISM

3RD AVENUE NORTH · 3RD AVENUE SOUTH

THE EATON HOUSE

COURTHOUSE

4TH AVENUE NORTH · 4TH AVENUE SOUTH

NORTH MARGIN STREET · SOUTH MARGIN STREET · BRIDGE STREET · MAIN STREET · CHURCH STREET

5TH AVENUE NORTH · 5TH AVENUE SOUTH

ST. PAUL'S EPISCOPAL CHURCH

COLUMBIA AVENUE · FAIR STREET · MARGIN STREET

CARNTON PLANTATION

MCGAVOCK CONFEDERATE CEMETERY

LOTZ HOUSE

CARTER HOUSE

SHORTER CHAPEL A.M.E. CHURCH

CHURCH STREET

NOT TO SCALE

© MOON PUBLICATIONS, INC.

still in private hands. A more detailed guide is the excellent *Touring the Middle Tennessee Backroads,* by Nashville judge Robert Brandt. Another good resource for the entire trail is the *Tennessee Antebellum Trail Guidebook,* by David R. Logsdon, which relates history and stories about houses and other points of interest.

HISTORY

Founded in 1799, the town was named for Benjamin Franklin. Many of the early settlers of Williamson County were Revolutionary War veterans who were given land for their service to their country. This patriotic spirit surfaced again during the Mexican War, when, it is said, every single, able-bodied man in this county joined the army. Such love of country—or willingness to get into a fight—caused Tennessee to be dubbed "The Volunteer State."

Ideal for farming, Williamson County, of which Franklin is the seat, became by the Civil War one of the wealthiest counties in the state. Using slave labor, plantation owners amassed fortunes with which they built large houses that still sit in the town and along surrounding roads.

Franklin lay in the way of Confederate General John Bell Hood's ill-fated effort to attack Nashville. Going against the judgment of his officer corps, on November 30, 1864, he ordered an attack on Union troops who were dug in at Frankin. The resulting battle was one of the bloodiest of the war, though not very well known except to Civil War buffs.

Williamson County has a rich musical heritage. Brothers Sam and Kirk McGee were one of the earliest duos on the Grand Ole Opry. Lasting through the years, they were the first act to play in the new Opryhouse in Nashville. Franklin is the birthplace of Jack Anglin, half of the country duo Johnnie & Jack, who reached success in the '50s and '60s. Robert Lunn, whose Opry specialty was the talking blues, also came from Franklin. Nowadays many country music figures live in Williamson County.

Tennessee Walking Horse fanciers revere Franklin as the home of Midnight Sun, two-time champion and legendary sire of a string of subsequent champions.

SIGHTS

Downtown

Franklin is best seen by foot. A good place to start is the **Williamson County Chamber of Commerce and Tourism,** on the square at the corner of Main St. and 2nd Ave. S, tel. (615) 794-1225. Here one can get brochures elaborating on the Battle of Franklin and local sights. Highlights of the latter include the **Courthouse,** which was built in 1859 and features four cast-iron columns.

Eaton House, an 1818 federal townhouse down from the square on 3rd Ave. N, was home to John and Peggy Eaton, whose courtship and marriage provoked endless scandal in Washington when John served as Andrew Jackson's secretary of war. Peggy was a beautiful widow whose father owned the boardinghouse in which Eaton lived while in Washington. The two were married only four months after Peggy's first husband died, and she was reputed to be pregnant with Eaton's child when the two were wed. She wasn't, but this ugly rumor set tongues wagging in the capital, and the Eatons were shunned by polite society. Knowing the pain of false gossip about marriages, Jackson championed the

FRANKLIN

Eatons, and this made things worse. Finally John Eaton resigned and returned to Franklin. Jackson was a frequent guest here. Now a law office, the house is not open to the public.

The **Hiram Masonic Lodge,** on 2nd Ave. S, is a Gothic structure built in 1823 for Tennessee's first Masonic organization. At that time it was the only three-story building in the entire state. In 1827 the state's first Episcopal church was organized here as well, and in 1830 Pres. Andrew Jackson, his secretary of war, and others negotiated a treaty here with the Chickasaw.

The story of the Civil War experiences at **St. Paul's Episcopal Church,** at the corner of 5th Ave. N and Main St., could be titled "Why They Hated the Yankees For So Long." The first and oldest Episcopal church in Tennessee, this church, built in 1831, was heavily damaged during the occupation by Northern troops. The pews, pulpit, and furnishings were hacked up for firewood or used as horse troughs. Organ pipes were tossed into the street, fires were built on the floor, and the tower was used as a smokestack. Luckily, the silver and church records were buried where the marauders could not find them, and after the war the church was restored. The slave balcony was taken down, and in 1915 Tiffany windows were installed. It is open to the public.

Another house of worship, **Shorter Chapel,** 255 Natchez St., tel. (615) 790-6611, is the oldest African Methodist Episcopal Church in the county. Slaves made the bricks before the war, soldiers used it as a hospital during the war, and freed slaves claimed it as their own after the war.

A more secular delight is the **Franklin Cinema,** 419 Main St., tel. (615) 790-7122, a restored 1936 movie house in which patrons can sit on couches or chairs and have pizza and beer while watching foreign or art films. The *Rocky Horror Picture Show* is on tap every Friday night at midnight.

Historic Houses Outside Town

Outlying places of interest begin with **The Carter House,** 1140 Columbia Ave., tel. (615) 791-1861, which holds a particularly poignant story of the Battle of Franklin. The house was built between 1828 and 1830, and by the time of the Civil War the Carter family consisted of the father, three sons, and four daughters. After the attack on Fort Sumter, the brothers all enlisted in the Confederate army. One was captured and released to come home, and one was shot at Shiloh and discharged. Tod, second of the brothers, was captured at Missionary Ridge, yet managed to get back in action in the army under Gen. John Bell Hood.

Following Hood's dream of taking Nashville, Tod marched toward his home. He had seen neither his family nor his home for three and a half years. The Union army, under Gen. John Schofield, dug in around the town of Franklin, using the Carter House as headquarters while the family took shelter in the basement.

Approaching his hometown, Tod could see Carter House behind the enemy lines. With the others, he charged the entrenched Federals, and with them he fell. When dawn rose on the horrible battle scene, word came to the family that Tod lay wounded on the Federal breastworks. Picking their way through the dead and the wounded, the family sought Tod. Finding him, they used an overcoat to carry him home, where despite their ministrations he died two days later.

The Carter House presents a video and model of the battle, a museum, and a guided tour of the house and grounds. Admission is $7 for adults, $5 for seniors, and $2 for children under 13.

Lotz House War Between the States and Old West Museum, 1111 Columbia Ave., tel. (615) 791-6533, was built in 1858 by Albert Lotz, a German woodworker and piano maker who with his family took shelter in the Carter House during the Battle of Franklin. Afterward the wounded from both sides were treated here. Now open to the public as a museum, the house

contains an extensive collection of uniforms, flags, weapons, and artifacts of the war, especially of Gen. Nathan Bedford Forrest, the "Wizard of the Saddle." Among items on display are his wedding silver, one of his wife's dresses, family Bibles from three generations, and photos. Other exhibits contain items from the Indian wars, such as weapons, photos, and battle shirts. Admission is $5 for adults, $4 for seniors, and $1.50 for children under 12. Visit online at www.lotzhouse.org.

While Carter House served as Union headquarters, **Historic Carnton Plantation,** at 1345 Carnton Lane, tel. (615) 794-0903, was a hospital for the Southerners. The house was built by a former mayor of Nashville about 1826 and was named for his father's house in Ireland, which in turn came from the Gaelic version of "cairn," a pile of stones to commemorate an event or individual. The name proved prophetic, for when John Bell Hood ordered the suicidal charges on the Union troops dug in at Franklin, the wounded and the dead were carried here. The bodies of four Confederate generals—including Irish-born Patrick Cleburne—were laid out on the back verandah.

Inside, the husband and wife of the house rolled up their carpets and tended to the wounded as best they could. Army surgeons sawed off arms and legs in the parlor, and blood stained the wooden floors.

Behind the house is the **McGavock Confederate Cemetery,** where are buried 1,481 bodies from the battle. The cemetery remains in private hands and is one of the largest Confederate

The son of Carter House almost made it home after an absence of three and a half years.

BRIAN BARDWELL

THE BATTLE OF FRANKLIN

The Battle of Franklin is not considered one of the important engagements of the Civil War—James McPherson's *Battle Cry of Freedom* gives it only two paragraphs—yet the toll was horrendous: Confederates alone suffered more than 6,000 casualties, with 1,750 dead, six generals killed, one captured, and five more wounded.

The battle took place late in the war. By the middle of November 1864, Union General Sherman had defeated the Confederate forces under John Bell Hood, burned Atlanta, and was sweeping toward Savannah. The situation facing the Confederacy could be compared to the physical condition of Hood, whose left hand was paralyzed from a wound at Gettysburg and who had lost his right leg at Chickamauga.

Despite the debilitation of his body, however, the general envisioned sweeping north through Tennessee, invading Kentucky, and then heading east to rendezvous with Lee and defeat the Northern forces. Hood moved into Tennessee and headed for Nashville, where 60,000 Northern troops awaited Hood's 40,000 men.

When 30,000 of the Northerners under the command of Gen. John Schofield came out to meet Hood, the Confederate general tried and failed to do an end run on them. Schofield's forces skirmished with Hood's at the Duck River in Columbia, then once more at Spring Hill. In preparation for the larger attack he knew would come, Schofield retreated during the night of November 29-30 and dug in at Franklin.

Franklin was a good place to do so. The Union had occupied the town for almost three years and had time to build substantial entrenchments. The Harpeth River off to the east prevented Southern troops from attacking on that side, and Schofield had plenty of artillery.

Hood made his headquarters on Winstead Hill, two miles south of town. His men faced a charge across open ground against well-dug-in defenders who were amply supported by artillery. The Southerners' own cannons were still on the road behind them. Nonetheless, shortly after 4 p.m. on the afternoon of November 30, Hood ordered his men to attack.

Their charge was more difficult than Pickett's famous one at Gettysburg, yet these men persevered for five hours. The Southerners rushed the fortifications 13 times. At one point troops under the command of Irish-born Patrick Cleburne broke through the federal lines but were driven back. Cleburne was killed in the process.

As midnight approached, the Union troops pulled back and headed for Nashville, where even greater fortifications would protect them. They left a scene of terrible carnage. Army surgeons working furiously at the Carnton plantation house south of town and piled up wagonloads of amputated limbs.

The battle of Franklin, followed by the defeat at Nashville and the loss of Savannah to Sherman, made most people in the South realize that their struggle was almost over, and that the Confederacy was doomed.

---

resting places in the country. Carnton Plantation is being restored to its pre-war appearance. Admission is $7 for adults, $5 for seniors, and $3 for children six to 12.

South of town along Hwy. 31 is the **Winstead Hill Lookout,** from which John Bell Hood launched the Battle of Franklin and from which he watched the defeat. Admission is free.

ENTERTAINMENT AND EVENTS

On the Stage
The **Bunganut Pig Pub and Eatery,** at 1143 Columbia Ave., tel. (615) 794-4777, offers live entertainment from blues to bluegrass every night.

Jammin' Java, 117-B 5th Ave. N, tel. (615) 591-4888, is a Christian coffeehouse with live music every night. Lunchtime brings forth salads and sandwiches.

The **Pull-Tight Players,** 202 2nd Ave., tel. (615) 790-6782, offer community theater. Call for information and reservations.

Main Street Festival brings more than 250 craftspeople, entertainment, and food to downtown the last full weekend in April. Call (615) 790-7094 for details.

House Tours
Heritage Foundation Town & Country Tour of Homes, on the first weekend in May, gives visitors a chance to tour National Register man-

sions that are open at no other time. Admission is $12 in advance and $15 the day of the tour. Call (615) 591-8500.

Carter House Candlelight Tour of Homes, tel. (615) 791-1861, on the first weekend of December takes visitors to homes, churches, and other buildings, all lit by candles and decorated.

Festivals and Fairs

Carnton Plantation Symphony on the Lawn and Picnic Competition, on the second Sunday in June, brings the Nashville Symphony to town. The annual picnic has a different theme every year, and diners are invited to bring their finest fixin's to compete. Call (615) 794-0903.

Franklin Jazz Festival brings traditional jazz, Dixieland, and big-band music to the town square on the first weekend in August. Admission is free. Call (615) 790-7094 for information.

Dickens of a Christmas, downtown on the second weekend of December, features carolers in Victorian costumes, horse-drawn carriage rides, and "living windows" of craftspeople. Call (615) 790-7094.

WHERE TO STAY

Bed and Breakfasts and Inns

Blueberry Hill, 4591 Peytonsville Rd., Franklin, TN 37064, tel. (615) 791-9947, sits on top of the hill with spectacular views of the surrounding hills and valleys. The original section of the house replicates federal architecture. The two guest rooms, with private baths, are furnished with four-poster beds, gas log fireplaces, loveseats, and televisions. Rates are $70-80 and include a full breakfast and snacks. Find them online at www.bbonlin.com/tn/blueberry. Moderate.

Magnolia House Bed and Breakfast, 1317 Columbia Ave., Franklin, TN 37064, tel. (615) 794-8178, was built on the site of the Battle of Franklin in 1905 and was adapted to a craftsman style in the early 1920s. The four bedrooms are furnished with antiques, and a sitting area has a TV, books, magazines, and games. The host serves breakfast in the formal dining room. Rates run $80-95 per night. Check them out online at www.bbonline.com/ten/magnolia. Moderate-Expensive.

Inns Nearby

Built in the mid-1800s, **A Homeplace Bed and Breakfast,** 7286 Nolensville Rd., Nolensville, TN 37135, tel. (615) 776-5181. A two-room suite on the second floor comes with wash basins in each room and a shared bath, canopy beds, and fireplaces in each room. The parlor suite has a fireplace, floor-to-ceiling bookcases and a private bath. Wheelchairs are available. The separate Victorian Cottage offers a private bath and a small kitchen. Rates are $75-85 and include breakfast. Moderate.

Old Marshall Inn, 1030 John Williams Rd., tel. (615) 591-4121 or (800) 863-5808, lies east of town off Hwy. 96. The house was built in 1865 and has been restored to offer two rooms and a suite. Rates are $85-150. See the inn online at www.rrv.net/web/marshall. Expensive-Premium.

Peacock Hill Country Inn, 6994 Giles Hill Rd., College Grove, TN 37046, tel. (615) 368-7727 for information and (800) 327-6663 for reservations, is an antebellum farmhouse and luxury country inn 18 miles southeast of Franklin on Farm One, a working cattle and horse farm. The inn has 10 new bedrooms with private baths that include whirlpools and showers. Some guest rooms have fireplaces, and a two-story 1850s log cabin is available. Rates run $125-225, including a full country breakfast by the fireside or on the porch. Fireside suppers are available with notice, and horses can be boarded overnight in the stables. See them online at www.bbonline.com/tn/peacock. Premium-Luxury.

Sweet Annie's Bed & Breakfast & Barn, 7201 Crow Cut Rd. SW, Fairview, TN 37062, tel. (615) 799-8833. Personal fitness workouts are available, as are a hot tub, and a pool in season. The house has two guest rooms that share a bath. Travelers with horses will find six stalls, paddocks, and a pasture. Two horses are available for riding. The spread is near the 800-acre Fairview Nature Park and convenient to the Natchez Trace riding trail. Room rate is $70 and includes a full country breakfast. Moderate.

Xanadu Farm, 8155 Horton Hwy., Triune, TN 37014, tel. (615) 395-4771, is for horse lovers. This cowboy country cottage was an old servant's quarters and is on a working horse farm in Triune, 13 miles east of Franklin. Outside is a rustic picnic shelter near a one-and-a-half acre pond stocked for fishing; hiking or horseback riding trails are nearby. But the real focus at Xanadu is horses. The barn is newly refurbished with 28 stalls. Guests can bring their own feed and hay or use Xanadu's. The staff will clean the stalls each day. Rate is $95 per night, including continental breakfast. Expensive.

Motels

Options are: **Best Western Franklin Inn,** Hwy. 96 East and I-65, tel. (615) 790-0570 or (800) 251-3200; **Budgetel Inns,** 4207 Franklin Commons Court, tel. (615) 791-7770 or (800) 428-3438; **Comfort Inn,** 4206 Franklin Commons Court, tel. (615) 791-6675 or (800) 228-5150; **Franklin Holiday Inn Express,** Hwy. 96 E and I-65, tel. (615) 794-7591 or (800) 465-4329; or **Best Western Goose Creek Inn,** I-65 and Peytonville Rd., tel. (615) 794-7200 or (800) 528-1234.

Camping

Goose Creek Inn, at I-65 and Peytonville Rd., tel. (615) 794-7200 or (800) 528-1234, has 10 RV sites next to the motel, none for tents. It's open all year.

FOOD

Barbecue

Herbert's Bar-B-Q, at 111 Royal Oaks Blvd., tel. (615) 791-0700, is famous for its corn light bread. The proprietor, who dishes up pork, ribs, and chicken barbecue, emphasizes that his place serves "inside meat"—no skin or fat.

West Side Ribs & Barbecue, 224 New Hwy. 96 W, tel. (615) 790-6787, serves barbecued beef brisket, chicken, ribs, turkey, and its famous stuffed baked potatoes.

All the Rest

Antonios, 119 5th Ave. N, tel. (615) 790-1733, serves Italian cuisine including veal Marsala, snapper Portuguese, pasta dishes, and fresh salmon on weekends.

Bunganut Pig Pub and Eatery, 1143 Columbia Ave., tel. (615) 794-4777, is a fun place to go. The complete menu includes shepherd's pie, fish and chips, and American fare such as steak, chicken, pasta, salads, and sandwiches. There's a full bar. Live entertainment from blues to bluegrass is offered every night.

Dotson's Restaurant, 99 E. Main St., tel. (615) 794-2805, serves plate lunches of country cooking seven days a week.

Dumplin's Bakery, in Maples Shopping Center at 1010 Murfreesboro Rd., tel. (615) 791-0051, features freshly baked cinnamon rolls, Danish, muffins, cookies, pies, healthful desserts, specialty cakes, and cheesecakes.

Fourth and Main, Main St. and 4th Ave., tel. (615) 791-0001, offers upscale cuisine with items such as portobello mushroom sandwiches and pan-glazed salmon. A very good place for lunch.

H.R.H. Dumplin's of Franklin, 428 Main St., tel. (615) 791-4651, serves lunch-only specials such as homemade chicken 'n' dumplings, casseroles, quiches, soups, salads, sandwiches, its famous rolls, and pies and cakes.

Magnolia, 230 Franklin Rd. at The Factory, tel. (615) 791-9992, is one of the more upscale restaurants this side of Nashville. Dinner entrees run $16-35 and include domestic lamb chops crusted with Creole mustard, served with roasted garlic and roasted red potatoes perfumed with rosemary. Upstairs is a cigar bar. No country cookin' here.

Merridee's Bakery and Restaurant, 110 4th Ave., tel. (615) 790-3755, is a "scratch bakery" and small restaurant. Baked goods are the specialty here, but the restaurant serves sandwiches and soups.

MORE PRACTICALITIES

Shopping

One of the more exciting developments in the Franklin area is **The Factory,** a renovation of a 46-acre industrial site that once cranked out MagicChef ranges north of Franklin along Hwy. 31. Now home to Magnolia, a very upscale restaurant, when completed it will house shops, a "light jazz" club, coffeehouse, art galleries, antique outlets, and a variety of other shops.

Earl's Fruit Stand, 95 E. Main St., tel. (615) 794-5212, sells fresh produce from local farms as well as jams, jellies, sorghum, and shrubbery. In October it kicks into overdrive, with a petting zoo, painted pumpkins, and at least one monstrosity of a pumpkin of more than 700 pounds.

Franklin Antique Mall, 251 2nd Ave. S, tel. (615) 790-8593, occupies a building that used to house a mill and, at the turn of the century, an ice house. Now it holds something like 18,000 square feet of antiques.

Franklin Booksellers, 118 4th Ave. S., tel. (615) 790-1349, is a good source of historical books about the area.

The Harpeth Antique Mall, 529 Alexander Plaza, tel. (615) 790-7965, brings together about 80 dealers. Next door is the **Heritage Antique Mall,** 527 Alexander Plaza, tel. (615) 790-8115.

Magic Memories, 345 Main St., tel. (615) 794-2848, offers a good supply of Civil War relics, such as saddles, swords, and buttons. A Southern sword goes for about $1000, while a similar Yankee item costs $800. The store also sells books, cards and prints.

Patchwork Palace, 340 Main St., tel. (615) 790-1382, is a quilter's paradise. More than 500 antique and not-so-old quilts are usually on hand, as are quilt-related crafts and folk art.

Rebel's Rest Civil War Museum and Artifact Shop, 212 S. Margin St., tel. (615) 790-7199, deals in high-end artifacts and other items—often in better shape than those in museums. The owner displays his personal collection of 2,796 kinds of bullets of the estimated 5,500 varieties used in the war. Also on display is a collection of tinware. Perhaps the most unusual item is a brass Parrott artillery fuse that collided with a 58 caliber Minie ball. Civil War buffs can buy authentic bullets, tinware, firearms, sabers, glassware, and bullets. An authentic Confederate uniform sells for $25,000.

Information

Williamson County Visitor Information Center, just off the square at 209 E. Main St., tel. (615) 591-8541 or (800) 356-3445, offers various brochures, including a walking tour of the town. Visit them online at www.phoenix.w1.com/franklin.

SOUTH TO SPRING HILL

Now home to an enormous General Motors plant that produces Saturn automobiles, Spring Hill is more famous in Civil War circles as one of the great lost opportunities of the lost cause.

Late in the war, after Atlanta had fallen and Union General Sherman's troops were pillaging their way toward Savannah, Confederate General John Bell Hood turned his army in a last-ditch effort and headed for Nashville. Between him and the capital of Tennessee was a Union army commanded by Gen. John Schofield, whose job it was to slow Hood down. Schofield retreated to Columbia, thinking Hood would attack him there.

In a shrewd move, Hood bypassed Schofield and got between the Union army and Nashville, then bedded his troops down for the night. He was in a good position—he could move on to Nashville or attack Schofield from the rear.

Schofield realized he had been outmaneuvered and frantically marched his troops north during the night in an effort to get back between Hood and Nashville. Fully expecting to get attacked when they approached the Southerners, the Union soldiers quietly walked so close past the encamped Confederates that they could easily hear conversations around the fires. The Yankees passed by unmolested, and Schofield's entire army got back into position. When the sun rose, the Yankees were in Franklin, where they would later devastate the hapless Hood.

Sights

Saturn Welcome Center, 100 Saturn Parkway, tel. (931) 486-5440, www.saturn.com, introduces visitors to the Saturn automobile manufacturing plant, built in 1986. Saturn now employs more than 8,200 people in its approximately 2,400-acre plant and has produced more than a million cars. It was designed to preserve the rural and historical surroundings, and this huge plant is almost invisible from Hwy. 31 because of the landscaping and building colors. Farming continues on the plant site, including more than 600 acres of planted corn, soybeans, barley, and shear. And more than 300 acres are planted in mixed grasses and alfalfa. Saturn received the "1987 Industrial Conservationist of the Year" award for its efforts to reduce the environmental impacts of the largest private construction project in the history of Tennessee. Admission is free. To reserve a spot on a tour, call (931) 486-5083.

Rippavilla, 5700 Main St. across from the Saturn plant, tel. (931) 486-9037, was built in 1852 and was used as headquarters by both sides during the Civil War. The day of the Battle of Franklin, Confederate General John Bell Hood and his staff had breakfast here, and before the day was over, five of those generals were killed. The house has been restored to its 1850s appearance with period furniture and includes a gift shop and a museum. Admission is $5 for adults, $4 for seniors, and $3 for children six to 12.

Nearby is **Oaklawn,** 3331 Denning Ln., tel. (931) 486-9037, a brick home built in 1835 and where Gen. John Bell Hood spent the night when an entire Union army sneaked past him. The house was bought in the 1970s by country crooners George Jones and the late Tammy Wynette, who inflicted shag carpeting on the floor where Civil War generals had walked. To install the carpet, the bottoms of the 140-year-old doors were sawn off and put out in the trash. A sharp-eyed local woman retrieved the strips of wood and triumphantly returned them when the house passed into the hands of a more history-minded owner. Now properly restored to the way it appeared on the fateful night while Hood slept, the view of Oaklawn offers visitors very little of anything from the 20th century. To get there from Rippavilla, go south on U.S. 31 for 0.2 mile, then turn left on Denning Lane. A 2.5-mile drive leads to the mansion. While this house is open to the public on occasion, most of the time it isn't, so visitors should not invade the driveway.

Events
Every September in odd-numbered years, the Sons of Confederate Veterans stages a large reenactment. As many as 50,000 spectators gather to watch 11,000 reenactors clash. This event is complete with authentic weapons and period costumes. Call (615) 791-6533 for details.

Accommodations and Food
Try the **Holiday Inn Express,** Hwy. 31, tel. (931) 486-1234 or (800) HOLIDAY.

Early's Honey Stand, on Hwy. 31, tel. (931) 486-2230 or (800) 523-2015, modestly claims to be "The South's Most Famous Old-Time Eating House." Here the visitor can load up on country ham, bacon, smoked sausage, ribs, and barbecue. Other items include jams and jellies, stone-ground flour and cornmeal, soups, and cheese.

Information
Maury County Convention & Visitors Bureau, no. 8 Public Square, Columbia, tel. (931) 381-7176 or (800) 381-1865, is open Mon.-Fri. 8 a.m.-5 p.m. Visit online at www.springhilltn.com.

COLUMBIA AND VICINITY

With its rich farmland, Maury County was quickly settled in the first decade of the 1800s. Within 20 years Columbia had aspirations of becoming the state capital, and by 1850 it was the third-largest town in the state, second only to Memphis and Nashville. Not having a navigable river held Columbia back, but by 1860 the county was the wealthiest in Tennessee, as the mansions still standing here demonstrate. One of the wealthiest families here was the Polks. James K. Polk became the 11th president of the country, and his cousins owned huge plantations outside of town.

William Faulkner once wrote that a mule will work patiently 10 years for the chance to kick its owner once. Many old-timers hereabouts would understand that statement, for Columbia used to be the mule capital of the world. Thousands of mules were traded each year, and it all culminated with **Mule Day,** which in 1939 boasted "1,000 girls on 1,000 mules." Although no longer celebrated with such de Millean spectacle, Mule Day is still Columbia's biggest event.

SIGHTS

James K. Polk Home
Most visitors to Columbia make a beeline to the Polk Home, 301 W. 7th St., tel. (931) 388-2354, www.jameskpolk, which was built by Polk's father in 1816 while the future president was off at college. James and Sarah Polk did not live for very long in the house, but it contains many pieces of their furniture and other items that they used. Admission is $5 for adults, $4 for seniors, and $1.50 for age six to 18.

THE DARK-HORSE CANDIDATE

Like all presidents from Tennessee so far, James K. Polk was actually born in North Carolina. He came to Tennessee in 1806, when he was 11 years old. He returned to North Carolina to go to the university there, then studied law with an attorney in Nashville.

In 1823 his political career began with his election to the Tennessee legislature, and it was through politics that he met his wife, Sarah Childress. She was well educated for a woman of that day and took an active role in her husband's career. The couple never had children, possibly because of a urinary tract operation that Polk underwent as a boy.

Polk was elected to a seat in Congress in 1825 for the first of seven terms, and he rose to become speaker of the house 1835-39. Polk was a strong supporter of Andrew Jackson, even to the point of backing New Yorker Martin Van Buren, Jackson's hand-picked successor, over Tennessean Hugh Lawson White for the 1836 presidential race. This struggle split the Democratic Party and led Jackson's opponents to create the Whig Party. Polk's loyalty to Jackson came back to haunt him, for in 1839 he was elected governor of Tennessee, but he lost the office in the next two elections largely because of the Whigs' efforts.

By 1844, the Democratic Party was still split, with Martin Van Buren of New York, John C. Calhoun of South Carolina, Lewis Cass of Michigan, and James Buchanan of Pennsylvania battling it out for the nomination. Delegates at the convention in Baltimore agreed that if no clear winner emerged the nomination would go to New Yorker Silas Wright, with Polk as the vice presidential candidate. Wright refused the nomination, however, and on the ninth convention ballot, Polk was unanimously elected. His name did not appear on the first seven ballots, and Polk became the first "dark-horse" candidate to win a presidential nomination.

Polk defeated Henry Clay for the presidency, becoming the only former speaker of the house ever to do so, but he did not carry Tennessee. Although he lacked any sort of mandate, he came to the White House aiming to stay one term and to accomplish four goals: to acquire California for the United States, to settle the boundary of Oregon, to reduce the tariff, and to set up an independent treasury. Setting a workaholic pace, he accomplished all four. His annexation of Texas began the two-year Mexican War, and the U.S. victory led to the acquisition of even more territory. During his administration the Department of the Interior, the naval academy, and the Smithsonian were founded.

At five feet six inches, James Polk was a short man, but he was renowned as "the Napoleon of the stump," a vociferous speaker who could readily dish out ridicule and sarcasm to his opponents. Because he was so short, his entry to a room during White House functions would often go unnoticed, to the great annoyance of his wife. She is said to be the person who established the custom of playing "Hail to the Chief" when the chief executive enters a room.

Polk left Washington utterly drained. Two portraits in the Polk home in Columbia show what four years in office did to his appearance. His term ended March 14, 1849, and a little more than three months later he died in Nashville. He was 53 years old. Sarah Polk returned to Nashville, where she lived until her death in 1891. During the Civil War, when so much destruction was done to local mansions, troops from both sides left the Polk house.

Polk is not one of the well-known presidents, but his sense of purpose and effectiveness rank him as one of the better ones. A 1996 poll of historians ranked Polk as one of the "near great" presidents, alongside Jefferson, Jackson, T. Roosevelt, and Truman. Not bad company.

Athenaeum

Down the street and around the corner is perhaps the oddest structure in two or three counties. The Athenaeum, 808 Athenaeum St., tel. (931) 381-4822, looks as if it were designed as a home for one of the Shriners' Grand Potentates. Built in 1835 for one of the ubiquitous Polk family members, the surprisingly small house combines elements of Moorish, Gothic, and Italianate styles. In 1851 it became the rectory of the Columbia Athenaeum School, which educated girls until closing in 1904. The Athenaeum is open for tours during the summer and can be rented for receptions, weddings, and meetings. Admission is $3 for adults, $2 for seniors and $1 children six to 18. Children under six get in free.

Tours

Antebellum Home Tours, run by the Maury County Convention & Visitors Bureau, tel. (931) 381-7176 or (800) 381-1865, offers tours for groups of eight or more. The tours can be customized to the interests of the group but usually include the interiors of at least three homes.

Sights Nearby

Elm Springs, 740 Mooresville Pike, tel. (931) 380-1844, a Greek revival home built in 1837, has an unusual feature for homes of that time— a second-story smokehouse built in an ell onto the main house. Meat was hung here to cure as smoke from the downstairs kitchen wafted through it. The home survived the Civil War through a slave's quick thinking. As Confederates approached from the South, Union troops were ordered to burn large structures so as to have a clear field of fire. A Yankee soldier placed a burning broom in a closet under the back stairs, but a female slave found it and put out the fire.

A Southern mansion in Mississippi was not so lucky. When troops came to burn the Clark family home in Attallaville, they let the family remove its furniture first, then put the house to the torch. Most of the Clark family furniture is now in Elm Springs, which serves as the headquarters of the Sons of Confederate Veterans and the Order of the Stars and Bars. Admission is free to SCV members and $3 for nonmembers. The house is open Mon-Fri. 9 a.m.-4 p.m.

RECREATION AND ENTERTAINMENT

Canoeing and Caving

Columbia's Duck River was never suitable for steamboats, but it's dandy for canoeing. Go east of town to **River Rat Canoe Rental,** 4379 Hwy. 431, tel. (931) 381-2278, to get on the water.

Southwest of Columbia in the community of Culleoka lies **South Port Saltpeter Cave,** 2171 Mack Benderman Rd., tel. (931) 379-4404 or (931) 388-8846. Said to be Middle Tennessee's largest cavern, it was used during the Civil War to produce nitrate for gunpowder and is now open for guided and unguided tours. Call ahead before going.

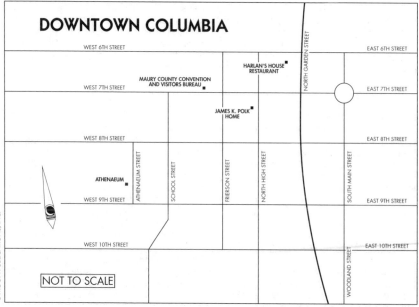

Birding

For 50 years the **Monsanto Ponds** site in Maury County was the world's largest producer of phosphates. From the beginning, the tailing ponds left by the mining attracted birds and other wildlife. Mining ended in 1986, and now 5,345 acres provide habitat for birds and animals. Birders have spotted more than 160 species here. Admission is free. To get there, go west of Columbia on Hwy. 50. Turn right onto Monsanto Rd. and follow the signs. Call (931) 380-9300 for more information.

Baseball

The **Columbia Mules** belong to the Big South League and offer professional baseball during a season that runs from mid-June through August. Home games are played at Columbia State Community College. Tickets are available at the Courthouse Annex, 1 Public Square. For information, call (931) 540-8466.

Events

Mule Day commemorates Columbia's most famous product. Held on the first weekend in April, it consists of a mule sale, parade, fiddler's contest, liar's contest, and checkers contest, among other things. Organizers solemnly warn potential parade participants that they can wear nothing that "would be repulsive or cause fear or anxiety to a large portion of the community and/or might incite people to violence." And they mean it. Call (931) 381-9557 for more details.

The **Spring Garden Plantation Pilgrimage,** tel. (931) 381-7176 or (800) 381-1865, is held on the third and fourth weekend in April.

Jazz in June plays on the Sunday closest to summer solstice.

Majestic Middle Tennessee Fall Tour, (931) 381-4822, is a self-driving tour that takes visitors to homes and churches. It's usually the last weekend in September.

The **Plantation Christmas Pilgrimage** takes place on the first weekend in December.

WHERE TO STAY

Bed and Breakfasts and Inns

Locust Hill, 1185 Mooresville Pike, Columbia, TN 38401, tel. (931) 388-8531 or (800) 577-8264, was built in 1840. The 6,000-square-foot house has double porches and is furnished with antiques and collectibles. Guests can choose from two guest rooms, one suite, and a renovated exterior kitchen/smokehouse. Rates are $80-100 and include a full country breakfast. Locust Hill is five minutes from downtown Columbia and 12 miles from the Saturn plant. Moderate-Expensive.

Oak Springs Inn, 1512 Williamsport Pike, Columbia, TN 38401, tel. (931) 381-3610, on the edge of Columbia next to a farm, is an updated two-story log cabin built in 1810. The three bedrooms have a queen, double, and single bed, respectively; the cabin has two bathrooms, and guests have access to a kitchen and fireplace. The cabin sits on the grounds of an antebellum home (circa 1840), which visitors may tour. The rate is $85 per night per person, including a full country breakfast. Luxury.

Inns Nearby

Ridgetop Bed and Breakfast. P.O. Box 193, Hampshire, TN 38641, tel. (931) 285-2777 or (800) 377-2770, is a contemporary house that especially welcomes bicyclists. It offers one guest room, an 1830 log cabin, and another freestanding building called The Loft. Each comes with private bath. The host serves a full breakfast. Rates run $65-85. Ridgetop is four miles east of the Natchez Trace Parkway on Hwy. 412 in Lewis County, two miles from the Maury County line. Moderate.

Sweetwater Inn, Campbell Station Rd., Culleoka, TN 38451, tel. (931) 987-3077, www.bbonline.com/tn/sweetwater, is a Gothic steamboat-style house built 1900-1903 during the American revival period. It sits on a knoll with panoramic views of the surrounding countryside. Each of the four guest rooms has a private bath. Two rooms are suites. Fresh flowers decorate the guest rooms, and coffee is served outside the door each morning. Rates are $100-125 and include a full three-course Southern gourmet, candlelight breakfast, afternoon refreshments, and evening dessert. The inn can provide lunches and suppers with notice. Expensive to Premium.

Motels

Among the choices are **Econo Lodge,** 1548 Bear Creek Pkwy., tel. (931) 381-1410 or (800) 424-6423; **James K. Polk Motel,** 1111 Nashville

Hwy., tel. (931) 388-4913 or (800) 348-8309; **Ramada Inn,** 1208 Nashville Hwy., tel. (931) 388-2720 or (800) 2RAMADA; and **Richland Inn,** 2407 Hwy. 315, tel. (931) 381-4500 or (800) 828-4832.

Camping
Travelers RV Park, tel. (931) 381-4112, has 65 sites, a pool, and a sports field. From I-65 take Exit 46 and follow the signs. It's open all year.

FOOD

Barbecue
Back Porch Barbecue, 200 W. 3rd St., tel. (931) 381-3463, serves pork, beef brisket, chicken, and ribs.

J.J.'s Barbecue, 1122 Hampshire Pike, tel. (931) 380-1756, smokes it all—pork, beef, chicken, turkey, ham, and ribs.

Nolen's Barbecue, 115 E. James Campbell Blvd., tel. (931) 381-4322, offers pork, beef, turkey, chicken, and ribs from the drive-in.

All the Rest
Bucky's Family Restaurant, 1102 Carmack Blvd., tel. (931) 381-2834, looks decidedly downscale, but the food is superb. Monday through Saturday, a diner can choose from four or five meats, 11 vegetables, two kinds of bread, two cobblers, and six kinds of desserts. Dessert and drink are extra—if diners have room for more food.

Public Square Eatery, 32 Public Square, tel. (931)388-2891, offers breakfast and lunch. Salads and sandwiches are the fare here, such as corned beef with Swiss for $3.45.

KT's on the Square, 34 Public Square, tel. (931) 388-8543, serves continental-style breakfast and lunch. Lunches include a meat-and-three-vegetable cafeteria-style plate. Short-order items are also available.

MORE PRACTICALITIES

Shopping
West of downtown is the **Oak Springs Inn and Gallery,** 1512 Williamsport Pike, tel. (931) 381-3610, a bed and breakfast with a barn that has been transformed into a gallery containing local folks' original art and crafts.

Columbia has lots of antique stores, among them the **Old Book Shop,** 1021 S. Main St., tel. (931) 388-6926, which is home to magazines and odd volumes and other items.

Sweet 14, at 808 S. High St. next to the Polk home, tel. (931) 380-2077, offers painted furniture, antiques, jewelry, vintage linens, floral arrangements, clothing, and artwork.

Information
Call or visit **The Maury County Convention & Visitors Bureau,** behind Rippavilla, the mansion across from the Saturn Plant north of the city on Hwy. 31. Call (931) 381-7176 or visit www.antebellum.com. Rippavilla is also the headquarters of the **Tennessee Antebellum Trail,** tel. (800) 381-1865, which covers historic properties from Nashville to Mount Pleasant. A gift shop and bookstore make this a good place to stop.

SOUTH ON HIGHWAY 43

THE POLK LEGACY

A three-and-a-half mile drive southwest of Columbia on Hwy. 243 brings the traveler to the territory of those members of the Polk family who left the most striking imprints on Maury County. This branch of the tribe descended from William Polk, a cousin to the president, who acquired an enormous tract of land by gambling with the governor of North Carolina. Colonial Americans apparently played a game called Rattle and Snap—the exact rules have been lost over the years—in which dried beans were shaken in the hand and then thrown forth with a snap of the fingers. However it was played, Polk won and the governor lost, and 5,648 acres changed hands. Polk divided the land among his four oldest sons by his second wife, Sarah, and all four brothers built mansions.

One of the four brothers was Leonidas Polk, who while being educated at West Point got to know a fellow Southerner named Jefferson Davis. Polk became an Episcopal priest and persuaded his brothers to build St. John's, an Episcopal plantation church that served the Polks and their servants. When the Civil War broke out, Leonidas Polk joined his college friend in beating his plowshare into a sword and became a major general in the Confederate army. Polk's military career came to an end when he encountered a Union artillery shell in 1864.

St. John's Episcopal Church

A pull-off on the east side of the road affords a view of the Polk family church, built 1840-42. A congregation worshipped there until 1915, and now the old church holds just one service per year on the last Sunday in May. Most of Tennessee's Episcopal bishops are buried behind the church in the cemetery.

Hamilton Place

Continuing south on Hwy. 243 and going 0.7 mile past Zion Rd., the visitor will see Hamilton Place on the right. A brick house with double-columned porches, this relatively simple structure was the first of the Polk brothers' homes, and was built in 1832 by Lucius Polk, who married a grandniece of Rachel Jackson in the White House. Most of the materials for the home came from the grounds: bricks were fired from clay there, stone was carved from the ground there, and the wood came from trees on the estate. The house is considered a classic example of Palladian architecture.

Rattle and Snap

The last and greatest of the Polk brother's houses is across the road and farther southwest. George Washington Polk's Rattle and Snap, named for the game by which his father won the land, rests at the top of a hill, the most magnificent antebellum mansion in Tennessee, if not the entire South. The capitals atop the 10 Corinthian columns were cast in Pittsburgh and Cincinnati, fireplaces were fashioned from marble, and the grounds were designed by a German gardener. Rattle and Snap was finished in 1845, and the Polk family had 15 happy years there before the war.

When the Civil War struck, marauding Union soldiers took a perverse delight in torching Southern mansions, and in 1862 a group with arson in mind stepped in the front door. The officer in charge noticed a Masonic ring on the life-sized portrait of the absent owner, and decided to spare the house. The Civil War ruined the Polk fortunes, however, and they lost the home in 1867. Over the decades the once-elegant Rattle and Snap became rundown to that point that in the 1930s and 1940s hay was stored in it and chickens roamed the once-elegant rooms.

The house was stabilized and renovated in the 1950s but not fully restored until Amon Carter Evans, former publisher of the Nashville *Tennessean,* bought the house in 1979 and assembled a team headed by Henry Judd, the retired chief restorationist for the National Park Service, and turned them loose to restore the house to its 1845 appearance. When research revealed that the downstairs doorknobs had been made from silver plate, Evans ordered silver plate replicas. To reconstruct a missing ell, an old church in Nashville that was being torn down provided 88,000 bricks of the proper vintage. Asked to comment on a report that all this work cost $6 million, Evans replied, "That is a conservative estimate."

The result is a house that is staggeringly luxurious. Wall coverings and draperies are true to the period, as are carpet patterns. The tables hold silver candelabra, and some of the chandelier replicas burn lard oil, as did the originals. Almost all of the original George Polk family furniture is long gone, but the house contains period pieces and a number of Polk items from nearby Hamilton Place.

Rattle and Snap offers more than just a house tour for visitors. Preparations are under way to build an interpretive center on the grounds, and local Civil War reenactors set up camp on the third Sunday of every month. By reservation, as many as 200 visitors can eat lunch there year round. The meal consists of homemade bread, vegetables grown in the plantation garden, and cobbler made from Rattle and Snap apples, all served on china with silver. Admission to Rattle and Snap is $8.50 for adults, $6 seniors, and $2.50 for children 6-12. Lunch, by reservation only, costs $10.95 for the cold lunch and $12.95 for the hot lunch. For more information, call (800) 258-3875 or (931) 379-5861, or visit online at http://edge.edge.net/~adevans/.

MOUNT PLEASANT

This literally pleasant place is a great place to stop for lunch or dinner. Lumpy's Malt Shop, on the square at 100 S. Main St., tel. (931) 379-9268, is a visual tribute to the '50s—lots of neon, black and white floor tile, pink flamingoes, and a glowing Wurlitzer jukebox loaded with oldies. A 1952 soda fountain is the centerpiece of the store, and customers sit amid antiques and displays. Mount Pleasant's first fire truck—a 1934 model—holds the floor near black and white televisions playing videos of *Leave it to Beaver* and other nostalgic TV shows.

"We don't serve anything that you couldn't get in 1952," said Glenn Lumpkins, a.k.a "Lumpy." His offerings include soda fountain favorites, hamburgers, and, for dinner, barbecue and prime rib. A room in the back is decorated with a World War II theme. Lumpy's attracts locals as well as day-trippers from a 100-mile radius. The place has had to expand three times since it opened in 1996.

Large phosphate deposits were discovered near Mt. Pleasant in 1895, and these were mined extensively for fertilizer and other uses for several decades. The Mt. Pleasant/Maury Phosphate Museum, 105 Public Square, tel. (931) 379-9511, recalls those days with exhibits of ore, equipment, clothing, and Civil War relics that were found during mining operations. Tours can be arranged by appointment. Admission is free.

SUMMERTOWN

Tennessee has known several deliberate communities, and **The Farm,** tel. (931) 964-3574, has been the most successful. Its story began in 1970, when college English professor Stephen Gaskin led a caravan of approximately 300 people from Berkeley, California, to a 1,750-acre tract northwest of Summertown. Here they set up a communal way of life in which those who joined gave everything they owned to a common treasury, built buildings themselves, and shared work. This incarnation of The Farm peaked in 1981 with 1,400 people.

As their communal forebears at Tennessee communities such as Ruskin had learned before them, it is very hard to make a living from the soil. In The Farm members' own words, "a recession, several business reverses, overcrowding, lack of experience, and mismanagement brought about severe financial crisis." In October 1983, the members reorganized their community, and now the population is about 180. They do no more large-scale farming—hay is the big crop. Several cottage industries operate at The Farm, including mushrooms, radiation detectors, and mail-order books.

Over the years The Farm has become noted for its first-class midwifery. The late Jessica Mitford, author of *The American Way of Birth,* referred to The Farm's Ina May Gaskin as the "acknowledged foremost theoretician and practitioner of the (midwifery) movement in America."

Although it would probably never occur to the residents to do so, The Farm ought to be put on the National Register of Historic Places. It wouldn't quite appeal to the Southern mansion crowd, but it gives a good sense of certain aspects of the '60s and '70s—ones that survive in few other places. A drive through The Farm reveals a lot of buildings of odd design, blissfully free of building codes. Several have solar collectors and some look unfinished; at one place the rusty framework of a geodesic dome sits forlornly in the woods. The residents seem to have succumbed to the time-honored Tennessee tradition of refusing to part with automobiles, trucks, and broken-down farm machinery.

Visitors are welcome at The Farm, although calling ahead is a good idea. To get there, take Hwy. 20 N out of Summertown. Turn right on Drakes Ln. and follow the signs. Those who come to The Gate receive a map of the community and a choice of various literature and catalogs. Admission is free, although guests can swim in the pond for $1. A primitive campground is available, and guests are welcome to shop at The Store.

Summertown holds the **Summertown Bluegrass Reunion** on the first weekend in September. No alcohol is allowed. Get information online at www.thefarm.org.

Duck River Orchards, along Hwy. 43 at 3 Monument Rd., tel. (931) 964-4040, offers a rarity amongst the orchards—espresso. This roadside stand sells a variety of things to take back home: jellies, candy, locally made crafts, and cider. During the harvest season, they sell 18 kinds of apples and 10 kinds of peaches.

ETHRIDGE

Farther along down Hwy. 43 is the town of Ethridge, home to a community of Amish, a German-speaking religious sect usually associated with Pennsylvania and Ohio. This group moved to Tennessee in the 1940s, and here close to 200 families farm and live in the old ways, using horses and buggies for transportation and disdaining electricity, telephones, and buttons on coats. They have no churches, meeting in one another's homes. Depending on the season, visitors to the Amish community will see roadside stands or signs advertising peanut brittle, baskets, bread, cedar chests, and furniture. While the residents are happy to talk to and engage in commerce with outsiders, visitors should remember that the Amish intensely dislike having their pictures taken.

An enormous technological leap from the Amish, **Granny's Network** is the brainchild of Sarah Evetts, a.k.a. "Granny," who runs a 10-watt television station at **Granny's Welcome Center,** 4001 Hwy. 43, tel. (931) 829-2433. Here she holds forth on items of interest to her local audience and will cheerfully interview sojourners who stop by. To those who ask, she will give a videotape of the interview. (She does charge for subsequent tapes.) Admission is free to the center, which contains a crafts store.

Amish Country Galleries, 3931 Hwy. 43, offers many objects made by local Amish craftspeople. Furniture, quilts, and baskets head the list of items available here.

LAWRENCEBURG AND VICINITY

Although Tennessee sent a large number of volunteers to the Mexican War, the two-year conflict and overwhelming U.S. victory is little noted with public monuments. Lawrenceburg's town square boasts an obelisk in honor of the war.

Nearby is a life-sized statue of David Crockett. The hero of the Alamo lived near here for about five years, and a state park marks the site. About a block and a half south of the statue is a replica of Crockett's cabin. The items inside are period pieces or replicas of items Crockett might have owned. The cabin is open every day. Admission is free.

Outside the larger cities, Catholic churches are scarce in Tennessee. This county, however, has three, all because of German immigrants who began coming here in 1870 to take advantage of inexpensive farmland. The **Sacred Heart of Jesus Church** was begun in 1887. Parishioners baked the bricks and craftsmen lovingly built the structure, which stands on Church Street.

Those who didn't go to church sometimes wound up in Lawrenceburg's jail, which was built in the late 1800s and used until 1974. Now the **Old Jail Museum,** on Waterloo St., tel. (931) 762-4509, houses a small museum related to the town. Admission is free, but reservations are needed.

David Crockett State Recreational Park

A half-mile west of Lawrenceburg, this 987-acre park marks the one-time home of David Crockett. He moved here in 1817 and built a mill, a powder mill, and a distillery along Shoal Creek. Quickly winning favor with his neighbors, he was elected justice of the peace, then town commissioner, then state representative. While he was off in Nashville serving in the legislature in 1821, a massive flood hit Shoal Creek and washed away most of his enterprises. Forced into bankruptcy, he moved near Rutherford farther west in the state.

The park contains an interpretive center dedicated to Crockett, with exhibits on frontier life, Crockett's industries in Lawrence County, his moves across Tennessee, and his political life. Also on exhibit are items thought to belong to the county's most famous resident.

Recreational amenities include a large swimming pool, fishing, bicycling, hiking, and boat rentals. The restaurant seats 240 people. For days and hours, see below. Call (931) 762-9408.

Entertainment and Events

Live local music plays on the second and fourth Saturdays every month at the Lawrenceburg City Administration Building. The **Tennessee Valley Jamboree** features bluegrass, country, and gospel music starting at 7 p.m. No alcoholic beverages are permitted, and admission is free.

Where to Stay

Granville House Bed & Breakfast, 229 Pulaski St., tel. (931) 762-3129, occupies a restored, antebellum home one block east of the square. The five large rooms all have private baths, and some have fireplaces and private balconies. The host serves a continental breakfast. The rate is $75 plus tax. Moderate.

Or try the **Richland Inn Lawrenceburg,** 2125 N. Locust Ave., tel. (931) 762-0061 or (800) 828-4829, rates $39-44. Inexpensive.

Two campgrounds at **David Crockett State Recreational Park** offer a total of 107 sites, each with water and electricity. Hot showers are available. Call (931) 762-9408.

Food

Big John's Barbecue, 904 N. Military Ave., tel. (931) 762-9596, lays out ribs and chicken.

The Brass Lantern, 2290 Hwy. 64, tel. (931) 762-0474, offers steak, seafood, pasta, barbecue, plate lunches, and sandwiches.

Rick's Barbecue, at 401 W. Gaines St., tel. (931) 762-2297, serves pork, beef, and chicken barbecue.

Some folks consider the restaurant at the nearby **David Crockett State Recreational Park,** tel. (931) 762-9541, the best in town. Country cooking is the fare.

Square Forty, 40 Public Square, tel. (931) 762-2868, serves steak, catfish, and riblets. The building dates to the turn of the century, with the original pressed tin ceiling and lots of antiques and paintings. It offers live piano music on Friday and Saturday.

Shopping

Mama J's Cabin, halfway between Lawrenceburg and Pulaski at 4716 Pulaski Hwy., tel. (931) 762-0678, occupies a structure fashioned out of two log cabins, one dating from 1845. Inside are antiques, jewelry, toys, and Christmas ornaments.

The Wood Shop, on Rt. 64 at the bottom of Powdermill Rd. three-quarters of a mile outside Lawrenceburg, sells Amish items, custom furniture, wood crafts, rocking chairs, swings, and lawn furniture.

Those looking for the perfect item for a recreation room should pull in at **Yesterdaze Collectibles** at 2140 Pulaski Hwy., tel. (931) 762-

8182. Robert Dwiggins offers perfectly restored jukeboxes, pinball machines, Coke machines, and gas pumps.

Information

The Lawrenceburg Chamber of Commerce, 1609 N. Locust Ave., tel. (931) 762-4911, is open Mon.-Fri. 9 a.m.-2:30 p.m. Find out more online at www.usit.net/lawrence.

LORETTO

This little town has several distinctions. First, it is home to one of the two independent telephone companies left in the state—the Loretto Telephone Company. The other is in Millington in West Tennessee. Second, the Loretto Casket Company, founded in 1950, is the oldest and largest casket company in the state. Finally, Loretto has a long tradition of dancing—an island of fun in a sea of Baptistry.

The dancing started when Loretto attracted a large number of German immigrants in the late 1800s. With them they brought their Catholic faith. The town was named for a shrine in Loretto, Italy, and the first priest in the church asked the Virgin Mary to protect Loretto from wind. Since then, locals claim, Loretto has never suffered a tornado.

As for the dancing, one local grande dame summed it up by saying, "Those Catholics know how to have a good time." Orchestras were imported from big cities such as Sheffield, Alabama, and dances were held in the Catholic school. Square dances took place every Saturday night and attracted people for miles around. This tradition continues with Loretto's annual Gone with the Wind Ball, open to visitors as well as locals.

Sights

The Sacred Heart of Jesus Church on Church St., tel. (931) 853-4370, is a Gothic brick structure built by its German congregation in the 1920s. It has beautiful stained-glass windows and stations of the cross. Admission is free.

The Loretto Milling Company, on 2nd Ave. S, has been run by the same family for more than 100 years. It now produces animal feed only.

CHOCOLATE GRAVY ON DIG DAYS

Forty Three Salvage and More, Hwy. 43, tel. (615) 853-4364, is aptly named. This enterprise, occupying the third and fourth buildings on the right as travelers come into Loretto, serves food fit for the King. Elvis would love it here.

The combination store and restaurant serves fried bologna and egg biscuits, but the item for which it is noted is chocolate gravy on biscuits. Here's the recipe:

Combine in saucepan one cup of sugar, one-half cup of flour, and two level teaspoons of cocoa. Add water—maybe two cups—until it begins to cook and thicken. If it starts getting too thick, add more water. Serve on hot biscuits.

The restaurant is open Mon.-Sat. 5 a.m.-8 p.m., Sunday 1-6 p.m. Anywhere from 15 to 20 people can fit in there, and they go through about two quarts of chocolate gravy on any given day. No reservations are necessary.

Once visitors have had breakfast, they are ready for Dig Days, held Wednesday, Saturday, and Sunday. A Dig Day is the ceremonial unwrapping of a 1,100- to 1,200-pound bale of clothing that arrives from points north. Inside the bale are new clothes, but customers have to dig through it to find the bargains. In addition to the clothes, truckloads of shoes arrive from time to time, and the store sells knick-knacks and jewelry. The proprietors also run a used car lot outside. To reach the salvage store or car lot, call (615) 853-4365.

The **Ralph J. Passarella Memorial Museum,** 133-134 S. Main St., tel. (931) 853-4351, commemorates the longtime co-owner of the Loretto Telephone Company. Although the museums two rooms contain a good deal of old telephone equipment, the collection also includes many antiques and curiosities. Chief among the latter is a wicker body basket once used by undertakers to transport a body to the funeral home. The museum is open by appointment. Admission is free, although donations are enthusiastically received.

The **Coca Cola Palace,** sitting on the corner of 2nd and Broad Streets, is a converted former general store now devoted to Coca-Cola memorabilia. Malcolm and Gail Walters, who live beside the Palace at 108 2nd Ave. S are generally available to show visitors around. Admission is free.

Events

Loretto's annual **Gone With the Wind Ball,** held on odd-numbered years in September, is open to visitors as well as locals. Dancers are encouraged to wear Old South clothing, but this is not mandatory. For further information, call Carolyn Thompson at (931) 853-4351.

A town with a German background has to have an **Oktoberfest,** and the one hereabouts is held the first full week in October and consists of a polka band, German food, and block parties. Call (931) 762-4911 for more details.

PULASKI

This town got its name from Casimir Pulaski, a Polish count who fought and died in the American Revolution. The original settlers hacked down 18-foot-high cane stalks to build the town, which is now the seat of Giles County on the Alabama border.

Pulaski never saw a major battle during the Civil War, yet it is remembered in the South as the place where Sam Davis was hanged. Davis, whose story is more fully told in "Smyrna" under "Nashville to Murfreesboro," below, was captured near Pulaski and executed as a spy.

Pulaski is far more notorious as the postwar birthplace of the Ku Klux Klan. December 1865 was a low point in Pulaski and much of Tennessee. The economy was ruined, the state was ruled by a governor intent on punishing former Confederates, and people in Pulaski and other places were apprehensive about all the former slaves who lived around them.

On Christmas Eve of 1865, in a law office at 207 Madison St., just off the town square, a group of young men dreamed up a social club to take their minds off their troubles. They named it the Ku Klux Klan, and invented costumes and initiation ceremonies and weird-sounding titles. While riding around bedecked with sheets and other ghostly garb, club members noticed with delight how their appearance terrified superstitious ex-slaves. It didn't take long for this amusement to transform itself into whippings, lynchings, and all manner of violence. The Klan moved on from Pulaski, but the stigma connected to the organization remains. For many years the building where the Klan was founded bore a large plaque commemorating the event. To symbolize his opposition to the Klan and what it stands for, however, the owner of the building removed the plaque, turned it around, and re-bolted it to the wall.

THE DAY THE TOWN STOOD STILL

The Ku Klux Klan was founded just off the town square in Pulaski in the late 1860s, and although the organization's headquarters soon departed the seat of Giles County for other places, the town's association with the birth of the Klan continued to haunt it. Various Klan incarnations through the years came to Pulaski to march and make hate-filled speeches, confident they were among friends.

Finally, Pulaski had enough. When an Aryan Nation group announced in 1989 it was coming to town for a rally, the townsfolk took a stand. More than 5,000 people signed a resolution condemning the group. More than 200 additional petitions were circulated across the state in opposition to the white supremacists.

The townsfolk took their most dramatic step, however, on October 7, 1989, when the Aryan Nations people arrived and found the town deserted—a very unusual situation on Saturday, normally the busiest day of the week. More than 180 merchants—virtually every one in Pulaski, including Wal-Mart—closed their doors and went home. When the group made its speeches, they echoed off empty buildings and rang through deserted streets. The Aryan Nation never came back.

Buoyed by this success, Pulaski organized Giles Countians United, a group composed of blacks and whites, Jews and Gentiles, who organized Brotherhood Weekend, an annual series of events aimed at bringing people together. Hate groups still occasionally come to town—free speech guarantees them the right to do so—but they can no longer assume they are welcome.

SIGHTS

The **Sam Davis Museum** stands at the site of his death, now Sam Davis Ave., and contains the leg irons he wore as well as other Civil War artifacts. To open the museum, call (931) 363-3789.

The **Giles County Courthouse** in the middle of the square is the grandest such building in Middle Tennessee, if not the entire state. Built in 1909, the courthouse has a cupola supported by Corinthian columns. A balcony inside encircles the third floor. Admission is free.

The **Giles County Historical Museum,** in the library at 122 S. 2nd St., tel. (931) 363-2720, features exhibits on the county's history containing Civil War artifacts and farming implements. Admission is free.

Built by a former Confederate general who became a governor of Tennessee, the **Brown-Daly-Horne House,** 318 W. Madison St. at the corner of 3rd and Madison Streets, tel. (931) 363-1582, began as a relatively simple structure but was transformed in the late 1890s to a Queen Anne-style house complete with a third-floor ballroom, dumbwaiter, exterior turrets, stained-glass window borders, and gabled roof. Completely restored, the building now houses a bank and has been placed on the National Register. Admission is free to see the interior, which is open during banking hours.

Outside Town

Just eight miles north of Pulaski on Hwy. 31 is **Milky Way Farm,** tel. (931) 363-9769, an estate built by Frank Mars, founder of the Mars Candy Company. When it was established in 1932, the farm consisted of 2,700 acres, 38 barns, and its own railroad siding. Championship cattle and Gallahadion, the 1940 Kentucky Derby winner, came from here. Now the Tudor mansion is used for corporate retreats and occasionally is open to the public. Once inside, visitors can ogle at the 21 bedrooms, 18 baths, and a 28- by 12-foot dining room table—perhaps the largest one in the state. Tours of the mansion are available for four or more people by appointment and cost $8 per person. Lunch is available for $20 per person for groups of more than 25, which includes admission. Dinner costs $25 per person.

Ten minutes west of Pulaski on Hwy. 64, the **Green Valley General Store,** tel. (931) 363-6562, sells an estimated 5,000 fried pies a month. This and fresh lemonade, homemade ice cream, and homemade cookies, along with canned fruits and sauces—and that's just the edibles. The store also stocks quilts and Amish goods, hats, and baskets. Next door is the flea market, known for its antique farm equipment, mostly horse-drawn. A large Amish community nearby is both the biggest supplier and buyer of the equipment. The flea market varies in size from a couple of acres to 10 acres. Auctions are held the third Thursday in April and October.

EVENTS

The **Brotherhood Parade,** held the Saturday before Martin Luther King Jr.'s birthday, marks Pulaski's declaration that racism and bigotry have no place here. The **Unity Service,** held in a church, is "the best church service you'll experience all year," according to a person who goes to every one.

The **Chili Cook-Off** is held in February at the National Guard Armory. Call the Giles County Chamber of Commerce for details at (931) 363-3789.

The Giles County Historical Society's **Walking Tour of Historic Homes** takes place in December. Call (931) 363-3789.

The **City Sidewalks Festival** brings an old-fashioned Christmas to Pulaski with a tour of five to six houses and carriage rides. Call (931) 363-3789.

PRACTICALITIES

Where to Stay
Try the **Best Western Sands Motor Hotel,** Hwy. 64 and I-65, tel. (931) 363-4501 or (800) 528-1234; or the **Richland Inn Pulaski,** 1020 W. College, tel. (931) 363-0006 or (800) 828-4834.

Valley KOA, tel. (931) 363-4600, has 60 campsites, a pool, and hiking trails. From I-65 take Exit 14 and follow signs. It's open all year.

Food
The **Heritage House Restaurant,** 219 S. 3rd St., tel. (931) 363-2313, is in the Gladish Garner House, a 1905 structure in which lunch and dinner are served Mon.-Friday. A full menu is provided, including grilled salmon and shrimp scampi. It also offers a buffet of Southern-style foods, such as ribs, catfish, chicken, and a barbecue plate.

Hickory House, 330 Patterson St., tel. (931) 363-0231, offers a country cooking buffet, barbecued ribs, and chicken.

Lawler's BBQ, on Hwy. 64 W, tel. (931) 363-3515, offers takeout only.

Reeves Drugstore, on the square at 125 N. 1st St., tel. (931) 363-2561, may be the only place left in the state that sells nickel Cokes from an old-fashioned soda fountain. It also serves deli food, sandwiches, salads, sodas, milk shakes, and ice cream.

Sarge's Shack, 14 miles east of town on Hwy. 64 at I-65 Exit 14, tel. (931) 363-1310, has a line of people waiting to belly up to the all-you-can-eat-catfish served on Friday night. This popular place also serves steaks, shrimp, charbroiled chicken, fish and chips, and country ham.

Tours and Information
Giles County Chamber of Commerce and Tourism, 100 South 2nd St., tel. (931) 363-3789, is open Mon- Fri. 8 a.m.-5 p.m. The chamber specializes in setting up custom tours for groups. See them online at www.usit.net/giles.

LYNNVILLE

North of Pulaski along Hwy. 31, Lynnville is a lovely town that once had to get up and move. After the Civil War the railroad came through about one mile east of the town. Realizing that if it were to prosper it had to be near the train, Lynnville moved beginning in 1860 to its present location beside the tracks.

Now with 59 buildings, several of them Victorian homes and churches, Lynnville is listed on the National Register of Historic Places and is making a concerted effort to attract visitors. The chief attraction is the **Lynnville Railroad Museum,** a new depot built to resemble the original structure. The museum contains an inoperable steam train, model railroad, a passenger coach, flatcar, and caboose, and is open April through October.

Across the street from the museum is **Soda Pop Junction,** a restored drugstore housed in an 1860 building, tel. (931) 527-0007. Here visitors can enjoy complete service from a 1940s vintage soda fountain while sitting in the old wire-backed chairs.

This a good town for a stroll, and visitors will find an art gallery and a growing number of shops to visit. For further information, call the **Giles County Chamber of Commerce** at (931) 363-3789 or look at www.lynnvillerailroad.com.

NASHVILLE TO MURFREESBORO

SMYRNA

In 1810 Smyrna was a farming community centered around the First Presbyterian Church, a building that burned down and was replaced by the current structure.

The **Sam Davis Home,** 1399 Sam Davis Rd., tel. (615) 459-2341, shows where the "Boy Hero of the Confederacy" grew up. This is not one of the ostentatious plantation homes, but it does show how a comfortable family lived in the mid-1800s. Visitors can see a museum and then tour the house and gardens. The house is decorated for Christmas, and theme exhibits are presented throughout the year. Admission is $4 for adults, $3.50 for seniors, and $2.50 for kids six to 12.

The **Nissan manufacturing plant,** 983 Nissan Dr., tel. (615) 459-1444, built in 1983, employs 6,300 people who build Altima sedans, Frontier pickups, and sport-utility vehicles. Locally, Nissan is considered a good neighbor, making $7 million in contributions to area programs and projects. It conducts tours each Tuesday at 8:30 a.m., 10 a.m., and 1 p.m.; and Thursday at 8:30 a.m. and 10 a.m. The hour-long tours start with a film about the start-up operations of the assembly plant. Trams carry visitors throughout the plant. For safety reasons, children under 10 and visitors wearing shorts or sandals cannot go on the tour. Tours are free, but reservations are required.

Events
Days on the Farm at the Sam Davis Home, 1399 Sam Davis Rd., tel. (615) 459-2341, takes place

THE BOY HERO OF THE CONFEDERACY

For those Southerners who make "The Lost Cause" into a religion, Sam Davis qualifies for sainthood. Born on a farm near Smyrna, he was only 18 years old when the war broke out. He enlisted in the Confederate army and became a member of Coleman's Scouts, a group who spied behind enemy lines.

While trying to take some information to Gen. Braxton Bragg, Davis was stopped by Union troops near the town of Pulaski. His boot was cut open, and sewn inside were papers that held details on Union forces and locations. Although Davis was wearing a Confederate uniform, he was put on trial and charged with spying. A guilty verdict meant death by hanging.

The Union command was more concerned about who provided the information than about executing Davis, and it offered him a horse and an escort if he would reveal where he got his papers. The young man steadfastly refused to do so, and the night before he died wrote a letter to his mother saying, "I do not fear to die."

The next day he sat on his coffin in a wagon and was driven to the gallows. A Union officer told him one last time, "Speak the name of your informant, and go home in safety."

Accounts vary as to what Davis replied, but it was something akin to: "If I had a thousand lives to live, I would give them all, rather than betray a friend or my country." This so impressed the commanding officer that he could not bring himself to give the order that would spring the trap. The condemned man finally gave the order himself, passing through the gallows floor and into history. He is buried on the grounds of the Sam Davis Home.

the first week in May over four days and presents living history, including music and demonstrations of mid-1800s farm life. Between 900 and 1,000 schoolchildren take part in this event. Admission is $3.50 for adults.

Heritage Days at the Sam Davis Home, 1399 Sam Davis Rd., tel. (615) 459-2341, takes place about the first week in October. Demonstrations deal with farm work of the mid-1800s. This annual event attracts hordes of area students and admission is $3.50 for everyone on Thursday and Friday. On Saturday the admission is $4.

Tennessee Aviation Days Air Show takes off each September at the Smyrna Airport and brings to town various high-performance aircraft. Participants have included the Warbirds of World War II, wing walkers, and modern jet fighters in the U.S. fighting forces. Call (615) 355-0494.

Where to Stay

Days Inn is located at 1300 Plaza Dr., tel. (615) 355-6161 or (800) 325-2525.

Nashville I-24 Campground, tel. (615) 459-5818, has 175 sites, a pool, cabins, and tenting. From I-24 eastbound take Exit 66B (westbound Exit 70) and follow signs. It's open all year.

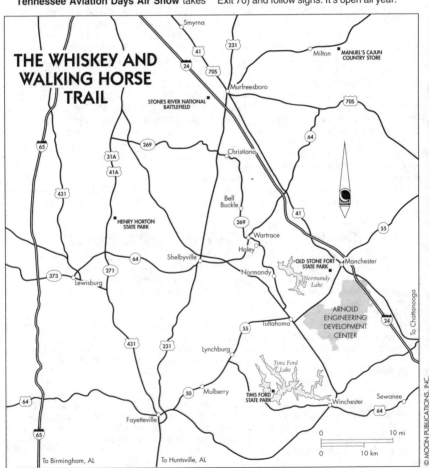

THE WHISKEY AND WALKING HORSE TRAIL

© MOON PUBLICATIONS, INC.

THE MISERABLE BATTLE OF STONES RIVER

Like the Battle of Franklin to the west, the Battle of Stones River never makes the short list of clashes that casual students of the Civil War can rattle off. The struggle was significant, however, for it proved that the South could not evict the invading Union army, thus setting the stage for the loss of Chattanooga and eventually Atlanta.

The action began in December of 1862. The Union army had occupied Nashville since February of that year, and Lincoln, needing some progress on the western front, was urging Gen. William Rosecrans and his 42,000 troops to move south. Facing him from Murfreesboro were 34,000 Southerners under the command of Gen. Braxton Bragg.

Neither army was in a hurry to fight. The weather was miserable—cold, pouring rain that turned fields and roads to mud. Each army was reasonably well-provisioned and relatively comfortable. On the day after Christmas 1862, Rosecrans at last came out for battle. By December 30 the two forces faced each other two miles northwest of Murfreesboro. The armies camped so close they could hear each other's bands. First a Union band played Northern songs, which were answered by a Confederate band playing Southern favorites. Toward the end of the impromptu concert a Union band struck up "Home Sweet Home." Other bands—Northern and Southern—joined in, and a choir of thousands of men on both sides sang the sentimental verses far into the night.

The two generals had come up with the same plan: attack the enemy's right. The next morning the Southerners attacked at dawn, surprising Union troops that were fixing breakfast and forcing the Union to cancel its plans and defend itself. Union forces, which had been strung out in a line, folded back on themselves like a blade into a pocketknife. This concentrated the fields of fire and reaped a harvest of death.

The din was so loud that soldiers snatched cotton still clinging to plants and stuffed it in their ears. They fought amid thick stands of cedar trees. General Rosecrans rallied his Union troops by riding up to them and shouting encouragement. On one of these rides a cannonball took off the head of an officer on horseback beside him. According to one account, the headless body stayed in the saddle for 20 paces before falling off.

New Year's Eve fell on a scene of terrible carnage. Men who had been singing the night before now cried out in agony as a chilling rain fell. Union and Confederate soldiers looked for comrades and offered help to the wounded of both sides. As the night wore on, escaped hogs ate some of the bodies, and many of the dead and wounded froze to the ground. Murfreesboro was swamped with wounded Confederates, and Union casualties had to endure a bumpy 30-mile ride back to Nashville.

Neither side attacked on the first day of 1863, but on January 2 Bragg ordered a group of Kentuckians commanded by John C. Breckinridge, a former vice president of the U.S. who had lost the 1860 presidential race to Lincoln, to attack a hill held by Union troops. Breckinridge protested that the charge would be suicidal, but Bragg insisted. When the Kentuckians attacked, their numbers were decimated.

On January 3, Bragg learned that the Union troops were getting reinforcements from Nashville. He decided to retreat. The Battle of Stones River had cost him 27% of his troops—9,239 killed or wounded. Rosecrans of the North had fared little better with 9,532 casualties, or 23% of his force. Neither side could claim victory, although both did so.

Bragg moved 25 miles south and set up positions along the Duck River, and Rosecrans advanced his army and occupied Murfreesboro. Both armies settled down to get over the effects of this terrible battle.

Food

The Omni Hut, on Hwy. 41 South, tel. (615) 459-4870, was a dream come true for Jim Wall, a World War II pilot who was stationed all over the Pacific. Between bombing runs on Japanese targets, he collected Polynesian recipes and, after retiring from the military, built this restaurant. The ambience is pure South Seas island. The decor includes a waterfall, tiki gods, and other Polynesian touches. The large menu includes traditional and uncommon South Seas dishes.

Rossi's Restaurant, 114 Front St., tel. (615) 459-7992, is a family-owned Italian restaurant that serves pizza, calzones, and other savory homemade dishes.

Asian Restaurant, 129 N. Lowry St., tel. (615) 223-0509, serves an all-you-can-eat buffet and menu items.

Information

The **Chamber of Commerce,** 315 S. Lowry St. at City Hall Bldg., tel. (615) 355-6565, is open Mon.-Fri. 9:30 a.m.-3:30 p.m. City Hall is open Mon.-Fri. 8:30 a.m.-4:30 p.m.

STONES RIVER NATIONAL BATTLEFIELD

Established in 1927, this 500+ acre national battlefield commemorates the Civil War battle of the same name. The clash at this site, which began New Year's Eve 1862, caused 23,515 casualties—one of the bloodier battles in Tennessee. While the park is open year round—visitors can participate in self-guided tours of the battlefield on any day—summer is the best time to go, for during those months the Park Service offers interpretive programs and demonstrations of military life. In July there is a Civil War encampment. The visitors center, 3501 Old Nashville Hwy., tel. (615) 893-9501, provides additional information about this battlefield and Fortress Rosecrans, which is in downtown Murfreesboro. A three-mile walking and bicycling trail connects the national battlefield with the fortress site. It's open 8 a.m.-5 p.m. year-round, except Christmas. No charge, but donations are accepted. See the site online at www.nps.gov/stri/.

MURFREESBORO

Murfreesboro was the capital of Tennessee from 1819 to 1825. This made great sense, for the town was about one mile from the geographic center of the state. The **Geographic Center of Tennessee** is just off Old Lascassas Pike, one mile from downtown, where an obelisk stands in a place that locals call, with just a bit of tongue in cheek, the "Dimple of the Universe."

The courthouse in which the legislature met, however, burned in 1822 and, seeking a better meetinghouse, the members moved the seat of government to Nashville. Locals implored them to come back, arguing that Murfreesboro was "deficient in those sources of amusement which in Nashville are supposed to distract the legislators from strict attention to their duty." Apparently liking the distractions, the legislators stayed put. A new **Rutherford County Courthouse** was built in 1859 and is one of the six or so antebellum courthouses still in use in the state. Murfreesboro saw action in the Battle of Stones River, which is detailed in a Special Topic above.

Middle Tennessee State University (MTSU) was founded in 1911 as a teachers' college and has grown to become the second-largest (the University of Tennessee is the biggest) and fastest-growing university in the state. Enrollment each fall numbers about 17,500. The university offers a variety of sports and cultural activities for visitors. Call (615) 898-2551 for information.

As Nashville expands outward, Rutherford County is the fastest-growing county in Tennessee. One of the positive sides of growth has been a wave of sophistication that has swept over Murfreesboro. In the last two or three years the restaurants in town have moved three or four notches up.

SIGHTS AND RECREATION

Cannonsburgh

The casual visitor to Middle Tennessee could gain the impression that all of the historically significant structures were built right before the Civil War. Few log buildings remain, for most of

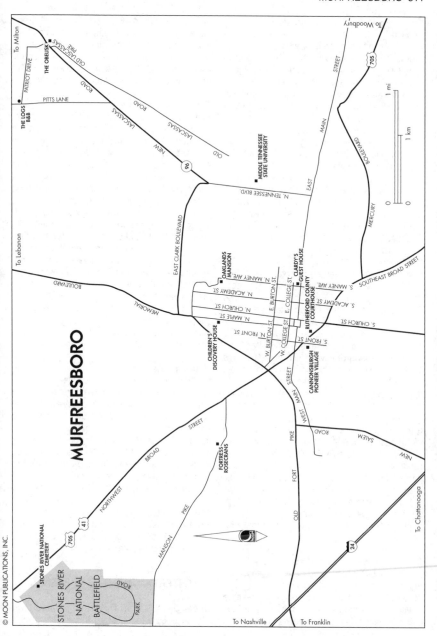

MURFREESBORO

STONES RIVER NATIONAL BATTLEFIELD

Stones River National Cemetery

Children's Discovery House

Oaklands Mansion

Fortress Rosecrans

Cannonsburgh Pioneer Village

Clardy's Guest House

Rutherford County Courthouse

Middle Tennessee State University

The Obelisk

The Logs B&B

To Milton
To Lebanon
To Nashville
To Franklin
To Chattanooga
To Woodbury

© MOON PUBLICATIONS, INC.

1 mi
1 km

them were demolished to make way for the fancier buildings. Murfreesboro was first called Cannonsburgh in honor of a local who became governor, but the name was changed to honor a Revolutionary War hero. The Pioneer Village of Cannonsburgh begins with a collection of buildings and artifacts that show what life was like before the days of the plantations, when this area was part of the frontier, and then marches forward to the year 1925 with other structures and items. Included are a gristmill, one-room schoolhouse, flatboat, log cabin, 1800s doctor office, and early automobile garage.

To get there, get off I-24 onto Hwy. 96 and go east for two miles. Turn right onto Broad St., stay in the right lane for a half-mile, then turn right onto Front Street. Cannonsburgh will be in the first block on the right. Admission is free. Call (615) 893-6565.

Oaklands

Oaklands, 900 N. Maney Ave., tel. (615) 893-0022, is a plantation manor that traces the economic rise and fall of a doctor and his family. The oldest part of the house was built about 1815 and consisted of only two rooms and a loft. As the family prospered they added to the house, and by the time of the Civil War Oaklands had a long driveway with majestic oaks leading to an Italianate house containing a spectacular freestanding staircase.

As the surrounding area changed hands during the Civil War, armies from both sides occupied the plantation. The Maney family provided hospitality to the officers of both sides—albeit reluctantly in the case of Northern troops—and guests included Confederate President Jefferson Davis. By 1882 the family had to sell the home, which passed through a series of owners and reached a low point in the 1950s, when it was abandoned.

Now the home has been restored to its appearance in 1862. About 30% of the furniture is original. Admission is $4 for adults and $2 for children.

Children's Discovery House

For youngsters weary of old Southern mansions, the Discovery House, 503 N. Maple St., tel. (615) 890-2300, is the place to go. This one-time house is now a hands-on museum in which kids can see permanent and traveling science and nature exhibits, play in water and sand, and have a good time while learning. They can try a flight simulator or see animals such as a pot-bellied pig, iguanas, ferrets, birds, and turtles. Admission is $3 for adults and 2.50 for kids. Visit online at www.digitalvantage.com/discovery.

Fortress Rosecrans

Fortress Rosecrans is the nation's largest earthen fort. After the Union's success at the battle of Stones River, the Union forces decided that it was strategically important to strengthen the supply line along the Nashville and Chattanooga railroad. Murfreesboro became an important depot, and Fortress Rosecrans was built in 1863 to protect that depot. Union troops and black laborers built 14,000 feet of earthworks surrounding approximately 200 acres. Approximately 30 acres of the original earthworks have been restored. A three-mile walking and bicycling trail connects the fortress with Stones River National Battlefield. The fortress is administered by the National Park Service; its visitors center at the national battlefield can provide more complete information about the fortress. To get to the fortress, take I-24 to Exit 78B, drive about a mile to Gulf Ln., and turn left. It's open daylight hours year-round except Christmas Day.

Naturalist Resort

Rock Haven Lodge, 462 Rock Haven Rd., tel. (615) 896-3553, is a 25-acre naturalist (nudist) resort for whose who strongly believe the biblical passage about taking no thought about what ye shall put on. Rock Haven operates from April 1 through October 31, offering a pool, hot tub, tennis, volleyball, shuffleboard, horseshoes, darts, Ping-Pong, and hiking. Take a peek online at www.cybernude.com/rockhaven.

A visit for the day costs $20 per couple, and those who would like to spend the night will pay $40-60 per night. Anyone belonging to the International Naturalist Federation receives a discount. A 100-site campground is on the grounds; the sites are available April 1-October 31.

ENTERTAINMENT AND EVENTS

Uncle Dave Macon Days brings more than 30,000 people together for three days of old-time music, dance, and arts and crafts competitions along with a bike race, good food, and children's activities. It's held on the second weekend in July at Cannonsburgh Pioneer Village, and admission is free. For information about the festival, call the chamber of commerce at (615) 893-6565 or (800) 716-7560.

Every year a **Civil War Encampment** takes place at Stones River National Battlefield on the second weekend in July. Demonstrations of camp life with period uniforms combine with the firing of a battery of cannons to give visitors a sense of how the soldiers who fought here lived. Call (615) 893-9501.

Cannonsburgh Harvest Day, on the last Saturday in October, offers music, dance, food, blacksmithing, and broom-making. Call (615) 893-6565 or (800) 716-7560 for information.

Tennessee International Folkfest, held each May, features folk groups and performers representing many countries and cultures. The folkfest includes performances, a parade, and a street festival. Call (615) 893-6565 or (800) 716-7560.

Pioneer Power Days, held in the little town of Eagleville in West Rutherford County, brings the South's largest exhibition of antique farm machinery on the weekend after Labor Day in September. Call (615) 274-6987 and ask for Buddy Woodson.

Mardi Gras takes place in July in Milton, just east of Murfreesboro, because residents thought that the usual time before Lent is just too cold. This combination Fourth of July and Mardi Gras celebration features a parade of horses, covered wagons, marching bands, old cars, new cars, decorated lawn mowers, and exuberantly costumed citizens. Activities continue all day, finishing up with Cajun music and dancing. This is small-town life at its best.

WHERE TO STAY

Bed and Breakfasts

Clardy's Guest House, 435 E. Main St., Murfreesboro, TN 37130, tel. (615) 893-6030, occupies an 1898 house four and one-half blocks from the town square. Three guest rooms are available, two with private baths and one with a shared. The interior of the house is decorated with Victorian antiques. A common area contains a television set and a VCR. Breakfast is continental plus. Moderate. Check out the Web site at www.bbonline.com/tn/clardy.

THE DIXIE DEWDROP

Warren County was the birthplace of perhaps the most colorful entertainer ever to appear on the Grand Ole Opry. The son of a Confederate army veteran, Dave Macon spent 14 years hereabouts, then moved with his family to Nashville. His family ran a hotel that was often host to traveling entertainers, and the young Macon would hang around musicians, listening to them talk and watching carefully as they rehearsed.

His father was murdered in Nashville, and the family moved to rural Cannon County, where Macon lived life like many others; he worked on a farm, got married, raised a family, and hauled freight on wagons pulled by mules.

When he was on the far side of 50, Macon began playing music professionally. He started locally, and before long "Uncle Dave Macon" was booked all over the South. His act was a combination of cornball comedy and boisterously played music with titles such as "Keep My Skillet Good and Greasy." Macon successfully combined folk music, songs he had heard black people sing when he was a boy, and the latest from Tin Pan Alley. He would introduce his numbers with a story or a joke. Audiences loved him.

In 1924 he made his first recordings in New York City, and his records could often be found alongside those of the Carter Family on the shelves of Tennesseans and others. When the Grand Ole Opry came along, 55-year-old Uncle Dave was ready. He had played on the Opry's WSM before, and he took to the new medium with confidence.

He remained with the Opry until a few months before he died in 1952. As country music got slicker and slicker, Uncle Dave served as a connection to the simpler times, and Nashville old-timers still tell stories about him. One of them, recounted in Charles K. Wolfe's excellent *Tennessee Strings,* tells how Uncle Dave once said of Bing Crosby, "He's a nice boy, but he'll never get anywhere until he learns to sing louder so people can hear."

Then there's Simply Southern Bed Breakfast, 211 N. Tennessee Blvd., tel. (615) 896-4988, which sits across the street from MTSU. Their Web site is www.bbonline.com/tn/simplysouthern. Moderate-Premium.

Motels

Among the numerous choices are the Inexpensive **Comfort Inn,** 110 N. Thompson Ln., tel. (615) 890-2811, rates $36-44; **Hampton Inn,** 2230 Old Fort Pkwy., tel. (615) 896-1172 or (800) HAMP-TON, rates $49-56; **Howard Johnson Lodge,** 2424 S. Church St., tel. (615) 896-5522 or (800) 446-7656, rates $32-49; **Shoney's Inn,** 1954 S. Church St., tel. (615) 896-6030 or (800) 222-2222, rates $40-55; and **Wayside Inn,** Hwy. 231 and I-24, tel. (615) 896-2320, rates $43-45.

Moderate-priced lodgings include **Holiday Inn Holidome,** 2227 Old Fort Pkwy., tel. (615) 896-2420 or (800) HOLIDAY, rates $53-65; **Quality Inn,** 118 Westgate Blvd., tel. (615) 848-9030, rates $30-75; and **Ramada Limited,** 1855 S. Church St., tel. (615) 896-5080 or (800) 272-6232, rates $30-65.

At the top of the heap is the **Garden Plaza Hotel,** 1850 Old Fort Pkwy., tel. (615) 895-5555, rates $59-109. Moderate-Expensive.

Buck-Naked Camping

The 25-acre naturalist resort **Rock Haven Lodge,** 462 Rock Haven Rd., tel. (615) 896-3553, has a 100-site campground on the grounds; the sites are available from April Fools Day until the first weekend in October.

FOOD

Bangkok Cafe, off the square at 113 N. Maple St., tel. (615) 896-8399, offers Pad Thai and other traditional Thai dishes.

Bunganut Pig Pub and Eatery, 1602 W. Northfield Blvd., tel. (615) 893-7860, is a fun place to go. The menu includes shepherd's pie, fish and chips; American fare such as steak, chicken, pasta, salads, sandwiches; and a complete bar. It offers live entertainment from blues to bluegrass every night.

The **City Cafe,** 113 E. Main St., tel. (615) 893-1303, has been serving plate lunches of country cooking since 1900.

Corkeys, 116 John R. Rice Blvd., tel. (615) 890-1742, is a branch of the famous Memphis barbecue eatery. It serves both wet and dry ribs, as well as great pork barbecue.

Demos' Steak and Spaghetti House, 1115 NW Broad St., tel. (615) 895-3701, has been voted "Best Restaurant" for two years in a row by *The Nashville Scene.* It also serves seafood and sandwiches.

The Front Porch Cafe, 114 E. College St., tel. (615) 896-6771, presents soups and sandwiches in a restored old home.

Sebastian's and Diana's Brewpub, 109 N. Maple St., tel. (615) 895-8658, makes its own lager and has American dishes to eat.

At **Marina's Italian Restaurant,** 125 N. Maple St., tel. (615) 849-8885, diners have to wait 20-25 minutes for their food. People don't object, because everything here is made fresh, and you can taste it. Try the oven-baked garlic chicken or traditional Italian dishes such as chicken Marsala. Marina's has one of the better wine cellars in town as well.

The Parthenon, at 1935 S. Church St., tel. (615) 895-2665, offers Greek dishes as well as American fare.

Farther Afield

Pope Taylor's Bar-B-que, 4409 E. Main St., tel. (615) 893-7191, is about four miles east of Murfreesboro on Hwy. 70 S toward Woodbury. This place has a great roadhouse atmosphere and pulled pork, ribs and chicken halves.

Manuel's Cajun Country Store, off Hwy. 96 on Milton Rd. in Milton, tel. (615) 273-2312, combines an eatery and shop featuring Cajun delights. This family operation, run by the lively Abe and Dottie Manuel, has son Tim cooking, while Shirley, Judy, Bobbie, and granddaughter Layla serve. Dishes include shrimp or crayfish etouffee; red beans and rice; fried alligator, shrimp, oysters, and catfish; and shrimp okra gumbo. All the seafood is brought up from Louisiana; extended family members in Louisiana trap the 'gators and get them up to Tim. On the shelves, visitors can find Cajun seasonings, Louisiana memorabilia, hot sauces, and Cajun coffee.

Visitors swing to live Cajun music at Manuel's

each Friday and Saturday night 6-9 p.m. Abe leads off with his fiddle or guitar while Dottie plays guitar and sings and daughter Shirley plays washboard. This musical family spawned brothers Joe and Abe Jr., who back Merle Haggard. When weather permits, the dancing moves outside onto the main street. This busy place serves hundreds of customers every weekend, and reservations are taken until 6:30 p.m.

Millers' Grocery: a Country Cafe, 7011 Main St., Christiana, tel. (615) 893-1878, between Murfreesboro and Bell Buckle, was a store for 80 years and is now a restaurant featuring what the owners call "country gourmet" food. Everything here is made from scratch, including award-winning desserts. Friday features an unbeatable combination—catfish and live bluegrass. Saturday and Sunday nights offer a buffet with two seatings. This place often sells out, so reservations are strongly suggested.

Visitors will find **Lynch's Restaurant and Dairy Bar** near Eagleville City Hall at the intersection of Hwy. 41A and Hwy. 99, tel. (615) 274-6427. Billy Lynch, former mayor of this tiny town, runs the restaurant himself. It is known for a meat-and-three-vegetable plate lunch, and ice cream and homemade pies.

SHOPPING AND INFORMATION

Murfreesboro has a large number of antique dealers, most of which are listed in Maud Gold Kiser's excellent *Treasure Hunter's Guide,* which is available at bookstores or by calling (615) 383-3411.

The Shoppes at River Rock lie off I-24 Exit 78 on Hwy. 96 W, tel. (615) 895-4966.

Yesteryear's, 3511 Old Nashville Hwy., tel. (615) 893-3470, sells Civil War relics such as swords, buckles, buttons, and guns, as well as memorabilia and letters.

Arts and Crafts
Studio S. Pottery, 1426 Avon Rd., tel. (615) 896-0789, produced the china now used in the White House and has done work for almost every president since Richard Nixon. Its work is decorative yet functional.

Information
The **Rutherford County Chamber of Commerce** can be found at 501 Memorial Blvd., tel. (615) 893-6565 or (800) 716-7560, in an 1853 log house. It's open Mon.-Fri. 8 a.m.-4:30 p.m. See them online at www.rutherfordcounty.org.

SOUTH OF MURFREESBORO

BELL BUCKLE

During the Civil War, various officers from the British Army came to peruse the proceedings. Colonel Arthur Freemantle witnessed a grand review of the Confederate Army of Tennessee in Bell Buckle in 1863, and he wrote the following: "Most of them were armed with Enfield rifles captured from the enemy. Many, however, had lost or thrown away their bayonets, which they don't appear to value properly, as they assert they have never met any Yankees who would wait for that weapon."

To those pulling in from the west, the tiny town of Bell Buckle seems to consist entirely of a short row of 19th-century shops facing the railroad tracks. "Is this all there is?" would be a very reasonable question at this point.

There is more to the town, as a drive down Webb St. proves. Bell Buckle was a thriving railroad town in the years after the Civil War, and in 1886 the town leaders made a very smart investment: They offered to subsidize the **Webb School**'s move from Maury County to here. The school accepted the offer and through the years became one of the leading boarding schools in the South, producing 10 Rhodes Scholars, governors of three states, and a host of alumni who love to come back and spend money. Visit online at www.the webbschool.com.

Today the school consists of about 240 students and 35 or so faculty. Visitors are invited to tour the **Junior Room Museum** on Webb Rd. at the edge of the campus. This museum depicts the original one-room schoolhouse. Admission is free, and the museum is open during school hours.

Despite the presence of the school, the town declined throughout this century, until Railroad Square got down to one store. That's when Anne White Scruggs came to town. A professional potter, she was looking for an inexpensive studio and bought two buildings for $4,000. "In the beginning," she recalls, "we'd have days we would only take in fifty cents. Bell Buckle is built on strong-willed people and risk-takers."

Scruggs' presence launched a renaissance for Bell Buckle, and today the town is noted for crafts, antiques, and festivals. In 1984 the National Quilt Convention was held here, bringing more than 20,000 people to this small place.

Sights

Bell Buckle is home to the **Louvin Brothers Museum,** 25 Railroad Square, tel. (931) 389-9655—what Charlie Louvin calls "the only new building in Bell Buckle." The Louvin Brothers, Charlie and Ira, were perhaps country music's greatest brother act. Their harmony took them to the Grand Ole Opry, where they sang songs such as "Must You Throw Dirt in My Face." Ira died in 1965, and Charlie continues to appear on the Opry.

The museum contains show clothing, mandolins and guitars—Charlie plays a Martin—old records, and a wide variety of printed material. Charlie is usually in the museum which is usually open on Saturday afternoons. In a refreshing contrast to the country souvenir store "museums" in Nashville, admission is free to the Louvin Brothers Museum.

The poet laureate of Tennessee, Margaret Britton Vaughn, runs **Bell Buckle Press** on Bell Buckle's historic Railroad Square, tel. (931) 389-6878. Few people ever get to see a poet in the flesh, and this one can quote verses and sell birdhouses at the same time. Other poets and literary types have gravitated to Bell Buckle, which may be on its way to becoming a Middle Tennessee Bloomsbury.

The **Seldom Scene Farm,** tel. (931) 389-6783, raises Tennessee Walking Horses and ostriches. Tours are offered by appointment only.

Entertainment

Bell Buckle Cafe swings with live music Thurs.-Sat. nights and Sunday afternoons. Admission is free. The **J. Gregry Jamboree,** a live concert and radio broadcast described as a cross between *Saturday Night Live* and Garrison Keillor's Lake Wobegon, is presented every Saturday afternoon 1-3 p.m. Call (931) 389-9693 or get more info online at www.bellbucklecafe.com.

Events

Details on all of the following can be had by calling the Bell Buckle Chamber of Commerce at (931) 389-9911. All events are on the third weekend of the month.

Daffodil Day, a celebration of spring, kicks off the season in March.

A **Moon Pie Festival** in June features the world's largest Moon Pie (in 1996 it stretched four feet across and was about eight inches thick), country music, contests, and games.

September brings a **Barbecue Cookoff,** with live music and plenty to eat.

Quilt Walk in September is a tour of the town with quilts displayed in homes and churches.

The **Webb School Art and Craft Festival** in October brings more than 800 exhibitors and a crowd of 70,000-80,000 to town.

The **Haunted Evening** in October brings the thrills of Halloween to Bell Buckle, and **Christmas Open House,** late in November, brings an old-fashioned Christmas to town.

Where to Stay

The **Bell Buckle Bed & Breakfast,** 17 Webb Rd., Bell Buckle, TN 37020, tel. (931) 389-9371, is owned by Bob and Anne Scruggs, the people responsible for the town's renaissance. They also own Bell Buckle Crafts, so this house is decorated to the nth degree. The Victorian home contains three guest rooms, two of which have private baths. Rates range $55-65 and include a heavy continental breakfast. Inexpensive-Moderate.

Food

The **Bell Buckle Cafe** on Railroad Square, tel. (931) 389-9693, offers barbecue, steak, chicken, and other dishes.

Bocelli, 15 Webb Rd., tel. (931) 389-6124, is a new Italian restaurant in Bell Buckle. Subs, pizza, and the like are the fare.

Shopping

Bell Buckle Antique & Craft Mall, around the corner from the row of shops on Liberty Pike, tel. (931) 389-6174, contains 50 exhibitors.

The **Bell Buckle Bookstore** on Railroad Square, tel. (931) 389-9328, carries new and used books. It has a good Civil War section.

Daffodilly, in the town's old drugstore at Railroad Square, tel. (931) 389-6663, offers collectible antiques.

Phillips General Store on Railroad Square, tel. (931) 389-6547, is an antique shop specializing in primitive and architectural pieces, folk art, antique dolls, and antique quilts.

Traditions and Bell Buckle Country Store, at the end of Railroad Square, tel. (931) 389-9555 or (800) 707-0483, is a Victorian shop selling all manner of jellies, vintage hats, jewelry, homemade sauces, and jams. Captain Rodney's Hot Pepper Jelly is shipped all over the world from here.

Arts and Crafts

Bell Buckle Crafts on Railroad Square, tel. (931) 389-9371, is the granddaddy of all the shops hereabouts. Inside are pottery, quilts, willow furniture, and wire sculpture. Visitors can also have their photos made while dressed in antique clothing.

Bingham's Fabrics Quilting & Crafts, 3 Webb Rd., tel. (931) 389-6908, is one of the finer quilt shops in the state. They have 800-900 bolts of cloth.

Information

Bell Buckle Chamber of Commerce, 26 Railroad Square, tel. (931) 389-9555, is open whenever Traditions and Bell Buckle Country Store are open. See them online at www.bellbuckle.com.

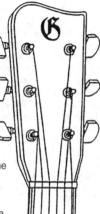

Est. 1965

Gallagher guitars logo

WARTRACE

This town's unusual name comes from "trace," an old word for road, and the fact that various Indians traveled up and down it to fight each other. Wartrace reached its peak as a railroad junction, when its one hotel was built. This hamlet is known as the "Cradle of the Tennessee Walking Horse," for the owner of the hotel trained a horse, Strolling Jim, who in 1939 became the first Tennessee Walking Horse Grand Champion. The event that eventually became the Walking Horse Celebration got its start in Wartrace, but was later moved to Shelbyville. (For more on Walking Horses, see "Shelbyville and Vicinity" later in this chapter.)

Eager to emulate the success of Bell Buckle, its neighboring town, Wartrace is beginning to recognize its heritage, spruce up its buildings, and attract visitors. Much of the downtown is listed on the National Register of Historic Places. A steady stream of musicians come to Wartrace to buy Gallagher guitars, which are handcrafted here.

The center of town is the **Walking Horse Hotel,** built in 1917. The first floor is the **Strolling Jim Restaurant,** the second floor has shops, and guest rooms occupy the third floor. This is a town on the way back.

Entertainment and Events

Gallagher Guitar Homecoming Festival, held every May, offers a chance for owners of these famous guitars to get together, listen to each other pick a little, and have a good time. The high point is a concert at the Cascade School. Call (931) 389-6455.

Where to Stay

Log Cabin, 171 Loop Rd., Wartrace, TN 37183, tel. (931) 389-6713, is a two-story, 4,000-square-foot cabin just outside of town in the middle of eight acres of farmland. The three guest rooms all have private baths. The house can sleep a total of 12 people. Rates are $65 and up and include a full breakfast, which the owner modestly calls "the best breakfast in Tennessee." Moderate.

The Walking Horse Hotel in the middle of town, tel. (931) 389-7050, is where many of the early decisions about developing the breed were made. The first grand champion, Strolling Jim, is buried behind the building, which displays Walking Horse memorabilia. The hotel, built in 1917, is on the National Register and contains seven rooms, all with private baths, and all with access to the verandah. One room, on the first floor, is handicapped accessible. The building has new central heat and air-conditioning. Rates are Moderate.

Food

Strolling Jim Restaurant, in the Walking Horse Hotel, tel. (931) 389-7050, offers a cuisine that retains the best of Southern cooking yet presents it with a modern, healthy approach. Lunch entrees range $5-7.

Wartrace Whistle Stop, 27 Main St., tel. (931) 389-6119, doesn't have fried green tomatoes, but it does offer ice cream, pizza, burgers, and cappuccino.

Just south of town, **Our House,** in Haley 15 miles west of I-24 Exit 97 toward Wartrace, tel. (931) 389-6616 or (800) 876-6616, has food so good that people from Huntsville, Alabama, regularly make a pilgrimage here. Typical entrees include blackened sea bass, broiled salmon with dill sauce, braised pork with blueberry sauce, and grilled rack of lamb. The seafood is fresh! Linens, china, and crystal complement the food and the decor. Reservations are necessary. To get there from Wartrace, take Vine St. east for 2.9 miles.

Shopping

If the visitor has ever had an urge to joint the growing number of Civil War reenactors, the **Blockade Runner,** 103 Blackman Blvd., tel. (931) 389-6294, is the place. Located in an old mill, this store carries everything needed to assume the persona of an 1860s lady or gentleman. A Confederate kepi cap costs $27.50, men's wool pants go for $71, and a shirt sells for $22. A woman's "work dress"—nothing fancy, now—sells for $169. Their entire catalog can be seen at www.blockaderunner.com.

Gallagher Guitars, 7 Main St., tel. (931) 389-6455, every year produces just over 100 acoustic instruments, which range in price $1700-3000—custom models can run as high as $10,000. Customers include Johnny Cash, Doc Watson, and Neil Diamond. Visitors can take a brief tour of the factory as well. See what they have online at www.dnj.com/gallagher.

The second floor of the Walking Horse Hotel contains gift shops and an antique mall.

Information

The Wartrace area keeps up a pretty informative website at www.volweb.utk.edu/schools/bedford/cascade/wartrace.

MANCHESTER

This town, the seat of Coffee County, sits at the edge of the Cumberland Plateau on the banks of the Duck River, which is the longest river completely in Tennessee. The town was named for Manchester, England, and local entrepreneurs hoped to make this place an industrial center that would live up to its namesake. They erected mills along the Duck River, and for a time Manchester enjoyed a lively business in cotton.

SIGHTS AND RECREATION

The **Manchester Walk/Drive Tour** points out historic houses, churches, and other buildings. Copies of the brochure are available at the chamber of commerce at 110 E. Main Street.

Museum Arrowheads/Aerospace Cultural Center, Exit 114 of I-24, tel. (931) 723-1323, is a five-acre site that includes nature walks and a 7,000-square-foot museum that houses antique dolls, toys, trains, quilts, an old general store, military displays, fossils, and Indian relics. Outside is a playground. Tours and special activities, such as storytelling and Civil War demonstra-

tions, are scheduled throughout the year.

Eli's Country Store, 1001 Hwy. 41, tel. (931) 728-4452, is a small museum in the back of Jiffy Burger where owner David Pennington displays his private collections of more than 3,000 toys from the 1920s through the '60s. Highlights include more than 400 cap guns and 22 pedal cars. Admission is free.

Rutledge Falls, where Crumpton Creek has cut through the Southern Highland Rim of Tennessee, is worth seeing. Visitors should drive southwest from the town square on Hwy. 55 for 4.1 miles, then turn right onto Belmont Road (some maps show this as Wilson Rd.). Go 1.2 miles to Cat Creek Road, then go left for 1.5 miles to Short Springs Road. Turn right at the Rutledge Falls Baptist Church onto Rutledge Falls Rd., where a parking area sits next to a large house with a gazebo. These falls are on private property, but the owners permit people to see them.

Entertainment and Events

The **Coffee County Fair** takes place in the third full week in September at the Coffee County Fairgrounds in Manchester.

Old Timer's Day has been going for more than three decades. Held in early October, it includes clogging, music, food, a parade, and a five-kilometer race.

WHERE TO STAY

Bed and Breakfast
My Grandmother's House, 704 Hickory Grove Rd., Manchester, TN 37357, tel. (931) 728-6293, is a log home built in 1837 in Franklin County. Moved to this site, it has been meticulously restored into a bed and breakfast with 10 rooms and 3,200 square feet. The house has three guest rooms, all of which share baths. The rooms, one of which comes with a nursery, have period antiques and family furniture. All of the light fixtures—all 23 of them—were fashioned by the owner, a tinsmith. The common room contains a fireplace and hand-stenciled floors. The host serves a full country breakfast. The rate is $55. Inexpensive.

Motels
You'll find a number of chain inns in the area. **Ambassador Inn** is on Interstate Dr., tel. (931) 728-2200 or (800) 237-9365. **Hampton Inn** is at I-24 and Hwy. 53, tel. (931) 728-3300. **Holiday Inn** is at I-24 Exit 114, tel. (931) 728-9651 or (800) 465-4329. **Scottish Inn** is at I-24 Exit 114, tel. (931) 728-0506 or (800) 251-1962.

Camping
KOA Manchester, tel. (931) 728-9777, has 87 sites. From I-24 take Exit 114 and follow the signs.

Whispering Oaks Campground, tel. (931) 728-0225, has 80 sites, a heated pool, fishing, hiking trails, limited grocery store, recreation hall, and playground. From I-24 take Exit 105 and follow the signs.

MORE PRACTICALITIES

Food
J & G Pizza, Hwy. 55/Rt. 3, tel. (931) 728-9696, serves very good Greek food in addition to pizza. This is the place for Greek salads and shish-kabob, as well as steaks and sandwiches.

Jiffy Burgers, 1001 Hwy. 41, tel. (931) 728-4452, dishes up country barbecue, burgers, and more. Don't skip the toy museum out back.

Shopping
North Side Clocks, 2032 MacArthur/Hwy. 55, tel. (931) 728-4307, is one of the finer timepiece shops in the state. Over 1,000 new, old, and antique clocks are for sale at any given time—so to speak—and repairs are done here as well.

Foothills Crafts, 800 Woodbury Hwy./Hwy. 53, tel. (931) 728-9236, is the shop for an association of more than 600 regional artisans and craftspeople. The building is stacked floor to ceiling with finely crafted wooden furniture, textiles, stained glass, prints, pottery, jewelry, sculpture, and more. The association also offers classes and seminars in crafts.

Information
The **Manchester Area Chamber of Commerce,** 110 E. Main St., tel. (931) 728-7635, is open daily 8 a.m.-4:30 p.m.

OLD STONE FORT STATE ARCHAEOLOGICAL AREA

Just northwest of Manchester on Hwy. 41, this 940-acre area along the Duck River was once thought to hold the remnants of a structure built by persons unknown. The "fort" encloses something like 50 acres with a perimeter measuring one and a quarter miles. Speculation held that Hernando de Soto, roving Vikings, or some obscure Welsh prince built the fort. Under closer examination, however, these theories faded away. Studies by the University of Tennessee date the structure to the Indians of the Woodland period—about A.D. 30-430. The purpose of the enclosure was probably ceremonial, but there is no conclusive proof of this.

Two forks of the Duck River cut into the Highland Rim here, resulting in a beautiful landscape. Remnants of old mills that once used the water power still stand in the park, which has excellent fishing as well. The area contains a visitors center and museum, 51 campsites, hiking trails, numerous beautiful waterfalls, picnic areas, and a nine-hole golf course. Call (931) 723-5073 for information or see it online at www.tnstateparks.com.

The **Old Stone Fort Arts & Crafts Festival** is held late in September. Call (931) 728-9236.

TULLAHOMA AND VICINITY

This town saw the Confederate army coming and going. General Braxton Bragg and his troops came back to Tullahoma after invading Perryville, Kentucky, and from here they headed north again to confront a Union army moving south from Nashville. After the disastrous Battle of Stones River in December 1862 and January 1863, the troops returned to Tullahoma, where they spent the rest of the winter. The Union army moved again, however, backing the Confederates out of Tullahoma and down into Georgia, where they clashed at the Battle of Chickamauga. A Confederate cemetery is sited in the back section of the Maplewood Cemetery.

SIGHTS AND RECREATION

Sitting on the rail line from Nashville to Chattanooga, Tullahoma bounced back from the Civil War more quickly than surrounding towns. The town's prosperity shows in the collection of Victorian homes that makes up the **Historic Depot District.** The chamber of commerce offers a brochure for a walking tour of the district.

Part of Tullahoma's 20th-century success was due to the location of Camp Forrest, an enormous, 10-square-mile army base named for Nathan Bedford Forrest and established in 1926. During World War II it became an induction center for Americans and, later, a prisoner-of-war camp for Germans. After the war, U.S. military leaders proposed studying jet propulsion, and a 40,000-acre site that included some of Camp Forrest was selected on which to build a research center. **Arnold Engineering Development Center,** tel. (931) 454-3000, ext. 3396, is its name, and since 1951 jet and rocket engines have been tested here. Tours are offered Mon.-Fri. during business hours and last about two and a half hours. Group sizes range 12-35 people. Visitors need reservations, but there is no charge.

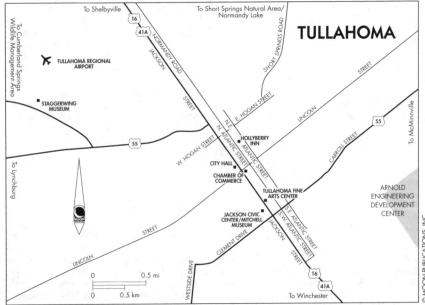

Softball and baseball fans should head for the **Worth Sports Company,** 2102 N. Jackson St., tel. (931) 455-0691 or (800) 282-9637, the world's largest manufacturer of softballs, baseballs, and bats. There are free tours for up to 20 people at 8 a.m. and 10 a.m. on Wednesday, but call first. See it online at www.worthsports.com.

South Jackson Civic Center, 402 S. Jackson St., tel. (931) 455-0620, in the first public school building in Tullahoma, houses the performing arts center and the Mitchell Museum. Call for a listing of the current performances.

Museums

The **Walter H. Beech Staggerwing Museum,** tel. (931) 455-1974, honors a particular kind of aircraft produced by the Beech Aircraft Company 1932-46. Staggerwings were biplanes whose upper wing was set farther back than the lower wing, or "staggered." This innovative design permitted the small planes to fly at 200 miles per hour at a time when commercial airliners flew at only 175-180 mph. "These were the Lear jets of the '30s," explained a trustee of the museum.

Using a Staggerwing, Louise Thaden won a 1936 transcontinental race. Approximately 800 Staggerwings were built, about 200 survive today, and about 100 still fly. The museum occupies a complex beside the Tullahoma airport and contains an example of every model of Staggerwing Beechcraft ever built, including the very first one. Admission is free for those 12 and under, and $4 for everyone else. The museum can be opened by special appointment, but admission then is $5 per adult. To get there, take Hwy. 130 off Hwy. 55, or you can visit the museum online at www.cyberair.com/museums/usa/tn/swm.html.

The South Jackson Civic Center's **Floyd and Margaret Mitchell Museum** depicts Tullahoma and regional history with Indian artifacts, antique clothing, military items from the Civil War that were unearthed from Tullahoma, an exhibit of Camp Forrest items, a handcrafted Civil War diorama, items from World War I and World War II, antiques, dolls, old photographs, tools, and even the contents of the cornerstone from the old high school. Admission is free, and the museum is open on the first Sunday afternoon of the month. To see it at other times, call (931) 455-5321 and press "0."

The **Tullahoma Fine Arts Center/Regional Museum of Art,** 401 S. Jackson St./Hwy. 41A, tel. (931) 455-1234, occupies an 1868 house and has permanent and touring exhibits. Some items are for sale. Admission is free.

Outside Town

Short Springs Natural Area is a 420-acre nature preserve that is noted for its wildflowers and unique botanical specimens. Hiking trails lead to two falls and Normandy Lake. Along the way are rugged rock outcroppings. This area with its underground water source was the old watershed for the community. To get there, go three miles out of Tullahoma on Short Springs Road. The chamber of commerce has further information, or call (931) 455-2648, ext. 109.

Millions of magazine readers through the years have seen the black and white photographs that illustrated Jack Daniel's ads. The first photographer of these was the late Joe Clark, and an exhibition of his work is on display in the library at Motlow College's Crouch Learning Center, west of town off Hwy. 55 at Ledford Mill Rd., tel. (931) 393-1660. Most of the subjects in the **Joe Clark Photo Display,** however, were photographed in East Tennessee. Admission is free. See the site online at www.mscc.cc.tn.us.

Entertainment and Events

The **Paul Pyle Dulcimer Festival,** held the Sunday after Father's Day each June, brings together makers and players of this classic Appalachian instrument. The musicians jam for several days before the actual festival. The jamming and the festival are held at the South Jackson Civic Center. Call (931) 455-6800.

Tullahoma Fine Arts & Crafts Festival takes place on the last weekend in May on the school grounds across from the Fine Arts Center. Booths and exhibits from 100 artists display artwork in a variety of disciplines: basket weaving, pottery, quilting, watercolors, and drawing. The artwork is juried and prizes are awarded to artisans in the different categories late Saturday on the festival grounds. The National Watercolors Society competition and the high school competition are simultaneously displayed in the Fine Arts Center. The festival covers about an acre and a half and draws approximately 8,000-10,000 people. Call (931) 455-1234.

PRACTICALITIES

Where to Stay

Hollyberry Inn, 302 N. Atlantic St., Tullahoma, TN 37388, tel. (931) 455-4445, is a turn-of-the-century Greek revival home with a 60-foot-long porch stretching across the front, complete with columns. Guests can enjoy a hot tub and whirlpool. Once the railroad superintendent's home, it's in the Historic Depot District and is on the National Register. Inside, the three guest rooms offer canopied beds and private baths. The master suite includes a fireplace, private bedroom, and Mark Hampton bed. Rates for the inn run $79-129 and include breakfast. Hollyberry Inn was a restaurant in times past and still serves gourmet meals with reservations. Moderate-Premium.

Motel options are the **Knotty Pine Motel,** 2323 N. Jackson St., tel. (931) 455-4493; **Steeplechase Inn,** 1410 N. Jackson St., tel. (931) 455-4501; and the **Veranda Hotel,** 100 W. Lincoln St., tel. (931) 455-7033.

Shipman Creek, west of Tullahoma, has had a mill since 1807. The building housing **Ledford Mill Bed & Breakfast,** Rt. 2, Box 152 B, Wartrace, TN 37183, tel. (931) 455-2546, the current incarnation, was built in 1884. The three-story mill was powered by a water turbine, which is much more efficient than the large mill wheels so beloved by photographers. Now one of the more unusual bed and breakfasts in the state, the three rooms all have their furniture beside the now-defunct milling machinery. The room at the top has two bedrooms and a balcony overlooking the creek and waterfall. Rates are $80-100. See them online at www.bbonline.com/tn/ledfordmill. To get there, take Hwy. 41A northwest from Tullahoma and turn left onto Ledford Mill Road. Follow the signs. The mill is open Tues.-Sat. 10 a.m.-6 p.m. and Sunday noon-6 p.m. Moderate-Expensive.

Food

Daddy Billy's Delicatessen, on N. Atlantic St. north of Anderson Street along the railroad, tel. (931) 455-6195, is allegedly haunted by three ghosts from the Civil War who "don't like it when furniture is moved." If patrons leave the furniture alone, the sandwiches are very good.

The Stuffed Goose, at 115 N. Collins St., tel. (931) 455-6673, serves chicken salad, fresh-baked bread, and light meals.

Leaving Tullahoma and heading northwest toward Shelbyville on Hwy. 41A/16, Shipman Creek Rd. goes off to the left just past the airport. Look for the sign to **Granny Fishes,** tel. (931) 857-4025. This place is famous hereabouts for fresh trout and catfish, frog legs, huspuppies, and homemade pies.

Shopping

The **Coca-Cola Company Store,** 1504 E. Carroll St./Hwy. 55, tel. (931) 454-1030, specializes in selling all sorts of memorabilia with the famous red and white logo.

Smiling Owl Gallery & Gifts, 111 Lincoln St., tel. (931) 455-0673, carries the works of regional artists: jewelry, pottery, glassware, and woodturning.

Information

Tullahoma Chamber of Commerce, 135 W. Lincoln St., tel. (931) 455-5497, is open 8:30 a.m.-4:30 p.m. You can visit them online at www.tullahoma.net.

NORMANDY

Before Prohibition, Tennessee had more distilleries than any other state in the country. In the 1800s, one of them was the **George Dickel Distillery,** tel. (931) 857-3124, which transformed spring water from Cascade Hollow into George A. Dickel's Cascade Whiskey. George died in 1894, and Prohibition put an end to the distillery. In 1956, the Schenley Distillers of Kentucky rebuilt the works and got back in the whiskey-making business. While not as famous as Jack Daniel's, a mere 20 miles away, George Dickel is made in pretty much the same fashion, mellowing the whiskey by dripping it through tall vats of charcoal made from sugar maple. The old-timers say that this "takes the hog tracks out of it." Whatever it does, the product is classified as Tennessee Sour Mash Whiskey, a product distinct from bourbon.

The George Dickel Distillery offers tours of its operations. To get there, take I-24 to Exit 105, then go south on Hwy. 41. Turn right onto

Hwy. 4291 toward Blanton Chapel Rd., then follow signs to the distillery.

Where to Stay
Parish Patch Farm & Inn, 1100 Courtner Rd., Normandy, tel. (931) 857-3017 or (800) 876-3017, sits on a 230-acre working farm and began its career as a corporate retreat. It has 21 guest rooms and two cabins, all with private baths, color television, and air-conditioning. Guests can stroll along the Duck River, swim in a pool, go birdwatching, bicycle, fish, hike, or work out in the exercise room. The inn also offers a playground for children. To get there, follow the directions for Courtner Mill Restaurant below. Rates are $68-185 and include breakfast. Moderate-Luxury.

Food
The **Courtner Mill Restaurant,** tel. (931) 857-3018 or (800) 876-3017, offers country dining in a scenic and historic atmosphere. The mill, built in 1848, holds 82 diners who can feast on dinners including Cornish game hens, frog legs, and rainbow trout. The specialty of the house is beefalo steaks, which are raised on the farm. Beefalos are a cross between buffalo and cattle, and the resulting meat has one-fifth the cholesterol of regular beef. To get there from Tullahoma, follow Hwy. 269 N for approximately seven miles.

TULLAHOMA TO FAYETTEVILLE

TIMS FORD STATE RUSTIC PARK

This 413-acre park sits on the banks of the 10,700-acre Tims Ford Reservoir between Tullahoma and Winchester. Fishing and other lake-oriented activities are the chief focus here, but visitors can also hike, bike, and enjoy a swimming pool and other recreation.

Accommodations include 20 cabins overlooking the lake. Each sleeps eight in two bedrooms and comes with a fireplace, outdoor balcony, and reasonably equipped kitchen. Cabins are available March 1-December 1 and cost $90 per night. Expensive. The campground offers 50 sites with tables, grills, and hookups, available on a first-come, first-served basis. Bathhouses have hot showers. For information and to make reservations, visitors should call (931) 967-4457 or (800) 421-6683.

LYNCHBURG

If the wind is right, visitors approaching this village can detect a sweet, slightly odd smell before coming into town. This is the aroma of sour mash—fermenting corn, rye, and barley malt—which is the principal ingredient of the **Jack Daniel Distillery,** tel. (931) 759-6180, home to Tennessee's most famous product. A long-running and highly successful ad campaign depicts Lynchburg as a place where time stands still, where various overall-wearing, hardworking good old boys crank out "sippin' whiskey, drop by drop."

It's true.

Lynchburg is a tiny town, and the distillery, the oldest registered one in the country, is the biggest game in town. Jack Daniel erected his distillery in 1866 below a large spring that produces superb, iron-free water. Free tours are given every day 8 a.m.-4 p.m. (closed Thanksgiving, Chrismas, and New Year's Day), and more than a quarter of a million people take one every year. They see a barrelhouse, where more than 20,000 barrels of whiskey are aged; the brickyard, where hard sugar maple is burned to produce charcoal; the bubbling, fermenting vats of sour mash; and the spring from which the water flows. The distillery serves no samples, although visitors can buy commemorative bottles for off-site consumption. Moore County is a dry county.

Lynchburg is so small and the distillery signs are so pervasive that directions are not needed. The tour is totally accessible—including the brewery from which Jack Daniel's 1866 Class Amber Lager flows. The closest place to buy the complete range of Jack Daniel's products is Tullahoma. Knock one back online at www.jack-daniels.com/.

The rest of Lynchburg centers on the town square, in the middle of which sits the 1885 Moore County Courthouse. Most of the businesses here are intent on separating tourists from their dollars, but an auto parts place and co-op still serve the locals. The **Historic Old Jail Museum,** which displays photographs of the town and the history of the jail, is open irregularly, but mostly during weekdays April-October. Admission is free, but visitors are expected to leave some sort of donation.

Entertainment

Bar-B-Que Caboose Cafe, on the square, tel. (931) 759-5180, offers country music and blue-grass jam sessions on Saturday mornings and every Saturday night, except in the wintertime.

Events

For information on all of the following, call the Welcome Center, tel. (931) 759-4111.

Spring in the Hollow is a one-day event held in early May with antique cars, arts and crafts, food, and music.

Frontier Days late in June recalls the days when Tennessee was the wild and woolly West. People in pioneer garb take their places in a nonmotorized parade amid music, food, and crafts.

Jack Daniel's Birthday Celebration, September 9, usually involves at least one country music headliner, local country music people, clogging, and crafts and food booths. About 5,000 people attend this annual event held on the square and in nearby Wiseman Park.

Jack Daniel's World Champion Invitational Bar-B-Que Cook Off is held late in September on the square and in Wiseman Park, where 20,000-25,000 barbecue fans show up to taste the offerings of 45 or so invited cooking teams. Other activities include arts and crafts, music, cloggers, and sometimes a tractor pull and greased pig contest.

Christmas in Lynchburg, on the first Saturday in December, starts with a parade and includes caroling and tours of old houses.

Where to Stay

The Cottage Haus, on Majors Blvd., Rt. 2, Box 114, Lynchburg, TN 37352, tel. (931) 759-4273, is the second cottage north of the only traffic light in town. This completely restored Victorian cottage, built about 1880, is furnished with antiques and lies within walking distance of the town square and the distillery. The two guest suites have private baths. Rate is $75 and includes a full breakfast served in the cottage. Moderate.

Goose Branch Farm Bed & Breakfast, Rt. 3, Box 140, Lynchburg, TN 37352, tel. (931) 759-5919, is exactly three miles from downtown Lynchburg. Guests can relax in a 100-year-old large farmhouse surrounded by large shady trees on about 57 acres of farmland complete with grazing cattle, a pond, two springs, and a creek. The two suites have private entrances and private baths. The rate is $60 per night. Inexpensive.

Lynchburg Bed and Breakfast, General Delivery, Lynchburg, TN 37352, tel. (931) 759-7158, is a big 1877 two-story house with two guest rooms, one with a queen-sized bed and one with two doubles. It's within walking distance of the Jack Daniel Distillery. Rates are $50-65 and include a special continental breakfast. Visit online at www.bbonline.com/tn/lynchburg. Inexpensive-Moderate.

Farther Afield

Mulberry House Bed & Breakfast, Rt. 1, Mulberry, TN 37359, tel. (931) 433-8461, midway between Lynchburg and Fayetteville on Hwy. 50, is a 115-year-old farmhouse with two guest rooms, both with private baths. It has a nice big porch to sit on. The rate is $50 plus tax and includes a continental breakfast. See them online at www.bbonline.com/tn/mulberry. Inexpensive.

Dream Fields Bed & Breakfast, General Delivery, Mulberry, TN 37359, tel. (931) 438-8875, is a Gothic revival farmhouse built in 1845. For more than 100 years it belonged to the family of Wiley Daniel, a brother of Jack Daniel. Guests can take walking trails over the 260 acres, stroll along creeks, or partake of the occasional hayride and music at the barn. Rates run $75-100. See them online at www.bbonline.com/tn/dreamfields. Moderate-Expensive.

Tucker Inn , Rt. 3, Box 110, tel. (931) 759-5922, lies between Lynchburg and Winchester out in the country. The inn offers a 15-mile view, full country breakfast, and private baths. Rates begin at $65 for rooms, and $150 to rent the entire inn. Moderate.

Food

For many years the only place to eat in Lynchburg was **Miss Bobo's Boarding House,** tel. (931)

759-7394, which is just a few steps west of the square on Main Street. First opened in 1908 in an 1867 house, it was a favorite of Jack Daniel himself. Nowadays the place serves country cooking to about 62 people at a time; they sit at large tables and introduce themselves to each other before dining. The food is served family-style, and everyone is instructed to pass the bowls and platters to the left. Meals include at least two meats, six vegetables, a drink, breads, and dessert. Reservations are absolutely necessary for weekends—some Saturdays get booked five months in advance—and aren't a bad idea for weekdays. Lunch—called "dinner" hereabouts in the fashion of country folks—is served Mon.-Sat. at 1 p.m. and costs $12 per person.

Countryside Restaurant, west of the square on Hwy. 50, tel. (931) 759-4430, serves country cooking. The lunch buffet offers meats, vegetables, breads, and homemade desserts. It's open Mon.-Sat. for all three meals.

Iron Kettle Restaurant, on the square, tel. (931) 759-4274, serves country cooking three meals a day Mon.-Saturday.

For lighter fare, **The County Seat Deli** on the square, tel. (931) 759-5994, offers submarine sandwiches, salads, and desserts. It's open seven days a week for breakfast, lunch, and supper.

Shopping
All of the following establishments are on the square.

Country By Nature, tel. (931) 759-6444, sells dried flowers, watercolors, prints, and items related to gardening.

The Lynchburg Hardware and General Store, tel. (931) 759-4200, offers all manner of items related to Jack Daniel: clothes, clocks, mirrors, jugs, playing cards, etc.

Lynchburg Pottery, tel. (931) 759-4737, features functional and decorative works thrown by Frank and Suzanne Inman.

If one wants to enjoy a belt in Lynchburg, it has to be one of the leather variety. The **Plainsman Leather Company,** tel. (931) 759-5066, sells locally made guitar straps, belts, holsters, and other leather items.

Information
The **Lynchburg Welcome Center and Metro Moore County Chamber of Commerce,** on the square, tel. (931) 759-4111, is open Mon.-Fri. 10 a.m.-5 p.m.

FAYETTEVILLE

Visitors to Lynchburg, which can get very crowded at times, owe it to themselves to push on to Fayetteville. This lovely town is the seat of Lincoln County, a name that sounds surprising in these highly Confederate parts. The county came into being in 1809 and was named for Gen. Benjamin Lincoln, who fought in the Revolutionary War.

In 1813 Tennesseans were mustered here under the command of Andrew Jackson to punish the Creek to the south for their involvement in the Fort Mims massacre in Alabama. One year later, some 2,000 troops assembled here, this time to fight the British at Mobile, Alabama.

Just before the Civil War a beautiful stone bridge was built over the Duck River here. Its six arches spanned 450 feet, and during the war Gen. William T. Sherman marched his troops across it to join General Grant in freeing Chattanooga. According to an old story, once his troops were across, Sherman ordered the bridge destroyed, but the Union officer sent to supervise the destruction was so impressed by the graceful structure that he refused to demolish it. A flood in 1969 finally did in the bridge, and only the abutments remain.

The center of town remains the Lincoln County Courthouse and surrounding square. The shops and restaurants around it are well worth the trip. Of particular interest are two adjoining pool halls—perhaps the only such juxtaposition in the entire state. At night the lights come up at the Lincoln Theater, an old movie theater that still shows films.

Sights and Recreation
The Borden Company built a canned milk plant here in the '20s, thus creating a demand for milk that sustained local dairy farms for decades. The old Borden plant, which closed in 1967, now provides a large space for the **Lincoln County Museum,** 521 Main St., tel. (931) 438-0339. Admission is free, but donations are cheerfully accepted. To visit the museum call the chamber of commerce for hours or to have it opened.

Fayetteville's historic district contains a great

the highly ornamental "steamboat Gothic" mansion

WYATT ANTIQUES

selection of old homes. One worth a detour is the steamboat Gothic mansion at the corner of Washington St. and N. Elk Avenue. Built in 1894, this highly ornamented house contains Wyatt Antiques (under "Shopping," below) and is an architectural delight; with downstairs rooms paneled in maple, walnut, and cherry lumber that was cut on a local farm and finished in Nashville. Those who wish to see the house's interior should affect an interest in the high-end antiques—$5,000 for a plantation desk, for example—or risk getting the cold shoulder from the proprietor.

Elk River Plantation, on Eldad Rd., tel. (931) 433-9757, is a working farm of about 130 acres. The owners raise emus—"the meat of the future"—llamas, water buffaloes, horses, mules, miniature donkeys, strawberries, alfalfa, and pumpkins. The plantation is open to the public for a variety of events, all listed below. The owners also run a bed and breakfast, listed below. To get there from Fayetteville, go east on the Hwy. 64 bypass, then go south on Eldad Road. The farm is on the right just over the hill.

Nine miles east of town on Hwy. 64 in the Kelso community is **Elk Canoe Rental,** tel. (931) 937-6886, where visitors can float down the placid and scenic Elk River. This place will rent the entire works—canoes, paddles, and flotation devices—and arrange for drop-off and pickup.

Entertainment and Events
The **Lincoln Theater,** on the north side of the square, tel. (931) 433-1943, is a 1950s movie house that hasn't changed much since the days of James Dean.

The **Lincoln County Fair,** held on the second weekend in September, is much like other Tennessee county fairs with one exception: This is the only all-weather sanctioned harness-racing track in the entire state. Call (931) 433-1235.

The last weekend in September is **Sozo,** a Greek word meaning "wholeness in Christ." Around here it means a battle of Christian bands at Elk River Plantation. More than 30 bands attend—the music varies from acoustic to those of whom it is only charitably said that they make a joyful noise—and perform on the three stages erected on the farm.

During **Pumpkin Patch Days,** held every weekend in October at Elk River Plantation, sorghum is produced by mule-power. Visitors can go on hayrides, pick their own pumpkins, and visit the log museum where early pioneer family skills are demonstrated. **Haunted Hayrides** also take place on the plantation Thurs.-Sun. in October.

Fayetteville: Host of Christmas Past, on the second Saturday in November, brings costumed carolers, carriage rides, live reindeer, and Santa Claus. Call (931) 433-1235 for details.

Where to Stay

Fayetteville Bed & Breakfast, 1111 W. Washington St., Fayetteville, TN 37334, tel. (931) 433-9636, is a country home, built circa 1915, with large a wraparound porch. One guest room is available with a private bath. Rates range $50-60 and include either a full or continental breakfast. Inexpensive.

Heritage House Bed & Breakfast, 315 E. College St., Fayetteville, TN 37334, tel. (931) 433-9238, is a brick colonial-style home near the historic district. Guests enjoy a swing and wicker furniture on the porch that stretches across the front of the home. Three guest rooms are available; two comprise a suite for a family. The guest room and the suite have private baths. Rates range $50-100 and include a continental-plus breakfast. Inexpensive-Expensive.

Old Bagley House, east of town at 1801 Winchester Hwy., Fayetteville, TN 37334, tel. (931) 433-3799, looks like a French or English country house, but parts of it predate the Civil War. Deer, wild turkeys, and butterflies frequent the property, which consists of 12.9 acres of land across from Motlow College campus. Each of the three guest rooms has a private bath, and guests can relax in a private parlor. The rate is $65 per night and includes a large breakfast. See the house online at www.bbonline.com/tn/tbbia/fayetteville. Moderate.

Old Cowan Plantation, Rt. 9, Box 17, Fayetteville, TN 37334, tel. (931) 433-0225, occupies an 1886 colonial home less than a mile from town. Three guest rooms are available, each with a private bath. A sitting room contains a fireplace and television. The host serves morning coffee on the verandah overlooking the countryside. Smoking is permitted in the common rooms and dining room. Rates begin at $42. To get to Old Cowan Plantation, go west on Hwy. 64 from the square, then turn right on Old Boonshill Road. Inexpensive.

Strawberry Hill House, 77 Eldad Rd., Fayetteville, TN 37334, tel. (931) 433-9757, on Elk River Plantation is a newly remodeled tenant house with English cottage decor inside. It includes an enclosed back porch, living room with working fireplace, and fully equipped kitchen. No breakfast is served; guests cook their own. The rate is $500 a week, but guests can stay for a single night if they wish. To get there from Fayetteville, go east on the Hwy. 64 bypass, then go south on the first road—Eldad Road—and the plantation sits on the right just over the hill. Moderate.

Motel options include the **Best Western Fayetteville Inn,** tel. (931) 433-0100 or (800) 528-1234; and the **Days Inn,** 1651 Huntsville Hwy., tel. (931) 433-6121 or (800) DAYS-INN.

Food

Despite the admonitions of *The Music Man's* Prof. Harold Hill, pool halls in Fayetteville are good places to go. **Honey's Restaurant,** tel. (931) 433-1181, and **Bill's Cafe,** tel. (931) 433-5332, are adjacent to each other at, respectively, 109 and 111 E. Market Street. Honey's claims to have invented "slawburgers"—hamburgers topped with a sweet-mustard slaw—although they are served at both places. Honey's, open Mon.-Sat. for all three meals, is more of a family place and the more polished of the two.

Cahoots, 114 W. Market St., tel. (931) 433-1173, occupies the town's old firehouse and jail. Diners sit in cells as they enjoy steaks, chicken, Mexican dishes, and salads.

O'Houlihan's, 101 Market St., tel. (931) 433-0557, occupies an 1890s grocery store whose shelves now contain antiques. It serves muffins, nice sandwiches, salads, and soups.

Mulberry Bay, 108A Mulberry Ave., tel. (931) 433-3192, housed in an old building that was the first car wash in town, is now beautifully decorated. It serves sandwiches, salads, and desserts.

Barbecue fans should head two miles west of town on Hwy. 64 to **Woodley's B.B.Q.,** tel. (931) 433-3044, which serves barbecue all week and ribs on Friday and Saturday.

Shopping

Marbles Mercantile, 125 Main St., tel. (931) 433-3024, sells perhaps the widest selection of marbles available in the state—buckets and buckets of marbles. Other items include pottery, whirligigs, cast iron banks, wind chimes, and folk art.

The gift shop at **Old Cowan Plantation,** tel. (931) 433-0225, sells items made by regional artists. Directions are listed above.

P. Fitz, 102 Main St., tel. (931) 433-8452, offers a lively collection of pottery, home accessories, cast iron items, and folk art.

Wyatt Antiques, 301 Elk Ave. N, tel. (931) 433-4241, occupies Fayetteville's famous "steamboat Gothic" mansion.

Information

The **Fayetteville-Lincoln County Chamber of Commerce,** 208 S. Elk Ave., tel. (931) 433-1235, is open Mon.-Fri. 8 a.m.-4:30 p.m. See them online at www.vallnet.com/chamber of commerce.

SHELBYVILLE AND VICINITY

Many towns in Middle Tennessee were plotted with a courthouse in the center of a square facing various businesses. Carroll Van West, in his very good *Tennessee's Historic Landscapes,* says that Shelbyville is believed to be the first town in the nation to have such a plan. Shelbyville was a Daniel of Northern sympathizers amid the lion's den of Confederates during the Civil War. Some folks referred to it as "Little Boston," quite an insult in those days.

SIGHTS

In the 1900s Shelbyville became known as "Pencil City." Cedar forests nearby and water power from the Duck River made it an ideal location for pencil factories. At least six companies in the area still manufacture pens, pencils, or erasers.

Shelbyville's greatest claim to fame, however, rests on a horse that rose from farms and fields to become a Middle Tennessee industry. The annual **Tennessee Walking Horse National Celebration** is held here every year. The **Tennessee Walking Horse Museum,** inside the Calsonic Arena on the Celebration Grounds at Whitthorne St., tel. (931) 684-0314, uses exhibits, video displays, and interactive devices to tell the story of Tennessee's favorite equine. The museum is open Mon.-Fri. 9 a.m.-5 p.m. Admission is $3 for adults, $2 for seniors, and $2 for children seven to 12.

The **Old Jail** was built in 1886 using four-foot by four-foot rocks hauled to the site in a wagon by "Big Tom" Martin, who is said to have weighed 300 pounds and to have arms eight inches longer than a normal man's. Now on the National Register, the Old Jail is behind the new jail. Visitors can see the outside only.

Tri-Star Vineyards and Winery, tel. (931) 294-3062, is owned by a family who made their own wine for more than 25 years before going professional. All that expertise now produces dry, semi-sweet, and sweet reds and whites, Tennessee muscadine, and various berry wines. To get there, go seven miles north of town off Hwy. 41A and turn left onto Halls Mill Road, then go a half mile and turn right onto Scales Road. Go another half mile and the winery will come into sight. It's open Friday and Saturday 10 a.m.-5 p.m. and Sunday noon-5 p.m.

Waterfall Farms, 2395 Hwy. 64 E, tel. (931) 684-7894, is a more-than-900-acre horse farm that welcomes visitors. Here Tennessee Walking Horses are bred, trained, and proudly displayed. The farm has three mare barns sheltering as many as 260 broodmares. These equine ladies receive occasional visits from one of the gentleman callers of "Stud Row," and the offspring's pedigree is intensely studied for early indications that this Walker might be a champion. The farm has an indoor riding ring, and visitors can see trainers working with horses year-round. Visitors are welcome during daylight hours, and admission is free.

ENTERTAINMENT AND EVENTS

The event in Shelbyville is the **Tennessee Walking Horse National Celebration,** which takes place on the 10 days preceding the Saturday night of Labor Day weekend. Competitions take place nightly at the 28,869-seat outdoor arena. During the day people wander around the 100+-acre Celebration Grounds, stopping at some of the 1,686 stalls to look at fine horses, talk with trainers, and buy all manner of horse tack and souvenirs. Tickets cost $7-15 and can be had by calling (931) 684-5915. They are generally available for every night of the celebration.

The **Spring Fun Show,** staged late in May is a good warm-up show for the larger Tennessee

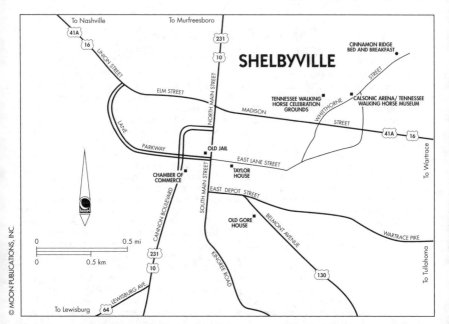

Walking Horse National Celebration. Call (931) 684-5915.

The **Gallagher Guitar Homecoming Festival** hosts an annual concert in Calsonic Arena in May. Call (931) 389-6455 for dates and headliners.

The **Great Celebration Mule Show** in late July offers pulling contests, costume classes, four- and six-mule hitches, and a look at Tennessee Walking Mules—high-stepping mules that result from a jack being bred to a Tennessee Walking Horse mare. Call (931) 684-5915 for information.

WHERE TO STAY

Bed and Breakfasts

Bottle Hollow Lodge, P.O. Box 92, Shelbyville, TN 37160, tel. (931) 695-5253, is a bed-and-breakfast inn out in the country between Shelbyville and Lynchburg on a ridgetop with a 30- to 35-mile view of the countryside. Its four guest rooms have private baths, and it is handicapped-accessible. Rates are $90 and include a full breakfast.

Cinnamon Ridge, 799 Whitthorne St., Shelbyville, TN 37160, tel. (931) 685-9200, is an early 1900s colonial-style home with five guest rooms, all with private baths. Rates range $55-65 and include a full breakfast and treats in the afternoon and evening. Visit online at www.bbonline.com/tn/cinammon. Inexpensive-Moderate.

Old Gore House, 410 Belmont Ave., Shelbyville, TN 37160, tel. (931) 685-0636, is a colonial-style home restored and decorated in period colors and antique furnishings. The gardens grow a huge variety of perennial flowering plants. The four bedrooms and two suites all have private baths, color TV, and telephones. Rates range $60-75 and include a full breakfast on the weekends. Their website is www.bbonline.com/tn/oldgore. Moderate.

The Taylor House, 300 E. Lane St., Shelbyville, TN 37160, tel. (931) 684-3894, is an 1890 Victorian house that sits in the historic district. Decorated in period antiques, the four guest rooms each have private baths. The host serves a classic country breakfast, and guests can relax in two common areas. Rates are $75-100. See the Web site: www.bbonline.com/tn/taylorhouse. Moderate-Expensive.

THE WORLD'S GREATEST SHOW AND PLEASURE HORSE

Motorists through Middle Tennessee, particularly south of Nashville, often see mailboxes or barns displaying a silhouette of a horse whose front leg is pulled up belly high and whose back legs seem to be taking enormous steps. These are Tennessee Walking Horses, a breed that means big business in these parts.

Often described as "the world's greatest show and pleasure horse," Walking Horses are a delight to ride. Unlike temperamental racehorses, Tennessee Walkers are docile animals whose natural gaits are easy on the rider. Indeed, some enthusiasts claim that the horses move so smoothly that riders can sip hot coffee—or Tennessee sippin' whiskey—from a cup while riding along.

Walking Horses were developed by breeders in Middle Tennessee to meet several needs. Plantation owners and overseers sought mounts that they could ride all day without getting saddle sore and horses that could cover a lot of ground and not get weary. Owners of small farms who could afford only one or two horses wanted ones that were strong enough to pull a plow yet easy to ride.

The Southern Plantation Walking Horse, as this breed came to be known, had a distinct gait called a "running walk." This seeming contradiction in terms is accomplished through overstriding, in which the rear foot of the horse steps over—overstrides—the imprint of the front foot by as much as 18-24 inches. The back legs of walking horses thus extend much farther forward than those of other breeds, and this produces the smooth ride that typifies the horse.

The first horse to naturally perform this running walk was born in 1837, and almost 100 years later a breeders association was founded in Lewisburg.

The first Tennessee Walking Horse Grand Champion was crowned in 1939, yet it took 15 years for the U.S. Department of Agriculture to recognize Tennessee Walkers as a separate breed. In the meantime, Walking Horses found favor with trail riders, pleasure riders, and an increasing number of people whose horses competed in show rings. Producing champions brought fame to trainers, money to owners, and excitement for fans.

At the annual celebration in Shelbyville, fans began to applaud and judges began to reward horses who could do "the big lick"—picking their front feet very high off the ground and reaching forward at the same time. Putting heavy horseshoes or boots on a horse could produce the big lick, but a relentless pursuit of the crowd-pleasing tactic brought a sad chapter to the industry. Trainers began "soring" horses using chains, or in the worst cases, chemicals, to irritate the skin and thus force the horse to pick its feet up higher. After much bad publicity, legal remedies, and a lot of controversy, widespread soring has largely ended, although unscrupulous trainers still get caught abusing their horses.

Today the Tennessee Walking Horse Breeders' and Exhibitors' Association has more than 16,000 members, one-third of whom live in Tennessee. Tennessee Walking Horses bring a lot of money into the state and a lot of pleasure to their owners.

TENNESSEE WALKING HORSE MUSEUM™

Motels

Try the **Best Western Celebration Inn,** 724 Madison St., tel. (931) 684-2378 or (800) 528-1234; or the **The Shelbyville Inn,** 317 N. Cannon Blvd., tel. (931) 684-6050.

Camping

Tennessee Walking Horse National Celebration, tel. (931) 684-5915, opens its grounds to camping during its events. Its 200 sites are on Whitthorne Street.

MORE PRACTICALITIES

Food

Richard's Cafeteria, 223 Lane Pkwy., tel. (931) 684-7288, offers breakfast from a menu and an all-you-can-eat lunch and dinner buffet seven days a week.

Pope's Cafe, on the square, tel. (931) 684-7933, is a place with a lot of character that serves good food—meat-and-three and burgers.

Many folks say **Prime Steak House,** 1057 Madison St., tel. (931) 684-0741, is the best place in town. The owner is Greek, so the Greek items on the menu are very good.

El Mexico, 713 N. Main St., tel. (931) 684-0874, is a relatively small place that offers great Mexican food.

Braylon's Family Restaurant, 423 Flack Rd., tel. (931) 684-3609, serves basic country cooking, and meat-and-three-veggies plates.

Shopping
Joe's Liquors and Wines, 633 N. Main St., tel. (931) 684-0777, has one of the more extensive collections of Tennessee sour mash whiskey in Middle Tennessee. Here are collectible Jack Daniels bottles, pints of the no-longer-made Lem Motlow whiskey, and other manifestations of the spirits world. Take a cybersip at www.cafes.net/joesliquors.

Information
Shelbyville's **chamber of commerce,** 100 N. Cannon Blvd., tel. (931) 684-3482, is open Mon.-Fri. 8 a.m.-noon and 1-4 p.m. Their Web site is www.shelbyvilletn.com.

HENRY HORTON STATE RESORT PARK

This 1,135-acre park sits beside the Duck River on the former estate of Henry Horton, the governor of Tennessee 1927-33. Here visitors can choose from a variety of recreational opportunities, including golf, canoeing, horseback riding, and swimming, as well as various sports fields and courts. Perhaps the most unusual offering is a professional multifield skeet and trap range. Visitors can use their own shotguns or rent one. Instruction is available as well. The park's restaurant has a seating capacity of 300 and is open year-round every day for breakfast, lunch, and supper. Call (931) 741-1200.

Accommodations begin with the **Horton Inn's** 72 air-conditioned units. Four of them are suites with kitchenettes. All units have two double beds, carpeting, television, and phones. They cost $75 per night. The park also has four cabins that each hold six people and come with air-conditioning, fireplaces, televisions, and phones. They

go for $90 per night. To make reservations, call (931) 364-2222 or (800) 421-6683. See them online at www.tnstateparks.com. Moderate.

LEWISBURG

The seat of Marshall County, Lewisburg was incorporated in 1837 and was named for Meriwether Lewis of Lewis and Clark fame. The thick cedar forests that so plagued Civil War soldiers who tried to fight among the bushy trees were put to use here by pencil factories. The **Sanford Corporation,** 551 Spring Place Rd., tel. (800) 835-8381 or (931) 359-1583, this country's largest pencil maker, has a factory here that employs more than 750 people. Visitors can tour the plant Aug.-March by appointment only.

The world headquarters of the **Tennessee Walking Horse Breeders and Exhibitors' Association** is in Lewisburg—take Exit 37 off I-65 S, then follow the signs; or call (800) 359-1574. Here visitors can view the Hall of Fame's pictures of all the World Grand Champions and may also see, by appointment, a 30-minute video showing the breed's aspects. Brochures with information about Walking Horses and the nearby barns that allow visitors are also available. The association provides a free copy of *Voice,* its magazine, and will arrange tours of horse barns for groups. See them online at www.twhbea.com.

Entertainment and Events
Big Jim's is east of town on Hwy. 50, tel. (931) 359-7125. Live music plays for those who like line dancing and other forms of boot-scootin'. The barnlike structure shelters a down-home atmosphere that swings with the sounds of old and new country music, with a little hip-hop and old rock thrown in for variety. For those new to country line dancing, lessons are offered every Thursday and Sunday 7-9 p.m. These lessons are a nice place for the whole family, kids too. An open dance follows the lessons and lasts until 10:30 p.m. Friday and Saturday are livelier by far and for adults only. Dancing lasts 6 p.m.-1:30 a.m. Be prepared for a huge crowd on Saturday night.

Oktoberfest, held in the town square, offers crafts, local music, and food on the first weekend in October.

Accommodations and Food

Motel options are **Best Western Walking Horse Lodge,** I-65 Exit 37, tel. (931) 359-4005 or (800) 528-1234; or the **Econo Lodge,** 3731 Pulaski Hwy., tel. (931) 293-2111 or (800) 424-4777.

Fountain Square Restaurant, on the square, tel. (931) 359-7488, serves country-cooking plate lunches.

Lawler's Barbecue, 1301 N. Ellington Pkwy., tel. (931) 359-5990, is a drive-through takeout establishment providing barbecued beef, pork, ham, and turkey.

Marvin's Family Restaurant, 740 N. Ellington Pkwy., tel. (931) 359-9490, offers a buffet that changes every day for lunch and supper; menu items are available too.

Information

The **Marshall County Chamber of Commerce,** 227 2nd Ave. N, tel. (931) 359-3863, is open Mon.-Fri. 8 a.m.-4 p.m. See their site online at www.lewisburgtn.com.

BETWEEN I-40 AND McMINNVILLE

EDGAR EVINS STATE RUSTIC PARK

This 6,280-acre park sits on the edge of Tennessee's Eastern Highland Rim, an area with steep bluffs and narrow ridges. In 1948 the Army Corps of Engineers built the Center Hill Dam, damming the Caney Fork River to create Center Hill Reservoir. The park was created in 1975 and named to honor the former mayor of nearby Smithville.

Like many Tennessee state parks, this one emphasizes recreation. Fishing and boating are popular here, as are picnicking and playgrounds.

At the marina visitors can rent boats or buy fishing licenses, food, fuel, and gifts at the store. The restaurant here serves three meals a day and is open year-round, except for Christmas and New Year's Day.

Accommodations include 34 cabins, each of which sleeps six people and comes with a

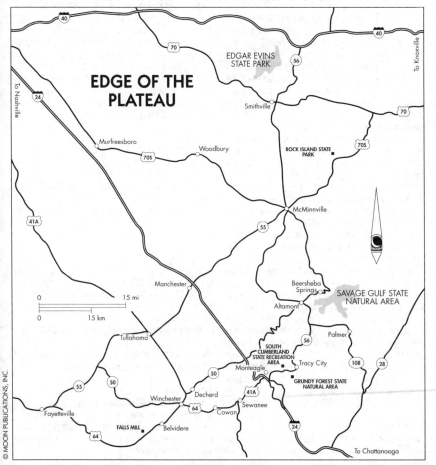

housekeeping kitchen. A swimming pool serves cabin guests only. The cabins stay open year-round, except from mid-December to mid-January, and cost $69.88 per night including tax. For reservations, call (615) 858-2114 or (800) 421-6683. Moderate. The park also has 60 campsites, open year-round and available on a first-come, first-served basis. Each comes with electrical and water hookups, and bathhouses offer hot showers. To get further information, call (931) 858-2446 or (800) 250-8619.

SMITHVILLE

This town might better be named Evinsville in honor of the prominent Evins family. Edgar Evins was a local businessman who had a hand in many operations in the town. He served as mayor and represented the town in the state Senate. His son, Joe Evins, continued the tradition of public service and extended it to a 30-year career in the U.S. Congress. While there, he looked out for his district and made sure that federal money flowed its way.

An example of this is the **Joe L. Evins Appalachian Center for Crafts,** on the shores of Center Hill Lake, tel. (615) 597-6801. It offers exhibits, items for sale, and classes on how to make them. A cafeteria serves lunch weekdays and on selected weekends. To get there, take Hwy. 56 northeast from town. Just before crossing Hurricane Bridge, turn right on Craft Center Road.

Back in town on the square is **F.Z. Webb & Son,** tel. (615) 597-4185, an old-fashioned drugstore that has been in the same family since 1881. The soda fountain is gone, but the store still sells coffee for a nickel a cup as well as locally made pottery, and visitors can gaze on pharmaceutical antiques such as a wooden label dispenser.

The **Smithville Fiddler's Jamboree & Crafts Festival** is one of the larger such events in the state. Held on the weekend closest to the Fourth of July, it features competitions in a wide variety of events—flat-pick guitar, dobro, junior buck-dancing, and country harmonica, to name a few. Craftspeople from more than 35 states usually show up. Call (615) 597-8500 for information.

Camping

Nearby Center Hill Lake has several recreation areas run by the Army Corps of Engineers. All are open May-Sept. and none have hookups. For information about camping and the area, call (931) 858-3125. The following four campgrounds lie along Hwy. 96 north of Smithville, and all offer lake swimming, fishing, canoeing, and boating.

Cove Hollow, tel. (615) 548-8781, offers 25 sites for tents and RVs. From I-40 take Exit 268 and follow signs.

Long Branch, near Silver Point across the lake from Smithville, tel. (615) 548-8002, has 57 sites for tents and RVs. From I-40 (Exit 268), go five miles south on Bob Steber Road, then two miles west on Hwy. 141.

Holmes Creek, tel. (615) 597-7191, is closer to town and has 97 sites. From the junction of Hwy. 56 and Hwy. 70, go five miles west on Hwy. 70, then five miles north on a county road. Holmes Creek is open May 1-September 15.

Ragland Bottom, east of town off Hwy. 70 toward Sparta, tel. (931) 761-3616, has 78 sites. From the junction of Hwy. 56 and Hwy. 70, go eight miles east on Hwy. 70, then one mile north on a county road. Follow the signs.

Food

Main Street Deli and Cafe, 406 W. Main St., tel. (615) 237-0404, has hot and cold sandwiches and homemade desserts.

Sundance, 107 E. Main St., tel. (615) 597-1910, has something different every day of the week. This place, inside a former 19th-century stable, sells vitamins as well as meals, and the food here is healthy but good.

Shopping

Recreation room fanciers should stop in at **Mary Lou's Curious Gifts,** 8950 Hwy. 70, tel. (615) 548-4059, to look over the jukeboxes and pinball games from days gone by. Mary Lou's also sells old records and neon signs.

Griffin's Fruit Market, on W. Broadway St., tel. (615) 597-5030, sells local home-grown tomatoes and other fruit and vegetables in season. It also has cider, honey, and other good things.

Information

The **Smithville/DeKalb County Chamber of Commerce,** in the courthouse on the square, tel. (615) 597-4163, is open weekdays 9 a.m.-3 p.m., closed Wednesday. See them online at www.dekalbtn.com.

WOODBURY

Just east of town is the highest mountain between the Appalachians and the Ozarks. Oddly enough, it is named Short Mountain.

The land on the Highland Rim here is not very fertile, and to make a living the residents got very good at making baskets and chairs, which were traded for goods that the farmers could not raise or grow. The basket patterns have been handed down for so many years that no one can name their origins. Some people speculate that when the Cherokees were marched through here on the infamous "Trail of Tears" that some of the women stayed behind to marry local men and brought the basketmaking with them. Wherever it came from, the tradition of high-quality craftwork continues in Cannon County in a greater concentration than about anywhere else in the state. Woodbury has in fact been named one of the 100 best arts towns in America.

The first stop should be **The Arts Center of Cannon County,** 1424 John Bragg Hwy., tel. (615) 563-ARTS. Here are exhibits of local crafts, some of which are for sale. Better yet, the center gives directions to makers of baskets, chairs, and quilts (see "Arts and Crafts" below).

Robert Mason Historical Museum, tel. (615) 563-ARTS, shares the building with the Arts Center. Permanent exhibits include the Confederate uniform of a member of Forrest's cavalry and a samurai sword. Admission is free.

Events and Entertainment
The **Arts Center** features wonderful cultural events varying from classical guitar concerts to theatrical productions.

White Oak Country Crafts Fair, held the second weekend in August, is a juried event bringing together the best local craftspeople. It includes demonstrations and food.

Billy Womack was a contemporary of Uncle Dave Macon and is fondly remembered with the **Billy Womack Bluegrass Celebration** in mid-October.

Food
Main Street Deli, 108 W. Main St., tel. (615) 563-6118, offers subs made with its own tuna, chicken, and seafood salads served on freshly baked bread. Pizzas, soup, and a salad bar are available as well, and diners can round off the meal with cheesecake and fresh pies.

Joe's Place, 108 Tatum St., tel. (615) 563-4140, features country cooking—plate lunches, sandwiches, and steaks.

D.J. Pizza and Steak, 805 W. Main St., tel. (615) 563-2821, serves Italian dishes in addition to the items for which it's named.

Arts and Crafts
Many of the people who do excellent craftwork in Cannon County invite visitors into their homes to look over their wares. The Arts Center is the best place to get information on who makes what. The following are just a few of the people who welcome visitors. Call ahead for directions.

Jake and Ruth Davis, tel. (615) 563-4498, make straight chairs and rocking chairs. A regular white oak chair sells for $60, a jumbo for $70, and a double chair for $125. The cross pieces are kiln-dried wood, whereas the legs are green. The older the chair gets, the tighter the legs hold onto the cross pieces.

Thelma Hibdon, tel. (615) 563-5445, is a fifth-generation white-oak basket maker, the daughter of Ida Pearl Davis, who has made baskets for the Smithsonian.

ROCK ISLAND STATE PARK

Many people who want to see waterfalls head for Fall Creek Falls State Park. While the falls there are the highest in the state, the water in them comes from creeks. At **Rock Island State Park,** on the other hand, the waters from three rivers come together to absolutely roar. In this 883-acre park, the Rocky, the Collins, and the Caney Fork all merge and pour into a gorge that drops 100 feet in the space of two miles. A dam holds back the Great Falls Reservoir and releases water that goes over the Great Falls—a cascade that is a photographer's delight.

The park certainly was a cinematographer's delight in Sylvester Stallone's *The Professional,* in which those Tennessee woods were passed off as the jungles of Columbia.

Asa Faulkner, an early capitalist, designed a three-story brick cotton mill here, and his son Clay and others completed it in 1892. The water powered the mill, which at one time produced 4,000 yards of cotton sheeting a day. It ran until 1902, when a bad flood stripped it of its water wheel. The building still sits in the park.

Across the road from the cotton mill is a stone structure known as the Spring Castle. Built about the time the dam was built, it was originally a spring house. This was a resort area for Middle Tennesseans wishing to escape the heat of the summer, and modern-day visitors will see why they found this place so appealing.

One fun thing to do is take a drive across a dam on what feels like a rickety bridge. The park also has a visitors center, boating and fishing on the lake, ball fields, tennis courts, and a natural sand beach. Four picnic areas are available, as are tours of nearby **Big Bone Cave,** a dry cave from which saltpeter was mined. No admission is charged for the tours, which should be arranged as far in advance as possible.

The park has 10 modern cabins, all built in a Victorian style with front and back porches and capable of sleeping 10 people. The cabins are very popular; from Memorial Day to Labor Day they must be rented by the week and cost $430 plus tax. At other times they cost $65 for weeknights and $85 on weekends. Moderate.

The park also has 50 year-round campsites and, unlike those in most Tennessee parks, these can be reserved ahead of time by calling (931) 686-2471 or (800) 421-6683. See them online at www.tnstateparks.com.

McMINNVILLE

Sitting on the edge of the Cumberland Plateau, McMinnville and the surrounding area are a prime location for plant nurseries. The elevation ranges from 976 feet in McMinnville to 1,892 feet on nearby Ben Lomond Mountain. Each 1,000 feet in elevation creates a climate equivalent to weather conditions 300 miles north, and thus local plants can be widely sold. Furthermore, the varying soils successfully duplicate those found both north and south of here, and nursery products can be grown on small farms. For those reasons, young trees and bushes and ornamental plants of all kinds roll out of here annually.

McMinnville is the birthplace of Dorothy Marie Marsh, the youngest of 10 children who picked cotton near here. Her mother, abandoned by her husband, opened a restaurant in the town, and by the time the little girl was 12 she had sung on the radio. She became known as Dottie West, a country star often remembered for the song "Country Sunshine." A member of the Grand Ole Opry, she sang many duets with Kenny Rogers and died as the result of a car crash in 1991. She is buried in McMinnville's Mountain View Cemetery.

Sights and Recreation
McMinnville boasts an unusually large library for a town its size, and thereby hangs a tale. William Magness, a wealthy resident, donated the library to the town in 1931. He provided room for books and added an apartment for himself and showers in the basement for the benefit of any locals who wanted to take a bath. Visitors will find the **Magness Community House and Library** at 118 Main St., though they can no longer use the showers.

Historic Falcon Manor, 2645 Faulkner Springs Rd. in McMinnville, tel. (931) 668-4444, is a bed and breakfast that occupies one of the finest homes in the county. Local entrepreneur Clay Faulkner operated a cotton mill outside of town and, growing tired of commuting, told his wife he would build her "the finest home in Warren County" if she would move closer to the mill. She consented, and the house was completed in 1896. Counting porches and verandahs, this Queen Anne-style Victorian mansion totals about 10,000 square feet. It later served as a hospital and is now an antique-filled bed and breakfast. Admission is $5 for adults and $3 for children under 12 years old. Visit online at www.falconmanor.com.

Cumberland Caverns, seven miles southeast of McMinnville off Hwy. 8, tel. (931) 668-4396, is one of the larger cave systems in the United States. It was discovered in 1810 by a hapless surveyor who climbed into a hole, lost his torch, and had to wait for rescuers to find him. The cave was mined for saltpeter during the War of 1812 and the Civil War, and some of the mining equipment still sits in the cave. The cave's biggest room is called the Hall of the Mountain King.

Visitors can take tours varying from the regular 90-minute tour to a 14-hour overnight "wild cave" adventure. For this visitors spend the night in the cave, hear a ghost story, and explore their way through about a mile of totally undeveloped passageways, including a crawl through some tight spaces. The adventure is for the young at heart and youth groups, as almost all visitors get wet and muddy slogging through the infamous Bubblegum Alley—where explorers come out of 18 inches of water onto a mudbank. Tours cost $9.50 for adults and $4.75 for children six to 15 years old. The overnights can be taken year-round and have a variety of prices. These tours are very popular (about 350 people spend the night each weekend), so reservations are required.

Halfway between McMinnville and Manchester, **The Cheese Store,** along Hwy. 55 in the Morrison community, tel. (931) 635-3004, makes a variety of cheeses: cheddar, hot pepper, Swiss, onion, and Monterey Jack. Many of the wineries in Tennessee sell cheese made here.

Where to Stay

Historic Falcon Manor, 2645 Faulkner Springs Rd., McMinnville, TN 37110, tel. (931) 668-4444, as described above, offers six guest rooms, some with private baths; all feature antiques. The inn sits on three acres of land with century-old trees that lend a country setting, but it's conveniently near town. Rates begin at $105 and include a tour of the mansion and full breakfast. Check in online at www.falconmanor.com. Expensive-Premium.

Motel options include **Best Western,** 1609 Sparta Hwy., tel. (931) 473-7338 or (800) 528-1234; **Holiday Inn Express,** 809 Sparta Hwy., tel. (931) 473-2159 or (800) HOLIDAY; and **Shoney's Inn,** 508 Sunnyside Heights, tel. (931) 473-4446 or (800) 222-2222.

Food

The **Amesbury Cafe & Bakery,** 127 Main St., tel. (931) 506-5281, has art on the walls and good food on the plates. This is a good place for soups and sandwiches as well as more substantial meals.

City Drugstore, at the corner of Main and Spring Streets, tel. (931) 473-2234, has a lunch counter for lovers of soda fountains. Chili is a favorite dish, while burgers and sandwiches round out the offerings.

The **Collection Cafe** sits in an antique mall at 216 E. Main St., tel. (931) 473-8000. The menu includes sandwiches, salads, herb teas, and high-grade coffee.

Gillentines, at the Scottish Inn on the Sparta Highway, tel. (931) 473-7757, offers steaks, catfish, and plate lunches.

Peking Restaurant, in the Plaza Shopping Center, tel. (931) 473-3630, is open for lunch and dinner seven days a week.

Fiesta Ranchera, 202 McMinnville Plaza on Route 56, tel. (931) 473-6423, is a great place to sample the wave of Mexican cuisine that has swept over Tennessee in recent years. Situated in a little mall, Fiesta Ranchera has a colorful, upbeat atmosphere that's just right to enjoy burritos, quesadillas, and other Mexican delights. They even have vegetarian dishes.

Information

The **Chamber of Commerce,** 110 S. Court Square, tel. (931) 473-6611, is also online at www.warrentn.com.

HIGHWAY 56 TO MONTEAGLE

SAVAGE GULF STATE NATURAL AREA

The name of this area makes it sound like some sort of fearsome place. "Savage" refers to the name of Samuel Savage, an early settler, while "gulf" is a peculiar Tennessee word for canyon. The Savage Gulf Natural Area is a part of the larger South Cumberland Recreation Area, which includes seven parks spread over four counties. The headquarters, tel. (931) 532-0001, is outside Tracy City.

This entire 11,500-acre area sits on the Cumberland Plateau, and Savage Gulf State Natural Area is made up of places where three streams have cut converging canyons into the plateau. Each of the three canyons is about five miles long, and at their deepest they extend 800 feet below the plateau. No one can drive down into any of the canyons, which means visitors will largely have the place to themselves. Here are some of the highlights.

The **Great Stone Door** is a 150-foot-long crack in a rock that suggests an enormous door that someone has barely opened. To get there, go to the town of Beersheba Springs and follow the signs to a ranger station and great views of the gulf. On some days visitors can see raptors riding thermals coming up out of the canyon. Indians used the Great Stone Door as a pathway down into the canyon, and modern-day visitors can as well. Maps available at the ranger station suggest good trails.

Greeter Falls begins the Big Creek canyon by taking a 50-foot plunge over a cliff. To get there, drive 1.1 miles from Altamont's square south on Hwy. 56 to Greeter Road. Turn left and go 0.1 mile to the trailhead. A half-mile walk leads to the falls.

Savage Gulf is on the eastern side of the area and contains more than 500 acres of virgin hardwood forest. The family who owned it resisted pressures to log this area, and thanks to them it is preserved today. To get to the ranger station, tel. (931) 779-3532, go south on Hwy. 56 through Beersheba Springs and Altamont, then take Hwy. 108 to the east—left—and go through the town of Gruetli-Lager, then turn left on Hwy. 399. Follow the signs. See it online at www.tnstateparks.com.

BEERSHEBA SPRINGS

Highway 56 from McMinnville climbs to the old resort town of Beersheba (BURR-shuh-buh) Springs. It was named for Beersheba Cain, who was traveling on horseback with her husband from McMinnville to Chattanooga when she wandered up an old Indian path and found a spring whose water contained a lot of iron. This became known as Beersheba's Spring, and in 1839 the area opened as a resort. A hotel was built at the top of the mountain, and, when stagecoaches would begin their climb up the mountain, the driver would blow his horn a number of times to indicate how many people on board would be present at dinner. By the time guests arrived, the meal would be well under way. Andrew Jackson was a frequent visitor to Beersheba Springs, as were many Nashvillians.

The hotel was expanded and "cottages"—rather large houses—were built. The place reached its zenith in the years just before the Civil War. Since those days the old hotel changed hands many times until its purchase in 1941 by the United Methodist Church, which still uses it for retreats. Most of the cottages are still there, and they and the hotel have a grand view of Savage Gulf and the Collins River Valley.

The **Old Brown Museum,** on the same side of the highway as the post office, tel. (931) 692-3522, is one of those places that exists through the efforts of a devoted individual, in this case Margaret Coppinger, who lives beside it. The museum contains old clothing, furniture, and exhibits relating to the Civil War, including a diary kept during those years by a local resident. Books and selections from the diary are available for sale. Admission is free, and the museum, open May-Sept., has no particular hours. Call for further information or pull up and blow the horn.

In the last weekend of August, the hotel grounds are the scene of the **Beersheba Springs Arts and Crafts Festival,** now into its third decade and involving 250 exhibitors from all over. Call the post office for info at (931) 692-3701.

Beersheba Porcelain, 1 Dahlgren, tel. (931) 692-2280, offers porcelain pieces created from a process that Phil Mayhew (a former arts professor) developed. Using higher temperatures, the process increases durability and the intensity of colors. Terri Mayhew creates porcelain and handcrafted silver jewelry.

Information

The best place for information on the area is online at www.nostalgiaville.com/hills/grundy/beer.

ALTAMONT

After seeing Beersheba Springs, a good place to spend the night is this little town, the seat of Grundy County, located farther along on Hwy. 56. The history of the area, such as the time Nathan Bedford Forrest and 1,000 troops camped here, is displayed in the **Courthouse Museum,** tel. (931) 692-3153, across the street from the new courthouse and behind the Manor Bed and Breakfast. This museum is housed in an 1830s log cabin that at one time served as the courthouse. Now it contains items from various periods in Grundy County history. Indian artifacts, Civil War items, and exhibits on the lumber and mining industries make up the collection. The museum is closed Jan.-March. Admission is free.

Where to Stay

The Manor on Hwy. 56, P.O. Box 156, Altamont, TN 37301, tel. (931) 692-3153, is listed on the National Register and has one of the largest libraries—more than 3,000 volumes—to be found in a bed and breakfast. The 1885 house that makes up the Manor was for years the home of a wealthy but eccentric woman who never married. On being told that if she died without a will "there would be a heck of a fight," she supposedly replied, "Let 'em fight."

The Manor has five bedrooms with four baths. The rate is $55 per room. The Manor also has a three-bedroom housekeeping cabin for $65 per night; guests who stay there prepare their own breakfasts. Inexpensive.

Had the intestate owner of the Manor lived longer, she could have gotten a will from the owner of Altamont's other bed and breakfast, an attorney. Like many fine homes in Tennessee, **Woodlee House,** P.O. Box 310, Altamont, TN 37301, tel. (931) 692-2368, was built in stages. The interior of the cabin wall now makes up one interior wall of the living room. Listed on the National Register, the house is filled with collections of books, quilts, coverlets, and miniature houses. The two guest rooms share a bath. The host serves a full breakfast. Alcohol is not permitted. The rate is $60 a night. Inexpensive.

Food

Zak's Pizza and Grill on Canyon Dr., tel. (931) 692-2132, serves takeout homemade pizza and side orders.

Arts and Crafts

The **Cumberland Craftsman,** tel. (931) 692-3595, on the grounds of a mill that operated 1901-68, is the place to go for folk art, woodcarvings, walking sticks, and other items. Ron Van Dyke is the artist and proprietor.

Information

See the area online at www.nostalgiaville.com/hills/grundy/alta.

TRACY CITY

Driving from Altamont to Tracy City, the visitor passes though an area that was extensively mined for coal after the Civil War. As in most mines here and to the east, the coal was converted to coke, a more efficient fuel. The work was hard, and this was the scene of many labor struggles. In the late 1800s owners used convict labor, thus holding down the wages of the rest of the workers. The miners finally revolted, commandeered trains, and shipped the convicts out. Labor unrest continued into the 1930s and led to the establishment of the **Highlander Folk School** about four miles west of Tracy City on Hwy. 41.

Highway 108 leads to the community of Palmer, where the **Miner's Museum and Her-**

HIGHLANDER SCHOOL

The coalfield struggles of the Southern Cumberland Plateau attracted two young Southerners, Myles Horton of Tennessee and Don West of Georgia. The two founded the Highlander School, a center for adult education, in the Summerfield community between Tracy City and Monteagle. The Highlander School soon became a center of activity for the labor movement, first in Tennessee and then all over the South.

People at Highlander put out pro-union newspapers, trained activists in union organizing, and brought in textile workers and others for seminars on topics such as how to become an effective shop steward. They accomplished their mission with music as well as with more conventional forms of instruction.

Through the years, the issues have changed, but the activism has never dimmed. Highlander took an active role in the civil rights struggles. Martin Luther King Jr. and Ralph Abernathy, among others, came to Highlander for support and to plan their acts of civil disobedience. Rosa Parks, for instance, attended Highlander shortly before she refused to give up her seat on a bus in Montgomery, Alabama. "We Shall Overcome" here became the anthem of the civil rights movement. In more recent times, Earth First! activist Judi Bari participated in Highlander workshops before launching the Redwood Summer—a radical environmental series of events.

Highlander became infamous in some circles in the 1960s when a photograph of Martin Luther King Jr. taken at Highlander was splashed on billboards and captioned "a Communist training school" by the John Birch Society. The House Committee on un-American Activities also investigated Highlander.

The school ended its Grundy County existence in 1959 when local law enforcement people raided it and found that beer was being sold to those in attendance. Although the sales were more of the put-some-money-in-a-box-when-you-get-a-beer variety, this proved the tool the authorities needed to seize the buildings and try to shut down the school. Highlander then moved to Knoxville and now operates in a rural site near New Market in East Tennessee.

Today Highlander works with community groups, primarily from Appalachia and the Deep South. "We bring people together to learn from each other," says the group's mission statement. This takes the form of residential workshops, training sessions, and other methods that develop leadership in issues such as fighting corporate pollution, bringing U.S. and immigrant workers together, and combating the increasing use of part-time, temporary, and contract workers.

Celebrating the 25th anniversary of the school in 1957 are, from left, Martin Luther King, Jr., Pete Seeger, Charis Horton (daughter of co-founder Myles), Rosa Parks, and Ralph Abernathy.

---

itage Center, adjacent to the library on Hwy. 108, tel. (931) 779-3593, displays a great number of artifacts from the days when this was a big coal mining area. The wide assortment of mining equipment covers pick-and-shovel days up to more modern days. On Labor Day the center always takes part in the town celebration. For information on this or any other aspect of Grundy County, visit **Sham and Shorty's,** a convenience store across from the bank on Hwy. 108 in town. Shorty has been the president of the Grundy County Chamber of Commerce and is the source of all knowledge in these parts.

Camping
Foster Falls, five miles east on Hwy. 150, no phone, has 26 sites with no hookups. It's open late April through mid-October.

Food
The **Dutch Maid Bakery,** 111 Main St., tel. (931) 592-3171, is the oldest family-owned bakery in the state. Among its delights are these breads: honey and nut, raisin, jalapeño, potato, six-grain, salt rising, and pumpernickel. Some of the recipes date to Swiss immigrants who came to these parts in the 1870s. The proprietors will give visitors a short tour if things in the store aren't too hectic. Look for the 1929 mixer.

Information
Contact the **Grundy County Executive's Office,** tel. (931) 692-3718, or see them online at www.nostalgiaville.com/hills/grundy.The **Dutch Maid Bakery,** listed above, also stocks a wide selection of brochures.

SOUTH CUMBERLAND STATE RECREATION AREA

This 11,500-acre area includes seven parks with 10 different entrances spread over four counties. Though spread around, these have much to offer the visitor, beginning with flora and fauna. The areas constitute four disparate ecological zones: plateau top, bluff, gorge, and aquatic. Wildlife includes red and gray foxes, coyotes, beavers, otters, white-tailed deer, possums, squirrels, and raccoons. Migratory birds join local wild turkeys and raptors throughout the area. Wildflowers are a delight from March into October.

Hikers can choose trails that vary from strolls to grueling climbs, that pass cliffs, waterfalls, swimming holes, caves, and streams. Others will marvel at historic structures such as coke ovens. Visitors should keep in mind that hunting is permitted in several of these areas and conduct themselves accordingly during the fall hunting season.

The South Cumberland State Recreation Area has no large campsites but offers a variety of backcountry sites. A permit is required for all backcountry camping, and guests must use designated sites, all of which contain primitive toilets. Permits are available at the headquarters or at the trailheads.

Free programs and guided hikes are offered at the headquarters, between Tracy City and Monteagle, tel. (931) 924-2956 or (931) 924-2980, which contains several natural history exhibits.

One of the more interesting is a 3-D map showing all the parks.

Grundy Lakes Day Use Area was donated to the state during the Depression after coal mining had ended. Here the Lone Rock Coke Ovens, run by convicts, transformed coal into coke. The area centers on Grundy Lake, and the entire park is on the National Register of Historic Places. The remains of a long row of coke ovens sit on the west side of the lake. Visitors cannot camp here, but they can hike, picnic, and swim. To get there, take Exit I-24 at Monteagle, go six miles on Hwy. 41 toward Tracy City, then turn left onto Lakes Drive to the park.

Grundy Forest State Natural Area is a 212-acre tract containing the northern terminus of the Fiery Gizzard Trail. The hike leads 12.7 miles to Foster Falls, but a two-mile jaunt down the northern end takes the hiker past a large rock shelter, a five-century-old hemlock tree, Blue Hole Falls and its accompanying swimming hole, the Black Canyon, and a group of house-sized boulders called The Fruit Bowl. And that's just the first two miles. To get to this area, go to Tracy City, just off Hwy. 41, and follow the signs.

Foster Falls TVA Small Wild Area gets its name from a waterfall that plunges 60 feet into a large pool. It marks the southern terminus of the Fiery Gizzard Trail. To get there, take Hwy. 41 E from Tracy City and look for the sign on the right.

Sewanee Natural Bridge State Natural Area used to belong to the University of the South. A short walk leads to a sandstone arch that is 27 feet high and spans 57 feet. To get there, take Hwy. 56 South from Sewanee and look for the sign on the left.

The Buggytop Trail, farther south down Hwy. 56 from Sewanee Natural Bridge State Natural Area, leads to **Carter State Natural Area.** The area's big feature is Lost Cove Cave, whose entrance Thomas Barr's *Caves of Tennessee* describes as "one of the most impressive cave mouths in the state. It is 100 feet wide and 80 feet high and opens at the base of an overhanging bluff 150 feet high. The cave stream cascades down from the mouth and drops 40 feet in less than 100 yards." The cave shelters rare and endangered species of bats and salamanders, which should be left alone. Occasionally rangers conduct tours of the cave.

The Buggytop Trail is only four miles roundtrip but drops 620 feet in elevation. The way back from the cave is a long pull. See them online at www.tnstateparks.com.

MONTEAGLE

The chautauqua movement began in 1874 on the shores of Lake Chautauqua in upstate New York, where Sunday-school teachers and others would spend most of a summer living in a wholesome environment, listening to lectures and concerts, and engaging in other uplifting activities. The trend spread across the country and came to the town of Monteagle in 1883 in the form of the **Monteagle Sunday School Assembly,** an annual, nondenominational gathering.

It was a great success here, for Monteagle, on the Cumberland Plateau, was cooler than most places farther south. Even better, it was far from worldly pleasures and yet accessible by railroad, the final leg of which was traveled on a small train called the Mountain Goat. Families built cottages—now numbering 163—on the 96-acre site and came there summer after summer. The adults attended classes and other events, and the children had a grand time.

One longtime veteran of the assembly recalls that not everyone who summered there always stuck to the straight and narrow. When asked if anyone ever partook of the bottled versions of spiritual comfort, he replied, "Well, you know what they say; if you find four Episcopalians, you'll always find a fifth."

Over the years the religious aspects of the gathering have been emphasized less and less, but the idea of a resort for families has stayed strong. Even though few now stay the entire summer, families—some of them for the fifth generation—still come to Monteagle and take part in the educational programs. The cottages have no shortage of tenants, and some are available for rent by calling (931) 924-2272. If visitors want to rent cottages, they must submit sublease applications, which include references. Other accommodations include two inns, listed below.

Sights and Recreation

The assembly is on the National Register, and its 19th-century buildings are a delight. Most are prime examples of carpenter Gothic and

Queen Anne architecture. Six wooden pedestrian bridges cross the gorges through the property, and the whole place is eminently walkable. The assembly grounds are private property, but visitors can buy one-day to entire-season admission tickets at the gate. For information call (931) 924-2286.

Wonder Cave, tel. (931) 467-3060, was discovered in 1897 by three Vanderbilt students who were tracking the source of unusually cool air that flowed down from a mountain. The cave was bought by R.M. Payne, a far-thinking man who in 1909 pushed a state law that protected caves. Payne gave tours of the cave with lanterns, whose flickering lights heightened the appeal of the various formations. Wonder Cave still gives one-mile tours with lanterns, the only such tours conducted in the Southeast. It has more formations per square inch than any other cave in the United States, with the exception of New Mexico's Carlsbad Caverns. Admission is $7 adults, $5 children (four to 12), and free for kids under four. To get there, take I-24 Exit 127 (the Pelham Winchester Exit), go east on Hwy. 50, and go south on Hwy. 41.

Monteagle Wine Cellars, Hwy. 64/41A on the west side of I-24, tel. (931) 924-2120 or (800) 556-WINE, produces wines as various as chardonnay and sweet red muscadine.

Entertainment and Events

The **Monteagle Arts and Crafts Show** takes place on the first weekend in August at the Monteagle Elementary School. Visitors will see artists, music, and good food.

Where to Stay

The **Adams Edgeworth Inn,** Monteagle Assembly, Monteagle, TN 37356, tel. (931) 924-2669, is the grande dame of country inns in this part of Tennessee. It was built in 1896 as an inn on the assembly grounds and is richly decorated in the Chautauqua cottage style, with watercolors and yards and yards of imported fabric. The library, containing more than 2,000 volumes, is a favorite gathering place for guests. The inn has 11 rooms plus three rooms in the carriage house. Rates range $70-185 and include a full continental breakfast. Moderate-Luxury.

The North Gate Inn, P.O. Box 858, Monteagle, TN 37356, tel. (931) 924-2799, also on the assembly grounds, offers seven guest rooms, each with a private bath. The inn is decorated with antiques, and each room has its own floral color. This place is larger than the usual bed and breakfast, and thus offers the guest a greater chance of meeting like-minded or interesting souls. Rates range $72-85 and include a large breakfast. Moderate.

Another motel in town is **Budget Host,** Rt. 1, tel. (931) 924-2221.

Jim Oliver's Smokehouse, Exit 135 off I-24, tel. (931) 924-2268 or (800) 489-2091, runs a lodge with 91 rooms and cabins. Rates range $24-166. Amenities include a swimming pool in the shape of a country ham, 20 acres of land, and tennis, horseshoes, hot tubs, and walking trails. Jim Oliver's Smokehouse offers camping, too. Open all year, it has about 30 RV sites—10 have electricity, water, and sewer, the rest have electricity and water—and about 15 grassy tent sites.

Laurel Trails Campground in Monteagle, tel. (931) 924-2738, is open year-round and offers about 10 hookups and about 32 acres of camping for tents, with a total of 20 campsites. The bathhouse is clean but rustic. To get there, go toward Tracy City on Hwy. 41 South; after about 0.8 miles turn left at the sign and follow the signs.

Food

The **Adams Edgeworth Inn,** Monteagle Assembly, tel. (931) 924-2669, offers gourmet dinners by reservation only. Entrees include such items as grilled chicken Florentine, and Alaskan salmon steaks in dill butter. Desserts might be strawberry brulee or Georgia pecan pie.

Jim Oliver's Smokehouse, Hwy. 64/41 west of I-24, tel. (931) 924-2268, attracts about 400,000 diners a year. They come for wonderful country ham—the place serves about 5,000 hams a year and an estimated one million biscuits—and world-class country cooking. The Smokehouse is open seven days a week for all three meals.

Shopping

Jim Oliver's Smokehouse Trading Post, Hwy. 64/41 west of I-24, tel. (931) 924-2268, is a good place to get antiques, country hams, Tennessee souvenirs, and you name it. A wedding chapel on the grounds is available for those wishing to tie the knot.

Sculpture in Wood, one mile south of Monteagle on Hwy. 41, tel. (931) 924-2970, is the studio/shop of Jess Betschart, a talented woodcarver and sculptor whose work is mostly religious figures and small animals. Examples of the former include nativity scenes and crucifixes, while animals that appear from his hands are chipmunks, raccoons, and possums.

Information

For visitor information call the **City of Monteagle,** tel. (931) 924-2265. Explore the city online at www.nostalgiaville.com/hills/grundy/monteagle, or www.fccc-tn.org.

SOUTH PITTSBURG

This town was founded by a group of investors in England who hoped that it would became an iron center much like its namesake. In 1896, a Pennsylvania native named Joseph Lodge established a foundry there that he named Blacklock Foundry in honor of the man who ran it. It burned in 1909 and out of the ashes rose Lodge Manufacturing, which has been making cast iron cookware for almost 100 years. They make skillets, Dutch ovens, griddles, cornstick pans, muffin pans, teakettles, and more. Their company website is www.lodgemfg.com.

The foundry isn't open to the public for safety reasons, but the **Lodge Discount Factory Outlet,** E. Fifth St., tel. (423) 837-5919, has factory seconds at great prices. Just off I-24 at Exit 152.

The best time to come is during the **National Cornbread Festival,** held the first weekend in May. This event brings 22,000 people to town to eat cornbread, listen to music, shop at 60+ crafts booths, and enjoy kids' events. For info, call (423) 837-0022.

South Pittsburg hired a marshal named Thomas Mix in 1907 to keep law and order among the sometimes rowdy iron workers there. The young man lasted less than a year, when he headed for Hollywood and a new career in the movies. Shortening his name, he became Tom Mix, star of more than 300 cowboy films.

WEST OF MONTEAGLE

SEWANEE

The prettiest college campus in Tennessee, if not the entire South, highlights this town on the edge of the Cumberland Plateau.

University of the South
The university was the inspiration of Leonidas Polk, Episcopal bishop of Louisiana, Confederate general, and one of the illustrious Polks of Columbia, Tennessee. Polk envisioned an Episcopal university for the South in the 1850s, and he and others decided it should be in the northern South away from the disease-plagued lowlands. The Sewanee Mining Company, hoping to stimulate traffic on its Mountain Goat rail line, donated a large tract of land atop the Cumberland Plateau for the college. Only a few buildings were on the site when the Civil War broke out, and these were destroyed.

After the war, work began again, but Southern fortunes on which university supporters had counted were largely ruined. The officials turned to England for the needed funds, and work on the university resumed, heavily influenced by the architecture of Oxford and Cambridge.

The result is a striking campus composed of buildings constructed with sandstone quarried on the 10,000-acre grounds, known as "the domain" and said to be the largest college campus in the country. **All Saints' Chapel,** completed in 1957, is anchored by Shapard Tower, from which rings the 56-bell Leonidas Polk Memorial Carillon, one of the largest such instruments in the world.

Today the University of the South is often referred to as "Sewanee" and enrolls more than 1,200 students in the College of Arts and Sciences and another 75 in the School of Theology.

The university buildings resemble those of Oxford and Cambridge.

It is owned by 28 dioceses of the Episcopal Church spread over 12 states.

Visitors are welcome to walk on the campus and see the buildings. To find the campus, turn north on University Ave. off Hwy. 64/41A. Services are held in All Saints' Chapel daily and Sunday, and visitors are welcome. The **Abbott Cotten Martin Ravine Garden,** known to the irreverent as "Abbo's Alley," lies to the west of the main campus and consists of a landscaped area containing wildflowers, a brook, stone bridges, and goldfish. A wonderful vista awaits at **Memorial View,** where a giant cross commemorates Sewanee war dead. To get there, take Tennessee Ave. off University Ave. and drive for about a mile. From here visitors can take a look at the Highland Rim, 1,000 feet lower in elevation. For information about cultural and sports activities, call (931) 598-1286.

St. Andrews-Sewanee School
This school is the latest incarnation of boarding schools in Sewanee. Tennessee writer and Pulitzer Prize-winning novelist James Agee spent 1916 through 1924 as a student at St. Andrews School, which was run by Episcopal monks. One of them, Father James Harold Flye, corresponded with Agee for the rest of the latter's life. These letters, which shed insight into the writer, were published after his death as *Letters of James Agee to Father Flye.*

St. Andrews is now a co-ed, Episcopal, college preparatory school for 240 boarding and day students. Visitors often come just to see the red-tile-roofed chapel. Piney Point, a 10-minute walk from the football field, offers a wonderful view from the edge of the Cumberland Plateau.

The school maintains an **Agee Room** with memorabilia connected to its most famous alumnus. The **Heritage Room** is a small museum recalling the school's history, including photos

THE KINDNESS OF STRANGERS

When the will of Tennessee Williams (1911-83) was probated, the University of the South learned that the playwright had left it a large sum of money. This became the seed money for the Sewanee Writer's Conference, an annual gathering of men and women of letters.

Tennessee Williams did not attend the University of the South, although his grandfather, the Rev. Walter E. Dakin, attended the University's School of Theology. Williams was offered an honorary degree shortly before he died, but he was sick and could not attend the ceremonies. No one knows if Williams ever laid eyes on the college.

The annual Writer's Conference is held in July. It includes workshops, readings, and lectures in fiction, poetry, and playwriting. Past participants include writers Russell Banks, Amy Hempel, Francine Prose, and Maxine Kumin, as well as agents, publishers, and editors. For details call (931) 598-1141.

taken by Father Flye. Admission is free. The school can be reached at (931) 598-5651.

Recreation
The old train track down the mountain to Cowan, once the roadbed of the Mountain Goat train, is now a challenging jeep road ideal for mountain bike aficionados. The dirt road parallels Hwy. 41A for a bit, and a good place to get on it is the historical marker for the Army of Tennessee.

Entertainment and Events
Shenanigans, Hwy. 41A, tel. (931) 598-5671, stages live music most weekends.

Held on the campus at Manigault Park, the **Spring Craft Show** coincides with commencement at the University of the South—usually the second weekend in May—and features works by local artisans. Call (931) 598-0301 for information.

The **Fall Craft Show** takes place in Convocation Hall on the Saturday before Thanksgiving. Call (931) 598-0301.

Where to Stay
Sewanee Inn, Hwy. 64/41A, tel. (931) 598-1686, is owned by the university and open to those

attending a function or in some way connected with the university.

Full Circle Bed & Breakfast, 4115 E. Roarks Cove, tel. (931) 598-5180, www.cafes.net/fullcircle, occupies a 150-acre farm that is three miles from Sewanee. Guests can choose from two rooms, each of which is furnished with antiques.

Food
Four Seasons, midway between Sewanee and Monteagle, tel. (931) 598-5544, offers country cooking.

Pearl's Cafe, 15344 Sewanee Hwy., tel. (931) 598-9568, offers a respite from country cooking. Here's the place for fried calamari, fresh Canadian mussels, and Jamaican jerk wings. One can drink imported beer while gazing at the artwork hanging on the walls—all for sale.

Quidnunc Cafe, 580 University Ave., tel. (931) 598-1595, serves pizza and sandwiches.

Shenanigans, Hwy. 41A, tel. (931) 598-5671, serves salads, soup, quiche, sandwiches, and imported and draft beer.

Arts and Crafts
The **Elvin King Gallery,** King Rd., tel. (931) 598-5867, is the only one in the state that describes itself as "a place surrounded by a bunch of old cars down in a field." It is also the home of one of the few people anywhere who can peel an apple with a chainsaw. Elvin King carves wood with a chain saw, transforming it into animals, bowls, and half-inch high mushrooms. To get to the gallery, go 2.5 miles south of Sewanee on Hwy. 56. Turn left onto King Rd.—if drivers go to Rattlesnake Rd., they have gone too far—and follow the road until the house and attendant cars come into view. Mr. King attends a lot of festivals on weekends, so the wise visitor will call ahead. This gallery keeps no particular hours. "We're around here most of the time," says King.

John Ray Pottery, tel. (931) 598-5184, has to be one of the more unusual such places in the state. John Ray apprenticed in Japan for more than five years with various potters, and on returning to this country set about building a 40-foot-long kiln in which his work is fired by wood. He produces pottery as various as four-foot-high urns and teapots and temple teacups. The pottery is eight miles from Sewanee, and visitors should call ahead for directions.

Hallelujah Pottery Gallery, Hwy. 41A in Sewanee, tel. (931) 598-0141, produces functional stoneware such as baking dishes, pitchers, and mugs. It features wood-fired, salt-glazed pottery, all of it one-of-a-kind.

Information
The **Franklin County Chamber of Commerce,** 1927 Decherd Blvd. in Winchester, tel. (931) 967-6788.

COWAN

The drive from Sewanee to Cowan, or vice versa, particularly on a snowy day, clearly demonstrates the obstacle that the Cumberland Plateau posed to travelers. This was particularly true for early Tennessee railroads, which had to climb the Plateau to get from Nashville to Chattanooga. At Cowan, the railroad officials decided to dig a tunnel through the mountain. Four hundred slaves worked on the three-year effort, which resulted in the 2,228-foot-long Cumberland Tunnel. By 1854, trains connected Nashville with Chattanooga and points south. One of the blunders that Confederate general Braxton Bragg made as he retreated from Tennessee was neglecting to destroy this tunnel. Unscathed, it served as a vital supply line to Union troops pushing toward Atlanta.

One of the participants in Bragg's retreat was Nathan Bedford Forrest, who with his escorts brought up the rear of the sad procession. An old woman was berating the retreating troops for their cowardice. As Forrest—much taller than average—passed, the woman shouted, "A big stout man like you running away! You ought to be ashamed of yourself! If old Forrest was here, he would make you stand and fight!"

Sights
The town's 1904 railroad depot in midtown is the site of the **Cowan Railroad Museum,** no phone, which includes a locomotive and caboose. Admission is free, but donations are accepted.

From here visitors can see the northern entrance of the Cumberland Tunnel. Even with the tunnel, however, the grades up the Plateau are so steep that additional engines were and are still attached to trains to help them get to the top.

One of the items that no doubt came on the train in the early 1900s was a **mail-order house** from Sears Roebuck, which still stands at 518 W. Cumberland Street. It is not open to the public.

McDonald Farm, 7745 Sewanee Hwy., tel. (931) 967-7137, is the home of a group of exotic animals—emus, rheas, ostriches, miniature donkeys, and others. One mile east of Cowan on the way to Sewanee, it is the third house on the left. Admission is free.

Recreation
Cowan is the downhill end of the old Mountain Goat railbed that leads up to Sewanee. Now a jeep trail, it is an excellent place to ride a mountain bike. To find the trail, park in the middle of town and ride on the right side of the railroad track toward the Cowan Tunnel. When the track enters the tunnel, the road goes over the tunnel and veers off to the left. Follow it uphill until reaching the campus of the University of the South.

Entertainment
Every other Saturday night, Cowan closes Tennessee Ave. for a **street dance** with live bands.

Accommodations and Food
Try **Rolling Acres Motel,** Hwy. 41A, tel. (931) 967-7428.

Buck's Market, 415 W. Cumberland, tel. (931) 967-6241, has won second place in a statewide barbecue competition. Get barbecue or ribs—wet or dry.

The Corner House Tea Room, 400 E. Cumberland, tel. (931) 967-3910, is a Victorian tea house that serves such items as chicken salad, pasta, seafood, and blackberry or peach cobbler.

Flo's Restaurant, 508 W. Cumberland, tel. (931) 967-9158, offers a country cooking buffet for breakfast and lunch, then shifts to à la carte for dinner. Shrimp and steak are some of the items available for dinner.

Information
Call **Cowan City Hall** at (931) 967-7318. The **Franklin County Chamber of Commerce** is located at 1927 Decherd Blvd. in Winchester, tel. (931) 967-6788.

WINCHESTER

This pleasant town originated as a stop on the mail route that ran from Virginia to New Orleans. The town was laid out in 1808 and was populated in the early days by veterans of the Revolutionary War and their offspring. David Crockett came here to sign up for the militia, and later Franklin Countians pushed for secession. No Civil War battles were fought here, but armies for both sides passed through and helped themselves to livestock, burned fence rails, and made the locals miserable.

Winchester was the site of Mary Sharp College, dubbed "The Pioneer Female College of the South." Its motto was "Educate the mothers and you educate the world." Founded in 1850, it lasted for almost a half century, and it was the first women's college in the country whose graduation requirements for women were the same as those set for men.

The most famous person to come from Franklin County was Frances Rose Shore, a singer who, while attending college at Vanderbilt, sang on a WSM radio show whose theme song was "Dinah." The young woman became known as Dinah Shore, star of stage and screen, seller of cookbooks, and fan of Burt Reynolds. She is fondly remembered in Winchester, where a prominent street bears her name.

Sights

Downtown Winchester holds several attractions for the visitor. First is the town square, which is anchored by a Depression-era courthouse whose design incorporates art deco elements. On one side of the square sits **Hammers,** a has-to-be-seen-to-be-believed store, and on the opposite side is the **Oldham Theater,** tel. (931) 967-2516, a movie palace that has occasional plays. A few steps off the square on 2nd Avenue NW leads to **Rainbow Row,** brightly painted 19th-century storefronts containing antique shops, a restaurant, a bookstore, and a gift shop.

A walk down Dinah Shore Blvd. leads to the **Franklin County Old Jail Museum,** 400 1st Ave., tel. (931) 967-0524. This town built its first jail in 1814, and the festivities surrounding the completion of the log structure reached such a euphoric state that the object of celebration burned to the ground. This version was completed in 1897 and now houses a museum containing frontier artifacts, more than 200 Civil War items as well as things from other wars, and exhibits related to Dinah Shore.

Entertainment and Events

The **Tennessee Tomahawks** belong to the Big South League and offer professional baseball during a season that runs from mid-June through August. The Tomahawks play home games at the Gamble Sports Complex. Tickets are available at 300 S. Jefferson Street. For information, call (931) 962-4922.

Those magnificent men and their flying machines of the **Experimental Aircraft Association** gather for a monthly fly-in breakfast at the Winchester Airport on the first Saturday of each month 7:30-10 a.m. Call (931) 967-3148.

The **"High on the Hog" Bar-B-Que Cookoff** heats up in mid-June at the Winchester City Park. Auxiliary events include 5K and 10K runs, arts and crafts, and carnival rides.

The **Arts & Crafts Fair** on the third weekend in September attracts participants from several states.

The second weekend in October brings the **Winchester Fall Festival,** which includes living history demonstrations, Civil War demonstrations, an Indian camp, arts and crafts, food, and music.

Where to Stay

The Antebellum Inn, 974 Lynchburg Hwy., tel. (931) 967-5550, occupies an 1850s home that overlooks Tims Ford Reservoir and is surrounded by lots of land. The three guest rooms all have private baths. Rates range $82-95. Moderate-Expensive.

Green Pastures, 114 Sharp Springs Rd., Winchester, TN 37398, tel. (931) 967-9509, is in an 1860 home on the National Register. Guests can choose from three bedrooms, one of which is handicapped-accessible. Two of the rooms have private baths. The innkeeper speaks Japanese. Rates are $75-120. Moderate-Premium.

Motel options include **Winchester Inn,** 700 S. College, tel. (931) 967-3846; or the **Royal Inn,** 1602 Dinah Shore Blvd., tel. (931) 967-9444.

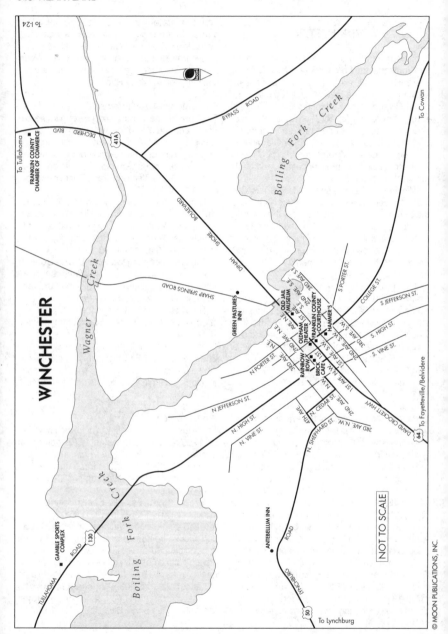

WINCHESTER

NOT TO SCALE

© MOON PUBLICATIONS, INC.

Fairview Campground on Fairview Rd., tel. (931) 967-4230 or (931) 967-1967, has 71 sites. It's open April-September.

Winchester Campground, on Hwy. 130, tel. (931) 967-2532, has 20 sites open May-October.

Food
The Antebellum Inn, 974 Lynchburg Hwy., tel. (931) 967-5550, offers dinners by reservation only Wed.-Sat. and brunch on Sunday. Guests can choose from dishes such as rack of lamb, Cornish hen, prime rib, and fresh seafood. The Green Door Pub, also in the inn, is the only place in the entire county with a full liquor license.

Brick Cafe, 103 2nd Ave. NW, tel. (931) 962-2233, sits in the middle of Rainbow Row and offers light breakfasts and gourmet sandwiches. Try the muffuletta—ham, salami, mortadella, and provolone with olive salad on a round bread loaf.

The Cookery, 301 S. College St., tel. (931) 962-9003, is a one-woman operation with limited seating, but the food makes it all worthwhile. Here diners can sample homemade chicken salad served on fresh-baked bread, peach cobbler, and other delights.

Cline's Barbecue, 1848 Decherd Blvd., tel. (931) 962-2001, features pork barbecue, dry ribs, chicken, and side orders. One of the sides is Crazy Taters, which consists of new potatoes, cheese, bell peppers, onions, and smoked sausage.

Green Pastures, 114 Sharp Springs Rd., tel. (931) 967-9509, offers macrobiotic, vegetarian, and seafood lunches and dinners by reservation only.

Hawks Steak and Pizza, 1106 Dinah Shore Blvd., tel. (931) 967-1111, makes steak and pizza and much more: barbecue, chicken, soup and salad bar, and desserts.

Mahogany's Barbecue, 706 S. College St., tel. (931) 962-0720, serves great barbecue sandwiches.

Rafael's Italian Restaurant, 2659 Decherd Blvd., tel. (931) 962-4997, offers dishes such as veal parmesan, Grecian chicken, lasagna, and more.

Shopping
Expressions, A Bookstore/Art Gallery, 113 2nd Ave. NW, tel. (931) 962-1622, has original art, mostly from Tennessee, as well as pottery, woodworking, metal sculpture, and books.

Gallery I, 1319 Dinah Shore Blvd., tel. (931) 967-0646, offers limited-edition prints, local works, china, and gifts.

Those who cannot get to Memphis to see A. Schwab's Dry Goods should stop at **Hammers General Store,** 102 1st Ave., tel. (931) 967-3787. The store contains tons of merchandise, some of it useful and some of it junk.

Rainbow Row, 101-115 2nd Ave., is a brightly colored series of shops and a restaurant in a restored 19th-century building just one block off the square. Among them is **Anderton & Co. Antiques and Folk Art,** 101-115 2nd Ave. NW, tel. (931) 967-8844. Even visitors who aren't particularly antique fans will like this place, which has a great selection of folk art as well.

Information
You'll find the **Franklin County Chamber of Commerce** at 1927 Decherd Blvd. in Winchester, tel. (931) 967-6788. See them online at www.fccc-tn.org.

HIGHWAY 64 WEST

Hundred Oaks Castle, one mile west of town on Hwy. 64 across from the Winchester Hat Company, was once a 30-room home. Built in 1891, it was for a time home to Albert S. Marks, the state's 21st governor. It burned in 1991, but the ruins are still remarkable.

David Crockett moved near here with Polly, his first wife, in 1812. She died three years later and is buried near Hwy. 64. A historical marker indicates the site of her grave.

Belvidere
Travelers who have passed through Pennsylvania will remember the barns built on the sides of hills or against banks so that wagons could drive right into the second story. Such barns are unusual in Tennessee, but can be seen around this small town, which was settled by Swiss and German families after the Civil War.

Other evidence of their presence is the **Swiss Pantry,** Hwy. 64 W, tel. (931) 962-0567, which is run by Mennonite women who produce an enormous variety of foodstuffs: 33 cheeses, 17 kinds of dried fruit, 22 candies, and 16 relishes. Here's where visitors can get Vidalia onion sweet BBQ sauce, Tupelo honey, smoked and peppered bacon, and horehound candy. The pantry is west of Belvidere on Hwy. 64.

Belvidere Market, 6334 Davy Crockett Hwy., tel. (931) 967-3872, is a combination restaurant and art gallery. The restaurant offers what it calls the "Belvidere Bomber"—a sandwich made of ham, turkey, bologna, lettuce, tomato, onions, pickles, and cheese served on white or wheat bread. The gallery features local crafts, pottery, and collectibles.

Falls Mill

This is not a town, but there's so much to see here that it deserves an entry of its own. To get there, go west from Belvidere on Hwy. 64 to the community of Old Salem. Go right on Salem-Lexie Rd., then follow the signs to the mill.

Most of the mills out in the country in Tennessee are designed to grind corn or wheat into, respectively, meal and flour. This three-story brick place was built in 1873 as a cotton and wool factory; indeed, the creek on which it sits is called Factory Creek. After the turn of the century it was transformed into a cotton gin, and after World War II the mill was changed into a woodworking shop. In the late 1960s it became a grist and flour mill.

This has to be one of the most beautiful mills in the state. A 32-foot overshot waterwheel powers the machinery, which grinds grain between large millstones. Stone works better than steel, so say aficionados, because stones do not get as hot as steel and thus do not partially cook the grain they grind. The slightly irregular surface of stone permits a coarser grind, thus delivering more flavor. Here one can buy yellow cornmeal, white cornmeal, grits—the only difference between grits and cornmeal is the size of the cracked corn—whole wheat flour, and rice flour.

Inside the mill is a museum of hand looms, spinning wheels, and 19th-century power looms and carding machines. A country store sells books, arts and crafts, and other items. Admission is $3 for adults, $2 for seniors, and $1 for children under 14.

And there's more. A reconstructed 1895 log cabin can hold up to four adults. Complete with full kitchen and bath, it has a sleeping loft, balcony, and air-conditioning. Rates start at $75. Information on all of the above can be had by calling (931) 469-7161 or, after 4 p.m., (931) 469-0259. Moderate.

ALONG I-40 EAST OF NASHVILLE

HERMITAGE

Due east of Nashville, this suburb takes its name from the grand home of the nation's seventh president.

The Hermitage
Sections of Andrew Jackson's majestic house, Lebanon Rd., tel. (615) 889-2941, were built 1819-21, but most of what visitors now see of The Hermitage was constructed while Jackson was living in the White House.

The Hermitage sits on 625 acres of land, and, unlike many historically significant buildings that nowadays find themselves beside fast-food outlets, this one preserves a sense of what Jackson's country setting was like when he lived here. Almost everything in the home belonged to Jackson. He and Rachel Donelson never had children, a fact that probably helped keep both The Hermitage and its contents intact.

Visitors go through a small museum displaying items owned by the Jacksons and then into The Hermitage and its grounds. The president and

his beloved Rachel are buried in the garden. Jackson was a slaveholder, and visitors can see the cabins in which his human possessions lived. Also in the tour is **Tulip Grove,** home to Old Hickory's nephew and private secretary, Andrew Jackson Donelson.

Donelson's wife, Emily, served as White House hostess during the Jackson years, and it was for her that Donelson built Tulip Grove, a brick Greek revival mansion, in 1834. On coming home to Tennessee after the years in Washington, however, 29-year-old Emily died of tuberculosis. The house now contains period antiques.

Admission is $8 for adults, $7 for seniors, and $4 for children six to 12. It has a cafeteria on the site, **Rachel's Garden Cafe,** offering breakfast and lunch. To get there, take I-40 to the Old Hickory/Hermitage Exit, bear left, then go about one mile to Lebanon Road. Turn right and go about a mile until the signs for the entrance, which is on the left.

Old Hickory
North of Hermitage along the Cumberland River stands the company town of Old Hickory. In 1918,

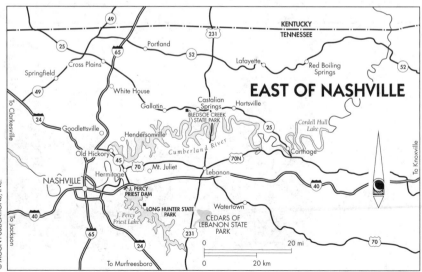

OLD HICKORY

Andrew Jackson, though born in South Carolina, is known to history as a Tennessean, and his career ran the length of the state. He began as a lawyer in Jonesborough, spent much of his life in and around Nashville, co-founded Memphis, and helped write the state constitution.

Jackson's fierce personality was evident from an early age, when as a boy he refused to shine the boots of a British officer and was struck across the face with a sword. His temper led him into arguments and duels; on one occasion he locked a man who had insulted an innkeeper in the inn's corncrib.

When he moved to Nashville, he boarded in the home of John Donelson, who had led the flotilla of boats carrying the people who originally settled the city. There the young Jackson met Rachel Donelson, living back at home to escape her abusive husband. Learning that her husband had applied to the Virginia legislature for a divorce, and thinking he had obtained one, the two were wed. In fact, Rachel's husband had only received permission from the legislature to seek a divorce, and, in a final affront to his wife, waited until she was wed and then received a divorce by claiming that Rachel had deserted him and committed adultery with Jackson. The Jacksons, learning of this to their horror, got married again, but for the rest of their lives, their enemies used this situation against them. They moved to a plantation east of Nashville called The Hermitage.

Jackson became one of Tennessee's first congressmen during George Washington's final term but served only one term. Elected in 1797 as a senator, he returned to the nation's capital but resigned the next year to come home to Rachel.

Tennessee was growing, and over the years Jackson involved himself in various land transactions. At times he prospered, and other times he felt the financial pinch. He maintained close ties to Tennessee politicians and partook of horse races whenever he could. Appointed a judge, he presided in trials in various towns and became well known throughout the state.

When the War of 1812 broke out, Jackson was ready. He had long hated the British and called for 50,000 men to join him in invading Canada. The federal government sent Jackson and his army in the other direction, however, to smite the Creek, who were allied with the British. The Tennesseans utterly defeated the Creek in Alabama, and Jackson became a hero to Tennesseans and other westerners.

Operating without orders, he continued south with his army, aiming to attack the Spanish at Pensacola, Florida. Learning that the British planned an attack at New Orleans, he hastily moved to Louisiana and, in a battle that took place

Andrew and Rachel Jackson Tomb

after the peace treaty was signed in Belgium, thrashed the British in a decisive battle. When news of this reached Washington and other eastern cities, Jackson became a national hero.

People began to talk of Jackson as presidential timber. Further military successes against the Seminoles in Florida added to his stature, and in 1823 he was again elected to the U.S. Senate. He ran for president in 1824, and when none of the four candidates received a majority of electoral votes, the election—the only time in American history—was settled in the House of Representatives. Through the efforts of Speaker of the House Henry Clay, Jackson lost to John Quincy Adams, who promptly appointed Clay secretary of state. Amid charges of a "corrupt bargain," Jackson resolved to run again and began his campaign immediately.

In 1828 it paid off. In the ugliest presidential race in the new country, Jackson ousted Adams from the White House. During the campaign, however, Adams's supporters had dragged out the old charges of adultery, and within weeks of Jackson's election, his beloved Rachel was dead—some said in part because of her intense embarrassment.

The election of Jackson marked a watershed in American politics. He was the first president from a state not bordering the ocean, and his victory marked a shift of power to those who had not had much of an opportunity to run the country. Jackson's taking the oath of office kicked off the wildest party ever held in the White House, with raw-boned Tennesseans and other westerners whooping it up and having a grand old time. The only thing that got them back outside was an announcement that the drinks were being poured there.

Jackson's presidency was noted for his response to an 1830 move in South Carolina to leave the Union over a tax it did not like. A staunch Unionist, he threatened to invade if South Carolina seceded. Perhaps the most shameful of his actions was standing by and letting Georgia lead the Cherokees on the Trail of Tears when the Supreme Court had ruled in favor of the tribe. Nonetheless, he fares well in history. A 1996 poll of historians ranked him as "near great," a tier below only Washington, Lincoln, and F.D. Roosevelt.

Elected to a second term by more votes than his first victory, Jackson solidified the control of the Democratic Party on national politics, and he was able to virtually hand-pick his successor, Martin Van Buren.

Jackson came home to The Hermitage, where he lived the remaining eight years of his life in exceedingly bad health. He still commanded great respect in Tennessee, and his counsel was sought until his death on June 8, 1845. Jackson and his wife had never had any children, and his home and furnishings were acquired by the state, giving today's visitors a wonderful look at Tennessee's most powerful politician.

---

in an all-out effort that foreshadowed World War II's construction of Oak Ridge, the DuPont Company built the world's largest smokeless gunpowder plant and surrounded it with a town for workers. Construction was quick: a six-room bungalow, complete with plumbing, was built in nine hours. Finished just in time for the armistice, the factory was mothballed, only to open again in 1923 as a manufacturer of rayon and cellophane.

Once again workers occupied the company homes, which were sold to their occupants beginning in the late 1940s. Today the **Old Hickory Historic District** shows the visitor the company housing and other buildings built during the DuPont era.

Events

The **Spring Garden Fair,** held in mid-May at the Hermitage, brings lectures, walks, birdwatching expeditions, and all manner of events relating to gardening.

Storytelling Days take place for three days in October, when professional storytellers ply their art in large tents on the Hermitage grounds.

Accommodations and Food

Try **Comfort Inn,** 5768 Old Hickory Blvd., tel. (615) 889-5060 or (800) 221-2222; **Hermitage Inn,** 4144 Lebanon Rd., tel. (615) 883-7444; or **Holiday Inn Express,** I-40 Exit 221, tel. (615) 871-4545 or (800) HOLIDAY.

All-you-can-eat country cooking fills the bill at **Hermitage House Smorgasbord,** 3131 Lebanon Hwy. 70, tel. (615) 883-9525.

Information

Go to **Donelson/Hermitage Chamber of Commerce,** 5651 1st Blvd. no. 703, tel. (615) 883-7896. Visit the chamber at their online site at www.donelsonhermitagechamber.org.

LONG HUNTER STATE RECREATIONAL PARK

Motorists on I-40 east of Nashville pass a long dam to the south of the interstate. This is J. Percy Priest Dam, which impounds Stones River to create J. Percy Priest Lake, on whose eastern shore stands this 2,315-acre park. Long Hunter is primarily a day-use park, with activities such as swimming, picnicking, and hiking. Some primitive camping is allowed, but the park has no cabins. Those wishing to camp must have a permit, which they can obtain at the visitors center.

Long Hunter contains trails and picnic areas especially accessible to handicapped visitors, including nature trails and fishing in Couchville Lake. To get to the park, take Hwy. 171 from either I-40 E or I-24 S. Call (615) 885-2422 or visit online at www.tnstateparks.com.

LEBANON

This town, the seat of Wilson County, got its name because the large cedar trees reminded early settlers of the cedars of Lebanon mentioned in the Bible. Several prominent Tennesseans lived here, including Andrew Jackson, Sam Houston, and three governors of the state, one of whom, elected when Tennessee was in the Confederacy, never took office because his capital was in the hands of the Union.

Deford Bailey, the first black entertainer on the Grand Ole Opry and one of its more popular performers, was born near here in 1899. An accomplished harmonica player, he was a visible symbol of country music's roots in the blues. Johnny Wright, half of country's famous Johnny and Jack duo, was born in Lebanon. Current stars Charlie Daniels and Reba McEntire live in Wilson County.

Sights

Visitors can glean a multitude of facts from the **Wilson County Museum,** 236 W. Main St., tel. (615) 444-9127, which occupies an historic home known as Fessenden House. The museum, begun in 1870 by a doctor who served in the Civil War, is open by appointment only. Admission is $2 for adults and $1 for children.

Fiddlers Grove, on the grounds of the Ward Agricultural Center, 945 Baddour Pkwy., tel. (615) 443-2626, consists of 20 buildings that illustrate the history of Wilson County. Structures such as a general store, doctor's office, and print shop contain items that relate to each. Normally admission is free, unless a special event is taking place on the grounds. The best time to see the grove is during the Wilson County Fair, when crafts and activity demonstrators transform the old buildings into a living village.

Cumberland University got its start in 1842, when most attorneys got their training by "reading the law" under the tutelage of another lawyer. The university's law school produced many prominent judges and lawmakers, but in this century the institution achieved a more dubious form of fame: Georgia Tech beat it 220-0 in a 1916 football game. The law school moved to Birmingham, Alabama, during the 1960s, and the university continues today as a four-year private college with just over 1,000 students.

Lebanon was home for 84 years to **Castle Heights Military Academy,** which had a 225-acre campus. Closed in 1986, it left a series of brick and stone castellated buildings, some of which are currently being used for businesses and offices.

Entertainment and Events

Chapel Playhouse, housed on E. Market Street in a former church that is the oldest brick building in Wilson County, is a community theater company offering five or six productions per year. Call (615) 449-2787 for tickets and information.

Details on all events are available from the chamber of commerce at tel. (615) 444-5503.

Wilson County Lifestyle Days takes place on the first weekend in May and consists of train rides, crafts, food, and flea markets.

Cedarfest, held on the third weekend in July, brings contests—fiddling, square dancing, and buck dancing—food, and music.

The **Wilson County Fair,** held the third week in August, attracts more than 120,000 people in nine days. Featured are a carnival, rural exhibits, and live entertainment.

A **Victorian Christmas** occurs on the third weekend in November. Carriage rides, house tours, and lights make up this seasonal festival.

FRANK BUSTER AND HIS MYSTERIOUS HEAD

Frank Buster's head appears on billboards all over Lebanon beckoning customers to **Cuz's,** his enormous antique emporium. For pedestrians in the town square, however, he offers a marketing technique—The Mysterious Critter—at least as old as Davy Crockett.

The attraction in his front window is a stuffed head resembling a Bigfoot kind of beast. According to a press release that Buster hands out, a couple leaving an extramarital tryst on nearby Sugar Flat Rd. was driving home when their truck—sounds like a country song so far—hit one of a pair of creatures. Getting out, the driver saw to his horror that he had killed one of them. Afraid he and his lover would get caught making whoopee, he dragged the hairy body into the bushes, then took his lady friend home and went home himself. Unable to sleep, he came back in the dawn's early light to bury the mysterious body.

At the last minute, according to the tale, he severed its head and took it to a taxidermist, who agreed to preserve it. The head stayed on a mantel for years before being sold to the entrepreneurial Mr. Buster.

The release ends on an ominous note: "But there continue to be spottings of the creature's mate up and down Sugar Flat Road. Residents of the area have complained that chickens, ducks, and turkeys often come up missing and the rumor is that if a dog barks at night, that dog will probably never be seen again . . . ."

At least that's the tale—and not a bad one at that. The head certainly makes passersby slow down and has drawn the attention of inquiring minds. One such soul, reporting in a "Bigfoot Field Researcher's Organization" website, suggests that this head is a hoax. He notes that the owner of the head himself lives on Sugar Flat Rd., and an analysis of the fur on the hirsute cranium by Dr. Henner Fahrenbach (a doctor!) reveals that it

comes from "a common rabbit." As for Buster, the Internet correspondent in Lebanon opines, "I get the feeling he doesn't think it a fake."

In the meantime, Frank Buster and his head, whatever its origin, continue to pull in customers. Perhaps the erudite Dr. Fahrenbach, after suitable analysis, would conclude that Frank Buster is an uncommon marketer.

If your own mind would like to inquire, see www.moneymaker.org/BFRR/REF/THEORIES/SM/mhead.htm.

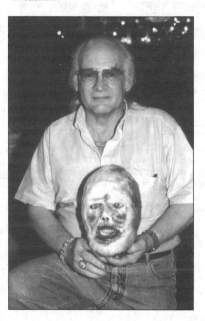

Frank Buster and the Head

Where to Stay

Watermelon Moon Farm, 10575 Trousdale Ferry Pike, Lebanon, TN 37087, tel. (615) 444-2356, is in what used to be the summer kitchen of an old plantation house. The antebellum house is on the National Register and has verandahs front and back. The cottage has its own bath and is decorated in a country style. Water-

melon Moon Farm is home to Country Plus, a wholesale business that produces hand-painted crafts. The rate is $60 per night. Moderate.

Motel options include **Best Western Executive Inn,** 631 S. Cumberland, tel. (615) 444-0505 or (800) 528-1234; **Budget Host Inn,** I-40 and Hwy. 231 S, tel. (615) 449-2900 or (800) BUD-HOST; **Comfort Inn,** I-40 and Hwy. 231 S, tel.

(615) 444-1001 or (800) 221-2222; **Days Inn,** I-40 and Hwy. 231, tel. (615) 444-5635 or (800) 325-2525; **Hampton Inn,** I-40 and Hwy. 231 S, tel. (615) 444-7400 or (800) HAMPTON, rates $48-58; **Holiday Inn Express,** 641 S. Cumberland, tel. (615) 444-7020 or (800) HOLIDAY; and **Shoney's Inn,** I-40 and Hwy. 231 S, tel. (615) 449-5781 or (800) 222-2222.

Campers can set up at **Countryside Resort,** tel. (615) 449-5527, which has 105 sites. From I-40 take Exit 232 and follow signs. It's open all year.

Shady Acre Campground, tel. (615) 449-5400, has 125 sites and is open all year. From I-40 take Exit 238 and follow signs.

Timberline Campground, tel. (615) 449-2831, lies off I-40 on Hwy. 321 South. It has 100 sites and is open all year.

Food

Allens Market, 725 York St., tel. (615) 444-9415, offers deli sandwiches and beer for lunch.

Cherokee Steakhouse, 450 Cherokee Dock Rd., tel. (615) 452-1515, sits next door to Reba McEntire's place. It offers all manner of steaks, seafood, chicken, and ribs for dinner only.

Meacham's Cafe, 1418 W. Main St., Suite K, tel. (615) 449-1200, serves Italian dishes, steaks, and seafood, as well as sandwiches and salads.

New City Cafe, 113 E. Main St., tel. (615) 444-7117, offers what it calls "upscale country cooking," which means it uses seasonings other than salt and pepper. Everything served here is made here, including the salad dressings.

The Perfect Cup Coffeehouse, 104 N. Maple St., tel. (615) 449-7939, specializes in espresso and cappuccino augmented by homemade desserts and Italian grilled sandwiches. It's only a half block from the square.

Elaine's Country Restaurant, 1103-$^1/_2$ N. Cumberland, tel. (615) 443-2135, offers farm-raised catfish, frog legs, fried oysters, steak, and various interpretations of country cooking.

Shopping

Lebanon is famous among antique-fanciers for its collection of dealers. While aficionados can easily spend the better part of a day in the downtown area, other dealers have shops on Hwy. 231. Of particular note are the following.

Coach House Antiques, 103 Public Square, tel. (615) 443-1905, deals in clocks, fine furniture, and lamps. This is a good place to get a pocket watch.

Cuz's Antique Center, 140 Public Square, tel. (615) 444-8070, stocks more than 150,000 square feet of American, French, and English antiques. It also offers more than 1,000 stained-glass items. Maud Gold Kiser, who literally wrote the book on antiquing in Middle Tennessee, says that this is the largest antique place "in the universe as we know it." Knife fans will want to stop to see the Fightin' Rooster Cutlery Company here, which has thousands of knives.

Information

Seek information at the **Lebanon/Wilson County Chamber of Commerce,** 149 Public Square, tel. (615) 444-5503.

CEDARS OF LEBANON STATE RECREATIONAL PARK

This 831-acre park adjoins an 8,056-acre state forest and natural area, and together they constitute the largest red cedar forest remaining in the country. "Red cedar" in this case is a misnomer, for the trees are actually junipers *(Juniperus virginiana).* Early settlers used this soft wood for everything from log cabins to roofing shingles. It splits easily, resists rot, and smells good. Moths will not infest woolens stored in cedar chests. Tennessee's pencil industry to the southwest of here came about because of the abundance of cedars.

In this park are cedar glades, places where the soil is too thin to support trees, even cedar trees. Prickly pear cactus and other unusual plants grow here, some of which—such as Guthrie's ground plum—are unique to this area. The Merrit Nature Center is open daily during summer.

Those whose interest in botany is confined to the grass on a playing field will find plenty to do in this park. Eight miles of hiking trails, 12 miles of horse trails, a large swimming pool, sports fields, and a Frisbee golf course await the visitor. Park-sponsored activities include summertime programs, hayrides, evening movies, and organized games.

Nine housekeeping cabins that can sleep six are available for $90 a night. During the summer these must be rented for at least a week. A group lodge complete with kitchen can accommodate 40 people. For reservations, call (615) 443-2769 or (888) 867-2757. The park offers 119 campsites, all with picnic tables and grills; 89 have hookups. The campground is open all year, with sites available on a first-come, first-served basis.

The park is six miles south of I-40 on Hwy. 231. For further information, call (615) 443-2769.

WATERTOWN

Due east of Cedars of Lebanon State Recreational Park lies Watertown, named for Wilson Waters, a Republican who freed his slaves before the Civil War. He founded the town on his farm, ran a store and a mill, and helped ensure that the railroad came through here.

It still does. Several times a year the Tennessee Central Railway Museum runs a train from Nashville to Watertown. For ticket information, call (615) 781-0262. Passengers find a charming little square with period lighting. The town is locally famous for its mile-long yard sale held every year in April.

Events
Many of the events in Watertown center occur when the excursion train from Nashville pulls into town. Among these are the following: **Mile-Long Yard Sale,** held in mid-April; **Swingin' Jazz Festival** in mid-July; **Fall Flea Market** and **Fall Foliage** in October; and **Christmas in the County** in early December.

Where to Stay
Watertown Bed & Breakfast, just off the town square at 116 Depot Ave., tel. (615) 237-9999, occupies a railroad hotel built in 1898. Guests can relax on hammocks and swings on the upper and lower verandah. Inside, five guest rooms await, four upstairs and one down. Each bedroom has a private bath—two have whirlpools—but the ones upstairs share a shower. The downstairs room also has a private bath, but it is across the hall. Guests enjoy a library and board games, and the hosts serve a full breakfast. Rates range from $55 for the downstairs room to $115-125 for the whirlpool rooms. Visit online at www.bbonline.com/tn/watertown. Inexpensive-Premium.

Food
The Barn, 105 Main St., tel. (615) 237-3008, has a hayloft facade outside and barn wood inside. Country cooking is the fare, with a buffet on weekends.

Depot Junction Restaurant, 108 Depot St., tel. (615) 237-3976, features a model train that chugs around the walls. Diners will find steak, seafood, country cooking, and homemade desserts.

Information
Find **Lebanon/Wilson County Chamber of Commerce** at 149 Public Square, tel. (615) 444-5503. Visit online at www.usagetaways.com/watertown.

NORTH OF I-40

CARTHAGE

The Cumberland River downstream from Nashville isn't exactly straight, but upstream from Music City it becomes absolutely serpentine. This reflects the increasingly rugged terrain through which the river flows. These same hills made it difficult to build railroads and good roads, thus making riverboats the main form of transportation hereabouts long after railroads had vanquished them from larger rivers. Carthage was a major port on the Upper Cumberland, and one of the people who ran a fleet of packet boats, as they were called, was Thomas Ryman. Ryman fell under the influence of an evangelist and was inspired to build a building in Nashville for religious services. Originally named the Union Gospel Tabernacle, it is now known as Ryman Auditorium, the original home of the Grand Ole Opry.

Carthage was the home of the Albert Gores, a father and son who served as congressmen, senators, and, in the case of Al Gore Jr., vice president. The latter, however, spent most of his time growing up in Washington, D.C., although he claims to be a Carthenagen at heart. The elder Senator Gore died December 5, 1998 at the age of 90. Given the number of lunatics running loose, this book will not give the location of the Gore family home.

Tennessee has a wonderful bunch of odd community names, and two of them are northeast of here. **Defeated** and **Difficult** were used to describe a trip in which some pioneers engaged in 1786. The Indians were defeated and the trip was difficult. Thus the names.

Recreation

Five miles up the Cumberland River from Carthage is **Cordell Hull Lake,** a Corps of Engineers project that was completed in 1973 and produces hydropower, extends river navigation as far as Celina, and offers an opportunity for recreation. This last benefit includes swimming, boating, picnicking, and hunting. The Cordell Hull visitors center at the dam, tel. (615)

735-1034, features exhibits on the animals of Middle Tennessee as well as explanations of hydropower. To get there, take Hwy. 233 N. from Carthage.

Events

Smith County Fall Heritage Festival, held on the town square in October, offers a pleasant combination of arts and crafts, demonstrations of blacksmithing and other old-time activities, and good food.

Where to Stay

Gibbs Landing Bed and Breakfast, 136 Gibbs Landing, Carthage, TN 37030, tel. (615) 735-2198, occupies a home that sits on five acres along the river and features a streamside walking trail, outdoor hot tub, covered verandah, and screened porch. Rates are $85-125. Visit online at www.bbonline.com/ten/gibbslanding. Expensive-Premium.

Other choices include **Cordell Hull Motel,** Hwy. 25, tel. (615) 753-1300; or the **Comfort Inn,** Hwy. 53 at I-40, tel. (800) 228-5150.

Food

B & B Drive-In, 421 Cookeville Hwy., tel. (615) 735-9657, has, according to one regular, "the best steak and grilled chicken you have ever put your teeth into." This used to be one of the hangouts of Al Gore Jr.

David and Leslie's, 4 Dixon Springs Hwy., tel. (615) 735-9990, has a long bar with stools. People come here for the hamburgers and fries.

La Villa, 67 Dixon Springs Hwy., tel. (615) 735-1331, offers one of the bigger menus to be found in these parts. Diners can choose among hickory-smoked barbecue, catfish, oysters on the half shell, ribs, steak, burgers, and country ham.

The Country Courtyard Restaurant, 4 E. Main St., tel. (615) 683-6441, features a country cooking buffet as well as a full menu.

The Timber Loft Restaurant, at the I-40 and Hwy. 53 interchange, tel. (615) 683-8697, offers a buffet of traditional Southern cooking.

Information

Smith County Chamber of Commerce is located at 130 W. 3rd Ave., tel. (615) 735-2093. Another source of information is the rest area on I-40 between Exits 258 and 268.

GAINESBORO

The second largest meteor crater in the United States lies west of town off Hwy. 53. **Flynn's Lick Crater** was created about 350 million years ago when some sort of celestial body slammed into the ground and displaced 0.3 cubic miles of land.

An early account of the "long hunters" who first explored Middle Tennessee tells of a party of men from French Lick—today's Nashville—killing 105 bears, 75 buffalo, and 80 deer near here.

Gainesboro is the seat of Jackson County, and visitors can see artifacts from riverboating days at the **Jackson County Museum,** which occupies a building on Montpelier that once housed the local newspaper. Call (931) 268-0971.

"Sock a little poke sallet to me," sang Elvis. "I need me a mess of it." He could eat his fill at the **Poke Sallet Festival,** held on the first weekend in May. This three-day event features all-you-can-eat poke sallet, a.k.a. pokeweed, which has leaves that, when boiled three or four times and adorned with vinegar, butter, and bits of bacon, are downright good. Other activities include an outhouse race, music, and crafts. For information call (931) 268-3447.

WHITLEYVILLE

This little community is the home of **Freestone Pottery,** 707 N. Fork Ln., tel. (931) 621-3456, wherein potters Tom and Sally Freestone create plates and other items adorned with Bible verses and hand-painted flower designs. To visit their studio, call ahead. Freestone pottery is also sold at Gainesboro Drugs on the Square in Gainesboro.

RED BOILING SPRINGS

Of the places in Tennessee where people would come to "take the waters," this was one of the more successful. It all started, according to local lore, when a pioneer who had some sort of eye problem bathed in the waters here and over time was healed. Word spread and others came, and the first hotel was built just before the Civil War.

In those days the water came out of the ground in artesian wells, but before long so many man-made wells were dug that the artesian pressure diminished.

Things really got rolling, so to speak, with the coming of the railroad to nearby Hartsville at the turn of the century. By 1918 the town had four hotels, and less than 10 years later it had eight hotels and more than a dozen boardinghouses. Guests could partake of five kinds of water: Red, Black, and White were so named for the color they would turn a silver coin. Freestone was said to have no minerals at all, while Double and Twist, the most memorable variety,0 got its name from a gastrointestinal effect so intense that it caused the drinker to double over and writhe on the ground.

Guests not occupied with doubling and twisting the night away could go dancing, bowling, roller-skating, or swimming; play tennis or shuffleboard, or choose from an assortment of baths, massages, and electrotherapy. Entertainer Dinah Shore came here as a girl, and the hotels catered to luminaries from Tennessee and elsewhere.

The same factors—the automobile and the Depression—that killed off other resorts did their work here. A flood in 1969 devastated the town, but the federal money that flowed in afterward mitigated some of the damage. Two covered bridges were built over the stream.

Luckily, three of the old hotels remain, and people still come here to take the waters, which is available from hand pumps throughout the town. Some just come to get away. One of the ways to begin is a **mineral bath and massage,** available only at Armours, one of the old hotels. The one-hour treatment, bath, and massage cost $40. To schedule a treatment, call (615) 699-2180.

Red Boiling Springs is also home to the world's first gas turbine electrical generator powered by sawdust. The sawdust, a by-product of the many lumber mills in the area, has almost no commercial value, but has been rendered productive by the Tennessee Valley Authority, which buys the electricity cranked out by the plant. The operation lies north of town on Lake Road.

Where to Stay
Built in 1924, **Armours,** 321 Main St., tel. (615) 699-2180, was the first brick hotel in town. Now

its 26 rooms have period furnishings and air-conditioning. This place is run by the founder of the Folk Medicine Festival, who makes it a point to introduce guests to each other. "We are educating a whole generation of people," said another hotel owner in town, "about a slower pace of life, rocking on a front porch, taking time to talk to people, and making new friends. We see a lot of creative people from Nashville—songwriters, singers, and producers—who come here to take it easy." Rooms cost $80 per night. Moderate.

The **Donoho Hotel,** 500 E. Main St., tel. (615) 699-3141, with its long, colonnaded porches on the first and second floors, is the very picture of a Southern resort hotel. It is owned by a couple who stopped at an auction to get a soft drink and wound up buying the hotel. Built in 1914, it has 59 rooms, 36 of which have private baths. The hotel also has Greta, described as a ghost or an angel who is sometimes seen in the dining room. She seems to like music and books and sometimes creates faint music of her own. Room rates include three meals served family-style at long, antique tables. With notification in advance, the hotel can accommodate special diets. Rates are $40 per person per night and include two meals. Moderate.

The building that now houses the **Thomas House,** 520 E. Main St., tel. (615) 699-3006, was built in 1890 from bricks baked in ovens behind the building. The wood inside is chestnut that was cut on the property. Guests have a choice of 27 rooms, all with private baths. Additional rooms display toys, Christmas decorations, and antique clothing, and an antiques store is on the premises. This inn has a great library. Outside is a swimming pool and tennis court. Smoking is permitted. Rates are $80 and include dinner and breakfast. Moderate.

Food
Armours, 321 E. Main St., tel. (615) 699-2180, serves family-style meals of country cooking year-round. Breakfast, lunch, and dinner are by reservation only. Meals here "recall Red Boiling Springs' boardinghouse days," said the owner. "People talk about themselves and what they have been doing."

The **Donoho Hotel,** 500 E. Main St., tel. (615) 699-3141, serves three meals a day by reservation only. Meals are served family-style—all one can eat. A typical dinner includes country ham, four vegetables, biscuits and gravy, and dessert.

The **Thomas House,** 520 E. Main St., tel. (615) 699-3006, also serves all three meals by reservation only. Country cooking is the fare, and on most nights the hotel features live entertainment. The innkeeper does a great Patsy Cline.

Arts and Crafts
The Little House Crafts and Gifts, 503 E. Main St., tel. (615) 699-2345, is the home of Comus and Blanche Moss, whose front yard has a little house from which his wares are sold. He is open "most of the time."

Mineral Springs Arts, 100 Main St., tel. (615) 699-2422, occupies the old bank building in town and sell quilts, original paintings, hand-painted gourds, and other crafts.

Farther Afield
Newberry and Sons Chairs, 1593 Jennings Creek Rd., tel. (615) 699-3755, are fifth-generation chairmakers in the community of Willette. They fashion chairs out of oak, walnut, and cherry wood, and put woven hickory bark bottoms and backs on some of them. They make rocking chairs, dining room chairs, baby rockers, and high chairs. The Newberrys live right beside the shop, which they will open about any time.

To get there from Red Boiling Springs, head south on Hwy. 56 and go about five miles to Gibbs Crossroads, then turn east on Hwy. 56/262, a.k.a. Willette Road. Go two miles to Highland Rim Truck Parts, a gas station. Here the road splits. Bear left on Hwy. 56 and go 1.5 miles to a gray building with a sign out front.

Shopping and Information
Quilts and More, 310 Milltown Ln., tel. (615) 699-2460, has 50-100 machine-quilted quilts on hand at any given time. I

The best sources of information here are the three inns or at City Hall, 166 Dale St., tel. (931) 699-2011. Or look online at www.redboiling-springs.com.

LAFAYETTE

This town, the seat of Macon County, contains **Key Park,** a dandy place for a picnic. A half block west of the town square, the four-acre park contains an 1824 log cabin housing the chamber of commerce. Those seeking an anthropological experience should head for the southeast corner of the public square, where a group of men gather on pleasant days to whittle and talk. These gentlemen are repositories of local lore, have opinions on a wide range of topics, and delight in telling lies to each other and to impressionable visitors.

Lafayette has produced two noteworthies. State Sen. John Butler introduced the bill making it illegal to teach the theory of evolution in Tennessee, the passage of which led to the Scopes Trial in Dayton. In 1992, Nera White became the first woman to be inducted into the National Basketball Hall of Fame. Teams on which she played won 11 Amateur Athletic Union Championships—eight of them in a row. White played for the USA All-Star team and led it to victories. She was named Most Valuable Player at the 1957 World Games.

A first-class piano restoration establishment is about as rare in these parts as a metaphysics bookstore. **The Piano Store and More,** 102 Public Square, tel. (615) 666-5706, is such a place. Step in here to see player pianos and others coming back to musical life.

The **Galen School Museum of Macon County,** tel. (615) 666-4167, is north of town in the Galen community. Built in 1920, the building has been renovated to show off the tongue-and-groove ceilings and walls. It contains a collection of tools, kitchen items, photos, and scrapbooks from the old days. Open by appointment only.

Events
Hillbilly Day, held the first weekend in June, begins with a Friday night all-you-can-eat catfish fry, then rolls into Saturday with music competitions in guitar, mandolin, and other instruments; buck dancing; and singing. Crafts and food are available as well. Call (615) 666-5885.

Where to Stay
Try the **Ellington Motel,** 518 Ellington Dr., tel. (615) 666-2593; or the **Hearthstone Inn,** 605 Hwy. 52 Bypass W, tel. (615) 666-7114.

Food
Grecian Steak House, 1213 Scottsville Rd., tel. (615) 666-2520, offers a country cooking buffet along with steak, seafood, sandwiches, and a salad bar.

McClards's Drug Store, 200 Public Square, tel. (615) 666-3613, still has an ice cream fountain. Stop here for milk shakes, soft drinks, and a few other items.

Old Hickory Bar B Q, Hwy. 52 Bypass, tel. (615) 666-6683, serves pork and chicken barbecue and hamburgers.

Tray's Garden, Hwy. 52 Bypass, tel. (615) 666-6688, serves Chinese food for lunch and dinner seven days a week.

Information
For information, look to the **Macon County Chamber of Commerce,** 208 Church St., tel. (615) 666-5885.

HARTSVILLE

Trousdale County farmers have long grown a lot of tobacco, and the **Trousdale County Living History Museum,** on White Oak St., tel. (615) 374-9343, shows how those 19th-century folks lived. Local buildings have been brought to Hartsville and organized to resemble a working tobacco farm. No admission fee is charged.

Across the street is the restored depot, whose oldest section was completed in 1892. Inside is the Depot Museum, which contains an antique harpsichord, Civil War pictures, and other relics from the town and surrounding area. To visit the museum, call the chamber of commerce at (615) 374-9243.

Just west of town stands a monument to one of the biggest failures of the Tennessee Valley Authority. An enormous concrete cooling tower marks the spot of the Hartsville nuclear power plant, which was conceived in the '60s as the agency embarked on the largest nuclear building program in the world. TVA vastly underestimated the costs of the project and vastly overestimated the demand for electricity, and the 17-reactor program had to be cut back. Billions of dollars were wasted, many of them here, where TVA had planned a four-reactor plant that would have been the world's largest. A beautiful view is spoiled daily by this example of agency hubris.

Where to Stay
Miss Alice's Bed and Breakfast, 8325 Hwy. 141, tel. (615) 374-3015, occupies an early 1900s farmhouse that has been fully restored and sits on 50 acres. Here guests can enjoy a hammock, deck, and walking trails. Two guest rooms are inside, one with a private bath. The rate is $65. Moderate.

The Williams Motel, 782 McMurray Blvd., tel. (615) 374-2589, has rooms for $35 a night. Inexpensive.

Food
Dillehay's Cafe, 102 E. Main St., tel. (615) 374-2069, serves country cooking. Plate lunches are the specialty here.

Crocco's Restaurant, 101 River St., tel. (615) 374-2900, serves appetizers, salads, steak, pizza, chicken, and pasta dishes.

Information
Find **Trousdale County Chamber of Commerce** on the second floor of the Trousdale County Courthouse, tel. (615) 374-9243.

OLD HWY. 25 WEST TO GALLATIN

Old State Hwy. 25 parallels the more modern Hwy. 25 through here, and motorists should stay on the older road as much as possible to enjoy a slower pace and a chance to look at some historic homes.

Castalian Springs
Heading from east to west, the traveler comes to the springs, an old salt lick that has been the scene of human habitation for more than 17,000 years. Evidence suggests that roving Ice Age people first came here about 15,000 B.C. Present-day visitors can see Indian mounds circa A.D. 1400 north of Hwy. 25 near the post office in this hamlet.

Castalian Springs was one of the first settlements in Middle Tennessee. When pioneers first came here, there were so many buffalo milling around that the visitors were afraid to get off their horses. Thomas Spencer arrived in 1777 and lived in a large hollow sycamore tree nine feet in diameter.

Wynnewood
This log structure to the south of Old Hwy. 25, tel. (615) 452-5463, is thought to be the largest log structure ever built in the state—142 feet long. Some of the logs are 32 feet long, and one can only imagine the effort it took to move and position these huge pieces of oak, walnut, and ash. Built in 1828 along with a racecourse, it served as a stagecoach inn and mineral springs resort. Among the guests was Andrew Jackson, who came to race horses. Admission is $3 for adults, $2.50 for seniors, $1.50 for kids 12-18, 50 cents for children under 12.

The **Wynnewood Celebration** takes place on the third weekend in October and offers food, music, Civil War and pioneer reenactments, and demonstrations.

Bledsoe's Fort Historical Park
Across the road from Wynnewood lies this park. Most of the original settlements in Middle Tennessee became the centers of towns, and their sites have long since drowned in asphalt and concrete. Not this one. Of the 12 settlements that made up the Cumberland Compact, the agreement that originally governed Middle Tennessee, this is the only one whose original site is preserved. The land has been grazed for 200 years, and an old cabin stands here. Archaeological diggings have produced artifacts on display at the Sumner County Museum in Gallatin. Bledsoe's Fort is not open on a regular basis, but efforts were under way to offer tours. For information, call Wynnewood, tel. (615) 452-5463, or simply cross the road and ask.

Just east of Bledsoe's Fort, a large Indian mound rises in the field. It is assumed this is a burial mound.

Cragfont
Cragfont, north of Hwy. 25, is as elegant as Wynnewood is rustic. General James Winchester, a Maryland native, brought craftsmen from Baltimore to the frontier to build him a showplace. Beginning work in 1798, the builders cut poplar, walnut, cherry, and ash lumber from trees on the property and quarried limestone for the exterior walls.

Every other structure in the area was made of logs, so Cragfont quickly became the finest house in Middle Tennessee. Among its guests were Andrew Jackson, Sam Houston, and the Marquis de Lafayette, the French hero of the American Revolution.

The house is furnished with authentic American federal antiques, including some pieces owned by the Winchester family. The basement of the house contains displays of farm and carpentry tools and a weaving room. Cragfont is open April 15 through October. Those wishing to see the house November 1 to April 14 should call (615) 452-7070. Admission is $3 for adults and 50 cents for children under 12. Children under six are admitted free.

Bledsoe Creek State Park

One of the smaller parks in the Tennessee system, this 164-acre area lies on a backwater of the Cumberland River. Once prime hunting ground for Indian tribes, it now offers hiking, camping, and lake access for visitors. The park has 126 campsites, all with hookups and access to hot showers, and is open all year. For further information about the park, call (615) 452-3706.

GALLATIN

This town earned a place in Tennessee's musical history as the home of Randy's Record Shop, at one time the largest mail-order record store in the country. By advertising on Nashville's WLAC, Randy Wood cornered the market on rhythm and blues records, introducing Chuck Berry and Bo Diddley to predominantly white audiences. In 1950, Wood opened Dot Records, a label that recorded Pat Boone, Billy Vaughn, and the Fontaine Sisters. The store closed in 1991.

Sights and Events

The *Historic Walking Tour* of the town, a brochure available from the chamber of commerce, shows off the town's treasures. First among them is **Trousdale Place,** 185 W. Main St., tel. (615) 452-5648. Two blocks from the Gallatin public square, this brick home was built in 1813 by John Bowen, a member of Congress. After his death the property was bought by William Trousdale, who served alongside Andrew Jackson at Pensacola and New Orleans in the War of

1812 and later in the Seminole War of 1836. He served in the Tennessee Senate and became the state's governor in 1849. Admission is $3 for adults, $2.50 for seniors, $1 for children 12-18, and 50 cents for children six to 11.

Adjacent to Trousdale Pl. is the **Sumner County Museum,** 183 W. Main St., tel. (615) 451-3738, whose 10,000 square feet feature a collection that begins with Indian pots, tools, and weapons and then moves into pioneer days and more recent times. Visitors can see a black mantilla that belonged to Andrew Jackson's wife Rachel, a tinsmith shop, a woodworker's shop, a blacksmith's shop, and a few Dot records. Admission is $1 for ages six and above, and 50 cents for children under six.

The Palace Theater, 142 N. Water St., is the oldest movie theater in the state. Opened in 1913, its silver screen showed the best of Hollywood until 1977. Efforts were under way to renovate the building and open it once more.

Main Street Festival, held the first Saturday in October, offers music, food, and arts and crafts.

Where to Stay

Hancock House, 2144 Nashville Pike, Gallatin, TN 37066, tel. (615) 452-8431 or (800) 242-6738, occupies a log building that served as a stagecoach stop and toll house beginning about 1878. The inn has seven bedrooms, one of which is a cabin, and all have private baths. Each room contains period antiques, fireplace, refrigerator, telephone, coffeemaker, and television. Three rooms have whirlpools. Rates are $90-200. Get info online at www.bbonline.com/hancock. Expensive-Luxury.

Motel options are **Comfort Inn,** 354 Sumner Hall Dr., tel. (800) 228-5150; or **Shoney's Inn,** 221 W. Main St., tel. (615) 452-5433 or (800) 222-2222.

Cages Bend Campground, eight miles southwest on Hwy. 31 E, tel. (615) 824-4989, has 49 sites but no hookups. It's open April through mid-October.

Food

El Rey Mexican Restaurant, 450 Cherokee Dock Rd., tel. (615) 230-7422, offers chiles rellenos, huevos rancheros, and the real stuff.

Shopping and Information

Gallatin has a great many antique stores. One of the larger ones is **Antiques on Main,** a mall containing about 200 dealers. Here are furniture, books, Civil War items, and much more.

The place to find information about the town is the **Gallatin Chamber of Commerce,** 118 W. Main St., tel. (615) 452-4000. See them online at www.gallatintn.org.

HENDERSONVILLE

This town was so small that it received no listing in the 1939 *WPA Guide to Tennessee.* This changed when the Army Corps of Engineers dammed the Cumberland River in the 1950s to create Old Hickory Lake. The town's population grew, and within two decades Hendersonville became the largest town in the county. Country music stars built some of the bigger homes.

Historic Houses

The tradition of building big homes began in 1784, when Daniel and Sarah Smith moved here to claim land that the state of North Carolina had given to Daniel for his work as a surveyor. He planned a grand home, then took off on one of his long surveying trips and left the supervision of the construction to Sarah, who had to cope with two children and Indian attacks along with the usual headaches of building a house.

The result, **Rock Castle,** on Rock Castle Ln. off Indian Lake Rd., tel. (615) 824-0502, is a prime example of the "glorified pioneer style," which combined Georgian and federal architecture styles. The house was built from limestone and wood that came from the grounds. Inside, it has unusual floor-to-ceiling black walnut cabinets as well as a few of the original pieces of furniture. Admission is $3 for adults, $2.50 for seniors, and $1.50 for children six to 12.

The Hendersonville Arts Council has its offices in **Monthaven,** 1154 W. Main St., tel. (615) 822-0789. This Greek Revival house, which contains Haven Gifts, was built around 1860.

Trinity City

Several country music stars have homes in Hendersonville, including Garth Brooks and Johnny Cash. The first country artist to open his house to the public was Conway Twitty, a rock 'n' roller turned country musician whose "Twitty City" proved a hit with fans. Twitty died in 1993, and Twitty City was sold to the Trinity Broadcasting Network, which now calls the place Trinity Music City, U.S.A., 1 Music Village Blvd., tel. (615) 826-9191.

The Trinity Network produces programs for more than 500 television stations and offers two options for visitors. The first is an overall tour of the operations beginning with the gift shop, an auditorium that looks like a transplanted European opera house, the LaVerne Tripp Ministries Recording studio, Twitty's mansion, and a memorial garden. No admission is charged for this tour or any other presentation at Trinity.

If a show is being taped that day, visitors are welcome to watch. Guests on various shows have included Glen Campbell, Ricky Skaggs, Lulu Roman, and Charlie Daniels. Admission is free.

The second option begins with a re-creation of the Via Dolorosa, the Jerusalem streets through which Jesus carried his cross. This leads into a theater in which a short film describes the work done at Trinity. From there it's off to a larger theater, billed as a "Virtual Reality Theater." The theater shows a movie about Jesus titled *The Revolutionary,* and during the showing the seats shake and viewers are bombarded by sound from a host of speakers. This film is shown hourly on the half hour.

A gift shop offers Twitty items, Bibles and books, T-shirts, souvenirs from Israel, and porcelain art objects. From late October through January 1, Trinity is open every night until 9 p.m., when the place is lit up with an estimated million light bulbs. Inside, *Christmas Around the World* plays daily.

As Conway Twitty views these latest developments from the great beyond, this incarnation of the former Twitty City must bring a smile to the man who went to number one with a song called "You've Never Been This Far Before." Visit Trinity online at www.tbn.org/tmc/tmc.

Events and Entertainment

B.R.A.S.S. stands for Bike Ride Across Scenic Sumner County, a series of rides that take place on the third weekend in August. The longest ride is 75 miles long. For registration information, call (615) 824-2818.

The Bell Cove Club, 151 Sunset Dr., tel. (615) 822-7074, sits on the shore of Old Hickory Lake and is the best place to hear music in this area. Friday and Saturday are showcases for bands, which may be rock, blues, or country. Sunday afternoon brings Songwriters Grill-Outs from 2 p.m. until 8 p.m., with tunesmiths offering their best work. Find out more online at www.telalink/~bellcove.

Where to Stay

Morningstar Bed & Breakfast, 460 Jones Ln., Hendersonville, TN 37075, tel. (615) 264-2614, sits on five acres with a fine view of sunsets and the Nashville skyline. Other outdoor amenities include a driving range for those so inclined, patio, and gazebo. Of the four guest rooms, two have private baths. The rooms have antique iron beds. Guests can enjoy a full breakfast in the dining room, on the gazebo, or the porch. Rates are $95-125. Find out more online at www.morningstarbb.com. Expensive-Premium.

Motel options are the **Hendersonville Inn,** 179 W. Main St., tel. (615) 822-4240; and the **Holiday Inn,** 615 E. Main St., tel. (615) 824-0022 and (800) HOLIDAY.

Food

Center Point Bar-B-Que, 1212 W. Main St., tel. (615) 824-9330, is so named because it is close to the center point between Nashville and Gallatin. Now it's the home of pork and chicken barbecue. Try the dry ribs and homemade pecan pie.

Fortune House, 410 Main St., tel. (615) 824-2006, offers the finest in Tennessee Mandarin cooking.

Closer to Nashville, **The Shack,** at 2420 Gallatin Rd. in Madison, tel. (615) 859-9777, is the sort of place where diners eat roasted peanuts and throw the shells on the floor while waiting on prime rib and seafood and chicken dishes.

Information

Find information at the **Hendersonville Area Chamber of Commerce,** 101 Wessington, tel. (615) 824-2818.

EAST OF I-65

White House

White House Inn Library & Historical Museum, 412 Hwy. 76, tel. (615) 672-0239, was built as a replica of the White House Inn, a 1796 structure that provided the name for this little community. The museum contains memorabilia of the town, a spinning wheel, a still, farming implements, and old photographs. Admission is free.

For a place to stay, try **Days Inn,** 1009 Hwy. 76, tel. (615) 672-3746 or (800) 325-2525.

Seek info at **Hendersonville Area Chamber of Commerce,** 101 Wessington, tel. (615) 824-2818.

Portland

Portland is big strawberry country and home of country artists Roy Drusky and Ronnie McDowell. The **Strawberry Festival** takes place on the third weekend in May. Call (615) 325-9032 for details.

Cold Springs School Museum, tel. (615) 325-6029, is a restored school built in 1857. When the Civil War broke out, it became the main building for Camp Trousdale and later a Confederate hospital. After the war it was used as a church and then reverted to being a school once more. The museum contains community artifacts and pictures of the various schoolteachers who presided here. The museum is open on summer Sunday afternoons. Admission is free.

For more information call **Portland's chamber of commerce,** 111 S. Broadway, tel. (615) 325-9032.

NORTH OF NASHVILLE

CROSS PLAINS

This charming village is the home of **Thomas Drugs,** tel. (615) 654-3877, which has been in business at the four-way stop since 1930. The surrounding populace still uses it as a drugstore, and visitors will delight in the old-fashioned soda fountain. Here one can sit at the fountain and order a phosphate, egg cream, or milk shake, or go whole-hog with a banana split. It also serves burgers and sandwiches. Unlike the folks at so many eateries these days, the people at Thomas Drugs will talk to customers, asking from where they have come and telling them about the area. The drugstore features the products of local artists and craftspeople.

West of Cross Plains is **Carr's Wild Horse/ Burro Center,** tel. (615) 654-2180, which serves

Stop in at the old-fashioned soda fountain at Thomas Drugs, in business since 1930.

as an adoption station for thousands of wild horses and burros that come from Western states for new homes in the East. Here as many as 250 animals—the overwhelming majority are horses, which cost only $125—await new owners. More than 17,000 horses and burros have come through this place, which welcomes visitors. To get to the center, go 1.1 miles north on Couts Rd. and follow the signs.

Shopping

Graves Market, 7781 Hwy. 25, tel. (615) 654-4800, occupies an 1870s building that is the oldest one in town. Inside are antiques, including china, glassware, silver, jewelry, documents, old advertisements, local crafts, and quilts.

Turner Station, 3352 Hwy. 25, tel. (615) 325-4610, carries primitive antiques, old advertising and calendars, country-style items, and some local crafts.

Around the corner from Thomas Drugs is the e.e. cummings of antique stores, **g. skippers antiques,** 4604 E. Robinson St., tel. (615) 654-3307, which sells furniture and glassware.

East of town is **Robin's Nest Orchard,** tel. (615) 654-3797, which produces apples, peaches, blackberries, and raspberries, most of which visitors can harvest themselves. A farm stand sells homemade doughnuts, fried pies, and specialty breads. When the apple crop ripens, the owners make fresh cider. From January to June the orchard is on a limited schedule, but July-Dec. it is open seven days a week. To get there from the center of Cross Plains, go one mile east on Hwy. 25, then go left on Cedar Grove Rd. for two miles.

SPRINGFIELD

This county seat is the home of two traditional Tennessee products—tobacco and whiskey. The former is still a mainstay of the economy, while the latter is only a memory.

Much of the tobacco grown hereabouts is cured in heated barns and called "dark-fired" to distinguish it from air-cured leaves. Plantations around here have grown the tobacco since before the Civil War, and in the early 1900s the "Black Patch Tobacco War" erupted over pricing. The larger growers banded together in an association to force a rise in prices they were offered. The American Tobacco Company, which bought most of the local product, tried to break the association's power by enticing small farmers to sell at an artificially high price.

Many of these farmers willingly accepted the higher paychecks, and this brought on nighttime visits from the "Silent Brigade," an organization that used Klanlike whippings, barn burnings, and destruction of tobacco fields. Unlike the Klan, however, black farmers belonged to the association and may have even taken part in the nocturnal activities. Several people died in the struggle, which ended when the tobacco company gave in and agreed to buy leaves only from association members.

Were it not for Prohibition, Robertson County might be as famous as Lynchburg. At one time more than 75 whiskey makers operated here, but none of them survived the passage of the 18th Amendment.

Where to Stay
Try **Best Western Springfield Inn,** 2001 Memorial Blvd., tel. (615) 384-1234 or (800) 528-1234; or the **Royal Inn,** 1508 Memorial Blvd., tel. (615) 384-4523.

Food
Torino's Greek and Italian Restaurant, 1701 Memorial Blvd., tel. (615) 384-6548, features dishes such as gyro platters and chicken Alfredo that reflect the two great food traditions that come together here.

Information
Springfield-Robertson County Chamber of Commerce is at 100 5th Ave. W, tel. (615) 384-3800.

GOODLETTSVILLE

This town, now a part of Nashville's sprawl, played an important role in the settling of Middle Tennessee. Kasper Mansker was one of the "long hunters"—so named because their hunting trips took them away from home for long periods of time—who first came here in 1772. The game was reportedly so thick that he killed 19 deer in one day, and he resolved to come back and settle here. He did so in 1779-80, building a fort for protection, but the pressure from the Indians was so great that he abandoned it and moved to the more secure area of Fort Nashborough. His second fort, built in 1782, was called Mansker's Station, and it provided the nucleus for the settlement that eventually became Goodlettsville.

Sights
Those interested in learning more about this should steer for **Mansker's Fort,** in Moss-Wright Park off Caldwell Ln., tel. (615) 859-3678. This reproduction of the first settlement in Goodlettsville is about one-third the size of the original and is staffed by people who dress and act as if they were living in 1779. The tour appropriately begins at the **Bowen Plantation House,** the oldest brick house in Middle Tennessee. Now it contains period furniture, and here guests see a video that introduces Mansker's Station.

A walk down the hill brings the visitor to the reconstructed fort. Inside are a blacksmith's shop, a tannery, and a tavern. This is living history, not a museum, so guests can go up the stairs and pick up any implements they see. Usually at least three reenactors are on hand, and on special occasions as many as 300 swarm over the place. These gatherings take place in March, during the Colonial Fair in early May; on the Fourth of July; and in September, October, and December. Admission is $3 for adults and $2 for students.

The historic **Stone Arch Bridge** lies off Hwy. 41. Go north past the place where the road goes under the railroad. Directly across the road from a KOA campground is a road leading into the Old Stone Bridge Industrial Park. Turn into the park and then go left onto a dirt road, which leads to the bridge. This structure is said to contain no mortar.

The **Museum of Beverage Containers & Advertising,** 1055 Ridgecrest Dr., tel. (615) 859-5236, purports to be the world's largest collection of soda and beer bottles and cans. The gift shop contains more of the same along with signs, trays, and bottle caps. Admission is $2; children under 12 get in free when accompanied by a paying adult.

Entertainment and Events

The **Long Hollow Jamboree,** 3600 Long Hollow Pike, tel. (615) 824-4445, presents live music on Tuesday, Friday, and Saturday nights. Usually it's country on Saturday, bluegrass on Friday, and open-mic on Tuesday.

Rook is a Southern card game in which "getting the bird" is not an affront. A **Rook Tournament** takes place in Goodlettsville during the first weekend in May.

The **18th-Century Colonial Fair** is a trip back in time to the 1750-90 days. Every event is juried, attracting the best in crafts, merchants, and reenactors. This is the place to buy colonial furniture, weapons, and leather goods, or to watch blacksmiths, hear music of that time, and enjoy the beggars, trollops, long hunters, and Indians. It's held for two days in May at Mansker's Station.

The **Fall Fiddlin' Jamboree** is a three-day event that takes place the third weekend in October and features competitions, food, and crafts.

Where to Stay

Terrawin, 304 Highland Heights Dr., Goodlettsville, TN 37072, tel. (615) 859-0041, is a large colonial-style brick house about 25 years old. The house has four bedrooms with baths down the hall. Guests can enjoy themselves in a large rec room. Children are welcome, and no alcoholic beverages are permitted. Rates are $50-75. Inexpensive-Moderate.

More Inexpensive-Moderate motel options are the **Baymont Inn,** 120 Cartwright Court, tel. (615) 851-1891 or (800) 428-3438; **Econo Lodge,** 320 Long Hollow Pike, tel. (615) 859-4988 or (800) 424-4777; **Red Roof Inn,** I-65 and Long Hollow Pike, tel. (615) 859-2537 or (800) 843-7663; and **Shoney's Inn,** 100 Northcreek Blvd., tel. (615) 851-1067 or (800) 222-2222.

Higher priced is the **Comfort Inn,** 925 Conference Dr., tel. (615) 859-5400 or (800) 221-2222.

Campers can set up at **Nashville North,** 780 North Dickerson Rd., tel. (615) 859-0075, offering 140 sites all year; or **Owls Roost Campground,** tel. (615) 643-0046, with 94 sites. From I-65 take Exit 104 and follow the signs. It's open all year.

Food

Cisco's Cafe, 503 S. Main St., tel. (615) 859-5693, always features three meats and six veggies from which to choose.

Rivergate Cooker, 317 Bluebird Ln., tel. (615) 859-2756, serves home-cooked food such as pinto beans and fried tomatoes as well as pasta, chicken, and burgers.

Mason's Restaurant, 901 S. Dickerson Rd., tel. (615) 859-7653, offers meat-and-three plates.

Shopping

Antique-lovers can spend a long time on N. Main St. in Goodlettsville. Among the antique stores are the Main Street Antique Mall, Antique Corner Mall, Goodlettsville Antique Mall, Sweet Memories, and others.

Quilter's Attic, 126 N. Main St., tel. (615) 859-5603, usually has 10-20 quilts, 1,500 bolts of cloth, and 300-400 books on hand at any given time. It also carries quilting notions and rug-hooking supplies.

The **Rivergate Mall,** 1000 Two Mile Pkwy., tel. (615) 859-3456, with more than 150 stores, is one of the larger shopping malls in the Nashville area.

Information

Goodlettsville Chamber of Commerce, 100 S. Main St., tel. (615) 859-7979, is open Mon.-Fri. 8 a.m.-4:30 p.m. Find out more online at www.goodlettsvillechamber.com.

NORTHWEST OF NASHVILLE

ASHLAND CITY

Many towns in these parts came into being because the Cumberland River eased the transportation of people and goods. Ashland City, by contrast, was founded in a place where the river refused to cooperate. Steamboats on the Cumberland ran aground at a shallow place called the Harpeth Shoals and were obliged to unload their cargo, steam past the shoals, then load everything up again. A community grew up there, was ambitiously dubbed a city, and remains a pleasant place to visit. A dam and set of locks solved the shoals headache in 1907, and these were replaced by a newer dam in 1950. The locks lie 12 miles northwest of town.

Bridge fanciers should drive northeast of town about three or four miles on Hwy. 49. Just as the road crosses Sycamore Creek, a gaze to the right will reveal the last remaining 1800s cable-stayed bridge in the country. The bridge led to a gunpowder works that for a time served the Confederacy.

Pat Head Summit, who coaches the Lady Vols basketball team at the University of Tennessee, grew up in Montgomery County and should have gone to Clarksville High School. That school, however, had no girls' basketball team, so her family moved across the line into neighboring Cheatham County, in the little community of Henrietta on Hwy. 12, so she could play on the girls' basketball team at Cheatham County High School in Ashland City. The future coach graduated from UT-Martin and played on the 1976 US Olympic team, which won a silver medal. She then became the first and only head coach of the Lady Vols

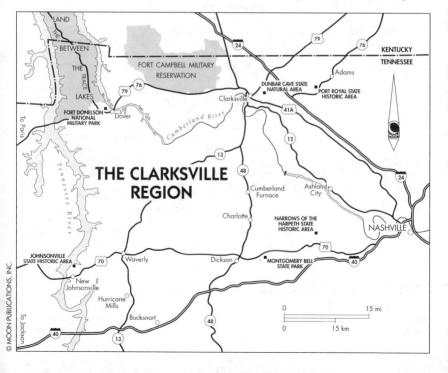

and has led them to a record number of NCAA championships.

Ashland City is the birthplace of Redd Stewart, country music vocalist and co-writer of "The Tennessee Waltz," perhaps the most famous song with Tennessee in the title. Cheatham County is also the birthplace of Amos and Gale Binkley, prominent members of an early Grand Ole Opry band called the Dixie Clodhoppers.

Where to Stay

The **Birdsong Country Inn Bed & Breakfast,** 1306 Hwy. 49 E, Ashland City, TN 37015, tel. (615) 792-4005, occupies a cedar log home built in 1914 by the family who owned Maxwell Coffee in Nashville. Now decorated with a combination of antiques and contemporary art, the inn is a great place to relax. Guests can stroll about the 10-acre property, then relax in a hot tub. Golf, tennis, and swimming are available just across the valley. The inn offers three rooms with private baths and a fourth room that can be a suite. The rates are $100 per night. Expensive.

Cheatham Lake has two campsites operated by the Army Corps of Engineers. **Lock "A" Recreation Area** is northwest of Ashland City. The campground offers 46 sites with electrical outlets, hookups, and water; there's a laundry, playground, game court, amphitheater, and boat-launching ramp. The cost per site ranges $14-18 per night depending on whether the site is on the river, inland, or for tents. It's open April 1 through October 31. Call (615) 792-3715.

The second campsite is **Harpeth River Bridge,** which has some riverside sites, a playground, a courtesy float to which boats tie up, and a boat-launching ramp. These $6-per-night sites are available on a first-come, first-served basis. The campground is open April 1 through October 31. Call (615) 792-4195.

Food

El Rey Restaurante Mexicano, at 104 S. Main St., tel. (615) 792-1330, offers Mexican food.

Bill's Catfish, 1.5 miles south of town on Hwy. 12, tel. (615) 792-9193, features catfish, its own barbecue, steaks, seafood, and chicken.

Stratton's Restaurant and Soda Shop, 201 S. Main St., tel. (615) 792-9177, has great burgers and fries and other fast food, all offered in a 1950s atmosphere.

River View Restaurant and Marina, across the river from town on Hwy. 49, tel. (615) 792-7358, offers diners a view of the passing river traffic while they enjoy steak, chicken, and seafood dishes.

Shopping and Information

Ashland City boasts a string of antique shops along Main Street. Among them is **B.J.s Attic,** 108 N. Main St., tel. (615) 792-7208, offering primarily furniture.

The **Cheatham County Chamber of Commerce** is located at 605A N. Main St., tel. (615) 792-6722. To find out more go to their Web site at www.cheatham.org.

ADAMS AND VICINITY

Sights and Recreation

The Bell Witch is this town's claim to fame, and visitors in search of this phantom should head immediately for **The Bell Witch Cave,** tel. (615) 696-3055, which can be reached by driving 0.7 miles south of town on Keysburg Road, then turning right at the sign and going 0.3 miles.

The cave has the usual unusual formations, but the operators note that curious events take place here as well. Weird noises are allegedly heard in the cave—a screen door creaking open or mysterious voices. Sometimes cameras refuse to function. The cave is open 10 a.m.-6 p.m. May-October. Admission is $4 per person; those five and under get in free.

Northwest of Adams on Hwy. 41 lies **Red River Valley Canoeing,** tel. (615) 696-2768, an enterprise offering canoes, camping, and the occasional country music concert.

Entertainment and Events

The nightlife in town centers on the **Bell Witch Opry,** no phone, a gathering of local talent that performs every Saturday night in the local school. The music is mostly bluegrass and country and the stage is open, as one regular put it, "to anyone who wants to pick and grin and sing." Occasionally someone gets up and belts out a classical piece, but not too often. Shows take place Saturday night 7:30-10:30 p.m.

The threshing of wheat and other grains—separating the grains from the rest of the plant—

THE BELL WITCH

Tennessee's most famous supernatural figure is the Bell Witch, an apparition who is never seen but whose presence is keenly felt. According to a long account in *WPA Guide to Tennessee*, the Bell family moved near Adams from North Carolina in 1804. They bought some property from a cantankerous neighbor, one Kate Batts, who later claimed she had been cheated in the transaction, and who on her dying day swore she would come back and "hant John Bell and all his kith and kin to their graves."

That's when things got lively in the Bell household. No one ever saw the witch or ghost or whatever she was, but she made her presence felt in constant mischief. She threw furniture and dishes, pulled the Bell family's noses and hair, poked them with needles, and yelled all night to keep them from sleeping.

As if that weren't enough, the witch attended local revivals, where she sang loudly and outshouted the other participants. Not overly pious, she would sometimes raid moonshiners' stills and come back to the Bell household to create more of an uproar than usual.

Andrew Jackson, he who had fought duels and the British, came up from Nashville with some friends to dispatch this terror. As the story is told, the Jacksonian ghostbusters rolled up to the Bell farm in a wagon whose wheel suddenly stopped and refused to turn. Jackson's cursing and mules straining produced nothing. Then a voice called out, "All right, General, the wagon can move on." And it did.

That night the witch further entertained the party by singing, swearing, throwing dishes, overturning furniture, and yanking the covers off everyone. After a sleepless night, Jackson left early for home, telling John Bell, "I'd rather fight the British again than have any more dealings with that torment."

The Bell Witch was heard from no more when John Bell died. His farmhouse was eventually razed, and since then, to the intense frustration of local boosters, the witch has yet to put in an appearance.

---

was a special time on Tennessee farms. Aside from railroad locomotives, threshing machines were the most impressive pieces of machinery that most country people ever saw. Most farmers did not own threshing machines, so someone who owned one of these behemoths would come to process their grain. A threshing crew, often made up of neighboring farmers, would arrive in the fields to do the work. Older threshing machines were powered by steam and rolled from farm to farm on massive steel wheels, belching smoke all the way. Women cooked huge meals to serve the crews, and the whole time was one of great excitement.

A sense of those days pervades the annual **Tennessee-Kentucky Threshermen's Show,** held in Adams in mid-July, when antique threshers, steam engines, and tractors are brought together. A tractor pull and a mule pull, arts and crafts, dancing, music, and storytelling are also included. Call (615) 696-2058.

The **Bell Witch Bluegrass Festival and Arts and Crafts Show,** tel. (615) 696-2058, is held in August. The name says it all.

Port Royal State Historical Area
Port Royal was once a thriving little town on the Red River, upstream from Clarksville. From here goods were shipped as far away as New Orleans. At one time local entrepreneurs tried to launch a silk business, planting thousands of mulberry trees to fuel the silkworms, but one of the organizers who was sent to England to buy machinery absconded with the money.

Modern forms of transportation bypassed Port Royal, and the town slowly died, leaving one of the few covered bridges remaining in the state. The state acquired 34 acres around the bridge, and the result is a beautiful little park for walking and picnicking. A museum keeps the memory of Port Royal alive. Admission is free, and the park is open 8 a.m. until sundown. Call (931) 358-9696.

CLARKSVILLE AND VICINITY

Downstream from and northwest of Nashville, Clarksville long benefitted from its location at the confluence of the Red and Cumberland Rivers, and today long barges still stop at the "Queen City" to do business. Tennessee's fifth-largest city, like Rome, is built on seven hills, and those out for a stroll can readily get their hearts pumping. One of the areas in town bears the name Dog Hill Architectural District. It seems that the local canines would howl whenever a steamboat or train blew its whistle.

In the downtown area lies the River District. Adjacent to the River District is the Riverwalk, a

symbol of Clarksville's rediscovery of its riverfront. On the north end are a playground and parking lot, which were to be joined by a river master's house, an amphitheater, and floating courtesy docks where boats can tie up. Plans for the southern end of the park called for a bell tower and pedestrian overpass above Riverside Drive. The Clarksville Area Chamber of Commerce offers a brochure giving routes for walking and driving tours of the city.

Tennessee grows a lot of tobacco, and the variety hereabouts, cured in heated barns, is called "dark-fired" to distinguish it from the air-

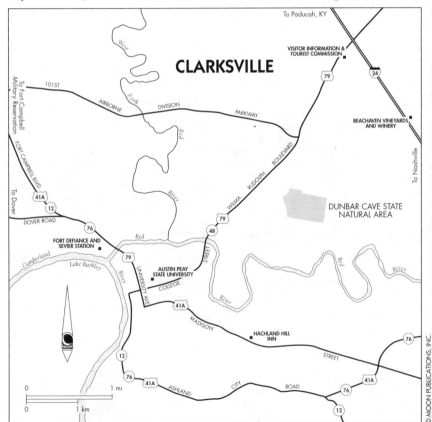

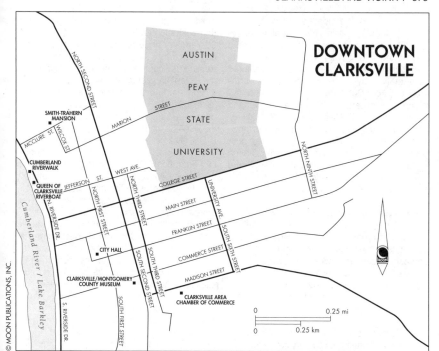

DOWNTOWN CLARKSVILLE

AUSTIN PEAY STATE UNIVERSITY

SMITH-TRAHERN MANSION

CUMBERLAND RIVERWALK

QUEEN OF CLARKSVILLE RIVERBOAT

CITY HALL

CLARKSVILLE/MONTGOMERY COUNTY MUSEUM

CLARKSVILLE AREA CHAMBER OF COMMERCE

Cumberland River / Lake Barkley

NORTH SECOND STREET
MARION STREET
MCCLURE ST.
WILCOX ST.
JEFFERSON ST.
WEST AVE
N. RIVERSIDE DR.
NORTH FIRST STREET
NORTH THIRD STREET
COLLEGE STREET
MAIN STREET
FRANKLIN STREET
SOUTH SECOND STREET
SOUTH THIRD STREET
COMMERCE STREET
MADISON STREET
SOUTH FIRST STREET
S. RIVERSIDE DR.
UNIVERSITY AVE.
SOUTH SIXTH STREET
NORTH NINTH STREET

0   0.25 mi
0   0.25 km

© MOON PUBLICATIONS, INC.

cured version produced farther east. Used in smokeless tobacco products and cigars, this crop is so economically important that the local newspaper is named the *Leaf Chronicle,* and Clarksville tobacco warehouses sell more than five million dollars' worth of the plant per year.

The city is more famous as the home of the late Wilma Rudolph, the first female runner to win three gold medals in an Olympics. As recounted in her autobiography, *Wilma,* her story is impressive. Childhood illnesses left her with a paralyzed leg, and at age six she could only hop. The little girl persevered, and she eventually competed in the 1956 and 1960 Olympics, winning her three medals in the latter. Rudolph died in 1993. Frank Sutton, a local boy who played Sergeant Carter on television's *Gomer Pyle, USMC,* was also from Clarksville and is buried there.

Clarksville is home to **Austin Peay State University,** which educates more than 7,000 students and brings a variety of cultural events to town. For information as to what is happening on campus, call (931) 648-7876 or go to www. apsu.edu.

SIGHTS AND RECREATION

Historic Buildings
The flamboyant building containing the **Clarksville-Montgomery County Historical Museum,** 200 S. 2nd St., tel. (931) 648-5780, was built as a post office and customs house in 1898. Exhibits feature quilts and coverlets, military matters, and a Victorian small-town avenue.

The **Smith/Trahern Mansion,** at the corner of Spring and McClure Streets, tel. (931) 648-9998, was built in 1858 for a wealthy tobacco merchant and features a widow's walk, a curved staircase, and period furniture. The house is often rented for weddings and parties on weekends. Admission is $1 for adults, free to children and students.

The New Providence community of Clarksville contains **Sevier Station,** on Walker St., tel.

(931) 648-5780, the oldest structure in Montgomery County. Built in 1792 by Valentine Sevier, the stone structure was designed to survive attacks, but late in 1794, Indians killed several members of Sevier's family who had ventured outside. Nearby on "B" St. stands the earthworks of **Fort Defiance**, tel. (931) 648-5780, which Southerners built along the Cumberland River during the Civil War to repel the Yankees. After Fort Donelson upstream surrendered, however, the fort's occupants got much less defiant and retreated to Nashville. Sevier Station and Fort Defiance have no visitors center and can be seen virtually anytime. There's not a great deal to see here, however.

Beachaven Vineyards and Winery

Located at 1100 Dunlap Ln., tel. (931) 645-8867, Beachaven produces wine of such quality that one of its entries bested 990 others in a 1993 contest. The offerings vary from chardonnay to muscadine to blackberry and strawberry wines. Tours and tastings are available daily year-round, and several free jazz concerts take place on the grounds every year.

Historic Collinsville

This restored nineteenth century settlement, tel. (931) 648-9141, lies 10 miles south of Clarksville along the Cumberland River. Ten structures give a glimpse of the life of a family from those times. One cabin dates to 1842 and contains period furnishings. An 1870 house and its contents shows how a family living there would have increased their standard of living 30 years later. Open from May through October. Admission is $4 for adults. Children under five are free. Find out more online at www.dogg.com/public/users/historiccollinsville.

Fort Campbell

Sitting astride the Tennessee/Kentucky state line, this is the largest military base in Tennessee. Established in 1942 and covering 105,068 acres—about one-fifth the size of the Great Smoky Mountains National Park—the Army base holds approximately 23,000 military personnel and about 5,000 civilian employees. Ten thousand family members live at the base, while another 28,000 family members live around it. Fort Campbell encompasses 48 ranges, five major drop zones, one assault landing strip, two demonstration areas, 48 maneuver areas, and 304 artillery firing points. Visitors to the base can hear troops singing cadence during physical training, helicopters overhead, and sometimes the distant firing of guns.

Fort Campbell is the home of the 101st "Screaming Eagles" Airborne Division, the world's only air assault division. Its paratroopers were the first Americans to set foot in France during the D-Day invasion, and the 101st has participated in every American war since and many other military operations. Other combat groups, such as the Green Berets, operate out of Fort Campbell; also based here are the infamous black helicopters so beloved by conspiracy fans. Find out more online at www.campbell.army.mil.

Civilians, especially those with kids, should make a beeline for the **Don F. Pratt Memorial Museum**, corner of 26th and Tennessee, tel. (502) 798-3215, which houses more than 50 years of Screaming Eagles history. The museum displays a World War II tank, German weapons, personal articles that belonged to Adolf Hitler, a glider, various weapons, and other artifacts. Outside and across from the museum are aircraft such as a C-47; a C-19, the so-called "Flying Boxcar"; an A-10 "Warthog"; and various helicopters. The museum is open daily 9:30 a.m.-4:30 p.m. Admission is free. To get there, go to Gate 4 and ask for a pass.

Dunbar Cave State Natural Area

Caves riddle this part of Tennessee, and one of the larger ones lies under the 110 acres making up this natural area within the Clarksville city limits. Indians first used the eight-mile-long cave, but it became most famous as a concert venue during the big-band era, when acts such as the Tommy Dorsey Band and Count Basie played to large audiences. Country singer Roy Acuff bought the property and resumed the concerts, this time with big-name country music stars. The state of Tennessee bought the cave in 1973 and opened it as a public park.

No camping is permitted in this park, but visitors can picnic, fish on a 15-acre lake, tour the cave, and see a small museum in the visitors center. The staff offers guided cave hikes during the summer every day. Call (931) 648-5526 for information, to secure reservations, and for times of tours the rest of the year. Hikes cost $2 per person. The tours cover culture, history, and geologic features such as stalactites and stalagmites. The cave is chilly; wear a jacket. The passageways are not paved, so shoes with good traction are recommended.

River Cruises

The *Queen of Clarksville* paddlewheeler, docked at McGregor Park on Riverside Dr., tel. (931) 647-5500, operates April-Oct. offering sightseeing and dinner/dance cruises.

ENTERTAINMENT AND EVENTS

The **Roxy Theatre,** 100 Franklin St., tel. (931) 645-7699, built in 1911 as a movie hall, now serves as home to the **Roxy Community Theater.** The season's of 10 productions include musicals, classic plays, and comedies.

The **Old Time Fiddler's Contest,** held in March at the Clarksville High School on Warfield Blvd (Hwy. 374), tel. (931) 648-0001, offers competitions in 14 categories.

The **Clarksville Rodeo,** tel. (931) 648-0001, is held in early August. Bareback riders, bull riders, calf ropers, and others compete for prizes.

Riverfest, held all over town early in September, includes art exhibits, a 5K run, country dancing, arts and crafts, concerts, drag racing, and food. Festival information is available at (931) 645-7476.

WHERE TO STAY

Inn

The **Hachland Hill Inn,** 1601 Madison St., tel. (931) 647-4084, sits on a wooded hill in downtown Clarksville alongside three cedar cabins built in the late 1700s. The inn is decorated with primitive antiques and has eight rooms with private baths. The three cabins respectively sleep 14, 10, or four people. Smoking is permitted in the cabins. Rate at the inn is $65 per night for two, and the cabins cost $65 for the first two people and $10 for each additional person. The rate for two couples in the four-person cabin is $65 per couple. See "Food and Other Practicalities" for details on food at this inn. Moderate.

Motels

Among the Moderate options in Clarksville are the **Econo Lodge,** 201 Holiday Rd., tel. (931) 645-6300 or (800) 424-4777; **Ramada Limited,** I-24 and Hwy. 79 N, tel. (931) 552-0098; **Ramada Inn-Riverview,** 50 College St., tel. (931) 552-3331 or (800) RAMADA; and **Winner's Circle Motel,** 4430 Fort Campbell Blvd., tel. (931) 431-4906.

More expensive are the **Days Inn,** 3065 Guthrie Hwy., tel. (931) 552-1155 or (800) 325-2525; **Holiday Inn I-24,** 3095 Guthrie Hwy., tel. (931) 648-4848 or (800) HOLIDAY; and **Hampton Inn,** 201 Holiday Rd., tel. (931) 552-2255 or (800) HAMPTON.

Camping

Clarksville Campground, tel. (931) 648-8638, offers 41 sites, a pool, and a playground. Take Exit 1 from the junction of I-24 and Hwy. 48, go north, and follow the signs. It's open all year.

Spring Creek Campground, tel. (931) 552-9790, has 50 sites and is open all year. From I-24 Exit 4, go one mile northeast on Hwy. 79 N and follow the signs.

FOOD AND OTHER PRACTICALITIES

Blackhorse Brewery and Pizza Kitchen, 134 Franklin St., tel. (931) 552-9499, brews four beers, which run from the house light ale to the dark Coalminer stout. It serves 18 gourmet pizzas, such as shrimp and scallops or bleu cheese and spinach. Or diners can build their own pizzas, choosing from more than 60 toppings. The Blackhorse also has a strong salad menu.

Brunie's Bar and Grill, 101 Legion St., tel. (931) 645-8414, is a friendly little place featuring German and American food. Diners can sit down to a dish of jaeger schnitzel or hamburger steak, and before the night is over Brunie herself will wander over and ask how things are going.

The Franklin Street Pub, 132 Franklin St., tel. (931) 552-3726, offers Irish greetings on its menus and serves barbecue. A long list of appetizers, including stuffed jalapeños, precedes dinners of steak, chicken, and pork chops. Billiards and darts are available to patrons, as are 60 kinds of beer.

The **Hachland Hill Inn,** 1601 Madison St., tel. (931) 647-4084, is a bed and breakfast that offers gourmet meals to nonguests as well—up to 300 at one time. Owner Phila Hach has written eight cookbooks, and her kitchen cranks out delights such as Moroccan leg of lamb, *coquilles* St. Jacques, and garden-fresh vegetables.

Moss's, 1208 College St., tel. (931) 465-9415, offers great "meat-and-three" food in an unassuming atmosphere.

The smell in **Red's Bakery,** 101 Riverside Dr., tel. (931) 647-5646, will make visitors hungry before they even get in the door. This is a great place for a country breakfast.

The **Sportsman's Restaurant & Lounge,** Sportsman's Ln., tel. (931) 431-4140, offers German and American food, including a sort of in-between item called Cow Poke Schnitzel. Lunch features a range of sandwiches.

Wilson's Catfish House, 2560 Wilma Rudolph Blvd., tel. (931) 552-2342, has been turning out fried fish and hushpuppies for over 50 years.

Nightlife
Brunie's Bar and Grill, 101 Legion St. downtown, tel. (931) 645-8414, has live jazz or blues on the weekend.

Information
The **Clarksville Tourist Commission Visitors Center** is at 180 Holiday Rd., just off I-24 Exit 4, tel. (931) 551-3572.

Our City, a local newspaper, has a Web site at www.ourcityonline.com.

WEST OF CLARKSVILLE

DOVER

This little town gives no clue today to the important role it played during the heyday of river traffic. Steamboats called here to deliver goods and to transport iron products made by the Cumberland Iron Works, which operated 14 furnaces hereabouts. Things went rapidly downhill during the Civil War, when the town came under attack by the Union army as it pounded Fort Donelson. (For a more detailed account, see "Fort Donelson National Military Park," below.)

Sights and Recreation
Civil War fans should go to the **Dover Hotel** at the end of Petty St., tel. (931) 232-5348, the place where Gen. Simon Bolivar Buckner met Gen. U.S. Grant and surrendered 13,000 Confederate troops. The hotel, also known as "Surrender House," was one of the few buildings left standing after the war. The hotel's exterior has been restored to its Civil War appearance and is open noon-4 p.m. Memorial Day to Labor Day.

Rice House, 314 Church St., tel. (931) 232-4535, offers something for a wide range of people. Built in the late 19th century and later transformed into a motor court, it is now an incubator for women's businesses, so the entrepreneurial enterprises in here change from time to time.

Two constants, however, are a gourd collection and an art gallery. The former consists of 25-30 specimens grown in Tennessee, some in their natural splendor, others modified into useful items—a punchbowl is perhaps the most unusual—and those that resemble something else. Don't miss the one that looks like a snake. The **Rice House Art Gallery** features local artists in changing exhibitions, including such displays as an arrowhead and Indian doll show.

Perhaps the most unheralded fact about Rice House is that it once housed Elvis Presley when he worked for a company that was wiring Dover's first factory. He stayed there for several weeks, going back to Memphis every weekend. "He was a sweet, handsome fellow," recalled one female fan, who said that Elvis had a guitar with him and often sang in a local "joint" in Dover's black community. "When we later found out who he was," she said with a laugh, "we went in the room he had been in and touched everything."

Reaching upstream from Dover to Cumberland City, **Cross Creeks National Wildlife Refuge** provides 8,862 square miles of habitat for migrating birds. About one-third of the refuge is hardwood forest, with the remainder of it wetlands and farmland. Visitors here can see all manner of waterfowl as well as hawks, ospreys, and bald eagles.

A visitors center with exhibits and a slide show stands three miles east of Dover off Hwy. 49, tel. (931) 232-7477. Admission is free, and no camping or fires are permitted.

Entertainment and Events

The **River Days Festival** takes place the Saturday and Sunday before Labor Day. Visitors can watch Civil War reenactments and displays, hear live music, buy crafts, and ride carnival rides. Call (931) 232-8290.

Where to Stay

PJ's Restaurant & Resort, 960 Brownfield Rd., tel. (931) 232-8954, has cabins and lies 17 miles southwest of Dover on the banks of Kentucky Lake.

Or try **Dover Inn Motel,** 1545 Donelson Pkwy., tel. (931) 232-5556; or the **Sunset Motor Inn,** east of Dover on Hwy. 79, tel. (931) 232-5102.

Camping

Boswell Landing, no phone, has 25 sites but no hookups. To get there, go nine and a half miles west on Hwy. 79, five miles north on Fort Henry Road, then follow signs. It's open all year.

Bumpers Mills Recreational Area, 13 miles northwest on Hwy. 120, tel. (931) 232-8831, offers 33 sites, lake swimming, boating, and fishing. It's open April-October.

Gatlin Point, tel. (502) 924-5602, is four miles north on the Trace. Follow the signs. It offers 25 sites, no hookups, and boating and fishing. It's open all year.

Piney Campground, nine and a half miles west on Hwy. 79, then two miles on Fort Henry Rd., tel. (931) 232-5331, has 382 sites, lake swimming, boating, fishing, and hiking trails. It's open March-November.

PJ's Resort, tel. (931) 232-8954, has 60 sites plus furnished rental units, offers boating, fishing, a pool, and restaurant, and is open all year. Go eight miles west on Hwy. 79 and follow the signs.

Leatherwood Resort, tel. (931) 232-5137, has wooded campsites with full hookups. Go west on Hwy. 79 eight miles and follow signs. It is open all year.

Food and Information

Cindy's Catfish House, 2148 Donelson Pkwy., tel. (931) 232-4817, features a lunch and dinner buffet.

Get information from the **Stewart County Chamber of Commerce** at 323 Watson Building, Spring St., tel. (931) 232-8290.

FORT DONELSON NATIONAL MILITARY PARK

Lying one mile west of the town of Dover on Hwy. 79, Fort Donelson National Military Park, tel. (931) 232-5706, marks the Union's first significant victory in the Civil War. A driving tour takes visitors to batteries that overlook the Cumberland River, which has been dammed to create Lake Barkley. An interpretive trail leads through the park as well. The National Cemetery contains 655 Union dead, 504 of whom are unknown. Admission is free. Find out more online at www.nps.gov/fodo/.

LAND BETWEEN THE LAKES

The thin strip of land between the Tennessee and Cumberland Rivers used to be home to about 800 families, whose farms surrounded four Tennessee and five Kentucky villages. Along came the Tennessee Valley Authority, which in 1961 proposed making the land into a national recreation area that would stimulate the local economy. More than half the land was already in federal hands, and Congress appropriated the money to buy out the land that belonged to the residents. They had no choice but to go, and many of them left angry and wondering what TVA was doing in the recreation business.

Land Between the Lakes, as it was named, is a 170,000-acre park offering recreation, education, and lots of sanctuary for wildlife. Admission to the park is free, although there are fees for camping, and the education centers all charge admission. Visitors should keep in mind that there are no restaurants in the park and plan accordingly.

As for recreation, visitors have a lot to choose from—fishing, hiking, off-road biking and driving, camping, picnicking, backcountry camping,

"UNCONDITIONAL SURRENDER"

The Tennessee and Cumberland Rivers, flowing northward out of Tennessee, provided a perfect means by which to invade the Confederacy. The South, realizing this, built two forts that stood back to back across a 12-mile neck of land that separated the two rivers. They didn't have long to wait.

An obscure general, Ulysses S. Grant, proposed a combination land and river attack on the forts. Fort Henry, a stockade lying on low land along the Tennessee River, fell in short order on February 6, 1862, and its defenders retreated to the Cumberland River's Fort Donelson near Dover.

Opening the Tennessee River was important, to be sure, but the Cumberland River led straight to Nashville, a real prize. Fort Donelson had its pluses and minuses. It was more of a stockade than a fort, yet it stood atop a 100-foot bluff in which the Confederates had dug trenches and prepared for a fight. When Union gunboats approached, the Confederate gunners blasted them with cannon fire and forced them to retreat.

Nonetheless, the Southerners were surrounded. They tried to break through the Union lines, but their commander decided in the confusion to pull them back, and Grant quickly took up the slack. The three Confederate generals decided that Simon B. Buckner, an old friend of Grant's who had once lent him some money, should offer to surrender. The other two generals slipped away with about 2,000 men.

Nathan Bedford Forrest, who commanded a cavalry battalion that he had raised and equipped with his own funds, refused to give up the fight, leading his 700 troops through the icy waters of Lick Creek to safety.

Buckner sent a message to Grant asking about terms of surrender. Grant's reply was succinct: "No terms except an unconditional and immediate surrender can be accepted." Buckner was in no position to negotiate and handed over his 13,000 troops, who spent the rest of the war in prison camps. Despite this, Buckner remained Grant's friend and was one of the former president's pallbearers in 1885.

After the Southern triumph at Bull Run, the North badly needed this victory. Abraham Lincoln appointed Grant to the post of major general, and newspapers hailed the new hero. The path to the South's heartland lay open.

DOVER PUBLICATIONS, INC.

shooting, hunting, archery, swimming, canoeing, and paddleboating.

The educational sites, approached from the Tennessee side, begin with **The Homeplace-1850.** Here TVA has collected 16 log structures from the region to give visitors a sense of life back in the days when family farms weren't flooded out by government agencies. Staff members dress in 1850 clothing and do chores relating to those times—cutting wood with old tools, tending livestock, cooking on a woodstove, spinning thread, or quilting. Even the vegetables in the garden are of the old-time variety.

As a reminder of times even further back, TVA maintains a herd of buffalo in an adjacent field. In 1998 *Family Fun* magazine named this place one of the top 10 living history exhibitions in the country. The Homeplace-1850 is open seven days a week, year-round. Admission is $3 for adults and $1 for children six to 17.

Crossing into Kentucky, the motorist soon comes to the **Golden Pond Visitors Center,** open seven days a week, year-round. Admission is free, although seeing the **Golden Pond Planetarium,** tel. (502) 924-2020, costs $2.75 for adults and $1.75 for children five to 12.

The **Woodlands Nature Center,** farther north on the shores of Lake Barkley, a.k.a. the Cumberland River, offers live animals—eagles, coyotes, deer, snakes, and raptors. Exhibits focus on the flora and fauna of the region. The nature center is open seven days a week March-Nov., and on weekends only the rest of the year. Admission is $2.50 for adults and $1 for children six to 17.

Events
Information on all the following festivals can be had by calling Land Between the Lakes, tel. (502) 924-5602. Or visit www.lbl.org.

April brings **Earth Week,** with environmental programs at Homeplace-1850, the Woodlands Nature Center, and the Golden Pond Planetarium.

May features the **Kentucky Lake Arts and Crafts Show,** with live music and food.

The **Four Rivers Folk Festival** is held each June at the Homeplace-1850. The two-day event brings forth folk and bluegrass music, various demonstrations, and storytelling.

In September **Kentucky's Western Waterland Arts & Crafts Festival,** one of the larger such events in the region, takes place.

The year's events come to an end with the **Apple Festival** at the Homeplace-1850. Visitors can sample all manner of apple products, watch cider presses, and enjoy crafts demonstrations and wagon rides.

Camping
Land Between the Lakes offers camping that varies from RV-friendly full hookups to solitary backcountry sites. The Tennessee options are as follows:

Piney Campground, on the Tennessee River (a.k.a. Kentucky Lake), tel. (931) 232-5331, has all of the amenities—lake access, full hookups, etc., for 322 of its 385 sites. It's open March-November.

Farther away and downstream is **Rushing Creek Campground,** tel. (502) 924-5602, which has almost as many amenities as Piney Campground; the chief omissions are boat launching ramps and nightly programs. It is open year-round.

Wranglers Campground, along Kentucky Lake on the Kentucky side of the park, is a horse owner's delight. In addition to full hookups and hot showers, it offers barns, hitching posts, and 35 miles of horse trails. It is open all year. Call (502) 924-2200.

Backcountry camping is available in a large number of places. For complete guidelines, check with the officials at one of the visitors centers.

WEST OF NASHVILLE

NARROWS OF THE HARPETH STATE HISTORIC AREA

This 200-acre place is home to two interesting sights—one natural and one man-made. As it flows toward the Cumberland River, the Harpeth River swoops back and forth across the land west of Nashville. At one place in Cheatham County, the river comes back and almost meets itself; the loops are separated by a bluff that narrows to 180 feet. Thus the name—the Narrows of the Harpeth.

Montgomery Bell was an early iron magnate in Tennessee who built up a healthy enterprise out of iron forges in the region. Indeed, it was cannonballs from Bell's forges that Andrew Jackson fired at the British in the Battle of New Orleans. Bell had a problem. Despite all the iron he produced, he lacked the ability to manufacture it into a wide range of products. For that he needed huge hammers that could pound red-hot iron into sheets or pieces that could be more easily transformed into tools and other goods.

Bell noticed that the Harpeth on one side of the narrows is 16 feet lower than on the other side of the bluff, and he reasoned that if he could cut a tunnel from one side to the other he would have an enormous source of water power. Using crude tools and black powder, sometime about 1818 Bell cut a large tunnel—16 feet wide, eight feet tall, and 100 yards long—through the bluff. It may have been the first tunnel in the country. Bell's workers, many of them slaves, took advantage of a natural arch to help hold the roof of the tunnel up, thus diverting enough water to spin eight large water wheels, which provided power for the hammers and bellows of the Patterson Forge.

In its heyday this forge ran day and night, four huge hammers ringing as they rose and fell and pounded out the iron. Bell's goods were carried by steamboat to Vicksburg and even to New Orleans. Bell died in 1858 and was buried within sight of his tunnel, and the Civil War brought an end to his enterprise.

Today the tunnel is virtually the only remnant of Bell's industry. When the waters of the Harpeth

are low, visitors can wade into the tunnel and inspect it closely. Other activities at the area include swimming in the river and picnicking. Call (931) 797-9052 for further information.

The community of **Pegram,** between the historic area and Nashville, puts on an annual March **fish fry** that attracts thousands of people. This event is a bit out of the way. Call the Cheatham County Chamber of Commerce, tel. (931) 792-6722, for more details. Find out more online at www.tnstateparks.com.

MONTGOMERY BELL STATE RESORT PARK

The 3,782-acre Montgomery Bell State Resort Park, tel. (931) 797-9052, lies between Nashville and Dickson on Hwy. 70. Like Tennessee's other state parks, this one benefitted from the attentions of the Civilian Conservation Corps during the Depression, and its work endures in the beautiful stone dams. The story of Montgomery Bell is recounted above under "Narrows of the Harpeth State Historic Area," and this park contains the remains of his 1815 Laurel iron furnace and the pits from which iron ore was dug.

A schism of the Presbyterian denomination took place here in 1810 amid the "Great Revival" that swept through American Protestantism at the turn of the century. Three ministers came to Samuel McAdow's cabin and, after an all-night session of prayer, decided to form the Cumberland Presbyterian Church, a group whose ministers, unlike those of the Presbytery from which it sprang, did not have to be formally educated. The park contains a replica of the cabin and an early 1800s chapel in which many weddings take place.

Montgomery Bell State Resort Park offers a host of leisure activities: golf, swimming, boating, fishing, hiking, tennis, and archery, as well as various athletic courts. The only place to eat in the park is the restaurant at the inn, which is open year-round offering three meals a day every day except two weeks around the Christmas and New Year's holidays. Find out more online at www.

state.tn.us/environment/parks/montbell or www. tnstateparks.com.

Where to Stay

The brand new **Montgomery Bell Inn,** tel. (931) 797-3101 or (800) 250-8613, contains 120 rooms and is open year-round. Overlooking 35-acre Acorn Lake, the inn is a popular place, and reservations must be made up to a year in advance. Rooms cost $68-72 per night plus tax. Moderate.

Nine two-bedroom cabins lie across a cove from the inn and connect to it via a rustic bridge. They are fully equipped for housekeeping and are open year-round. During the summer, cabins rent by the week, but during the off-season visitors have only a two-night minimum. Cabins cost $90 per night plus tax. Expensive.

The park campground offers 120 sites, 92 of which have water and electrical hookups. Hot showers are available for all, and the campground is open year-round.

DICKSON AND VICINITY

Although the county with which it shares its name was chartered in 1803, Dickson is a relatively new town, one that came into being because of a railroad built by Union soldiers. After the turn of the century, it became a manufacturing center.

Dickson is the birthplace of Frank Clement, who was the youngest governor of Tennessee and who holds second place in number of years in that office. He burst on the national scene by making the keynote address at the 1956 Democratic Convention but rendered the speech in a histrionic, pre-TV style more suited to revival tents. One acerbic newspaper reporter wrote that Frank Clement "last night slew the Republican party with the jawbone of an ass."

Entertainment and Events

Live country music pours forth from the **Grand Old Hatchery,** 113 Main St., tel. (931) 446-2575, every Saturday night. This establishment used to be the fifth-largest chicken hatchery in the United States, but in 1985 it transformed itself into a place to incubate musical careers. Performers have ranged in age from four to 94 and have come from all over the world. Tryouts are on Friday night. The show begins at 7 p.m. each Saturday. Performers—some professionals and some amateurs—are accompanied by a nine-piece house band. This family-oriented place serves no alcohol and welcomes kids. Admission is $3 for adults, $1.50 for seniors, and free for kids under 12. Clogging and Western line dancing classes are scheduled during the week.

Old Timer's Day, with arts and crafts, a flea market, and contests, is held in downtown Dickson

on the first Saturday in May. The festivities begin with a two-hour parade that steps off at 10 a.m.

WHERE TO STAY

Bed and Breakfasts and Inns

East Hills Bed & Breakfast Inn, sitting on more than four acres of land on Hwy. 70 E at 100 E. Hill Terrace, Dickson, TN 37055, tel. (931) 446-6922, is a charming Southern house built in the late 1940s. Guests can relax on the pillared front porch or walk to a nearby lake. The inn's four big rooms feature private baths. No alcoholic beverages are allowed. The rooms cost $65-95. Moderate-Expensive.

The Inn on Main Street, at 112 S. Main St., Dickson, TN 37055, tel. (931) 441-6879, occupies a turn-of-the-century home with a porch and verandah that extend the full width of the house. Furnished with period antiques, the inn contains one suite and two rooms. The suite comes with a private bath, and the rooms each have a vanity and sink. Rates run $55-105 depending on the room and the season. The inn's first floor is handicapped-accessible. Find out more online at www.bbonline.com/tn/innmain. Moderate-Expensive.

Motels

A host of franchise motels line Interstate 40 hereabouts. Try the **Comfort Inn,** 2325 Hwy. 46, tel. (931) 446-2423 or (800) 221-2222; **Econo Lodge,** 2338 Hwy. 46, tel. (931) 446-0541 or (800) 424-4777; or **Holiday Inn,** 2420 Hwy. 46, tel. (931) 446-9081 or (800) HOLIDAY.

THE RUSKIN COLONY

It all began with Julius Augustus Wayland, a man from Indiana with a noble-sounding name and even nobler visions of how society should be run. His principles took shape in the Ruskin Colony, an experiment in socialism eagerly followed by thousands of people around the country.

As described in John Edgerton's excellent *Visions of Utopia,* Wayland lived in a time of great economic uncertainty in the United States. The stock market crashed in 1893, and populists such as William Jennings Bryan found many people willing to listen to new ideas of government and economics. A well-to-do man, Wayland in 1893 began publishing his own newspaper, *The Coming Nation,* in which he took socialism as defined by English thinkers, particularly John Ruskin, put it in easy-to-understand language, and printed weekly editions.

The Coming Nation boomed; within six months 13,000 people paid 50 cents for a year's subscription, and by the spring of 1894 circulation topped 50,000. Wayland had long wanted to set up a community based on cooperation and socialism, and in 1894 his representatives bought 1,000 acres in Dickson County near a hamlet called Tennessee City. He called it the Ruskin Colony. As in Rugby, a colony founded on idealistic principles in East Tennessee, the founders' philosophical vision was clearer than their agricultural one; the land they bought had very poor soil.

Nonetheless, about three dozen people from all over the country came to the colony. They bound themselves legally into a corporation, built a building in which to print *The Coming Nation,* built homes for themselves, and set out to live the cooperative life. All work, whether hoeing corn or setting type, was valued at the same rate. Members paid for various goods with scrip issued by the corporation, and prices were expressed in hours. A pound of coffee cost seven hours of work, a quart of peanuts cost one hour, and a pair of men's pants cost 37 hours.

In the beginning, the colony boomed. The eager Ruskinites set up a kiln and planing mill, and they manufactured and sold items such as suspenders, wool pants, chewing gum, cereal, and a patent medicine. Almost 100 people lived in the colony by fall 1894.

Having that many idealists together, however, proved a challenge. The hard workers began to notice that slackers got paid the same as those who strove industriously. And people complained that Wayland, despite all his talk of socialism, retained ownership and control of his newspaper. He donated the ownership of *The Coming Nation* to the colony, yet tried to retain editorial control. Wayland quarreled with his former followers until he had had enough. In the summer of 1895 he left the colony, moved to Kansas, and started another newspaper.

In the meantime, the colonists decided to move to literally greener pastures. They bought 800 acres north of Tennessee City, property that contained two enormous caves. By 1897 they had built Commonwealth House, an enormous, three-story structure holding the printing operation and topped by a 700-seat auditorium. Here things hit a peak. The colony owned 75 buildings, telephones, a gristmill, machine shop, cafe, laundry, bakery, commissary, school, and a variety of cottage industries. The colonists used the large cave on their property for a cannery.

Two hundred fifty residents from 32 states and several foreign countries came to Ruskin, and the place hummed with activity. Increasingly, however, it also hummed with controversy. Some of the newcomers proved more radical than the founders and complained about the way things were run. A few disdained marriage and advocated "free love," and accounts of this school of thought did nothing to enhance Ruskin among the locals.

The colony ended amid a ton of bickering. The fact that the colony was incorporated led various shareholders to attack other shareholders in the courts. After a series of court proceedings, a judge declared that the litigants had irreconcilable differences and ordered that the assets be sold at auction and distributed to the shareholders.

Ruskin lives on as the name of a cave at the Ruskin Cave Trophy Trout Ranch enterprise. Commonwealth House still stands on the Great Caves property, though it is well off the road and in such bad shape that visitors cannot go inside.

Camping

KOA Dickson/Nashville, tel. (931) 446-9925, offers 81 sites, a pool, and tours. From I-40 take Exit 172 and follow the signs. It's open all year.

Tanbark Campground, tel. (931) 441-1613, has 24 sites. Take Exit 163 at the junction of I-40 and Hwy and follow the signs. It's open all year.

FOOD

The Catfish Kitchen, 2.5 miles east of town on Hwy. 70, tel. (931) 446-4480, offers Tennessee's favorite fish as well as other seafood , frog legs, and steaks.

East Hills Restaurant, 702 E. College St. at the intersection of Hwy. 46 and Hwy. 70 E, tel. (931) 446-6922, is famous for its fresh-cooked vegetables and homemade pies. Carnivores can chow down on steaks, ribs, catfish, and fried chicken.

Fossie's BBQ, 603 E. Walnut, tel. (931) 446-8674, serves homemade barbecue with all the usual sides.

Wang's China, 107 W. Christi Rd., tel. (931) 446-3388, offers Chinese dishes, including a lunch and supper buffet.

And in nearby White Bluff, **Hog Heaven Barbeque,** 4142 Hwy. 70 E, tel. (931) 797-4923, serves great barbecue, full breakfasts, plate lunches, and homemade desserts.

The Perfect Pig Bar-B-Que and Grill, also in White Bluff at 4491 Hwy. 70 E, tel. (931) 797-4020, offers daily specials, burgers, chicken, and steaks.

SHOPPING AND INFORMATION

Those in need of a chocolate break should stop at **Sweetwater Station,** 123 N. Main St., tel. (931) 441-1682, for a great selection of homemade confectioneries. Choose from imported and locally produced sweets. The station is open Mon.-Sat. 9:30 a.m.-5:30 p.m.

Arts and Crafts

Creative Gallery I, at the entrance to Montgomery Bell State Park, tel. (931) 797-3101 ext. 260, sells a wide variety of crafts, among them hand-thrown pottery, grapevine wreaths, homemade jellies and jams, lye soap, and photographs.

Information

Get in touch with the **Dickson County Chamber of Commerce** at 119 Hwy. 70 E in Dickson, tel. (931) 446-2349.

NORTHWEST OF DICKSON

To get to the following take Highway 46 or Exit 172 and go about 10 miles out of Dickson.

Jewel Cave

This cave offers formations in abundance. The many colors of the stalactites and stalagmites and other features led to the cave's name. Admission to the Jewel Cave costs $5.50 for adults and $4.50 for children ages 6 to 12. Jewel Cave is open from April through the fall. For further information, call (931) 763-0389.

Ruskin Cave Trophy Trout Ranch

Ruskin Cave takes its name from the colony of socialists who owned it and used it for a cannery. Though Ruskin does not have the formations that most cave visitors want to see, it contains an enormous spring that sends forth two million gallons of water per day, which now contain large trout. Anglers can fish here for $20 per hour—more on the weekends. Call (931) 763-6269. Wildlife such as Watusi cattle, buffalo, llamas, and camels can also be seen, as well as a rock house built for country musician David Allen Coe. Admission to the wildlife area costs $5 for adults and $2 for kids.

NORTH OF DICKSON

Charlotte

North of Dickson lies a small town once prominent in the state. Established in 1804 as the county seat, Charlotte sat on an important stagecoach route, and Andrew Jackson and Thomas Hart Benton practiced law here. Such was the town's stature that it was proposed as the state capital, losing to Nashville in 1843 by only one vote.

To this town in the winter of 1862 came Nathan Bedford Forrest and his troops after escaping capture at Fort Donelson. According to the tale, Forrest's men happily filled the taverns and availed themselves of the products therein. Forrest, a teetotaler who was eager to move on, kept riding his horse up to the saloons, sticking his head in the door while still on horseback, and ordering that no more whiskey be served to his troops. In a final effort to rally his men, Forrest and a few of his more sober troopers rode to a hill east of town, where they fired guns and gave the Rebel yell. The revelers, fearing the Yankees had followed them, leapt on their horses and rode off to what they assumed was another battle. In a couple of minutes, not one of them was left in Charlotte.

The Civil War and getting bypassed by the railroad greatly impeded the town, but it held onto its position as county seat, despite numerous efforts to move it to Dickson. The courthouse here, built in 1833, is the oldest one in use in the state. Among the buildings to see is the Charlotte Cumberland Presbyterian Church, built in 1850 and still containing many of its original furnishings.

Cumberland Furnace

This town, farther north on Hwy. 48, is where the iron industry in this part of the state began. Montgomery Bell, of park fame, built the fledgling industry hereabouts before selling out. The Civil War halted production, but it resumed after the war and continued as recently as World War II—a remarkable run. The town is listed on the National Register as a Historic District.

A brochure put together by Cumberland Furnace Historic Village, Inc., gives the visitor a walking tour of the town. Highlights include a former furnace owner's mansion on the hill, the old train depot, and some buildings present when Nathan Bedford Forrest's troops camped here in 1862.

SOUTH OF DICKSON

Bon Aqua

This former resort community is home to an interesting clothing company as well as a good place to eat. The **Bon Aqua Clothing Company,** 10296 Hwy. 46, tel. (931) 670-3589 or (888) 8-GUSSET, is out to reform the world of jeans, one crotch at a time. David Hall and his cousin Jeff took conventional jeans and added a triangular or diamond-shaped piece of cloth in the crotch. This addition, called a gusset, relieves the strain that causes normal jeans to rip or wear out. The jeans are attracting a wide following and can be ordered by mail or in stores. See Bon Aqua on the Web at www.gusset.com, or call for a list of outlets.

The Beacon Light Tea Room, 6343 Hwy. 100, tel. (931) 670-3880, was named for an aviation beacon erected in the 1930s across the road from the restaurant. The light is no more, but the food here has not changed since those days. People come here for country ham, fried chicken, hot biscuits, and homemade preserves. Breakfast is served anytime.

WEST TO THE TENNESSEE RIVER

BUCKSNORT

The **Bucksnort Budget Inn** and a service station mark the Bucksnort Exit on I-40, a rural spot in Hickman County. Originally, this area was known as Old Furnace, named for the nearby old iron furnace. When I-40 was built, Bucksnort was the unforgettable name selected to identify the exit. The original Bucksnort was a store and mill run by the Spence family in the 1830s about a mile west of Old Furnace. It got its unusual name because it sold whiskey; its motto was "For a buck you can get a snort." The store remained in business until the 1920s. To get to the site of the original Bucksnort, get off I-40, and turn onto the dirt road that runs alongside Sugar Creek and the interstate. Proceed for about a mile. All that remain are the rocks that formed the foundation of the store.

HURRICANE MILLS

This is a one-woman town. Country music icon Loretta Lynn and her husband bought a large farm here in 1967, and with it came a mill and the tiny town of Hurricane Mills. In 1975 the couple opened a campground on the property, and since then Hurricane Mills has attracted a steady stream of her fans. Part of the lure of coming here is the chance to see Lynn, who frequently comes out to greet admirers and sign autographs.

The "ranch" covers 6,500 acres, and admission to the grounds and various shops in Hurricane Mills is free. However, those wishing to tour the Lynn home—the original farmhouse, museum, and reconstructed Butcher Holler cabin—must pay $12.50 plus tax. Children under six are admitted at no charge.

Lynn no longer lives in the house—she lives in a home not visible from any roads—but her furniture and decorations look as if she has just stepped out. Visitors are led through the kitchen and other rooms on the first floor of the house

and can see for themselves the relatively simple tastes of Lynn and her longtime husband, "Mooney," who died in 1996.

The museum contains items such as the dress she wore when she first sang on the Grand Ole Opry, every award she's won in country music, scripts from movies and television shows, and letters from presidents and other famous people.

Across the road and on the side of a hill sits a house that is a reminder of how far Lynn has come. As her most famous song and biographical movie declares, she was a "Coal Miner's Daughter." Newspaper is used for wallpaper, the woodstove in the kitchen is the one used in the movie, and the exterior of the house has no paint. Down the hill is a walk-through depiction of a coal mine, complete with authentic tools. Visit online at www.thelynns.com/hmills.

Events
The ranch hosts diverse events though the year, among them motocross motorcycle competitions, trail rides, and an Indian powwow. Loretta Lynn performs two to three times a year, always during the summer. Other concerts present gospel and country music. Get further information about the events by calling (931) 296-7700.

Where to Stay
Motel options are **Best Budget Motel,** I-40 and Hwy. 13, tel. (931) 296-1202; **Best Western of Hurricane Mills,** I-40 and Hwy. 13, tel. (931) 296-4251 or (800) 528-1234; **Days Inn of Hurricane Mills,** I-40 and Hwy. 13, tel. (931) 296-7647 or (800) 325-2525; and **Super 8 Motel,** I-40 and Hwy. 13, tel. (931) 296-2432 or (800) 800-8000.

Loretta Lynn's Ranch, tel. (931) 296-7700, offers 465 campsites with full amenities. From I-40 take Exit 143 and follow signs. The campground is open April-October.

Buffalo River KOA, Exit 143 at the junction of I-40 and Hwy. 13, tel. (931) 296-1306, has 60 sites and is open all year.

THE WIZARD OF THE SADDLE

Historian Shelby Foote has said that the Civil War produced two authentic geniuses—Abraham Lincoln and Confederate Cavalryman Nathan Bedford Forrest. Of all the Civil War generals, Forrest remains the most controversial, one whose deeds and misdeeds are still argued today.

Born in 1821 on a farm in Bedford County, he grew up with little schooling but with a good head for business. He moved farther west, living for a time in Mississippi, then achieved prosperity as a slave trader in Memphis. When the war broke out, Forrest signed on as a private. He was 40 years old.

As the Southern armies took shape, Forrest raised his own cavalry battalion, paying for it out of his own pocket. Although he had never been in a battle before, he quickly became one of the most feared Southern commanders, eventually rising to the rank of lieutenant general—the only man on either side to rise so far from the rank of private. Forrest used his mounted force to cover ground quickly and to strike when unexpected, usually dismounting before battle. He refused to surrender at Fort Donelson, fought at Shiloh, and saw action in Tennessee, Mississippi, Alabama, and Georgia.

Forrest used some simple axioms to guide his actions. "Fighting means killing" was one of these that he took to heart. During the war he personally killed 31 men and had 29 horses shot out from under him. He captured 31,000 prisoners and thought nothing of shooting his own men if they tried to run from battle. "Keep up the skeer" (scare) was another slogan. He relentlessly pursued Union forces, chasing and attacking one force for hundreds of miles.

When Gen. William T. Sherman was storming through Georgia toward the sea, Forrest hit the Union supply lines, leading his cavalry against gunboats on the Tennessee River and utterly destroying the federal warehouses at New Johnsonville. These attacks led Sherman to write that his adversary was "the very devil" and "There will never be peace in Tennessee until Forrest is dead."

Late in the war, Forrest overran Fort Pillow, a Mississippi River stronghold of Union troops, many of whom were black. According to Northern reports, Forrest's men needlessly killed at least 300 of the troops in the fort. Southerners vehemently denied

Confederate general Nathan Bedford Forrest

that version of the "Fort Pillow Massacre," as Northern newspapers dubbed it. They insisted that the Union troops died because they refused to give up.

When the war ended, Forrest entertained the notion of refusing to surrender and riding off to Mexico, but he finally laid down his arms and gave all his men a printed copy of his final orders. The final paragraph contained the following:

I have never, on the field of battle, sent you where I was unwilling to go myself; nor would I now advise you to a course which I felt myself unwilling to pursue. You have been good soldiers; you can be good citizens. Obey the laws, preserve your honor, and the government to which you have surrendered can afford to be, and will be, magnanimous.

This lofty-sounding advice, no doubt crafted in part by one of his staff, was not followed by Forrest himself, for late in 1866 he became the Grand Wizard of the fledgling Ku Klux Klan. In 1871 he was summoned to Washington to testify in Congressional hearings on the organization. During the hearings he claimed no Klan affiliation whatsoever. By then, this may have been true, for he and others thought that the Klan's increasing violence might bring a return to martial law in Tennessee and elsewhere. He had apparently resigned his post and urged that the Klan disband.

Forrest never prospered after the Civil War, and biographer Jack Hurst groups the final years of the general's life into a section called "Penitent." While living in Memphis, Forrest participated in the decoration of Union graves and accepted an invitation to attend a barbecue hosted by local blacks. In 1875, after a lifetime of indifference to religion, he became a Christian. Two years later at the age of 56, he died in his home on October 29, 1877. One of the last people to see him alive was Jefferson Davis.

Forrest is buried in downtown Memphis under a statue of him mounted on a horse. Vandals regularly deface his grave, which is not mentioned in any of the official Memphis tourist publications.

JOHNSONVILLE STATE HISTORICAL AREA

By November of 1864, the South was headed for defeat. General Sherman had just burned Atlanta and was marching for the sea. His supply lines, which began in Louisville, Kentucky, stretched longer and longer as he moved toward Savannah. Johnsonville—named for Andrew Johnson, then military governor of Tennessee—was the crucial link in the chain. Here supplies were transferred from steamboats to railroad cars and then shipped south following Sherman's army. It was this weak link that Confederate Cavalry General Nathan Bedford Forrest resolved to smash.

Commanding a force of 3,000 men and 10 cannons, he sneaked up along the west side of the Tennessee River, set up a gauntlet, and blasted away at Union boats that approached. He captured badly needed supplies and several Union boats, then attacked Johnsonville with two of them. At the same time, his men moved artillery pieces directly across the river from the docks.

When the bombardment was over, the damage was impressive: four gunboats, 14 steamboats, 17 barges, and quartermaster stores worth an estimated $6.7 million. Forrest lost only two men, with nine wounded, and made military history in becoming the only cavalry to engage and defeat a naval force.

The attack, costly as it was to the Union, had little effect on Sherman, who had resolved to live off the land as he scourged the South. Nonetheless, on hearing of this tremendous loss, Sherman said, "That devil Forrest must be hunted down if it costs 10,000 lives and bankrupts the Federal treasury!"

The creation of Kentucky Lake in the 1940s flooded the battle site, leaving only the higher elevations. The Johnsonville State Historical Area occupies this high ground. Here visitors can tour a small museum and walk among what is left of the Union rifle pits and other defensive works. Admission is free, and the area is open daily 8 a.m. until sunset. Call (931) 535-2789 or find out more online at www.tnstateparks.com.

ALONG THE NATCHEZ TRACE

THE NATCHEZ TRACE PARKWAY

The Natchez Trace was one of the country's first interstate highways. Following game trails, Indians tramped back and forth along it to trade or wage war on each other. Europeans, beginning with Hernando de Soto, traveled it as well.

The Trace reached its heyday in the early 1800s, and most of the travel on it was one-way. In the days before steamboats, virtually all traffic on rivers was downstream. Tennesseans and others would build flatboats, crude crafts that drifted with the current, and use them to ship hides, corn, whiskey, or whatever. When the boatmen got to Natchez or New Orleans, they found buyers for their goods, sold their boats for lumber, and set out to walk the 600 miles home.

It was a perilous trek, for robbers knew that the northbound travelers were carrying money. For this and other reasons, the Trace shifted paths from time to time and followed a myriad of routes.

In 1800 the federal government designated the Trace a mail route and later improved it as a military road. Andrew Jackson and his troops marched down the Trace to whip the British in New Orleans, then marched up it in triumph. Steamboats, which could easily go upstream, finished off the Trace about 1815.

Efforts to commemorate the old Trace began about 1900, but it took the Depression and the need to put people to work that led to today's Parkway. Much like its Blue Ridge counterpart along the crest of the Appalachians, the Natchez Trace Parkway provides a limited access road that offers a pleasant drive for motorists and a great ride for bicyclists.

Sights

Only one-fifth or so of the Trace is in Tennessee, but it offers some interesting sights. The first is a bridge that carries the Parkway over Hwy. 96—well worth getting off the Parkway to take a good look. The first post-tensioned, segmental concrete arch bridge in the U.S. is 1,648 feet long and is supported by three pier columns and two soaring arches. One arch spans 582 feet, while the second stretches 460 feet. On conventional arched bridges, the section containing the road is connected to the arches by vertical columns. The designers of the Parkway bridge, to escape the cluttered appearance characteristic of a row of columns, came up with a bridge that omitted these columns entirely. The weight of the bridge rests on the very top of the arch, resulting in a striking bridge that cost $12 million.

The **Old Trace,** at Milepost 403.7, is a 2,000-foot section of the original Trace on which visitors can walk. The **Grave of Meriwether Lewis** is at Milepost 385.9, and thereby hangs a tale.

Meriwether Lewis of Lewis and Clark came to spend the night of October 10, 1809, at a "stand"—one of the rude inns offering shelter to travelers on the Trace. The innkeeper heard a shot in the night, and a wounded Lewis tried to come in her cabin. She refused to open the door, and the next morning Lewis died in his room. His death was ruled a suicide, and he was buried on the grounds. The grave of one of the greatest explorers in the history of the country is marked with a simple monument.

Entertainment and Events
Meriwether Lewis Arts and Crafts Fair, held the second week in October on Main Street, brings together local and regional craftspeople at the Meriwether Lewis monument on the Natchez Trace Parkway.

Information
The **Natchez Trace Parkway headquarters** is in Mississippi and can be reached at (800) 305-7417 or (601) 680-4025. The **Natchez Trace**

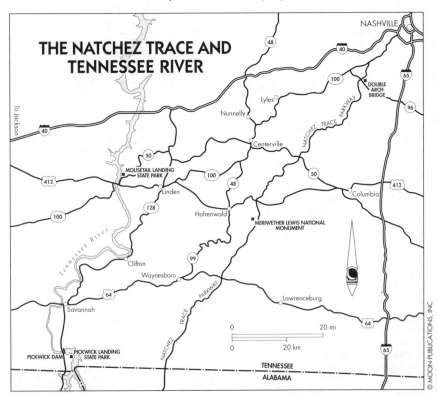

NATCHEZ TRACE PARKWAY

The bridge that carries the Parkway over Hwy. 96 is the first of its kind in the U.S.

Bed & Breakfast Reservation Service can help plan auto or bicycling trips, tel. (800) 377-2770. Find out more online at www.nps.gov/natr/. Bicyclists should look at www.millsaps.edu/~parksjf/ tips/html.

LEIPERS FORK

The rolling countryside here is home to a great many gentleman farmers, most of whom enclose their acreage—or have others do it—with beautiful fences. This used to be the northern terminus of the Natchez Trace Parkway, and it's still a good place to pull off the road and get out of the car.

Where to Stay
Namaste Acres Barn Bed & Breakfast, 5436 Leiper's Creek Rd., Franklin, TN 37064, tel. (931) 791-0333, is a Dutch colonial country home. A pool beside a large, outdoor deck overlooks grazing horses and a scenic mountain view. Franklin Quarters costs $65 per night, while Leiper's Loft goes for $75. A full country breakfast is included in the rate. No charge for children five and under. Horses stay free in the large open pasture. Moderate.

Food and Music
Puckett's Grocery Store 4142 Old Hillsboro Rd., tel. (931) 794-1308 is a wonderful old store that serves hamburgers made from meat they grind themselves. That, deli sandwiches, and homemade desserts make this a good place to have lunch.

Green's Grocery, on Rt. 46 not far from the Natchez Parkway, tel. (931) 790-4072, is another place that has more than its name suggests. It's actually a restaurant/nightclub that offers country cooking—along with "free range possum wings" and, later on, entertainment very similar to that offered by Bluebird in Nashville—songwriters playing their creations.

PRIMM SPRINGS

Like Red Boiling Springs to the Northwest, this little community was one of those places that people went to "take the cure" or just have a good time in the 1800s and the early part of the 1900s. Five kinds of water were available—black sulfur, white sulfur, lime, calomel, and arsenic.

The old hotels are gone, but **Heartland Manor Bed & Breakfast,** 7621 S. Harpeth Rd., tel. (931) 799-1326 or (800) 484-1326 (pin # 9367), offers three bedrooms, two of which have private baths. Guests can also enjoy a pool, exercise room, full gourmet breakfasts, a rec room with a pool table, and more. Rates are $85-125. You can find out more at www.bbonline.com/tn/heartland. Expensive-Premium.

CENTERVILLE

This is the seat of one of the more rural counties in the state. Even now, the county has just one caution light. Hickman County is the birthplace of Beth Slater Whitson, a prolific songwriter best known for her 1908 "Let Me Call You Sweetheart."

Centerville is more famous for producing another sweetheart, the late Sarah Colley, who became Minnie Pearl, one of the most famous characters on the Grand Ole Opry. Colley based her modest "I'm so proud to be here!" routine on the behavior of girls she had observed all over the South while working with a theatrical company. Much of her humor revolved around her attempts to "land a feller," and she often set her stories in the local Grinders Switch community. Although she affected an unsophisticated routine, she was the product of a Nashville finishing school and in her off-stage life was a distinguished lady. She died in 1996.

Hickman County produced three prominent country music sidemen: Ernest Ferguson, a mandolin player who played in several bands; Howdy Forrester, a fiddler who backed Bill Monroe and Roy Acuff; and Paul Warren, another fiddler who played alongside Kitty Wells, Flatt & Scruggs, and Johnnie & Jack.

Details on these and other facets of local life can be seen at the **Hickman Country Museum** in the chamber of commerce building, 117 N. Central Avenue. Admission is free.

Where to Stay
McEwen Farm Log Cabin Bed and Breakfast, P.O. Box 97, Duck River, TN 38454, tel. (931) 583-2378, is out in the country between Centerville and the Natchez Trace Parkway. Lodging is available in two log cabins built with logs used in the 1820s construction of the original buildings

Minnie Pearl's hat was her trademark.

on this working farm. Guests can also stay in a restored Victorian train depot of the North Carolina & St. Louis line. The host provides a continental breakfast. Guests can cook in the cabins and the depot. The rate is $85 per night, with a charge of $10 per person for each additional person up to six people. Expensive.

Or try the **Grinders Switch Inn,** 107 N. Central Ave., tel. (931) 729-5195.

Food
Breece's Cafe, 111 S. Public Square, tel. (931) 729-3481, has been in the same location since 1939. Diners can get a meat and four vegetables for $3, then add on homemade pies or blackberry cobbler.

Fish Camp Restaurant, 406 Hwy. 100, tel. (931) 729-4401, specializes in two Tennessee favorites: catfish and barbecue. The catfish is served as fillets or fiddlers—the whole fish minus the head—and diners can also choose from hickory-smoked barbecue, steaks, chicken, and seafood. It's located one mile north of the town square.

Manley's, 139 N. Central Ave., tel. (931) 729-2948, features country cooking—plate lunches, a buffet, and steaks, catfish, barbecue, and chicken.

Shopping and Information
Remember When, 108 S. Public Square, tel. (931) 729-0052, sells antique furniture and lamps.

Hickman County Chamber of Commerce, 117 N. Central Ave., tel. (931) 729-5774. Find out more by going online to www.nostalgiaville.com/hills/hickman.

HOHENWALD

This pleasant little town was settled in 1878 by German immigrants, who gave it a name that means "high forest." A group of Swiss settlers who had found slim pickings in Nebraska arrived 16 years later, and the town maintains a European feel to this day.

Hohenwald is the birthplace of **Tootsie Bess,** the late owner of Tootsie's Orchid Lounge, a famous watering hole next to the Ryman Auditorium in Nashville.

Sights and Recreation

A good place to begin is the **Hohenwald Depot,** built in 1885 at 112 E. Main St. and now home to the Lewis County Chamber of Commerce.

Compared to many small-town museums that consist of unlabeled relics and dusty junk, the professionalism of the **Lewis County Museum of Natural and Local History,** 108 E. Main St., tel. (931) 796-1550, is a pure delight. Visitors here have the opportunity to see one of the largest single hunter's collections of exotic game mounts in the country. Cape buffalo, Persian ibex, and African dik-diks are some of the animals bagged by Dan Maddox, whose collection forms the centerpiece of this museum. While "great white hunters" may not be in vogue anymore, this museum offers a chance to examine well-mounted specimens seldom seen outside of much larger institutions. Other exhibits include Lewis County artifacts. Admission is $2 for adults and 50 cents for children.

Willis Furniture Company, 995 Centerville Hwy., tel. (931) 796-4517, two miles north of town on Hwy. 48, offers a huge collection of ornamental cement items for one's yard. The best sellers hereabouts are fountains, frogs, and alligators.

Buffalo River Canoeing, whose office is at 18 W. Linden, tel. (931) 796-3622 or (800) 339-5596, rents canoes for the nearby Buffalo River.

Entertainment and Events

Maifest in early May reflects Hohenwald's German heritage with a parade, German music and food, and events such as a tractor pull.

Oktoberfest Heritage Festival on the second weekend of October, offers German music and food and a variety of events.

Where to Stay

Try **Shadow Acres Motel,** Hwy. 48 N, tel. (931) 796-2201.

Hohenwald's finest hostelry, the **Swan View Motel,** proudly sits at 1240 Columbia Hwy., tel. (931) 796-4745. Swan Creek runs through the end of the field and offers pleasing views. Bike riders and motorcyclists often fill up the place, where rates are $35 a night. A gem mine is in the works across the street.

Buffalo River Canoeing, whose office is at 18 W. Linden, tel. (931) 796-3622 or (800) 339-

5596, offers primitive camping all year along the Buffalo River.

Natchez Trace Parkway, seven miles east on Hwy. 20, tel. (800) 305-7417, has 32 campsites with no hookups. It's open all year.

Food

Big John's BBQ, 426 E. Main St., tel. (931) 796-2244, serves barbecue and steaks, chicken, and seafood.

General Cafe, corner of Main and Maple, tel. (931) 796-3990, offers country cooking plate lunches.

Swan View Restaurant, 1240 Columbia Hwy., tel. (931) 796-4745, has been in business for more than 20 years and claims to serve the best catfish and hushpuppies to be found anywhere.

Shopping

Hohenwald's Main St. junk stores are famous for **Dig Days**—occasions when large bundles of clothing arrive from distant cities. The compacted bundles, which weigh as much as 1,000 pounds, are placed on the floor, the wires are snipped, and customers literally dig in. Sharp-eyed diggers, who arm themselves with pillowcases to stash their finds, sometimes emerge with brand-new designer clothes, cashmere coats, and men's suits. Once the diggers are done, the proprietors separate the clothing, hang it up, and offer it for sale.

A & W Salvage, 336 E. Main St., tel. (931) 796-3026, has digs on Wednesday, Saturday, and Sunday. The wires are snipped at 8 a.m. on Wednesday and Saturday and at 1 p.m. on Sunday. Dig in.

Dig Days at **Lawson's Stores,** 100 E. Main St., tel. (931) 796-4380, start at 8 a.m. on Wednesday and Saturday.

Information

Go to **Lewis County Chamber of Commerce,** 995 Centerville Hwy., tel. (931) 796-4517. Or see www.visitlewis.com for one of the best Web sites for a small town.

WAYNESBORO

The county seat of the second largest county in the state, Waynesboro is the hometown of country singer Mark Collie, whose debut album was *Hardin County Line.*

Visitors who have had too much driving and country cooking should stay for a week at **Tennessee Fitness Spa,** between Waynesboro and Hohenwald off Hwy. 99, tel. (931) 722-5589 or (800) 235-8365. Healthy meals, lots of exercise, and classes get people in a fit frame of mind and body. Facilities include a 10-person hot tub, aerobics gym, weight room, covered pool, and hiking trails. Rates run $350-2,400 per week, and the program runs Sunday to Sunday. Find out more online at www.tfspa.com.

The grounds of the spa contain a geologic wonder—a double span natural bridge. A stream carved out one bridge and then turned and cut out another one. These bridges are on private property, so visitors should call ahead. Sunday afternoon, when spa guests come and go, is the worst time to try to see it.

Recreation
Crazy Horse Canoes, 12 miles north of town on Hwy. 13, tel. (931) 722-5213, offers float trips on the Buffalo River April-September.

Buffalo River Trail Rides, P.O. Box 591, Waynesboro, TN 38485-0591, tel. (931) 722-9170, offers trail rides for those who have their own horses. No rental steeds are available. Rides last for one week and include live entertainment and meals.

Where to Stay
Try the **Sims Motor Lodge,** Hwy. 64 W, tel. (931) 722-3655.

Buffalo River Trail Rides, P.O. Box 591, Waynesboro, TN 38485-0591, tel. (931) 722-9170, has camping spaces along the Buffalo River.

Crazy Horse Park on Hwy. 13 N, tel. (931) 722-5213, offers shaded campsites, swimming, fishing, a store, and a restaurant.

Food and Information
Emerald's Restaurant, on the square, tel. (931) 722-5611, serves lunch and dinner every day. Country cooking is the fare, and the walls are lined with old photos of the town. This is a surprisingly nice place, one that attracts diners from far-flung towns.

Wayne County Chamber of Commerce, Wayne County Courthouse, tel. (931) 722-9022, www.nostalgiaville.com/hills/wayne, is open weekdays except Wednesday 8:30 a.m.-4 p.m.

NORTH ALONG THE TENNESSEE

SAVANNAH

Originally a group of cabins on a bluff, Savannah is the largest town on the Tennessee River as it makes its second pass across the state. Main Street leads right down to the river, where a ferry used to take travelers to the west bank. The Cherokee came through here during their Trail of Tears march on the way to Oklahoma.

Sights
The **Savannah Historic District** stretches for two miles and includes 16 impressive homes, most built 1860-1930. A map available at the chamber of commerce can show the route; the chamber also offers a brochure for the **Historic Savannah Walking Trail.**

On April 6, 1862, word came to a man eating breakfast in the **Cherry Mansion** that the Battle of Shiloh had begun. He stood up and said, "Gentlemen, the ball is in motion. Let's be off." And with that, Gen. U.S. Grant climbed aboard a steamer in Savannah and headed up the Tennessee River. Visitors can walk the grounds of the mansion and make arrangements with the chamber of commerce office, tel. (800) 552-FUNN or (901) 925-2363, to tour the house.

The best place to get oriented here is the **Tennessee River Museum,** 507 Main St., tel. (800) 552-FUNN or (901) 925-2363, which has five exhibit areas pertaining to the river and the area. More than 200 fossils are displayed along with Indian artifacts and weapons from the Civil War. Admission is $2 for adults; all others get in free. The museum shares space with the Hardin County Chamber of Commerce, which has the same hours.

Queen and Alex Haley Sr., the grandparents of *Roots* author Alex Haley, lived on a small farm outside of Savannah. He ran a ferry across the river while she worked as a maid in the Cherry Mansion. Queen was dramatically featured in a television miniseries of the same name; the couple is buried on the hill behind the courthouse.

The Saltillo Ferry, north of town on the Pitts Bend of the river, crosses the Tennessee to Saltillo. The ferry runs on demand during daylight. To get there, take Hwy. 128 north of town and turn left on the Saltillo Ferry Road.

Recreation
Pickwick Landing State Park, covered in the Western Plains chapter of this book, is just south of Savannah.

Eleven miles east of town on Hwy. 64 is **Indian Creek Canoe Rental,** tel. (901) 925-7990, offering three-hour, five-hour, all-day, and overnight trips on the Buffalo River.

Entertainment and Events
Information on all of these is available from the Hardin County Tourism Office at tel. (800) 552-FUNN or (901) 925-2364.

Ride the River offers bicyclists a chance to pedal 30, 50, or 100 miles on the last weekend in April.

The **Tennessee River City Bluegrass Festival,** on the first weekend in July, brings forth local pickers and regional favorites.

The **National Catfish Derby Festival** runs for most of the summer, with various events held on different weekends. Events include arts and crafts; gospel, country, and bluegrass music; and a catfish-skinning contest. The Catfish Cookoff and the World's Best Hushpuppy Competition are the highlights.

The **Hardin County Fair** is the first weekend in September at the Hardin County Fairgrounds.

Where to Stay
White Elephant Bed and Breakfast Inn, 304 Church St., Savannah, TN 38372, tel. (931) 331-5244 or (800) 458-2421, is a two-story Queen Anne-style Victorian home built in 1901. On one and a half grassy acres, it is five blocks from the Tennessee River and downtown Savannah. Inside are two parlors, fireplaces, and antique furnishings. The two guest rooms are furnished with antiques and each has a private bath. The host serves a full country breakfast. Rates are

$75-85. Find out more online at www.bbonline.com/tn/elephant. Moderate.

The Botel, south of Savannah below Pickwick Dam, tel. (901) 925-4787, is one of the more unusual lodgings in the state. The "Botel" is a lodging boat built in 1900 and used by the Corps of Engineers to house people working on dams, levees, etc., up and down the river. The 140-foot-long boat now holds 12 rooms plus a restaurant. Four "cooking units" are on the shore. Rooms and units begin at $36 per night. Inexpensive.

Other options are **Days Inn,** Pickwick Rd., tel. (901) 925-5505 or (800) 325-2525; **Savannah Lodge,** Pickwick Rd., tel. (901) 925-8586; **Savannah Motel,** Hwy. 64 and Adams, tel. (901) 925-3392; or **Shaw's Komfort Motel,** Wayne Rd., tel. (901) 925-3977.

The Botel, on Hwy. 128 and Botel Rd., tel. (901) 925-4787, also offers 20 RV sites at Kentucky Lake, a restaurant, golfing, and houseboats for rent.

Savannah RV Park on Hwy. 226, tel. (901) 925-8767, has 18 sites. It's open all year.

Food
Christopher's Restaurant, 1012 Pickwick Rd., tel. (901) 925-9285, serves catfish, chicken, steak, and barbecue.

The Hickory Pit, 411 Main St., tel. (901) 925-2268, offers barbecue and burgers as well as barbecue bologna.

Woody's, 705 Main St., tel. (901) 925-0104, occupies one of the oldest buildings in Savannah, the former mercantile for the town. The original brick walls can be seen inside along with a 125-year-old soda fountain. The food varies from burgers to filet mignon and also includes chicken, ribs, and seafood.

Shopping and Information
The **Savannah Art Guild,** 112 Williams St., tel. (901) 925-7529, operates a gallery featuring the work of members. It's open Mon.-Sat. 9 a.m.-4 p.m.

The **Hardin County Chamber of Commerce,** 507 Main St., tel. (800) 552-FUNN or (901) 925-2363, is open Mon.-Fri. 9 a.m.-5 p.m. and (during daylight saving time) Saturday 10 a.m.-4 p.m. and Sunday 1-4 p.m. Or go online at www.hardincountytn.com.

DID THE DESERT FOX COME TO CLIFTON?

Lawrence Wells wrote a novel called *Rommel and the Rebel* that puts into fiction the recurring tales that Erwin Rommel, the German "Desert Fox" of World War II, came to the U.S. to study the Civil War and came to Tennessee to examine the cavalry tactics of Confederate General Nathan Bedford Forrest.

Forrest and his troopers rode into Clifton in November of 1862 and built flatboats to cross the Tennessee River. Reaching the other side, they sank the boats and rode off to harass Union troops and supply depots in West Tennessee. Headed back, they refloated the flatboats and crossed the river again, this time to the cheers of Cliftonians.

That much is fact. The rest is a collection of memories from old people, missing hotel registers, and perhaps fanciful thinking. In a 1995 article in *The Oxford American* magazine, Wells wrote of interviewing an 82-year-old Clifton woman who recalled that Rommel was riding the first motorcycle she had ever seen.

Rommel was reported to have visited novelist Thomas Stribling, who along with his wife spoke fluent German, and who recounted in his autobiography that one day Rommel appeared out of the blue, introduced himself, and chatted on the porch about Forrest.

Much like Forrest and his cavalry against the Union, Rommel bedeviled the British in North Africa with his tanks. In 1944 he took part in an attempt to assassinate Adolf Hitler and was forced to swallow a lethal dose of poison as a result.

Wells traveled to Germany and talked to Manfred Rommel, son of Erwin, who flatly denied that his father was ever in America. He admitted that his father rode a motorcycle and traveled to Italy to study tactics, but insisted he was never in America, much less Clifton.

Wells ended his article with the following: ". . . indeed, to anyone with a reverence, not to say, a vulnerability, for the past, Clifton's ghostly motorcyclist, whoever he was—anonymous wanderer or future war hero—lives on in their imaginations. They can still hear the rumble of his motorcycle, the click of polished knee boots as he bows to the Striblings, the rhythmic creak of the porch swing, questions asked in Prussian-accented English, answers given in West Tennessee English."

CLIFTON

Until a new bridge crossed the Tennessee River, Clifton was home to one of the last ferries in the state. One of the more famous river crossings without a ferry was made on New Year's Day of 1863 by Confederate general Nathan Bedford Forrest, who, pursued by Union troops, moved approximately 2,000 men, their horses, six artillery pieces, and a wagon train over the river to Clifton. The river at that time was about three-quarters of a mile in width; most of the horses made the crossing by swimming, and the entire force came across the cold water in about 10 hours.

Sights

The town's most famous resident was novelist Thomas S. Stribling, who was born here in 1881 and wrote many novels while living here. Stribling's books about the South were closer to those of Erskine Caldwell than to any sort about mansions and magnolias. He won the Pulitzer Prize in 1933 for *The Store*. The **Stribling Museum,** in his Water St. house overlooking the river, contains original furniture, clothing, and books.

Clifton has a large mural, about 40 by 80 feet, depicting the town's glory days. The **Clifton Motel and Museum,** in the Clifton Motel just outside of town on Hwy. 114, tel. (931) 676-3632, contains a collection of Indian artifacts, Civil War relics, and other materials depicting old times in Clifton. Admission is free.

A great many out-of-towners come to Clifton to live, some of them for years. Clifton is home to the **South Central Correctional Center,** a privately owned prison housing approximately 1,000 inmates. No tours are given.

Events

The **Horseshoe Bend Festival,** held in July, features boat races, a carnival, music, barbecue, and dancing. Call (931) 676-3311 for details.

Where to Stay

Pillow Street Bed and Breakfast, 305 W. Pillow St., Clifton, TN 38425, tel. (888) 305-0305, occupies a restored 1870 house overlooking the river. Guests can take it easy on the balcony. The five rooms all have private baths, and a full country breakfast is served daily. Rates are $55-85. Inexpensive-Moderate.

Or check out the **Clifton Motel,** Hwy. 114, tel. (931) 676-3632.

Food

Riverside Restaurant, 410 Water St., tel. (931) 676-3944, specializes in fish—catfish, shrimp, and grilled salmon. It also serves frog legs, six kinds of steak, chicken, and wonderful hushpuppies. It overlooks the river.

In the sea of fried catfish and the flow of cholesterol that characterize country cooking, **River View Restaurant,** Water and Main Streets, tel. (931) 676-3770, offers a healthy alternative. Here diners will find a daily buffet of homemade breads, vegetables, and salads, all low in fat and salt, and totally free of preservatives. This place is famous for its Tennessee River mud balls, a concoction of carob, toasted almonds, and toasted coconut.

Information

City Hall, 130 Main St., tel. (931) 676-3370, is the most reliable source of information about Clifton.

MOUSETAIL LANDING STATE RUSTIC PARK

Downstream from Clifton lies this 1,249-acre park. It supposedly got its name when a local tannery caught fire during the Civil War. Mice in great numbers poured from the conflagration, giving rise to the name.

The mice are long gone, and today's visitor will find hiking trails, a swimming pool, 26 campsites, and backcountry camping. Call (901) 847-0841, or go online at www.tnstateparks.com.

MEMPHIS
INTRODUCTION

In his wonderful *It Came from Memphis,* which takes a look at Memphis music from the 1950s forward—and does not spend all its time on Elvis—Robert Gordon presents a great perspective on the city: "If aerial photographs could reveal energy the way infrared photographs reveal heat, Memphis would be surrounded by vectors pointing toward it: This is the place."

Memphis is the largest city in Tennessee. Its economic influence reaches across West Tennessee, down into Mississippi, and across the river into Arkansas; one can travel 200 miles in any direction before reaching another city its size. Some argue, convincingly, that Memphis is actually the capital of northern Mississippi.

For a long time, Memphis was the place where rural people, black and white, came when they hit the right combination of money and gumption. The itinerant bluesmen out of the Delta made the journey, as did countless sons and daughters who wanted to get off the farm and away from little towns. Elvis Presley's parents came from Mississippi with thousands of others.

Memphis was ready for all of them. Early on, Beale St. was a place for blacks at which segregation diminished, if just for an afternoon. Planters came to sell cotton. People with money came, and still come, to Memphis to buy everything from furniture to wedding gowns.

These people rubbed up against each other in a way that made the music happen. Whites heard blacks and imitated their music and clothing. Blacks played for whites, adapting the music to what would sell. Studios recorded blacks and whites, finally hitting the right formula that became rock 'n' roll, a formula that a young man named Elvis would sell to the world.

Now Memphis focuses on its music, not in the industry-sponsored vision of Nashville, but in its own peculiar fashion, a fashion that, for today's traveler, becomes a joyful discovery. For those who come to Tennessee for the music, this *is* the place.

HISTORY

The First Settlers

The site of Memphis, at the edge of the western plains of Tennessee, was occupied by people as early as 3,000 years ago. The bluffs above the Mississippi River offered protection from floods as well as from enemies. Archaeologists estimate that the first permanent village was built about A.D. 1,000, and a series of villages were built there during the next 600 years.

When Hernando de Soto, the Spanish explorer of the southeast, came through here in 1541, he described powerful rulers and populous towns on the bluffs. He and his troops spent some time here replenishing supplies and building boats with which to cross the river. Yet when Marquette and Joliet came downstream 132 years later in 1673, they also traded with Indians, but reported no such large villages.

During the 1700s, trade on the river increased as Tennesseans and others drifted downstream past what was by then called the Chickasaw Bluffs. This land lay between the English colonies and Spanish territory to the southwest, and both sides had reason to claim it. James Robertson, later dubbed "The Father of Tennessee," brought troops here in 1782 and began giving goods to the Chickasaw in an effort to win their allegiance. Twelve years later John Overton set up a trading post for the same reason. The Spanish, uneasy at these approaches, sought to establish a fort in 1795 but were forced to retreat.

North Carolina, wanting to reward its Revolutionary War soldiers, began promising them land in what is now West Tennessee. Of course North Carolina had no right to do this, but that did not

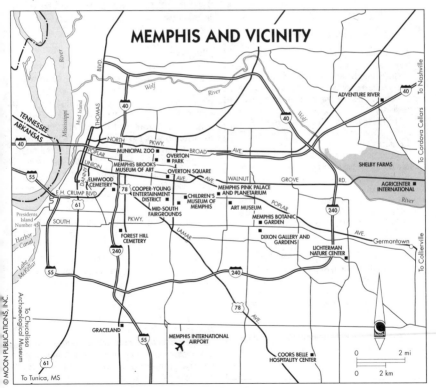

MEMPHIS AND VICINITY

dissuade it from going ahead and doing it anyway. This development led the federal government to make the Chickasaw Indians one of those "offer you can't refuse" deals for the entire area of West Tennessee. Andrew Jackson and others negotiated with the Indians, telling them that the federal government could not keep the eager North Carolina land-seekers out.

Wild West

In 1818 the Chickasaw signed away their lands, and the Jackson Purchase, as it was known, opened up the Wild West of Tennessee. Settlers poured in, and the next year a trio of land speculators—Jackson, Judge John Overton, and Gen. James Winchester—established the town of Memphis. They took the name from the ancient capital of Egypt, a word said to mean "place of good abode."

MUST-SEE HIGHLIGHTS

G raceland is where Elvis Presley lived and died.

The Hunt-Phelan Home, displaying history and good taste, gives a quiet viewpoint of a side of Memphis history that is often downplayed these days.

The River Walk on Mud Island enables the visitor to walk the length of the Mississippi in five blocks.

Beale Street's Center for Southern Folklore combines gift shop and museum with enthusiastic employees in a joyful interpretation of the South.

The Memphis Music Hall of Fame is the single best place in Memphis to get a handle on the city's tremendous contribution to popular culture.

The Rendezvous has a back alley entrance to Memphis's most astonishing restaurant.

The National Civil Rights Museum shows how far Americans have come, and accomplishments yet to attain.

Shangri-La Records will delight lovers of Memphis Music—the old, the new, and the weird.

The Peabody Hotel Lobby is the best place in the universe to have a gin and tonic on a hot afternoon. It doesn't get any better than this.

It quickly became a place for a good time. Flatboatmen on their way downstream were happy to pull in and blow off a little steam. Landowners arrived with gangs of slaves to cut down the hardwood forests and turn the rich soil into plantations. Indians traded furs for liquor, and gamblers did their best to separate one and all from their money.

The 1830 federal census counted only a couple hundred people. By 1840, 2,000 were on hand, and 10 years later more than 8,800 people called Memphis home. By 1850, according to Robert Corlew's *Tennessee, A Short History,* local plantations produced 150,000 bales of cotton valued at $7.5 million, most of which moved through Memphis on its way to market. Ten years later traders sold three times that amount. Because of the large amount of international shipping, Memphis gained a customs office in 1850. By 1857, a railroad connected Charleston to Memphis, and by 1860, 33,000 people lived by the river.

Civil War

When the Civil War hit Tennessee, Memphis was isolated from the rest of the state when Union troops fought their way down the Tennessee River, their struggle culminating at the battle of Shiloh. Their victory forced a Confederate retreat from Fort Pillow, which guarded the river north of the city. Memphis's last chance came when Union and Confederate gunboats fought it out on the river. Memphians watched from the bluffs above as the boats, using rams much like Roman galleys, slammed into each other. When it was all over, a Union force came ashore and erected its flag at the post office. General Grant moved into the Hunt-Phelan Home. Memphis was in Union hands, where it would remain for the rest of the war.

This proved not entirely bad. Memphians did not undergo a siege, as did Vicksburg farther downstream, nor was Memphis shelled and burned, a fate suffered by Atlanta and other cities. Indeed, merchants made a lot of money selling cotton and trading for goods that could be sold to both North and South.

The most colorful episode of Memphis's Civil War history came late in the war in August 1864, when Confederate Nathan Bedford Forrest staged a daring raid on the city where he once

THE WRECK OF THE *SULTANA*

W hen it comes to maritime disasters, most of us tend to think of the *Titanic,* which sank in 1912 with a loss of 1,503 lives. America's worst inland maritime disaster, however, took place on the Mississippi on the night of April 27, 1865, eight miles north of Memphis.

The Civil War had just ended. The *Sultana,* a side-wheeler with a licensed capacity of 345 passengers, took on a vast number of Union troops at Vicksburg who wanted to get home in a hurry. Some of them were former prisoners of war—a good many hailed from East Tennessee—and the authorities were reluctant to turn anyone away. Consequently, the *Sultana* was grossly overloaded with as many as 2,485 passengers—the exact figure will never be known.

The river was in flood stage, and the steamboat was laboring upstream in the middle of the river when one of the boilers blew up at 2 a.m., tearing the ship in two. The explosion and burst of steam instantly killed scores of people, and the resulting fire threatened everyone else. Thinking they were close to shore, many jumped into the muddy water.

In actuality, it was over four miles in either direction to land, and the survivors grasped for pieces of wood or anything that would keep them afloat. Weakened from months or years in prison, many of them were too weary to survive. When another boat arrived 90 minutes later, for too many it was too late.

Between 500 and 600 survivors were taken to Memphis hospitals, and hundreds of bodies floated to the city. Estimates of the deaths range from 1,450 to 1,900, and many, their identification impossible to determine, were buried in mass graves.

The wreck of the *Sultana* did not get much notice in the press of the day or in history books. Lincoln had been dead only 11 days when the disaster took place, and so it never got the attention of subsequent maritime horrors. Survivors of the wreck formed a society and held regular reunions, and the last member died in 1930. You'll find a site devoted to the wreck at www.sultana.com.

---

served as alderman. Hoping to capture three Union generals and to free Southerners held in a prison, Forrest and his men galloped into town at 4 a.m. They captured no generals—although one had to scamper in his nightgown to a nearby fort—and didn't free any prisoners, but the troopers were cheered by the locals, particularly the women, who, while wearing nightgowns of their own in the dawn's early light, flung open doors and windows and gave the riders a seldom-seen and much-appreciated look at feminine pulchritude.

Pestilence

Memphis came through the war relatively unscathed, but disease brought it to its knees during the next 15 years. Cholera and yellow fever struck in 1867, and yellow fever returned in 1872 and far worse in 1878. In the words of the *WPA Guide to Tennessee,* "Memphis became a pesthole. As deaths mounted, the streets were deserted except for the 'dead wagons.' Bodies lay rotting in the streets where they had fallen. The criminal element of the city ran wild. Looting and killing, terrific drunken brawls, gun battles, and rape were common. Not more than 20,000 people remained in the city; 14,000 were Negroes, of whom 946 died. The higher fatality was among the 6,000 whites, of whom 4,206 died."

The disparity of deaths between black and white populations came about because blacks possessed a natural immunity that had come with them from Africa. As in the Civil War, however, what brought tragedy to some brought opportunity for others. Property values plummeted, and many speculators, former slave Robert Church among them, bought land and homes from the fleeing residents.

The situation got so bad that Memphis declared bankruptcy, gave up its charter, and legally ceased to exist for 12 years. Citizens set about making sure the epidemics would never return by putting in an effective sewage system, stopping the practice of drinking river water, and draining ditches that had produced clouds of disease-carrying mosquitoes. Among the ones to buy the bonds that financed all this was Robert Church.

Recovery, the Blues, and Racial Conflict
The people returned—totaling 64,589 by 1890—and with them came prosperity. A railroad bridge

BANNED IN MEMPHIS?

Comparing the current brochures and tourist information now given to visitors with the highlights of Memphis listed in the 1939 *WPA Guide to Tennessee* reveals some of the same attractions: the Magevney House, the Cotton Exchange Building, and Overton Park, to name a few.

Many of the parks and monuments that relate to the Confederacy mentioned in the *Guide,* however, have seemingly vanished from present-day travel literature. They still stand in Memphis but show up on no maps or brochures. Here are a few of the monuments to what, at least in Memphis, might be called the Truly Lost Cause.

Confederate Park

This park between N. Front Street and Riverside Dr. commemorates the Battle of Memphis, a sort of demolition derby of gunboats that ended when Memphis fell into Union hands. At one time this park contained Civil War cannons, but in a burst of World War II patriotism the city donated them for scrap to support the war effort. They were replaced with artillery pieces from World War I, thus providing an anachronism alongside the statue of Jefferson Davis.

Elmwood Cemetery

The oldest cemetery in Memphis, and still in use, 80-acre Elmwood is just off Crump Boulevard at 824 S. Dudley Street. Nineteen Confederate generals lie here, as do more than 1,000 of the soldiers they commanded. Part of the cemetery is called "No Man's Land," for it was in that place that the victims of the yellow fever epidemics were buried in trenches. Normally no one else is buried here, but not too long ago a 103-year-old black man who had driven the death wagons as a boy during an epidemic requested that he be laid to rest among the people he had carried. Permission was granted.

The grounds of the cemetery are open daily 7 a.m.-4 p.m. The office, housed in a Victorian Gothic cottage on the National Register, is open Mon.-Fri. 8 a.m.-4 p.m. and Saturday 8 a.m.-2 p.m. Here visitors can obtain a map, rent an audiocassette tour, or take part in guided tours. Call (901) 774-3212. Visitors are reminded that funerals still take place here and should comport themselves accordingly.

Gayoso Hotel

The facade of this old hotel can still be seen at the corner of Peabody and Front Streets. Built in 1844, it was used as a headquarters by both North and South during the Civil War, but is most remembered as one of the objectives of Nathan Bedford Forrest's 1864 raid on the city. His brother, William Forrest, rode his horse into the hotel lobby to capture a Union general who lived there. Luckily for the general, he had chosen that night to sleep somewhere else.

Jefferson Davis Park

The site of the park is believed to be the place where Hernando de Soto built boats with which to cross the Mississippi. It had no particular historical connection with the president of the Confederacy but was set off to honor him after the war. Now it is occupied by the Tennessee Welcome Center.

Site of the Jefferson Davis Home

The one and only president of the Confederacy lived in Memphis after the war 1867-75 while he was the president of a local insurance company. The house in which he lived stood at 129 Court Avenue.

Forrest Park

This park, at Manassas and Union Ave., serves as the lightning rod for those who would like to downplay Memphis Confederate history. It consists of a statue of Nathan Bedford Forrest, Memphis slave trader, alderman, famous Confederate general, and infamous early leader of the Ku Klux Klan. The statue faces south because, according to some, Forrest said he would never turn his back on the South. The general and his wife are entombed beneath the statue, which often attracts graffiti and other vandalism.

The general and his wife were originally buried in Elmwood Cemetery, but in 1905 they were moved to Forrest Park. His birthday, July 13, 1821, is regularly commemorated by the Sons of Confederate Veterans and various admirers, while others, most notably the Memphis branch of the NAACP, have mounted efforts to have his remains placed elsewhere. This would require the permission of his descendants, who have so far declined.

across the Mississippi was built in 1892, and the next year Memphis got its charter back. It remained the center of the cotton business and also became the greatest hardwood lumber center in the world.

The money in Memphis trickled down to the black population. It was during this time that Beale St. became the center of black life. Black professionals who had been educated in the North came to Memphis to practice their trade. Robert Church founded the Solvent Bank and Trust and became the South's first black millionaire. In 1923 the Universal Life Insurance Company, one of the largest black-owned insurance companies, was chartered. Many rural blacks moved to Memphis, and with them they brought a strange kind of new music called the blues. W.C. Handy, a local bandleader and cornet player, wrote the first tune with the word "blues" in the title. His "Memphis Blues," originally written as a campaign song, was followed by the "St. Louis Blues," and popular music was changed forever.

In 1916 a grocer named Clarence Saunders opened a store with a funny name and a revolutionary *modus operandi*. Piggly Wiggly was the first grocery store in the country in which customers took a basket and helped themselves to the items they needed. One year later Saunders owned 25 stores, three years later 162 stores, and by 1923 there were 1,267 Piggly Wigglys. Saunders built a large house with pink marble, quickly dubbed "The Pink Palace" by locals, but because of various setbacks lost his stores and died penniless.

The early 20th century saw the rise of Edward Crump, a Mississippian who was elected mayor of Memphis in 1909, 1911, and 1915. "Boss" Crump, as he became known, refused to enforce Tennessee's law prohibiting the sale of alcoholic beverages, and the Tennessee legislature passed the Ouster Law to remove him from office. Crump lost this battle but built a political machine so formidable that it ran Shelby County for years and exerted considerable influence across the state. Crump made an alliance with Republicans in East Tennessee, granting them control of patronage in their area in return for their support. Crump and his cronies thus controlled most statewide elections until Gordon Browning and Estes Kefauver beat them in the Democratic primary of 1948.

Memphis is the largest city for several hundred miles in any direction, and it attracted its share of entrepreneurs. In 1952 Kemmons Wilson came up with the idea of a franchise motel. Naming it after a popular Bing Crosby movie, he called his creation a Holiday Inn.

The summer of the year "Boss" Crump died, a young man walked into Sun Studios and on July 5, 1954, recorded a song called "That's Alright." In a few short years, Elvis became the biggest star to come from Memphis and indeed from all of Tennessee and was credited with luring white audiences to what had heretofore been considered black music. Stax/Volt Records brought names such as Otis Redding, Rufus Thomas, Booker T and the MGs, Karla Thomas, and Johnny Taylor to national attention.

Musically the races may have come closer together in the 1950s, but in other ways they were far apart, particularly in Memphis, which had the largest black population in the state. Sit-ins took place here in 1960, and a biracial Committee on Community Relations helped desegregate the city. Like other American cities, Memphis underwent great transformations after World War II, and the racial conflict accelerated white flight from downtown. Not since the days of yellow fever had white people so deserted downtown Memphis. Urban renewal efforts beginning in the 1960s leveled many of the abandoned and sub-standard buildings, leaving much of Beale Street off by itself amid fields of grass.

The Murder of Martin Luther King, Jr.

In 1968, the sanitation workers went on strike. Although the usual labor issues—more money and a better working environment—were involved, this strike became in and of itself a civil rights movement, for most of the workers were black, and the city government that employed them was white. The Reverend Martin Luther King, Jr. and other civil rights leaders encouraged the sanitation workers. Marchers clashed with police and the city was scarred with violence and property damage.

While King was in town getting ready for a second march, he spoke at the Mason Temple. In a final, eerily prescient sermon, he said, "I don't know what will happen now. We've got some difficult days ahead. But it doesn't matter with me now. Because I've been to the moun-

dent, died in 1977, seemingly a symbol for the city.

Memphis Nowadays
Memphis had begun its comeback in the 1970s—Federal Express was founded here in 1972—but things began to happen, oddly enough, after Elvis died. A renovated Peabody reopened in 1981, Graceland began welcoming the public in 1982, and the stream of people making Elvis pilgrimages gave Memphis a renewed sense of its musical heritage.

The novels and films of John Grisham have also contributed to a greater national awareness of Memphis. Filmed versions of *The Firm* and *The Client,* with scenes of Mud Island's tram and other local landmarks, put Memphis back on the popular culture map. *Mystery Train,* a film by Jim Jarmusch, looks at the odder types drawn to Memphis, and *The People vs. Larry Flynt* and *The Rainmaker* added to the city's cinematic hits.

A revival of Beale St. coincided with an upswing in interest in the blues, and with its growing number of festivals and attractions Memphis is returning as a tourist destination. The 32-story Pyramid offers a unique presence on the city's skyline, and the National Civil Rights Museum has transformed the Lorraine Motel from a place of shame and sadness to a center for education and renewal. The new home of the Memphis Redbirds will bring even more people downtown.

Today Memphis is the 18th-largest city in the country, the undisputed pork barbecue capital of the world, and a town that, as in the days of the flatboatmen, knows how to have a good time. More than 150 festivals and celebrations commemorate everything from Elvis to zydeco music. It is the South's largest medical center, anchored by the medical school of the University of Tennessee; one of the top 10 wholesaling and distribution centers in the U.S.; and the most musical place in the most musical state.

Dr. Martin Luther King, Jr. delivered his "I've Been to the Mountaintop" sermon shortly before his murder in 1968.

taintop. . . . I've seen the Promised Land. I may not get there with you. But I want you to know tonight that we as a people will get to the Promised Land. So I'm happy tonight. I'm not worried about anything. I'm not fearing any man. Mine eyes have seen the glory of the coming of the Lord."

The next day about dinnertime as King, Jesse Jackson, and others were standing outside his room on the second floor of the Lorraine Motel, James Earl Ray fired a rifle from the window of a building across the street and killed King.

This proved to be the low point for Memphis. Businesses and those who could afford to fled downtown. The Peabody Hotel closed in 1975. Elvis Presley, Memphis's most celebrated resi-

SIGHTS AND RECREATION

THE LAY OF THE LAND

In Memphis, unlike the other three major cities in Tennessee, visitors can see most of the big attractions without using an automobile. The following describes several interesting areas, from north to south. Detailed information about the individual attractions appears in the appropriate category later on.

The best way to get around downtown is on the **Main Street Trolley,** tel. (901) 274-6282, which runs up and down Main St. and makes a five-mile loop around Riverside Drive. The antique-looking cars provide a useful form of transportation as well as an experience in and of themselves. The price of a ticket is 50 cents one-way, a bargain, and the cars are fun to ride.

Pyramid and the Pinch
Anchoring the north of Memphis stands the most stupendous structure in all of Tennessee. The 32-story Pyramid is the third largest such edifice in the world, and an impressive, if some-

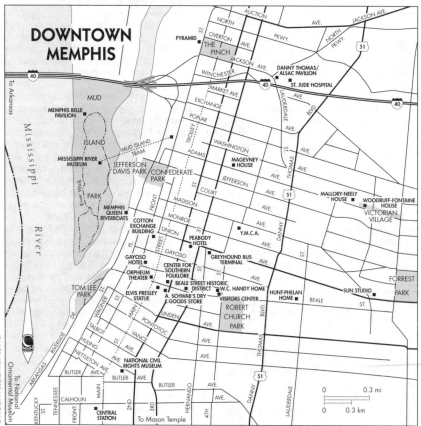

DOWNTOWN MEMPHIS

what bizarre, addition to the Memphis skyline.

In the frontier days of the 1830s, the people who lived north of Market St. were derisively called "pinch guts," for they were so malnourished they had to tighten their belts so far they "pinched their guts." The place where they lived has been known ever since as "The Pinch," now Front St. and Second Avenue.

The Pinch became a neighborhood for German Jews; a remnant survives as the **Slavehaven/Burkle Estate,** a stop on the Underground Railroad. Irish fleeing the potato famine were the next influx, and their presence is remembered each March with St. Patrick's Day celebrations hereabouts. Visitors enjoy walking in the area, stopping in at High Point Pinch nightclub, Irish pubs such as T.J. Milligans, Pig in the Pinch, the North End Restaurant, the antique stores, and other neighborhood pleasures.

Looking to the east down Jackson St. from the Pinch, the visitor can see a golden dome. This is part of **St. Jude Children's Research Hospital,** where a small museum and the tomb of Danny Thomas await the visitor.

Victorian Village Historic District

The residential areas of Memphis used to begin just a few streets away from the river, but over the years the commercial district has expanded and wiped out most of the old houses. Just a few are left on Adams St., and these make up the Victorian Village Historic District. Here stands **Magevney House,** one of the oldest homes in the city, and just down the street are the **Mallory-Neely House** and the **Woodruff-Fontaine House,** beautiful homes that reflect the taste of the wealthy families who lived in them. Several other Victorian houses hold court in the neighborhood, but these are not open to the public.

Mud Island

No one in the Civil War ever saw Mud Island. According to the 1939 *WPA Guide to Tennessee,* the island formed in 1910 when a Spanish-American War gunboat headed upstream had to anchor in Memphis for six to eight months to await high water. As it sat there, an eddy deposited sand and gravel against the hull, and when the boat left town the deposits stayed and grew to the point that the island threatened the port of Memphis. Until the Mississippi was

dammed upstream, Mud Island was subject to flooding, and between floods thickets of willow trees sheltered several moonshiners.

Now Mud Island contains the **Mississippi River Museum,** a look at Memphis and the influence of the river on it; **River Walk,** an enormous scale model of the Mississippi; and the *Memphis Belle,* perhaps the most famous bomber from World War II. An outdoor theater hosts many concerts.

Visitors can get to Mud Island by taking a tram that departs from the intersection of Front and Adams Streets.

Cotton Row Historic District

If cotton was king in the South, Memphis was where he reigned. Seeds and supplies for the white fibers were sold here, bales of cotton were shipped from here, and the money that came back to the planters was very often spent here. Although much of the cotton industry has moved farther west, Memphis still sells more cotton on the spot market than anywhere else in the country.

The center of the cotton trade hereabouts is on Front St., and a good place to begin walking is **Confederate Park,** at W. Court St. on the bluff overlooking Riverside Drive. Walking south on Front St., the visitor comes to a series of buildings with particular architectural features. Before cotton is sold it must be graded, or classified, and before 1950 this required natural light—thus large windows. Cotton bales are big items, and the buildings needed large doors for moving cotton in and out.

The **Falls Building,** 20-22 N. Front St., only served cotton brokers. W.C. Handy first played his "St. Louis Blues" in the rooftop garden.

The **Cotton Exchange Building,** 84-86 South Front St., was and is the center of the Memphis cotton business. Visitors can step into the lobby but cannot lay eyes on the Exchange room. "I think they play more checkers than they want people to know," confessed one who was privileged to see the inner sanctum. On the other side of the street is the **Front Street Deli,** where Lee Busby dispenses cold drinks, good food, and advice to those visiting his city.

Visitors are welcome at the **Turley Cotton Company,** 64 S. Front St., tel. (901) 527-5449, where the employees often take time to explain what they are doing. Cotton samples are on display, and visitors can look at a cotton "snake"— a miscellaneous collection of graded cotton samples thrown into a hemp bag to be reginned and recycled. This place is open Mon.-Fri. 9 a.m.-5 p.m. Sharing the building is the **We're Nuts Pecan Company,** offering another traditional Southern product.

A few steps away from Front St. stands **The Peabody Hotel,** 149 Union Ave., tel. (901) 529-4000, the grande dame of Memphis hotels, and a place once said to be the northern terminus of the Mississippi Delta. Tourists—especially children—love its twice-daily parade of ducks to and from the fountain.

Beale Street
The most famous street in Memphis, if not the entire state of Tennessee, Beale St. begins at the Mississippi River bluff and runs east for a mile or so. In the days of segregation, Beale St. was the center of black life and black culture. Here folks could get a haircut, get drunk, get clothes, get

saved, get life insurance, get lucky, and get entertained—or do several simultaneously.

Beale St. enjoyed its heyday from about 1880 until the Depression. Aside from serving the large black population in Memphis, Beale St. attracted many rural blacks who would put on their finest clothes and come to town on weekends. **Church Park,** the only public park to which blacks could go, was established near Beale St. and 4th Avenue.

The street is most celebrated for the musicians who flocked here. W.C. Handy played here often; his home is now a museum, and a statue of him presides over the street. Others who stayed or played include B.B. King—who got his "B.B." from being called the "Beale Street Boy"—Jimmy Lunceford, Furry Lewis, Albert King, Muddy Waters, Alberta Hunter, and Memphis Minnie McCoy. In the early 1950s, a young high school student named Elvis came here to buy clothes. His statue now stands on Beale Street as well.

But by the '50s, Beale St. was a shadow of what it used to be. The gradual end of segregation no longer confined blacks to specific areas, and their dollars flowed elsewhere. Thousands had gone north, and with them went many of the musicians. The greatest threat came from urban renewal, which in Memphis took the form of bulldozers knocking down dilapidated housing, rooming houses, and the community surrounding the once-vibrant street.

Indeed, visitors to today's Beale St. Historic District will note that the street seems off by itself, surrounded by vast parking lots and open spaces. In his *Tennessee's Historic Landscapes,* Carroll Van West says that some 530 neighborhood buildings were demolished, leaving only about 65 to carry on the legacy of Beale Street.

Beale St. began its comeback in 1983 when millions of dollars flowed into restoration projects. The city of Memphis, learning from Graceland the blessings that throngs of music-lovers can bring, saw Beale St. as a means of bringing people downtown again. The city has relentlessly promoted the place, maintained a strong police presence here, and converted the urban-renewal plains of destruction into parking lots.

And out-of-towners love it. A good first stop is the **Center for Southern Folklore,** a delightful place offering insight into various expressions of

Southern culture. **A. Schwab's Dry Goods** lends a folksy look at shopping in a time long gone.

Church Park is a good place to sit down. Then it's on to the **Beale Street Baptist Church,** the **Memphis Music Hall of Fame,** the **W.C. Handy Home,** and, farther east, the historic **Hunt-Phelan Home.** At night, Beale St. offers several places to eat and catch some music. **Blues City Cafe, B.B. King's, The New Daisy,** and **Rum Boogie Cafe** all feature live entertainment. A statue of W.C. Handy, the father of it all, stands in **Handy Park.**

Just south of Beale is the **Gibson Guitar Factory,** which makes the hollow-bodied electric guitars of the kind loved by bluesmen and rockabillies.

Overton Square

Farther east along Madison Ave. is Overton Square, three blocks of restaurants and shops in midtown. **Playhouse on the Square,** the city's only professional repertory company, is here, as are more than 15 restaurants that vary from outdoor patios to formal dining. The food includes alligator chili, specialty pizzas, French crepes, and Mexican dishes. The rise of Beale St. has siphoned most of the nightlife from here, but the restaurants still hold the fort.

Cooper-Young Entertainment District

Five miles from the river is the intersection of Cooper St. and Young Ave., the epicenter of the Cooper-Young Entertainment District, which attracts those who like a walk on the alternative side. A good place to begin is the **Cooper Street Gallery,** followed by a delightfully irreverent **First Church of the Elvis Impersonator,** a coin-operated shrine in **Java Cabana.** When it is time to eat, hit the **Young Avenue Deli.**

MUSICAL SIGHTS

Memphis is the most musically diverse place in Tennessee, and it is a joy to partake of the wide choice of museums and live entertainment options. Compact disc and record stores are listed in "Shopping" under "More Practicalities," below.

Center for Southern Folklore

This place, 130 Beale St., tel. (901) 525-3655, is nearly impossible to categorize. A rare combination of museum, performance center, art gallery, bookstore, gift shop, and magnet for interesting people, the center's stated purpose is "documenting and presenting the people and traditions of the South through films, books, records, exhibits, and public events." Exhibits blend into the gift shop so smoothly that visitors don't realize they are getting educated on Southern music, literature, and art. Excellent tours of Beale Street and the Delta operate from here. Admission is free.

This early 1920s photo of Beale St. musicians is on display in the Maurice "Fess" Hulbert Collection in the Center for Southern Folklore.

TENNESSEE TOURIST DEVELOPMENT

Church of the Full Gospel Tabernacle

This church, 787 Hale Rd., tel. (901) 396-9192, is home to the Reverend Al Green, whose services at 11 a.m. on Sunday reflect the talent that took him to the top of the soul charts. He found a higher calling, however, and gave up—well, mostly—show business for the straight and narrow. Visitors are welcome, but they should remember that this is a church and dress and act appropriately. Eat a good breakfast—by noon this preacher is just getting warmed up.

Gibson Guitar Plant

Hollow-bodied electric guitars have produced some of the most famous music to emerge from Memphis. Scottie Moore played one with Elvis, and B.B. King's Lucille is a hollow-body. Now that kind of guitar will itself be produced in Memphis at the **Gibson Guitar Plant.** Located one block south of Memphis between Second and Third Streets, the plant offers a tour of the factory, a 325-seat cafe with live music, and various interactive exhibits.

In 2000, the plant will become the home of the Smithsonian Rock and Soul Museum exhibit, which opened in Washington, D.C. and subsequently toured the country. Find out more online at www.gibson.com.

Memphis Music Hall of Fame

For music fans, the Hall of Fame, 97 S. 2nd St., tel. (901) 525-4007, is itself worth a trip to Memphis. This place pays homage to Memphis music from slave days until the present. Exhibits begin with stark-looking slave shackles and collars and a 1783 map showing slave routes, and the visitor is immersed in recordings of classic blues artists scattered among 18 videos showing rare movie footage of performers such as Bessie Smith, Furry Lewis, and Robert Timothy Wilkins, a 1920s performer often called "the original Rolling Stone."

Instruments on hand include Gus Cannon's banjo, and guitars played by Memphis Minnie, B.B. King, Johnny Shines, Howlin' Wolf, Johnny Cash, and Carl Perkins. The hall also boasts the largest collection of Elvis memorabilia outside of Graceland. Most of the original recording equipment from Sun Studios is here, as are two of the saxophones used on Jackie Brenston's "Rocket 88," recorded in Memphis and generally regarded

as the first rock single. The hall also contains all four instruments belonging to Booker T and the MGs and a Jerry Lee Lewis piano. Admission is $7.50 for adults, and $2.50 for kids 6 to 12.

Sun Studio

Sun Studio, 706 Union Ave., tel. (901) 521-0664, is where it all began. Sam Phillips here recorded a shy truck driver who wanted to make a record for his mother, and on subsequent visits the once and forever King of Rock 'n' Roll took flight. The studio attracts gawkers during the day and, at night, earnest artists who fervently hope that the old luck will strike again. The Irish group U2 came here in 1988 and laid down tracks that became five songs on *Rattle and Hum.*

Visitors—an astonishing number from Europe—get a 30-minute guided studio tour, which consists of stepping into the studio, hearing a spiel, and listening to clips of songs recorded

Sam Phillips made musical history in the 1950s at Sun Studio, where he launched the careers of R&B and rock'n'roll musicians, Elvis Presley among them.

MURRAY LEE/STATE PHOTOGRAPHIC SERVICES

IN THE FOOTSTEPS OF THE KING

The individual associated with Memphis more than any other person is Elvis Aaron Presley, who was born in Tupelo, Mississippi, and moved to Memphis as a teenager. Except for his years in the Army and his numerous performances in concerts, movies, and television shows, he never left Memphis, eventually settling in a mansion called Graceland.

Elvis sold an estimated one billion records, enough to give every single person in America four Elvis albums or singles. In the U.S. he had 111 albums or singles that sold enough copies to be certified gold, platinum, or multiplatinum.

Perhaps no one could withstand that kind of success and the resulting adulation. To do something as simple as go to a movie, Elvis had to rent a theater and see it at night. Through it all, according to those who knew him, Elvis remained a person whose greatest pleasure was sitting around a piano and harmonizing with friends. Those wanting the definitive book on Elvis—and there are scores from which to choose—should seek out Peter Guralnick's two-volume biography. The first book, *Last Train to Memphis,* was published in 1994, and the second volume *Careless Love,* came out in late 1998. The first takes Elvis from birth until he enters the Army, and the second chronicles the long decline. Both are outstanding.

Elvis died on August 16, 1977, at the age of 42, a victim of his lifestyle and, some argue, a management that primarily focused on money and kept him isolated. Fans began arriving within hours of his death, and Memphis and the country marveled at the devotion and sense of loss these people dis-

played. He was initially entombed in a mausoleum at Forest Hill Cemetery, but the presence of fans convinced the family to move his and his mother's remains to Graceland.

The strip mall across from Graceland almost overnight became a tacky series of Elvis souvenir shops, many of them hawking bootleg Elvis paraphernalia. The fans continued to come, especially on the anniversaries of his birth and death. Vernon Presley, Elvis's father, died in 1979, and the last relative to live in Graceland, Elvis's grandmother, Minnie Mae, died a year later.

Priscilla Presley, Elvis's wife, decided to open Graceland to the public, and the first visitors came on June 7, 1982. The next year, Graceland took over the shopping center across the street and, once the tenants' leases expired, transformed it into a major part of the Graceland complex, which has become the greatest tourist attraction in Memphis. The White House is the only house in America that receives more visits.

A trip to Graceland is worth taking, if for no other reason than to see one's fellow pilgrims. Guests—whether punk rockers, beehive-coiffed fundamentalists, bus tours of senior citizens, or curious teenagers—tend to speak in hushed tones as they walk through the mansion and gaze into places such as the Jungle Room, a denlike room containing heavy, hand-carved wooden furniture upholstered in fake animal fur. They reverently look up close at one of Elvis's jumpsuits or marvel at the wallful of gold records. Visitors are treated with respect and not rushed through, and the whole experience is unlike anything else in the country.

Graceland has become a shrine for millions of Elvis fans

Graceland

The legacy of The King consists of museums and exhibits at his mansion Graceland, 3734 Elvis Presley Blvd., tel. (800) 238-2000 or (901) 332-3322. To see the whole works, go for the **Platinum Tour,** which includes everything and costs $17 for adults, $15.30 for seniors, and $11 for children five to 12. This tour takes two to three hours.

Graceland Proper is a tour of the mansion, including the Jungle Room, the gravesite, and various outbuildings. This costs $9 for adults, $8.10 for seniors, and $4.75 for children five to 12. **The Elvis Presley Automobile Museum** displays cars, motorcycles, and other vehicles owned by Elvis and costs $5 for adults, $4.50 for seniors, and $2.75 for children five to 12. **The Lisa Marie Jet and Hound Dog II Jetstar Planes Tour** depicts the way Elvis traveled, for which visitors fork out $4.50 for adults, $4.05 for seniors, and $2.75 for children five to 12. Then there's **Sincerely Elvis,** a museum offering a look at personal items: home movies, snapshots, riding tack, sports equipment, and stage outfits. This costs $3.50 for adults, $3.15 for seniors, and $2.25 for children five to 12. The one free item at Graceland is a 21-minute film on the life and music of Elvis.

The rest of the Graceland complex includes gift shops and restaurants. Graceland is open seven days a week except Nov.- Feb., when the mansion tour is closed on Tuesday. The aircraft and other museums, however, are open every day except New Year's Day, Thanksgiving, and Christmas. The ticket office is open 7:30 a.m.- 6 p.m. Memorial Day weekend through Labor Day, and 8:30 a.m.-5 p.m. the rest of the year. The last mansion tour begins when the ticket office closes, and the self-paced tours stay open two hours after the ticket office closes.

Pilgrims can see the grave of Elvis for free most mornings for 90 minutes before the paying visitors start coming in. Walk-up time ends 30 minutes before that day's tours begin.

Favorite Spots around Town

Several of the following are more fully described in the appropriate section in the Memphis chapter. True devotees should pick up a copy of Sharon Colette Urquhart's *Placing Elvis: A Tour Guide to the Kingdom,* published by the Paper Chase Press of New Orleans.

Elvis attended his senior prom at the **Peabody Hotel** and bought records at **Poplar Tunes.** The owners have maintained this downtown store as it looked in the '50s—complete with photos of Elvis. **Sun Studio** was the site of his first recording.

The **Overton Park Shell,** 1928 Poplar Ave., was the site of a famous 1954 Elvis performance in which with just two songs he blew away Slim Whitman, the headliner. Elvis used to rent **Libertyland Amusement Park,** site of his last public appearance, for all-night fun with his girlfriends and cronies. His favorite ride was the Zippin Pippin, now the oldest operating wooden roller coaster in the country. He would ride it again and again. One of the cars he used to ride in has been preserved, and guests are welcome to sit in it and have their photos taken.

Events and Information

Elvis Presley's Birthday Tribute takes place January 6-8 at Graceland. The schedule of events varies from year to year, so call for specifics, tel. (901) 332-3322 or (800) 238-2000.

The second week in August brings **Elvis Week,** a.k.a. "Death Week," built around the anniversary of his death on August 16, 1977. This is a giant reunion for his fan clubs and includes a variety of activities and Elvis movies every night. This is your chance to see the only Graceland-sanctioned Elvis impersonator competition; Elvis Week culminates with a candlelight vigil over his grave. Send for a brochure or call (901) 332-3322 or (800) 238-2000 for additional information. The only authorized Elvis Web site is www.elvispresley.com.

Elvis in 1968

ELVIS PRESLEY ENTERPRISES, INC.

here. Vintage instruments, microphones, and photos of the stars adorn the walls. Sun Studio also operates a cafe, which serves "'50s food"—cheeseburgers, barbecue, Dixie Fried Banana Pie, and the King's favorite sandwich—fried peanut butter and banana on white bread.

At night this place reverts to its role as a recording studio. Admission is $8.50 for adults. Anyone under 12 is admitted free. The restaurant and upstairs gift shop are free. Find out more online at www.geocities.com/Nashville/5826 or www.sunstudio.com.

W.C. Handy Museum

This house, on Beale St. at 4th St., tel. (901) 522-1556 or (901) 527-3427, is the small home of the man who published the first piece of music with "blues" in the title. Born in Alabama, Handy made his musical name in Memphis as a composer and bandleader. Long after he died, this house was moved to Beale Street as part of its gentrification. Admission is $2 or $1 for kids.

The Jerry Lee Lewis Ranch

Possibly the only one of Elvis's contemporaries who can still play the way he tore it up in the '50s, Jerry Lee Lewis has now opened his home to the public. It is in Nesbit, Mississippi, just a few minutes from the Tennessee border.

Visitors to the 35-acre "ranch" can see the house, one lake, 17 dogs, 13 cars, a Harley-Davidson motorcycle, a piano-shaped swimming pool, and a horse. That's the outside. Inside, where "The Killer" actually lives, guests are escorted—would anyone walk through this house unescorted?—into the living room, various halls, and the den, all presided over by his sixth wife. They can see the kitchen but cannot go in it, and the bedrooms—where Jerry Lee might be sleeping when guests come through—are also off limits. Very rarely, Jerry Lee comes out and greets guests, but they should not count on this happening.

Call (601) 429-1290 between 9 a.m. and 5 p.m. to make reservations for the tours. Tickets cost $15 per person—man, woman, or child. Group rates are available.

To get to the ranch, take I-55 south into Mississippi. Get off at the Pleasant Hill Rd. Exit and go left—east—to a four-way stop at the intersection of Getwell Road. Continue straight to another four-way at Malone Road. Go right, and the ranch is on the right. A large fence covered with graffiti surrounds the property, and the wooden gates have pianos on them.

HISTORIC SITES

Houses of Worship

The **Beale Street Baptist Church,** 379 Beale St., tel. (901) 522-9073, was the first church in Memphis built by blacks for a black congregation; it demonstrates the economic power generated by former slaves right after the war. People still worship here, and visitors are welcome.

Mason Temple Church of God in Christ, 930 Mason St., tel. (901) 578-3800, is the headquarters of the Church of God in Christ, the largest black Pentecostal denomination in the country. Services are no longer held regularly here, but people still come to see where the Reverend Martin Luther King Jr. gave his final sermon, the "I've been to the mountaintop" speech. Admission is free.

Burkle Estate/Slavehaven

The estate, 826 N. 2nd St., tel. (901) 527-3427, is a small house built by German immigrant Jacob Burkle, whose home is believed to have served as a station on the Underground Railroad in slavery days. A secret room in the basement has a tunnel that may have provided escaped slaves with a path to freedom.

Kids and adults alike are intrigued by the trap door and hidden room here. Admission is $5 for adults, $4 for seniors, and $3 for children six to 18.

Hunt-Phelan Home

If visitors have time for only one historic home, the Hunt-Phelan Home, 533 Beale St., tel. (901) 344-3166 or (800) 350-9009, is the one to see. On the east end of Beale St.—far from the sounds of the blues—it is the last of what used to be a neighborhood of antebellum mansions. The house, built sometime between 1828 and 1840 on what was then the frontier, has a tunnel through which residents could escape any Indian attacks. The home had running water, forced air heat, and gas lights before any other house in the area.

Jefferson Davis was a frequent guest in the house before the Civil War, and during that conflict U.S. Grant took over the house, using it as his headquarters and planning the campaign against Vicksburg while sitting at the library table. When Grant left, a series of Union officers including William T. Sherman stayed there, and the kitchen was used as a hospital for Union soldiers. Immediately after the war the house was used as one of the first Freedmen's Bureau's schools.

After exacting a promise not to charge the federal government for the years it used the house, Pres. Andrew Johnson—who had been a guest in the house before the war—pardoned William Hunt and returned his house to him. Hunt spent years putting it back in shape. Over the decades the house presided over many changes in the neighborhood and reached a low point in the 1960s when it was included in the Beale St. Urban Renewal project and earmarked for destruction. The owner used his political connections to get the second President Johnson to remove this historic house from the project and thus save it.

After a $1 million renovation, the house was opened to the public in 1996. Managed by the same people who run Graceland, the Hunt-Phelan Home includes antiques dating from 1608. Admission for adults is $10, seniors and students $9, and children five to 12 $6. Find out more online at www.huntphelan.com.

More Historic Houses

Magevney House, 198 Adams Ave., tel. (901) 526-4464, is a modest home once owned by Memphis's first Irish immigrant and one of the older buildings left in the city. No Southern mansion, it is the site of the first Mass celebrated in the city and features 1830s period furnishings. Admission is free, but donations are cheerfully accepted. Visit online at www.memphismuseum.org.

Mallory-Neely House, 652 Adams Ave., tel. (901) 523-1484, shows how Memphians with money spent it. This mansion was built about 1852, extensively remodeled in the 1880s and 1890s, and decorated with original furnishings. Admission is $5 adults and $4 for seniors. Young folks kindergarten- to college-age get in free. Find out more online at www.memphismuseum.org.

Woodruff-Fontaine House, 680 Adams Ave., tel. (901) 526-1469, stands beside the Mallory-Neely House in the Victorian Village Historic District. This mansion was erected in 1870, has 16 rooms, and contains period furnishings and changing exhibits. Occasionally special events such as mystery dinners and plays take place in the house. Admission is $5 for adults, $4 for seniors, and $2 for students.

MUSEUMS

History

The National Civil Rights Museum, 450 Mulberry St., tel. (901) 521-9699, is in the Lorraine Motel, where Martin Luther King, Jr. was felled by an assassin's bullet. Using state-of-the-art technologies combined with artifacts and documents, the museum tells the story of the Civil Rights

The National Civil Rights Musuem preserves a lunch counter sit-in.

movement and presents a vivid picture of discrimination. A good example of this is a 1950s-era bus in which, when visitors sit down, they hear harsh voices commanding them to move to the back. If the would-be bus rider stays in the seat, he or she feels and hears the rapping of a cane on the seat's back.

The museum is a sobering place, but one that should be on anyone's short list of things to see in Memphis. Admission is $6 for adults, $5 for seniors and students with ID, and $4 for children 4 to 17. Find out more online at www.civilrightsmuseum.org.

The **Mississippi River Museum's** 18 galleries contain displays on Memphis and regional history from prehistoric times to the present. (See "Mud Island," below.)

Art

The **Art Museum** of the University of Memphis is housed in the Communications and Fine Arts Building at 3750 Norriswood, tel. (901) 678-2224. It displays Egyptian as well as West African art. The chief example of the former is the mummy Iret-Iruw. Other galleries exhibit contemporary works. Admission is free.

The Dixon Gallery and Gardens, 4339 Park Ave., tel. (901) 761-5250, features collections of French and American Impressionism, 18th-century German porcelain, and European and American pewter. The gallery hosts traveling exhibits as well. The gardens consist of 17 acres containing a formal English garden, a woodland garden, and a cuttings garden. Admission is $5 for adults, $4 for seniors, $3 for students with ID, and $1 for children 5 -11. Check it out online at www.dixon.org.

Memphis Brooks Museum of Art, Overton Park, 1934 Poplar Ave., tel. (901) 722-3500, is the oldest art museum in the state and one of the larger ones in the South. Given to the city by the widow of Samuel Brooks in 1915, the museum displays pieces by Renoir, Thomas Hart Benton, and Rodin along with paintings, sculpture, prints, drawings, photographs, antiquities such as Greek vases, and African and Latin American art. The museum also offers lectures and film and performance series.

The permanent collection is too large to display all at once, so exhibits are changed from time to time, and the museum also hosts traveling exhibitions. Admission to the permanent collection is $5 for adults, $4 for seniors, and $2 for students with ID and kids 7-17. Find out more online at www.brooksmuseum.org.

Nathan and Dorothy Shainberg Gallery at the Memphis Ave. Jewish Community Center, 6560 Poplar Ave., tel. (901) 761-0810, changes its exhibits of sculpture, pottery, paintings, and lithographs monthly. It's handicapped-accessible.

Science

Chucalissa Archaeological Museum, 1987 Indian Village Dr., tel. (901) 785-3160, is run by the anthropology department of the University of Memphis and sheds light on the original residents of the bluff. On the site of an actual Indian village, it has been reconstructed to demonstrate Indian life in the 1400s. Visitors get guided tours and can see present-day Choctaw Indians demonstrate ancient crafts and ways of life. Admission is $5 for adults and $3 for seniors and children four to 11.

Memphis Pink Palace Museum and Planetarium, 3050 Central Ave., tel. (901) 320-6320, began in 1923 as the palatial home of Clarence Saunders, the founder of Southern favorite Piggly Wiggly, the nation's first self-serve grocery store. Saunders went broke and the city took his house. The city's best natural history museum, this complex contains fossils, rocks and minerals, a planetarium, and an IMAX theater. Cultural aspects of Memphis and the surrounding area are on exhibit as well. The Pink Palace is open seven days a week. Admission is $6 for adults, $5.50 for seniors, and $4.50 for children three to 12. Find out more online at www. MemphisMuseums.org.

Specialty

The Children's Museum of Memphis, 2525 Central Ave., tel. (901) 458-2678, offers hands-on fun and learning. Kids can climb over a fire truck, try a wheelchair, and enjoy special demonstrations. Admission is $5 for adults and $4 for seniors and children 12 and under. Kids must be accompanied by an adult. See it on the Internet at www.cmom.com.

The **Downtown Police Station Museum,** 159 Beale St., tel. (901) 528-2370, probably has the best security system of any museum. This free museum inside a police station displays an old jail cell, police uniforms, confiscated weapons, photos of "Machine Gun" Kelly, and the extradition order for James Earl Ray, convicted assassin of Martin Luther King, Jr. It's open 24 hours a day.

The **Fire Museum of Memphis,** 118 Adams St., tel. (901) 320-5650, occupies the refurbished 1910 Fire Engine House Number 1 at 118 Adams Street. The museum's displays will include equipment, artifacts, uniforms, and photos regarding fire fighting. Admission is $5 for adults and $4 for seniors and children 3-12. It's on the Web at www.firemuseum.com.

The **National Ornamental Metal Museum,** 374 Metal Museum Dr., tel. (901) 774-6380, pays tribute to metalsmithing, be it working with exquisite gold or hammering red-hot iron on an anvil. This place displays items varying in size and complexity from handmade nails to a beautiful outdoor iron gazebo. Visiting artists do their work while guests watch, and exhibits change from time to time. Admission is $3 for adults, $2 for seniors, and $1 for kids five to 18. Find out more online at www.metalmuseum.org.

MUD ISLAND

Mud Island, out in the Mississippi, was a gift to Memphis from the river, which began depositing sediments early in this century. The island offers a 52-acre park with several attractions for visitors. It is open spring, summer, and autumn (approximately April-Oct.), with separate schedules for each season. Call ahead for specifics. For all the attractions including the monorail to the island, the admission is $8 for adults and $6 for children and seniors. Admission to the grounds only—everything but the museum—is $4 for adults and $3 for children. The park includes the following: the Mississippi River Museum; River Walk, a five-block-long scale model of the river; the *Memphis Belle* Pavilion; gift shops; and restaurants. To get to Mud Island, catch the monorail at Front and Adams Streets. Call (901) 576-7241 or (800) 507-6507 with questions.

The *Memphis Belle* B-17 bomber flew 25 missions over Germany in World War II without any crewmen getting hurt, then it starred in a 1943 documentary meant to lift spirits stateside. The story was updated for *Memphis Belle,* a 1980s film. The old plane, restored and sitting under a white canopy, now fights only the pigeons, who fly sorties against it regularly. See it online at www.memphisbelle.com.

River Walk is a five-block-long scale rendition—30 inches to one mile—of the 1,238-mile-long Mississippi River, complete with flowing water. Would-be Paul Bunyans can stroll upstream or downstream, learning about the river and its cities and points of interest along the way. The "Gulf of Mexico" in this model is a swimming pool.

The **Mississippi River Museum** has 18 galleries containing displays on Memphis and regional history from prehistoric times to the present. Among the offerings are 35 scale models of riverboats—flatboats, keelboats, packet steamers, ironclads, and so on. Some of these models are six to eight feet long. The museum has full-sized replicas of parts of boats such as a city-class Civil War ironclad and a packet boat, complete with grand salon, pilot house, and foredeck, through which visitors can walk—kids love it. And music lovers will appreciate the way the museum traces the evolution of music from field hollers to blues to ragtime to rock. Exhibits include one of Elvis's performance jumpsuits and a replica of a honky-tonk.

MORE SIGHTS

The Peabody Hotel

This hotel, 149 Union Ave., tel. (901) 529-4000, is the grande dame of Memphis hotels, a place once said to be the northern terminus of the Mississippi Delta. What began as a 1930s drunken afternoon prank—putting live ducks in the lobby fountain—has become a twice-daily exercise with ceremony exceeded only by Masonic rites. At 11 in the morning the ducks march in and at 5 they march out. It's as simple as that. Admission is free, and visitors can subsequently retire to one of the Peabody's watering holes for libations of the stimulant or depressive variety.

The Peabody Memorabilia Room, near the northwest corner of the mezzanine beside the Alonzo Locke Room, contains old menus, photos, tableware, and original documents donated by guests of the hotel. Together these offer a look at high society of the Old South and a grand old hotel. The Peabody is open all the time. Find out more online at www.peabodymemphis.com.

The Pyramid

The Pyramid, One Auction Ave., tel. (901) 521-9675, is arguably the most distinctive such multipurpose building in the country. This 32-story pyramid—the third largest in the world, behind a couple in Egypt—contains a 22,500-seat arena used for sports events, concerts, and other gatherings. Tours go through the building, through sports locker rooms and dressing rooms for star performers. Because of demands on the building, tour hours vary. Admission is $4 for adults, $3 for seniors and children four to 11.

Delectables

Agricenter International, Inc., 7777 Walnut Grove Rd., tel. (901) 757-7777, consists of a demonstration farm and exhibition facilities that have frequent shows open to the public. The **Red Barn** operates as a farmer's market from May well into December. Its website is www.agricenter.org.

Coors Belle Hospitality Center, Coors Memphis Brewery, 5151 E. Raines Rd., tel. (901) 368-BEER, gives guests a look at how this Colorado-based elixir is packaged. After the tour, adults can quaff two choices of Coors products. Admission is free. For directions, call (901) 375-2100.

Due east of Memphis lies **Cordova Cellars,** tel. (901) 754-3442, a winery that produces chardonnay, merlot, apple cider, and other beverages. To get there, take I-40 E to the Germantown S Exit—Exit 16—and turn right onto the Germantown Parkway. Go 2.7 miles, then turn left onto Macon Rd. at the traffic light. Go 2.2 miles through the Cordova community to the winery's driveway.

Danny Thomas-ALSAC Pavilion, St. Jude Children's Research Hospital

A young entertainer with seven dollars in his pocket got down on his knees in a Detroit church before a statue of St. Jude, the patron saint of lost causes, and asked the saint to "show me my way in life." At another turning point in his life, he again prayed to the saint and pledged to someday build a shrine to St. Jude.

The young man was Danny Thomas (1914-91), whom those of a certain age remember as the star of a popular television show called *Make Room For Daddy,* a spin-off of which was *The Andy Griffith Show.* In the 1950s he began to look for a way to make good on his pledge and, though he had no connection to Memphis, he decided to build a children's hospital here. Thomas, who came from a Lebanese family, joined other Arab-Americans in raising money to help fund a research hospital devoted to curing catastrophic diseases in children of the world.

The hospital, 332 N. Lauderdale, opened its doors in 1962 and focuses on pediatric leukemia, solid tumor forms of cancer, and biomedical research. Since then it has treated more than 13,500 children from around the world regardless of race, religion, creed, or ability to pay. Thomas died in 1991, having lived to see his hospital—and his pledge to St. Jude—become one of the best-known hospitals in the country.

The American Lebanese Syrian Associated Charities (ALSAC) has full responsibility for all of the hospital's fundraising efforts. At the pavilion, visitors can tour a museum featuring various aspects and memorabilia of Thomas's life, and can visit his gravesite. Admission is free. For a tour of the hospital, call ahead to (901) 495-3661. Find the hospital on the Internet at www.stjude.org.

PARKS AND ZOOS

Tom Lee Park, on the riverfront south of Beale St., commemorates the 1925 heroics of Tom Lee, a black laborer who took a small boat and rescued 32 people from a sinking steamboat. Lee made repeated trips to the stricken craft, even though he could not swim.

Memphis Botanic Garden, 750 Cherry Rd., Audubon Park, tel. (901) 685-1566, is a 96-acre park of outdoor gardens featuring beautiful flowers, exotic plants and trees, and sculptures. Admission is adults $2, seniors $1.50, children $1, and under six free. Admission is free on Tuesday 12:30 p.m.-closing.

Lichterman Nature Center, 5992 Quince Rd., tel. (901) 767-7322, is a great place to learn about wildlife and four kinds of West Tennessee habitat: forest, field, marsh, and lake. Various trails lead through the 65 acres there, and guided tours take place on weekends. More than 1,000 injured animals are brought here every year for rehabilitation, and visitors can see some of these. Admission is $2 for adults, $1 for seniors and children ages 3 to 18.

Memphis Zoo, 2000 Galloway, Overton Park, tel. (901) 276-WILD, spent $30 million providing habitats such as Primate Canyon, Cat Country, Animals of the Night, and so on. These habitats are designed to reflect cultural elements of the animals' native countries. Thus North African species are shown around what looks like an abandoned temple à la Indiana Jones. Admission is $8 for adults, $6 for seniors, and $5 for children two to 11. Free on Tuesday afternoons. Find out more online at www.memphiszoo.org.

At 4,500 acres, **Shelby Farms** in the eastern part of the city has to be one of the largest urban parks in the country. It offers hiking trails that wind through hardwood forests and orchards; a 60-acre lake ideal for windsurfing, canoeing, and sailing; a herd of buffalo; and picnic areas. The wildlife here includes an estimated 217 species of birds.

AMUSEMENT PARKS

Libertyland Amusement Park, 940 Early Maxwell Blvd., tel. (901) 274-8800, is a theme park that features 23 rides, live music, an assortment of places to eat, and things to see. This was the park that Elvis used to rent for all-night fun with his friends, riding a wooden roller coaster called the Zippin Pippin over and over. One of the roller coaster cars on which he used to ride has been preserved, and guests can sit in it and have their photos taken. Elvis's last public appearance before he died was at Libertyland. Admission to all rides is $16 for adults and kids. The $7 ticket pays for admission to the park, all shows, and kiddy rides. Those 55 and over get in free. Preview the park online at www.memphisnet.com/libertyland.

CRUISES AND TOURS

On the Water
The boats of **Memphis Queen Line Riverboats,** foot of Monroe Ave. at 45 Riverside Dr., tel. (901)

SOUTH OF THE BORDER GAMBLING

In many ways Memphis is considered the capital of northern Mississippi, but the enormous number of casino ads directed at visitors can easily make them think they are already in Mississippi. The success of these ventures is an extension of the Southern-in-general-and-Tennessee-in-particular attitude toward vice: You can have it, but we don't want to hear about it.

Gambling is forbidden throughout Tennessee, yet in many counties country clubs and fraternal organizations—Elks, Moose, etc.—have slot machines that are ignored by the local constabulary unless a spectacular raid is needed to bolster reelection efforts. Often the same counties will ban alcoholic beverages, a prohibition endorsed by Baptists and bootleggers alike.

Mississippi is taking this attitude and riding it all the way to the bank. In 1989 the Mississippi state legislature voted to allow riverboat gambling on navigable waters. The key word here is "navigable," which has been interpreted to mean large trenches barely deep enough to float barges. Indeed, if these vessels threatened to sink and any passenger leaped off, he or she would probably hit dry land.

The first casinos opened in 1992, and since then a host of others, including Harrah's, Bally's, and Circus Circus, have opened and set about parting Memphians and visitors from their money. Anyone arriving in Memphis will be barraged with billboards and ads touting various casinos.

Is it worth a trip? If you have never been to a casino, by all means go. The worldly travelers who have been to Atlantic City or Nevada, however, will find these places a bit tame. To get there, take Hwy. 61 or I-55 and head south. Anyone who cannot find the casinos has no business going there.

Tunica County used to be the poorest county in the entire country, but now the money is pouring in, leaving Memphis leaders to dream and scheme of ways to bring all that gambling money back home. Don't be surprised if some obscure Indian tribe surfaces to claim Mud Island, is granted instant recognition from the Memphis City Council, and opens casinos as soon as possible.

527-5694 or (800) 221-6197, offer rides that include sightseeing cruises, dinner cruises, and daylong excursions to Helena, Arkansas. Prices range $11-35. Find out more online at www.memphisqueen.com.

Sightseeing Tours

For the absolute best popular culture tour of Memphis and the surrounding area, book passage on **American Dream Safari,** (901) 527-8870, an outfit that offers tours in a 1955 Cadillac to the haunts of the King, trips through the Mississippi Delta, or custom trips tailored to the interests of visitors. Owner Tad Pearson knows the way to Al Green's church, juke joints, and the roots of the blues.

The tour isn't cheap—the least expensive is $45 per person for a three-hour excursion, but well worth it. Put on sunglasses and a stylish hat, and you'll be the center of attention wherever you go. Visit it at www.memphismojo.com/bluesride.

Heritage Tours, 280 Hernando St., tel. (901) 527-3427, is the first black-owned tour company in the state of Tennessee, and it offers perhaps the best historical tour of Memphis. The three-hour tour passes or stops at 30 or more historical sights, including Beale St., Church Park, and many lesser-known sites. Unlike the official tourist publications, these guides do not ignore the Confederate history of Memphis. "We're glad they lost," said one guide, "but it's history nonetheless." Book reservations by calling the telephone number above or by going to the W.C. Handy House on Beale St. at 4th Street.

Blues City Tours, 325 Union Ave., tel. (901) 522-9229, offers a variety of tours—Graceland, shopping, and gambling.

Germania Travel Consultant, 3482 Fox Hunt Dr., tel. (901) 794-0347, offers English and German or French language tours of Memphis and the surrounding area. Customers can choose from walking or escorted tours. Find out more online at www.freeyellow.com/member2/traveletc.

Stardust Gray Line of Memphis Tours, Inc., 2050 Elvis Presley Blvd., tel. (901) 346-8687, has a wide variety of tours, including Mud Island, Elvis haunts, and one called "Blues, Booze, and Barbecue."

guarding the gates of the Memphis Zoo

ENTERTAINMENT AND EVENTS

STAGE AND SCREEN

Venues

Blues City Cultural Center is at 205 N. Main St., tel. (901) 525-3031.

The **Mud Island Amphitheater** showcases name entertainers during warm weather. Concerts are advertised in local newspapers.

The **Orpheum Theatre,** 203 S. Main St. at Beale St., tel. (901) 525-3000, was constructed in 1888 as the Grand Opera House. It has been beautifully restored with chandeliers, tapestries, and gilt architectural features, and now it hosts concerts and other productions.

Music and Dance

Name bands play live bluegrass most Friday nights at **The Harvester Lane Bluegrass Show,** 2984 Harvester Ln. in Frayser (north Memphis). The show is performed in the 250-seat old union hall; no drinking or smoking is permitted. To find out the schedule, call (901) 358-3486.

Ballet Memphis performs four programs a year at the historic Orpheum Theatre, 203 S. Main St. at Beale St. tel. (901) 763-0139. Find out more online at www.balletmemphis.org.

Memphis Symphony Orchestra, 3100 Walnut Grove Rd., Suite 501, tel. (901) 324-3627, stages a host of concerts at sites around the city. Its Elvis Week concert is always a big hit. Get more information on the Internet at www.memphissymphony.org.

Opera Memphis, University of Memphis, South Campus, Building no.47, tel. (901) 678-2706, stages four operas or musicals a year in addition to concerts.

Theater

Circuit Playhouse, 1705 Poplar Ave., tel. (901) 726-4656, presents 10 plays a year, titles such as *Jeffrey, Voices of the South,* and *Sylvia.* The

---

MAKING THE SCENE AT THE MAP ROOM

The corner of Main and Madison downtown is the Map Room, tel. (901) 579-9924, an eclectic combination of bookstore, library, restaurant, tearoom, place to get a beer, live music venue, and collecting point for unusual souls. Here the visitor can sign up for the Manhole Cover Tour, Ghost Tour, and a few other offbeat ramblings through Memphis. Some nights the best thing to do is just watch the people who show up. Definitely hip. See the website at www.memphismaproom.com.

at the Map Room (left to right): Jade Pagoda, Darla Devlin, Beverly Lynn, and Valentina Violett

MEMPHIS RADIO

Memphis has two radio stations of which visitors should take particular note, one FM and one AM.

WEVL is a volunteer-run, public station with the sort of eclectic programming one would expect in this most musical of cities. At 90.0 on the dial, this station dishes up bluegrass, blues, old-time country music, acoustic, and so on. See the station's website at www.wevl.com.

At 1070 on the AM band, WDIA was the first all-black formatted radio station in the South; since 1948 generations of people have listened to its blues, gospel, and disc jockeys. This station had a profound effect on early rock 'n' roll musicians in the area, who were influenced by on-air personalities such as B.B. King and Rufus "Do the Funky Chicken" Thomas.

WDIA still has great music.

---

shows here tend to be a bit more experimental than those of some of Memphis's other theaters.

The more than 400 volunteers of **Germantown Community Theatre,** 3037 Forest Hill Rd., tel. (901) 754-2680, help work up seven shows a year—straight plays, musicals, and comedies.

Germantown Performing Arts Centre, 1801 Exeter Rd., tel. (901) 757-7256, books concerts, dance, and theatrical productions. Call for tickets or information.

Playhouse on the Square, 51 S. Cooper St., tel. (901) 726-4656, is Memphis's only professional repertory theater group. The Playhouse presents eight productions per year, shows such as *Ain't Misbehaving, Steel Magnolias,* and *Three Tall Women.*

Theatre Memphis, 630 Perkins Extended, tel. (901) 682-8323, has two venues, one seating 435 and the other seating 100. The larger house offers mainstream plays and musicals, while the smaller theater leans more toward the avant-garde.

At the Movies
Be sure to visit **Union Planter's IMAX Theater,** Memphis Pink Palace Museum, 3050 Central Ave., tel. (901) 763-4629 (information), (901) 320-6362 (reservations), or (901) 320-6320 (general office). IMAX movies use enormous film—

one frame is the size of a playing card—projected onto a huge screen and backed with a blow-back-your-hair sound system.

FESTIVALS AND EVENTS

Memphis has a wider range of events than any place in Tennessee. What follows are just the highlights. For complete information, call the numbers listed at the end of this chapter.

January
Elvis Presley's Birthday Tribute takes place January 6-8 at Graceland. The schedule of events varies from year to year, so call for specifics, tel. (901) 332-3322 or (800) 238-2000.

February
Beale Street Zydeco Fest, held sometime around the second weekend in February, features zydeco music—the infectious dance music invented by black Creole folks. Most of the

---

THE LUCY OPRY

Memphis is as far in Tennessee as one can get from the geographic origins of bluegrass music, but fanciers of that high, lonesome sound can get their fill at the Lucy Opry, held every Friday night the Frayser community north of Memphis. While the occasional local plays, this place books name performers along the lines of the Osborne Brothers and Jim and Jesse. Admission is charged.

This "opry" used to be held in the town of Lucy—thus the name—but now is held in a UAW Hall at 2984 Harvester Lane. To get there from downtown, go east on Union Ave. until it intersects with Thomas St., a.k.a. Hwy. 51. Go north for five miles, then turn left onto Whitney Ave., and a half mile later turn right onto E. Harvester Lane. It is just a couple hundred yards to the Hall.

Coming on the Interstate? Take I-240 north of Memphis to the Millington Exit—2A—and go north on Hwy. 51. Turn left at the second traffic light, then go six or seven blocks and then right on Harvester. For more information, call (901) 358-3486, (901) 357-6432, or (901) 357-1221.

artists come from Louisiana. This is a one-day deal running 3 p.m.-5 a.m. Visitors can buy a wristband that will let them into all 12 of the clubs on Beale Street.

April

Spring Memphis Music Festival is the kick-off for the musical season. Held indoors and out along Beale Street in early April, it's a one-day event that features more than three dozen local musicians. Visitors buy wristbands that permit them to club-hop among the 12 clubs and attend the outdoor festivities. The festival runs 3 p.m.-5 a.m.; a main stage is erected in Handy Park with a concert 1-9 p.m. Call (901) 526-0110.

Crossroads, held annually in April, is a three-day music festival for up-and-coming musicians to strut their stuff in front of the music industry and the general public. The artists are categorized in 10 genres, including country, blues, alternative rock, gospel, metal, urban, rap, and singer/songwriter. After buying admission wrist tags (less than $10), visitors can flit from club to club on Beale St. and Marshall Avenue. Crossroads also offers outdoor events such as a street party, gospel tent, etc. For specifics, call (901) 526-4280.

May

Cotton may no longer reign as king hereabouts, but vestiges of those days remain in two Memphis events. The **Carnival Memphis,** which used to be the Cotton Carnival, was organized by planters and, somewhat akin to Mardi Gras in New Orleans, features balls and krewes that are by invitation only and largely limited to people of the Caucasian persuasion.

The **Cotton Maker's Jubilee,** however, held late April through mid-May, is a wide-open event centering on African-Americans. The Carnation Ball in April culminates with the crowning of the king and queen of jubilee. The largest black parade in the country steps off in early May. The Barbecue Cooking Contest is held in May, and visitors can also participate in the Las Vegas Cruise and Club Room Party on the Mississippi. There is also a midway. For tickets to any of these events or for additional information, call (901) 774-1118.

Memphis in May International Cultural Festival is a monthlong shindig that salutes a different country every year. Somehow the orga-

nizers work in the World Championship Barbecue Cooking Contest, the Sunset Symphony and the Sunset Symphony Rehearsal picnic, the Beale St. Music Festival, and the International Weekend. Typically, the festival organizers bring a performing artist, such as the Thai Ballet, from the honored country for the international weekend. Visitors can select from a huge variety of events promoted by the festival. Call (901) 525-4611 for more information.

W.C. Handy Blues Awards is the Oscars of the blues world. The event is organized by the Blues Foundation and typically held in May at the Orpheum Theatre. Be sure to stay for the jam session afterward. Visitors can also participate in a two-day symposium, a Keeping-the-Blues-Alive banquet, and a moonlight cruise on the Mississippi. Call (901) 527-2583 for details.

July

Memphis Music & Heritage Festival, sponsored by the Center for Southern Folklore, celebrates regional music, food, and arts and crafts. This three-day outdoor event is usually held the third weekend in July at Court Square downtown. A huge heritage tent offers crafts demonstrations; three music stages present regional music such as blues, bluegrass, zydeco, rockabilly, and gospel; and crafts and food vendors shout their wares. This is an excellent event, and admission is free. Call (901) 525-3655.

August

The second week in August brings **Elvis Week,** a.k.a. "Death Week," built around the anniversary

---

A WORD ABOUT THE WEATHER

The astute observer will note that Memphians have their big festivals in the spring and fall. Summertime is beastly hot—temperatures of 100° combined with 95% humidity are not at all rare. This can take the starch out of even the most determined visitor—especially children.

The best times to visit are May and October. The winters aren't very cold—Memphis seldom gets enough snow to make a snowman—but rain can come almost anytime.

of his death on August 16, 1977. This is a giant reunion for fan clubs and includes a variety of activities and Elvis movies every night; this is the time to see the only Graceland-sanctioned Elvis impersonator competition. The event culminates with a candlelight vigil over his grave. Send for a brochure or call for additional information, tel. (901) 332-3322 or (800) 238-2000.

The **Memphis Blues Festival,** held the second Saturday in August, is a laid-back, lawn chairs-and-blankets kind of concert in Tom Lee Park against the banks of the Mississippi River. Visitors can listen to bands perform on multiple stages. No coolers are permitted, but beer and food are sold on site. For information, call (901) 398-6655; for tickets, call TicketMaster at (901) 525-1515.

September

September brings one of the best events in town. The annual three-day **Cooper-Young Festival,** held at the intersection of Cooper and Young Streets, features live music, crafts, and various bohemian activities. Historically this was a not-very-thriving blue-collar neighborhood that was reinvigorated with a circle of art shops, **Java Cabana** coffeehouse, and its famous chapel—The First Church of the Elvis Impersonator. Be sure to put a coin in the slot. This is a big neighborhood festival with quality arts and crafts celebrating the revitalization of the area. It is well done. Call (901) 272-3056 for more information.

The **Zoo Rendezvous** in early September is a fundraiser for the Memphis Zoo. This is an elegant adult party with food, dancing, music, decorations, and flowers. Tickets are in the range of $100 apiece (it *is* a fundraiser). Call TicketMaster to order tickets, or, for information, call (901) 276-9453.

The **Annual Labor Day Weekend Blues Bash** is the end-of-the-summer salute offering three days and nights of blues on Beale St., lots of outdoor bands, and food vendors. Visitors buy wristbands to participate in the activities. Call (901) 526-0110.

For a lot of tomfoolery and a variety of goat-related competitions, attend the **International Goat Days Festival** late in September. This fun family event is held in USA Stadium in Millington, a northern suburb of Memphis. It includes a pancake breakfast, goat chariot races, a whistling competition, egg tosses, and pill (dried goat droppings) flipping. Admission is free. Call (901) 872-4559.

December

The last night of the year brings the **Count Down on Beale.** Beginning about 8 p.m., outdoor New Year's Eve revelers listen and dance to two or three musical acts at the main stage erected in Handy Park. Then the Blue Note—a lighted neon musical note—rises to signify midnight. Fireworks follow in the park. Admission is free at the park, and revelers who prefer to party inside the clubs can buy a wristband to get into any and all of the 12 clubs on Beale Street. Call (901) 526-0110 for information.

SPECTATOR SPORTS

The **Memphis Redbirds** are unusual in baseball in that they are the only professional team run on a nonprofit basis. Part of the profits from the team are spent teaching baseball and softball to Memphis children. A part of the St. Louis Cardinals organization, the AAA-level team will play the 1999 season at Tim McCarver Stadium at the Fairgrounds, but will open the 2000 season in a brand new downtown park. **Autozone Park** is in downtown Memphis at the corner of 3rd St. and Union Ave. and seats only 14,320, ensuring a good seat for everyone. For ticket information call (901) 721-6000. Find out more online at www.memphisredbirds.com.

The **Memphis Riverkings** play AA-level professional hockey in the Central Hockey League Oct.-March. This popular team plays in the Mid-South Coliseum at the fairgrounds. For tickets call (901) 278-9009 or TicketMaster outlets, or charge them by calling (901) 525-1515. Find them online at www.riverkings.com.

The **AXA/Equitable Liberty Bowl Football Classic,** at the Mid-South Fairgrounds, seats 62,384 people for the annual December postseason bowl game. For tickets, call (901) 795-7700.

University of Memphis basketball and football teams compete in Conference USA, Division 1. The basketball team plays at the Pyramid Arena, while the football team competes at the Liberty Bowl Memorial Stadium. For tickets call the University Ticket Office, tel. (901) 678-2331. See the team on the Internet at www.gotigersgo.com.

NIGHTLIFE

The following restaurants and nightclubs were researched and reviewed by Fredric Koeppel, the restaurant and book critic for the *Memphis Commercial Appeal.* He writes nationally about wine, locally about classical music and art exhibitions, and, when it comes to the finer things in life, singlehandedly anchors the northern end of the Mississippi Delta.

Alex's Tavern, 1445 Jackson Ave., tel. (901) 278-9086, has been a hangout for Rhodes College—formerly Southwestern—students for decades. It serves great hamburgers, has one of the best jukeboxes in the city, and offers live music Tuesday-Saturday. It's open 24 hours every day and charges a small cover for weekend performances.

Americana Club, 4090 Winchester, tel. (901) 368-0994, is one of those airplane-hangar-sized spaces where thousands of cowboys and cowgirls do the hoe-down or the mashed potato or whatever they call those dances one does in a line together to such songs as "Rocky Top." Cover charge Friday and Saturday.

At **B.B. King's Blues Club,** Beale St. at 2nd St., tel. (901) 524-5464, the legendary bluesmeister himself shows up at his namesake club two or three times a year. Otherwise, various local and nationally known groups provide the music. The club is open daily, serves lunch and dinner, and charges a cover for name groups.

Barrister's, 147 Jefferson St., alley entrance, tel. (901) 523-9421, has a firm hold on new music, featuring not only the alternative sounds by emerging out-of-town groups but occasional offbeat film festivals, happenings, and the "gay matinee." Admission fees and cover charges apply.

Blues City Cafe, 138-140 Beale St., tel. (901) 526-3637, is a restaurant that serves steaks, ribs, sandwiches, and great pecan pie; it opens into The Band Box, where local and national groups provide blues and rhythm 'n' blues every night. Cover charges are nominal.

Earnestine & Hazel's, 531 S. Main St., tel. (901) 523-9754, across from the to-be-renovated Amtrak station, has served as grocery, restaurant, and whorehouse, all within living memory. Now there's no getting in the place after midnight on weekends. It's best to disguise oneself as someone between the ages of, oh, 22 and 23.

Hernando's Hide-a-way, 3210 Old Hernando Rd., off Brooks Road, tel. (901) 398-7496, must be the only old-fashioned roadhouse left in this corner of the state. It's where Jerry Lee Lewis used to go when he wanted to tickle the ivories just for fun. There's a cover charge on weekends.

High Point Pinch, 111 Jackson Ave., one block east of the Pyramid, north of the Convention Center, tel. (901) 525-4444 or (901) 525-4445, offers standard pub grub, lots of imported

IF BEALE STREET COULD TALK

In many people's minds, Memphis is so intimately identified with music that "Memphis blues" (a phrase taken from the title of a W.C. Handy song written decades ago) and "Memphis soul" are taken almost as expanded definitions. So much music has come out of the city that the first and biggest temptation facing anyone discussing Memphis music is to make grandiose and hyperbolic assertions about its importance. You know the sort of thing—calling a style "America's Music" or "America's Gift to the World," or anointing a performer or composer as the "father" (or, much more rarely, the "mother") of something or other, all in the sort of chamber of commerce histories, tourist brochures, or liner notes. And why not? After all, you are talking about B.B. King, Elvis Presley, Johnny Cash, Otis Redding, Jerry Lee Lewis, Isaac Hayes . . . and that's only picking some of the most famous names from a list that goes on and on. This sort of hand-waving exaggeration does have one advantage: It sidesteps any question that "Memphis music" is one particular thing. But is that true? What does the driving rockabilly of Carl Perkins's "Dixie Fried" have to do with the sweet soul of Al Green's "Call Me," the wrenching heartbreak of James Caar's "Rainbow Road," or the aching pop of the Box Tops' "The Letter"? What joins any of them to Furry Lewis or Rufus Thomas—or to Mud Boy and the Neutrons or the Grifters?

I'd Rather Be Here

In his "Beale Street Blues," a song that forever captures and mythologizes the excitement and danger of Memphis's nightlife ("business never closes 'til somebody gets killed"), Handy wrote of the blind man on the corner who sings, "I'd rather be here than any place I know."

Thousands, maybe even millions, have taken this (or something else that echoes its spirit) as a beckoning call to come to Memphis and hear, or maybe even make, that music for themselves. Memphis shares with New Orleans not just the blues but a sense that something at the heart of the city is just strange, eccentric, outside, of no other place, and that sense permeates the music that has been made here.

But what really makes "Memphis music" is a gritty bareness of emotion, an earthbound honesty that prevails over whatever else is going on. No one would ever confuse, although each is sublime in its own way, most soul records made in Detroit or

Philadelphia, or most country records made in Nashville, with recordings from Memphis. At times this rawness can be coarse—writer Greil Marcus once perfectly extrapolated the spirit in the lyrics of the primal Elvis Presley recording as, "That's all right, Mama, that's all right for you . . . eat shit."

While one cannot overestimate the desire of those involved in making music in Memphis to make it—remember Sun Records owner/producer Sam Phillips's famous remark (whatever he said exactly), "If I could find a white man who could sing like a black man, I would make a billion dollars"—Memphis has always been more of a music town than a music business town, with a sense that the place has a unique spirit that can't be exactly copied or entirely suppressed or prettied up, even when someone is trying to.

The "Real" Memphis

That sense both draws the tourists and the pilgrims and creates some fairly incongruous circumstances for them and the natives. The "revitalization" of Beale Street (and parts of downtown generally) and its transformation into a tourist destination are astonishing and even disorienting to anyone who remembers it not only as a barren wasteland (deserted, boarded-up buildings, where there were buildings) but also as literally nonexistent—the asphalt itself torn up, leaving nothing but the earth underneath, no "street" at all. It would probably be incomprehensible to anyone who knew the city in the early part of the century, in Beale's legendary days. Some purists certainly insist that the music there and elsewhere in the city today isn't "authentic," just a Disney version of the blues—but B.B. King has his own club now, and who could be so ungenerous as not to wish him that and any other good thing he could possibly have? These same people, a few years back, were lamenting that nobody was paying any attention at all to the music. And they would maintain that no outsider ever truly experiences the "real" Memphis. In the sort of insular parochialism that is certainly not unique to Memphis, or even the South, they would say that the real spirit can't be captured.

They Wrote About Memphis

Fortunately, some wonderful writers have certainly tried, turning their hands to the musicians and the music associated with Memphis. Peter Guralnick's work is consistently outstanding: it exhibits the enthusiasm of a lifelong fan expressed through meticulous research and a finely honed critical sense. His *Last Train to Memphis* is the definitive biography of Elvis Presley's early years. The second volume, *Careless Love,* covering the years until Elvis's death in 1977, came out in December 1998. As the title suggests, *Sweet Soul Music* describes the development of soul in general and the explosion in the black music industry in Memphis in the 1960s and early '70s in particular, including the rise and fall of the Stax/Volt record labels. *Feel Like Going Home* and *Lost Highway* contain insightful portraits of blues and country musicians, famous and neglected alike, many of them intimately connected with Memphis.

Robert Gordon's *It Came From Memphis* provides an offbeat history of the Memphis music scene from the days when wildman disc jockey Dewey Phillips's hipster rants (on his radio show *Red Hot and Blue*) brought first rhythm and blues and then rock 'n' roll to black and white audiences alike—and of what some in the audience did with the experience.

Greil Marcus has written some of the most insightful commentary on Elvis, especially in *Mystery Train,* and his *Dead Elvis* explores the posthumous neo-religious Presley subculture cult. All provide detailed guidance to particular recordings. Any one is a good place to start.

Move Out to Move Up

Despite the clubs, the crowds, and the Elvis devotees, Memphis seems, oddly, not an outstandingly good place to try to make a living as a musician. There has been no real music industry presence in Memphis since the '70s—certainly nothing on the order of that in Nashville—although there is still a lot of studio business, with everyone from internationally famous superstars such as U2 to hopeful regional favorites such as the band Joe, Mark's

Brother still hoping to find someone who will catch lightning in a bottle as Sam Phillips, Jim Dickinson, Chips Moman, and other producers did for bands years ago. But in truth, their hopes are much like those of the tourists—to come and be touched by, or connected to, some bygone glory. Many local musicians resent what they see as the industry's willingness to occasionally exploit the city's sense of identity without really investing in anything that fosters it—and the city's willingness to let it happen. After a lifetime of struggling to make a career in his hometown, one (who was finally leaving town for Nashville) said that being from Memphis was "just something to put on your resume" when trying to get jobs elsewhere. Succinctly voicing his feeling that the city merely talks a good game in presenting itself as a music center, another said, "This town is so full of it."

Take Me to the River

And yet, standing next to the river, the sun going down red over the flat Arkansas horizon, it is possible to feel that there is something there, that there is, at the risk of serving up so much (barbecued) baloney, some magic in the air that the tourist promotions are only the shadows of, some music that would be playing even if no one other than the musicians themselves were there to hear it. At the end of his masterful, joyous version of Handy's song, Louis Armstrong (who knew a thing or two about playing the blues himself) sings,

I'm goin' to the river, baby by and by,

Yes I'm goin' to the river, and there's a reason why:

Because the river's wet,

And Beale Street's done gone dry.

It remains to be seen whether or not this is true. But people are still going to the river. The best thing you can do is go and listen for yourself.

—*Franklin Jones*

---

beer, and local live music on weekends. Call to see if a cover charge is in force.

Huey's is a 26-year-old Memphis restaurant chain known for blues, brews, and burgers (and a little jazz on the side). On Sunday 4-7 p.m. musicians perform live jazz, and 8 p.m.-midnight, blues. No cover. The eateries are **Huey's Midtown,** 1927 Madison Ave., tel. (901) 726-4372; **Huey's East,** 2858 Hickory Hill Rd., tel. (901) 375-4373; and **Huey's Cordova,** 1771 N. Germantown Rd.,

tel. (901) 754-3885; 77 N. 2nd St. (across from The Peabody), tel. (901) 527-2700.

The New Daisy, 330 Beale St., tel. (901) 525-8979, supplies a constant diet of local and national groups (and boxing) in a small arena setting. Various cover changes and ticket prices apply; it's open Tues.-Saturday.

Newby's, 539 South Highland St., tel. (901) 452-8408, near the University of Memphis serves food and a bewildering variety of live music

Wed.-Saturday. The kitchen stays open very late. There's a cover charge for bands.

Otherlands, 641 S. Cooper St., tel. (901) 278-4994, is a mellow coffee bar and exotic gift store. This nonsmoking cafe serves Caravali Coffee—a Seattle blend—fresh pastries, and a new soup every day. Occasionally live music is performed—acoustic, folk, Celtic, jazz guitar, etc. The store carries home furnishings and clothing from India, Africa, South America, and local artisans.

P & H Cafe, 1532 Madison Ave., tel. (901) 726-0906, offers beer, terrific cheeseburgers, a dim, smoky pool room, and the flamboyant, many-hatted Wanda Wilson, the best-known barkeeper in town. This haven for writers, artists, actors, and journalists sports huge caricatures of notorious local political figures on the ceiling; Michelangelo comes to mind.

At **Raiford's Hollywood Disco,** 115 Vance, tel. (901) 528-9313, one can see the spires of downtown Memphis from the front door, but patrons still have to check their weapons at this late, late-night glittery dance-'n'-rap palace. It's best on Friday and Saturday nights.

Rum Boogie Cafe, 182 Beale St., tel. (901) 528-0150, is home to live rhythm 'n' blues, Memphis-style, with a backbeat you can't lose. One of Beale Street's liveliest clubs, it serves full lunch and dinner every day and offers music every night. Nominal cover charges apply.

Sleep Out Louie's, 88 Union Ave., tel. (901) 527-5337, is a bar that proves yuppies can not only survive but thrive in Memphis, though they get a bit older every year. Lunch and dinner are served every day; live entertainment is offered on Friday and Saturday. Occasional warm weather alley parties bring out thousands.

Six One Six, 600 Marshall Ave., tel. (901) 526-6552, treads the fine line between alternative rock and mainstream alternative but definitely leans toward the latter. The motto—"The Closest Thing to New York"—ain't exactly true, but this aging veteran of the Memphis club wars keeps rolling along. Dancing till dawn is the program. Cover charges escalate to actual ticket prices.

Wild Bill's Club, 1580 Vollintine, tel. (901) 726-5473, is a discreet storefront in a quiet neighborhood, but go inside and do the blues ever take one away. Call on Friday, Saturday, or Sunday to see if Big Lucky Carter is in residence.

Wolf's Corner, 530 S. Main St. across from Earnestine & Hazel's, tel. (901) 525-4538, is an old corner bar where a handful of lucky old black men listen to the best jukebox in the world. The fact that there are only 25 records on the box makes the experience not only authoritative but mystical. The place seems like it's always open.

Gay and Lesbian Hangouts

Memphis's gay and lesbian scene is not as out front as in other places.

Amnesia, 2866 Poplar Ave., tel. (901) 454-1366, barely contains within its walls the city's liveliest gay/transvestite scene and its greatest, indeed epic, drag show. It offers live music occasionally. Call about scheduled events and cover charges.

J-Wags, 1268 Madison Ave., tel. (901) 725-1909, is a longtime Memphis watering hole with drag shows and beauty contests Wed.- Saturday.

WHERE TO STAY

BED AND BREAKFASTS

Reservation Services
Bed and Breakfast About Tennessee, P.O. Box 110227, Nashville, TN 37222, tel. (615) 331-5244 or (800) 458-2421, is the oldest and the largest reservation service in the state. It represents B&Bs across the state, including almost 10 in Memphis. Call for information or reservations.

Bed and Breakfast In Memphis, P.O. Box 11141, Memphis, TN 38111-1141, is a reservation/broker service for about 15 area B&Bs and carriage houses. The rates for the B&Bs are $95 and up. The service also assists in extended stays for relocation and business travelers. For information or reservations call (901) 458-5866; for reservations only call (800) 327-6129.

In Memphis
Quite possibly the best place to stay in Memphis is **Talbot Heirs Guesthouse,** a boutique hotel directly across from the Peabody Hotel at 99 S. 2nd St., tel. (901) 527-9772, www.talbot-house.com. Here await nine guestrooms, all of which have private baths and fully functional kitchens, two phone lines with data ports, and superb concierge service. Guests have included Hal Holbrooke, David Copperfield, and Francis Ford Coppola. Rates $150-$250. Luxury.

Arbor House, 323 N. McLean Blvd., tel. (901) 278-3060, in the city's historic district bordering Overton Park, the zoo, and Brooks Art Museum, is one of the most elegant bed and breakfasts in midtown. Built in 1920, it is decorated in Victorian antiques, with a pool and gardens in the back. Arbor House has three guest rooms with private baths and one guesthouse in the back near the gardens. Rates run $80-90 and include a full breakfast served on antique china and crystal. Moderate-Expensive.

Lowenstein-Long House (also known as Bed and Breakfast in a Castle), 217 N. Waldron Blvd., tel. (901) 527-7174, is a turn-of-the-century Victorian mansion known for its elegant simplicity. The four guest rooms—one with a small adjoining room—all have private baths and cable TV. Rates are $75-80 and include a full breakfast. Find out more online at www.bbonline.com/Lowenstein. Moderate.

HOSTELS

The International Youth Hostel, 1084 Poplar Ave., tel. (901) 527-7174, offers perhaps the lowest-priced accommodations in the city. Singles cost $12 per night and a double private room costs $32.

HOTELS AND MOTELS

The major national chains are well-represented, sometimes in duplicate or triplicate, in Memphis. (See "Where to Stay" under "Accommodations and Food" in the On the Road chapter for a list of franchise accommodations.) Among the other options in Memphis, good bets are:

Moderate
Choices are **Memphis Inn,** I-240 at Perkins Rd. Exit, tel. (901) 794-8300 or (800) 770-INNS; **Memphis Inn,** I-40 and Sycamore View, 6050 Macon Cove, tel. (901) 373-9898 or (800) 770-INNS; and the **Wilson Inn East,** I-40 Exit 18, tel. (901) 372-0000 or (800) WILSONS.

Expensive
Choose from **Brownestone Hotel,** 300 N. 2nd, tel. (901) 525-2511 or (800) 468-3515; **Country Suites By Carlson,** 4300 American Way, tel. (901) 366-9333 or (800) 456-4000; **Wilson Inn-Memphis Central,** I-240 at Perkins Rd., tel. (901) 366-9300 or (800) WILSONS; **Wilson World Graceland,** 3677 Elvis Presley Blvd., tel. (901) 332-1000 or (800) WILSONS; and the **Wilson World Hotel,** I-240 at Perkins Rd., tel. (901) 366-0000 or (800) WILSONS.

Premium
Those willing to spend a little more can stay at the **The Peabody Memphis,** 149 Union Ave., tel. (901) 529-4000 or (800) PEABODY, grande

dame of Memphis hotels and home of the daily duck parade.

Other good choices are **Crowne Plaza Memphis,** 250 N. Main, tel. (901) 527-7300 or (800) 2-CROWNE; **Adam's Mark Hotel,** 939 Ridge Lake Blvd., tel. (901) 684-6664 or (800) 444-ADAM; **Embassy Suites,** 1022 S. Shady Grove Rd., tel. (901) 684-1777 or (800) EMBASSY; **French Quarter Suites Hotel,** 2144 Madison Ave., tel. (901) 728-4000 or (800) 843-0353; **Homewood Suites,** 5811 Poplar Ave., tel. (901) 763-0500; and **The Ridgeway Inn,** 5679 Poplar Ave., tel. (901) 766-4000 or (800) 822-3360.

CAMPING

Agricenter International, Inc., 7777 Walnut Grove Rd., tel. (901) 757-7777, doesn't sound as if it were a campground, but this place has room for something like 293 RVs. It's open year-round.

Elvis Presley Boulevard RV Park, tel. (901) 332-3633, lies within walking distance of Graceland. It offers tent sites and full hookups. Take the boulevard exit from I-55, I-40, or I-240 and follow signs. It's open year-round.

KOA Memphis East, eight miles east on I-40 Exit 20 at 3291 Shoehorn Dr. in Lakeland, tel. (901) 388-3053, has 100 sites with full amenities. It's open all year and offers tours to Graceland, riverboats, and Mud Island.

KOA Memphis/Graceland-Elvis Presley Boulevard RV Park, 3691 Elvis Presley Blvd., tel. (901) 396-7125, is across the street from Graceland. It offers 72 full hookup sites, four cabins, a pool, and a convenience store, and is open all year.

Mississippi River RV Park, 870 Cotton Gin Pl., tel. (901) 946-1993 or (800) 827-1714, lies close to the Mississippi River. It has 31 sites with full hookups, tour bus pick-up sites, and a free shuttle to Beale Street. It's open year-round.

FOOD

The following material was assembled by Fredric Koeppel, restaurant and book critic for the *Memphis Commercial Appeal,* the local newspaper.

BARBECUE

The Ritual
As far as barbecue is concerned, Memphis is Heaven, Mecca, and Nirvana rolled into one. Before listing some of the barbecue places, a bit of explanation is in order. Most of the barbecue here is pork. A few infidels cook beef, and the more health-minded appreciate chicken, but for most people in Memphis, barbecue and pork are synonymous. Usually barbecue hereabouts comes from two cuts of meat—shoulders and ribs.

Barbecue has its own language: cognoscenti express their preferences among "white" or "brown" meat, "pulled" or "chopped," and "wet" or "dry." The first four terms refer to pork shoulders. "White" is interior meat uncolored by smoke or sauce. It tends to be more tender, but not as strongly flavored as "brown" meat, which is chewier. Those who specify neither will usually get a mixture of both. "Pulled" pork is meat so tender

that it can be pulled from the bone by hand and put on a plate or on a sandwich. This usually results in larger chunks. "Chopped" pork has been cleaved into submission.

Diners who order ribs will often get this question: "Dry or wet?" "Dry" ribs have no barbecue sauce on them. Often they have been cooked with a "rub" consisting of spices such as salt, pepper, cumin, and chili powder, which, if done right, seals in the juices and makes the best ribs in the world—especially for diners with handlebar mustaches. "Wet" ribs have been basted with sauce during their final hour or so on the grill. These require plenty of napkins but are worth it.

Traditional side dishes include slaw, which some patrons will add to a barbecue sandwich; baked beans, sometimes with bits of barbecue in them; potato salad; and bread.

The Dispensers
Bar-B-Q Shop, 1782 Madison Ave., tel. (901) 272-1277, specializes in ribs and pulled pork shoulder. It's open for lunch only on Monday, and lunch and dinner Tues.-Saturday.

Corky's, 5259 Poplar Ave., tel. (901) 685-9744, may not be funky and may not be down-home, but it does offer what one has to assess as one of the best pulled pork shoulder barbecue sandwiches in the world. The ribs, well, they don't quite compete.

Cozy Corner, 745 N. Parkway, tel. (901) 527-9158, *is* funky and down-home, and its barbecue Cornish game hen is one of the unique treats that make Memphis the city it is. Pork shoulder sandwiches and pork ribs are also excellent.

Gridley's has two locations at 6430 Winchester Rd., tel. (901) 794-5997, and 6065 Macon Rd., tel. (901) 388-7003. Ribs are the specialty of the house.

Interstate Bar-B-Q & Restaurant, 2265 S. 3rd St., tel. (901) 775-2304, brings a consensus to Memphians who love to argue about barbecue restaurants; few would disagree that these are the best ribs in town and, therefore, in the world.

Little Pigs BBQ, 671 S. Highland St., tel. (901) 323-9433, serves up excellent pulled pork sandwiches, ribs, chicken, and grilled cheese sandwiches.

Neely's Bar-B-Que, 670 Jefferson Ave., tel. (901) 521-9798, and 5700 Mt. Moriah Rd. Exit, tel. (901) 795-4177, doesn't surprise by the excellence of its product; it's run by the nephews of Jim Neely, owner of Interstate Barbecue. In addition to excellent pork shoulder sandwiches and ribs, try the barbecue spaghetti (an odd Memphis tradition) and the smoked sausage.

Payne's Bar-B-Que has two locations: 1393 Elvis Presley Blvd., tel. (901) 942-7433, and 1762 Lamar Ave., tel. (901) 272-1523. Both serve shoulder and wet ribs for lunch and dinner.

Rendezvous, 52 S. 2nd St., tel. (901) 523-2746, has dry ribs so fine that when Elvis played Vegas he reportedly had them flown in. Now Cybill Shepherd does the same thing for friends in Los Angeles. Perhaps that's why FedEx began in Memphis. To get to this place, go through an alley across from the Peabody Hotel. The visitor will step into a place whose walls are lined with antiques and Memphis memorabilia. It seats 700 and serves dinner only.

TOP OF THE HEAP

Aubergine, 5007 Black Rd., tel. (901) 767-7840, offers exquisite contemporary French cuisine prepared under the direction of chef Gene Bjorklund, who works wonders with foie gras, sweetbreads, veal shank, and all manner of fish. His lunchtime sautéed trout with caper beurre blanc and mashed potatoes is simple and memorable. Fairly reasonable midday prices give way to hefty tabs at night.

Chez Phillippe, in The Peabody Hotel downtown, tel. (901) 529-4188, is the city's most formal, most thoughtfully detailed restaurant—and its most expensive. Chef Jose Gutierrez's exquisite, artfully presented dishes reflect his French background and the influence of the American South; diners won't find hushpuppies with shrimp Provençal anywhere else. The wine list is high-toned, and so is the impeccable service.

Cielo, 679 Adams Ave., tel. (901) 524-1886, occupies an 1880s house in Victorian Village. The unforgettable decor mixes Sleeping Beauty with the Jetsons, and the food, under chef Don Fox, is as eclectic as all-get-out, lassoing influence from the Caribbean, the Southwest and Southeast Asia. The restaurant is the creation of the energetic Karen Blockman Carrier, resident genius at Automatic Slim's (see entry below). A wonderful little bar upstairs with a small separate dining room is decorated with work by legendary local artists and features excellent martinis.

Erling Jensen: The Restaurant, 1044 S. Yates Rd., tel. (901) 763-3700, is named for the chef who used to be at La Tourelle (see entry). Jensen, a quiet man steeped in European tradition but imbued with New World fervor, turns out sumptuous, luxurious, and very expensive fare in a 1950s house turned into an elegant and whimsical restaurant that also offers the best wine list in town. Fish and seafood dishes are particularly inventive, and desserts will knock you out of your chair.

Koto, 22 S. Cooper St., tel. (901) 722-2244, is a collaboration between Erling Jensen (previous entry) and Jimmy Ishii, owner of several Sekisui Japanese restaurants: "Ko" is Copenhagen; "To" is Tokyo. Chef Jennifer Hood concocts an ever-changing menu of intriguing, sometimes challenging, and frequently delicious fare that combines many disparate elements in beautiful spare presentations. The small restaurant is almost painfully aware of its elegance and hipness but remains an oasis of comfort and attentive service.

La Tourelle, 2146 Monroe Ave., tel. (901) 726-5771, combines a serene environment, smooth friendly service, and fabulous food for one of the city's great dining experiences. Chef Lynn

Kennedy-Tilyou creates dishes such as salad of grilled quail, red cabbage, and shredded sweet potato. Her rack of lamb is the best in town.

Marena's, 1545 Overton Park Ave., tel. (901) 278-9774, whose interior was decorated by local artists, is one of the most intimate and beautiful restaurants anywhere. It offers Mediterranean cuisine, with a monthly changing menu that features food from one European country and one North African or Near Eastern country. Garlic, olive oil, and rosemary dominate. Visitors should take their own wine. Marena's is in a quiet neighborhood far from the usual business haunts.

EASIER ON THE WALLET

Steaks and Seafood

Cafe Society, 212 N. Evergreen St., tel. (901) 722-2177, is midtown's most popular lunch place, and evenings can be a squeeze too. A small, comfortable bar and a large, slightly cold room are both warmed by excellent service. Food leans toward French-American preparations, with emphasis on veal, beef, fish, and seafood. Fish items at lunch are particularly good. Prices are reasonable to moderately expensive. The place offers sidewalk dining during nice weather. It's open for lunch Sun.-Fri., for dinner daily.

On Teur, 2015 Madison Ave., tel. (901) 725-6059, easily qualifies as the city's most eccentric restaurant, but what the chef does with fish and seafood and intensely pure and flavorful sauces will make the diner forget that the little restaurant stands next to a convenience store and that the outside deck is on a parking lot. Prices are reasonable. Teur's serves lunch and dinner Mon.-Saturday.

Pete & Sam's Restaurant, 3886 Park Ave., tel. (901) 458-0694, is the kind of place where the great-grandchildren of the original customers still eat. Forget the forgettable southern Italian cuisine, except for the rich and sumptuous lasagna, and go straight for the best steaks in Memphis, as well as terrific cracker-thin pizzas. Patrons should take their own wine. It's open for dinner every night.

Southern and Eclectic

Arcade Restaurant, 540 S. Main St., tel. (901) 526-5757, which opened in 1919, is the city's oldest continually operating restaurant. It serves breakfast every weekday morning and all day Saturday and Sunday. Lunch is typical Southern plate-style fare with particularly good soups. A different chef at night turns out delicious (and more expensive) renditions of Southern food such as roasted chicken with Tennessee bourbon sauce and pecan-crusted trout. It's open every day and serves dinner Tues.-Sunday.

Ellen's Soul Food Restaurant, 601 S. Parkway E, tel. (901) 942-4888, universally known as Miss Ellen's, serves the best meat loaf, smothered chicken and pork chops around, bolstered with plates of fried cornbread pancakes. Friday is chitlins day. It's open Mon.-Fri. for lunch and early dinner.

Jarrett's Restaurant, 5687 Quince Rd., in Winchester Square shopping center, tel. (901) 763-2264, offers a reasonable buffet lunch several cuts above the ordinary buffet, but the restaurant shines at night with its eclectic American menu featuring smoked trout ravioli, mixed grill of sausages, crab cakes, grilled chicken, duckling in two styles, and a knockout cappuccino crème caramel. Prices are moderately expensive. It's open for lunch Mon.-Sat., dinner every day.

Ethnic

Asian Palace, 2920 Covington Pike, tel. (901) 388-3883, is the best Chinese restaurant in the region. The menu is uniquely ingenious and nonrepetitive, and the fare is bright and fresh and delicious. Don't miss the clams with black bean sauce, the duck broth and the steamed fish, whatever the fish may be. It's open for lunch and dinner daily.

Automatic Slim's Tonga Club, 83 S. 2nd St., tel. (901) 525-7948, leads the vanguard of hip, lively restaurants in Memphis. The constantly evolving Southwestern-Louisiana-Caribbean menu features jerk chicken and pork dishes, Caribbean voodoo (seafood) stew, *huachinango* (crispy whole red snapper), molasses-glazed lamb chops and, at lunch, a variety of two-fisted sandwiches. Various salsas, fruit sauces, and peppy accompaniments keep the spice and heat levels high. It's open for lunch Mon.-Fri., for dinner Mon.-Saturday.

Cafe Samovar, 83 Union Ave., tel. (901) 529-9607, serves authentic Russian dishes including borscht, beef stroganoff, veal *soblinka, luli kabob, kulebyaka,* chicken and lamb kabobs, Norwegian salmon with champagne and caviar sauce, and Journey to Russia appetizer samplers. Desserts are large and rich. The atmosphere is festive and folklike. The café is open for lunch Mon.-Sat. and dinner Tues.-Saturday.

Delhi Palace, 6110 Macon Rd., tel. (901) 386-3600, is particularly good with curry dishes, especially lamb, and with a multitude of colorful and spicy vegetarian items. The Indian breads are tempting in their variety and flavors. Service is friendly and helpful for guiding neophytes through the intricacies of the cuisine. It's open for lunch and dinner daily.

King's Palace Cafe, 162 Beale St., tel. (901) 521-1851, continues to offer the only good food in the dining desert of Beale Street. The emphasis is on such Cajun and Creole fare as gumbo, shrimp, and crawfish etouffee as well as on steaks, chicken, and ribs. It's open for lunch and dinner every day.

Molly's La Casita, 2006 Madison Ave., tel. (901) 726-1873, presents typical American-Mexican fare, perhaps, but made untypical by freshness and attention to detail. Particularly good are the charcoal-grilled red snapper, the chicken fajita enchiladas, and any dishes served with the profoundly intense ranchero sauce. Molly's is open every day for lunch and dinner.

Ronnie Grisanti & Sons, 2855 Poplar Ave. in Chickasaw Crossing shopping center, tel. (901) 323-0007, specializes in fare from southern Italy, though Ronnie's sons Judd and Alex, now the chefs, are turning more to their northern Italian heritage. The restaurant is comfortably intimate, and decorated with artworks that vary from beautiful to bizarre. It's open Mon.-Sat. for dinner.

Salsa, 6150 Poplar Ave. in Regalia shopping center, tel. (901) 683-6325, serves fresh versions of Tex-Mex fare, along with a few unusual inventions from the chef, in a clean, bright room gleaming with color and polished wood. Salsa makes excellent margaritas and is open Mon.-Sat. for lunch and dinner.

Sekisui of Japan, 50 Humphreys Blvd. in the Humphreys Center, tel. (901) 747-0001, and 25 Belvedere in Midtown, tel. (901) 725-0005, offers the freshest, most authentic sushi in Memphis, as well as soups and salads, teriyaki items, innovative dishes that owner Jimmy Ishii calls "Pacific Rim" specialties, and (at the Humphreys location) a *robata bar* for grilled snacks and entrees. It's open for lunch Mon.-Fri. and dinner every day.

Tsumani, 928 S. Cooper, tel. (901) 274-2556, is the city's newest entry into the Pacific Rim category. Chef Ben Smith offers terrific and exotic fish and meat dishes enlivened with Asian and tropical touches in a hipoid-funko setting designed by his artist-sister. The cuisine is supported by a remarkably suitable and inexpensive wine list. It's open Mon.-Sat. for dinner.

All the Rest
Boscos Pizza Kitchen & Brewery, 7615 W. Farmington, Saddle Creek shopping center (Germantown), tel. (901) 756-7310, serves a variety of standard and innovative pizzas baked in a wood-fired oven, pastas such as fettuccine Alfredo, soups, salads, appetizers, and calzones, along with filet mignon and grilled and rotisseried selections. Four varieties of beer are brewed on the premises—one of them the renowned "Boscos Famous Flaming Stone Beer," a concoction whose brewing process includes heating granite stones to 900° and dropping them into the unfermented beer. The intense heat causes sugars to caramelize on the stone and gives the beer a great flavor. Boscos is open for lunch and dinner every day.

Lulu Grille, 565 Erin Dr. (off Poplar) in White Station Plaza, tel. (901) 763-3677, though a bit spare in the decor line, is one of the most pleasant restaurants in Memphis. It offers typical American bistro-type food, focusing on salads, pastas, pizza, fish, and chicken—always fresh and well-prepared. Outdoor dining is available in balmy weather. It's open for lunch and dinner every day.

DOWNRIGHT REASONABLE

Acapulco, 3681 Jackson, tel. (901) 386-1199, is probably as Mexican as a Mexican restaurant can get in Memphis. Both restaurant and neighborhood are unprepossessing, but be prepared for gigantic tostadas and burritos filled with meat and eggs, *carne asada,* chile verde, or *barbacoa,* a Mexican version of barbecue. The food is simple, down-home, authentic, and delicious. Open for lunch and dinner daily.

Belmont Grill, 4970 Poplar Ave., tel. (901) 767-8836, offers the elements everyone wants in the perfect bar and grill: darkness, friendly waitresses, a great sound system, and a terrific hamburger, this version served on a French roll with bacon and a choice of cheeses. It also serves excellent chicken wings and is open from lunch until early morning every day.

Bombay Cafe, 3700 Ridgeway Rd. at Winchester in Hickory Ridge Commons, tel. (901) 368-1002, is a husband-and-wife-run establishment that serves delicious down-home northern Indian cuisine at incredible prices; nothing on the menu is more than $6.99. From curries that flirt with danger to smooth, mild lentil and potato dishes, Bombay Cafe does an admirable job. The restaurant is stuck back in a corner of a suburban shopping center, but seekers of fine food will not let that circumstance put them off. It's open for lunch and dinner daily.

The Cupboard, 1495 Union Ave., tel. (901) 276-8015, emphasizes fresh vegetables in its roster of typical home-cooked fare. Try chicken and dressing, beef tips with noodles, and pork chops. Also try the excellent cornbread, mashed potatoes, and fried chicken. It's open daily for lunch, Mon.-Fri. for early dinner.

Front Street Deli, 77 S. Front St., tel. (901) 522-8943, is open Mon.-Fri. for breakfast and lunch, and Saturday for lunch only. It serves great hoagies as well as salads and desserts. Note to University of Tennessee alumni: this place has the same kind of steamed sandwiches that come from Sam and Andy's in Knoxville.

Huey's, 1927 Madison Ave., tel. (901) 726-4372, has expanded to two suburban locations, but this original midtown bar remains truest to the Huey's laid-back spirit. Forget everything else on the brief menu and go straight for one of the plumpest, juiciest, meatiest hamburgers ever eaten. Then take the cellophane-tasseled toothpick and use a straw to blow it up to the ceiling, joining thousands of others. Huey's is open from lunch until 3 a.m. every day.

Jasmine Chinese and Thai Restaurant, 3024 Covington Pike, tel. (901) 386-2974, offers Thai dishes—forget the Chinese—whose innocent appearance on the plate conceals the heat and spice to make diners cough and hiccup and ingest massive quantities of water. And that's the mild version. It's great and delicious stuff for those with cast-iron stomachs. Jasmine is open for lunch and dinner every day.

Memphis Pizza Cafe, 2089 Madison Ave. in Overton Square, tel. (901) 726-5343, can provide salads, calzones, and sandwiches, but best are the fresh and vivid pizzas, especially the vegetarian rendition and the "Eclectic," with basil, garlic, and cheese. It's open for lunch and dinner every day.

Saigon Le, 51 N. Cleveland, tel. (901) 276-5326, features Vietnamese fare so fresh, so vivid, and so good that patrons can't believe how cheap it is. A family-run restaurant with Mom in the kitchen and the kids and husbands and wives (and a few babies) in front, Saigon Le manages to move huge crowds through the dining room with never a slip in the excellence of the food. Soups are terrific, with the curry tofu soup nudging the divine. It's open Mon.-Sat. for lunch and dinner.

Yellow Rose Cafe, 56 N. Main in the Lincoln-American Building, tel. (901) 527-5692, offers simple breakfasts and excellent lunch plate specials in the Southern fashion. It's open Mon.-Fri. for breakfast and lunch.

MORE PRACTICALITIES

SHOPPING

Fine Arts and Crafts

Albers Fine Art Gallery, 1102 Brookfield Rd., tel. (901) 683-2256, features the sculptural furniture of Philadelphia's Peter Pierobon and the colored-pencil still lifes of Memphian Cora Ogden. The gallery also handles contemporary art by regional and national artists, such as the late Walter Anderson.

Cooper Street Gallery, 964 S. Cooper St., tel. (901) 272-7053, a contemporary art gallery, features local artists and includes owner Jay Etkin's studio.

Willis Gallery, 156 Beale St., tel. (901) 526-3162, features African artifacts and African-American Impressionistic Realism art.

Ledbetter Lusk Gallery, 4540 Poplar Ave., tel. (901) 767-3800, offers the work of contemporary Southern artists.

Lisa Kurts Gallery, 766 S. White Station Rd., tel. (901) 683-6200, carries contemporary American art with an emphasis on Southern artists, displayed in monthly exhibitions. The gallery also specializes in American paintings of the 19th and 20th centuries.

Madison Avenue Art Gallery in Carrefour Mall, 6645 Poplar Ave., tel. (901) 759-9402, sells a variety of media, including oil and acrylic paintings, mixed-media, sculpture, fine crafts, handcrafted jewelry, and pottery from approximately 270 tri-state and national artists.

Marshall Arts, 639 Marshall Ave.—one block west of Sun Studios and directly east of the Heartbreak Hotel, tel. (901) 522-9483, is an alternative arts space with exhibits of painting and sculpture and the occasional piece of performance art. Open on Saturdays 1-5 p.m. or by appointment.

At **Tobey Gallery,** 1930 Polar Ave. in Overton Park, tel. (901) 726-4085, student and professors at the Memphis College of Art occasionally display fiber, painting, and sculpture pieces.

Music

Memphis Music Shop and Souvenirs, 149 Beale Street, tel. (901) 454-9690, has a great collection of blues CDs and tapes.

Pop Tunes, 308 Poplar Ave., tel. (901) 525-6348, was known as Poplar Tunes in the 1950s, when a regular customer from the nearby Lauderdale Courts housing projects made purchases here. There's not much to see now—only a smattering of Elvis photos on the wall. Other, much less historic, locations are 4195 Summer Ave., tel. (901) 324-3855, and 2391 Lamar Ave., tel. (901) 744-0400.

River Records, 822 S. Highland St., tel. (901) 324-1757, is for the fan who seeks rare records. "We have about 500,000 records," said one clerk, "78 blues albums from the '20s, 45s from the '50s, and you name it." The shop offers rare Elvis records and related memorabilia and sells other CDs, comic books, posters, etc..

Rod & Hank's Vintage Guitars, 45 S. Main St., tel. (901) 525-9240, carries an ever-changing stock of used and vintage instruments. See them online at www.rhguitars.com.

Shangri-La Records, 1916 Madison Ave., tel. (901) 274-1916, is both a record store and an independent recording label. The record store carries a lot of vinyl. The bathroom is a museum to the 1970s, complete with Kiss masks and a *Welcome Back, Kotter* beanbag chair. This place sells bricks from the old Stax studio building for $10. It also stocks a large section of Memphis music. Get a catalog if you can't go there, or see them online at www.shangri.com.

Specialty Shops

Afrikan Emporium, 3984 Elvis Presley Blvd., tel. (901) 396-3999, sells African-imported art and clothes for men, women, and children as well as woodcarvings and artifacts.

Flashback—The Vintage Department Store, 2304 Central Ave., tel. (901) 272-2304, sells vintage clothing, furniture, and collectibles from the 1920s-1970s. I

The Memphis City Store, 340 Beale St., tel. (901) 543-5336, sells memorabilia such as Memphis street signs, fire boxes and firefighters' clothing, Memphis shirts and hats, and novelty items.

Otherlands, 641 S. Cooper, tel. (901) 278-4994, a coffee bar, is also an exotic gift store.

LISTENING TO MEMPHIS MUSIC

The CD reissue revolution has resurrected many records of Memphis music that were difficult to find or out of print and has also brought to light a lot of previously unreleased music. Much of this is readily available, from the lavish RCA box sets of Elvis material to the Rhino reissues from the Stax/Volt catalogue.

One less familiar series that should not be overlooked—and is very much worth seeking out—is that of **Memphis Archives**, P.O. Box 171282, Memphis, TN 38187, tel. (800) 713-2150, whose stated goal is "to preserve our rich American musical heritage by making historical recordings available." Its releases are a treasure, covering every aspect and style of Memphis music, including (to name only a few) the W.C. Handy Blues Band's recordings of the composer's work, collections of country blues, early regional big bands, and jug bands.

It has also issued CDs of the Memphis Blues Caravan shows from the 1970s and contemporary artists the Memphis Sheiks. The focus is on Memphis, but not exclusively—other terrific collections include *Tin Pan Alley Blues, 1916-1925; Blue Ladies* (an anthology of female vocalists); and pianist Art Tatum's *California Melodies*, a fine set of 1940 radio broadcasts. Memphis Archives' aims are worthy and its products excellent—check them out. Music lovers won't be disappointed by people who offer transcendental pleasures such as Robert Wilkins's "Old Jim Canaan," Tampa Red's "Jim Jackson's Jamboree," or Jack Teagarden's version of "Beale Street Blues."

—*Franklin Jones*

The store carries home furnishings and clothing from India, Africa, South America, and local artisans. Shoppers can find textiles, mirrors, jewelry, clothing, pottery, and more.

Rainbow Works, 387 S. Main St., tel. (901) 521-0400, sells stained glass, jewelry, and art glass that is made on site.

A. Schwab Dry Goods Store, 163 Beale St., tel. (901) 523-9782, seems a museum at first; merchandise for sharecroppers of another time is in abundance here, as are T-shirts, postcards, and associated frippery. Perhaps the most unusual goods are the voodoo potions and oils alleged to help one find love or luck—or both. For a bit of fun, browse in this section and listen to other customers making their decisions. Schwab's has been in business in this same location since 1876.

Vintage Mania, 2151 Young Ave., tel. (901) 274-2879, sells vintage clothing and housewares.

We're Nuts Pecan Company, 62 S. Front St., tel. (901) 521-6887, sells wholesale (and a little retail) cracked and shelled pecans. The denizens of the adjacent cotton company swear that this is the best possible name for this establishment.

Those who can't make it through the day without the *New York Times* will find happiness at **World Wide News,** downtown at 124 Monroe Ave., tel., (901) 523-9970.

Malls

Chickasaw Oaks Plaza, 3092 Poplar Ave., tel. (901) 794-6022, looks like a mall from the 1700s. Fifteen or so stores hold forth here.

Hickory Ridge Mall, Winchester Rd. at Hickory Hill Rd., tel. (901) 367-8045, has 100+ stores.

Mall of Memphis, I-240 at Perkins Rd., tel. (901) 362-9315, has more than 100 places to spend money.

Oak Court Mall, Poplar Ave. at Perkins Rd., tel. (901) 682-8928, has two major department stores and 80 smaller shops. Unusual among malls, its center is a small park containing animal sculptures.

Raleigh Springs Mall, 3384 Austin Peay Hwy., tel. (901) 388-4300, has 72 shops and restaurants.

Saddle Creek Shopping Center, 5855 River Bend Rd., tel. (901) 761-2571, sits in Germantown, home of the upscale shoppers.

GETTING AROUND

The **Memphis Area Transit Authority** , a.k.a. MATA, offers citywide bus service, van service for disabled folks, and the tourist-oriented Main St. Trolley. For information on routes, schedules, and fares, call (901) 274-1757.

Rent-A-Wreck, tel. (901) 525-7878, offers a low-priced option for renting a set of wheels.

Taxis include **Yellow Cab,** tel. (901) 577-7777.

INFORMATION

The **Tennessee Welcome Center,** 119 N. Riverside Dr., does not have a phone number but is open 24 hours a day with information about Memphis as well as the rest of the state. See them online at www.memphistravel.com.

Give Me Memphis Hotline, tel. (901) 681-1111 or (800) 820-3035, offers information 24 hours a day on topics such as weather, events, music, and entertainment. Anyone wanting faxed material on Memphis should call (800) 57-FAX-ME.

Walking Tour 1998 is a handy booklet available at the Memphis Convention & Visitors Bureau. Tours include "Beale Street," "Victorian Village," "Ghost Tour of Memphis," and "Elvis Presley."

Links to various Memphis entities can be found at www.ci.memphis.tn.us/cityguide/links.

Finally, **The Memphis Flyer,** a local weekly, has a Web site that sheds light on the local scene at www.memphisflyer.com.

Home of the blues, Beale Street is one of the most famous streets in America.

THE WESTERN PLAINS
INTRODUCTION

The Southern Plains

The first travelers, prehistoric Indians, came hundreds of miles to this part of Tennessee to build enormous structures of earth for purposes still unclear. The Natchez Trace rang with the sound of boatmen walking back from their travels downstream, carrying gold and silver and watching out for robbers. Andrew Jackson marched this way to smite the British in New Orleans. Others came to hack a new life out of the hardwood forests that covered the fertile ground.

Nathan Bedford Forrest and his troops rode here, and Gen. William T. Sherman slashed a plantation-home staircase in anger and frustration. Troops clashed at Shiloh, the first big battle of the Civil War, and in two days more Americans died than in all previous American wars combined.

This is a land of heroic figures. A railroad engineer left Jackson and rode into legend as he tried to stop a speeding locomotive. A sheriff, walking tall, ran a nest of criminals out of his county.

The world's largest coon hunt cuts loose here, as do the National Field Trials for birddogs. People in McNairy County eat their slugburgers, and the smoke from barbecue pits rises over almost every town. Visit online at www.tast.tn.org.

The Northern Plains

Two rivers serve as bookends for West Tennessee: the Tennessee flowing north and the Mississippi flowing south. Between them lies the flattest land in the state, a place of big, hot, long fields of cotton that to someone hoeing or picking could seem as if they reached from horizon to horizon.

This is the place where the most severe earthquake in American history created a lake. It is a place of Doodle Soup and catfish: steaks, fillets, or "fiddlers"—whole fish minus their heads. It was the last Tennessee home of David Crockett and the place where a young boy named Alex Haley first heard tales of his African ancestors.

Above all, this is a place of distinctive music, birthplace to Tina Turner, Carl Perkins, bluesmen such as Sleepy John Estes, and to hundreds of choirs whose voices rose, and still rise, on Sunday to sing songs of faith.

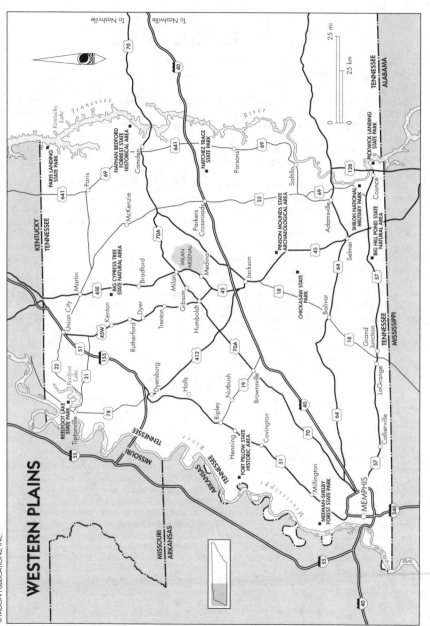

© MOON PUBLICATIONS, INC.

WESTERN PLAINS

THE BARBECUE TRAIL

COLLIERVILLE

This charming place, like Franklin south of Nashville, is a place whose leaders have seen the encroaching suburbs of a large city and have taken steps to preserve the architecture and feeling of the past. This effort is just in time, for Collierville claims to be the fastest-growing town in the state.

Collierville was a small town along the railroad tracks east of Memphis, but it was significant enough to attract the attention of Union General William T. Sherman, who occupied the town in 1863. Confederate cavalry could not dislodge his forces from the depot, although they did manage to appropriate his horse for the Southern cause. Collierville was all but burned to the ground.

Mississippi Fred McDowell, contrary to his nickname, was born east of here in Rossville in 1904. His blues centered on bottleneck guitar and a voice that sounded as if he gargled gravel. His "You Gotta Move" appeared on the Rolling Stones's *Sticky Fingers* album.

Sights

When the town was rebuilt in the 1870s, the planners laid it out in the town-square manner as if it had a courthouse in the center. No courthouse is here, so the focus of the town is a bandstand in the center of the park. In a nod to the "Hell no, we ain't forgetting" school of the Lost Cause, the sidewalks in the park are laid out to resemble the design of the Confederate battle flag. Bluesman W.C. Handy led concerts in this park.

Rail fans will enjoy the train here. A 1912 steam engine, 1938 lounge car, diner, theater car, 1945 Pullman sleeper, and caboose sit on tracks near the old depot. These are owned by Memphis Transportation Museum, which opens them to the public. Admission is $6 for adults and $3 for kids four to 12. For further information, call (800) 850-5514.

St. Nick Farms and Zoological Park, 10928 E. Shelby Dr., tel. (901) 853-3492, is home to various exotic animals, including Tom II, the Bengal tiger mascot of the University of Memphis, along with snow leopards, mountain lions, and other beasts. It's open on Saturday 1-3 p.m.

MUST-SEE HIGHLIGHTS

The little town of **Counce** boasts the greatest collection of barbecue restaurants of any place in the state.

Pinson Mounds, south of Jackson, leads the visitor to marvel at the Indians who, basket by basket, piled soil into a mound that today is seven stories tall.

Paris's **World's Biggest Fish Fry** is a small-town festival at its best. Don't miss the catfish races.

Visitors can see the roots of one of the state's most beloved writers at Henning's **Alex Haley Home.**

Reelfoot Lake, in the northwest corner of the state, has bald eagles, eerie cypress trees, dark water, and a violent story of creation through the country's strongest earthquake.

Union City's **Dixie Gun Works,** has a collection of old guns on display, new guns, and even cannons for sale.

Gus's World Famous Hot & Spicy Chicken just outside of Memphis, offers absolutely no pretensions and wonderful fried chicken.

Brownsville's folk art masterpiece, **Mind Field** is worth a detour off I-40. Its creator, who lives out back, is as interesting as the structure.

Wild Onion Ridge Music Heritage Park in Nutbush is the way to reach Sharon Norris, who can explain West Tennessee roots music with her wonderful tours of Tina Turner's hometown.

Shiloh National Military Park marks the first big battle of the Civil War, where more men fell than in all previous American wars put together.

Trenton's illuminated teapots make up one of the more unusual and beautiful collections in the state.

Bolivar's **Western Mental Health Institute** has some of the most striking architecture on this end of the state.

or by appointment for groups. Admission is $3 per person.

Events

Fair on the Square, held on the first weekend in May, is one of the bigger and older arts and crafts gatherings hereabouts. It features food, music, and kids' pastimes.

The **Sunset on the Square Concert Series,** Thursday evenings in June and July, begins at 7 p.m. and presents big band, country, Dixieland, and other kinds of music.

The **Fall Festival Arts and Crafts Show** on the last weekend in October is a smaller version of the Fair on the Square.

Dickens on the Square Christmas Festivities take place on the first weekend in December and offer carriage rides, live music, an English-style marketplace, and children's games with Styrofoam "snowballs."

Where to Stay

Azalea Ridge, 342 Peterson Lake Rd., Collierville, TN 38017, tel. (901) 853-3421, is a ranch-style home with two guest rooms furnished in Victorian antiques. Both rooms share a bath. The property contains 300-400 azaleas, which burst into full color in April. The hosts serve a full country breakfast, and the rate is $65. To get there from downtown Collierville, go down Walnut St. to Hwy. 57, go west to the first traffic light, then go right onto Peterson Lake Road. Moderate.

Other options in town are **Comfort Inn,** 1230 W. Poplar Ave., tel. (901) 853-1235; and **Sunset Inn,** 154 Hwy. 72 W, tel. (901) 853-2229.

A bit farther down Hwy. 57 in Rossville is the **Mebane-Nuckolls-Perkins Home,** which offers luncheons and tours by reservation and is also a bed and breakfast. Built 1848-1860, the house has some dramatic stories. Rates are $100 per night. Visit online at www.bbgetaways.com/Mebane-NuckellsHouse. Expensive.

Food

Cafe Grill Steakhouse, 120 Mulberry Ln., tel. (901) 853-7511, serves American dishes, and they know their town. A sign described Certified Angus Beef as "the BMW of steaks."

Captain John's Bar-B-Q, 106 Hwy. 72 E, tel. (901) 853-8004, serves barbecue and other items three meals a day every day.

The Silver Caboose, 132 E. Mulberry St., tel. (901) 853-0010, has hot plate lunches and serves fresh turnip greens year-round. Dinner items include appetizers of charbroiled shrimp followed by dishes such as filet mignon and grilled salmon. Finish off with the frozen pecan balls.

White Church Antiques & Tea Room, at 196 Main St., tel. (901) 854-6433, serves "country French cuisine," including pasta, seafood, pork loin, steak, and salad.

Shopping

Collierville boasts a wide variety of antique stores, some of which are noted below. A Main St. Collierville brochure lists 20 antique outlets as well as a dozen gift shops and galleries.

Hewlett & Dunn Jean & Boot Barn, on the Square at 111 N. Center St., tel. (901) 853-2636, sells clothing, footwear, and tack and has a wonderful collection of old radios on the wall.

Remember When Antiques, 110 E. Mulberry St., tel. (901) 853-5470, has some merchandise that requires a long memory indeed; the goods date from 1830 to 1940. Among its antiques are Civil War memorabilia and a special area devoted to military saddles.

In the **White Church Antiques & Tea Room,** on the Square at 196 Main St., tel. (901) 854-6433, more than 40 dealers set up in an old Victorian Congregational church.

Information

Main Street Collierville, 151 Walnut St., tel. (901) 853-1666, is open 9 a.m.-5 p.m.

MOSCOW

This little town lies along the Wolf River, which in recent years has been discovered by canoers and kayakers. No whitewater here, but instead a chance to see ducks, beavers, and deer up close. Between here and LaGrange the river flows into a swamp and a lake, thus inspiring the name "Ghost River," for it wasn't clear just which way the Wolf went. The canoe route is now marked, however. Visit online at www.bp-basecamp.com/wilderness/tn_wolfriver or www.kesler.biology.rhodes.edu/wolf.

To get on the water, go to **Wolf River Canoe Trips** at 1600 Old Stateline Dr., tel. (901) 877-

3958. This place offers canoe rentals and shuttle service for trips ranging from three to nine hours.

Fine dining awaits in Moscow, one block off Hwy. 57 at 18 Charleston Street. There lies **Tea for Two,** tel. (901) 877-3883, a small Victorian cottage that is the home of high-end lunches and dinners. Dinner menu prices range from $15 to $38, and items include pork tenderloin stuffed with apricots. This place often has live piano and dulcimer music.

LAGRANGE

This lovely town, dating from 1824, was one of the first established in West Tennessee and was the first entire town in Tennessee to be placed on the National Register. Many antebellum homes lie along the highway, although at this writing none is open to the public. One of them, **Woodlawn,** noted by a historical marker, was built in 1828. Unlike most of the houses here, which face north or south, this one looks east—seems the owner didn't want to have to stare at the railroad tracks.

The decade before the Civil War marked the peak of LaGrange, a bustling town with the LaGrange Female College and LaGrange Synodical College for Men. The latter produced only one class of graduates in 1861, and every one of them volunteered for the Confederacy. When the War came, Woodlawn was temporarily used as a headquarters by Union general William Sherman. General U.S. Grant and his wife also spent time in LaGrange. The men's college was destroyed, as were some 40 homes.

Today LaGrange is a pleasant place to visit. The first stop should be **Cogbill's General Store & Museum,** 14840 LaGrange Rd., tel. (901) 878-1235, which is run by the mayor of LaGrange, Lucy Cogbill. Her grandfather was the original storekeeper, and she carries merchandise from 104 artists and antique dealers, most of them local folks. One is Armsterd Peeler, a folk artist who paints scenes on pine planks.

GRAND JUNCTION

This town grew up at the crossroads of two railroads about 1854, and over the years its fortunes rose and fell with the trains. The Union army occupied the town during the Civil War, when most of the buildings were burned. A persistent local legend holds that Thomas A. Edison once operated the telegraph here.

The area's most influential visitor was Hobart C. Ames, a Yankee who came to town in the 1890s to do two things: shoot birds and spend money. The Massachusetts industrialist—his company made shovels and tools—bought a plantation home built in 1847 and through purchases and leases amassed some 25,000 acres. More than 200 families worked the fields, raising cotton and prize-winning cattle. Ames served as president of the National Field Trial Champion Association, a group that judged bird dogs, for 43 years. It was only natural that the national championships for dogs be held at **Ames Plantation.**

Ames and his wife usually spent only four months a year in Tennessee. When he died in 1945, his widow put the plantation in a trust to benefit the University of Tennessee, which made the 18,567-acre place the largest land research facility in the state. And it is still the epicenter of the bird dog world.

Those who wish can tour the Ames house on the fourth Thursday of each month March-Oct., and by appointment. Some 19th-century homes and farm buildings have been restored and can be seen when the house is open. If a guide is available, visitors can go in the buildings. Admission is $2 per person. Call (901) 878-1067. To get there, drive north of Grand Junction on Hwy. 18 toward Bolivar and turn left onto Ellington Road. Visit online at www.ames plantation.org.

The **National Bird Dog Museum,** Hwy. 57, tel. (901) 878-1067, was built to honor the 36 distinct breeds of pointing dogs, spaniels, and retrievers. Displays mostly consist of paintings and photos of celebrated dogs, although saddles, videos of dogs working, and Ames memorabilia are on hand as well. A new Wildlife Heritage Center contains exhibits of quail, pheasant, and other game birds in their habitat. Hunt the museum down online at www.fielddog.com/foundation/museum.

Events
The **National Field Trials** take place in mid-February, a time when dog fanciers come from all over to hobnob with each other and to watch

the dogs hunt for quail and other birds. Most of this is done from "the gallery," hundreds of people who follow the action while on horseback. Admission is free. Visitors bring their own horses, saddle up, and ride off. Those who have no horses will not see a great deal. For further information, call (901) 878-1067.

Where to Stay

A little farther up Hwy. 18 toward Bolivar is **Avent-Rogers,** tel. (901) 764-2714, occupying an 1898 Victorian, two-story house with lots of gingerbread. Inside are two guest rooms that share a bath. One room is decorated with antiques and the other with "comfortable country" furniture. The rate is $75 per night. Moderate.

Shopping

Tennessee Pewter Company, 133 Madison Ave., tel. (901) 764-2064, makes and sells over 500 spun pewter products such as tabletop services, goblets, bowls, candleholders, tumblers, coffee sets, salt and pepper shakers, and steins. The company also produces cast pewter (melted and poured into molds) for jewelry, collectibles, letter openers, and key rings. More than 400 items are available, including a bust of Nathan Bedford Forrest. Visitors can see pewter being spun or cast whenever the place is open, but the best days to see the operations are Tuesday and Wednesday, when the complete staff is on site. Online at www.tnpewter.com.

BIG HILL POND
STATE NATURAL AREA

Eight miles south of Selmer on Hwy. 57, this 4,218-acre park sits at the confluence of the Tuscumbia and Hatchie Rivers and is less developed than other state parks. Wildlife abounds here.

The park features hiking trails, a 73-foot observation tower with a 360-degree view, and 165-acre Travis McNatt Lake. The "pond" in the park's name came from a railroad embankment that restricted the drainage of the surrounding wetlands and created a 35-acre lake. The park has 30 camping spaces with no electrical hookups. In the winter the water is turned off and the bathhouse closed, but the campground is still open. Call (901) 645-7967 or visit online at www.tnstateparks.com.

COUNCE

Highway 57 leading through Counce should be designated "Tennessee's Barbecue Highway," for along this road is the greatest concentration of barbecue places in the state.

Counce is home to the **Tenneco Packaging Company Arboretum,** on the grounds of the mill just off Hwy. 57, tel. (901) 689-3111. The arboretum grows trees and shrubs native to Tennessee, Alabama, and Mississippi. Visitors can walk along a trail that leads past 73 kinds of trees, many of them labeled. It's open during daylight hours. Admission is free.

Where to Stay

Try the **Hampton Inn,** corner of Hwy. 57 and Old South Rd., tel. (901) 689-3031 or (800) HAMPTON.

Food

Mr. D's BBQ, Hwy. 57, tel. (901) 689-3736, keeps it simple: barbecue with a few side dishes.

Pickwick Catfish Farms Restaurant, Hwy. 57, tel. (901) 689-3805, specializes in smoked catfish and offers all-you-can-eat fried catfish, ribs, and shrimp.

Price's Bar-B-Q, Hwy. 57, tel. (901) 689-5248, specializes in hickory-smoked barbecue, baby back ribs, and catfish.

The Red Wood Hut, Hwy. 57, tel. (901) 689-3260, offers a hot buffet for lunch along with sandwiches, hot melts, and steaks. The folks here smoke their own pork barbecue.

The Ribcage, Hwy. 57, tel. (901) 689-3637, serves ribs and barbecue as well as smoked turkey, ham, and chicken.

Information

Hardin County Tourism, 507 Main St., Savannah, can be reached at (800) 552-3866 or (901) 925-2364.

PICKWICK LANDING
STATE RESORT PARK

This park covers 1,392 acres, but the focus here is the water. Pickwick Dam impounds the Tennessee River to create Pickwick Lake and has locks for pleasure and commercial river traffic to use.

Visitors can golf on a par 72, 18-hole course, go swimming in the lake, go boating, or go fishing. The marina offers rental boats and slips for mariners who are passing though. A restaurant in the inn is open seven days a week for all three meals year-round and serves country cooking.

Accommodations begin with the inn, whose 75 single and double rooms range from $42 to $60, depending on time of the year and day of the week. Inexpensive. Ten two-bedroom housekeeping cabins are on the grounds, each with central heat and air, TV, and a fireplace. These cost $90 per night year-round and can only be rented by the week in the summer. Expensive. Seniors get a 10% discount on lodging. The inn and cabins are extremely popular, and they should be reserved as far ahead as possible by calling (901) 689-3135 or (800) 250-8615.

Forty-eight campsites all come with electrical and water hookups and a central bathhouse. Campsites are allocated on a first-come, first-served basis. The Bruton Branch Primitive Area, across the lake from the main park, has a modern bathhouse and campsites with no hookups. Its phone is (901) 926-1082.

General information about the park can be had at tel. (901) 689-3129 or on the Internet at www.tnstateparks.com.

Food Nearby
Jon's Pier, Hwy. 57 S, tel. (901) 689-3575, serves prime rib, ribs, and seafood. It's about four miles below the dam and about one and a half miles from the Mississippi state line on the Counce side of the water. Jon's is open for dinner Mon.-Sat., and in the summer is also open on Sunday.

The **Wharf Restaurant,** on Hwy. 4, tel. (901) 925-9469, is on the river one mile below the dam on the Savannah side. Open noon-9 p.m. Thurs.-Sun., its dinners include fish, steak, and seafood.

SHILOH NATIONAL MILITARY PARK

Many Civil War parks, particularly the ones near large cities, occupy only a part of the historic ground. This one, fortunately, covers something like 96% of the Shiloh battlefield. Visitors can drive a 9.5-mile auto tour route or, better yet, ride a bicycle along it.

The visitors center at the park is open daily 8 a.m.-5 p.m. Visitors can walk the battlefield or take a self-guided auto tour. The park staff offers talks, tours, and demonstrations from time to time. Admission is $2 for those over 16 or $4 for a family. Call (901) 689-5696. Visit online at www.nps.gov.

Nearby
Those who would like to own a piece of the Civil War should visit **Ed Shaw's Gift Shop,** Hwy. 22 S, tel. (901) 689-5080, which sells relics of the Shiloh battle—bullets, buttons, belt buckles, etc. Minié balls—bullets from rifles—sell for 75 cents apiece. Other bullets go for 22 cents to $1. Indian artifacts and souvenirs are on hand as well. Check it out online at www.hardincounty.com/edshawsgifts.

ADAMSVILLE

This town was home to two men whose behavior in elected office is still discussed—one with honor and one without.

The Buford Pusser Home and Museum, 342 Pusser St., tel. (901) 632-4080, commemorates the famed sheriff of McNairy County, whose crusade against lawless elements has become a part of popular culture.

Pusser, who was six and a half feet tall, worked as a professional wrestler before moving back to

The South brought 62 cannons to Shiloh for the largest concentration of artillery firepower ever seen in a North American battlefield.

SHILOH

The battle that took place here April 6 and 7 in 1862 was the first big battle of the Civil War. Forty thousand Union troops under U.S. Grant had come down the Tennessee River on their way to the state of Mississippi, stopping at a little hamlet called Pittsburg Landing to await the arrival of an army under D.C. Buell. Moving toward them was a Southern army of 44,000 men commanded by Albert Sidney Johnston, who aimed to destroy the Union troops before any reinforcements arrived.

Neither force had seen much combat. Grant's troops were so green that he decided to drill them rather than fortify his positions. This was a critical mistake. The Southerners had raw troops as well, but they were eager for battle.

Grant was eating breakfast nine miles downstream in Savannah when thousands of Southerners giving the Rebel yell poured through the woods and onto the Northern troops. Grant heard the cannon and ordered a steamboat to take him to Pittsburg Landing. Gen. William T. Sherman was in the thick of battle—one that relentlessly pushed back his troops.

The South's General Johnston thought he had the battle won. He rode up near the front, hoping to spur his troops onward. The air hummed with bullets, several of which clipped the general's clothing. One cut an artery in his leg, a wound so slight that Johnston didn't take it seriously until his loss of blood made him almost pass out. Aides lifted him from his horse to the ground, where he soon died.

Confusion reigned. Southern and Northern troops wandered around in the thick forest, getting separated from their regiments and fighting a thousand individual fights. The Union forces finally regrouped along a country lane, known as the Sunken Lane, and there repelled the repeated Confederate attacks that befell them. The fighting was so fierce that the area in front of this lane was dubbed "The Hornet's Nest." Finally, the Southerners rolled up 62 cannons—the largest concentration of artillery firepower ever seen on a North American battlefield—and forced the Union troops to retreat. Their valiant six-hour stand along the Sunken Lane had given Grant enough time to form another line, and the Confederates, now under Braxton Bragg, were too weary to pursue them.

During the night, the Union reinforcements crossed the Tennessee River to join the battle, and the next morning the Union army moved forward, recrossing ground it had given up the day before. Theirs was a gruesome march, for it took them past the dead and wounded from the day before. Some of the bodies had been partially eaten by hogs. By noon, the Southerners could see that they were losing, and they retreated toward Mississippi. The next day Grant sent Sherman in a half-hearted pursuit, but troops under Nathan Bedford Forrest dissuaded him from accomplishing anything.

Shiloh was the first big battle of the Civil War, and it showed both sides just how terrible this conflict was going to be. Grant, who had thought that a convincing victory would make the Confederates give up, realized that it would take a total conquest to bring the South to its knees. The South, which had hoped that the North would lack the will to pursue the war, saw a fearsome resolve on the part of its commanders.

One of every four men in the Battle of Shiloh was killed or wounded—some 21,000 in all. More Americans died at Shiloh—an estimated 3,477—than in the Revolutionary War, the War of 1812, and the Mexican War put together. Ironically, "Shiloh" is a Biblical word meaning "place of peace."

his hometown and becoming a law officer. Elected sheriff in 1964, he took on the job of ridding the county of a group of criminals who, run out of Alabama, had established themselves near the state line in south McNairy County. In battling the mob, Pusser was shot eight times, knifed seven times, and once fought off six men at once, sending three to jail and three to the emergency room. In 1967 a car pulled alongside Pusser's and fired shots that killed his wife and blew away much of his jaw. Eventually, he prevailed.

Pusser served three terms as sheriff, and his story was made into the very successful *Walking Tall* series of movies. In August of 1974 he died in the crash of his new Corvette. His home is now a museum devoted to his exploits. Admission is $2 for adults and $1 for children six to 18.

The late Ray Blanton was a member of Congress who then served as governor of Tennessee from 1975 to 1979. In general his administration ran the state well, except for the actions of a few ill-chosen cronies. Blanton's successor, Lamar Alexander, was sworn in early when it was discovered that the lame-duck Blanton staffers were taking bribes to commute the sentences of dozens of felons, many of them murderers and armed robbers. The governor was not charged with this offense, but he did serve time in prison for his involvement in illegal efforts to sell state liquor licenses. A subsequent U.S. Supreme Court ruling overturned his fraud conviction, and a Tennessee court restored his citizenship. He ran again for his old seat in Congress, telling people, "The voters know I was railroaded and falsely accused." They might have known this, but they did not vote for him in sufficient numbers.

Events
Buford Pusser Festival, held the weekend before Memorial Day, remembers the legendary lawman with carnival rides, arts and crafts, and other events. Call (901) 632-4080 for details.

SELMER

Several restaurants in Selmer serve a hamburger called a "cereal burger" or "slugburger," a way that originated in Corinth, Mississippi, of making ground beef go farther by mixing it with soybean grit and other ingredients. How did it get its other-than-appetizing name? "Oh, those kids," said one restaurant worker. "They started calling them that."

Pat's Cafe, Court and 3rd St. in Selmer, tel. (901) 645-6671, opens at 5 a.m.with full-throttle country breakfasts. Lunch consists of sandwiches and salads—slugburgers if so desired—and the place closes down at 2 p.m. It's open Mon.-Saturday.

Pappy John's Original BBQ, Hwy. 45 S, tel. (901) 645-4352, serves pork barbecue and ribs. It's open Mon.-Sat. for all three meals.

Risner's Steak House, junction of Hwy. 45 and Hwy. 57, Eastview, tel. (901) 645-5648, has a special that few restaurants in Tennessee offer—all the quail one can eat. This deal is offered every Thursday night, while Friday and Saturday nights feature hickory-smoked ribs. It's open every day for all three meals.

Wink's Diner, 137 S 2nd St., Selmer, no telephone, makes slugburgers so good that it serves

an average of 400 per day, compared to only 30 or so hamburgers. "I sell a world of them," said Wink, who also offers sandwiches and other items. Wink's is open Mon.-Sat. 5:30 a.m.-4 p.m.

Accommodations
Overnight options are the **Southland Motor Lodge,** 515 E. Poplar Ave., tel. (901) 645-6155; or **Days Inn,** 631 Mulberry Ave., tel. (901) 645-4801.

Information
Contact **McNairy County Chamber of Commerce** at 114 Cypress St., tel. (901) 645-6360, or see the chamber online at www.centuryinter. net/mccc.

SALTILLO

One of the last remaining ferries on the Tennessee River connects this little town with the eastern shore. The ferry runs Mon.-Sat. every week. If it happens to be on the other side of the river, motorists should blow their horns for service.

Where to Stay
At **Parker House Bed and Breakfast,** Hwy. 69, tel. (901) 278-5844, guests have a choice of two antique-furnished bedrooms with shared baths. The hosts serve a full country breakfast. Rates are $75 per night. Moderate.

Saltillo Marina Campground on Riverview has 18 sites. It is open in wintertime, but has no water. Call (901) 687-7353.

Food
Vittles Restaurant on Oak St., tel. (901) 687-3335, is an island of gourmet dishes amid a sea of country cooking. More than 50 varieties of sandwiches and 25-plus gourmet burgers are on the menu here, as are chicken cordon bleu, pasta, and three kinds of chicken wings. It's open Mon.-Sat. for lunch and dinner.

Information
Hardin County Chamber of Commerce, 507 Main St., Savannah, is open Mon.-Fri. 9 a.m.-5 p.m., and, during daylight saving time, Saturday 10 a.m.-4 p.m. and Sunday 1-4 p.m. Call (800) 552-3866 or (901) 925-2363.

JACKSON

Next to Memphis, this is the largest city in West Tennessee. Founded in 1821 and named after Andrew Jackson, it owes its prominence to the presence of the railroads and its location between Memphis and the Tennessee River. The tracks came to town three years before the Civil War, and by the time fighting broke out Jackson became a target for northern armies. It was occupied by the North in 1862.

After the Civil War, the railroads worked on connecting the Deep South with the Midwest, and this directly benefitted Jackson. The homes in the **East Main Street Historic District** reflect this prosperity, which also extended to the large numbers of freed slaves who settled in Jackson to work for the railroad. **Lane College,** established in 1882, was one of the first colleges established for black people by black people. It still educates students.

Musically, Jackson has been home to significant figures. Blues fans know of two "Sonny Boy" Williamsons, both of whom played harmonica—or harp, to blues folk. The first one, John Lee Williamson, was born here and is remembered for his virtuoso harmonica playing. He played with Sleepy John Estes and other locals but did his most significant work in Chicago. Among his songs is "Good Morning Little School Girl."

Big Maybelle was a blues shouter in the '50s and '60s, while Bertha Dorsey was one of the very few black women to experience success in country music. Recorded under the name Ruby Falls, her songs appeared during the '70s, as did those of Jackson native Kenny Vernon, best known for the duet "Picking Wild Mountain Berries."

The most famous Jackson musician, however, is Carl Perkins, who lived and owned a restaurant in Jackson until his death in January 1998.

Last but not least, Jackson is home to the branch of Procter & Gamble that makes Pringles potato chips.

THE KING OF ROCKABILLY

C arl Perkins was born in 1932 to a sharecropping family outside of Tiptonville, near Reelfoot Lake. His extended family moved to Bemis, a factory town south of Jackson, when he was 14, and he began playing with his brothers in a band called "The Perkins Brothers."

Carl was signed to a contract in 1955 by legendary Sam Phillips of Sun Records, where he met Elvis Presley and Johnny Cash. The three toured together, and back in the studio Perkins recorded his own composition, "Blue Suede Shoes," supposedly inspired when Perkins played at a dance during which a young man kept telling his partner not to step on his shoes. The song was the first record to top the pop, country, and rhythm and blues charts, and Perkins began to look like the next Elvis. Unlike Elvis, he could write his own material.

Then tragedy struck. On the way to New York City to appear on the *Ed Sullivan Show,* the band's car crashed in Delaware, breaking Carl's neck and causing injuries that later led to the death of one of his brothers. It was Elvis who wound up singing "Blue Suede Shoes" on the *Ed Sullivan Show.*

That accident stunted Perkins's career, and he was surpassed by fellow Sun artists Johnny Cash and Jerry Lee Lewis. Despite his troubles, he continued writing songs, and he always had a strong following in Europe. The Beatles recorded three of his songs—"Honey Don't," "Everybody's Trying to Be My Baby," and "Matchbox." He moved into country music, reaching a pinnacle in 1971 when Johnny Cash recorded his famous "Daddy Sang Bass."

Perkins died in January 1998 after a series of strokes. He was 65 years old.

SIGHTS AND RECREATION

When Jackson was installing its first modern waterworks in the early 1880s, it tapped an artesian well and water began flowing out of the ground. Named the **Electro Chalybeate Well,** it became the centerpiece of a park and attracted many who believed that the waters possessed curative powers. The park is now gone, but the city has restored

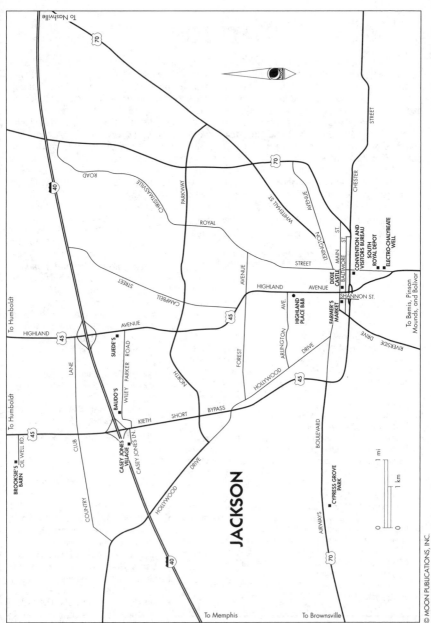

JACKSON

To Nashville

To Humboldt

To Humboldt

To Memphis

To Brownsville

To Bemis, Pinson Mounds, and Bolivar

BROOKSIE'S BARN

OIL WELL RD.

CASEY JONES VILLAGE

BAUDO'S

SUEDE'S

CYPRESS GROVE PARK

HIGHLAND PLACE B&B

FARMER'S MARKET

DIXIE CASTLE

CONVENTION AND VISITORS BUREAU

SOUTH ROYAL DEPOT

ELECTRO-CHALYBEATE WELL

CLUB

COUNTRY

LANE

WILEY PARKER ROAD

CASEY JONES LN.

HOLLYWOOD DRIVE

KIETH

SHORT

BYPASS

NORTH

FOREST

AVENUE

CAMPBELL

STREET

HIGHLAND

AVENUE

ROYAL

STREET

CHRISTMASVILLE

ROAD

PARKWAY

WHITEHALL ST.

AVENUE

LEXINGTON

MAIN ST.

BALTIMORE

CHESTER

STREET

HIGHLAND

AVENUE

STREET

ARLINGTON AVE.

HOLLYWOOD

DRIVE

AIRWAYS

BOULEVARD

RIVERSIDE DRIVE

SHANNON ST.

1 mi

1 km

0

0

© MOON PUBLICATIONS, INC.

the old fountain and built a gazebo over it. Visitors can still drink the water, absolutely free, next to the Jackson Utility Division's water operations center on S. Royal Street.

The **South Royal Depot**, on Royal St., tel. (901) 425-8223, is one of two railroad museums in Jackson. Restored to its 1907 appearance, it contains exhibits of Jackson railroad history. It's open Mon.-Sat. 10 a.m.-3 p.m.

The most famous railroad person hereabouts was an engineer who grew up in Cayce, Kentucky. Although his given name was Jonathan Luther, his co-workers knew him as "Casey" Jones, and on a dark night in Mississippi he passed into popular history when his train rear-ended another train. The **Casey Jones Home and Railroad Museum**, tel. (901) 668-1222, features the engineer's home as its centerpiece. The house was moved from its original location, and now it contains a museum with various items such as the watch Casey carried on his fatal run, the hearse that carried him thereafter, and a railroad engine of the kind that he operated. The museum is open seven days a week 8 a.m.-9 p.m. Admission is $3.50 for adults, $3 for seniors, and $2.50 for children six to 12. The village also contains an old country store and restaurant as well as the Casey Jones Station Inn.

In his *Tennessee: Historical Landscapes,* Carroll Van West gives considerable space to the **Bemis** community south of Jackson. In the early years of the 20th century, Northern capital flowed into Tennessee to build factories, and across the state paternalistic companies set up planned communities to house their workers. The company here was the Jackson Fiber Company, which made cotton bags, and it set up a village complete with homes, stores, churches, and many other features necessary for a good life. Three thousand people lived in Bemis as late as 1940, and the company began selling the houses to workers in 1965. To tour the area, drive down Highland Ave. (Hwy. 45) three miles south of the courthouse and turn right.

Cypress Grove Nature Park, tel. (901) 425-8364, sits three miles west of Jackson along Hwy. 70/1. This 165-acre park has a 6,000-foot-long boardwalk that takes visitors through a cypress forest, an open meadow, along two lakes, and past several enclosures containing various raptors. For those who cannot make it to Reelfoot Lake, this is a good place to see cypress trees, those water-loving hardwoods whose knobby "knees" stick up out of the water. Fishing is allowed from the shore of the lakes, but most people come here to see the birds and other wildlife. Depending on the season, visitors can see hummingbirds, migratory waterfowl, and owls. Herds of deer live in the park, as do generous varieties of insects. The park is open all year 8 a.m.-5 p.m., till 7:30 p.m. during daylight saving time.

Events
Shannon Street Blues Festival, held in June at the West Tennessee Farmer's Market, honors Sonny Boy Williamson.

Casey Jones Old Time Music Festival, a celebration of string music, is held in early September at the amphitheater behind the Casey Jones Village. Categories include guitar, dobro, bluegrass banjo, and buckdancing. For information, call (901) 686-7342.

BRIAN BARDWELL

The Casey Jones Home preserves the memory of the legendary railroad engineer.

Sports

Jackson is home to the **West Tenn Diamond Jaxx,** who play AA baseball at Pringles Park, 4 Fun Place, tel. (901) 664-2020. An affiliate of the Chicago Cubs organization, they play from early April through early September. Visit them at www.diamondjaxx.com.

WHERE TO STAY

Bed and Breakfasts

Highland Place Bed & Breakfast, 519 N. Highland Ave., Jackson, TN tel. (901) 427-1472, occupies a stately 1911 three-story brick colonial built in the classic revival style. It has been remodeled from top to bottom and was selected as the Designer Showhouse for West Tennessee in 1995. The three guest rooms all have private baths. Two interesting architectural features are the cherry-paneled library on the first floor, complete with a working fireplace—there are three in all throughout the house—and the tiger-striped oak planks used throughout the house. Rates range $75-95 and include a gourmet breakfast. Other meals may be served by arrangement. Moderate-Expensive.

Motels

Jackson offers a generous range of national chain hotels. (See "Where to Stay" under "Accommodations and Food" in the On the Road chapter for a list of franchise accommodations and their toll-free reservation numbers.)

For something different, try the **Casey Jones Station Inn,** I-40 and Hwy. 45 Bypass, tel. (901) 668-3636 or (800) 628-2812. Sleep in one of the 50 rooms in a motel-like place, or choose lodging in one of the four railroad cars—two cabooses or two other railroad cars. Rates run $36.95-69.95 for single occupancy and include a deluxe Southern breakfast bar with country ham, sausage, Virginia ham, chocolate gravy, and redeye gravy. Inexpensive-Moderate.

The **Inn at Jackson,** 1936 Hwy. 45, tel. (901) 668-4100 or (800) 4CHOICE, offers rooms for $50-55. Inexpensive.

Moderate-priced is the **Garden Plaza Hotel,** 1770 Hwy. 45 Bypass S, tel. (901) 664-6900 or (800) 3GARDEN; rates are $65-75.

Camping

Johnson Mobile Village and RV, 2223 Hollywood Dr., tel. (901) 668-2487, offers 14 RV spaces in a mobile home park near the interstate with level paved, open sites. It's open all year. From Hwy. 40 (Exit 79) go a quarter-mile south on Hwy. 20.

FOOD

Baudo's Restaurant, 559 Wiley Parker Rd., tel. (901) 668-1447, serves Italian and American cuisine Mon.-Fri. for lunch and dinner, and dinner only on Saturday. For those who want to try their hand at "Blue Suede Shoes" or other songs, Baudo's features karaoke each Thursday at 9 p.m. Comedy showcases are every Friday and Saturday night at 9:30 p.m.

Brooksie's Barn, 561 Oil Well Rd., tel. (901) 664-2276, was built by a gentleman who used to haul his rig and compete in barbecue contests—and win. He built this barn and has been serving barbecue, catfish, hushpuppies, ribs, and fried chicken ever since. He's open Tues.-Sat. for lunch and dinner and on Sunday for lunch only.

Burgers Up, 600 Old Hickory Blvd., tel. (901) 664-7286, reminds diners of what hamburgers were like before they were hijacked by the fast-food fiends. Each patty of beef here is shaped by hand. Milk shakes are made from whole milk, ice cream, and, if one requests a flavored version—real strawberries. It's open Mon.-Sat. for lunch and dinner.

The **Catfish Cabin,** 1290 S. Highland Ave., tel. (901) 422-1001, has one fan who warns patrons not to fill up on "the Absolutely Magnificent God's Own Perfect hushpuppies." Doing so would preclude enjoying the catfish, which is served all-you-can-eat or as a straight dinner. Catfish Cabin also serves steak, country ham, chicken, shrimp, oysters, snapper, and lobster tails. The late Carl Perkins was one of the owners of this place, and photos and other memorabilia of his hang on the walls. It's open for dinner only Mon.-Thurs. and for lunch and dinner the rest of the week.

China Cafe, 31 Bowling Dr., tel. (901) 664-8277, offers a full menu as well as a buffet of Cantonese, Mandarin, and Szechuan dishes for lunch and dinner seven days a week.

Lotta Steaking Going On" and "Boppin' the Blues Bar B Cue." If this restaurant were in Nashville, it would be called a museum. On display are guitars, gold records, and lots of photographs—Carl Perkins with Paul McCartney, Clint Black, Elvis, George Harrison, and other admirers. It's open Mon.-Sat. for lunch and dinner and Sunday for lunch.

SHOPPING AND INFORMATION

Shopping
Jackson boasts 14 antique stores. A brochure describing them is available at the chamber of commerce.

The **Cheese Factory,** in Jackson's Casey Jones Village, tel. (901) 664-8580 or (800) 960-3054, makes cheddar, Colby, flavored cheeses, and spreads. One of the more popular is a country ham-and-cheddar spread. It also sells gourmet meats, preserves, and specialty sauces. It's open Mon.-Sat. 9 a.m.-6 p.m. and on Sunday 12-5 p.m.

Brooks Shaw & Son's Old Country Store, in Casey Jones Village, tel. (800) 748-9588, displays more than 15,000 Southern antiques along with candy, collectibles, and souvenirs.

The **West Tennessee Farmer's Market,** at Shannon St. and Market Dr., has an enclosed building as well as open sheds. In addition to seasonal produce, the market offers quilt shows, blues festivals, and the odd political rally.

Wildlife in Wood Studio, in the gazebo at Casey Jones Village, tel. (901) 668-2782, contains wildlife carvings in wood, original paintings, and prints. Visitors can watch the artist, Dee Moss, at work. The studio is open Mon.-Fri. 9 a.m.-5:30 p.m. and Saturday by appointment.

Information
The Jackson/Madison County Convention and Visitors Bureau is in the Civic Center at 400 S. Highland Ave. Call (800) 498-4748 or (901) 425-8333.

The **Old Country Store Restaurant,** Casey Jones Village, tel. (901) 668-1223, is a 500-seat place open every day for breakfast, lunch, and dinner. Buffets of country cooking are the feature here, although diners can order a la carte.

Pig House Barbecue, 1024 Campbell St., tel. (901) 423-8566, sells sublime barbecue sandwiches—no ribs—and a few side orders amid a bunch of University of Tennessee paraphernalia. It's open every day 10 a.m.-8 p.m.

Reggie's Barbecue, 104 West Chester St., tel. (901) 422-3330, is one of the few barbecue places hereabouts to offer beef barbecue in addition to the more conventional pork and chicken. Reggie's also offers "rib tips," the part where ribs connect with the backbone. A third reason to stop here is barbecued bologna. It's open Mon.-Thurs. for lunch and dinner.

Suede's, 2263 N. Highland Ave. not very far from the I-40 exit, tel. (901) 664-1956, was owned by the late rockabilly and country great Carl Perkins, featuring dishes such as "A Whole

SOUTH OF JACKSON

PINSON MOUNDS STATE ARCHAEOLOGICAL AREA

Tennessee's first three-story building wasn't built until 1823, yet this 1,162-acre area contains a seven-story structure that has stood for at least 1,600 years. At 72 feet high, Saul's Mound is the second-highest Indian mound in the United States—the highest is Monk's Mound in East St. Louis.

The Area's museum, which was brilliantly designed to resemble a mound itself, assembles what tantalizingly little knowledge anthropologists have about the people who worked so hard to build these structures. The mounds are piles of earth, probably carried basket by basket from surrounding land. The archeological evidence assembled so far suggests that most of the mounds were built during the first three centuries A.D.

While a few of the mounds contain burial remains, most seem to have been used for ceremonies. When Joel Pinson, part of a group of surveyors mapping land acquired from the Chickasaw in the Treaty of 1818, found the mounds in 1820, the Indians in the area at that time denied building them and claimed to have no knowledge of anyone who did.

Visitors can walk up a staircase leading to a platform atop Saul's Mound, which in its heyday was no doubt higher than its current 72 feet.

From the platform the visitor can see other mounds and get a sense of the immensity of this site, which consists of at least 15 mounds, an earthen geometrical enclosure, and a habitation area of more than 400 acres.

The museum contains an 80-seat theater along with video and educational displays describing the people who built Pinson Mounds. A walk-through display focuses on the various cultures that make up Tennessee's prehistoric past. Pinson Mounds is open Mon.-Sat. 8 a.m.-4:30 p.m. and on Sunday 1-5 p.m. It is closed weekends Dec.-February. Admission is free. The area contains picnic tables and hiking trails, but no camping is permitted. Call (901) 988-5614 or visit online at www.tnstateparks.com.

HENDERSON

This town is the seat of Chester County, which in 1882 became the last county created in Tennessee. Following the Civil War, a large family named Hurst moved into the western part of the county, becoming so predominant that the area was termed "Hurst Nation." Perhaps they had to stick together, for during the war they supported the Union.

The 1939 *WPA Guide* reports that this was once the moonshine center for West Tennessee: "Under the leaves in the hollows (the moonshiners)

Saul's Mound, 72 feet high, is the second-tallest Indian mound in the United States.

stashed away the fresh corn and let it charter (char) for months. When aged, the deep red liquor was clear of verdigris (fusel oil) and held a bead the size of number five shot. There were no 'rabbit eyes on it to pop off' (big bubbles that foam and burst as soon as the bottle is shaken). Certain brands were known as 'creeping likker,' because they kicked 'slow and powerful.'"

The unidentified writer of the preceding sounds like he did considerable research on that topic. Chances are he was not a graduate of **Freed Hardeman University,** which is affiliated with the Church of Christ and serves 1,300+ students. The University maintains a museum of its memorabilia in the administration building. See it on the Internet at www.fhu.edu.

Anglers may want to stop off at the **Harville Manufacturing Company,** which produces more than 50 varieties of soft plastic fishing lures. These and others are for sale at **Hugh's Tackle Box,** 121 Front St., tel. (901) 989-5846. One of the better sellers is the six-inch Chicken Foot.

Six miles east of town at the intersection of Hwys. 100 and 22, you'll find Joyner's Bar-B-Que, with ribs, pork, and chicken.

CHICKASAW STATE RUSTIC PARK

This state park occupies 1,280 acres of the Chickasaw State Forest, a 14,384-acre tract of timberland that stands on some of the highest ground in West Tennessee. Like many Tennessee parks, the emphasis is on recreation: swimming, picnicking, boating, fishing, tennis, basketball, archery, horseback riding, square dancing, evening movies, and campfires.

Accommodations include a group lodge, cabins, and camping. The lodge, which stays open all year, can accommodate groups up to 40 people. Thirteen housekeeping cabins, complete with fireplaces, can sleep four or six people. These are open all year as well. To make reservations, call (901) 989-5141 or (800) 421-6683.

The park has 110 campsites, 70 of which have hookups, and hot showers and flush toilets are available in campground bathhouses. The camping season opens in March for RVs, in May for tents; it ends in November for tents and one month later for RVs. The horse camping section is open all year, and if campers have no horse and there is still space, they can stay.

MERCER

The little railroad town of Mercer is southwest of Jackson on Hwy. 138, and the building that was home to the town's store is now the **Mercer Cafe and Mercantile Company,** 1704 Hwy. 138, tel. (901) 423-8611, a restaurant that draws patrons from a wide area. The two-story brick building is more than 100 years old, and inside, the ceilings, complete with original pressed tin, are almost 20 feet high. The restaurant is decorated with copies of old pictures from local families, a photo of a fondly remembered black midwife, and items such as an antique ice crusher.

The food varies from first-class hamburgers and cheeseburgers to steak, pork chops, and chicken. Friday is fish-fry night—catfish complete with hushpuppies, white beans, coleslaw, and fried dill pickles. The restaurant is open for all three meals Mon.-Sat. and for lunch on Sunday.

BOLIVAR AND VICINITY

Bolivar came into being as the town of Hatchie, named for the river of which the town was the head of navigation. Located in lands bought from the Indians, it began as a trading post. Town boosters dreamed that the Mississippi and Tennessee Rivers would be joined by a canal that would go right beside the town, but it never happened. The town's name was changed in 1825 to honor Simon Bolivar, the liberator of Colombia and Venezuela—the first town in the country to be so named.

Hardeman County, of which Bolivar is the seat, produces more hardwood lumber than any other county in Tennessee. The entire area was covered with hardwood forests when planters arrived in the early 1800s, and their slaves cleared the large cotton fields that still produce today.

McAnulty's Woods, a conservation site in the town, is thought to be the only virgin forest remaining in West Tennessee.

After the Civil War, many of the freed slaves entered into work contracts with planters and other employers. A fascinating Web site, www.ccharity.com/freedmens/contracts, gives the exact wording and spelling of some of these documents in Hardeman County.

Sights

The Bills-McNeal District begins with **The Little Courthouse** was built of logs in 1824. When the county government moved into larger quarters, the logs were covered with clapboards and the erstwhile courthouse was transformed into a federal home that's now used as the county museum. Part of its collection consists of some silver spoons commissioned by an early lawyer whose first client paid him in silver. It's open by appointment only. Admission is $3 per person or $5 if visitors also take in The Pillars. Call Evalyn Harris at (901) 658-3390 for information.

The Pillars, at the corner of Bills and Washington Streets in Bolivar, was home to John Houston Bills, who kept a private journal from 1843 to 1871. Then, as now, good help was hard to get; the builders of the town's first brick home installed the eight fluted Doric columns upside down. That didn't bother the guests, however, who included James K. Polk, David Crockett, and Sam Houston. It's open by appointment only. Admission is $3 per person. Call Evalyn Harris at (901) 658-3390.

General Sherman's behavior at Magnolia Manor foreshadowed his later treatment of Southern property.

Also in town are two historic churches. **Bolivar Presbyterian,** at Market St. across from the Post Office, was organized in 1852 and is the oldest brick church in the county. During the Civil War, General Lew Wallace, later the author of *Ben Hur,* worshiped here. **St. James Episcopal Church** was built in 1870 in the Victorian Gothic style.

When most West Tennesseans think of Bolivar, they think of "being sent to Bolivar," for on the western end of the town stands **Western Mental Health Institute,** whose 1889 administration building is a great example of Victorian Gothic Revival. The Institute covers several hundred acres, and in past days the patients raised much of their food, had a uniformed baseball team, and participated in all manner of activities. The number of patients peaked in 1965 at 3,757, and now stands at 247. Patients come from all of West Tennessee except for Shelby County.

According to the official history of the Institute, Elvis Presley spent some time here in the late '50s, but only as a truck driver hauling away some bricks from a demolished smoke stack. Tours of the Institute can be arranged by making a reservation a week ahead. Call (901) 658-5141, extension 280.

Where to Stay

Magnolia Manor, 418 N. Main St., Bolivar, TN 38008, tel. (901) 658-6700, was built by slaves in the late 1840s from brick made on the site. Modeled on an English country home, the Georgian house was occupied during the Civil War by Union Generals Grant, Sherman, Logan, and McPherson. According to a tale still told in the house about the occupation, General Sherman mightily offended the hostess during a meal with some remark to the effect that all Southern women and children should be exterminated. She abruptly left the table and was found weeping on the back porch by General Grant. When he learned the source of her distress, he ordered Sherman to apologize. The future torcher of Atlanta did so, but was so irked that he slashed at the solid walnut stairway with his sword. The mark of that anger is still there. The house contains two suites and two other rooms, all of which share baths. Rates range $85-95. Expensive.

A couple of motel options are the **Aristocrat Motor Inn,** 108 Porter St., tel. (901) 658-6451; and **The Bolivar Inn,** 626 W. Market St., tel. (901) 658-3372.

Food

Joe's Restaurant, on the Square on Market St., tel. (901) 658-7255, serves all three meals Mon.-Saturday. The dinner specialty is seafood and steaks.

Also in Bolivar is **Richard's Bar-B-Q,** on W. Jackson St., tel. (901) 658-7652, which advertises that its barbecue is as "sweet and tender as a mother's love." Diners can choose from ribs, chicken, steaks, and even barbecued bologna.

Shopping

Wren's Nest Antiques, 308 Bills St., tel. (901) 658-3235, offers antiques, paintings, and china.

Information

The **Hardeman County Chamber of Commerce** is located at 500 W. Market St., tel. (901) 658-6554.

WHITEVILLE

Heading out of Bolivar on Hwy 100, the traveler comes to this little town, which has three wonderful sources of food.

Backermann's Bakery & Cheese Shop, Hwy. 64 W one mile from Whiteville, tel. (901) 254-8473, is a Mennonite bakery that also carries bulk foods, lunchmeats, and cheese. The bakery generally has on hand eight kinds of yeast bread and six kinds of pies and cookies.

Anderson Fruit Farms, in Whiteville on Hwy. 64, tel. (901) 658-5524, grows and sells a great deal of fruit and vegetables. Pears, apples, and peaches come from some 12,000 trees, and other crops such as corn, peas, strawberries, cantaloupes, watermelons, and blackberries are offered for sale at the farm store. During the fall the Andersons produce more than 15,000 gallons of apple cider. Try the fried pies, which are made daily by the women of the local Pentacostal church.

Cafe 100, outside Whiteville at the intersection of Hwy. 64/15 and Hwy. 100, tel. (901) 254-9409, offers three meals every day starting at 5 a.m. It serves plate lunches Mon.-Friday.

SOMERVILLE

This town, in the center of West Tennessee's plantation area, was the scene of a little-remembered episode of the Civil Rights Movement. When African-Americans sought to vote in 1959, the whites who ran the county banded together to wage economic warfare in an effort to prevent this from taking place. Merchants would not sell to blacks, physicians would not treat them, and anyone who attempted to register to vote was fired from his or her job. Once that year's cotton crop

was gathered, plantation owners evicted some 400 families, who banded together in "Tent City" to brave the cold weather. This determination to vote won the group national attention, and the Federal government brought suit against landowners and merchants. The ensuing ruling ordered them to stop standing in the way of anyone wanting to vote. Learn more online at www.picard.tnstate. edu/~library/digital/tent.

Somerville has many historic homes, and the best time to see them is in late October during the **Architectural Treasures of Fayette County Tour.** Volunteers are working to restore the Hanum-Rhea House, ca. 1832, for use as the Fayette County Museum and Cultural Center on North Street. For information on the tour, call (901) 465-8690.

Right on the square in town stands **Farmers Hardware,** a wonderful old-fashioned store that occupies a building erected in 1875. The owner, while poking around in the place, once found some .28-caliber bullets last manufactured in 1862. The store has a hole in the ceiling; it seems they used to assemble carriages upstairs and then lower them to the showroom floor.

Events

Hogmania Barbecue Contest takes place in September. For information, call (901) 465-8690.

Where to Eat and Shop at the Same Time

Me and My Tea Room sits in the **Magic Woods** antique store and specializes in lunch. The *pièce de résistance* here is Hidden Treasure, a chicken breast in phyllo dough. Call (901) 465-0077.

Information

Call **Fayette County Chamber of Commerce** at. (901) 465-8690 or visit them online at www. fayettecountychamber.com.

WILLISTON

The road runnning from Somerville to Moscow goes through Williston, home of **Pleasant Retreat Bed & Breakfast,** 420 Hotel St., tel. (901) 465-4599. This 1850 home is furnished with antiques. Rates are $75 per night. Visit online at www.bbonline.com/tn/pleasantretreat. Moderate.

Events

Vic Rhodes Traditional Music Fest, a celebration of old-time string music, is held in the middle of May at the Williston Airport. Categories include guitar, dobro, bluegrass banjo, and buckdancing. For information more information about the festival, call (901) 686-7342 or see www.geocities.com/Nashville/9158/index.

NORTH OF JACKSON

TO ALAMO

Motorists on Hwy. 412 in Crockett County northwest of Jackson sometimes do a double-take when they look into a field and see buffalo. This is **Hillcrest,** a farm on which the same family has lived for five generations. In addition to the American bison, owner Claude Conley stocks zebras, wildebeests, scimitar-horned oryxes, and other exotic animals. Visitors are invited to stop and look at the animals. No formal tour is given and no admission is charged, but sometimes guests can be shown around. Call (901) 696-4423 or (901) 696-5501.

Food

The **Olympic Steakhouse,** at the intersection of Hwy. 412 and Hwy. 70/79, tel. (901) 663-3294, offers lunch and dinner seven days a week. It serves catfish, barbecue, steaks, and chicken. Lunch features a country buffet, and Friday and Saturday nights have a seafood buffet.

Allen's Bar-B-Q at 774 Hwy. 412 outside of Alamo, tel. (901) 696-4620, has steaks, catfish, sandwiches, barbecue, chicken, and shrimp. It's open Mon.-Fri. for lunch and dinner.

HUMBOLDT

In West Tennessee, this town is synonymous with strawberries and a long-running festival that commemorates the red berries.

It also was the home of the late Jesse Hill Ford, author of *The Liberation of Lord Byron Jones.* The 1965 novel told the story of a black mortician who, seeking a divorce from his unfaithful wife, names a white police officer as her lover. The mortician's white lawyer tips off the policeman, who murders the mortician. The book became a best-seller and a 1970 movie and brought fame to Ford, but it infuriated the people hereabouts, who knew it was based on real people and actual events.

Ford got his comeuppance, at least in Humboldtian eyes, when he was charged with murder in the death of a black man who parked one night along Ford's long driveway. Because of a racial dispute surrounding high school football, Ford's son—the captain of the team—had received threats, and Ford feared that the driver of the car was there to ambush his son. The writer claimed that he fired his rifle just to hold the car there until police arrived, and, after a trial that received national coverage, he was acquitted. Ford died in Nashville in 1996.

Sights

City Hall contains two museums worth a stop. The **Strawberry Festival Historical Museum** exhibits relate to the 50-plus years of the celebration, but also to the history of Humboldt and surrounding area. Exhibits include an old telephone switchboard, black history book, and doctor's bag. Admission is free.

The **West Tennessee Regional Center for the Arts** occupies the second floor. More than 175 objects, including oil paintings, watercolors, sculptures, prints, lithographs, pastels, and silk screens, make up the collection, which was assembled by Dr. and Mrs. Benjamin Caldwell. Admission is $2. Both museums are open Monday, Wednesday, and Friday 9 a.m.-4 p.m.

T.G. Sheppard, the country singer-songwriter who hit a peak during the 1980s, is remembered as Billy Browder hereabouts, where he first saw the light of day in 1944.

Events

The **West Tennessee Strawberry Festival** is held the first full week in May and includes fireworks, gospel singing, country-western dancing, storytelling, a checkers tournament, parade, quilt show, five- and 10-kilometer runs, and a beauty pageant.

Where to Stay
Motel options are the **Heritage Inn,** 3350 E. End Dr., tel. (901) 784-2278; and **Regal Inn Motel,** 618 N. 22nd Ave., tel. (901) 784-9693.

Food
Armour's Barbecue, 607 W. Main St., tel. (901) 784-9450, serves barbecue and ribs. It's open Tues.-Sat. for lunch and dinner.

Kappis Steak House, 600 Hwy. 45 Bypass, tel. (901) 784-2077, serves a lunch and dinner buffet plus full menu Tuesday-Sunday. Kappis's Friday night seafood buffet is a local favorite.

Sam's Barbecue, 500 W. Main St., tel. (901) 784-9850, offers takeout only but is still worth a stop. It's open Mon.-Sat. for lunch and dinner.

Gordon's, 3100 E. End Dr., tel. (901) 784-4465, serves all three meals every day with steaks, catfish, and country ham.

Wall St. Grill, 2120 N. Central Ave., tel. (901) 784-1214, features steaks, sandwiches, soups, and salads for lunch and dinner every day.

Information
Humboldt Chamber of Commerce, 1200 Main St., tel. (901) 784-1842, is open Mon.-Fri. 8 a.m.-5 p.m.

And Nearby
Gibson, a village northwest of Humboldt along Hwy. 76/79/Alt. 40, is the home of **Laster's Bluegrass Opry,** a monthly gathering of musicians who play in the gym of what used to be Gibson High School. Held on the fourth Saturday of the month, this free concert—they do pass the hat—always has three bluegrass bands. Square dancers kick things off at 7 p.m., and different bands appear every month. For further information, call Donna or Buddy Laster at (901) 784-2054.

MEDINA

The **Tennessee Woods Art Gallery,** 585 Hwy. 45 E, tel. (901) 783-3265, offers life-sized nativity scenes, cypress log tree houses, and "mountain men" fashioned by chain saws and

other woodcarving tools. The gallery sells clocks and other crafts as well.

The gallery shares a building with **Big Bad Wolf Barbecue,** tel. (901) 783-5175, which offers barbecue and side orders Mon.-Sat. for lunch and dinner.

MILAN

During World War II Tennessee was often chosen for defense-related facilities. One that survives is the **Milan Army Ammunition Plant,** which Martin Marietta Ordnance Systems operates on 22,000 acres east of town. Here 10 production lines crank out items ranging from 40 mm cartridges to 155 mm artillery shells. An ebullient publicity brochure proclaims, "The Milan Army Ammunition Plant—it's the one place you should contact for your ammunition or other explosive-related requirements when you want immediate attention and on-schedule delivery of high-quality product."

West Tennessee Agricultural Museum, Hwy. 70A/79 N in Milan, tel. (901) 686-8067, is one of the better museums on this end of the state. Its building was designed to accommodate the museum, which presents a chronological look at agriculture in the region. Beginning with the Indians, its displays move to the era of settlers, subsistence farmers, cotton plantations, and early mechanized farming. It's open Mon.-Fri. 8 a.m.-4 p.m. and Saturday noon-4 p.m. Admission is free.

Events
One of the missions of agricultural colleges is to demonstrate crops and techniques that will preserve the land, enhance profits, or somehow make farming better. An example of this is "no-till" farming, in which annual plowing, which can lead to erosion, is replaced by chemical herbicides that "burn down" weeds—better living through chemistry.

The **No-Till Field Day** hereabouts has evolved into a festival with events that appeal to those who wouldn't know a plow from a disc. Held on the fourth Thursday in July, it leads into a weekend filled with a beauty pageant—Miss Milan No-Till—trap shooting, country music concert, arts and crafts, and horse show. For information, call (901) 686-7362.

Accommodations and Food
Try **Ramada Limited,** Hwy. 45 E/70, tel. (901) 686-3345 or (800) 2RAMADA.

At **Hig's Restaurant,** 1027 Oakwood Dr., tel. (901) 686-9901, diners can order from the menu or partake in the lunch and dinner buffet. Hig's serves chicken, steaks, and different kinds of fish, but its specialty is catfish. It's open Mon.-Sat. for lunch and dinner.

BRADFORD AND VICINITY

This little town claims to be the "Doodle Soup Capital of the World." Doodle Soup seems to be one of those dishes, such as Indian pudding in New England and mountain oysters in Colorado, that far more people talk about than actually eat. To make it, according to aficionados, one bakes a chicken, then mixes the drippings in the baking pan with one cup of vinegar and one cup of water. Season with red hot pepper to taste, bring to a boil, and serve over crackers or biscuits. The traditional accompanying dishes are mashed potatoes, peas, and fruit cocktail. One woman said she anoints her baked chicken with Doodle Soup, while another said with a sniff, "I never eat the stuff; it's too greasy for me." For further information, call the Bradford City Hall at (901) 742-2271.

Where to Stay
Bradford Bed and Breakfast, P.O. Box 100, tel. (901) 742-3143, is a guest apartment in the home of the town's sole physician. Outside are a private tennis court and lovely grounds, and inside is a complete kitchen, sitting room, and bedroom with a queen-sized bed and private bath. No alcoholic beverages are allowed. The rate is $45 per night. Breakfast includes homemade bread or muffins. A gourmet dinner is available by arrangement. Inexpensive.

SKULLBONE

About three miles east of Bradford on Hwy. 105 is the community of Skullbone, which gets its name from a particularly rough sort of 19th-century prize-fighting in which the combatants would face each other and trade punches to the head. Hitting anywhere below the collar wasn't con-

sidered sporting. John L. Sullivan is said to have fought here.

Skullbone was put on the map by an inspired local promoter, who got Governor Browning to issue a proclamation in 1953 recognizing "the Kingdom of Skullbonia" as "a worthy successor to the rugged frontiersmen who built its early traditions." **Hampton's General Store,** tel. (901) 742-3179, is about all that is left of the kingdom, but it is a pleasant place to stop, have a cold drink, and read the clippings on the wall. The store needs no address; one cannot miss it. It's open Mon.-Sat. 6 a.m.-7 p.m., and Sunday 2-5 p.m.

KENTON

The town of Kenton is **"The Home of the White Squirrels,"** a group of albino gray squirrels that has been nurtured over the years into a sizable population. Protected by statute and the efforts of locals, the squirrels jump from tree to tree all over town. During the summers, a local advises, the squirrels are best viewed early in the morning or in the evening. Seems they don't like the heat.

The town has **Kenton White Squirrel Homecoming** around the Fourth of July, complete with gospel singing, grand parade, and fireworks. For more information, contact or go by the Kenton City Hall, 108 N. Poplar, tel. (901) 749-5767.

RUTHERFORD

This little Gibson County town was the last Tennessee home of David Crockett, from which he departed to go off to the Alamo and glory. A replica of his cabin, built with some of the original logs, is two blocks north of the town's sole traffic light. It is open June-Labor Day 9 a.m.-5 p.m., and it contains period tools, furniture, and other items. Admission is $2 for adults and $1 for children.

The town holds an annual **Davy Crockett Days Celebration,** a weeklong festival that culminates on the first Saturday in October. Visitors can watch or partake of gospel music, a street dance, white bean and ham hock dinner, tall tales contest, and demonstrations of horse shoeing, spinning, and broom-making. For information, contact the Rutherford City Hall, 206 East Main St., tel. (901) 665-7166.

Food
City Cafe, 203 E. Main St., tel. (901) 665-7508, serves breakfast and lunch Mon.-Saturday. It offers down-home country cooking and has a luncheon buffet.

R&J Restaurant, 455 N. Trenton, tel. (901) 665-6999, specializes in barbecue and ribs. It's open Mon.-Sat. for lunch and dinner.

DYER

Three miles north of Dyer on Hwy. 45 W stands Gibson County High School. On the school grounds, history students have built the **Pioneer Homeplace,** a collection of 19th-century hewn log structures. Eight log buildings were put together by the students, who dress in period clothing and interpret their history for visitors.

The buildings include a "dog-trot" house, smokehouse, corn crib, livestock barn, and welcome center. Students who work on the project, which dovetails with their classes, learn how to spin wool yarn and make lye soap, baskets, brooms, and quilts.

Although the Homeplace usually caters to groups, individuals are welcome to tour the buildings. Call the high school at (901) 692-3616 and ask for Mike Ramsey, the teacher who inspired it all. Admission is 50 cents per person.

TRENTON

This town is home to the world's largest collection of *veilleuses-théières,* or lighted teapots. Dr. Frederick C. Freed, a Trenton native who taught medicine in New York, fell in love with this particular kind of teapot, which came about as a way of warming tea while providing light in sick-

rooms or nurseries. In the early 19th century, artists took this idea and produced teapots that were works of art, some depicting people, buildings, and scenes out of literature. Dr. Freed assembled his 1750-1860 teapot collection over 40 years, buying 525 of them in antique shops from places such as Singapore, Sri Lanka, Egypt, and all over Europe.

When the teapots were given to the city, Trenton had no appropriate place for the collection, but this was rectified with the construction of a new City Hall at 309 S. College Street. Now the walls of the city council room are lined with glass shelves containing the collection. Admission is free, and visitors can view the teapots whenever the building is open and no one is using the room—usually weekdays 8 a.m.-5 p.m. Call (901) 855-2013.

Entertainment and Events
The **Nite-Light Theatre** offers three productions a year of works such as *Anything Goes* and *Hello Dolly,* as well as children's fare. Call (901) 855-2129 to reach a tape recording listing upcoming shows, or call (901) 855-2382 to reach a person who can answer questions.

The second full week in May brings the **Teapot Festival,** complete with bean dinner, crafts fair, fireworks, tractor pull, and barbecue chicken sale.

Accommodations and Food
Stay in the **Carrie Belle Manor,** 655 N. College St., tel. (901) 855-0321.

The Majestic Steak House and Pizza, 2050 Hwy. 45 Bypass, tel. (901) 855-4808, serves steak, pizza, spaghetti, and catfish for lunch and dinner seven days a week.

Information
Greater Gibson County Area Chamber of Commerce, 2051 Hwy. 45 Bypass, tel. (901) 855-0973, is open Mon.-Fri. 8 a.m.-4:30 p.m.

JACKSON TO THE TENNESSEE RIVER

PARKERS CROSSROADS

Confederate general Nathan Bedford Forrest cut quite a swath—several of them, actually—in West Tennessee. He was successful because most of the time he was able to pick the place and the time to engage his enemies. Parkers Crossroads was a place where his luck almost ran out.

Forrest was known as the "Wizard of the Saddle," but most of the time his men fought dismounted while others held their horses to the rear of the battlefield. While attacking Union soldiers at Parkers Crossroads, Forrest received word that his horse-holders were under attack by an unexpected Union force. When asked what orders to give, he yelled, "Charge both ways!" They did, and he and his troops escaped to bedevil Union forces for the rest of the war.

At least that's the story. The most recent biographer of Forrest claims this tale is apocryphal, and anyone who wishes to argue with locals can begin at the **Cotton Patch Restaurant,** Parkers Crossroads (Exit 108) off I-40, tel. (901) 968-5533. This delightful place combines Civil War exhibits with a wonderful down-home restaurant, open for all three meals daily. It has a full menu but specializes in barbecued pork, catfish, and country ham. Visit online at www.bushwacking.com/cottonpatch.htm.

NATCHEZ TRACE STATE RESORT PARK

Visitors familiar with the Natchez Trace Parkway in Middle Tennessee may find the name of this park puzzling. The early land route from Natchez, Mississippi, to Nashville followed a myriad of paths though the forests and cane-brakes of the wilderness. When fear of robbery ran high, travelers would take this section of the route, called the Western Trace.

This 14,073-acre park sits amid the 48,000-acre Natchez Trace State Forest and provides a wide variety of wilderness and recreation experiences. Much of the land came into state hands because the farmers who lived here had more or less farmed it to death. By the 1930s the land was acquired by the U.S. Department of Agriculture, which began projects aimed at restoring the land and demonstrating soil conservation practices in hopes of preventing further devastation.

The third-largest pecan tree in North America, cleverly named the "Big Pecan Tree," grows here. Legend holds that one of Andrew Jackson's men carried a pecan from the Battle of New Orleans and gave it to a local, who planted it. The tree was measured in April of 1973 and found to be 18 feet two inches in circumference, 106 feet high, and spreading 136 feet. Locals

Union troops of the 14th Indiana Volunteer Infantry fire their muskets and fill the air with black powder smoke in a re-creation of a Civil War battle.

COURTESY OF AUBREY WATSON

announced that this was the largest pecan tree in the world, and soon found their tree topped by tree measurers from Virginia and Louisiana, whose claims dropped the Natchez Trace tree to third place. Since then, no one has gotten around to measuring the tree again.

Recreational opportunities abound here. The park has four lakes full of fish, and a swimming beach is open during summer. Hiking trails—one long enough for an overnight—lead through the park, as do trails and roads for off-road vehicles. Other activities include playgrounds, sports fields, archery, and croquet.

The **Pin Oak Lodge** contains a restaurant open seven days a week for all three meals April-Oct., and on weekends through November. Accommodations begin with the lodge, which has 20 rooms that cost $56-60. Extra guests are charged $6 per night. Housekeeping cabins sleep four, have fireplaces and air-conditioning, and come with all linens and fully equipped kitchens. They cost $65 and are enormously popular. Make reservations up to one year ahead by calling (901) 968-8176 or (800) 250-8616. Inexpensive-Moderate.

This park has three campgrounds with a total of 143 sites, each with a picnic table and hookups. Bathhouses have hot showers, and all campsites are on a first-come, first-served basis. One of the campgrounds stays open all year.

For information about the park, call (901) 968-3742 or go online to www.tnstateparks.com.

PARSONS

The Decatur County Fairgrounds south of Parsons on Hwy. 69 is the staging point for the **World's Largest Coon Hunt,** which is held on the second weekend in April. Coon hunting basically consists of turning a bunch of dogs loose in the woods, whereupon they sniff around until they find the scent of a raccoon and follow it in search of the animal. Raccoons usually lead the dogs on a merry chase and then take refuge in a tree. All this takes place at night, when raccoons are most active.

Human coon hunters either build a fire and sit around it listening to the dogs or try to keep up with them through the woods. For this festival, country music is played into the wee hours and a good time is had by all. The money raised in this fashion is donated to St. Jude's Children's Research Hospital in Memphis. For further information and rules about entering the competition, call (901) 847-4202.

object of the chase

THE TENNESSEE TO THE MISSISSIPPI

CAMDEN

This Tennessee River town is home to the state's cultured pearl business and the source of seed pearls for similar operations in Japan. The Tennessee River harbors 24 species of pearl-producing mussels, and the best of these are cultivated in wire nets that hang from floating plastic pipes. Keeping them close to the surface of the water accelerates pearl production, which usually takes three years. Tennessee River pearls occur in varying colors and shapes, and all have a beautiful luster. They are sold throughout the country.

The **Birdson Resort/Marina** outside of Camden cultivates freshwater pearls for export to Japan and for use in jewelry in this country. Mussel divers work April-Nov., but visitors can see a pearl jewelry store and museum daily 8 a.m.-5 p.m. Rings, brooches, pins, and other jewelry as well as individual pearls are for sale, and a 350-gallon aquarium contains live mussels for close inspection. Admission is free.

Groups of 15 or more can take A Pearl of a Tour, which lasts three to seven hours and includes a ride on the river, lunch, and a diving demonstration. Call one month ahead to make arrangements. To get to the pearl operation, take Exit 133 off I-40 and go nine miles north on Birdsong Rd. to the Birdsong Resort/Marina. Call (901) 584-7880.

On March 5, 1963, a small plane crashed near Camden, killing country legend Patsy Cline, Cowboy Copas, and Hawkshaw Hawkins.

Entertainment and Events
Fiddler's Bluegrass Championship is held annually in the Holladay community south of Camden on the third Saturday in April. Fiddlers, mandolin players, and bands compete. A dance is held the night before. Call (901) 584-3145 for information.

Harmon's Creek Heritage Festival, held on Labor Day weekend, draws up to 10,000 people to the area around Phifer's Country Store in Eva. Among the attractions are antique tractors, cars, and engines; barbecue; five bands; a flea market; and children's activities. The affair begins on Friday and runs through Sunday afternoon. Call (901) 584-9855.

Spring Festival in Big Sandy, tel. (901) 593-3213, takes place downtown on the Saturday before Memorial Day. The event kicks off with a parade about 10 a.m. followed by local country bands and singing groups, balloon tosses, wheelbarrow races, an ice cream eating contest, and a pet show. Usually there is a special event, such as a parachute demonstration. The day ends with a street dance in the evening.

The **Waterfowl Festival** takes place in Big Sandy in late August. The big attraction is the duck blind drawing (hunters hope to win a chance to hunt from the duck blind on the opening day of hunting season). The festival features a duck calling championship and retriever demonstrations, and the crafts include duck carvings. Call (901) 593-3213 for more details.

Where to Stay
Try the **Passport Inn,** 30 Old Rt. 1 Rd., tel. (901) 584-3111 or (800) 238-6161.

For campers, **Beaverdam Resort,** 1280 Lodge Rd., tel. (901) 584-3963, has 11 sites and is open all year.

Birdsong Resort and Marina, on Birdsong and Camden Roads, tel. (901) 584-7880, has 50 sites, a pool, boating, fishing, and hiking trails. It's open all year.

Food
Country and Western Steakhouse, 189 Extension St., tel. (901) 584-3026, specializing in steak and pond-raised catfish, serves lunch and dinner seven days a week.

The Catfish Place, Hwy. 641, tel. (901) 584-3504, offers all three meals seven days a week. It runs specials all week long, with catfish served every day—fiddlers (whole fish minus the head) or fillets.

1850 Log House, two miles north of the traffic light on Hwy. 641 N, tel. (901) 584-7814, serves dinner Wed.-Sat. with fish, shrimp, steak, and chicken dishes.

Information
Benton County/Camden Chamber of Commerce, 202 W. Main St., tel. (901) 584-8395, is open Mon.-Fri. 8 a.m.-4 p.m.

NATHAN BEDFORD FORREST STATE HISTORIC AREA

This 2,587-acre park, on the west bank of the Tennessee River, complements the Johnsonville State Historical Area on the east bank of the river in commemorating one of the more amazing feats of warfare—the only known defeat of a naval force by a cavalry group. (The battle is described in "Johnsonville State Historical Area" under "West to the Tennessee River" in the Heartland chapter.)

Nathan Bedford Forrest directed his attack from Pilot's Knob, a longtime river landmark that stands at 740 feet, the highest point in West Tennessee and about 450 feet higher than the

T.J. Whitfield "took in many a ton of shells" in his musseling days.

average height of the surrounding county. Now this area contains more than 20 miles of hiking trails, lots of access to Kentucky Lake, picnicking, and camping.

The **Tennessee River Folklife Center,** tel. (901) 584-6356, is an interpretive center at the Nathan Bedford Forrest State Park devoted to people who made their living from the river. Exhibits include *Old Betsy,* a mussel-gathering boat built and used by T.J. Whitfield, one of the last of the old-time musselmen. Subjects covered include commercial fishing, log rafting, music, and religion, and items displayed include baskets, tools, and audio recordings of people who recall the old days. The center's schedule changes, so call ahead to make sure it is open. Admission is free. Visit online at www.tnstateparks.com.

Events
Summer Song Festival, Saturday night of the Fourth of July weekend, is a gospel sing with live local bands at the Eva Beach area.

Tennessee River Folklife Festival, held the first Saturday in October at the Eva Beach area, demonstrates different life skills needed in days of yore, such as quilting, making lye soap, gathering edible and medicinal plants, shooting rifles, caning chairs, making baskets, and blacksmithing. Sometimes displays cover commercial fishing and musseling. Area country, bluegrass, and gospel musicians provide the entertainment.

Camping
The park has two campgrounds with a total of 53 sites. One campground has 38 sites with hookups and hot showers, while the other offers more primitive camping. Sites are available on a first-come, first-served basis and are open all year. Call (901) 584-6356.

PARIS AND VICINITY

The anonymous writer of the Paris section of the *WPA Guide to Tennessee* described how Isham G. Harris, a Paris native who was governor when the Civil War broke out, reacted when asked to send troops to the Union. "He replied: 'Tennessee will not furnish a single man for coercion, but 50,000, if necessary, for the defense of our rights or those of our Southern brethren.'" Then, in a masterpiece of under-statement, the writer added, "Harris was a leader in the movement for secession."

Paris also can lay claim to two country musicians. Rosan Gallimore, a.k.a. Rattlesnake Annie, was born north of here in the Puryear community. A friend of Willie Nelson, she has achieved great success in Europe. Hank Williams Jr., who puts on one of the best shows in country music, has lived in Paris since July 4, 1986. His fan club and Hank Williams Jr. Enterprises operate out of Paris, too. Call (901) 642-7455.

Bocephus, as Hank Jr. was nicknamed by his father, confesses on one of his albums that "I ain't crazy 'bout nothin' but women, money, and blues." The last of the three can be found at **The Big Apple** on Hwy. 641, tel. (901) 247-5798, in the nearby community of Puryear.

Sights

Harris was one of three Tennessee governors to come from this town, the seat of Henry County. The buildings on the east, north, and west of the square constitute one of the oldest stretches of 19th-century court square buildings in the state, if not the entire South. Visitors can pick up a brochure describing a walking tour of the town at the Paris-Henry County Heritage Center, 614 Poplar St., tel. (901) 642-1030.

Paris is home to the world's largest replica of the **Eiffel Tower.** Sixty-five feet tall and built of wood and steel at Christian Brothers University in Memphis, it was erected and given to the city in 1993. The tower stands in Memorial Park and is open daily year-round. Admission is free. To get there, take Volunteer Drive, which connects Hwy. 79 on the east side of town with Hwy. 641.

Entertainment and Events

Paris is about 15 miles from the Tennessee River (Kentucky Lake), yet it has capitalized on the river in a way that towns on the banks would envy. The **World's Biggest Fish Fry** takes place during the last full week in April, a time when approximately 100,000 people come to town to consume more than 13,000 pounds of fish. Between meals, they watch a parade, go to a rodeo, listen to music, shuffle over to the "Down & Dirty Dirt Dance," see crafts shows, and attend a beauty pageant.

One of the more unusual events is the Catfish Race, in which selected catfish race down 15-foot-long Plexiglas troughs of water on the courthouse lawn. Call (901) 642-3431 or (800) 345-1103.

Lakefront Resorts

Buchanan Resort, 14 miles east of Paris, tel. (901) 642-2828 or (800) 225-6302, offers a motel, cottages, lodges, and camping. Amenities include a swimming pool, tennis, and superb fishing. Take Hwy. 79 to Buchanan Boat Dock Rd. and follow signs. Rates run the gamut from Inexpensive to Luxury, ranging $48-195 per night for double occupancy.

Cypress Bay Resort, Rt. 2, Box 131, tel. (901) 232-8221, has eight cottages that sleep seven to 10 people. Two-bedroom cottages cost $30 per night for two people, three-bedroom cottages cost $48; each additional person costs $5. Inexpensive.

Motels

Try the **Best Western Travelers Inn,** 1297 Wood St., tel. (901) 642-8881 or (800) 528-1234, rates $40-58 (Inexpensive); or the **Hampton Inn,** 1510 E. Wood St. (Hwy. 79), tel. (901) 642-2838 or (800) HAMPTON, rates $41-63 (Inexpensive-Moderate).

Camping

Big Eagle, no phone, has 43 sites with no hookups. It's open mid-April through September. Take Hwy. 79 east of Paris and follow signs.

Buchanan Resort, tel. (901) 642-2828, has 56 sites. It's open mid-March through October, with a pool, boating, and fishing. Take Hwy. 79 to Buchanan Boat Dock Rd. and follow signs.

KOA-Paris Landing, tel. (901) 642-6895, has 75 sites. It's open April-September. Take Hwy. 79 to East Antioch Rd. and follow signs.

Food

Ace's Pizza, 1053 Mineral Wells Ave., tel. (901) 644-0558, with a big-screen TV and Chicago theme, serves wonderful Chicago-type pizza. It's open Mon.-Sat. for lunch and dinner.

Hong Kong Chinese Restaurant, 1021 Mineral Wells Ave., tel. (901) 644-1810, serves a daily lunch buffet and a weekend buffet in addition to menu selections.

Knott's Landing Restaurant, 209 N. Poplar St., tel. (901) 642-4718, serves excellent catfish, hushpuppies, and white beans. It's open Mon.-Sat. for three meals a day.

Redmons's Bar-B-Que, 101 N. Caldwell St., tel. (901) 642-9381, is a wonderful, family-owned business whose decor includes lots of local memorabilia. It's open Mon.-Sat. for all three meals.

Tom's Pizza & Steak House, 2501 E. Wood St., tel. (901) 642-8842, is open Tues.-Sun. for lunch and dinner.

Big Apple Cafe, Hwy. 641 in Puryear, tel. (901) 247-5798, serves Mexican food and deli sandwiches. It's open every day for lunch and dinner except Sunday and stages live blues every Saturday night starting at 9:30 p.m.

At the **Old Oak Tree Restaurant,** Buchanan Boat Dock Rd. (at the Buchanan Resort) in Springville, tel. (901) 642-8810, a 75-foot-tall red oak grows through the roof of the dining room, and diners have a beautiful view of Kentucky Lake. The restaurant is known for its catfish and is open for three meals a day, March-Oct. every day of the week.

Shopping
Downtown Paris has seven antique stores. **The Old Depot Antique Mall,** 203 N. Fentress St., tel. (901) 642-0222, is one block from Courthouse Square in the former train station. Here buyers can peruse furniture, railroad artifacts, artwork, fine glassware, linens, musical instruments, and paper collectibles including old advertisements, Civil war newspapers, old *Life* magazines, postcards, Elvis memorabilia, paper dolls, railroad books, and time schedules.

West Tennessee isn't as famous for country ham as East Tennessee, but **Clifty Farm,** 1500 Hwy. 641 S, tel. (901) 642-9740, upholds tradition by producing thousands of the cured delicacies a year. It is open Mon.-Fri. 7 a.m.-4 p.m.

Sally Lane's Hand Made Candies, a half-mile east of town on Hwy. 79, tel. (901) 642-5801, sells more than 100 kinds of confections, such as peanut brittle, pink and green mints, pecan logs, pralines, and sugar-free candy.

Information
Paris/Henry County Chamber of Commerce, 105 E. Wood St., tel. (901) 642-3431 or (800) 345-1103, is open Mon.-Fri. 8 a.m.-4:30 p.m.

PARIS LANDING STATE RESORT PARK

This 841-acre park lies 16 miles northeast of Paris on the shores of Kentucky Lake. The activity here focuses on the lake, the second largest man-made lake in the U.S. after Lake Mead on the Arizona-Nevada border. The park also includes a swimming pool, an 18-hole golf course, and recreation and nature programs. A full-service marina, tel. (901) 642-3048, offers 212 slips, a free boat launch ramp, and a full-service store with food and fuel.

With 100 rooms, the **Paris Landing Inn,** tel. (901) 642-4311 or (800) 250-8614, is the largest one in the state park system. Rooms cost $64-68. Moderate. Ten new cabins sleep 10 people; each includes three bedrooms, two baths, fully equipped kitchen, great room, fireplace, central heat and air, and a balcony overlooking the lake. One cabin is handicapped-accessible. A two-night minimum stay is required before Memorial Day ($130.24/night). Between Memorial Day and Labor Day cabins are let on a weekly basis only ($781.44). Call for reservations. Premium.

The campground has 46 sites, all with hookups and access to hot showers. Sites are available on a first-come, first-served basis, open all year. From December to March, camping is available only to self-contained vehicles. See the park on the Internet at www.tnstateparks.com.

McKENZIE

The **Gordon Browning Museum,** 640 N. Main St., tel. (901) 352-3510, commemorates the Carroll County native who served as governor 1937-39 and again for two terms 1949-53, becoming the only governor in the state to return to office after a 10-year hiatus. The Republicans nominated country singer Roy Acuff to run against him in 1949, to no avail. Browning was also the first governor to occupy Tennessee's governor's mansion.

The museum contains memorabilia that Browning collected in his more than 50 years of public service. One item is the first Tennessee driver's license; Browning was governor in 1938, the year the state started requiring licenses. The museum is open weekdays except Wednesday

9 a.m.-4 p.m. and on Saturday noon-3 p.m. Visit online at www.carroll.aeneas.net/~gbm/index.

Accommodations and Food

Try the **Briarwood Inn,** 635 N. Highland Dr., tel. (901) 352-1083.

At **Hig's Restaurant,** 25185 Hwy. 22, tel. (901) 352-7532, diners can order from the menu or partake of the lunch and dinner buffet. Hig's serves chicken and steaks and different kinds of fish, but its specialty is catfish. It's open for lunch and dinner Tues.-Sat. and lunch only on Sunday.

Catfish Restaurant, 525 N. Highland Dr., tel. (901) 352-5855, serves catfish, grilled chicken, steaks, and sandwiches, and it offers a salad bar and lunch and weekend buffet. It's open every day except Tuesday for lunch and dinner.

Information

Carroll County Chamber of Commerce, 141 E. Main St., Huntingdon, tel. (901) 986-4664, is south of McKenzie in the county seat. It's open Mon.-Fri. 8 a.m.-4 p.m.

MARTIN

This town did not exist during the Civil War but was incorporated in 1874 at the behest of William Martin, a prominent local tobacco farmer who persuaded the railroad to lay tracks through his property.

In 1927 a junior college was created here, and it has grown through the years and become a branch of the University of Tennessee. Now approximately 5,600 students attend the college, which has four-year status. See it online at www.utm.edu.

Where to Stay

Motel options include the **Econo Lodge of Martin,** 853 University St., tel. (901) 587-4241; and the **University Lodge,** Hwy. 431 at Hwy. 45 Bypass, tel. (901) 587-9577 or (800) 748-9480.

Food

Rich's Cafe, 241 S. Lindell St., tel. (901) 587-9028, serves full meals as well as sandwiches. It is open seven days a week for lunch and dinner.

Hearth Restaurant, 615 N. Lindell St., tel. (901) 587-9700, offers a full menu and a buffet and is the most upscale of the four restaurants listed here. It specializes in good country cooking and is open seven days a week for all three meals.

Cafe Yamato, 113 St. Charles St., tel. (901) 587-5770, open for lunch and dinner Mon.-Fri. and for dinner only Saturday and Sunday, serves Chinese food.

K-N Rootbeer Drive-in, 241 N. Lindell St., tel. (901) 587-2551, serves standard drive-in fare, including sandwiches, french fries, soft drinks, and ice cream cones. It's open Mon.-Sat. for lunch and dinner.

Information

Weakley County Chamber of Commerce is in Dresden at 110 W. Maple St., tel. (901) 364-3787. It's open Mon.-Fri. 8 a.m.-5 p.m.

BIG CYPRESS TREE STATE NATURAL AREA

This 330-acre natural area was named for an enormous cypress tree that at one time was the largest bald cypress in the United States and the largest tree of any kind east of the Mississippi. Reaching a height of 175 feet, it had a trunk that was 40 feet in circumference and 13 feet in diameter. In 1976, alas, a bolt of lightning struck the tree, whence it fell to the ground and smoldered for two weeks. Foresters estimated that the tree had stood for 1,350 years.

It is very difficult to see the remnants of the tree, for the stump is on the far side of the Obion River, and state officials in Nashville have never seen the wisdom of paying for a bridge to reach a stump. Visitors with their own canoes are welcome to cross the river, provided they can get to it. The low-lying ground is frequently very wet nine months of the year. Those confined to the shore, however, will find evidence of a variety of wildlife that inhabits the area, including deer, turkeys, quail, rabbits, raccoons, bobcats, coyotes, ducks, squirrels, and plenty of snakes.

The Middle Fork of the Obion River, which was "channelized" by the Corps of Engineers, crosses the hardwood bottomland forest. If visitors ignore the damp ground, profusion of reptiles, clouds of insects, and disappearance of the area's namesake, this is a pleasant place to go. Visitors will find no crowds. No camping is permitted in the area. Call (901) 235-2700 or get information on the Web at www.tnstateparks.com.

UNION CITY

This town was not named in honor of Northern troops; the name instead refers to the junction of two rail lines.

Sights

The **Obion County Museum,** 1004 Edwards St., tel. (901) 885-6774, comes up with a new theme every season. Exhibits include a log cabin and a horse-drawn hearse. It's open Sat.-Sun. 1-5 p.m. year-round. Admission is free.

Union City is famous to gun collectors as the home of **Dixie Gun Works,** Hwy. 51 S., tel. (901) 885-0700. Founded by the late Turner Kirkland, who began collecting guns when he was a boy, the Gun Works at any given time has about 1,500-2,000 antique firearms on hand for visitors to inspect. The company also imports and sells replicas of antique guns, many of which are used during black powder hunting season. There is no charge for visiting the gun room, which is open during the hours listed below.

The **Old Car Museum,** part of the Gun Works building, displays a collection centering on 36 antique cars, all of which are in running condition. Highlights include a 1924 Marmon Touring Car, a 1936 Packard limousine, and a 1909 Maxwell. The museum also exhibits an 1850 log cabin gunshop, 70 farm engines, three high-wheeler bikes, and an assortment of car horns and hubcaps. The Gun Works/Museum is open Mon.-Fri. 7 a.m.-5 p.m. and Saturday 8 a.m.-noon. Admission is $2 for adults or $5 for an entire family.

Where to Stay

Try the **The Hampton Inn,** 2201 Reelfoot Ave., tel. (901) 885-8850 or (800) HAMPTON; or the **Super 8 Motel,** 1400 Vaden Ave., tel. (901) 885-4444.

Food

The **Dixie Barn Restaurant,** 1315 Old Troy Rd., tel. (901) 885-3663, serves home-style food and fried catfish. It's open for all three meals Mon.-Sat. and for breakfast and lunch on Sunday.

The **Corner Barbecue,** 1425 E. Reelfoot Ave, tel. (901) 885-9924, offers the standard barbecue and trimmings. It's open for all three meals seven days a week.

Catfish Galley, 1001 Marshall Ave., tel. (901) 885-0060, is open seven days a week for lunch and dinner. It serves seafood, catfish, chicken, soups, salads, sandwiches, appetizers, and desserts, and also offers a children's menu.

Flippens Hillbilly Barn, four miles north of Hornbeak on Shawtown Rd. between Union City and Reelfoot Lake, tel. (901) 538-2933, contains a restaurant and market known for its jams, jellies, and fried pies. The restaurant is full service and offers fish, country ham, and sandwiches. The restaurant is open for breakfast and lunch Tues.-Thurs., for all three meals Fri.-Sat., and for lunch only on Sunday.

New Jade Restaurant, Reelfoot Shopping Center, tel. (901) 885-9999, offers Chinese food daily for lunch and dinner. Diners can choose from the luncheon or dinner buffet or order from the menu.

Olympia Steak and Pizza, 1705 W. Reelfoot Ave., tel. (901) 885-3611, serves lunch and dinner daily. Diners can partake of a luncheon buffet, or, for dinner, have a salad bar and order from the menu.

Searcy's Cafeteria, 306 S. 1st St., tel. (901) 885-0332, features homestyle food and homemade pies. It's open Mon.-Wed. for all three meals and Thurs.-Fri. for breakfast and lunch.

Snappy Tomato Pizza Company, 509 S. 1st St., tel. (901) 885-7627, serves pizza, salads, and subs. It's open for lunch and dinner seven days a week.

P.V.'s Hut, 209 E. Florida Ave., tel. (901) 885-5737, offers burgers, barbecue, great homemade potato salad, and spaghetti. It's open Tues.-Sat. for lunch and dinner.

Shopping and Information

The outlet stores at **Factory Stores of America,** 601 Sherwood Dr., tel. (901) 885-6465, are open daily year-round.

Obion County Chamber of Commerce, 215 S. 1st St. in Union City, tel. (901) 885-0211, is open Mon.-Fri. 8 a.m.-4:30 p.m.

REELFOOT LAKE AND VICINITY

REELFOOT LAKE STATE RESORT PARK

Reelfoot Lake State Resort Park is the most unusual lake in Tennessee, well worth a detour to see. The lake extends 14 miles long and five miles wide and covers some 15,000 acres. Sometimes the edge of the lake merges into wetlands and is difficult to discern. A relic of the New Madrid earthquake, Reelfoot Lake averages 5.2 feet in depth, and the deepest place in the lake is only 18 feet deep. The lake contains thousands of cypress trees with knobby "knees" that stick out of the water and tangled roots that intertwine under the water.

"Reelfoot," according to Indian legend, was the name of a local chief who abducted a local Indian maiden, thus causing the earthquake, which, the legend adds, swallowed up the chief's entire tribe. It hardly seems fair.

The shallow water, the trees, and the climate have conspired to create some of the best fishing in the country. Some 57 species of fish live here, among them largemouth bass, bream, and crappie—the latter so numerous that they are commercially fished with nets. During peak fishing season, which runs April-Oct., the park and surrounding towns fill with anglers.

Birdwatchers are attracted as well, for more than 250 species of birds visit the lake during the course of a year. Heading the list of birds to see are bald eagles, which winter in the park until mid-March. The harder the winters farther north, the more eagles show up at Reelfoot Lake, but usually at least 100 are on hand. The park has set up extensive programs to help visitors see the magnificent birds. The best place to get oriented is the visitors center, which is on the southwestern end of the lake.

Eagle tours take place Dec.-March. Buses leave the visitors center at 10 a.m. for the two-hour tours, which cost $3 per visitor. **Pontoon boat cruises** begin in May and end October 1. These last one to three hours and cost $4-6. Reelfoot Lake is the only state park with its own airstrip.

The town of Tiptonville and various landowners got to Reelfoot Lake before the park was created, so the place is a mixture of private and public land. This can be a bit disconcerting for those accustomed to entering a park gate and leaving the commercial world behind. Visit online at www.tnstateparks.com.

Events
This park offers an extensive series of events, details of which are available at the visitors center. Here are the highlights:

Crappiethon USA, usually held in April, involves the release of 1,000 tagged crappies. Lucky anglers win prizes for catching the right fish.

The cypress trees of Reelfoot Lake shelter multitudes of fish in their twisted roots.

THE NEW MADRID EARTHQUAKE

The strongest earthquake ever to occur in North America split the land in the winter of 1811-12 along the New Madrid Fault, which was named for a village in southeast Missouri. Tremors and small earthquakes in December gave an eerie indication of what was to follow.

On February 8, 1912, the big one hit. A quake that current-day experts estimate would have hit 8.8 on the Richter scale shook the earth, causing a 14-mile stretch of land to drop 50 feet in elevation. It was so sparsely settled that there was little loss of life, and, for the same reason, few eyewitnesses. One Eliza Bryan, a resident of New Madrid, described that the water "gathered up like a mountain, rising, 15 to 20 feet perpendicularly [while] fissures in the earth vomited forth sand and water, some closing immediately." Hardwood forests were flattened as if by a giant fist. The earth itself rippled with shock waves, and the poor souls who experienced it thought they were seeing the end of the world.

At least they were on land. The passengers and crew on the maiden voyage of the steamboat *New Orleans* were making their way downstream from Pittsburgh bound for New Orleans when they steamed right into the epicenter of the quake. Edward T. Luther, writing in *Our Restless Earth,* describes what happened to the boat. The voyage was unlike any before or since: The pilot steered through tidal waves, dodging clumps of ripped-out trees and avoiding collapsing riverbanks. The boat fell over waterfalls that had never been there before and escaped from whirlpools that swirled into newly opened holes in the riverbed. Amazingly, the *New Orleans* survived its Mississippi whitewater nightmare, and spectators greeted it with cries of disbelief when it pulled into Natchez, Mississippi.

Luther cites the composition of the alluvial soil as one culprit of the destruction. Carried from the Rocky Mountains and the Appalachians for eons, the sand and gravel mix was saturated with water to within 20 feet of the surface, and, when the shocks came, this soil behaved like a bowl of Jell-O in the hands of a toddler.

The Mississippi River flowed backward for 48 hours into the depression, filling it with water that became Reelfoot Lake. The world did not end, although clocks stopped in Boston. Reports later came in reporting shock waves as far away as Venezuela and Canada.

The **Reelfoot Waterfowl Festival** is held in mid-August and features a duck-calling contest.

September brings the **Roundhouse Music Reunion** with '50s-style music.

The **Arts and Crafts Festival** takes place in October.

Where to Stay

The park's wonderful 20-unit **Airpark Inn,** tel. (901) 253-7756 or (800) 250-8617, rests on pilings and extends out into the lake among tall cypress trees. Walking along one of the piers late on a summer night vividly brings to mind all those *It Came From the Black Lagoon* movies. The inn has 12 rooms that sleep two, and these rent for $56 a night. The remaining eight suites accommodate up to six people, and these cost $75. The park also has a five-unit hotel at the spillway of the lake, and rooms here cost $56-75. Lodging in the park is enormously popular and should be reserved as far in advance as possible. Inexpensive-Moderate.

Those who wish to sacrifice their bodies to the bugs—at least during summer—can choose one of the park's two campgrounds, offering a total of 120 sites. One is near the inn and the other lies at the south end of the lake. Both have bathhouses, and the one near the inn is open all year. Sites are available on a first-come, first-served basis.

Food

There is no shortage of eateries around the lake. The **Airpark Inn** has a 100-seat restaurant serving country cooking and looking over the lake. It is open seven days a week for three meals from January through the first weekend in October.

TIPTONVILLE

This town, one of the closest in Tennessee to the Mississippi River, sits on the Tiptonville Dome, a ridge that, in the days before levees, kept the town above floodwaters.

The proximity of Reelfoot Lake assures that the town is inundated with anglers every year, leading one observer on a particularly intense weekend to note that it looked as if the town were having a Bubba Convention.

The late Carl Perkins, country and rockabilly artist, was born here in 1932 in a sharecropper's shack. A museum in a similar house on Carl Perkins Parkway S, a.k.a. Hwy. 78, displays photos and a guitar as well as the sort of furnishings that a 1930s house would have had. The museum is open Fri.-Sun. 1-5 p.m., and admission is $1. Look for a large sign south of town on Hwy. 78 between Robertson and Church Streets. If no one is there, call Perkins Tire at (901) 253-7653, and Carl's cousin Hubert will dispatch someone to open the house.

Fishing Camps and Cabins

Reelfoot Lake attracts a great number of hunters and fishing fanatics; obtain a complete listing of cabins from the **Reelfoot Lake Tourism Development Council** at tel. (901) 538-2666.

At **Blue Bank Cypress Point Resort,** near the Reelfoot Lake spillway off Hwy. 21/22, tel. (901) 253-6878, 14 rooms are available at Blue Bank near the restaurant, and 32 rooms at Cypress Point down on the water. From the last week in March until the first week in June, the resort is available only for fishing packages. The resort also offers hunting packages and bald eagle-watching tours. The restaurant is open for lunch and dinner seven days a week. It serves fresh-cut steaks, catfish, crappie, ham, chicken, and pork chops. The resort facilities include a marina, boats to rent, pontoon boats, game room, swimming pool, large playground, and picnic area. Rates are $45 and up. Inexpensive-Moderate.

Boyette's Resort, about three miles east of Tiptonville on Hwy. 21, tel. (901) 253-6523, has 14 cabins; rates are $35-95. This is next to Bo's Landing. (See below.) Inexpensive-Expensive.

Gooch's Resort, located two miles east of Tiptonville on Hwy. 21/22, tel. (901) 253-8955, has a modern motel with all rooms facing the lake and a guest house that can accommodate groups of eight to 10 people. Rates are $30-45, and the resort offers a bait shop, swimming pool, boats for rent, guide service, and camping—see below. Inexpensive.

Where to Stay

The setting is the real feature at **Back Yard Bird's Lodge Bed & Breakfast,** Rt. 1, Box 286, Airpark Rd., Tiptonville, TN 38079 tel. (901) 253-9064, a two-story dwelling with a view of the lake. The lodge sits on the Mississippi flyway on the lake and a short distance from the Mississippi River. It is a good place for fishermen, birdwatchers, honeymooners, canoeists, and photographers. On one memorable day 200 pelicans and 100 cormorants rested in the yard alongside the banks of the lake. Visitors can choose from two guest suites, both with private baths and private entrances on the lake side. The suites come with fully equipped kitchens and sitting areas with color TV. The lodge also has boat slips and a bait shop. The hosts offer a bird locator service for eagles in winter (Oct.-March), songbirds, and waterfowl. A full breakfast is served on a glassed-in dining porch. The rate is $50 per night. To get there, go north from Tiptonville on Hwy. 78 about seven miles. Turn right on Hwy. 213/Airpark Road. The lodge is two miles on the right. Inexpensive.

Sweet Dream Bed & Breakfast, 431 Wynn St., or 1441 Church St. (mailing address) in Tiptonville; tel. (901) 253-7653, is a cottage behind the Caldwell-Hopson House, an 1890s Queen Anne-style Victorian home. The cabin, which is decorated in country Victorian, has a dining room, living room, upstairs bedroom, and bath with a claw-foot tub. Breakfast consists of homemade breads and casseroles. The rate is $85 per night. Moderate.

For campers, **Bo's Landing,** about three miles east of Tiptonville on Hwy. 21, tel. (901) 253-7809, has 25 RV sites and eight primitive tent sites. Rates are $5-10 per night, and it is open all year. Bo's also has a boat ramp, boat rental, fishing guides, and bald eagle tours. Food is available at the deli seven days a week for all three meals.

Gooch's Resort, two miles east on Hwy. 21/22, tel. (901) 253-8955, has 16 RV hookups and tent sites close to the lake. Eagles roost in the trees around the resort, whose campground is open year-round.

Food

Boyette's Dining Room, Hwy. 21, tel. (901)

253-7307, serves catfish, chicken, ham, and steak for lunch and dinner seven days a week.

Marcia's Kountry Kupboard, 300 Hwy. 78 S, tel. (901) 253-8822, offers plenty of kountry kooking seven days a week for breakfast and lunch.

Information
Call or visit the **Obion Country Chamber of Commerce,** 215 1st St. in Union City, tel. (901) 885-0211; or the **Reelfoot Lake Tourism Development Council,** at the junction of Hwy. 21/22 at Reelfoot Lake, tel. (901) 538-2666.

SOUTH ALONG THE MISSISSIPPI

DYERSBURG

This is the largest Tennessee town along the Mississippi north of Memphis. It was settled as far up the North Forked Deer River as steamboats could come. This access to the Mississippi made Dyersburg a trading center, one that was enhanced when the railroad came through.

From 1942 to 1945 the Dyersburg Army Air Base trained bomber crews for service in World War II. The name of the base was misleading, for it was actually near the town of Halls.

Where to Stay
Good choices are the **Comfort Inn,** I-155 Exit 13, tel. (901) 285-6951 or (800) 221-2222, rates $39-47; **Days Inn,** I-155 Exit 13, tel. (901) 287-0888, rates $38-46; and **Holiday Inn,** Hwy. 52 Bypass and Hwy. 78, tel. (901) 285-8601 or (800) HOLIDAY, rates $49-57. All are inexpensive.

Food and Information
The Airport Restaurant, on Airport Rd. in Dyersburg, tel. (901) 286-2477, serves breakfast and a lunch buffet only. It's open Mon.-Fri. 6 a.m.-2 p.m. and Sunday 11 a.m.-2 p.m.

The Dyersburg/Dyer County Chamber of Commerce, 2455 Lake Rd., tel. (901) 285-3433, is open Mon.-Fri. 8 a.m.-5 p.m.

HALLS

This little town saw its population surge in World War II with the construction of the Dyersburg Army Air Base. The Second and Third Army (there was no Air Force at that time) trained 7,700 crewmen for action in Europe and the Pacific.

President Harry Truman visited the base during the war, and afterward it was decommissioned.

Those glory days are commemorated every year with the **Air Show.** For each one, World War II "warbirds" fly in from all over the country to line up beside current military aircraft. Held on the last weekend in August, the event costs $3 in advance for those 12 and up and $4 at the gate. Children under 12 are free with a paying adult. For information, call (901) 836-7448.

Pig Out Bar-B-Q Place, Winchester St., tel. (901) 360-9635, serves shoulder sandwiches and ribs Mon.-Sat. for lunch and dinner.

RIPLEY

The rich soil hereabouts is ideally suited for growing tomatoes, and this fact is celebrated with the **Tomato Festival** on the first weekend in July. Activities include, besides tomato tasting, gospel music, arts and crafts, barbecue contest, pistol-shooting contest, baby-crawling contest, and country music.

Ripley was for many years the home of Noah Lewis, a blues harmonica player who recorded with Gus Cannon's Jug Stompers.

Lauderdale Cellars, 196 S. Washington St., tel. (901) 635-4321, is one of Tennessee's younger wineries and specializes in fruit wines for all tastes. It sells a particularly intriguing table wine made from locally grown tomatoes, which customers find most fun to take home and use to test the knowledge of self-appointed oenophiles. They also sell 12 other kinds of wine, including cabernet sauvignon and chardonnay. The winery is open for tastings and tours Mon.-Sat. 10 a.m.-6 p.m. and Sunday 1-6 p.m. Winter hours are Mon.-Sat. 11 a.m.-5 p.m. A gift shop stocks wine-related and agricultural items.

Accommodations and Food

Try the **Days Inn,** 555 Hwy. 51 Bypass, tel. (901) 635-7378.

Blue & White Cafe, 197 S. Washington St., tel. (901) 635-1471, presents a daily lunchtime buffet of country cooking. It's open Tues.-Sun. for breakfast and lunch.

Catfish Plus, 1320 Hwy. 51 Bypass, tel. (901) 635-7570, has a luncheon buffet and a seafood buffet Thurs.-Sat. nights. It's open daily for lunch and Mon.-Sat. for dinner.

Information

Lauderdale County Chamber of Commerce, 103 E. Jackson Ave., tel. (901) 635-9541, is open Mon.-Fri. 8:30 a.m.-4:30 p.m.

HENNING

Alex Haley, author of *Roots, The Autobiography of Malcolm X,* and other books, spent part of his boyhood in the railroad town of Henning. The **Alex Haley Home,** 200 S. Church St., tel. (901) 738-2240, was built by his grandfather, Will Palmer, who ran a mill and lumberyard and was prosperous enough to build a 10-room house. It was here that the young Haley heard stories about his ancestors—Chicken George, Kizzy, and Kunta Kinte—people who would become household words when *Roots* became the most popular miniseries ever shown on television.

While millions of Americans watched *Roots,* all assuming it to be true, the book never withstood the examination of historians. According to an article in the *Tennessee Encyclopedia* by Richard Marius, Haley was sued twice for plagiarism, and one of the more gripping parts of the book, the point at which Haley meets a *griot* in Gambia who recounts the story of Haley's very ancestor, doesn't hold up. It seems that the elderly storyteller knew in advance what the American author wanted to hear, and conveniently told it to him. For all his literary sins, however, Haley can be credited with getting this country to think about the horrors of the slave trade and its effects on his people, fictional or real.

The museum contains copies of all his books, many of which are for sale. Personal items are on display, as is furniture that was in the house when Haley was a boy. The author, who died in 1992, is buried under the front lawn. The house is open Tues.-Sat. 10 a.m.-5 p.m. and Sunday 1-5 p.m. Admission is $2.50 for adults and $1 for children six to 18.

Lauderdale County Chamber of Commerce, 103 E. Jackson Ave. in Ripley, tel. (901) 635-9541, is open Mon.-Fri. 8:30 a.m.-4:30 p.m.

FORT PILLOW STATE HISTORIC AREA

This 1,646-acre tract lies on the First Chickasaw Bluff, which once overlooked the Mississippi River. Over the years the river moved its bed about a mile to the west. Fort Pillow is the only Confederate bulwark along the Mississippi in Tennessee that is open to the public.

The visitors center contains nature exhibits and information about the park. Travelers can walk a mile roundtrip from the visitors center over a suspended bridge to see the battlefield. A museum offers a video, slide presentations, and exhibits about the battle of 1864. The gift shop sells Civil War memorabilia.

Hikers can take advantage of three wooded trails, one five miles long, one 10 miles long, and one a seven-mile backpacking trail. If backpacking, register at the visitors center. There is no cost, but for safety reasons the staff needs to keep track of backpackers. The fishing area is a 25-acre man-made lake with crappie, bass, bluegill, and catfish. There are 40 camping sites and a large group tent area that holds up to 200 people and contains a pavilion with a stove and picnic tables. Fort Pillow and the campground are open year-round. To get there from Covington, drive north eight miles to Henning on Hwy. 51, then go west 18 miles on Hwy. 87/207. For more information, call (901) 738-5581 or visit online at www.tnstateparks.com.

COVINGTON AND VICINITY

The seat of Tipton County is the third-largest city in Tennessee along the Mississippi. Unlike Dyersburg, Covington did not have any water access to the big river, and it owes its size to the coming of the railroad in 1873. Money flowed into the town, and the **South Main Historic Dis-**

THE FORT PILLOW MASSACRE

Of all the Civil War sites in the state of Tennessee, this one is without a doubt the most controversial. The Confederates built this fort on a high bluff above the Mississippi to help defend Memphis from attack by gunboats, but they abandoned it in 1862 when Corinth, Mississippi, fell to Union forces. Union troops occupied the fort, which, after the North captured the Mississippi River, ceased to be of much strategic importance.

By April 1864, Nathan Bedford Forrest, who was harassing Union supply lines, turned toward the fort, which he knew contained supplies and fresh horses.

It also contained 507 of the kind of troops that Southerners hated the most—Unionists from East Tennessee and blacks. The first group, called "homemade Yankees," was beneath contempt, but the hatred of the second was more intense. Slave owners had always feared a rebellion by blacks, yet they paradoxically claimed that blacks would never prove to be good soldiers. Whenever Southerners had encountered black troops before, they refused to treat them as legitimate prisoners of war. Instead, Confederates considered them stolen property and promptly sold them back into slavery.

The occupants of Fort Pillow were accused of sending foraging expeditions into the surrounding countryside, where the soldiers allegedly robbed residents and helped themselves to livestock, furniture, and anything they wanted.

On April 12, Forrest's troops surrounded the land side of the fort and demanded an uncondi-tional surrender. The Union troops refused—twice—so he attacked. A Union gunboat stood offshore, but its shells had little effect on the battle. When the Southerners breached the fort, the defenders made a desperate run down the bluff toward the gunboat, which pulled away, leaving them between the river and the guns of Forrest.

According to Northern reports, Forrest's men massacred at least 300 of the troops in the fort. The truth of that account of the "Fort Pillow Massacre," as Northern newspapers dubbed it, was vehemently denied by Southerners, who insisted that the Union troops died because they refused to give up.

One surviving Southern account reads as follows: "The poor, deluded Negroes would run up to our men, fall on their knees and with uplifted hands, scream for mercy, but were ordered to their feet, and then shot down."

Whatever spurred the deaths, the outcry led Congress to investigate. General Sherman was ordered to investigate the incident and, if the situation warranted, retaliate. He did nothing, leading some to argue that the whole thing was wartime propaganda.

The Fort Pillow attack diminished the reputation of Nathan Bedford Forrest, who made a chilling comment in his report of the battle. "The river was dyed with the blood of the slaughtered for 200 yards," he wrote. "It is hoped that these facts will demonstrate to the northern people that Negro soldiers cannot cope with Southerners."

---

trict, now on the National Register, shows how the townspeople of the 1880s-1900 spent it. One of the more unusual structures is the **Lowenhaupt-Simonton House** at 432 S. Main Street. It seems that a Mississippi riverboatman retired here and built a house of the kind more commonly seen in Louisiana. The house is not open to the public.

The **Tipton County Museum Veterans Memorial and Nature Center,** 751 Bert Johnson Ave., tel. (901) 476-0242, has the longest name of any such establishment in the state. This new facility, adjacent to Cobb-Parr Park, offers a look at military history with artifacts and uniforms as well as a look at nature both in the museum and along a nearby wooded trail. No admission charged.

The art deco **Ruffin Theatre** on W. Pleasant Ave., tel. (901) 476-9727, serves the town as the center of cultural activities such as concerts, plays, and dance presentations. Old-timers recall a talent show in the early 1950s in which a certain young man from Memphis blew away the competition. Call for information about what's playing now.

This is cotton country, as evidenced by the presence of **Tennessee Gins,** 800 Tennessee Ave., which operates during October and November. Call L.C. Thomas for tours, tel. (901) 476-7842.

Those beneath a certain age will light up with the knowledge that Covington is the "Blow Pop Capital of the World." Charms's Blow Pops, for candy neophytes, are lollipops with bubble gum centers. Alas, the Charms Company has neither a tour nor a company store.

The **Seldom Rest Ostrich Farm,** tel. (901) 837-8504, is south of Covington on Gilt Edge Rd., and here visitors can see the enormous birds and talk with their owners, David and Patricia Busby. This is a family hobby, not a business, so call ahead to arrange a convenient time to come by. To get there from Covington, drive south on Hwy. 51 to the only traffic light in the south part of the county (about 20 minutes south of Covington). Turn right onto Munford-Atoka Ave., then turn right onto Munford-Gilt Edge Road. The farm is on the right and the ostriches are in the field behind the chain-link fence.

Recreation

Cobb-Parr Park (corner of Hwy. 51 N, and Bert Johnson Ave.) is an 80-acre park and nature preserve and the site for many community festivals and activities. It includes a picnic area, playground, tennis courts, baseball fields, horse stables, and walking paths.

Glenn Springs Lake is a 310-acre fishing lake operated by the Tennessee Wildlife Resources Agency. The lake is stocked with bluegill, largemouth bass, sunfish, black crappie, and blue catfish. Visitors must have a fishing license and a permit, which they can buy at the full-service store right at the lake. The lake is open 30 minutes before sunrise until 30 minutes after sunset year-round. To get there take Hwy. 59 West, turn left on Glenn Springs Rd., then turn left onto Grimes Road. The lake is on the right.

Entertainment and Events

Heritage Day Festival, held during the last weekend in September, consists of tours of historic homes, crafts demonstrations, music, dance, and carriage rides. Call (901) 476-0426.

The **Tipton County Barbecue Festival,** begun in 1973, claims to be the oldest barbecue festival in the world. Held annually the third Thurs.-Sat. of July at the Cobb-Parr Park (corner of Hwy. 51 North and Bert Johnson Avenue) in Covington, it includes a cookers' showmanship contest, arts and crafts, games and rides, and a truck pull. Admission to the grounds is $2. Call (901) 476-9727.

Christmas City consists of 30 biblical and wintertime scenes illuminated by more than 130,000 lights on the 20-acre Rose of Sharon campground. It is open from Thanksgiving to New Year's, and admission is free. From Hwy. 51, take Hwy. 59 West and turn left on Candy Lane. The campground is on the right. Call (901) 837-7095.

Where to Stay

Havenhall Farm Bed & Breakfast, Hwy. 59 S, 183 Houston Gordon Rd., Covington, TN 38019, tel. (901) 476-7226, offers a three-bedroom barn apartment with full bath, large den, and fully equipped kitchen. The apartment is furnished with antiques and quilts. Outside is an 80-acre farm with 40 kinds of trees and various wildlife. Guests can fish, jog on a trail, use an exercise room, and swim in a pool. Horseback lessons are available, too. Smokers are welcome. The rate is $75 for double occupancy. Moderate.

Or choose between the **Best Western,** 873 Hwy. 51 N, tel. (901) 476-8561 or (800) 528-1234; and the **Comfort Inn,** 901 Hwy. 51 N, tel. (901) 475-0380 or (800) 221-2222.

Food

Buffalo Willy's, 224 N. College St., tel. (901) 476-2322, is open Mon.-Sat. for lunch and dinner. It serves burgers, french fries, steak, sandwiches, and the specialty, Buffalo Willy's hot wings.

Country Kitchen, 899 Hwy. 51 N., tel. (901) 476-1591, is open seven days a week for three meals; it serves breakfast all day long and offers a full menu of country cooking.

Gilt Edge Barbecue, 12 miles west of Covington in the little community of Gilt Edge, tel. (901) 476-7207, is open Tues.-Sun. for all three meals. It serves pork barbecue, ribs, sandwiches, and a full menu. To get there, go west on Hwy. 59. It is on the left side.

Little Porky's Pit Bar-Be-Que, 524 Hwy. 51 N, Covington, tel. (901) 476-7165, is open Mon.-Sat. 6 a.m.-9 p.m. It serves hamburgers, shrimp, catfish, grilled chicken, and barbecue.

Papa's Country Catfish, 1015 Hwy. 51 N, tel. (901) 475-1405, is open Mon.-Sat. for lunch and dinner. It offers a lunch and dinner buffet that includes a variety of dishes. Catfish is a choice every dinner and all day on Saturday.

Shopping and Information
Gift Gallery, 113 A Court Square W, tel. (901) 476-4438, offers home interior items, china and crystal, holiday decorations, brass and silver accents, and table linens.

Covington-Tipton Chamber of Commerce, 106 W. Liberty Ave., tel. (901) 476-9727, is open Mon.-Fri. 8 a.m.-4:30 p.m.

MASON

This town has two culinary landmarks that make it necessary to come here for lunch and dinner, or perhaps on two consecutive evenings, to get the entire experience.

If there were such a thing as a fried chicken juke joint, **Gus's World Famous Hot & Spicy Chicken** would be it. Coming from Memphis, this place is on the right side of Hwy. 70, tel. (901) 294-2028.

Some people will step inside, take one look at this place, and head right back out the door. The building is long and not the most immaculate-looking place in the world. The air is heavy with frying oil. Anyone who leaves this place without eating, however, will miss the best fried chicken in Tennessee, if not the entire universe. And right up front is one of the best blues and soul jukeboxes

in the state, with selections from Bobby Bland, John Lee Hooker, and James Brown.

Just east of Gus's is **Bozo's Hot Pit Bar-B-Q Restaurant,** 342 Hwy. 70, tel. (901) 294-3400, which is as noted in legal circles as it is in culinary ones. The restaurant was founded in 1923 by Thomas Jefferson "Bozo" Williams. Never mind how he got that nickname. Through the years, the restaurant prospered, and in 1982 the owners decided to register the name "Bozo's" as a federal trademark. Enter one Larry Harmon, a.k.a. Bozo the Clown, who holds rights to his alter ego's name and who decided to oppose the application on the technicality that it was a local restaurant and had no interstate patrons and thus could not register a trademark. People in West Tennessee don't cotton to out-of-town clowns, legal or otherwise, and called on friends and family from all over the country to write affidavits stating that they were out-of-state customers of the restaurant. The clown took it on the chin in court, then again on appeal, and pushed the case all the way to the Supreme Court, which in its wisdom refused to hear it. The name remains.

Now for the food: Bozo's serves barbecue plates, burgers, fried chicken, fried shrimp, and great vegetables.

BROWNSVILLE AND VICINITY

This pleasant town bills itself as "the Heart of the Tennessee Delta" and is working hard to promote its rich musical heritage. Heading the list of blues players is the late Sleepy John Estes, whose country blues songs were often about his personal experiences. He lost sight in one eye as a child, and later was given his nickname because he liked to take naps. He recorded from 1929 through the '40s, then returned to settle down in Brownsville when he became completely blind.

What happened later is best described by fellow West Tennessean Franklin Jones. "Sleepy John Estes lived for most of his life in Brownsville and was very important to the 1960s blues-rediscovery white northerners, because he was to them sort of like the coelacanth was to paleontologists—a living example of a species, in this case, Delta bluesmen, considered long extinct. Many eager-eyed music writers have Sleepy John stories, and for them hunting for and actually finding him was a watershed moment in life. The line from his song, 'I'm goin' to Brownsville, take that old right hand road,' took on almost religious meaning."

Estes, who lived in a series of shacks and died in 1977, was largely ignored by white Brownsville and often played with the late Hammy Nixon and Yank Rachel, who accompanied him on, respectively, harmonica and mandolin. In the 1960s and 1970s, it wasn't unusual for Estes and Nixon to jet off to perform concerts in Tokyo or Berlin or Washington, D.C.

Son Bonds, another bluesman, was born here, as was country musician Alex Harvey, who helped pen the Kenny Rogers hit, "Reuben James." He also co-wrote "Delta Dawn" and "No Place But Texas."

Now the town is scrambling to recognize its blues tradition. Better late than never, say blues fans.

SIGHTS

Blues-Related Sights

One of the houses that Sleepy John Estes lived in has been turned into a museum that sits beside the library at 1011 E. Main Street. Admission is free, and the house is open by appointment only. Call (901) 772-2193.

The house was to be moved in 1999 to the **Tennessee Delta Heritage Center,** located off I-40 at Exit 56 at 121 Sunnyhill Cove. The Center contains three sets of exhibits, the Cotton Museum, the Hatchie River Ecosystem, and the Music Museum. No phone at press time. For info, call (901) 772-2193.

genuine article: Billy Tripp of Brownsville

Mind Field, a work in progress, won't be finished for a quarter-century.

BILLY TRIPP

Mind Field

Brownsvillian Billy Tripp, a sort of folk artist with a welding rod, has erected *Mind Field,* a 40-foot-high steel sculpture that is a work in progress. In a published interview, Tripp claims that he expects the work to take 20-25 more years to finish. In the meantime, there's plenty to see. It contains steel cut-outs of Tripp's hands and feet, a basketball goal, skulls and cross-bones, and hearts. He charges no admission to see *Mind Field,* which is on Hwy. 70 one block from the town square. Visitors are not allowed to walk through the work, but they are welcome to stand outside of it and gaze. Tripp lives in a welding shop behind *Mind Field,* and if he is not busy is happy to discuss his work. He has just self-published a novel, *The Mind Field,* which is available for sale in the chamber of commerce office for $17.

Felsenthal Lincoln Collection

Before the Civil War, Haywood County, of which Brownsville is the seat, had the highest proportion of slaves in the state, so it seems somehow appropriate that a small museum devoted to the Great Emancipator is located here. Morton Felsenthal's grandfather gave one of the eulogies at Lincoln's Washington, D.C., funeral and then began a collection of memorabilia of the 16th president. The Felsenthal Lincoln Collection contains signed Lincoln documents, lithographs, books, and an 1860 campaign token. Other items include toy soldiers and a collection of three-inch statues of every president from Washington to Nixon.

More Sights

The Felsenthal Collection is in the same building as the **Haywood County Museum,** 127 N. Grand Ave., tel. (901) 772-4883. The museum displays area history in 25-year segments. Exhibits contain uniforms from various wars, antique tools, photos from times gone by, and a rural post office. The two are open Sunday 2-4 p.m. and Monday, Wednesday, Thursday, and Friday 10 a.m.-4 p.m. Admission is free at both places.

Temple Adas Israel is a rare item in these parts—a Jewish temple in a rural Southern town. Moreover, it is the oldest temple in continuous use in the state. It stands at the corner of Washington and College Streets, where it has stood since 1882.

Hatchie National Wildlife Refuge

A staple of movies for a time was the Southern prison escape film, in which two prisoners—usually one black and one white—break out of the big house while shackled together and have to escape through the swamps. If anyone wanted to remake one of those epics, the Hatchie National Wildlife Refuge could serve as the setting.

This is the one river left in the lower Mississippi Valley that has not been "channelized"—straightened out—by a federal government with good intentions but bad ideas. The 11,556 acres here abound with wildlife: 200 species of birds, including red-shouldered hawks, barred owls, and wild turkeys; 50 species of mammals, including deer, beavers, river otters, and squirrels; and a great many reptiles, amphibians, fish, and invertebrates.

This area often floods, and sections of it are closed Nov. 15 through March 15 to provide sanctuary for waterfowl. To get information on what is open, visitors should go to the headquarters, which are on Hwy. 76 just south of I-40 Exit 56, tel. (901) 772-0501. It is open weekdays 7:30 a.m.-4 p.m.

EVENTS AND PRACTICALITIES

Tennessee Peach Festival, held in June, celebrates the fruit with the selection of Miss Tennessee Peach, a Walking Horse show, tractor pull, arts and crafts, and music.

Motels
Try the **Comfort Inn,** 2600 Anderson Ave., tel. (901) 772-4082 or (800) 221-2222; **Days Inn,** I-40 Exit 56, tel. (901) 772-3297; **Guesthouse Inn,** I-40 Exit 66, tel. (901) 772-9500 or (800) 21-GUEST; or **Holiday Inn Express,** 120 Sunny Hill Cove, tel. (901) 772-4030 or (800) HOLIDAY.

Food
Backyard Bar-B-Q, 703 E. Main St., tel. (901) 772-1121, serves lunch and dinner Mon.-Sat. consisting of barbecued ribs, chicken, and pork, and sandwiches and side orders.

City Fish Market, 223 S. Washington St., tel. (901) 772-9952, sells fresh fish most of the week. On Friday and Saturday, however, the staff starts to cook and the place fills up with customers. From 9 a.m. to 6 p.m. the air is filled with the smell of fried fish and hushpuppies. No pond-raised catfish are served here; the fish on this menu are the genuine article.

Curley and Lynn's, 1016 N. Washington St., has no phone but serves very good barbecue.

Local farmers and townsfolk hold court every morning at **The Hibachi,** 471 Dupree St., tel. (901) 772-3184, which offers all three meals Mon.-Saturday. It has a full menu, including plate lunches, sandwiches, and buffets at lunch and Friday night.

The Hickory Pit, 690 Dupree St., tel. (901) 772-9926, serves barbecue and ribs Mon.-Sat. for lunch and dinner.

Olympic Steak House, 326 W. Main St., tel. (901) 772-5555, features steak, Italian dishes, and seafood accompanied by a large salad bar. It's open for lunch and dinner seven days a week.

Sweat's Pool Room and Cafe, across from the courthouse at 27 Lafayette St., tel. (901) 772-7016, is the gathering place for local politicians. Meals are served at a big U-shaped counter where everyone can keep an eye on everyone else. Sweat's has different plate lunches and specials Mon.-Saturday.

United China, 5 Court Square, tel. (901) 772-3989, serves Chinese, lunch and dinner daily.

The name of **ZZ's Kream Kastle,** 16 Grand Ave. S, tel. (901) 772-3132, suggests some kind of ice cream place, but ZZ's is more than that. It serves a wide variety of food, including salads, cheeseburgers, spaghetti, lasagna, pizza, fresh doughnuts and brownies, and jumbo stuffed baked potatoes. It's open seven days a week for lunch and dinner.

Information
Brownsville-Haywood County Chamber of Commerce, 121 W. Main St., tel. (901) 772-2193, occupies a building that was a Carnegie library built in 1910. It's open Mon.-Fri. 8 a.m.-4:30 p.m.

NUTBUSH

According to local lore, Nathan Bedford Forrest named this place. Tina Turner was born here, which was commemorated in the song "Nutbush City Limits." Calling this hamlet a city was most generous, yet it has had a musical heritage far richer than many larger towns. Part of that heritage is the Woodlawn Church, which was the first house of worship for freed slaves in these parts. From Brownsville, the church is on the left on Hwy. 19, Nutbush's main drag.

The community here produced and listened to a variety of musicians, among them Bootsie Whitelow and Sleepy John Estes. Much of the musical heritage of Nutbush is unmarked, however, and the visitor needs a knowledgeable guide. That would be Sharon Norris, music historian, entrepreneur, and tour guide, who is per-

TINA TURNER

The entertainer who the world knows today as Tina Turner was born November 26, 1939, on the Poindexter farm in Nutbush. Named Anna Mae Bullock, the second child of Richard and Zelma Bullock grew up as a sharecropper's daughter.

"I don't remember being poor," she says in a passage from her 1986 autobiography, *I, Tina.* "My father was always the top man on the farm; all the sharecroppers answered to him, and he answered to the owner. . . . We always had nice furniture in our house, and Alline [her sister] and I always had our own separate bedrooms. And we had animals—the cows and pigs and chickens and horses—and I knew people who didn't."

She grew up climbing trees, accompanying her father during hunting season, and enjoying other rural pleasures. When World War II broke out, her parents, taking advantage of newfound opportunities for blacks, took wartime jobs across the state in Knoxville. In Knoxville the little girl first sang professionally; when her mother took her shopping, Anna Mae would sing for the salesclerks, who would give her quarters.

At the end of the war, the family moved back to West Tennessee, returning to Nutbush and then moving to other rural communities. Anna Mae worked in the fields, weeding cotton, picking cotton, and picking strawberries. Her parents split up, and she lived with a variety of relatives, attending school in Ripley, becoming a cheerleader for the black high school, and then transferring to Brownsville, where she continued as cheerleader, played on the girls' basketball team, and appeared in talent shows and school plays.

Tina Turner's family was neither more nor less musical than anyone else's. She was exposed to church music in the Woodlawn Missionary Baptist Church and the Spring Hill Baptist Church, where she was the youngest member of the choir. She listened to country music on the radio, and to WDIA, the black station out of Memphis that broadcast B.B. King and other stars. She also heard the performances of local musicians such as Sleepy John Estes and Bootsie Whitelow.

When she was 16 years old, Anna Mae left Tennessee to go live with her father in Detroit, and then she joined her mother in St. Louis. One of the hotter bands playing at the time was the Kings of Rhythm, driven by the guitar playing of a young man named Ike Turner. He held an audition for a female singer, and Anna Mae got the job. She might have come from the country in West Tennessee, but musically she was shaped in one of the greatest concentrations of talent in the state.

Ike and Tina Turner became perhaps the most famous husband-wife act in rhythm and blues and later rock. After finally leaving Ike, who proved to be an abusive husband, Tina went on to even higher achievements in the entertainment world.

---

haps the best person in West Tennessee to talk to about music. Her **Wild Onion Ridge Music Heritage Park** offers concerts and a small museum of the area's music. It is open by appointment only.

The very best approach is to take one of her tours. The **Tina Turner Tour** begins in Brownsville and goes from there to Nutbush and Ripley. This tour, which can last from two and a half to five hours, includes Tina's birthplace, the Ripley and Brownsville neighborhoods that influenced her music, her high school, the churches she attended, and the Tina Turner Child Abuse Center. This tour costs $35 per carload, and you must make reservations.

The **Musical Heritage Tour** includes Sleeping John Estes's grave, Hammy Nixon's homeplace, and the old haunts of these and other bluesmen. One of the stops is the Woodlawn Church. This tour costs $35 per carload, and you must make reservations.

To reach Ms. Norris, call (901) 772-4265 or (901) 772-8157 or go to www.nutbush.com.

BOOKLIST

HISTORY

Corlew, Robert. *Tennessee, A Short History.* Knoxville: University of Tennessee Press, 1990. This condensation of a four-volume work is the definitive history book about the state.

Egerton, John. *Visions of Utopia.* Knoxville: University of Tennessee Press, 1977. Focuses on Nashoba, Rugby, Ruskin, and the "new communities" of Tennessee's past.

Johnson, Mattie Ruth. *My Melungeon Heritage.* Johnson City: Overmountain Press, 1994. A personal account of coming from a Melungeon family.

Kennedy, N. Brent. *The Melungeons, The Resurrection of a Proud People—The Untold Story of Ethnic Cleansing in America.* Macon: Mercer University Press, 1994. If there is a point book for militant Melungeons, this is it.

Klebenow, Anne. *200 Years Through 200 Stories.* Knoxville: University of Tennessee, 1996. These 200 essays illuminate history by focusing on individuals, from the Cherokee Attakullakulla to the Carthenagen Albert Gore, Jr.

Manning, Russ. *The Historic Cumberland Plateau.* Knoxville: University of Tennessee Press, 1993. A very good guide to this distinctive area between East and Middle Tennessee.

Neely, Jack. *Knoxville's Secret History.* Knoxville: Scruffy City Publishing, 1995. Looking at topics as various as colonial days and the death of Hank Williams, this talented writer illuminates Tennessee's oldest city. His *Secret History II,* published in 1998, offers more of the same.

McPherson, James. *Battle Cry of Freedom.* Oxford: Oxford University Press, 1988. A one-volume history of the Civil War.

Ward, Geoffrey. *The Civil War.* New York: Alfred A. Knopf, 1990. The companion volume to the Ken Burns Civil War documentary.

West, Carroll Van, editor. *The Tennessee Encyclopedia of History & Culture.* Nashville: Rutledge Hill Press, 1998. This 1,193-page compiliation of essays from all manner of scholars and experts is indispensable for learning about Tennessee.

Yellin, Carol Lynn and Janann Sherman. *The Perfect 36—Tennessee Delivers Woman Suffrage.* Memphis: Serviceberry Press, 1998. This delightful book shows how Tennessee became the state that caused the 19th Amendment to become law. Illustrated with photos, political cartoons, and newspaper articles of the day, it weaves a fascinating story.

DESCRIPTION AND TRAVEL

Brandt, Robert. *Touring the Middle Tennessee Backroads.* Winston-Salem, NC: John F. Blair, 1995. Written by a Nashville judge, this book interweaves historical tales with descriptions of towns, buildings, and other evidence of the past.

Osborne, Roger and Michael Gray. *The Elvis Atlas.* New York: Henry Holt, 1996. The ultimate guidebook for people following the pathways of the King.

Sakowski, Carolyn. *Touring the East Tennessee Backroads.* Winston-Salem, NC: John F. Blair, 1993. This book should be on the front seat of any history buff driving though East Tennessee.

Smith, Reid. *Majestic Middle Tennessee.* Gretna, LA: Pelican Publishing Company, 1982. A historic look at the mansions of Middle Tennessee.

Urquhart, Sharon Colette. *Placing Elvis: A Tour Guide to the Kingdom.* New Orleans: Paper Chase Press, 1994. A guidebook to the Memphis and Tupelo haunts of Elvis.

WPA Guide to Tennessee. Knoxville: University of Tennessee Press, 1986. A reprint of the 1939 guide written by the Federal Writers' Project of the Work Projects Administration— a Depression effort aimed at putting writers to work and supplying guidebooks for states. This book, full of the pride and prejudices of the time, gives a wonderful view of Tennessee—small towns and large.

MUSIC

Escott, Colin. *Good Rockin' Tonight.* New York: St. Martins, 1991. The story of Sun Studios, where it all began.

Gordon, Robert. *It Came From Memphis.* Boston and London: Faber and Faber, 1995. A wandering path through Memphis music since the 1950s, focusing on the great and near-great.

Guralnick, Peter. *Feel Like Going Home.* New York: Harper and Row, 1971. This book offers portraits of various blues and rock performers, among them Jerry Lee Lewis.

Guralnick, Peter. *Lost Highway.* New York: Harper and Row, 1979. Guralnick hits a home run with tales of country performer Ernest Tubb, bluesman Big Joe Turner, and rockabilly Sleepy LaBeef.

Guralnick, Peter. *Sweet Soul Music.* New York: Harper and Row, 1986. A great look at the rise of soul music and the Memphians who made it.

Marcus, Greil. *Mystery Train.* New York: Plume, 1990. A classic on the roots of rock 'n' roll. *Rolling Stone* calls this the best book ever on rock.

McCloud, Barry. *Definitive Country: The Ultimate Encyclopedia of Country Music and its Performers.* New York: Berkeley Publishing Group, 1995. This is the book in which to look up both the famous and the obscure.

McKee, Margaret and Fred Chisenhall. *Beale Black and Blue: Life and Music on Black America's Main Street* Baton Rouge: Louisiana State University Press, 1993. Interviews and reflections on Beale Street's heyday.

Palmer, Robert. *Deep Blues.* New York: Penguin Books, 1981. This look at Delta blues sheds light on the Memphis music scene.

Santelli, Robert. *The Big Book of Blues.* New York: Penguin Books, 1993. This book has a biographical entry on anyone who was anyone in the blues.

Tosches, Nick. *Country.* New York: Scribners, 1977. A look at the underside of country music—tales they'll never tell you at the Country Music Hall of Fame.

Wolfe, Charles K. *Tennessee Strings.* Knoxville: University of Tennessee Press, 1977. A thin but authoritative book on country music.

Zimmerman, Peter Coats. *Tennessee Music.* San Francisco: Miller Freeman Books, 1998. This combination travel book and music guide to the state is a must for roots music lovers.

FICTION AND LITERATURE

Agee, James. *A Death in the Family.* New York: Grossett and Dunlap, 1967. The best Knoxville novel.

Ford, Jesse Hill and George Garret. *The Liberation of Lord Byron Jones.* Athens: University of Georgia Press, 1993. Based on events that took place in the West Tennessee town of Humboldt, this novel was eventually made into a film.

Grisham, John. *The Client.* New York: Doubleday, 1993. Another of this Mississippi writer's string of hits.

Grisham, John. *The Firm.* New York: Double-day, 1991. This tale of a law firm with ties to the mob became a movie filled with Memphis scenes.

Haley, Alex. *Roots.* New York: Doubleday, 1976. The fascinating tale of this writer's ancestors, slaves and otherwise.

Marius, Richard. *After the War.* New York: Alfred A. Knopf, 1992. This novel takes flight from the story of Marius's father, who came from Greece to Tennessee and ran a foundry in Lenoir City.

Marius, Richard. *The Coming of Rain.* New York: Alfred A. Knopf, 1969. Set in a fictional version of Lenoir City, this book captures the turmoil of a small town.

Marshall, Catherine. *Christy.* New York: McGraw Hill, 1967. The inspiring story of a young woman who goes to teach school in a remote East Tennessee town. It later became a television show and a musical performed in the Smokies.

Taylor, Peter. *A Summons to Memphis.* New York: Ballantine Books, 1987. This account of a New York editor's summons home to help his spinster sisters prevent the remarriage of their aging father offers a look into the complex family lives of well-born Tennesseans in the middle of this century. This beautifully written story won the Pulitzer Prize and the Ritz-Paris Hemingway award.

Twain, Mark and Charles Dudley Warner. *The Gilded Age.* New York: Nelson Doubleday, 1873. The Tennessee land owned by the Clemens family plays a role in this novel, which gave its name to the post-Civil War years.

Wells, Lawrence. *Rommel and the Rebel.* Oxford, MI: Yoknapatawpha Press, 1992. This imaginative novel, building on the legend that the "Desert Fox" of World War II fame traveled through the South in the 1930s studying the tactics of Nathan Bedford Forrest, has Rommel playing tennis at midnight with William Faulkner. A great read.

Young, Thomas Daniel. *Tennessee Writers.* Knoxville: University of Tennessee Press, 1981. A quick look at Tennessee authors from David Crockett on up.

BIOGRAPHY

Derr, Mark. *The Frontiersman: The Real Life and the Many Legends of Davy Crockett.* New York: William Morrow and Company, 1993. An effective counterweight to the Crockett myth promoted by the Disney organization and others.

Escott, Colin. *Hank Williams: the Biography.* Boston: Little, Brown and Company, 1994. A very good biography of one of country music's greatest.

Guralnick, Peter. *Careless Love: The Unmaking of Elvis Presley.* Boston: Little, Brown and Company, 1999. The sad demise of the King as told by his best biographer.

Guralnick, Peter. *Last Train to Memphis.* Boston: Little, Brown and Company, 1994. This is the book on Elvis. To be the first of a three-book set, this one takes the King up to the time he left for Army duty in Germany. Based on meticulous research and a keen sense of American popular music, Guralnick's opus rises above the flotsam of Elvis books on the market.

Hurst, Jack. *Nathan Bedford Forrest.* New York: Random House, 1993. The latest biography of the Confederacy's greatest cavalry leader, Ku Klux Klan leader, and source of controversy even today.

Parton, Dolly. *My Life and Other Unfinished Business.* New York: Thorndike Press, 1995. Dollywood's tycoon tells of her rise from mountain girl to singing star.

Summitt, Pat Head. *Reach for the Summitt* New York: Broadway Books, 1998. The life story of the second—so far—winningest basketball coach in America, the coach of the University of Tennessee Lady Vols.

Trefousse, Hans L. *Andrew Johnson: a Biography.* New York: Norton, 1989. A fine recounting of an underappreciated president.

Turner, Tina, with Kurt Loder. *I, Tina.* New York: William Morrow and Company, 1986. The recollections of the most important female singer to come from West Tennessee.

ARCHITECTURE

West, Carroll Van. *Tennessee's Historic Landscapes.* Knoxville: University of Tennessee Press, 1995. With photos and astute commentary, this book leads the traveler though big cities and small towns in search of architectural treasures.

THE OUTDOORS

Coleman, Brenda D. and Jo Anna Smith. *Hiking the Big South Fork.* Knoxville: University of Tennessee Press, 1993. This book contains topographical maps and descriptions of the trails.

Manning, Russ and Sondra Jamieson. *Tennessee's South Cumberland.* Norris, TN: Mountain Laurel Press, 1994. This handy book pulls together the spread-out areas of the southern Cumberland Plateau.

Manning, Russ and Sondra Jamieson. *Trails of the Big South Fork.* Norris, TN: Mountain Laurel Press, 1995. This handbook fits into backpacks and guides the traveler along the roads and trails.

ODDS AND ENDS

Egerton, John. *Southern Food.* Chapel Hill: University of North Carolina Press, 1987. Combining recipes, fine writing, and great photos, this book takes a satisfying look at country cooking.

Kiser, Maud Gold. *Treasure Hunter's Guide.* Nashville: The Gold-Kiser Company, 1995. This thorough guide to Tennessee's antique stores also includes restaurants, bed and breakfasts, history, and the longest paragraphs this side of the Mississippi border.

Jones, Lind Brooks. *The Table at Gray Gables.* Nashville: Cumberland House Publishing, 1998. A collection of recipes, narratives, and other matters pertaining to Rugby by a native who runs one of the better inns in the state.

Luther, Edward T. *Our Restless Earth.* Knoxville: University of Tennessee Press, 1977. A short and very readable guide to the geology of Tennessee.

Verghese, Abraham. *My Own Country.* New York: Simon and Schuster, 1994. An amazing book written by a doctor from India who finds himself in Johnson City, Tennessee, treating AIDS patients. His stories about the patients are touching, and his accounts of life in East Tennessee are sometimes hilarious.

West, Carroll Van. *The Tennessee Encyclopedia of History and Culture.* Nashville: Rutledge Hill Press, 1998. If readers like the historical bits in *Tennessee Handbook,* they will love this 1,193-page volume, which is filled with fascinating short articles from a great many luminaries.

Wilson, Charles Reagan, and William Ferris, *Encyclopedia of Southern Culture.* Chapel Hill: University of North Carolina Press, 1989. This stupendous book—1,634 pages long—addresses mint juleps, sacred harp singing, kudzu, and other Southern items with scholarship and wit.

Womack, Bob. *The Echo of Hoofbeats.* Shelbyville, TN: The Walking Horse Publishing Company, 1973. The history of walking horses and the celebration thereof.

INDEX

BARBECUE JOINTS

BREWERIES

Big River Grille & Brewing Works: 276
Blackhorse Brewery and Pizza Kitchen: 375
Blackhorse Pub & Brewery: 102, 108
Blackstone Restaurant & Brewery: 276
Boscos Pizza Kitchen and Brewery: 429
Calhoun's: 102
Coors Belle Hospitality Center: 414
Great Southern Brewing Company: 102, 106
Hops: 102
Market Street Brewery and Public House: 276
Sebastian's and Diana's Brewpub: 314
Smoky Mountain Brewery and Restaurant: 131
Southern Brewers Association Beer Festival: 234

Bristol International Raceway: 36-37
Bristol White Sox: 37
British rule: 7-8; *see also specific place*
Broadway Dinner Train: 260
Brotherhood Parade: 306
Brown, Clarence: 89
Brown-Daly-Horne House: 305
Brownlow, William G.: 10, 72
Brownsville: 471-474
Broylesville: 75
Brushy Mountain Prison: 174
Bryan College: 187
Bryan, William Jennings: 187-188
Buckner, Simon B.: 378
Bucksnort: 385
buffalo: 52, 61, 242, 362, 415, 452
Buffalo Mountain Park: 64
Buffalo Springs Trout Hatchery: 50
The Buford Pusser Home and Museum: 440-442
Buggytop Trail: 340-341
Bullhead Trail: 153
Bull Run Fossil Plant: 173
Bulls Gap: 84
Burgess Falls State Natural Area: 195
Burn, Henry Thomas: 202
Burnside, Gen. Ambrose: 91, 98
burros: 366
bus service/tours: Bus Tours of the Smokies 124; Memphis 416, 432; Nashville 260
Buster, Frank: 355
Butcher, Jake: 92-93

Butler: 59
Butler, Sen. John: 361
Byrdstown: 181

C

Cades Cove: 150-152, 157
Camden: 458-459
Campbell, Archie: 84
candy factories: 93, 126-127, 195, 461
Cane Creek Park: 195
Cannonsburgh: 310-312; Harvest Day: 313
canoeing and kayaking: general discussion 19; Adams 370; Big South Fork National River and Recreation Area 168; Duck River 297; Elk River 326; Henry Horton State Resort Park 331; Hiwassee River 214; Hohenwald 391; Merrimack Canoe Company 193; Moscow 437-438; Ocoee River 212; organized tours 136; Pickett State Rustic Park 180-181; Riverpark 227; Savannah 393; Shelby Farms 415; Waynesboro 392; *see also specific place*
Carbo's Smoky Mountain Police Museum: 118, 121
Carden's Bluff: 58
Carmack, Edward Ward: 255-256
Carnegie, Andrew: 63
Carnival Memphis: 419
Carnton Plantation Symphony on the Lawn and Picnic Competition: 292
Carousel Theater: 99-100
carriage rides: 138, 292, 306
Carroll Reece Museum: 62
Carr's Wild Horse/Burro Center: 366
Carson-Newman College: 87
Carter Family: 33, 35-36; Carter Family Fold 43; Carter Family Memorial Music Center 35-36
The Carter House: 289-290; Candlelight Tour of Homes 292
Carter Mansion 56; Christmas at the Carter Mansion 58
Carter State Natural Area: 341
Carthage: 357-358
car travel: avoiding traffic 118, 125, 146; highway system 23, 29-30, 53, 199, 217, 387; Nashville 249; *see also* scenic drives; *specific place*
Carver's Orchard: 134
Casey Jones Old Time Music Festival: 445
Cash, Johnny: 33

CAMPGROUNDS AND RV PARKS

CIVIL WAR

HIKING AND BACKPACKING

MUSIC FESTIVALS AND EVENTS

MUSIC MUSEUMS

ELVIS PRESLEY

SCHOOLS, COLLEGES, AND UNIVERSITIES

SINGERS AND MUSICIANS

THEATER/PERFORMING ARTS

Trinity City: 364
Tri-Star Vineyards and Winery: 328
trolleys: Gatlinburg 125-126; Memphis 403;
    Nashville 282
Trousdale County Living History Museum: 361
Trousdale Place: 363
Tubb, Ernest: 261, 266
tuberculosis: 48, 191
tubing: 138
Tuckaleechee Caverns: 138
Tullahoma: 320-322; Fine Arts
    Center/Regional Museum of Art 321; Fine
    Arts & Crafts Festival 321
tunnels: Cumberland Gap Tunnel 54; shortest
    tunnel in the world 33
turkeys: 148
turkey vultures: 5
Turley Cotton Company: 404-405
Turner, Federick Jackson: 53
Turner, Tina: 474-475; Wild Onion Ridge
    Music Heritage Park 436, 475
Tusculum: 76-77
TVA: Chattanooga 220; environmental issues
    6; Hartsville nuclear power plant 361;
    history of 11, 184-185; Knoxville 92; Land
    Between the Lakes 377-379; Norris 162-
    163; see also dams; specific place
Twin Arches Trail: 167
Twin Rocks Nature Trail: 186
Twitty, Conway: 364

U

Unaka Mountain Wilderness: 69
Uncle Dave Macon Days: 18
Unicoi County Heritage Museum: 68
Union City: 463
Union Station Grand Hotel: 249
Unity Service: 306
universities: see schools, colleges, and
    universities
University of Tennessee: Arboretum 172-173;
    Arena 234; Fine Arts Center 234; Music
    Hall and Opera Theatre 99
Upper Room Chapel and Museum: 251, 258
uranium: 172

V

Vanderbilt, George: 67
Vanderbilt University: 245, 251, 265; Fine Arts
    Gallery 258
Van Vechten Gallery: 258

UNUSUAL CLAIMS TO FAME

Annual Tomato War: 50
Biblical Wonders of the Twentieth Century:
    214
Blow Pop Capital of the World: 469
Catfish Race: 460
Doodle Soup Capital of the World: 454
Eiffel Tower: 460
Elephant Hanging: 67-68
Great New Market Wreck: 87
Home of the White Squirrels: 454
Last Battle of the Revolutionary War: 219
Last English Colony in America: 175
Lost State of Franklin: 70-71, 79
Mind Field: 472-473
New Madrid Earthquake: 465
Peter's Hollow Egg Fight: 58
Richard Petty, bust of: 144
Shortest Tunnel in the World: 33
Third-Largest Pecan Tree in North America:
    456-457
World's Biggest Fish Fry: 18, 436, 460
World's Largest Collection of Lighted
    Teapots: 455
World's Largest Coon Hunt: 457
World's Largest Flea Market: 202
World's Longest Yard Sale: 193

Vardy Historic Community: 48-49
Vaughn, Margaret Britton: 316
Verghese, Abraham: 61
Vic Rhodes Traditional Music Fest: 452
Victorian Christmas: 354
Victorian Village Historic District: 404, 411
Virgin Falls Pocket Wilderness: 196
Volunteer Landing: 95
Volunteer State: origin of name 9; Veterans
    Hall of Fame 96

W

Wachtel, Rev. A.E.: 50
Walker, Dr. Thomas: 52, 54
walking tours/nature trails: Bicentennial Mall
    259; Cotton Row Historic District 404-405;
    Cove Lake State Recreational Park 164;
    Ducktown Green-Gold Conservancy 214;
    Gallatin 363; Historic Loudon Walking Tour
    200-201; Historic Savannah Walking Trail
    392; Horse Creek Recreation Area 82;

ABOUT THE AUTHOR

Jeff Bradley was born and raised in Kingsport, Tennessee, a town that once sentenced an elephant to death. He attended the University of Tennessee at Knoxville, emerging with a degree in journalism. He wrote on East Tennessee for *The New York Times* and simultaneously served as a stringer for *Time* and *Newsweek*.

In 1979 he was invited by fellow Tennessean Richard Marius to teach writing at Harvard, where he shared an office with Franklin Jones, a writing instructor from West Tennessee. The three of them frequently told more snake stories at dinner parties than most New Englanders heard in a lifetime.

Now a resident of Boulder, Colorado, he writes books and magazine articles, camps year-round with Troop 171, and periodically whangs away on a guitar.

LOSE YOURSELF IN THE EXPERIENCE, NOT THE CROWD

For more than 25 years, Moon Travel Handbooks have been the guidebooks of choice for adventurous travelers. Our award-winning Handbook series provides focused, comprehensive coverage of distinct destinations all over the world. Each Handbook is like an entire bookcase of cultural insight and introductory information in one portable volume. Our goal at Moon is to give travelers all the background and practical information they'll need for an extraordinary travel experience.

The following pages include a complete list of Handbooks, covering North America and Hawaii, Mexico, Latin America and the Caribbean, and Asia and the Pacific. To purchase Moon Travel Handbooks, check your local bookstore or order C/o Publishers Group West, Attn: Order Department, 1700 Fourth St., Berkeley, CA 94710, or fax to (510) 528-3444.

MEXICO

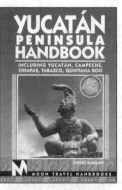

"These books will delight the armchair traveler, aid the undecided person in selecting a destination, and guide the seasoned road warrior looking for lesser-known hideaways."
—*Mexican Meanderings* Newsletter

"From tourist traps to off-the-beaten track hideaways, these guides offer consistent, accurate details without pretension."
—*Foreign Service Journal*

Archaeological Mexico	**$19.95**
Andrew Coe	420 pages, 27 maps
Baja Handbook	**$16.95**
Joe Cummings	540 pages, 46 maps
Cabo Handbook	**$14.95**
Joe Cummings	270 pages, 17 maps
Cancún Handbook	**$14.95**
Chicki Mallan	240 pages, 25 maps
Colonial Mexico	**$18.95**
Chicki Mallan	400 pages, 38 maps
Mexico Handbook	**$21.95**
Joe Cummings and Chicki Mallan	1,200 pages, 201 maps
Northern Mexico Handbook	**$17.95**
Joe Cummings	610 pages, 69 maps
Pacific Mexico Handbook	**$17.95**
Bruce Whipperman	580 pages, 68 maps
Puerto Vallarta Handbook	**$14.95**
Bruce Whipperman	330 pages, 36 maps
Yucatán Handbook	**$16.95**
Chicki Mallan	400 pages, 52 maps

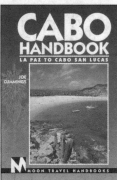

"Beyond question, the most comprehensive Mexican resources available for those who prefer deep travel to shallow tourism. But don't worry, the fiesta-fun stuff's all here too."
—*New York Daily News*

LATIN AMERICA
AND THE CARIBBEAN

"Solidly packed with practical information and full of significant
cultural asides that will enlighten you on the whys and
wherefores of things you might easily see but not easily grasp."

—*Boston Globe*

Belize Handbook	**$15.95**
Chicki Mallan and Patti Lange	390 pages, 45 maps
Caribbean Vacations	**$18.95**
Karl Luntta	910 pages, 64 maps
Costa Rica Handbook	**$19.95**
Christopher P. Baker	780 pages, 73 maps
Cuba Handbook	**$19.95**
Christopher P. Baker	740 pages, 70 maps
Dominican Republic Handbook	**$15.95**
Gaylord Dold	420 pages, 24 maps
Ecuador Handbook	**$16.95**
Julian Smith	450 pages, 43 maps
Honduras Handbook	**$15.95**
Chris Humphrey	330 pages, 40 maps
Jamaica Handbook	**$15.95**
Karl Luntta	330 pages, 17 maps
Virgin Islands Handbook	**$13.95**
Karl Luntta	220 pages, 19 maps

NORTH AMERICA AND HAWAII

"These domestic guides convey the same sense of exoticism
that their foreign counterparts do, making home-country
travel seem like far-flung adventure."

—*Sierra Magazine*

Alaska-Yukon Handbook	**$17.95**
Deke Castleman and Don Pitcher	530 pages, 92 maps
Alberta and the Northwest Territories Handbook	**$18.95**
Andrew Hempstead	520 pages, 79 maps
Arizona Handbook	**$18.95**
Bill Weir	600 pages, 36 maps
Atlantic Canada Handbook	**$18.95**
Mark Morris	490 pages, 60 maps
Big Island of Hawaii Handbook	**$15.95**
J.D. Bisignani	390 pages, 25 maps
Boston Handbook	**$13.95**
Jeff Perk	200 pages, 20 maps
British Columbia Handbook	**$16.95**
Jane King and Andrew Hempstead	430 pages, 69 maps

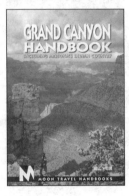

Canadian Rockies Handbook		**$14.95**
Andrew Hempstead		220 pages, 22 maps
Colorado Handbook		**$17.95**
Stephen Metzger		480 pages, 46 maps
Georgia Handbook		**$17.95**
Kap Stann		380 pages, 44 maps
Grand Canyon Handbook		**$14.95**
Bill Weir		220 pages, 10 maps
Hawaii Handbook		**$19.95**
J.D. Bisignani		1,030 pages, 88 maps
Honolulu-Waikiki Handbook		**$14.95**
J.D. Bisignani		360 pages, 20 maps
Idaho Handbook		**$18.95**
Don Root		610 pages, 42 maps
Kauai Handbook		**$15.95**
J.D. Bisignani		320 pages, 23 maps
Los Angeles Handbook		**$16.95**
Kim Weir		370 pages, 15 maps
Maine Handbook		**$18.95**
Kathleen M. Brandes		660 pages, 27 maps
Massachusetts Handbook		**$18.95**
Jeff Perk		600 pages, 23 maps
Maui Handbook		**$15.95**
J.D. Bisignani		450 pages, 37 maps
Michigan Handbook		**$15.95**
Tina Lassen		360 pages, 32 maps
Montana Handbook		**$17.95**
Judy Jewell and W.C. McRae		490 pages, 52 maps
Nevada Handbook		**$18.95**
Deke Castleman		530 pages, 40 maps
New Hampshire Handbook		**$18.95**
Steve Lantos		500 pages, 18 maps
New Mexico Handbook		**$15.95**
Stephen Metzger		360 pages, 47 maps
New York Handbook		**$19.95**
Christiane Bird		780 pages, 95 maps
New York City Handbook		**$13.95**
Christiane Bird		300 pages, 20 maps
North Carolina Handbook		**$14.95**
Rob Hirtz and Jenny Daughtry Hirtz		320 pages, 27 maps
Northern California Handbook		**$19.95**
Kim Weir		800 pages, 50 maps
Ohio Handbook		**$15.95**
David K. Wright		340 pages, 18 maps
Oregon Handbook		**$17.95**
Stuart Warren and Ted Long Ishikawa		590 pages, 34 maps

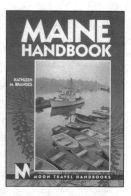

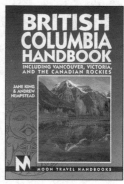

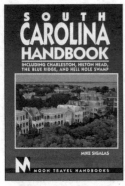

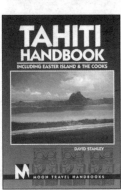

Pennsylvania Handbook	**$18.95**
Joanne Miller	448 pages, 40 maps
Road Trip USA	**$24.00**
Jamie Jensen	940 pages, 175 maps
Road Trip USA Getaways: Chicago	**$9.95**
	60 pages, 1 map
Road Trip USA Getaways: Seattle	**$9.95**
	60 pages, 1 map
Santa Fe-Taos Handbook	**$13.95**
Stephen Metzger	160 pages, 13 maps
South Carolina Handbook	**$16.95**
Mike Sigalas	400 pages, 20 maps
Southern California Handbook	**$19.95**
Kim Weir	720 pages, 26 maps
Tennessee Handbook	**$17.95**
Jeff Bradley	530 pages, 42 maps
Texas Handbook	**$18.95**
Joe Cummings	690 pages, 70 maps
Utah Handbook	**$17.95**
Bill Weir and W.C. McRae	490 pages, 40 maps
Virginia Handbook	**$15.95**
Julian Smith	410 pages, 37 maps
Washington Handbook	**$19.95**
Don Pitcher	840 pages, 111 maps
Wisconsin Handbook	**$18.95**
Thomas Huhti	590 pages, 69 maps
Wyoming Handbook	**$17.95**
Don Pitcher	610 pages, 80 maps

ASIA AND THE PACIFIC

"Scores of maps, detailed practical info down to business hours of small-town libraries. You can't beat the Asian titles for sheer heft. (The) series is sort of an American Lonely Planet, with better writing but fewer titles. (The) individual voice of researchers comes through."

—*Travel & Leisure*

Australia Handbook	**$21.95**
Marael Johnson, Andrew Hempstead,	
and Nadina Purdon	940 pages, 141 maps
Bali Handbook	**$19.95**
Bill Dalton	750 pages, 54 maps
Fiji Islands Handbook	**$14.95**
David Stanley	350 pages, 42 maps
Hong Kong Handbook	**$16.95**
Kerry Moran	378 pages, 49 maps

| Indonesia Handbook | $25.00 |
| Bill Dalton | 1,380 pages, 249 maps |

| Micronesia Handbook | $16.95 |
| Neil M. Levy | 340 pages, 70 maps |

| Nepal Handbook | $18.95 |
| Kerry Moran | 490 pages, 51 maps |

| New Zealand Handbook | $19.95 |
| Jane King | 620 pages, 81 maps |

| Outback Australia Handbook | $18.95 |
| Marael Johnson | 450 pages, 57 maps |

| Philippines Handbook | $17.95 |
| Peter Harper and Laurie Fullerton | 670 pages, 116 maps |

| Singapore Handbook | $15.95 |
| Carl Parkes | 350 pages, 29 maps |

| South Korea Handbook | $19.95 |
| Robert Nilsen | 820 pages, 141 maps |

| South Pacific Handbook | $24.00 |
| David Stanley | 920 pages, 147 maps |

| Southeast Asia Handbook | $21.95 |
| Carl Parkes | 1,080 pages, 204 maps |

| Tahiti Handbook | $15.95 |
| David Stanley | 450 pages, 51 maps |

| Thailand Handbook | $19.95 |
| Carl Parkes | 860 pages, 142 maps |

| Vietnam, Cambodia & Laos Handbook | $18.95 |
| Michael Buckley | 760 pages, 116 maps |

OTHER GREAT TITLES FROM MOON

"For hardy wanderers, few guides come more highly recommended than the Handbooks. They include good maps, steer clear of fluff and flackery, and offer plenty of money-saving tips. They also give you the kind of information that visitors to strange lands—on any budget— need to survive."

—US News & World Report

| Moon Handbook | $10.00 |
| Carl Koppeschaar | 150 pages, 8 maps |

| The Practical Nomad: How to Travel Around the World | $17.95 |
| Edward Hasbrouck | 580 pages |

| Staying Healthy in Asia, Africa, and Latin America | $11.95 |
| Dirk Schroeder | 230 pages, 4 maps |

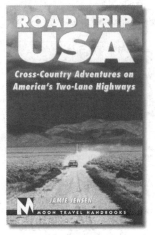

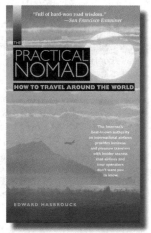

WHERE TO BUY MOON TRAVEL HANDBOOKS

BOOKSTORES AND LIBRARIES: Moon Travel Handbooks are distributed worldwide. Please contact our sales manager at info@moon.com for a list of wholesalers and distributors in your area.

TRAVELERS: We would like to have Moon Travel Handbooks available throughout the world. Please ask your bookstore to contact us for ordering information. If your bookstore will not order our guides for you, please contact us for a free catalog.

> **Moon Travel Handbooks**
> **C/o Publishers Group West**
> **Attn: Order Department**
> **1700 Fourth Street**
> **Berkeley, CA 94710**
> **fax: (510) 528-3444**

IMPORTANT ORDERING INFORMATION

PRICES: All prices are subject to change. We always ship the most current edition. We will let you know if there is a price increase on the book you order.

SHIPPING AND HANDLING OPTIONS: Domestic UPS or USPS priority mail (allow 10 working days for delivery): $6.00 for the first item, $1.00 for each additional item.

UPS 2nd Day Air or Printed Airmail requires a special quote.

International Surface Bookrate 8-12 weeks delivery: $5.00 for the first item, $1.00 for each additional item. Note: We cannot guarantee international surface bookrate shipping. We recommend sending international orders via air mail, which requires a special quote.

FOREIGN ORDERS: Orders that originate outside the U.S.A. must be paid for with an international money order, a check in U.S. currency drawn on a major U.S. bank based in the U.S.A., or Visa, MasterCard, or American Express.

INTERNET ORDERS: Visit our site at: www.moon.com